T0367922

# Treynor
# on Institutional
# Investing

# Treynor on Institutional Investing

JACK L. TREYNOR

John Wiley & Sons, Inc.

Published by John Wiley & Sons, Inc., Hoboken, New Jersey.
Published simultaneously in Canada

Wiley Bicentennial Logo: Richard J. Pacifico

For general information on our other products and services or for technical support, please contact our
Customer Care Department within the United States at (800) 762-2974, outside the United States at
(317) 572-3993 or fax (317) 572-4002.

Wiley publishes in a variety of print and electronic formats and by print-on-demand. Some material
included with standard print versions of this book may not be included in e-books or in print-on-demand.
If this book refers to media such as a CD or DVD that is not included in the version you purchased, you
may download this material at http://booksupport.wiley.com. For more information about Wiley products,
visit www.wiley.com.

*Library of Congress Cataloging-in-Publication Data:*

Treynor, Jack L.
    Treynor on institutional investing / Jack L. Treynor.
        p. cm.—(Wiley finance series)
    Includes index.
    ISBN 978-0-470-11875-7 (cloth)
    ISBN-13 978-0-470-11875-7
    1. Institutional investments.   2. Portfolio management.    I. Title.
    HG4521.T685 2007
    332.67′253—dc22

                                                                            2007026266

10  9  8  7  6  5  4  3  2

*To Betsy Glassmeyer Treynor,*
*who changed my life from black and white to Technicolor.*

# Contents

# Foreword

## Jack L. Treynor: An Independent Mind

This book, a collection of the writings of one of the most independent minds to tackle the financial market landscape, captures a number of ways in which the ever-provocative Jack Treynor influenced and touched the professional investment community over a period of decades. He reached many of us in two ways: (1) through published pieces of foresight and analysis that are now well recognized, and (2) through the individual guidance and advice that he has given to many of us. The book is part of a growing trend to recognize the many, and important, accomplishments of this esteemed practitioner.

If there is one way to sum up the contributions made by Treynor (and Walter Bagehot, his pseudonym for articles in CFA Institute's *Financial Analysts Journal [FAJ]* ), it was captured in Perry Mehrling's book on the late Fischer Black.[1] Treynor is credited by many scholars with drawing Black into the world of finance, and the two collaborated and counterpointed for years. Speaking in 1997 at a meeting of the International Association of Financial Engineers, Nobel Laureate Paul Samuelson suggested that a "Hall of Fame of Theoretical Finance" list should include Myron Scholes, Robert Merton (who would go on to be awarded Nobel Prizes), and Fischer Black (who died before he could receive a Nobel). In the middle of his speech, after mentioning the innovation of the capital asset pricing model (CAPM) for which William Sharpe had won the Nobel Prize in 1990, another Nobel Prize winner, Franco Modigliani, rose and said, "What about Treynor? You forgot Treynor!"

He knew Treynor had developed a CAPM in 1962, because Treynor had shown the model to him, and Modigliani regretted that he had not seen its potential and encouraged Treynor to pursue it. "I made a mistake with Treynor," he has noted. Treynor discovered the CAPM as a part of a journey to find better answers to the question of what was the appropriate discount rate to be used in capital-budgeting projects.

Ultimately, Black would write a letter of appreciation to Treynor as he was stepping down as editor of the *FAJ*, which read:

> *Your own research has been very important. You developed the capital asset pricing model before anyone else. But perhaps your greatest contribution has been through the work of others as Editor of the* Financial Analysts Journal. *Balancing academic interest, readability, and practical interest in a unique way, you guided issue after brilliant issue toward publication. I hope the profession will be able to repay you in some way.*[2]

CFA Institute, representing the investment profession, broadly, owes a huge debt to Jack Treynor. In 1981 as Treynor's term with the *FAJ* was coming to a close, Charley Ellis, CFA wrote:

> *Financial analysts have been striving for many years to develop a strong profession. A profession depends explicitly upon a comprehensive body of knowledge. Great progress in developing our professional knowledge has been made, but not without the stress of working it out piece by piece and stage by stage. Jack has been a leader in the process of developing our knowledge and our understanding, and he has taken us with him.*[3]

It is long past time for his writings to be gathered into a book that should grace the shelf of every investment professional.

Since the mid-1980s, Treynor has been president of Treynor Capital Management in Palos Verdes Estates, California. Following a major in mathematics from Haverford College, a stint with the U.S. Army, and an MBA with Distinction from the Harvard Business School (after which he stayed on at H.B.S. as a case writer for Bob Anthony in accounting), he was hired by the Operations Research Department at Arthur D. Little in 1956. Subsequently, he was hired by Donald Regan (the same Regan who later became U.S. Treasury Secretary) at Merrill Lynch to provide quantitative investment services to institutions. From 1969 to mid-1981, he presided as editor of the *FAJ* of what is now CFA Institute. After he left the *FAJ*, from 1981 to 1985, he was general partner and chief investment officer at the investment management firm of Treynor-Arbit Associates.

In 1985, Treynor earned from CFA Institute the prestigious Nicholas Molodovsky Award, which is presented periodically to individuals who have made outstanding contributions to change the direction of the investment profession. In 2007, he received from CFA Institute our highest commendation—the Professional Excellence Award for exemplary achievement, excellence of practice, and true leadership that have reflected honor upon the investment profession to the highest degree. He is a Distinguished Fellow of the Institute for Quantitative Research in Finance and has received the Employee Benefit Research Institute's Lillywhite Award.

Treynor is the coauthor of two books and more than 90 papers published in, among others, the *Harvard Business Review, Journal of Business, Journal of Finance, Journal of Investment Management, Journal of Portfolio Management,* and *FAJ*. He has taught investment courses at Columbia University and the University of Southern California and has served as director for several investment companies.

This book is more than a valuable collection of some of the leading-edge thoughts of the day by a gifted individual. It is a celebration of a practitioner who, arguably, had more influence over the profession than any other. It celebrates a person whose prime characteristic is an independence of views. In Treynor's own words, his true interest always "was the analytical problem behind investment decisions."[4] Or as Black wrote, "You started me out in finance and showed me the beauty of the way markets balance bulls and bears, speculators and investors. You taught me to look for buried treasure rather than surface nuggets in the unexplored wilds of research."[5]

In fact, Treynor was capable of connecting dots from far enough afield to the seeming point of eccentricity. How else to characterize someone who would bring a jar of red beans into his classroom at the University of Southern California to make a point? He would ask the students to guess how many beans were in the jar. Although the guesses ranged widely, Treynor was able to show that the average guess was close to perfect.

Surface nuggets are illusory. As a result, Jack would test an investment idea by telling others about it. If they easily understood the idea and agreed with the implied conclusion, he would presume the idea was already reflected in the security's price and move on. If they didn't see the point, he would conclude that the view was not impounded in the security's price and would pursue the idea further. I must admit I used the same tactic—usually on relatively sophisticated but unsuspecting investors—when I was in active management. So, of course, you can imagine my delight and disappointment when my old U.S. Equity team admitted that they were using *me* in the same manner after I was promoted to chief investment officer. When I was that one step farther away from the action, I no longer had the "edge." Let that be a warning.

Much of Treynor's work was being done at a time when academia was generally focused on a theory of market efficiency. On that subject, Treynor's statement is what sustains many an applied manager today:

> *[A]lthough the market is highly competitive, market efficiency as such should not prevent active investors from outperforming the market, by capitalizing on either inefficiencies in the propagation of information or inefficiencies in valuation.* [6]

Treynor's broad contribution can be seen in the way the material of this book is organized. Many know that his work goes well beyond capital asset pricing and the performance measurement extension. The headings of this book give evidence to this breadth:

Risk

CAPM

Performance Measurement

Economics

Trading

Accounting

Investment Value

Active Management

Pensions

Cases

Miscellaneous

Treynor makes important contributions in a number of areas that are fundamental to the investment management profession as a whole and CFA Institute in particular. His work addresses most of the ten topic areas that are the foundation for the CFA Program's examinations. Articles addressing the need to measure risk, valuation, capital asset pricing, capital budgeting, bond quality, active versus passive management, earnings quality, and options theory are but a few covered by this prolific writer. But his work extends beyond core topics and speaks to the whole of the investment business. For example, the CFA Institute Centre for financial Market Integrity is organized into four areas: standards of practice, capital markets policy, investment performance standards, and corporate disclosure. Treynor has made analytical contributions to each of these areas, which are traditionally thought of as advocacy.

In his early editorials and articles in the *FAJ* on stewardship, Treynor argued that investment practitioners, to be worthy of being called *professionals*, needed to move away from a focus on the securities industry toward a focus on the ultimate customer. He was critical of the emphasis on persuasion rather than performance. The principle, he believed, should not be what could be sold in the market for the benefit of Wall Street but the intrinsic value of the investment to the end user—whether beneficiary of a pension plan or mutual fund investor. We at CFA Institute also believe that the ultimate owner should be the prime beneficiary of the work we do.

With William Priest and Patrick Regan, Treynor correctly predicted the difficulties our pension system would face under ERISA and the Pension Benefit Guaranty Corporation, both created in 1974.[7] His early work on performance estimation was geared toward giving clients some rational means by which to look through the clutter of all the numbers to make inferences of skill on the part of investment managers, which is a foundation of the CFA Institute's work with Global Investment Performance Standards (GIPS). And his early papers on the accounting-driven nature of earnings statements, versus the investor need for statements that showed the economic rent firms were capturing, were a bulwark on which our voice for the financial statement user could be based. Moreover, he has written on securities law and regulation.

Equally important to Treynor's public contributions, but impossible to quantify, is the individual guidance and advice that he gave to individuals. Many of us can share stories of how Jack Treynor helped and influenced us on a personal scale, even though most of us doubt that he would even remember us. Allow me to share a couple of my own stories.

As the new volunteer head of the Candidate Curriculum Committee for economics at CFA Institute in the mid-1980s, I was struggling to find relevant material of an economic nature for the company research element of our examinations. From an economist's viewpoint, security analysis seemed to sit in a bit of a wasteland between economic theories of supply and demand and accounting approaches to financial statement analysis. Where were the economically principled articles to help a security analyst actually estimate cash flows? I called around and, of course, was directed to Jack Treynor. His first thought was to look at the appendix of John Burr Williams's 1938 gospel on valuation, in which the competitive position and evolution of the General Motors Company were described.[8] From that book, our discussion led to Michael Porter, Mike Spence, and Barry Nalebuff.[9] We accurately concluded there was, seemingly, a lack of supply–demand analysis in the practitioner world. We had great theory, but Jack also provided the applications.

The firm Treynor-Arbit evolved in 1985 out of American National Bank, a mid-sized gem in Chicago (American National was a pioneer in index fund investing with Rex Sinquefield). I was working down the street at First Chicago. When I took over the investment management function of domestic equities, two external firms had a large impact on what I subsequently attempted to do. One was Treynor-Arbit, with its extremely rigorous and nearly academic (by practitioner standards) approach to uncovering and documenting errors the market was making in understanding and pricing of industries and groups of securities. Here was a model of research, in my mind, that I could borrow from. And I did. It helped that I knew a few of Treynor and Hal Arbit's analysts.

Finally, in 1988, while I was working on a chapter on capital markets for Maginn and Tuttle's textbook, I needed to think particularly carefully, for various reasons, about the relevance of technical analysis.[10] No disrespect intended, but most books and articles on technical analysis at the time lacked rigor and care—despite the fact that much quantitative management is, essentially, sophisticated technical analysis. Treynor's presentation and writings on technical analysis provided a thoughtful way to get one's arms around this oft-used paradigm. This instance provides a valuable lesson: If you really understand deeply the nature of research and markets, you can understand how even easily dismissed theories have elements of value.

This book contains many wonderful articles. You could not do better than to sit down and enjoy them today, years after they were written, both for the perspective they provide and the timeless nature of some of them. I'm sure you'll see as you work through this volume the great independent mind that is Jack Treynor.

We also and always hope you use this book to continue your commitment to fair and free capital markets built on a foundation of trust and bred from the integrity of market participants and professionals like you.

Jeff Diermeier, CFA
President and chief executive officer
CFA Institute
April 2007

## Notes

1. *Fischer Black and the Revolutionary Idea of Finance* (Hoboken, NJ: John Wiley & Sons, 2005).
2. "An Open Letter to Jack Treynor" (July–August 1981): 14.
3. "Jack Has Never Been Easy" (July–August): 25.
4. "Ideas for the People Who Make Decisions," *FAJ* (July–August 2005): 6–8; reprinted in *Bold Thinking on Investment Management* (Charlottesville, VA: CFA Institute, 2005): 238–240.
5. "An Open Letter to Jack Treynor," *FAJ* (July–August 1981):14.
6. "What Does It Take to Win the Trading Game?" *FAJ* (January–February 1981): 57.
7. See *The Financial Reality of Pension Funding under ERISA* by Jack L. Treynor, Patrick J. Regan, and William W. Priest, Jr. (Homewood, IL: Irwin, 1976).
8. *The Theory of Investment Value* (Cambridge, MA: Harvard University Press).
9. Porter's influential books at that time were *Competitive Strategy: Techniques for Analyzing Industries and Competitors* (New York: Free Press, first published in 1980) and *Competitive Advantage: Creating and Sustaining Superior Performance* (New York: Free Press, first published in 1985). A. Michael Spence won the Nobel Prize in Economics in 2001 for work on the dynamics of information flows and market development. Barry

Nalebuff is coauthor with Avinash Dixit of *Thinking Strategically: The Competitive Edge in Business, Politics, and Everyday Life* (New York: Norton Paperback, 1993; first published in 1991).

10. The book was *Managing Investment Portfolios: A Dynamic Process* by John L. Maginn and Donald L. Tuttle; the third edition includes editors Jerald E. Pinto and Dennis W. McLeavey (Charlottesville, VA: CFA Institute, 2007).

# Preface

**M**uch of the pressure on investment institutions comes from two facts:

1. Results are made public.
2. For every winner there is a loser. Every investor can benefit from a rising market, but what he gains from trading, his counterparty loses.

Not surprisingly, money managers haven't been willing to stand pat with comfortable rituals. They want to know what works—and what doesn't work.

Because most retail investors can't afford to own enough stocks to be well diversified, they can't readily measure the market component of their return. So they don't know whether they are gaining or losing from their trading. Without a meaningful learning experience, retail investors make the same mistakes over and over again.

Since most institutional portfolios—mutual funds, pension funds, endowment funds—hold dozens, if not hundreds of stocks, they are reasonably well diversified, making it easier to distinguish between the two kinds of gains and losses. Perhaps it isn't entirely accidental that institutional investors have been steadily advancing their understanding of the investment problem. As the gap in understanding relative to retail investors has widened over the last 40 years, institutional investing has exploded into a profession that manages more than \$26.5 trillion[1] in the United States alone.

Many retail investors with demanding jobs reach a point in their careers where their own investment portfolio has become too important to ignore any longer. They know they are good at making business or professional decisions, but they sense that investment decisions are different. Fortunately, money management isn't rocket science. Whether they want to make conversations with an advisor more rewarding or prepare themselves for responsibilities on the boards of pension, endowment, or mutual funds, this book can be helpful.

The articles draw on the author's experience as a management consultant, money manager, and fund director.[2] First published in the *Harvard Business Review*, the *Journal of Business*, the *Journal of Finance*, the *Journal of Portfolio Management*, the *Journal of Investment Management*, and, of course, the journal the author edited for many years—*Financial Analysts Journal*, more than 16 of the papers in this book have been included in anthologies of finance and investing.

JACK L. TREYNOR
*Palos Verdes Estates, CA*
*April 2007*

## Notes

1. Pazarbasioglu, Ceyla; Mangal, Goswami; Jack, Ree. "The Changing Face of Investors," *Finance and Development, A quarterly magazine of the International Monetary Fund,* March 2007.
2. The author's consulting experience included casework for Philco, United Fruit, Royal Dutch Shell, the Irish Sugar Company, American Brake Shoe, British Aircraft Corporation, Minneapolis Honeywell, and others. He was a money manager for Treynor-Arbit Associates and fund director for over 30 years with Eaton Vance and its predecessor firms.

# Acknowledgments

The following is a very incomplete list of people I am indebted to, often learning far more from them than they could possibly learn from me.

Harvard Business School—to Robert N. Anthony who invited me to be a case writer.

Arthur D. Little, Inc.—to Phil Donham and Bruce Henderson, for giving me the opportunity to work on management consulting cases at Arthur D. Little, Inc. and to Bill Ackerman, a consultant to ADL on the United Fruit Case.

Merrill Lynch—to Jim Corbett.

*Financial Analysts Journal*—to Nick Molodovsky and especially Frank Block, for taking the gamble on me for the *Financial Analysts Journal*.

Eaton Vance—to Don Dwight, Sam Hayes, and Lynn Stout.

Research Affiliates—to Rob Arnott.

MIT—to Franco Modigliani, for inviting me to come to MIT, choosing my courses, and breaking my paper into two parts—the right part and the wrong part.

The Center for Research in Security Prices (CRSP) at the University of Chicago—to Jim Lorie and CRSP.

Yale—to Howard Phelan and John Ecklund.

London Business School—to Dick Brealey and Steve Schaefer.

Northwestern University—to Robert Korajczyk and Al Rappaport.

The Institute for Quantitative Research in Finance—to Roger Murray, Jim Farrell, Gifford Fong, and Peter Williamson.

CFA Institute—to Don Tuttle and John Maginn.

And to Fischer Black.

J. L. T.

# Introduction

## How a Profession Preserves Its Vitality

The word "professional" has many meanings. The dictionary definition coming closest to what we mean when we speak of the "professional" security analyst is "engaged in a calling requiring specialized knowledge and often long and intensive academic preparation." Even this definition seems somehow inadequate. What is it that the security analyst has in common with doctors, lawyers, engineers, and architects? The following characteristics, at least:

1. They draw on a body of formal knowledge to solve practical problems that often require going beyond that knowledge into gray areas where powers of observation, analysis, judgment, and so forth, play an important role.
2. The professional's client is entitled to expect that the professional would treat him as he would treat himself. In other words, the relationship between client and professional is not an arm's-length business relationship.
3. All these professionals have in common a sense of mission, a drive for self-improvement that goes beyond merely attempting to enhance their own individual earning power.

The first of these characteristics is perhaps less well known than the others, yet it may be the most important. The responsibility of the true professional does not stop with what is known. The professional who considers that his responsibility stops when he has exhausted the accepted techniques in his field may have a high income, and several academic degrees after his name, but his role in society is indistinguishable from that of a plumber.

On the other hand, it is precisely because the problems he is trying to solve go beyond the capabilities of present knowledge to solve them that he and his fellow professionals are constantly pressing forward in their search for new knowledge.

Nothing is more deadly to the vitality of a professional than defining his activities in terms of a set of comfortable rituals, rather than in terms of the great unsolved problems his clients have hired him to solve (this tendency is, of course, merely a special case of what Professor Ted Levitt in his famous *Harvard Business Review* article called "Marketing Myopia").

Because the solutions are never adequate to the practical problems, it is characteristic of a profession that there is a continuing tension between theory and practice. Sometimes this tension becomes so uncomfortable that both theoreticians and practitioners wish they could cease having anything to do with each other. Both theory and practice can survive that kind of schism, but the pale flame of professionalism cannot.

And it is a pale flame. For what distinguishes a profession from other human endeavors is not the average professional, but the exceptional professional. The latter is always far more important to his profession than his small numbers would suggest. What fraction of all doctors are brain surgeons? What fraction of all lawyers argue cases before the Supreme Court? What fraction of all engineers can invent a Wankel engine or a laser? The essence of the professional is the tireless pursuit of an ideal, and that ideal is approached by very few men.

The quintessentially professional activities in any profession tend to be of, by, and for the exceptional man. The average professional supports these activities, not because they have immediate practical value for him, or because they are tailored to his immediate capabilities and needs, but because they strengthen the common bond of professional aspiration that runs from the least of the men in his profession to the greatest.

Security analysis is a very young profession. In any profession so young there is always some danger that the average man in the profession will lose his sense of mission—his willingness to put the client first, his commitment to client welfare that goes beyond mere practice of accepted technique, his determination to advance the state of knowledge. A Greek philosopher would probably say that, among other things, a profession is a state of becoming. The tension between theory and practice is not too high a price to pay to keep the pale flame of professionalism burning.

# Risk

R isk is about events that we can't foresee. Is there nevertheless some underlying connection between the frequency of past events and the frequency of future events? Between the magnitude of past risks and the magnitude of future risks? Can connections between past and future risks be quantified in some useful way that is not itself risky?

Paradoxically, the risks that are hardest to quantify are the risks of least concern to the institutional investor. The key is the tendency for certain kinds of risks to occur together—i.e., the degree of correlation between the risks. Although uncorrelated risks are the easiest for an institutional investor to diversify, so-called "market" risks, which can't be diversified away, are the easiest to quantify.

J.L.T.

# CHAPTER 1

# Using Portfolio Composition to Estimate Risk

In recent years a number of financial scholars have commented on the marked degree of co-movement in the prices of securities. Statistical techniques have been applied to measuring the character and degree of co-movement by Donald Farrar, Hester and Feeney, and Benjamin King. Perhaps the best known model of stock prices that recognizes and incorporates the co-movement phenomenon is that of William Sharpe. In Sharpe's model fluctuations in the price of a particular common stock have two causes: (1) fluctuations in the general market level and (2) fluctuations unique to the stock in question. More complicated models than Sharpe's have been proposed and the Sharpe model has occasionally been criticized as being too simple to fit reality (see for example Benjamin King's discussion[1]). Nevertheless, its simplicity gives it great appeal.[2]

We are not the first to apply simple financial models to practical problems involving risk measurement. Marshall Blume tested the applicability of the Sharpe model to the problems of predicting the risk character of simulated rather than actual portfolios.[3] James Fanning, now of Rockefeller Brothers, and Marc Steglitz of Bankers Trust have measured risk in actual common stocks defined in terms of a related, but different, model and applied the results to estimating the risk character of actual portfolios containing these stocks. Although the present paper has benefited substantially from the work of Fanning and Steglitz, in terms of model and approach, we are much closer to Blume than Fanning and Steglitz.

Sometimes it is possible to identify stock price changes with particular news events. Even though the events that cause price changes sometimes seem to be unique, it is nevertheless useful to think of the events that affect prices as drawn at random from a large population, some of which can cause large price changes and some small, many of which have a high degree of uniqueness or individuality, but that, taken as an entire population, have a character that demonstrates some continuity

Copyright © CFA Institute. Reprinted from the *Financial Analysts Journal* with permission. September–October 1968.

This chapter was coauthored with William W. Priest, Jr., Lawrence Fisher, and Catherine A. Higgins.

We are grateful to Marvin Lipson for programming the computer runs, the results of which are reported here. The data for the study were taken from "Price Relative" tapes supplied to us by the Center for Research in Security Prices, the Graduate School of Business, the University of Chicago.

over time. Labor unions will continue to strike; countries will continue to declare war or to make undeclared war; the Fed will continue by turns to tighten up and loosen the money supply; and soforth. Some of these events are felt throughout the economy and have their impact to a greater or lesser degree on the prices of most common stocks. The impact of other events is specific to at most a few companies or industries.

The Sharpe model specifies that price fluctuations in a particular common stock will be the sum of fluctuations due to fluctuations in the market index and fluctuations unique to the stock in question.[4] The risk character of the stock is completely specified under the assumptions of the Sharpe model by specifying two parameters: The first is sensitivity of the stock to market fluctuations. It is common knowledge, however, that price fluctuations in individual common stocks are not completely explained by a market index. We call the portion of price changes left unexplained by a market index the *residual* price changes. The second risk parameter in the Sharpe model is a number that expresses the average magnitude of the residual fluctuations. In Sharpe's model, residual fluctuations are assumed to be independent from one security to another.

Some companies are more sensitive to the impact of events affecting the market index than others. Rapidly growing companies, companies that manufacture capital goods, companies with high fixed costs, and highly levered companies all tend to be more sensitive than companies for which these factors are absent. Companies for which several of these factors are present simultaneously are likely to be particularly sensitive.

The second parameter in the model—the measure of the magnitude of residual fluctuations—tends to be larger for companies in which technological changes in products or processes are taking place very rapidly. It also tends to be larger for one-product companies, companies for which style is an important factor and for companies whose fortunes depend on a single executive. Widely diversified companies and companies with a balanced management team will tend to demonstrate less residual variability than others. A high level of fixed costs or a highly levered capital structure will, of course, amplify specific risk in the same way that it amplifies market risk.

Exhibit 1.1 demonstrates the meaning of the risk parameters for individual stocks in graphical terms. The horizontal axis measures the change in a market index (Fisher's Combination Investment Performance Index[5]). The vertical axis measures the change in the value of the security in question. Both are measured as the ratio of value at the end of a month (including intervening dividends) to value at the beginning. A straight line has been fitted to the data points in Exhibit 1.1. The slope of the line is a measure of the sensitivity of the value of the security to fluctuations in the market index. The spread of data points around the line of best fit is a measure of residual variability.

The important distinction between market variability and residual variability in the individual security is that they affect portfolio returns in different ways. Sensitivity of a portfolio to variations in the market index is the average of the sensitivities of the individual securities held, weighted by the amounts. Residual variability in individual securities, on the other hand, tends to combine in such a way that it looms relatively less important in a portfolio (in comparison with market variability) than in the securities which comprise it. The spread is measured in terms of a number statisticians call the *residual variance*, which in terms of the present application is

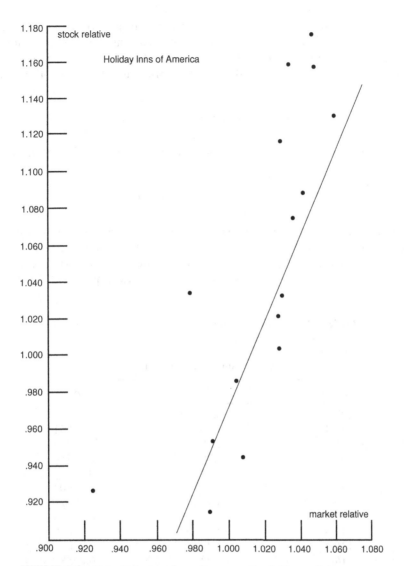

**EXHIBIT 1.1**　Price Relatives for a Common Stock Versus Price Relatives for "The Market"

an average of the squares of the (residual) fluctuations over the time period covered by the sample. Under the assumptions of the Sharpe model, there is a very simple rule for determining how specific risk in individual securities combines to determine specific risk in the portfolio: The residual variance for the portfolio can be expressed in terms of residual variance $\sigma_i^2$ for the individual stocks. Letting $x_i$ equal the number of shares of the ith stock held in the portfolio and assuming that the relevant measures are expressed on a per-share basis, we have

$$\text{Residual variance} = \Sigma x \sigma_i^2 \qquad\qquad (1.1)$$

In like fashion we can define *market variance* as the average over time of (squared) fluctuations in portfolio value due to market fluctuations. Letting regression-slope coefficients $B_i$ measure sensitivity of prices of individual stocks to fluctuations in the general market, and a variance $\sigma_m^2$ describe the variability of the general market, we have

$$\text{Market variance} = [\Sigma x_i B_i]^2 \sigma_m{}^2 \qquad (1.2)$$

Finally, expressions (1) and (2) can be combined to estimate total portfolio variance $\sigma^2$. We have

$$\sigma^2 = [\Sigma x_i B_i]^2 \sigma_m{}^2 + \Sigma x_i{}^2 \sigma_i{}^2 \qquad (1.3)$$

Equation 1.3 will hold only approximately since the residual variances for individual stocks are not strictly independent. As previously noted, a number of writers have challenged the Sharpe model on the assumptions underlying the way specific risks in individual securities combine in a portfolio. Nevertheless Equation 1.3 is probably

**EXHIBIT 1.2**  Exponentially-Smoothed Estimates of Market Volatility ($B$) and Residual Variance ($\sigma^2$)

| Month | B | $\sigma^2$ |
|---|---|---|
| | Holiday Inns of America, Inc. | |
| 3/64 | 0.663 | 0.00643 |
| 4/64 | 4.604 | 0.01051 |
| 5/64 | 4.307 | 0.00880 |
| 6/64 | 4.300 | 0.00754 |
| 7/64 | 4.314 | 0.00656 |
| 8/64 | 3.797 | 0.00604 |
| 9/64 | 3.132 | 0.00571 |
| 10/64 | 2.725 | 0.00528 |
| 11/64 | 3.025 | 0.00670 |
| 12/64 | 2.812 | 0.00635 |
| 1/65 | 2.923 | 0.00589 |
| 2/65 | 3.073 | 0.00548 |
| 3/65 | 2.961 | 0.00520 |
| 4/65 | 2.938 | 0.00489 |
| 5/65 | 3.006 | 0.00461 |
| 6/65 | 2.943 | 0.00436 |
| 7/65 | 1.742 | 0.00505 |
| 8/65 | 1.746 | 0.00479 |
| 9/65 | 2.036 | 0.00535 |
| 10/65 | 2.194 | 0.00581 |
| 11/65 | 2.356 | 0.00579 |
| 12/65 | 2.423 | 0.00572 |
| 1/66 | 2.391 | 0.00551 |
| 2/66 | 2.410 | 0.00529 |
| 3/66 | 2.427 | 0.00527 |

**EXHIBIT 1.3** How Market Risk Varies: Examples from the U.S. Market

| Ranked by $B_i$ | | |
|---|---|---|
| 1. | Holiday Inns | 2.427 |
| 2. | Warner & Swasey | 2.088 |
| 3. | Admiral | 2.025 |
| 4. | Collins Radio | 1.954 |
| 5. | General Instru. | 1.898 |
| 6. | Vornado | 1.817 |
| 7. | Piper Aircraft | 1.798 |
| 8. | Beckman Instru. | 1.763 |
| 9. | Fairchild Camera | 1.717 |
| 10. | Northwest Airlines | 1.687 |
| 11. | Commonwealth Oil | 1.679 |
| 12. | Max Factor | 1.624 |
| 13. | Phila & Reading | 1.609 |
| 14. | Raytheon | 1.595 |
| 15. | Bell & Howell | 1.595 |
| 16. | Avon | 1.589 |
| 17. | Texas Instru. | 1.575 |
| 18. | TWA | 1.524 |
| 19. | Pan Am World Airways | 1.517 |
| 20. | Financial Federation | 1.506 |
| 21. | Ampex | 1.505 |
| 22. | First Charter Financial | 1.504 |
| 23. | Control Data | 1.500 |
| 24. | Crowell Collier | 1.498 |
| 25. | Foxboro | 1.496 |
| 26. | Universal Oil Prod. | 1.479 |
| 27. | EJ Korvette | 1.472 |
| 28. | William H. Rorer | 1.446 |
| 29. | Magnavox | 1.438 |
| 30. | Polaroid | 1.425 |
| 31. | Eastern Airlines | 1.404 |
| 32. | Cerro | 1.398 |
| 33. | Reynolds Metal | 1.394 |
| 34. | National Airlines | 1.378 |
| 35. | Perkin Elmer | 1.378 |
| 36. | Zenith Radio | 1.358 |
| 37. | Cons. Electronics Inds. | 1.375 |
| 38. | Rayonier | 1.449 |
| 39. | Celanese | 1.357 |
| 40. | Xerox | 1.352 |
| 41. | Revere Copper & Brass | 1.350 |
| 42. | Motorola | 1.344 |
| 43. | Litton Inds. | 1.337 |
| 44. | Penn RR | 1.332 |
| 45. | Ginn & Co. | 1.320 |
| 46. | Douglas Aircraft | 1.308 |
| 47. | Indian Head Mills | 1.307 |
| 48. | Mallory | 1.306 |
| 49. | Sunstrand | 1.303 |
| 50. | Delta Airlines | 1.302 |
| 51. | I T & T | 1.296 |
| 52. | Carter Products | 1.291 |
| 53. | General Precision | 1.290 |
| 54. | Sperry-Rand | 1.290 |
| 55. | Western Airlines | 1.277 |
| 56. | Hewlett Packard | 1.262 |
| 57. | ACF Inds. | 1.242 |
| 58. | Great Northern Paper | 1.233 |
| 59. | Owens Corning | 1.207 |
| 60. | Kayser Roth | 1.205 |
| 61. | Grace | 1.194 |
| 62. | Kaiser Alum. | 1.191 |
| 63. | Frito Lay | 1.17 |
| 64. | Air Prd. & Chem. | 1.157 |
| 65. | Allis Chalmers | 1.157 |
| 66. | Whirlpool | 1.156 |
| 67. | Pfizer Chas. | 1.133 |
| 68. | Corning Glass Works | 1.123 |
| 69. | General Dynamics | 1.120 |
| 70. | Bigelow Sanford | 1.115 |
| 71. | Texas Oil & Gas | 1.114 |
| 72. | Wetson & Co. | 1.105 |
| 73. | Pennzoil | 1.098 |
| 74. | National Can | 1.093 |
| 75. | Schering | 1.092 |
| 76. | Union Bag Camp Paper | 1.078 |
| 77. | Burroughs | 1.072 |
| 78. | Mueller Brass | 1.059 |
| 79. | Allied Supermarkets | 1.054 |
| 80. | MGM | 1.048 |
| 81. | Bethlehem Steel | 1.045 |
| 82. | Fibreboard Paper Prds. | 1.039 |
| 83. | Olin Mathieson | 1.035 |
| 84. | Harbison Walker | 1.030 |
| 85. | Chesebrough Ponds | 1.022 |
| 86. | Southern Co. | 1.019 |
| 87. | Aluminum Co Amer. | 1.011 |
| 88. | W. Virginia Pulp & Paper | 1.000 |
| 89. | Caterpillar Tractor | 0.985 |
| 90. | Beaunit | 0.982 |
| 91. | Crown Cork & Seal | 0.978 |
| 92. | Tidewater | 0.978 |
| 93. | Chrysler | 0.966 |
| 94. | Montgomery Ward | 0.953 |
| 95. | Texas Gulf Sulphur | 0.945 |
| 96. | Cons. Cigar | 0.936 |
| 97. | Ex-Cell-O | 0.936 |
| 98. | Westinghouse Electric | 0.932 |
| 99. | Upjohn | 0.920 |

**EXHIBIT 1.3**　(*Continued*)

| | | | | | |
|---|---|---|---|---|---|
| 100. | Holt Rinehart & Winston | 0.914 | 117. | Marathon | 0.752 |
| 101. | Wesco Financial | 0.911 | 118. | Allied Chemical | 0.738 |
| 102. | Grumman | 0.904 | 119. | Gulf Oil | 0.727 |
| 103. | Halliburton | 0.893 | 120. | McDonnell Aircraft | 0.721 |
| 104. | Florida Pwr. & Light. | 0.888 | 121. | Socony Mobil Oil | 0.665 |
| 105. | Cone Mills | 0.887 | 122. | Texaco | 0.661 |
| 106. | Colgate Palmolive | 0.851 | 123. | Monsanto | 0.649 |
| 107. | Union Oil Cal. | 0.850 | 124. | Sunbeam | 0.639 |
| 108. | Merck | 0.850 | 125. | S. Carolina Elec. & Gas | 0.610 |
| 109. | Columbia Brdestg. | 0.837 | 126. | Central Southwest | 0.607 |
| 110. | Bobbie Brooks | 0.825 | 127. | Abbott Labs | 0.593 |
| 111. | Gillette | 0.819 | 128. | Standard Oil Cal. | 0.587 |
| 112. | Lockheed | 0.805 | 129. | Petrolane Gas Service | 0.576 |
| 113. | United Fruit | 0.782 | 130. | Beneficial Finance | 0.565 |
| 114. | Coastal States Gas Prod. | 0.774 | 131. | Gulf States Utilities | 0.549 |
| 115. | United Carr | 0.764 | 132. | Southwestern Public Sve. | 0.451 |
| 116. | IBM | 0.757 | 133. | AT&T | 0.403 |

the simplest model which has any reasonable hope of predicting the risk character of a diversified portfolio.

The values for the regression coefficients and residual variances are obtained by regressing price change histories for individual common stocks against a suitable market average. From these values and composition data, a model of the risk character of the portfolio is constructed. Predictions of a change in the value of the portfolio (given the change in market level) are compared with the actual change in order to test this model.

Our basic idea (in which we were anticipated by the work of Fanning and Steglitz, and also by that of Marshall Blume) is that if we knew the risk parameters for individual common stocks then we could estimate the risk character of a portfolio instantaneously—even though the composition was continuously changing. In order to test this idea we have studied all the common stocks held in an actual mutual-fund portfolio during a period of more than two years. The price history of each common stock was traced back as far as conveniently possible—in some cases, up to 40 years. From the price and dividend histories for the common stocks, we made running estimates of the risk parameters for each common stock held. Then, once a month for each month during the test period, we made an instantaneous estimate of the risk character of the mutual fund portfolio, based on its composition at the end of that month. Our estimate of *market* risk for the portfolio enabled us to predict how rapidly the value of the fund would change as the market level fluctuated. Our estimate of *residual* risk for the fund gives an estimate of the amount by which the true market value of the fund will differ from our predictions. For each month of the test period we estimated both risk parameters for the fund and observed the actual change in market level and the actual change in the value of the fund. How well we succeeded in predicting the observed changes in the value of the fund, given the actual changes in market level, is discussed at the end of this paper.

**EXHIBIT 1.4** How Specific Risk Varies: Examples from the U.S. Market

| Ranked by Residual Variance | | |
|---|---|---|
| 1. | Control Data Corp. | 0.02116 |
| 2. | Fairchild Camera & Instru. | 0.02071 |
| 3. | Texas Gulf Sulphur | 0.01576 |
| 4. | Texas Instru. | 0.01453 |
| 5. | Admiral Corp. | 0.01431 |
| 6. | EJ Korvette | 0.01344 |
| 7. | Collins Radio | 0.01326 |
| 8. | Wesco Financial Corp. | 0.01244 |
| 9. | Xerox Corp. | 0.01217 |
| 10. | Financial Federation | 0.01200 |
| 11. | General Instru. Corp. | 0.01145 |
| 12. | First Charter Finan. Corp. | 0.01045 |
| 13. | Ampex Corp. | 0.01011 |
| 14. | Cons. Electronics Inds. | 0.00946 |
| 15. | Beckman Instru. | 0.00939 |
| 16. | Commonwealth Oil Refining | 0.00900 |
| 17. | Raytheon Co. | 0.00893 |
| 18. | Vornado Inc. | 0.00892 |
| 19. | Max Factor & Co. | 0.00878 |
| 20. | Polaroid Corp. | 0.00874 |
| 21. | Magnavox Co. | 0.00861 |
| 22. | Crowell-Collier | 0.00820 |
| 23. | William H. Rorer | 0.00812 |
| 24. | Douglas Aircraft Co. | 0.00780 |
| 25. | Zenith Radio Corp. | 0.00765 |
| 26. | Texas Oil & Gas | 0.00762 |
| 27. | General Dynamics | 0.00752 |
| 28. | McDonnell Aircraft Corp. | 0.00730 |
| 29. | TWA Inc. | 0.00725 |
| 30. | Bell & Howell Co. | 0.00717 |
| 31. | Hewlett Packard Co. | 0.00711 |
| 32. | Crown Cork & Seal | 0.00705 |
| 33. | Piper Aircraft Corp. | 0.00697 |
| 34. | Universal Oil Prds. | 0.00694 |
| 35. | Northwest Airlines | 0.00692 |
| 36. | Perkin Elmer Corp. | 0.00691 |
| 37. | Carter Prod. Inc. | 0.00688 |
| 38. | Mueller Brass Co. | 0.00686 |
| 39. | Eastern Airlines | 0.00685 |
| 40. | Reynolds Metals | 0.00679 |
| 41. | National Can Corp. | 0.00668 |
| 42. | Foxboro Co. | 0.00666 |
| 43. | Pan Am Wld Airways | 0.00666 |
| 44. | Phil. & Reading Corp. | 0.00660 |
| 45. | National Airlines | 0.00659 |
| 46. | Allied Supermarkets | 0.00648 |
| 47. | Delta Air Lines Inc. | 0.00645 |
| 48. | General Precision | 0.00636 |

| | | |
|---|---|---|
| 49. | Ginn & Co. | 0.00628 |
| 50. | Kaiser Alum. & Chem. | 0.00622 |
| 51. | Pennzoil Co. | 0.00619 |
| 52. | Beaunit Corp. | 0.00613 |
| 53. | Kayser Roth Corp. | 0.00603 |
| 54. | Lockheed Aircraft | 0.00603 |
| 55. | Litton Inds. | 0.00590 |
| 56. | Grumman Aircraft | 0.00582 |
| 57. | Western Airlines | 0.00578 |
| 58. | Bobbie Brooks | 0.00576 |
| 59. | Sunstrand Corp. | 0.00573 |
| 60. | Motorola Inc. | 0.00571 |
| 61. | United Fruit | 0.00565 |
| 62. | Great Northern Paper Co. | 0.00564 |
| 63. | Schering Corp. | 0.00558 |
| 64. | Sperry-Rand Corp. | 0.00540 |
| 65. | Wetson & Co. | 0.00540 |
| 66. | Cerro Corp. | 0.00539 |
| 67. | Southern Co. | 0.00537 |
| 68. | Chrysler Corp. | 0.00532 |
| 69. | Cons. Cigar Corp. | 0.00529 |
| 70. | Holiday Inns of Amer. | 0.00527 |
| 71. | Tidewater Oil Co. | 0.00515 |
| 72. | Bigelow-Sanford Inc. | 0.00504 |
| 73. | Air Prod. & Chem. | 0.00501 |
| 74. | Indian Head Mills | 0.00498 |
| 75. | Burroughs Corp. | 0.00493 |
| 76. | Warner & Swasey Co. | 0.00489 |
| 77. | Holt Rinehart & Winston | 0.00488 |
| 78. | Revere Copper & Brass | 0.00482 |
| 79. | MGM | 0.00480 |
| 80. | Whirlpool Corp. | 0.00476 |
| 81. | Celanese Corp Amer. | 0.00475 |
| 82. | Owens Corning Fiberglass | 0.00465 |
| 83. | Corning Glass Works | 0.00449 |
| 84. | Sunbeam Corp. | 0.00447 |
| 85. | Rayonier Inc. | 0.00439 |
| 86. | Alum. Co. Amer. | 0.00433 |
| 87. | Petrolane Gas Srv. Inc. | 0.00429 |
| 88. | Intern. T & T | 0.00428 |
| 89. | Gillette Co. | 0.00406 |
| 90. | ACF Inds. | 0.00404 |
| 91. | Penn. RR | 0.00404 |
| 92. | Columbia Brdestg. | 0.00402 |
| 93. | W. Virginia Pulp & Paper | 0.00402 |
| 94. | Avon Prod. | 0.00401 |
| 95. | Frito Lay | 0.00396 |
| 96. | Fibreboard Paper Prds. | 0.00394 |
| 97. | Merck & Co. | 0.00387 |
| 98. | Mallory Pr. & Co | 0.00373 |

**EXHIBIT 1.4**   (*Continued*)

| | | | | | | |
|---|---|---|---|---|---|---|
| 99. | Caterpillar Tractor | 0.00363 | 117. | Olin Mathieson Chem. | 0.00274 |
| 100. | United Carr Inc. | 0.00359 | 118. | Gulf Oil | 0.00267 |
| 101. | Bethlehem Steel | 0.00356 | 119. | Westinghouse Electric | 0.00267 |
| 102. | Abbott Lab | 0.00354 | 120. | Grace WR & Co. | 0.00255 |
| 103. | Upjohn Co. | 0.00353 | 121. | Union Oil of Cal. | 0.00245 |
| 104. | Coastal States Gas Prd. Co. | 0.00352 | 122. | IBM | 0.00242 |
| 105. | Chesebrough Ponds Inc. | 0.00341 | 123. | Florida Pwr. & Light | 0.00234 |
| 106. | Ex-Cell-O | 0.00340 | 124. | Beneficial Finance | 0.00232 |
| 107. | Cone Mills | 0.00336 | 125. | Socony Mobil Oil | 0.00225 |
| 108. | Colgate Palmolive | 0.00330 | 126. | Texaco | 0.00217 |
| 109. | Halliburton Co. | 0.00331 | 127. | Gulf States Utilities | 0.00216 |
| 110. | Monsanto Co. | 0.00329 | 128. | S. Carolina Electric & Gas | 0.00203 |
| 111. | Allis Chalmers Mfg. | 0.00327 | | | |
| 112. | Marathon Oil Co. | 0.00323 | 129. | Central S. West | 0.00200 |
| 113. | Union Bag Camp Paper | 0.00318 | 130. | Allied Chem. Corp. | 0.00185 |
| 114. | Montgomery Ward | 0.00309 | 131. | Southwestern Public Svc. | 0.00181 |
| 115. | Pfizer Chas | 0.00294 | | | |
| 116. | Harbison Walker Refractories | 0.00291 | 132. | Standard Oil of Cal. | 0.00174 |
| | | | 133. | AT&T | 0.00091 |

Although the risk character of a fund may change quickly if the composition of the fund changes, our scheme assumes that risk parameters for individual common stocks change relatively slowly. In most cases the assumption seems valid to us, since they change through the gradual evolution of products, manufacturing processes, and markets. The risk character of a company's common stock may change quickly, however, if the company enters into a wide-ranging diversification program or undergoes a profound change in capital structure. The essence of the measurement problem is that they are measured subject to random fluctuations in the data and that reliable estimates can be obtained only with samples large enough to "average out" these random fluctuations to some degree. Unfortunately, over time, the underlying parameters that we are attempting to measure are themselves changing. Thus we are confronted with an inescapable dilemma: If we confine our samples to very recent data, possible error due to random fluctuations in sample data may be excessively large. If, on the other hand, we include in our sample a longer time span, we may be including data that are no longer relevant because of changes over time in the risk character of the common stock in question. In principle, there are ways of weighting more and less recent data that are optimal in the sense of minimizing the combined effects of both problems. We are currently experimenting with techniques that select optimum weights automatically. For this study, however, we used exponential smoothing techniques with arbitrary weights (see Appendix 1.1).

Using exponential smoothing we obtained running (that is, continually changing) estimates of the risk character of a large group of common stocks covering as much as 40 years. Exhibit 1.2 shows how estimates of the risk parameters for a single common stock have behaved over time.

Perhaps the most striking thing about our estimates of risk parameters for individual common stocks is the range of values encountered in our modest sample. Exhibit

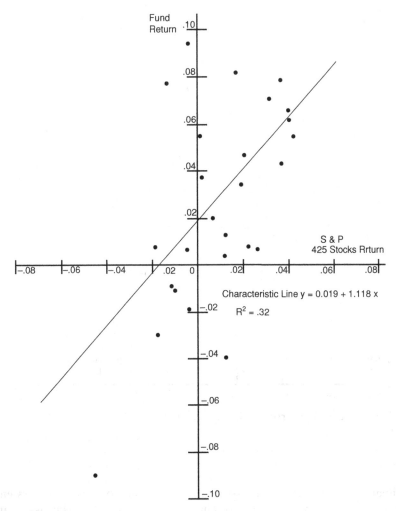

**EXHIBIT 1.5** Fund Return versus Market Return

1.3 shows current estimates for market risk of stocks in the sample. A regression-slope coefficient $B_i$ equal to 1 implies that the stock in question has an average degree of market risk, and that if the market rises or falls 10 percent other things equal the stock in question will rise or fall respectively 10 percent. Values $B_i$ in Exhibit 1.3 range from less than $\frac{1}{2}$ to more than $2\frac{1}{2}$. In other words some stocks in Exhibit 1.3 have more than 5 times as much market risk as some others. Clearly the degree of market risk in a portfolio is determined, not only by the proportions devoted to common stock and fixed income securities respectively, but also by the kind of common stocks held.

Exhibit 1.4 shows current estimates of $\sigma_i^2$, the spread in residual risk for the common stocks studied. Here too the range is impressive. As one might expect there is some tendency for stocks that rank high in Exhibit 1.3 to rank high in Exhibit 1.4.

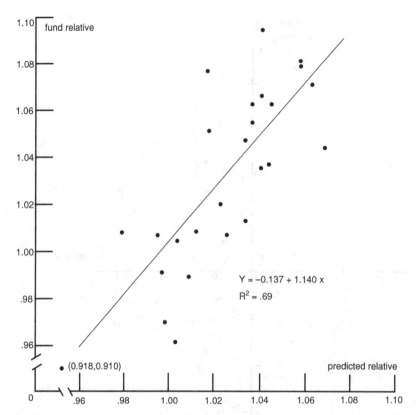

**EXHIBIT 1.6**   Fund Return versus Predictions Based on Risk Character of
Stocks Listed

Ultimately our interest in the risk character of common stocks derives entirely
from their possible impact on the risk character of a portfolio. The risk character
of the mutual fund portfolio considered in this study[6] is displayed in Exhibit 1.5.
The rate of return for an appropriate market index (the same Fisher Index referred
to above) is measured along the horizontal axis and a rate of return for the fund is
measured on the vertical axis. (The scatter diagram in Exhibit 1.5 covers 27 consecutive months of investment results for the fund.) The slope of the regression line fitted
to these points (the Characteristic Line) is a measure of the average level of market
risk in the fund over this period. If the actual level of market risk in the fund had
been maintained constant over the period, then the dispersion of month-to-month
results around the line of best fit would be a measure of the degree of specific risk
in the fund. If on the other hand, the actual degree of market risk in the fund was
changing from month to month, then the dispersion of the data around the line of
best fit overstates the degree of specific risk in the fund. It is obviously necessary to
accumulate data over a substantial period of time in order to measure market risk in
a fund using the Characteristic Line technique.

Exhibit 1.6 compares actual month-to-month results for the fund with results
predicted, using the technique described in this paper. A comparison of Exhibit 1.5

and 1.6 shows that our forecast of investment results for the fund is improved by using risk estimates for the individual common stocks held. In fact, roughly half the variance left unexplained by the Characteristic Line is accounted for by allowing for changes in the composition of the fund (hence changes in the risk character of the fund) over the sample period. We conclude that our risk-measuring technique is producing numbers that are both meaningful and useful—not only for estimating portfolio risk after the fact but also for estimating the impact on fund risk of making contemplated changes in the composition of the fund.

## APPENDIX 1.1

The following formulas indicate schematically how we used Exponential Smoothing to get continuously-updated estimates of risk parameters for individual common stocks. Let $x_i(t)$ be the rate of return for the ith stock in period $t$ and define $\bar{x}_i(t)$ implicitly as our estimate of the current expected value around which $x(t)$ is fluctuating. Let $\mu(t)$ be the rate of return for an appropriate market index and define $\bar{\mu}(t)$ analogously to $\bar{x}(t)$. Then define the covariance matrix $\sigma_i^2$ by

$$\sigma_i^2 = \begin{pmatrix} \sigma_{ii}^2 & \sigma_{i\mu}^2 \\ \sigma_{i\mu}^2 & \sigma_{\mu\mu}^2 \end{pmatrix} = \begin{pmatrix} (x_i - \bar{x}_i)^2 & (x_i - \bar{x}_i)(\mu - \bar{\mu}_i) \\ (x_i - \bar{x}_i)(\mu - \bar{\mu}) & (\mu - \bar{\mu})^2 \end{pmatrix} \tag{1.4}$$

and define $\sigma_i^2(t)$ implicitly by the relation

$$\sigma^2(t) = \alpha\sigma^2(t) + (1 - \alpha)\bar{\sigma}^2(t - 1)$$

where $\alpha$ is the same smoothing constant as before. Then our estimates of the regression parameters $\beta_i(t)$ and $\sigma_i^2(t)$ are given by

$$\beta_i(t) = \frac{\sigma_{i\mu}^2(t)}{\sigma_{\mu\mu}^2(t)} \tag{1.5}$$

$$\sigma_i^2(t) = \sigma_{ii}^2(t) - \beta_i^2(t)\sigma_{\mu\mu}^2(t) \tag{1.6}$$

It can be seen from these formulas that, when the true values of $\beta_i$ and $\sigma_i^2$ are changing along a steady trend, our estimates will tend to lag somewhat behind the true values.

## Notes

1. "Market and Industry Factors in Stock Price Behavior," *Journal of Business*, Volume 39, Number 1, Part II ("Supplement," January, 1966), pp. 139–190.
2. It should be noted that in conversation with one of us (Fisher) in 1964 or 1965, Harry Markowitz expressed the opinion that the degree of clustering of fluctuations found by

King would not cause portfolios to show riskiness substantially different from that estimated using the Sharpe model.

3. Unpublished monograph *The Empirical Adequacy of Portfolio Theory*, submitted to *Journal of Business*, July, 1968.

4. Sharpe's model was nearly anticipated by M. F. M. Osborne in his celebrated paper "Brownian Motion in the Stock Market," (*Operations Research*, Vol. 7, March–April, 1959). Osborne considered an "ensemble consisting of 1,000 pennies and one gold piece." The outcome of the toss of the gold piece affected the prices of 1,000 stocks; the effect of the outcome of tossing each of the 1,000 pennies was unique to a single stock.

5. Described in "Some New Stock Market Indexes," *Journal of Business, loc. cit.*, pp. 191–225.

6. The "fund" studied was the portion of Diversified Growth Stock Fund that was invested in common stocks listed on the New York Stock Exchange. These stocks comprised over 90 per cent of the net assets of the fund throughout the period studied (December 31, 1964 to March 31, 1966).

# CHAPTER 2

# Business versus Statistical Price Risk

**F**inance literature often makes a distinction between business risk and price risk. The notion of business risk presumably relates to the possibility of such misfortunes as new product failures, competitive threats, technological obsolescence, strikes, and so forth, that can affect the earning power of a company. Price risk, on the other hand, relates to the uncertainty surrounding the future value of the company's shares. In the young tradition of modern capital theory, price risk is usually estimated by reviewing the history of past price fluctuations—up, as well as down.

One risk is specific, the other general; one deals with the future, the other with the past; one is one-sided, the other two-sided; one deals with events, the other expectations; one tends to focus on events internal to the company, the other on events in the capital markets. One usually thinks of business risk in terms of potential unfavorable effects on a company's cash flow. To the extent that price fluctuations reflect changes in the consensus estimate of the cash flow, the company's earning power and its share price mirror the same events.

Events often affect price before they affect earning power, because the individual investors who make up the market consensus strive to correct their views as soon as possible. And even if an event affects earning power once and once only, a shifting consensus on the event can generate a whole series of (two-way) adjustments in share price. But business risk and price risk—particularly that portion of price risk independent of general market fluctuations—refer largely to the same events, recorded at different times and in different ways.

Which is more useful to the investor in assessing investment risk—a list of specific events that may affect future earning power unfavorably, or a measure of past price variability? Since investors will remain unaware of the possibility of some events until they happen, an explicit inventory of foreseeable business risks will generally underestimate the true magnitude of future price risk. Because risky events may be more numerous or more consequential in the future than in the past, the magnitude of past price fluctuations can lead to low estimates of the magnitude of future fluctuations; but past price variability is at least as likely to lead to high estimates.

---

# CHAPTER 3

# Specific Risk

**S**ome managers are attacking the problem of managing a conventional equity portfolio by dividing it into two complementary components—a passive (or nearly passive) core portfolio virtually devoid of specific risk and a highly active noncore portfolio containing a high level of specific risk but offering a high level of abnormal return. ("Abnormal return" is the amount of return expected in excess of the return on a diversified portfolio with the same market sensitivity, and "specific risk" is a measure of the uncertainty surrounding that return.) At a different level, some clients who employ fund managers are parceling their portfolios into active and passive sub-portfolios—sometimes managed by the same fund manager, sometimes by different managers.

The core/noncore concept has genuine merit at both levels. The writer is troubled, however, by one idea that has caught on with some clients employing the concept. These clients believe that, whereas the function of passive portfolios is diversification, the function of active portfolios is maximizing abnormal return without regard for risk. They argue that, because it is accomplished in the passive portfolio, diversification is irrelevant in the active portfolio.

If active portfolios could justifiably ignore it, specific risk in the individual security would be unimportant, since passive portfolios containing hundreds of stocks would be insensitive to it. But the truth is otherwise. As long as a client has a passive portfolio, the amount of *systematic* risk in his active portfolio is irrelevant because he can offset any addition to that risk by scaling down his passive portfolio. On the other hand, the client can always increase the abnormal return of his overall portfolio merely by incurring more *specific* risk—i.e., by shifting funds from passive to active—with the practical limit to the abnormal return of the client's total portfolio being the amount of specific risk he chooses to bear. It follows that performance in an active portfolio entails not maximizing abnormal return, but maximizing abnormal return per unit of specific risk.

Specific risk is a two-edged sword: When anticipated by research, it can contribute to an active portfolio's performance; when not anticipated, it can contribute to the portfolio's risk. Research will rarely anticipate more than a fraction of the forces affecting a security's specific risk. Although slightly more complicated than diversification in passive portfolios—since it involves abnormal return as well as specific risk—diversification across securities in active portfolios is the manager's only

---

weapon against the specific risk he incurs in his quest for abnormal return. Indeed, measured in terms of the ratio noted above, the active portfolio's performance is directly affected by how well the manager diversifies.

Diversification has at least two different meanings—weighting holdings so the the portfolio (1) behaves like the market (in practice, like a market index, whose behavior may or may not resemble the true market) or (2) makes the greatest possible contribution to portfolio performance. For an active portfolio, the second kind of diversification is never irrelevant.

# CHAPTER 4

# On the Quality of Municipal Bonds

**M**uch of what municipalities spend is spent without a clear *quid pro quo*, merely to help people deemed unable to help themselves. At the same time, the fact that many municipalities are getting into financial trouble suggests that a limit is being reached. What sets the limits on a city's power to tax? To borrow?

The power to tax and the power to borrow are not independent financial resources for the city. They are, rather, two aspects of the same resource. The measure of this common resource is the aggregate market value of the city's real property. The financial consideration in the city's decisions is thus their impact on this value. This is not to argue that every decision should be guided exclusively by financial considerations, or that eleemosynary projects are inappropriate to a city. On the other hand, allocation of limited resources among a number of such projects can be made rationally only if the demands for each project on the scarce resources are measured properly.

The fundamental criterion for the municipal bond investor is not willingness to pay, as measured by the current level of taxes, but ability to pay. In measuring this ability, the aggregate market value of the city's taxable real estate plays a role analogous to equity in the balance sheet of the private corporation. Black and Scholes have explained how the market value of the debt claims on a corporation will vary with variations in the value of the underlying corporate assets. Analogy suggests that the market value of municipal claims will vary with the value of the city's taxable real estate. When one uses the Black-Scholes option curve to estimate this value, no reference to bond ratings is necessary. There is no longer anything "qualitative" about the quality of municipal bonds.

Today the city is more important in American society than ever before. In the last 50 years, our country has changed from a predominantly agricultural society to a predominantly urban society. Service industries are becoming steadily more important relative to manufacturing industries, and most service industries are located in cities. Finally, cities are our primary instruments for social welfare and social change.

In view of the size of the social problems in the urban environment, it is not surprising that slum clearance and welfare programs have become important items in city budgets. Every American city feels responsibility toward its poor, underprivileged citizens and every city will offer help to these people within its means to provide. Every city would like to be able to afford museums and parks, as well as jails and sewers. If they could offer employers and citizens clean, quiet, rapid public transportation, clean air, crime-free streets, and a variety of cultural opportunities, few cities would fail to attract new business enterprise, broaden their tax base, generate additional employment opportunities for their populace, and progress toward that enriching diversity of economic activity that, according to Jane Jacobs, is the key to their economic success.[1]

Yet, for many cities, this state of bliss is a never-never land, which seems as far away now as it did years and many billions of municipal expenditures ago. After years of expending much of what they have had to spend without a clearly established "quid pro quo," many municipalities—including some of the largest—are getting into financial trouble. It is easy to say that they could avoid financial trouble by borrowing and spending wisely. But what is wisely?

If you ask a mayor to identify his financial resources, he will probably cite two— the power to tax and the power to borrow. When he answers in these terms, he is merely begging the ultimate question: What sets the limits on a city's power to tax? To borrow?

This article attempts to prove the following points:

(1) Taxing and borrowing are not independent financial resources for the city, but rather two aspects of the same resource. The measure of this common resource is the aggregate market value of the city's real property. It follows immediately that the financial objective in the city's spending decisions is maximizing this measure.
(2) The relevant cost of capital in reckoning the economic impact of municipal projects is not the cost of municipal borrowing, but the discount rate implicit in the valuation of municipal real estate.

This article is directed both to citizens and their delegated representatives and to lenders. It addresses both the question of how to invest municipal monies wisely and the question of what determines the quality of municipal bonds. Its main thesis is that cities are at root economic—not eleemosynary—organisms, and that a city can exhaust its resources through unwise spending just as readily as private corporations can. If it is to avoid this fate, it must subject its expenditures to the same kind of financial criteria that sophisticated corporations apply. The investor interested in municipal securities should apply these same criteria.

## HOW CITIES COMPETE

In the same way that man must work to eat, a city must export to survive. Conventional cities produce no agricultural products, gasoline, heating oil, and so forth. In its quest for money with which to buy essential (and nonessential) imports, a city must sell its export goods at a price that generates some margin in excess of the cost of imported raw material. Value added does not, however, give us an entirely satisfactory measure of economic health. It might have served for ancient cities that depended almost exclusively on slave labor. But labor in modern cities is free to migrate from city to city in search of the highest real wage. A city that cannot pay a competitive wage will lose its supply of workers to other cities.

**EXHIBIT 4.1**   Efficiency of Market for Labor Measured in Terms of After-Tax Income

| State | Per Capita Income Before Taxes | Per Capita Income After Taxes |
|-------|-------------------------------|-------------------------------|
| California | $7,911 | $5,898 |
| New York | $7,537 | $5,206 |
| Massachusetts | $7,258 | $4,857 |
| North Carolina | $5,936 | $5,006 |

*Source:* Michael Knight, "Taxes Hurt Massachusetts Jobs," *New York Times*, March 26, 1979.

Broadly speaking, therefore, one may say that cities compete with each other in two markets:

1. A market for goods
2. A market for labor

We will assume that both markets are perfectly elastic. The assumption of a perfectly elastic labor supply facing the individual city may seem extreme in view of the well known reluctance of people to move in the face of moving costs, disruption of social ties, schooling, and the like. In this respect, one should bear in mind that this article addresses the problems of formulating and evaluating the city's long-range financial decisions. The longer the range, the more elastic (presumably) the labor supply curve becomes. Workers may hang on for a year or two, or even five; but whether they will persist in the face of a lower real wage for 20 years is doubtful. (See, for an illustration, Exhibit 4.1.)

## The Tax Burden

The competitive nature of the markets for goods and labor has important implications for the city's power to tax. It will prevent employers operating in the city from shifting any part of a tax burden imposed on them by the city forward onto export customers, or backward onto import suppliers. Conversely, if the city imposes sales taxes that raise the price of goods purchased by labor, then employers must raise wages until labor's real income is once again competitive. The same is obviously true for city income taxes. Any tax—income or sales—on an export industry or its employees will tend ultimately to be absorbed by the owners of the industry.

But what about those service enterprises that sell only to local citizens, hence don't have to face the competitive pressures of export markets? The prices those industries charge affect citizens' real wages. The higher the prices, the more both export and local service industries will have to pay their employees. A tax burden imposed on local service enterprises will be distributed between both export and local service enterprises in a way that cannot be determined without reference to specifics, but whether the burden falls on the former or the latter, sales and income taxes tending to reduce the real income of labor in the service industries are ultimately shifted to the owners of capital.

If the notion of "capital investment" is broadened to include vacant lots, it is distinguishable from "real estate" only insofar as "capital investment" includes such portable capital goods as trucks and machine tools. Real property is virtually coextensive with that portion of a city's economic wealth that cannot escape the city's taxes, and it includes residential, commercial, and industrial buildings—which is to say, all fixed capital investment in both export and service industries.

## Optimal Taxing and Pricing

We will assume that a city's policies for setting taxes and prices for municipal services are optimal in the sense of maximizing the aggregate rents on real property. There is, of course, a rich and important branch of municipal finance dealing with the pricing of municipal services. In general, changes in the prices of these services can profoundly influence the welfare of a city's inhabitants and, of course, the level of rents on its real property. But the prices of municipal services should not be raised merely because the city happens to need more money, or lowered because it happens to need less.

Under the assumptions of optimal pricing and taxing, all municipal taxes—in whatever form—ultimately amount to taxes on land rents. The only distinction between real estate and other municipal taxes is that the owner will subtract the former from his gross rents in reckoning the value of the property to him, whereas the other taxes diminish the gross rents (in the ways discussed above). For simplicity, it will be convenient to treat all taxes as leaving gross rents unaffected—like real estate taxes. Thus changing the level of taxes leaves gross rents—and the allocation of resources—unchanged, so that our rent figures will always measure economic scarcity value, separated from any question of tax policy.

## No Free Lunch

The "no free lunch" (NFL) property of efficient capital markets states that the value of the sum of two or more future cash flow streams (i.e., the future cash flow stream that results from summing the individual flows, period by period) is the sum of the market values of the individual streams. This property applies independently of the risk character of the flows. In particular, it applies when some of the flows are certain and some are uncertain.

The NFL property implies that no market value gain will result from a merger of two companies, absent synergy affecting the combined flows. It implies that, disregarding tax effects, the gross market value of a firm will be independent of how claims on the firm are divided between debt and equity.[2] In short, it is merely an expression of John Burr Williams' celebrated Conservation of Value Principle.[3]

## THE VALUE OF A CITY

The appendix to this chapter applies this general property of efficient capital markets to cities characterized by the following assumptions:[4]

1. Property is valued net of taxes. In particular, future changes in taxes are fully anticipated in property values.

2. If the city remains solvent, it will meet its obligations sooner or later. Thus future tax revenues will be absorbed either in meeting operating expenses or in servicing debt, so they must be large enough to cover both.

3. Any refinancing of municipal obligations will not reduce their present value.

4. Lenders to the city will balk when the value of the city's gross aggregate cash flow before transactions with lenders (including debt service) no longer exceeds the value of its outstanding debt. The aggregate flow contemplated here is the aggregation of the (explicit or imputed) rental streams on individual properties subject to the city's taxing power less the stream of future expenditures (excluding debt service) required to operate the city—e.g., to pay policemen, firemen, teachers, and so forth. Without some minimal level of these expenditures, of course, the city would cease to function and the value of taxable property would collapse. Because such a collapse is not in the interest of lenders, the aggregate rents subject to the city's taxing power overstate the cash stream available to secure their loans. This assumption merely says that lenders will balk when the value of debt outstanding threatens to exceed the value of their underlying security.

5. The individual property owner will abandon his property when the stream of future taxes is heavy enough to drive the value of his property to zero, or below. In other words, if the owner can increase his net wealth by abandoning his property, he will do so.

For any city characterized by these assumptions, we can make two statements about the aggregate market value of the real property subject to its taxing power. (1) It equals the present value of the future rental streams of taxable property less the value of the municipal burden—the stream of future expenditures necessary to operate the city plus the cash flow stream required to service outstanding debt. (It would not, of course, be possible to talk about the first stream independently of the city's taxing policy, were it not for the assumption, previously noted, that rents are unaffected by taxes and other fees for municipal services.) (2) It equals the value of the city as security for further borrowing, hence the city's resources for further spending. If the city's financial goal is consequently maximizing the aggregate value of taxable property, the interest rate on the city's bonds will rarely, if ever, be the proper discount rate for computing the gain or loss from municipal projects. Capital asset pricing theory suggests that the effective discount rates implicit in the values of contractual and noncontractual cash flow streams will not in general be the same, since the latter cash stream will often have a substantial element of systematic risk.

These statements tell us that future city expenditures have a direct impact on the market value of private property, regardless of how they are financed. Municipal expenditures alleged to benefit the city economically do so if and only if they increase the value of the city's private property.

The second statement tells us how much the city can increase its debt before exhausting its borrowing power, provided that expending its proceeds buys the city nothing in terms of an increase in property rental or a decrease in its cost of operations. It is thus the fundamental measure of the city's financial resources.

It is in principle possible for a city to drive the market value of some parcels to zero, while taxing others only lightly. Since it is in the city's interest to avoid forcing abandonment of any property as long as possible, however, its taxing policy is not efficient unless it reduces the market value of all taxable parcels to zero simultaneously. In this case, the market value of every parcel will be positive whenever the aggregate market value is positive. Conversely, when the aggregate market value equals zero, the city has exhausted both its power to raise taxes and its power to borrow in general obligations.

## Eleemosynary Spending

We are not arguing that every urban decision should be guided exclusively by the financial criterion, or that eleemosynary functions are inappropriate to a city. But a city's financial resources are limited. Allocation of limited resources among a number of projects can be made rationally only if the demands of each project on these scarce resources are measured.

A great many urban projects with no specific eleemosynary features are undertaken in the name of urban improvement. If measured according to the criterion proposed here, grievously expensive subway lines, bridges and roads that could not justify themselves in terms of their net impact on aggregate real estate values would not be undertaken.

## IMPLICATIONS FOR BOND QUALITY

What does all this imply for the investor in municipal obligations? What does it have to do with bond quality? The main implication is that the fundamental criterion for the municipal bond investor is not *willingness* to pay—as measured by the current level of urban taxes—but *ability* to pay. In measuring this ability, the aggregate market value of the city's taxable real estate plays a role in municipal finance analogous to equity in the private corporation. The level of the city's taxes merely says something about *when* the city is going to pay off its financial obligations, without saying anything about *whether* it has the ability. A change in current tax rates changes the "when," but has no effect on the "whether."

Investment risk for the holder of municipal obligations arises because the market value of municipalities' underlying real estate assets—like the value of other real assets—is subject to unpredictable fluctuations. Black and Scholes have explained how the market value of the debt claims on a corporation will vary with variations in the value of the corporate assets.[5] A curve tracing the functional dependence between the equilibrium value of an option and the current value of the underlying asset plays a central role in their theory.

There is an exact analogy between the application of the Black-Scholes option curve to corporate obligations and its application to municipal obligations. In the application of that curve to municipal bonds, the aggregate market value of the city's real estate plays, as previously noted, a role strictly analogous to corporate equity in their discussion of corporate debt. For every possible value of the underlying real assets, there will be a unique equilibrium value for the municipality's general obligations. When one uses the Black-Scholes curve to estimate this value, no reference to bond ratings is necessary. There is no longer anything "qualitative" about the quality of municipal bonds.

# APPENDIX 4.1

## The "No Free Lunch" Property

Let small letters represent future (generally uncertain) cash flows; let the tilde over a small letter represent a stream of cash flows over time; and let V() represent the present value of the (vector) argument inside the parentheses. Then, for any constants $\alpha$ and $\beta$, the "no free lunch" (NFL) property can be expressed as:

$$V(\alpha \tilde{x} + \beta \tilde{y}) = \alpha V(\tilde{x}) + \beta V(\tilde{y})$$

The NFL property is applied to cities characterized by the following assumptions.

## Assumptions

The following definitions are used:

$\tilde{t}_i$ = the (in general, uncertain) stream of future taxes on the ith parcel of real property,

$\tilde{y}_i$ = the future stream of gross rents to be generated by the ith parcel,

$\tilde{u}$ = the future stream of out-of-pocket expenditures required to operate the city (excluding debt service) and,

$\tilde{d}$ = the future stream of payments required to service the city's outstanding debt (interest and principal).

Note that $\tilde{t}$, $\tilde{y}$, $\tilde{u}$ and $\tilde{d}$ are all vectors, with individual components corresponding to future points in time.

Investors in the real estate market value property net of taxes; hence, for the ith parcel we have:

$$V_i = V(\tilde{y}_i + \tilde{t}_i) \tag{4.1}$$

We also assume that if the city remains solvent, sooner or later it must levy enough taxes to meet its obligations, so:

$$\Sigma_i \tilde{t}_i = \tilde{u} + \tilde{d} \tag{4.2}$$

This assumption merely says that future tax revenues will be absorbed in one of two ways—meeting operating expenses or servicing debt—and that ultimately (which is to say, in present value terms), the stream of tax revenues must be large enough to cover both.

Any refinancing of municipal obligations replacing $\tilde{d}$ by, say, $\tilde{d}^1$ has the property that:

$$V(\tilde{d}^1) \geq V(\tilde{d}) \tag{4.3}$$

In other words, refinancing will not reduce the present value of the city's debt burden. (V(d) should, of course, be reckoned net of the cash flow consequences of any assets owned by the city.)

Lenders to the city will balk when or before:

$$V(\tilde{d}) \geq V(\Sigma_i \tilde{y}_i - \tilde{u}) \qquad (4.4)$$

The argument on the right-hand side is the city's aggregate cash flow before capital transactions (including debt service). The present value of this cash flow measures the gross value of the city as security for lenders. The left-hand side is, of course, the market value of the city's outstanding debt. Assumption 4.4 says merely that lenders will balk when the value of the outstanding debt threatens to exceed the value of their underlying security.

Finally, the taxpayer will abandon property i when:

$$V(\tilde{y}_i - \tilde{t}_i) \leq 0 \qquad (4.5)$$

which is to say, when taxes on his property are heavy enough to drive its market value to zero or below.

## Proof

Applying the NFL property to 4.1, we have for the market value of the ith parcel:

$$V_i = V(\tilde{y}_i - \tilde{t}_i) = V(\tilde{y}_i) - V(\tilde{t}_i) \qquad (4.6)$$

Summing over the city's taxable property, we have:

$$\Sigma_i V_i = \Sigma_i V(\tilde{y}_i) - \Sigma_i V(\tilde{t}_i) \qquad (4.7)$$

Applying the NFL property to 4.7, we have:

$$\Sigma_i V_i = V(\Sigma_i \tilde{y}_i) - V(\Sigma_i \tilde{t}_i) \qquad (4.8)$$

Substituting from 4.2 and applying the NFL property again, we have:

$$\Sigma_i V_i = V(\Sigma_i \tilde{y}_i) - V(\tilde{u} + \tilde{d})$$
$$= V(-\tilde{u} + \Sigma_i \tilde{y}_i) - V(\tilde{d}) \qquad (4.9)$$

The left-hand member $\Sigma_i V_i$ is the aggregate market value of the city's real estate. As noted in 4.4, the term $V(-\tilde{u} + \Sigma_i y_i)$ is the value of the city as security—the net cash stream generated from operations of the city taken as a whole, with private and public activities lumped together. The term $V(\tilde{d})$ is the value of the city's outstanding debt, which under Assumption 4.3 cannot be reduced by refinancing. It follows from 4.4 that the city's borrowing power is exhausted when the former approaches the latter. But equation 4.9 says that, when these terms are equal, the aggregate value of the city's real property will be zero. The measure of the city's remaining borrowing power is the aggregate market value of its real estate.

On the other hand, 4.5 says that taxpayer i will abandon his property when:

$$V_i = V(\tilde{y}_i - \tilde{t}_i) \leq 0$$

Equation 4.9 is, of course, a statement about aggregates, whereas 4.5 is a statement about the individual real estate parcel. The text notes that a city is taxing inefficiently unless it distributes the burden in such a way that the market value of all taxable property is driven to zero at the same time. When the above equation is satisfied for every property, however, we have:

$$\Sigma_i V_i = 0$$

hence the right-hand member of 4.9 must be zero. At this point—in other words, a wholesale property abandonment—the city exhausts its power to borrow. In this sense, the city exhausts its power to tax and to borrow at the same time.

## Notes

1. Jane Jacobs, *The Economy of Cities* (New York: Vintage Books, 1970).
2. Franco Modigliani and Merton Miller, "The Cost of Capital, Corporation Finance and the Theory of Investment," *The American Economic Review*, June 1958.
3. John Burr Williams, *The Theory of Investment Value* (Cambridge: Harvard University Press, 1938).
4. Our use of the "no free lunch" property does not imply that we think capital markets are perfectly efficient. Rather, we think that those who make municipal decisions and those who assess the quality of municipal obligations would be well advised to avoid assuming actual capital markets depart from efficiency in any systematic way that can be reliably forecast.
5. Fischer Black and Myron Scholes, "The Valuation of Option Contracts and a Test of Market Efficiency," *Journal of Finance*, May 1972.

# CHAPTER 5

# Time Diversification

*To maintain constant dollar risk, an investor concerned with his terminal wealth must sell when the stock market rises and buy when it falls. Although an asset with constant dollar risk doesn't exist in nature, it can be approximated with actual investment positions.*

**M**any investors are primarily concerned with their wealth at the end of their careers. Yet most of our theory is concerned with the current year's investment choices. How does each year's investment result affect the investor's terminal wealth? How do the gains and losses from the early years interact with the gains and losses from the later years? In particular, do they add or multiply?

## A PARABLE

Suppose you personally had the following experience:

At the beginning of a 50-year investment career, you borrowed $1.00 and invested it. Fifty years later, you pay off the loan. Assume the riskless rate of return is zero.

Over 50 years, the borrowed dollar appreciated to $117.39. So the accounting at the end of your career is

| | |
|---|---|
| Gross wealth | $117.39 |
| Pay off loan | $1.00 |
| Net wealth | $116.39 |

Now, suppose that instead of borrowing you received a $1.00 bequest from your late, lamented Aunt Matilda. Then, you could account for the terminal impact of the bequest as follows:

| | |
|---|---|
| Net wealth with own dollar | $117.39 |
| Net wealth with borrowed dollar | $116.39 |
| Terminal impact of inheritance | $1.00 |

If you took the same dollar investment risk with or without the bequest, your terminal wealth differed by the original dollar, appreciated at the riskless rate of zero.

---

Reprinted from the *Journal of Investment Management*, Vol.1, No. 3 (2003).

Was the dollar worth $117.39 50 years later? Or merely $1? If the latter, then the remaining $116.39 was the reward for taking 50 years of risk.

As the parable suggests, it is not obvious how their wealth and risk-taking interact to determine the investors' wealth at retirement.
Let

$u$ = market's rate of return
$v$ = investor's rate of return
$r$ = riskless rate
$h$ = dollars currently invested
$w$ = initial wealth
$\beta$ = level of relative (systematic) risk
$h\beta$ = level of dollar (systematic) risk

If $u$ and $v$ are rates of return, then $u - r$ and $v - r$ are rates of *excess* return—rates of return to risk taking. For a perfectly diversified asset, beta ($\beta$) is of course the ratio of its excess return to the market's excess return. In other words

$$\beta = \frac{v - r}{u - r}$$

Transposing, we have the so-called "market model":

$$v - r = \beta(u - r)$$

$$v = \beta(u - r) + r$$

The dollar gain or loss to an investor who invests an amount $h$ in the risky asset is

$$hv = h\beta\,(u - r) + hr$$

If he had wealth $w$, then his dollar investment in the riskless asset was

$$w - h$$

for a riskless gain of

$$r\,(w - h)$$

and a total dollar gain/loss of

$$h\beta\,(u - r) + hr + wr - hr = h\beta\,(u - r) + wr$$

We see that the investor's dollar gain or loss consists of two terms: One that does not depend on his risk and one that does not depend on his wealth.


## THE BUY-AND-HOLD INVESTOR

Many finance scholars (Ibbotson-Sinquefield; Cornell; Dimson, Marsh and Staunton) believe the risk in the US stock market's rate of return is roughly stationary across time. At the end of this paper, we offer some evidence. But of course if the risk in rate of return is stationary, then the dollar risk is proportional to the market level.

Now consider a buy-and-hold investor, who invests his/her wealth in the stock market and then lets it ride as the market level fluctuates: He/she will experience constant relative risk. But this means that the *dollar* risk—the risk of his/her dollar gain or loss from the market's excess return—will fluctuate with his/her wealth.

Buy-and-hold investors do not lever. If they did, they would be constantly buying and selling in order to offset the effects of market fluctuations on their desired leverage. But when the market level fluctuates, the beta of a diversified asset does not change. So, for buy-and-hold investors, the only thing that changes is the value of their portfolio. Over a short time period (a year, say) the market model holds: Investors get the riskless return on their current wealth, plus a risky excess return equal to their constant beta times their current wealth times the excess return on the market. Restating the model in terms of the investor's wealth at times $t$ and $t - 1$ we have

$$W_t - W_{t-1} = h_t \beta_t (u_t - r) + r\, W_{t-1}$$
$$W_t = h_t \beta_t (u_t - r) + (1 + r)\, W_{t-1}$$

Under constant relative risk, each period's exposure to stock market risk is proportional to that period's beginning wealth. We then have

$$W_t = W_{t-1} \beta (u_t - r) + (1 + r)\, W_{t-1}$$
$$W_t = W_{t-1} [\beta (u_t - r) + (1 + r)]$$

Letting

$$q_t = \beta (u_t - r) + (1 + r)$$

we have

$$W_t = W_{t-1} q_t, \qquad W_{t-1} = W_{t-2} q_{t-1}$$
$$W_t = q_t q_{t-1} W_{t-2}$$
$$W_T = q_T q_{T-1} \cdots q_1 W_0$$

Under buy-and-hold investing, the growth factors for the individual years multiply. So a bad year—a 40 percent loss, say, in any one year—means a 40 percent loss in terminal wealth.

When the market level is high investors, being richer, feel more able to bear the higher dollar risk. So, they may feel comfortable focusing on relative risk. But this special case tends to obscure the more general truth that terminal wealth depends on the dollar gains and losses in the individual years of the investor's career.

## TIME DIVERSIFICATION

We had for the general case

$$W_t - W_{t-1} = h_t \beta_t (u_t - r) + r\, W_{t-1}$$

Gains or losses from past risk-taking affect this year's beginning wealth. But it appreciates at the riskless rate. This year's reward to risk depends only on this year's risk.

Let the dollar gain or loss from risk taking in year $t$ be

$$z_t = h_t \beta_t (u_t - r)$$

Then, the investor's wealth $W_T$ satisfies

$$W_t - W_{t-1} = z_t + r\, W_{t-1}$$

$$W_t = z_t + (1+r)\, W_{t-1}$$

$$W_{t-1} = z_{t-1} + (1+r)\, W_{t-2}$$

$$\vdots$$

$$W_1 = z_1 + (1+r)\, W_0$$

The terminal wealth $W_T$ equals

$$z_T + (1+r)\, z_{T-1} + (1+r)^2\, z_{T-2} + \cdots + (1+r)^T\, W_0$$

Let $Z_t$ be the gain or loss in year $t$ on investing \$1.00 in the stock market. Then, we have

$$z_t = h_t \beta_t Z_t$$

Unless he plans to market time, the investor will want each of the individual years to have the same potential impact on his terminal wealth "portfolio." Optimal balance requires

$$W_T - W_0 (1+r)^T = \sum_0^T (1+r)^{T-t} h_t \beta_t Z_t = \sum_0^T Z_t$$

In order to have the same dollar impact on terminal wealth, each year's $Z$ must have the same weight. But, unless the riskless rate of return $r$ is zero, the terminal impact of one year's gain or loss depends on the time lag separating it from the terminal year. In order for each of the $Z_t$, with presumably equal risks, to have the same potential impact on the risky portion of the investor's terminal wealth (the expression on right-hand side), the current-dollar risk $h_i B_t$ must vary enough over time to offset this effect. So, we have

$$h_t \beta_t = \frac{1}{(1+r)^{T-t}} = (1+r)^{t-T}$$

Note that, if the effective riskless rate is positive, the investor's dollar risk $h_t \beta_t$ should actually increase as he ages.[1]

We have seen that for the buy-and-hold investor there is no such thing as time diversification. But, if investors make whatever trades are necessary to sever next year's bet from last year's outcome, then their gains and losses from each individual year add (algebraically) rather than multiply. Impacts from the individual years on their terminal wealth are

1. Cross sectionally diversified, so that all their risk bearing is fully compensated (under the CAPM);
2. Mutually uncorrelated.

Unless investors are rash enough to predict that the prospects for next year are different from the prospects for last year, they should be making roughly the same dollar bet on both years. In order to do so, however, they will need to sell every time the market rises and buy every time it falls. They will need to do a lot of buying and selling.

On the one hand, the potential for time diversification is there, even if the buy-and-hold investor cannot realize it. On the other, the cost of trading back to a constant level of dollar risk every time the stock market rises or falls may be daunting. Is this why hardly anyone has tried time diversification?

## RISK AND REWARD

Consider one year's rate of return on the US stock market. It has a certain distribution, with a certain standard deviation and a certain mean. Even if that distribution is indeed roughly stationary across time, we can measure only the actual rates of return for past years. The investors' probability of terminal loss—of arriving at the end of their career with less wealth than they started out with—depends on both the market risk and the market premium, the expected reward for taking this risk. Because its error can be reduced by subdividing the time sample more finely, estimating the standard deviation is not a problem. Dimson and his co-authors of *The Millenium Book*[2] estimate real annual rates of return on the market at 20.3 percent and 20.1 percent for the United States and United Kingdom, respectively.

But sample error is a potential problem for estimates of the mean. Take the authors' 100 year sample: The standard deviation of the sample mean is

$$\frac{0.20}{\sqrt{100}} = \frac{0.20}{10} = 0.02$$

**EXHIBIT 5.1**  Terminal Reward versus Terminal Risk*

| Career length | Market premium per year | | | |
|---|---|---|---|---|
| | 0.04 | 0.05 | 0.06 | 0.07 |
| 16 | 0.64 | 0.80 | 0.96 | 1.12 |
| 25 | 1.00 | 1.25 | 1.50 | 1.75 |
| 36 | 1.44 | 1.80 | 2.16 | 2.52 |
| 49 | 1.96 | 2.45 | 2.94 | 3.43 |
| 64 | 2.56 | 3.20 | 3.84 | 4.48 |

Standard deviation of terminal wealth

| Career length | 0.04 | 0.05 | 0.06 | 0.07 |
|---|---|---|---|---|
| 16 | 0.80 | 0.80 | 0.80 | 0.80 |
| 25 | 1.00 | 1.00 | 1.00 | 1.00 |
| 36 | 1.20 | 1.20 | 1.20 | 1.20 |
| 49 | 1.40 | 1.40 | 1.40 | 1.40 |
| 64 | 1.60 | 1.60 | 1.60 | 1.60 |

Expected career gain/standard deviation of terminal risk

| Career length | 0.04 | 0.05 | 0.06 | 0.07 |
|---|---|---|---|---|
| 16 | 0.80 | 1.00 | 1.20 | 1.40 |
| 25 | 1.00 | 1.25 | 1.50 | 1.75 |
| 36 | 1.20 | 1.50 | 1.80 | 2.10 |
| 49 | 1.40 | 1.75 | 2.10 | 2.45 |
| 64 | 1.60 | 2.00 | 2.40 | 2.80 |

*Expected dollar gain over career for a lifetime risk equivalent to one "terminal dollar."

The Central Limit Theorem applies to the dispersion of means of randomly drawn samples. There is roughly one chance in three that when a normally distributed sample mean is 0.06 (6 percent), the true universe mean is less than 0.04 or more than 0.08. Although they can benefit greatly from reflecting on Dimson's numbers, we think investors have to make their own judgment about the market premium. Accordingly, we include in Exhibit 5.1 a range of market premiums, as well as a range of possible career lengths.

## TERMINAL DOLLARS

The terminal impact of the dollar gains and losses of particular years depends on the riskless interest rate. Unless investors' riskless rates are zero, a current dollar corresponds to a different number of terminal dollars, depending their age. But if they are time diversifying, then they want their potential gains and losses at different ages to have the same terminal impact. So it is useful for them to measure their current risk in terms of what it represents for their terminal wealth—to measure their current risk in terminal dollars. Then, they can time diversify by maintaining a fixed number

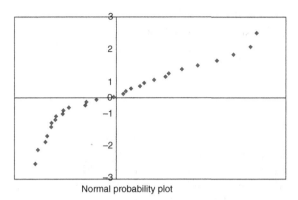

Normal probability plot

**EXHIBIT 5.2**　Rate of Return on U.S. Market
1971–2000

of "terminal dollars" worth of current risk. In Exhibit 5.1, for example, the expected gains and associated risks are expressed in terms of one dollar of terminal risk.

The first two panels in Exhibit 5.1 sum up market premium and market risk across investment careers varying from 16 to 64 years. Then, the third panel computes ratios of terminal reward to terminal risk. This is done for a range of assumptions about the hard-to-measure market premium.

The risk that investors will be worse off at the end of their career for having taken stock market risk depends on this ratio. If terminal risks are normally distributed, for example, that probability is 0.0036—three chances in 1000—for the most favorable case (a 64 year career length and a 7 percent risk premium).

Dimson estimates the real riskless rate at 1.2 percent per annum for the century 1900–2000. It is curious that this number is in the range of what many mutual funds charge shareholders. The effective rate for the time-diversifying investor should also allow for trading costs and taxes. But we defer further discussion until we get to inflation.

## CONSTANT DOLLAR RISK

Is there such a thing as a financial asset with constant dollar risk? Such an asset would permit the investor who owned it to achieve time diversification without trading.

All commercial risk measurement services focus on *relative* risk—surprise in an asset's value, divided by its beginning value. The only justification for such commercial measures is that the probability distribution of the ratio is stationary (see Exhibit 5.2). But then dispersion of the asset's dollar risk—surprise in its dollar value—fluctuates with fluctuations in the asset's value.

These comments apply to both individual common stocks and portfolios, including portfolios intended to proxy the value of the whole stock market. Let the stock market level—the value of the market portfolio—be $x$ and the value of an asset with constant dollar risk be $y$, and let $dx$ and $dy$ represent dollar surprise in $x$ and $y$, respectively. If both assets are completely diversified, then, the market level $x$ determines the value of $y$. Let the relation between the two values be

$$y = f(x)$$

We ask: What functional dependence of $y$ on $x$ translates the constant relative risk of $x$ into the desired constant dollar risk of $y$?

When the functional relation between $y$ and $x$ is such that, for all market levels, we have

$$dy = \frac{dx}{x}$$

The right-hand side is of course the rate of return on the market. As noted, many finance scholars believe its risk is stationary. The left-hand side and the right-hand side being equal, they will necessarily have the same probability distribution. In particular, if the right-hand side—the relative return on the stock market—is stationary across time, the left-hand side will also be stationary. But, whereas the right-hand side is the *relative* change in $x$—$dx$ divided by the level $x$—the left-hand side $dy$ is the *dollar* change in $y$. So if, as the market level $x$ fluctuates, its relative risk is truly stationary, then the dollar risk in $y$ is also stationary.

If we take indefinite integrals of both sides, we have

$$y = \ln x + \ln k$$

where $\ln k$ is a constant of integration, or

$$y = \ln kx$$

The asset with constant dollar risk is the asset whose value varies with the logarithm of the market level.

## INFLATION

We do not have the option of investing in the real market level. The values of the market and our log approximation are nominal values. But the risk we want to maintain constant over time—as the price level changes—is the *real* risk. If, as we have argued, the risk in nominal market return is stationary, then the risk of nominal dollar gains and losses in the log portfolio is also stationary. But this means that if, for example, the price level is rising, then the risk of real dollar gains and losses is falling.

Let $x$ be the nominal market level and $y$ be the nominal value of a portfolio that varies with the logarithm of the market level, and let the respective real values be $x'$ and $y'$, where the price level is $p$. We have

$$x' = \frac{x}{p}, \quad y' = \frac{y}{p}$$

For investment surprises we have

$$dx' = \frac{dx}{p}, \quad dy' = \frac{dy}{p}$$

The logarithmic portfolio is defined by a relation between nominals

$$dy = \frac{dx}{x}$$

Substituting, we have

$$pdy' = \frac{pdx'}{px'} = \frac{dx'}{x'}$$

We see that, if surprise in the rate of return on the real market level is stationary, surprise in the nominal rate of return will also be stationary.[3] But if surprise in the nominal value of the logarithmic portfolio is stationary, surprise in its real value

$$dy' = \frac{dy'}{p}$$

will not be. This means that if, for example, the price level is rising over the investors' career, the real risk in their logarithmic portfolio is falling.

Consider, first, the case where the real riskless rate of interest is zero. To offset the effect of inflation, investment positions in recent years in the investor's career should be rescaled relative to early years, with the rescaling from year to year equaling that year's inflation rate.

Then, consider the case where inflation is not a problem but the riskless interest rate is positive rather than zero. Then, investment positions in recent years should be rescaled relative to early years, with the rescaling from year to year being equal to the riskless interest rate.

We see that inflation causes the late nominal gain/loss to have less impact than an early gain/loss and the same is true for the real riskless rate. On the other hand, management fees, trading costs and taxes cause an early gain/loss to have less impact on terminal wealth than a late gain/loss. So, their annual rate of attrition subtracts from the sum of the real rate and the inflation rate—from the nominal interest rate. If the gain from trading just offsets management fees and the portfolio is not subject to taxes, the terminal impact of a current dollar of nominal gain or less will appreciate at the nominal interest rate.

## AN APPROXIMATION

The logarithmic asset is probably not available in today's security markets. But it can readily be approximated using assets that are. Consider the following Taylor series expansion of the logarithmic function, where $a$ is greater than zero:

$$\ln \frac{x}{a} = \left(\frac{x-a}{a}\right) - \frac{1}{2}\left(\frac{x-a}{a}\right)^2 + \frac{1}{3}\left(\frac{x-a}{a}\right)^3 - \cdots$$

Although the accuracy of the approximation increases with the number of terms retained in the series,[4] we retain only the first two. Expanding these terms we have

$$\ln\left(\frac{x}{a}\right) \approx 2\left(\frac{x}{a}\right) - \frac{1}{2}\left(\frac{x}{a}\right)^2 - \frac{3}{2}$$

The investor who seeks time diversification is actually concerned with the corresponding risks. How well does the risk of the right-hand side approximate the risk of the left-hand side? The dollar risk on both sides depends on a product. One factor in the product is the rate of change with respect to the market level $x$. We have for the respective sides

$$\frac{d}{dx}\ln\left(\frac{x}{a}\right) = \frac{1}{a}\left(\frac{1}{x/a}\right) = \frac{1}{x} \approx \frac{1}{a}\left(2 - \frac{x}{a}\right)$$

The other factor in both products is the dollar risk in $x$. But if $dx/x$ is stationary, then the dollar risk in $x$ is proportional to the (known, nonrisky) value of $x$.

If we invest in the approximation portfolio when $x$ equals $a$, then, the above rate of change is $1/a$ for both the logarithmic portfolio and the approximation. But the risk in the approximation drifts away from the log portfolio as the market level $x$ moves away from $a$.

## THE ROLE OF BETA

We have noted that beta is a measure of how much an asset's value changes when the general market level changes—that, specifically, it is the ratio of two rates of excess return. Define $x$ as the market level, $y$ as the (fully diversified) asset's value and level of relative risk by the Greek letter $\beta$. Then, we have

$$\frac{dy/y}{dx/x} = \beta,$$

$$\frac{dy}{y} = \beta\frac{dx}{x}$$

Taking the indefinite integral, we have

$$\ln y = \beta \ln x + \ln k$$

where in $k$ is a constant of integration. Taking antilogs we have

$$y = kx^\beta$$

We see that a diversified asset's value is linked to the market level by a power that equals its beta. Our truncated Taylor series approximation to the logarithmic function of the market level contains two powers of the market level $x$. Evidently, the terms containing these powers correspond to investment positions in diversified assets with betas of 1 and 2.

## ACCURACY OF THE APPROXIMATION

How bad are the errors in the approximation portfolio? Let

$$
\begin{aligned}
a &= \text{beginning market level} \\
x &= \text{market level at the end of the year} \\
dx &= \text{change in market level} \\
\sigma_{dx} &= \text{standard deviation of change} \\
y &= \text{value of approximation portfolio} \\
dy &= \text{change in value of approximation} \\
\sigma_{dy} &= \text{standard deviation of change}
\end{aligned}
$$

As noted, its dollar risk is the product of its rate of change with respect to the market and the dollar risk in the market. The first column in Exhibit 5.3 displays a range of possible ratios of the ending market level $x$ to the beginning market level $a$. The second column shows the resulting new market levels. The third column shows the standard deviation of the market's dollar risk for the following year—assuming its relative risk, the standard deviation of its rate of return, is still 20 percent.

The fourth column shows the rate of change of the approximation portfolio with respect to change in the stock market level. The fifth column is the product of the third and fourth columns. Because the third column measures dollar risk in the market level, and the fourth column measures its rate of change with respect to that level, the fifth column measures dollar risk in the approximation portfolio.

The dollar risk in the ideal, logarithmic portfolio is 20 percent of the initial market level $a$, no matter what the subsequent change in market level. But the approximation is imperfect. The fifth column shows how its dollar risk drifts progressively farther from the correct, constant value as the new market level $x$ moves away from

**EXHIBIT 5.3**   Approximation Errors

| $x/a$ | $x$ | $\sigma_{dx}$ | $dy/dx$ | $\sigma_{dy}$ | % Error |
|---|---|---|---|---|---|
| 1.30 | 1.30$a$ | 0.26$a$ | 0.70/$a$ | 0.1820 | 9.00 |
| 1.25 | 1.25$a$ | 0.25$a$ | 0.75/$a$ | 0.1875 | 6.25 |
| 1.20 | 1.20$a$ | 0.24$a$ | 0.80/$a$ | 0.1920 | 4.00 |
| 1.15 | 1.15$a$ | 0.23$a$ | 0.85/$a$ | 0.1955 | 2.25 |
| 1.10 | 1.10$a$ | 0.22$a$ | 0.90/$a$ | 0.1980 | 1.00 |
| 1.05 | 1.05$a$ | 0.21$a$ | 0.95/$a$ | 0.1995 | 0.25 |
| 1.00 | 1.00$a$ | 0.20$a$ | 1.00/$a$ | 0.2000 | 0.00 |
| 0.95 | 0.95$a$ | 0.19$a$ | 1.05/$a$ | 0.1995 | 0.25 |
| 0.90 | 0.90$a$ | 0.18$a$ | 1.10/$a$ | 0.1980 | 1.00 |
| 0.85 | 0.85$a$ | 0.17$a$ | 1.15/$a$ | 0.1955 | 2.25 |
| 0.80 | 0.80$a$ | 0.16$a$ | 1.20/$a$ | 0.1920 | 4.00 |
| 0.75 | 0.74$a$ | 0.15$a$ | 1.25/$a$ | 0.1875 | 6.25 |
| 0.70 | 0.70$a$ | 0.14$a$ | 1.30/$a$ | 0.1820 | 9.00 |

the beginning level *a*. (It may be worth noting, however, that the dollar risk of the approximation portfolio is always less than or equal to the correct value.) The sixth column expresses the errors as percentages of the correct dollar risk.

Exhibit 5.3 shows that a 20 percent move up or down in the market level changes the dollar risk in the approximation portfolio by only 4 percent. To trade back to constant dollar risk every time their portfolio changed 4 percent, conventional investors would have to trade

$$\left(\frac{0.20}{0.04}\right)^2 - 5^2 = 25$$

that is, 25 times as often. (If the dispersion of random fluctuations over a time interval varies with the square root of its length, the length of the time interval varies with the square of the stipulated dispersion.) Is this why conventional investors do not attempt to time diversify?

## REBALANCING

We have seen that, when the market has moved up or down one standard deviation, or 20 percent, the new standard deviation for the approximation portfolio is no longer 20 percent of the original dollar investment, but merely 18.2 percent. (Roughly one year in three, the market moves more than 20 percent.) When the market level *x* moves away from the "beginning" level *a*, two things happen:

1. The approximation breaks down as the risky positions' 4:1 ratio breaks down.
2. The scale, or magnitude, of net risk moves away from beginning net risk.

There are many combinations of the two risky positions that will satisfy the 4:1 condition and, hence, restore the logarithmic character of the portfolio. Also, there are many combinations that will restore the original net risk. But one, and only one, combination of the two positions can satisfy both conditions. If the investor changes the "beginning" market level *a* in this ratio to the current market level *x*, the ratio reverts to its original value of 1. But when the values of the risky positions were based on a ratio value of 1, they

1. Were in the accurate 4:1 ratio
2. Had the desired level of net dollar risk that the investors wanted to maintain over their lifetime

What the new value of *a* does not do is retain the same net investment in the two risky positions they had before we changed the ratio back to 1. This is where the third, constant, "riskless" term in the Taylor series formula comes in: When we are making the trades in the risky assets dictated by the change in the ratio, these trades free up or absorb cash, which then flows to or from the third, riskless, position. (Obviously, changes in the value of the riskless position do not change the portfolio's risk[5] so if, after these trades, the risky positions have the correct risk, so has the portfolio.)

**EXHIBIT 5.4**  Calculations for Approximation Portfolio 1977–2000 (see text)

| Year | U.S. market index | |
|---|---|---|
| 1977 | 169 | |
| 1979 | 179 | $179/169 = 1.0592,\ 1.0592^2 = 1.1218;\ 2(1059) - 1/2(1122);\ 2118 - 561 = 1557;\ 1557 - 1500 = 57$ |
| 1980 | 210 | $210/169 = 1.243,\ 1.243^2 = 1.544;\ 2(1243) -1/2\,(1544);\ 2486 - 772 = 1714,\ 1714 - 1500 = 214$ |
| 1981 | 225 | $225/210 = 1.0714,\ 1.0714^2 = 1.1479;\ 2(1071) - 1/2(1148);\ 2142 - 574 = 1568,\ 1568 + 214 - 1500 = 282$ |
| 1982 | 208 | $208/210 = 0.990,\ 0.990^2 = 0.9810;\ 2(990) - 1/2(981);\ 1980 - 491 = 1489,\ 1489 + 214 - 1500 = 203$ |
| 1983 | 281 | $281/210 = 1.3381,\ 1.3381^2 = 1.7905;\ 2(1338) - 1/2(1790) = 2676 - 895 = 1781;\ 1781 + 214 - 1500 = 495$ |
| 1984 | 283 | $283/281 = 1.007,\ 1.007^2 = 1.014;2(1007) - 1/2\,(1014);\ 2014 - 507 = 1507,\ 1507 + 495 - 1500 = 502$ |
| 1985 | 324 | $324/281 = 1.1530,\ 1.1530^2 = 1.328;\ 2(1153) - 1/2\,(1328);\ 2306 - 665 = 1641,\ 1641 + 495 - 1500 = 636$ |
| 1986 | 409 | $409/281 = 1.456,\ 1.456^2 = 2.119;\ 2(1456) - 1/2\,(2119);\ 2912 - 1059 = 1853,\ 1853 + 495 - 1500 = 848$ |
| 1987 | 516 | $516/409 = 1.2616,\ 1.2616^2 = 1.5917;\ 2(1262) - 1/2\,(1592);\ 2524 - 796 = 1727,\ 1727 + 848 - 1500 = 1075$ |
| 1988 | 478 | $478/409 = 1.169,\ 1.169^2 = 1.366;\ 2(1169) - 1/2\,(1366);\ 2338 - 683 = 1655,\ 1655 + 848 - 1500 = 1003$ |
| 1989 | 577 | $577/409 = 1.411,\ 1.411^2 = 1.990;\ 2(1411) - 1/2\,(1990);\ 2822 - 995 +1827,\ 1827 + 848 - 1500 = 1175$ |
| 1990 | 609 | $609/577 = 1.0554,\ 1.0554^2 = 1.114;\ 2(1055) - 1/2(1114);\ 2110 - 557 = 1553,\ 1553 + 1175 - 1500 = 1228$ |
| 1991 | 695 | $695/609 = 1.141,\ 1.141^2 = 1.302;\ 2(1141) - 1/2(1302);\ 2282 - 651 = 1631,\ 1631 + 1228 - 1500 = 1359$ |
| 1992 | 765 | $765/695 = 1.1007,\ 1.1007^2 = 1.2116;\ 2(1101) - 1/2(1212);\ 2202 - 606 = 1596,\ 1596 + 1359 - 1500 = 1455$ |
| 1993 | 806 | $806/695 = 1.160,\ 1.160^2 = 1.345;\ 2(1160) - 1/2(1345);\ 2320 - 672 = 1648,\ 1648 + 1359 - 1500 = 1455$ |
| 1994 | 841 | $841/806 = 1.0434,\ 1.0434^2 = 1.0887;\ 2(1043) - 1/2(1088);\ 2086 - 544 = 1542,\ 1542 + 1507 - 1500 = 1549$ |
| 1995 | 1000 | $1000/841 = 1.189,\ 1.189^2 = 1.414;\ 2(1189) - 1/2(1414);\ 2378 - 707 = 1671,\ 1671 + 1549 - 1500 = 1720$ |
| 1996 | 1235 | $1235/1000 = 1.2350,\ 1.2350^2 = 1.5252;\ 2(1235) - 1/2(1525);\ 2470 - 763 = 1707,\ 1707 + 1720 - 1500 = 1927$ |
| 1997 | 1593 | $1593/1235 = 1.290,\ 1.290^2 = 1.664;\ 2(1290) - 1/2(1664);\ 2580 - 832 = 1748,\ 1748 + 1927 - 1500 = 2175$ |
| 1998 | 1987 | $1987/1593 = 1.2473,\ 1.2473^2 = 1.5558;\ 2(1247) - 1/2(1556);\ 2494 - 778 = 1716,\ 1716 + 2175 - 1500 = 2391$ |
| 1999 | 2513 | $2513/1987 = 1.2647,\ 1.2647^2 = 1.5995;\ 2(1265) - 1/2(1600);\ 2530 - 800 = 1730,\ 1730 + 2391 - 1500 = 2621$ |
| 2000 | 2728 | $2728/2513 = 1.0856,\ 1.0856^2 = 1.1784;\ 2(1086) - 1/2(1178);\ 2172 - 589 = 1583,\ 1583 + 2621 - 1500 = 2704$ |

In Exhibit 5.4, the beginning market level is arbitrarily set at 1000. Then, the long position is

$$2(1000) = 2000$$

and the short position is

$$\frac{1}{2}(1000) = 500$$

So, the net value of the two risky positions (the "risky equity") is then

$$2000 - 500 = 1500$$

Each rebalancing returns the risky equity to 1500. But offsetting transfers to or from the riskless asset preserve the investor's total equity.

Exhibit 5.4 shows how the approximation portfolio would have functioned using actual US stock market data for end-of-year levels from 1977 to 2000. Although, given the limited data, rebalancings could not be triggered by daily market closes, there were 11 rebalancings during this period.

Exhibit 5.4 devotes three stages of calculation (separated by semicolons in the third column) to each year (except 1978). For the current value of $a$, the first stage calculates the ratios $x/a$ and $(x/a)^2$. The second stage applies the coefficients in the approximation formula to the respective ratios, and then multiplies all three terms in the formula by 1000. (For example, the initial value of the riskless term becomes $-1500$.) The third stage calculates the new risky equity, and the change since the last rebalancing.

Rebalancing makes the third stage of calculation more complicated. Since each rebalancing wipes out the difference between the current risky equity and the original investment (in this example, 1500), the third stage also calculates the new value of the riskless asset, reflecting the cash freed up or absorbed in returning the risky positions to their original values.

The value of the approximation portfolio to the investor includes the net value of both his risky positions and the accumulating sum of these (algebraic) additions to the riskless asset. Thus, the three-stage entry for a rebalancing year reflects both the effect of rebalancing, which takes place at the beginning of that year, and the effect on the two risky positions of the subsequent change in market level between the beginning and the end.[6]


## THE EVIDENCE

The last three decades of the century included several painful market collapses as well as a celebrated bull market. The nominal market level increased 16 times, the real level four. Surely this period is a worthy test of whether

1. The risk in the market's rate of return is really stationary.
2. The dollar risk in the logarithmic portfolio is really stationary.

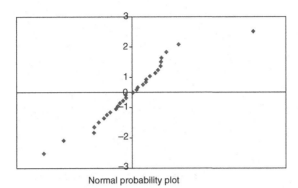

Normal probability plot

**EXHIBIT 5.5**  Year-to-Year Changes in the Dollar Value of a Portfolio that Varies with the Logarithm of the U.S. Market (1972–2000)

In order to test whether risks were stationary, we need to be able to measure *ex ante* risk *ex post*. Actuaries use a special kind of graph paper called "probability paper" to do this. Its vertical axis is conventional, with horizontal lines equally spaced. But its horizontal axis is variously compressed and stretched so that, when drawings from a normal sample are ranked from lowest to highest and then accorded equal probability increments (rather than equal distances) on that axis, they plot as a straight line. Depending on the chosen scale of the conventional vertical axis, the slope of that line reflects the sample's dispersion.

The point, of course, is that if the sample is drawn from a universe with different dispersions—if, across time, the risk is not stationary—then, the sample cannot plot as a straight line.

Were the two risks really stationary over the sample period? Exhibit 5.2 displays the data for the market's rate of return. Exhibit 5.5 displays the data for the year-to-year change in the dollar value of the logarithmic portfolio.

Did the approximation portfolio really track the logarithmic portfolio? Exhibit 5.6 displays the data for the dollar values. Exhibit 5.7 displays the data for the year-to-year changes in dollar value of the two portfolios—in other words, for their risks.

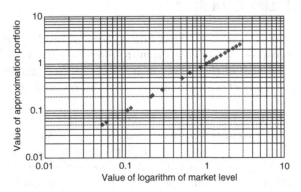

**EXHIBIT 5.6**  U.S. Experience 1980–2000

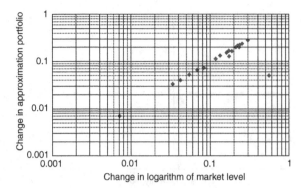

**EXHIBIT 5.7**   U.S. Experience 1972–2000

## IMPLEMENTING THE APPROXIMATION PORTFOLIO

As the market level goes up, the value of the short position increases, even as the value of the long position increases. Rebalancing entails reducing the long and short positions after the stock market has gone up and increasing the long and short positions after the stock market has gone down.

Brokers who borrow the stock the investor sells short will demand "margin"— valuable assets to protect them in case the investor is unable to cover because the market has risen too much. If the investors deposit their long position with the broker, their margin does not start to shrink until the market level has doubled (five standard deviations). It does not run out until the market level has quadrupled ($3 \times 5 = 15$ standard deviations of annual stock market return). But, in the meantime, the investor has rebalanced to less risky positions, over and over.

On the other hand, when the market falls the investors lose margin. But they do not lose all of it until the market level reaches zero. The 4:1 target ratio assures that the long position will always provide more margin for the short position than even the most timid broker would require.

## SHOULD RISK DECLINE WITH AGE?

We have argued that, if their real riskless rate is zero—or just large enough to offset trading and other costs—investors who want to time diversify should take the same dollar risk in the last year of their investment career as they take in the first. Does not this prescription conflict with the intuition that an old investor should take less risk than a young investor?

We have seen that, if they have time diversified, investors approaching the end of their career are likely to be richer than when they began. But then the same dollar risk at the end of their career represents a smaller relative risk; and relative risk is the way most investors—especially conventional investors—think about risk.

Is time diversification (constant dollar risk) just an unfamiliar way of expressing a familiar intuition?

## Notes

1. Obviously, the investor's savings at various points in his career also contribute to terminal wealth, appreciated forward at the effective riskless rate. Let his savings in year $t$ be $\Delta t$. Then, their contribution to terminal wealth is

$$s_0 (1+r)^T + s_1 (1+r)^{T-1} + \cdots + s_T = \sum s_t (1+r)$$

2. Dimson, E., Marsh, P., and Staunton, M. (2000). *The Millenium Book.* ABN-AMRO and the London Business School.
3. Past inflation has the same effect on the units of measure for the numerator and denominator. Current inflation adds algebraically to both market gains and losses, but affects the mean of these numbers rather than the dispersion.
4. There are other power series approximations—even other Taylor series approximations—to the logarithmic function.
5. When we use year-end data for the market level, we restrict our opportunities for rebalancing back to an accurate approximation of the logarithmic asset. In practical applications, changes in the market level can be followed and responded to almost continuously.

   When increasing approximation error forces us to rebalance back to our original investment positions, these positions should be scaled up from those of the previous rebalancing by a factor reflecting appreciation over the interval between rebalancings. (If the price level is inflating very rapidly, rescaling does not have to wait for the next rebalancing. Then, however, the investor incurs additional trading costs.)
6. Question: If rebalancing restores the original dollar risky positions at rebalancing, why is this not evident in JLT's 22 year example using actual U.S. stock market data? Answer: Whereas rebalancing occurs at the beginning of the year, the worksheet numbers are based on market level at the end.

# Two

# CAPM

**M**any investors are uncomfortable with bearing risk. The Capital Asset Pricing Model (CAPM) addresses the question: How will that discomfort be reflected in the way a rational market chooses its discount rates? Which risks will require an extra element of expected return? How much?

If they aren't correlated with other risks, many investment risks that loom large for an individual company, or even for an industry, will have little impact on the market portfolio.

*But some risks affect so many stocks—so many industries—that they contribute significant risk to the market portfolio. A rational stock market will reward investors for bearing these so-called* systematic *risks.*

William Sharpe's 1963 paper on the Diagonal Model contained a single risk factor to which all stocks were sensitive, albeit in varying degrees, as well as an additional source of risk specific to each stock. Because the latter diversified and the former didn't, the former explained market fluctuations.

In using a single factor to explain the distinction between systematic risk and specific risk, Sharpe's paper introduced what came to be called the Market Model. However, as he would be the first to point out, more than one macro variable can have enough impact to affect the overall market. The CAPM makes no assumptions about the number of systematic factors. Instead, the CAPM argues that different factors will carry different risk premiums, depending on their impact on the value of the market portfolio.

J.L.T.

# CHAPTER 6

# Toward a Theory of Market Value of Risky Assets

The objective of this study is to lay the groundwork for a theory of market value that incorporates risk. We consider a highly idealized model of a capital market in which it is relatively easy to see how risk premiums implicit in present share prices are related to the portfolio decisions of individual investors. In a real market institutional complexities, frictions, taxes, and certain other complications that are absent in our model may have a significant effect on share prices. The aim here, however, is not to present a fully developed apparatus for computing the cost of capital in practical problems. The present aim is merely:

- To show that, under our assumptions, optimal portfolio-balancing behavior by the individual investor leads to Proposition 1 of the famous Modigliani-Miller paper.
- To explore the manner in which risk affects investment value.
- To introduce the concept of insurability. Insurable risks have a negligible effect on the cost of capital.

We will develop a mathematical definition of insurability based on the assumptions of our market model, according to which it is a matter of degree whether a risk is insurable or uninsurable; nevertheless, we shall argue that it is often useful to treat risk as falling cleanly into one class or the other.

The assumptions required for the model we are about to introduce have much in common with the assumptions of the portfolio theorists (e.g., Markowitz, Tobin, Sharpe, and Farrar). The more familiar assumptions are:

1. There are no taxes.
2. There are no frictions, such as brokerage costs, to inhibit buying and selling.
3. The effect of the individual investor's decisions on prices is small enough to be disregarded.
4. Investors maximize expected utility, with primary concern for the first and second moments of the distribution of outcomes.
5. Investors are assumed to be averse to risk.

---

Originally published as part of the anthology *Asset Pricing and Portfolio Performance*, edited by Robert A. Korajczyk, Risk Books, 1999.

In addition, we assume that:

6. A perfect lending market exists.
7. Investors have perfect knowledge of the market, which we interpret to mean that every investor knows:
   a. Present prices
   b. What every other investor knows that might have some bearing on future investment values

If we further grant equal intelligence and equal effort to all investors, Assumption 7 is tantamount to assuming that investors agree in their forecast of future values. The emphasis in our study of the effects of risk is therefore on shifts in the market consensus over time, rather than on differences among investors at a particular point in time.

In a paper published in the February 1958 *Review of Economic Studies*, James Tobin introduced the concept of dominance. Tobin envisaged an investor who was free to select his portfolio from a set of risky assets and one riskless asset: cash. He showed that one set of relative proportions of the risky assets would dominate all other possible combinations, in the sense that for any given level of risk it gave the investor "the highest possible expectation of return available to him at that level of risk" (p. 83). In an optimal portfolio, therefore, "the proportionate composition of the noncash assets is independent of their aggregate share of the investment balance." An investor's attitude towards risk will be reflected in the fraction of the value of his portfolio held in cash, rather than in the proportionate composition of the noncash assets.

Tobin's concept of dominance, slightly altered, is the starting point for this study. In fairness to him, it must be admitted that the present development of the idea, although similar in many respects, is not entirely faithful to the original. In particular we have assumed away interest-rate risk, which was the only risk Tobin chose to consider. By focusing on interest-rate risk, Tobin sought to derive results for liquidity preference theory. His reason for limiting choice to cash and fixed-return assets was: "Among these assets cash is relatively riskless, even though, in the wider context of portfolio selection, the risk of changes in purchasing power, which all monetary assets share, may be relevant to many investors." Our investor diversifies to cope with equity risk, however, rather than interest-rate risk. Tobin points out that analysis of the portfolio problem in terms of the dominant set is possible only so long as a riskless asset is available. In proposing to apply the dominance concept to the problem of choosing between fixed-return assets and equity assets, therefore, we are implicitly assuming away price-level risk as well as interest-rate risk.

The justification we offer for assuming away price-level and interest-rate risk is that, although important in other contexts, in the U.S. economy they are both small in comparison with typical equity risks. The difference, which is a matter of common knowledge, is an order-of-magnitude difference. In assuming away interest-rate risk, we are also assuming away any motive on the part of the investor to hold more cash than he requires for transaction purposes. Although Tobin's condition that a riskless asset be available is not strictly met in our problem, the dominance concept is nevertheless useful in understanding the demand for equities, in which the risks are so large compared to the risks in cash and bonds that the latter seem almost riskless by comparison.

Another aspect of the present study which diverges from the Tobin paper is the absence of positivity constraints. The individual investor is free to borrow or lend, to buy long (or sell short) as he chooses, so long as his own capital—the margin of safety for his creditors—is not wiped out.

We consider, then, a market in which there are shares in a number of equities available to investors. Like Markowitz and Tobin, we consider time broken up into arbitrary short periods within which the composition of individual portfolios is held constant. In the present study, in which a single short time interval is under consideration, the focus is on the portfolio choices of investors at the beginning of the period, and the consequences of the choices for the prices of equity shares at the beginning of the period. From the point of view of the individual investor, the values of shares at that point in time are known (since, according to assumption 3, his own transactions have no effect on equity prices). The values (price plus the value of distributions during the interval) at the end of the current period are unknown and are therefore random variables. Assumption 7 implies that all investors share the same subjective probability distribution of the future (or terminal) value of shares. Denote the present (certain) price of a share in the $i$th equity by $v_i(0)$. Denote the future value of the ith equity by $v_i(1)$, and let the expected value of $v_i(1)$ be $\bar{v}_i(1)$. Then define the risk premium $a_i$ for the $i$th equity by

$$v_i(0) = b\bar{v}_i(1) - a_i$$

where b is a one-period discount factor defined in terms of the lending rate r by

$$b = \frac{1}{1+r}$$

The significance of defining risk premiums in this way becomes clear when we prove the following simple theorem.

Let $x_i$ be the number of shares of investment i held in the portfolio of an investor with (equity) capital C. Then expected performance is

$$rC + \frac{1}{b}\sum_i x_i a_i$$

In other words, the expected yield to the investor is the sum of (1) a return on his capital at the risk-free lending rate, which is independent of how he invests, and (2) an expected return for risk-taking, which depends only on the risk taken and is independent of his capital. Unless he hoards cash, the investor will receive a return on his capital at the risk-free lending rate no matter how he invests his money, plus a risk premium, the expected value of which depends *only* on the risk premium for the respective investments and the position he elects to hold in each. The risk-premium concept is thus a useful one for talking about the portfolio problem under our assumptions, since, together with the uncertainty associated with a given investment, it is the relevant investment parameter.

The proof is straightforward. Expected yield P is the expected future value minus present value. Expected future value is the algebraic sum of the future values of equity shares and any debt. Suppose that the current value of the investor's equity is C and that he elects to hold $x_i$ shares of investment i, currently priced at $v_i(0)$. Then the difference between the value of his equity and the value of his shares must be reconciled in the lending market. The future value of the debt is the present value of the debt, appreciated at the lending rate.

**Proof:**

Expected yield is

$$(1+r)\left[C - \sum_i x_i\, v_i\,(0)\right] + \sum_i x_i\, \bar{v}_i\,(1) - C$$

$$= rC - (1+r)\sum_i x_i\, v_i\,(0) + \sum_i x_i\, \bar{v}_i\,(1)$$

$$= rC + \sum_i x_i\,[\bar{v}_i\,(1) - (1+r)\, v_i\,(0)]$$

But we defined

$$v_i\,(0) = b\bar{v}_i\,(1) - a_i$$

whence

$$b\bar{v}_i\,(1) - v_i\,(0) = a_i$$

$$\bar{v}_i\,(1) - \frac{v_i\,(0)}{b} = \bar{v}_i\,(1) - (1+r)\, v_i\,(0)$$

$$= (1+r)\, a_i$$

Substituting in the expression for expected yield, we have

$$rC + \sum_i x_i\,[(1+r)\, a_i] = rC + \frac{1}{b}\sum x_i a_i$$

Let us consider the behavior of an investor who is attempting to find an optimal balance between uncertainty and expected performance. It should be clear that:

- With reference to the individual investor's optimization problem, the level of expected performance is determined by the value of $\mu$, defined by

$$\mu = \sum_i a_i\, x_i$$

- From our assumption that all investors are risk averters it follows that, for the level of expected performance which an optimal combination possesses, uncertainty is minimized.

The set of combinations with this property will dominate all other combinations in the sense of Tobin. Investors may differ, depending on their capital and attitudes toward risk, in the absolute amount of the dominant combination of risky investments they undertake, but if their (probabilistic) forecasts of future value agree, then the proportionate composition of the risky assets must be the same.

Like the portfolio theorists previously mentioned, we use variances and covariances to characterize the uncertainty in the yield of shares. Define the covariance matrix $A_{ij}$ by

$$A_{ij} = E\left[(v_i(1) - \bar{v}_i(1))(v_i(1) - \bar{v}_i(1))\right]$$

where E denotes the expected value of the expression in brackets. Then the error variance $\sigma^2$ in a portfolio containing $x_i$ shares of the ith equity is

$$\sigma^2 = \sum_{ij} x_i A_{ij} x_j$$

We shall refer occasionally to the inverse of $A_{ij}$, which we denote by $B_{ij}$:

$$\sum_j A_{ij} B_{jk} = \delta_{ik}$$

To find the optimal proportions, we minimize the portfolio variance subject to the constraint that expected yield

$$rC + \frac{1}{b} \sum_i x_i a_i$$

is equal to an arbitrary constant. For a given investor equity the constraint becomes

$$\mu = \sum_i a_i x_i = k$$

The objective, then, is to minimize

$$\sum x_i A_{ij} x_j = \sigma^2$$

subject to

$$\mu = \sum x_i a_i = k$$

Applying the method of Lagrange multipliers, we obtain

$$\sum_j A_{ij} x_j = \frac{\lambda}{2} a_i$$

whence we have

$$x_j = \frac{\lambda}{2} \sum_i B_{ji} a_i$$

Substituting, we get

$$\sum_j a_j x_j - k = \frac{\lambda}{2} \sum_{ji} a_j B_{ji} a_i - k = 0$$

or

$$\lambda = \frac{2k}{\sum_{ij} a_j B_{ji} a_i}, \quad x_j = \frac{\lambda}{2} \sum_i B_{ji} a_i$$

Referring back to relation

$$\sum A_{ij} x_j = \frac{\lambda}{2} a_i$$

we multiply through by $x_i$ and sum on i:

$$\sum x_i A_{ij} x_j = \frac{\lambda}{2} \sum x_i a_i = \frac{\lambda}{2} k = \sigma^2$$

The resulting expression for $\sigma^2$ enables us to write the ratio $\mu^2/\sigma^2$ as

$$\frac{\mu^2}{\sigma^2} = \frac{k^2}{(\lambda/2) k} = \frac{2k}{\lambda}$$

But we have

$$\lambda = \frac{2k}{\sum_{ij} a_j B_{ji} a_i}$$

so that for $\mu^2/\sigma^2$ we get

$$\frac{\mu^2}{\sigma^2} = \sum_{ij} a_j B_{ji} a_i$$

which is independent of specified expected performance k.

All efficient combinations have the same ratio of risk premium to standard error. The efficient set is a straight line on the diagram, passing through the origin (see Exhibit 6.1). The way in which constant-utility curves map on to the $k-\sigma$ plane will depend on the investor's capital and the lending rate, as well as his tastes. For an investor who is averse to risk, utility generally rises as one moves from southeast to northwest on the diagram. Tangency of the locus of efficient combinations (the "opportunity locus") with a utility isoquant will determine expected risk premium, $\mu$, for the investor in question.

For the $m$th and $n$th investors, respectively, the optimal combinations are given by

$$x_{j, m} = \frac{\lambda_m}{2} \sum B_{ji} a_i$$

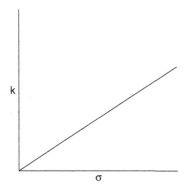

**EXHIBIT 6.1**  The Efficient Set

and

$$x_{j,n} = \frac{\lambda_n}{2} \sum B_{ji}a_i$$

For the jth equity we have

$$\frac{x_{j,m}}{x_{j,n}} = \frac{\lambda_m}{\lambda_n}$$

The holdings of any two investors are thus identical, up to a factor of proportionality. Although the meaning of the symbols is different, except for the $x_i$, the preceding development is closely parallel to Tobin's.

Let $x_i$ be the number of shares demanded by investors in the aggregate, and let $\wedge$ be defined by

$$\wedge = \sum_n \lambda_n$$

Then we have

$$x_j = \sum_n x_{j,n} = \frac{1}{2} \left[ \sum_n \lambda_n \right] \cdot \sum_i B_{ji}a_i$$

$$= \frac{1}{2} \wedge \sum_i B_{ji}a_i$$

The market clearing condition is

$$x_j = \breve{x}_j$$

where $\breve{x}_j$ is the number of shares of the jth equity outstanding. If the market is to clear, the risk premiums $a_i$ must satisfy

$$\frac{1}{2} \wedge \sum B_{ji}a_j = \breve{x}_j$$

Solving for $a_k$, we obtain

$$a_k = \frac{2}{\wedge} \sum A_{kj} \breve{x}_j$$

The summation is the covariance of the *k*th equity with the market as a whole. Define $k_n$ as the expected performance of the portfolio of the nth investor:

$$k_n = \sum_i x_{i,n} a_i$$

Then expected performance K for the market as a whole is

$$k = \sum_n k_n = \sum_{i,n} x_{i,n} a_i = \sum_i \breve{x}_i a_i$$

Using this equation and the preceding one, we can eliminate $\wedge$ from the expression for the $a_k$:

$$\sum \breve{x}_k a_k = \frac{2}{\wedge} \sum_{kj} \breve{x}_k A_{kj} \breve{x}_j = \breve{K}$$

$$\frac{2}{\breve{K}} \sum_{kj} \breve{x}_k A_{kj} \breve{x}_j = \wedge$$

Hence, we have for the equilibrium values of the $a_k$:

$$a_k = \breve{K} \frac{\sum A_{kj} x_j}{\sum \breve{x}_k A_{kj} \breve{x}_j}$$

In our idealized equity market, therefore, the risk premium per share for the *i*th investment is proportional to the covariance of the investment with the total value of all the investments in the market. Apparently it is a mistake to expect the risk premium to depend only on the sheer magnitude of the risk. If the uncertainty in the ith stock is small, or if the uncertainty is not small, but orthogonal to the market as a whole, then the risk premium will be small. The latter possibility would result in a small risk premium even for a "large" risk. This suggests that it may be useful in capital budgeting problems to distinguish between risks that, by their nature, can reasonably be assumed to be independent of fluctuations in the general level of the market and those which cannot. Investments that are risky only in the former sense are called insurable risks and have a cost of capital equal to the lending rate. The appraisal problem is not trivial, however, for uninsurable risks.

It should now be clear that positivity constraints on the $x_i$ in the portfolio problem considered first are unnecessary, since ideally the investor will hold shares in each equity in proportion to the total number of shares available in the market—and the latter share quantities are always positive.

A second observation about the result is that, in principle at least, it suggests a way of estimating risk premiums. The $A_{ij}$ can be estimated by taking covariances among stock-price time series, and the $x_j$, the number of shares of the $j$th stock outstanding, are readily available. Only K remains undetermined. A discussion of the econometric problems involved in measuring K and the $A_{ij}$ is outside the scope of this study.

The third point regarding the result is that it is consistent with market value linearity in the following sense: Consider, in the simplest case, two investments with (uncertain) future values $v_1(1)$ and $v_2(1)$, and a weighted combination with (uncertain) future value $v(1)$:

$$v(1) = \alpha_1 v_1(1) + \alpha_2 v_2(1)$$

If

$$v(0) = \alpha_1 v_1(0) + \alpha_2 v_2(0)$$

for all $v_1$ and $v_2$ then weak linearity exists. If the covariance of $v_1$ with the market is $\Sigma A_{1j} x_j$ and the covariance of $v_2$ with the market is $\Sigma A_{2j} x_j$, then the covariance of $v = \alpha_1 v_1 + \alpha_2 v_2$ with the market is

$$\sum (\alpha_1 A_{1j} + \alpha_2 A_{2j}) x_j = \alpha_1 \sum A_{1j} x_j - \alpha_2 \sum A_{2j} x_j$$

Referring back to the original definition of the risk premium, we have, as the expression for present value:

$$v_i(0) = b v_i(1) - a_i$$

$$= b v_i(1) - \sum_j A_{ij} x_j \left( \frac{K}{\sum_{ij} x_i A_{ij} x_j} \right)$$

Applying the expression to $v(1) = \alpha_1 v_1(1) + \alpha_2 v_2(1)$, we have

$$v(0) = b \bar{v}(1) - \sum (\alpha_1 A_{1j} + a_2 A_{2j}) x_j \left( \frac{K}{\sum_{ij} x_i A_{ij} x_j} \right)$$

$$= b [\alpha_1 \bar{v}_1(1) + \alpha_2 \bar{v}_2(1)] - \left[ \sum \alpha_1 A_{1j} x_j + \sum \alpha_2 A_{2j} x_j \right] \left( \frac{k}{\sum x_i A_{ij} x_j} \right)$$

$$= \alpha_1 v_1(0) + \alpha_2 v_2(0)$$

hence the market-value linearity condition is satisfied. If the condition is not satisfied, then there is no assurance that the total present market value of a firm will generally be independent of how the future value is partitioned into claims.

As the following theorem shows, one-period linearity is sufficient to guarantee that Proposition 1 of the Modigliani and Miller paper applies to any pattern of future earnings over time, and without restriction of those earnings to a particular risk class.

Let the future earnings for a firm at t = 1, 2, ..., n, be represented by F(t). A capital structure is a set of claims $F_i(t)$ on the future earnings. Now for any given $t \neq 0$, F(t) and, in general, $F_i(t)$ may be uncertain, as viewed from $t = 0$. The residual or equity claim in the set is so defined that $\Sigma_i F_i(t) = F(t)$, for all t. (The residual claim on earnings at a particular given point in time may of course be negative.) Define $V_i(t)$ as the value at time t of $V_i(t+1)$, and define

$$V_i(t) = v_i(t) + F_i(t)$$

Then for every claim $F_i(t)$ there corresponds a present value $v_i(0)$. Similarly, any other capital structure may be represented by a set of claims $F'_i(t)$ and a corresponding set of present values $v'_i(0)$. We have immediately that

$$\sum F_i(t) = \sum F'_i(t) = F(t)$$

We shall now prove that if one-period linearity applies and

$$\sum F_i(t) = \sum F'_i(t)$$

then

$$\sum v_i(0) = \sum v'_i(0)$$

If

$$\sum v_i(t) + F_i(t) = \sum v'_i(t) + F'_i(t)$$

then

$$\sum V_i(t) = \sum V'_i(t)$$

since by definition

$$V_i(t) = v_i(t) + F_i(t)$$
$$\sum V_i(t) = \sum v_i(t) + F_i(t)$$

Now we are given

$$\sum F_i(t) = \sum F'_i(t) = F(t)$$

Using the weak linearity property, we have that if

$$\sum V_i(t+1) = \sum V'_i(t+1)$$

then

$$\sum v_i(t) = \sum v'_i(t)$$

Hence, adding equals to equals we have

$$\sum v_i(t) + F_i(t) = \sum v'_i(t) + F'_i(t)$$
$$\sum V_i(t) = \sum V'_i(t)$$

Proof of the main theorem follows by induction, since we have shown that if

$$\sum V_i(t+1) = \sum V'_i(t+1)$$

then

$$\sum V_i(t) = \sum V'_i(t)$$

provided only that beyond some finite time T, all nonequity claims are identically zero. Then for any nonequity claims, and any $t = T$,

$$V_i = V'_i = 0$$

whence we have for $t = T$

$$\sum V_i(t) = V(t) = \sum V'_i(t)$$

since, in the absence of other claims, the respective equity claims, hence the value at time T of the respective equity claims must be identical.

# CHAPTER 7

# Portfolio Theory Is Inconsistent with the Efficient Market Hypothesis

**P**rofessional investors' criticisms of modern capital theory tend to focus on the assumption that markets are efficient. But capital theory and the efficient market hypothesis are actually unrelated ideas; one can accept and use the former without accepting the latter.

One possible reason for the widespread tendency to associate them is the assumption in the early versions of the capital asset pricing model that all investors hold the same expectations. This assumption was intended, not to express a judgment about the way the world is, but rather to help readers focus on the really important aspects of the model by eliminating irrelevant complexities. As John Litner pointed out, the difference between the model with and without so-called homogeneous expectations is slight: Relaxing this assumption merely requires replacing the homogeneous expectations with the appropriately weighted mean of individual investors' expectations.

If modern capital theory does not require market efficiency, its logical progenitor, portfolio theory, actually contradicts the efficient market hypothesis. Even if an investor has absolute confidence in a new piece of information, the relevant security will still be subject to specific developments as surprising to the investor as they are to the market consensus. According to portfolio theory, the diversifiable risk an investor adds to his portfolio by taking an active position in a security increases with the square of his position.

The square-law effect assures that there will always be some position beyond which the security's marginal contribution to the portfolio's risk-reward ratio will be less than that offered by some other asset. If he behaves in accordance with portfolio theory, therefore, the investor will never devote more than a fraction of his active portfolio to any one security. It cannot generally be assumed that the resulting position will be large enough to drive a security's price to a level consistent with the new information.

Unless new information reaches all investors simultaneously, portfolio theory is logically incompatible with strong-form market efficiency.

---

# CHAPTER 8

# In Defense of the CAPM

**M**any textbooks repeat two common complaints about the Capital Asset Pricing Model (CAPM):

1. Evidence that it takes more than one factor to explain the shared, or systematic, risk in securities refutes the CAPM.
2. In demonstrating that the risk premium on an asset depends only on its systematic factor loadings, Arbitrage Pricing Theory (APT) provides investors with a result of great practical value that the CAPM does not provide.

It may not be coincidental that some of the same books that make the first complaint don't actually discuss the CAPM. Some discuss the market model, and some discuss (usually without attribution) the Vasicek-McQuown pricing model. Both build on William Sharpe's Diagonal Model paper, which suggested (following up on a footnote in Harry Markowitz's book) that systematic risk could usefully be accounted for by a single factor.[1]

Vasicek and McQuown's argument proceeds as follows. Assume a single systematic risk factor exists, such that residual risks can be uncorrelated both with this factor and with each other. By taking appropriately long positions in some securities and appropriately short positions in others, the individual investor can hedge away all systematic risk. Thus he won't bear systematic risk unless it competes successfully with residual risk for inclusion in his portfolio. But if he includes enough positions (long *or* short) in his portfolio, he can drive the portfolio's residual risk to zero. Now, if residual risk is priced, this offers him an infinite reward-to-risk ratio. In order for market risk to compete successfully, it must offer an infinite expected return. Otherwise the investor will choose not to hold *any* systematic risk, and the market won't clear.

The market model takes the assumptions of the Diagonal Model and the result of the Vasicek and McQuown model and concludes that the actual, *ex post* systematic return—surprise plus risk premium—of every asset will be proportional to the asset's market sensitivity. Both Vasicek and McQuown and the market model thus assume a single systematic factor; but the CAPM in its various forms (Sharpe, Treynor, Lintner, Mossin, Black) makes no assumption about factor structure. In particular, it does not make the one-factor, Diagonal Model assumption that Vasicek and McQuown and the market model make.

Actually, a CAPM that abandons the assumptions of homogeneous expectations (as Lintner did) and riskless borrowing and lending (as Black did) doesn't make many other assumptions. All it *does* assume is that asset risk can be adequately expressed in terms of variances and covariances (with other assets); that these measures exist; that investors agree on these risk measures; and that investors can trade costlessly to increase expected portfolio return or reduce portfolio variance, to which they are all averse. Short-selling is permitted.

There is thus nothing about factor structure in the CAPM's *assumptions*. But there is also nothing about factor structure in the CAPM's *conclusions*. Factor structure is about surprise—in particular, the nature of correlations between surprises in different assets. In the Diagonal Model, a single factor accounts for all correlation. In richer, more complex factor structures, correlations in asset surprises can be due to a variety of pervasive, market-wide influences. The conclusion of the CAPM—that an asset's *expected* return is proportional to its covariance with the market portfolio—makes no assertions about the *surprise* in that asset's return. Because expected return and surprise are mutually exclusive elements in *ex post*, actual return, there can be no conflict between the CAPM and factor structure.

This point is the key to the second complaint. In order to demonstrate that APT's principal conclusion—that an asset's risk premium depends only on its systematic factor loadings—also holds for the CAPM, we can assume a perfectly general factor structure without fear of tripping on either the assumptions of the CAPM or its conclusions.

Consider a market in which *absolute* surprise for the ith asset, $x_i$, obeys:

$$x_i = \sum \beta_{ij} u_j + e_i \tag{8.1}$$

where $u_j$ are the systematic factors in the market and $e_i$ is a residual unique to the ith asset. The absolute surprise for the market as a whole, x, is simply the sum of absolute surprises for the individual assets;

$$x = \sum x_i = \sum \beta_{ij} u_j + \sum e_i$$

The CAPM asserts that any risk premium of the ith asset depends only on its covariance with the market—i.e., on the expectation of the following product:

$$\left( \sum \beta_{ij} u_j + e_i \right) \left( \sum \beta_{hk} u_k + \sum e_h \right) \tag{8.2}$$

Bearing in mind that the u's and e's are surprise, and assuming that all covariances between e's and between u's and e's are zero, we have for this expectation:

$$E\left[ \sum \beta_{ij} \beta_{hk} u_j u_k + e_i^2 \right] \tag{8.3}$$

or

$$\sum \beta_{ij} \left[ \sum \beta_{hk} \sigma_{jk}^{\ 2} \right] + s_i^{\ 2} \tag{8.4}$$

where

$$\sigma_{jk}^{\ 2} = E \left[ u_j u_k \right] \tag{8.5}$$

and

$$s_i^{\ 2} = E \left[ e_i^{\ 2} \right] \tag{8.6}$$

We see that an asset's covariance with the market portfolio (absolute surprise with absolute surprise) has two terms—one for systematic factors and one for the asset's unique surprise. A key issue is the relative size of these two terms.

We can, of course, make all the covariance terms in the systematic part zero by choosing a set of factors that are orthogonal. Then the covariance expression becomes:

$$\beta_{i1} \sum \beta_{h1} \sigma_{11}^{\ 2} + \beta_{i2} \sum \beta_{n2} \sigma_{22}^{\ 2} \tag{8.7}$$

Among the many possible choices of orthogonal factors, we can choose one in which only one factor correlates with the market portfolio. Assign the factor index to the factors so that the first term in the bracketed expression is the variance term for that factor. Then we can ignore for the moment the other systematic terms and focus on the first and last terms in the covariance expression, Equation 8.7. Factoring the respective terms into standard deviations gives us:

$$(\beta_{i1} \sigma_1) \left( \sum \beta_{h1} \sigma_1 \right) + \ldots + (s_i)(s_i) \tag{8.8}$$

Consider the first term. One factor reflects the absolute factor weight of the asset, the other the absolute factor weight of the market portfolio. The former is of the same order of magnitude as the standard deviation of the asset's unique risk; the latter is orders of magnitude larger (see Exhibit 8.1). This is because all the systematic risk in the market portfolio's absolute gain or loss is reflected in the market's factor weight, whereas the unique risk in the second term is that for a single asset. But this means that the systematic product is orders of magnitude larger than the unique product.

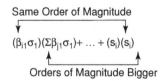

**EXHIBIT 8.1**  Systematic versus Unique Risk

To keep our exposition simple, we chose a special set of systematic factors. Had we chosen different systematic factors, the market portfolio could have been correlated with most or all of them, rather than merely one. Then the systematic portion of an asset's covariance with the market would have nonzero terms for more than one factor. Spreading it across several factors, however, won't diminish the magnitude of the aggregate systematic portion. Whether one systematic factor or several are correlated with the market portfolio, then, the systematic portion of an asset's covariance with the market will be orders of magnitude bigger than the unique portion.

If we drop the unique term and relax the assumption that only one systematic factor correlates with the market, then the expression within brackets in Equation 8.4 will in general have a different value for each of the systematic factors. But the value *doesn't depend on i*—the index that distinguishes between individual assets. What is *outside* the brackets is the factor loadings $\beta_{ij}$ for the ith individual asset on the factors $u_j$ in the factor structure. But this is the principal conclusion of APT—that an asset's risk premium should depend only on its factor loadings. Any corollaries that flow from this APT result also flow from the CAPM.

One of the differences between APT and the CAPM is the specification by CAPM of how systematic factors should be priced in relation to each other. The expression in brackets in the first term of Equation 8.4 is, to some constant of proportionality, the price of risk. The value of the expression, hence that price, is generally going to be different for different factors. APT can't specify the value of this expression; therefore it can't specify how factors will be priced in relation to each other.

What the APT *does* do is weaken the assumptions necessary to reach this conclusion. APT appeals to the older, better established tradition of arbitrage arguments exemplified by Modigliani and Miller's 1958 paper. APT joins the idea of specifying security risk in terms of a factor structure (Farrar's 1960 doctoral thesis at Harvard; Hester and Feeney's contemporaneous work at Yale) with Modigliani and Miller's arbitrage argument. Some may argue that, in effect, APT substitutes systematic risk *factors* for Modigliani and Miller's risk *classes*. Others may argue that the real provenance of APT is not Modigliani and Miller, but rather Vasicek and McQuown, with multiple risk factors substituted for their single risk factor.

This writer has no desire to take a position in such controversies. His only purpose is to clear up certain misunderstandings regarding the CAPM.

## Note

1. This material will appear as an appendix to the second edition of the *Guide to Portfolio Management* by James L. Farrell Jr., to be published by McGraw-Hill Book Company.

# Three

# Performance Measurement

If the purpose of performance measurement is to learn from our mistakes, then we need to separate luck from skill. *You buy a stock and its market price subsequently doubles.* But if you learn that the market level also doubled, then your rate of return was merely average. Now suppose your stock is twice as sensitive to market fluctuations as the average stock. Then your stock selection was worse than average. Using rate of return to measure skill in stock selection can be more confusing than helpful to investors.

When a mutual fund holds 100 stocks, the luck in stock selection is greatly reduced, but the luck in the market effect isn't. We can remove the latter luck by estimating the fund's historical sensitivity to market fluctuations and applying that sensitivity to what the market actually did.

Chapter 10, introduces the ideas of

1. Using a portfolio's history to measure its sensitivity to market risk.
2. Applying that measure to what the market actually did, in order to estimate, period by period, the portion of return that was actually market return.
3. Subtracting the "lucky" market return from total return in order to isolate the contribution from stock selection.

Some stock portfolios are more sensitive to the market factor than others. But once this sensitivity—now called *beta*—has been estimated, market effects can be removed from the manager's historical returns. What's left—now called *alpha*—is his or her performance in stock selection.

According to Chapter 11, "outguessing the market" means outguessing the market factor—in terms of our framework, raising the sensitivity of the manager's portfolio to that factor before the market goes up and lowering it before the market goes down. (Work by academic researchers suggests that diversified portfolios are often sensitive to more than one market factor. Fortunately, both performance measures apply to multiple market factors.)

J.L.T.

# CHAPTER 9

# The Coming Revolution

**W**hether a portfolio has performed well or badly, and whether particular advice contributed to or detracted from the portfolio's performance should be a matter of objective fact. The reason it isn't is that other factors—for example, what the market does—are commonly more important than the manager's selection decisions. Hence luck is a big factor in portfolio results.

An important consequence has been that the ultimate customer for investment skills has rarely known whether he was getting a good investment product or a bad one. The securities industry has responded to this state of affairs by emphasizing persuasion, rather than performance. The test of an investment idea has been whether it would sell, rather than its intrinsic value.

Although salesmanship is important in many industries, it has rarely, if ever, been as important in other industries as in the investment industry.

The emphasis on saleability has put a low ceiling on the degree of complexity or subtlety considered acceptable in investment thinking. If, for example, an auto manufacturer's main concern in making design decisions were how well showroom salesmen could defend them to the customer, we would still be driving Model T's. No design change that required any specialized technical knowledge relating to aerodynamics, metallurgy, thermodynamics, etc., for its justification would ever have been undertaken. Perhaps this ceiling explains why, compared to almost any other industry, the technology of investment management has progressed so little in the last forty years.

A new body of ideas explaining the behavior of security prices has grown up in the last decade, and one of the by-products is new and powerful methods of *measuring portfolio performance*. Half a dozen performance measurement services, offered by brokers and others, are based on these methods. The recent study by Friend, Blume and Crockett (Mutual Funds and other Institutional Investors, McGraw-Hill, 1970) used these methods. The SEC study of institutional trading is soon to be published, and in it the investment management industry is likely to find its performance subjected to measurement based on these same methods. The issues raised by the SEC study in particular are going to force the industry to come to terms with the new methods.

The rapid growth of institutions is replacing millions of amateur customers for investment advice with thousands of professional customers. By concentrating wealth in a much smaller number of portfolios, it makes the application of modern performance measurement methods practical. The time is soon coming when the value of advice, and the portfolio manager's success in using advice to improve portfolio results, will be measured as a matter of course.

There is at least an outside chance that the result will be a revolution in the way institutional customers think about the value of investment advice and its application in portfolio management. One consequence may be a more receptive climate for new ideas, and a genuine search, at every level of investment management, for ways to improve the quality of the investment product.

The impact on the rate at which the quality of investment thinking improves can scarcely be overestimated.

# CHAPTER 10

# How to Rate Management
# of Investment Funds

*The performance of mutual, trust, and pension funds can be quantitatively compared despite market fluctuations and different risk policies.*

Investment management has become an important industry in the United States. The responsibilities of investment managers are enormous, and their potential rewards are great. In order to reward management for good performance in this field, however, it is necessary to be able to recognize it. Unfortunately, pension funds, trust funds, and mutual funds all share one serious problem: To the extent that they are heavily invested in common stocks, the return achieved in any one period is subject to wide fluctuations which are beyond the control of investment management. The result has been that, although many believe the quality of investment management is important, no one has devised a satisfactory way to measure its impact on performance.

In this article we shall look at a new way to rate the performance of a fund's investment managers. The comprehensiveness of this rating is a question for the reader to decide for himself, depending on how he thinks about the "quality" of investment management. Most readers are likely to agree, however, that at least one dimension—and a critical one—of the quality of the investment management is analyzed by this new method.

## ANALYZING RISK

It is almost ironic that the presence of market risk should pose such a serious problem. The assets controlled by investment managers are remarkably liquid. To a degree almost unmatched in other enterprises, the investment manager is free to act independently of the investment decisions of his predecessors. Furthermore, although there are varying institutional restrictions placed on the investment manager's decisions, by and large he competes directly with other investment managers, buying and selling securities in the same market. If it were not for the problems created by market risk,

---

therefore, performance comparisons in the investment management industry would be more meaningful than in many other industries.

Actually, of course, there is more than one kind of risk in a diversified fund. There is a risk produced by general market fluctuations—the volatility of the stock market. There is also a risk resulting from fluctuations in the particular securities held by the fund. In any event, here are important practical consequences of either or both of these risks:

1. The effect of management on the rate of return on investments made in any one period is usually swamped by fluctuations in the general market. Depending on whether, during the period in question, the general market is rising or falling, the more volatile funds (stock funds) will look better or worse than the less volatile funds (balanced funds). As the Wharton Report points out, the difficulty is not solved by averaging return over a number of periods.[1] For any sample interval of reasonable length, average return is still dominated by market trends.
2. Measures of average return make no allowance for investors' aversions to risk. The importance of fluctuations in one or a few stocks from the investor's point of view is apparent when one considers that, after all, if this kind of risk were not important, investors would not diversify. It is sometimes argued that because the importance attached to risk varies from investor to investor, no absolute measure of fund performance is possible.

## Overcoming Difficulties

In order to have any practical value, a measure of management performance in handling a trust fund invested in equities or in handling pension or mutual funds must deal effectively with both problems. It should tend to remain constant so long as management performance is constant—even in the face of severe market fluctuations. Also, it should take into account the aversion of individual shareholders or beneficiaries to investment risk. The method to be described here overcomes both difficulties.

This article has three parts. The first describes a simple graphical method for capturing the essence of what is permanent and distinctive about the performance of a fund, including the effects of fund management. The second develops a concept of fund performance which takes investment risk into account. The third develops a measure for rating fund-management performance which can be applied directly, using the graphical technique developed in the first part. For the statistician, Appendix 10.1 details certain relationships used.

## THE CHARACTERISTIC LINE

The first main step to obtaining a satisfactory performance measure is to relate the expected rate of return of a trust, pension, or mutual fund to the rate of return of a suitable market average. The device for accomplishing this is the *characteristic line*. Let us examine its nature and significance.

## Application to Funds

If the rate of return—taking into account both market appreciation and dividends—is plotted for a fund invested substantially in common stocks, wide swings from period to period are often evident. It is not generally known, however, that most managed

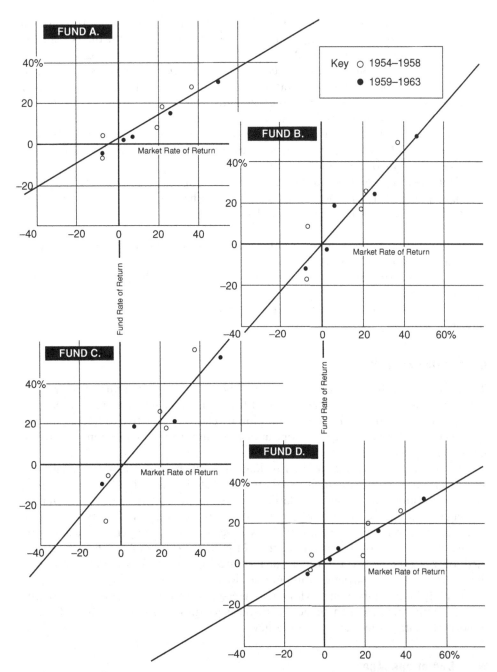

**EXHIBIT 10.1**   Characteristic Lines

funds actually demonstrate a remarkably stable performance pattern over time when viewed in terms of the simple graphical device that I call the characteristic line.

Exhibit 10.1 summarizes the performance history of four actual managed funds:

■ The horizontal and vertical axes in these figures are measured in terms of percent rate of return. (For both individual funds and market averages, rate of return is computed by dividing the sum of dividends, interest, and market appreciation on the funds available at the beginning of the year by the value of the funds available at the beginning of the year. Any increase in asset value during the year due to infusion of new funds is eliminated, as is any reduction due to distributions to beneficiaries or shareholders. Rates of return defined in this way are obviously approximations, because the value of funds available for investment typically fluctuates more or less continuously throughout the year.)

- The horizontal axis measures the corresponding rate of return recorded for a general *market* average (the Dow-Jones Industrial Average); the vertical axis shows the rate of return for the *fund*.
- Each point represents a year in the ten-year interval ending January 1, 1963. The open points represent the five years in the latter half of the ten-year interval; the filled points, the years in the former half.

Although the funds exhibited wide swings in rate of return over the ten-year interval, the rate of return in each year fell into a straight-line pattern, which remained virtually fixed throughout the ten-year interval. This line—the characteristic line—can be fitted by eye or by statistical methods. The significant thing about it is that it tends to be stationary over time, despite wide fluctuations in short-term rate of return.

## Information Revealed

The characteristic line contains information about both expected rate of return and risk. The slope of the line measures volatility. Thus, a steep slope means that the actual rate of return for the fund in question is relatively sensitive to fluctuations in the general stock market; a gentle slope indicates that the fund in question is relatively insensitive to market fluctuations.

The slope angle of the characteristic line obviously provides a more refined measure of a fund's volatility than the usual categories of "balanced fund," "stock fund," or "growth fund." The range of volatilities observed in actual practice is enormous. Among mutual funds, for example, I have found that volatilities range from roughly one-third to about two. A volatility of two means that a one-percent increase (or decrease) in the rate of return demonstrated by the Dow-Jones Average is accompanied, on the average, by a two-percent increase (or decrease) in the rate of return demonstrated by the particular fund in question.

For any individual investor who is risk-averse, the observed differences in volatility are surely large enough to be worth measuring. The differences also disclose important contrasts in management policy.

## What Deviations Mean

As users of the characteristic-line method will discover, the plotted points in a typical chart will not all lie on the characteristic line. What this means is that not all of the risk in the fund in question is explained by fluctuations in the general market level.

As pointed out earlier, one can consider that investment risk in a diversified fund is the sum of responses to (1) general market fluctuations and (2) fluctuations peculiar to the particular securities held by the fund. If a fund is properly diversified, the latter risk, which tends to be causally unrelated one security from another, tends to average out. The former risk, being common to all common stocks in greater or lesser degree, does not tend to average out.

If the management of a fund attempts to maintain a constant degree of volatility, then the slope of the characteristic line will tend to measure that volatility. If there are excessive deviations from the characteristic line, we have a strong indication that:

- Either the fund is not efficiently diversified to minimize risk unrelated to the general market (in which case the owner or beneficiary incurs additional risk without any compensating prospects of additional return).
- Or, perhaps inadvertently or perhaps as a matter of deliberate policy, management has altered the volatility of the fund. By increasing fund volatility when it is optimistic and decreasing volatility when it is pessimistic, management can speculate for the fund beneficiaries on fluctuations in the general market.

The appropriateness of such action is an interesting question but outside the scope of this article. It is worth noting, though, that in a sample I have taken of 54 American mutual funds, four out of five demonstrate fairly clear-cut characteristic-line patterns, with correlation coefficients equal to or exceeding 90 percent.

Possibly this pattern indicates wide agreement that causing fund volatility to vary greatly leaves the individual owner unable to rely on a stable estimate of the risk in the portion of his personal portfolio represented by the fund in question. His ability to strike what for him is the optimal overall portfolio balance between expected return and risk is then impaired. But if, in retrospect, fund management has speculated successfully with the volatility of a fund, it is conceivable that beneficiaries may consider the disadvantage more than offset by the improved rate of return.

Suppose the characteristic line itself shifts. This may happen when fund volatility remains constant but fund performance varies widely from year to year. A sweeping change in the personnel constituting fund management, for example, might be accompanied by a sudden shift in fund performance.

## Comparing Performance

The characteristic line also contains information about management's ability to obtain a consistently higher return than the competition's. If, for example, two trust or mutual funds demonstrate precisely the same volatility, their respective characteristic lines would have the same slope, but one line would be consistently higher than the other (unless they coincide). For instance, suppose a certain fund had exactly the same slope as Fund A in Exhibit. 10.1. If its characteristic line were plotted on the chart, it would run parallel to Fund A's but higher or lower. The fund with the higher line would demonstrate consistently higher performance—in good years and bad.

Although the problem of comparing performances of fund management is obviously not so simple when the slopes differ, the characteristic line does contain, as we shall see presently, the information necessary to make such comparisons.

## Implications for Control

The characteristic line has implications for management control, too. No matter how widely the rate of return for a fund may fluctuate, management performance is unchanged so long as the actual rate of return continues to lie on the characteristic line. One can establish control limits on either side of the line; points falling within these limits are assumed to represent a continuation of past management performance, while points falling outside the limits require special scrutiny. Without the characteristic line it is virtually impossible to tell whether the rate of return demonstrated in a given year represents a real change in the quality of fund management. With it, early detection of important changes becomes possible.

In summary, therefore, the graphical method provides a simple test of:

1. The extent to which a fund has adhered, purposely or not, to a single characteristic line.
2. The degree of volatility associated with the fund.
3. The success of fund management in maintaining a high rate of return under a variety of market conditions.

## PERFORMANCE MEASURE

We turn now to a second line. This one deals not with an individual fund but with a *portfolio* containing a certain fund. The purpose of the line is to relate the expected return of a portfolio containing the fund to the portfolio owner's risk preferences. This line can be called the *portfolio-possibility* line. We shall see that the slope of this line is a measure of fund performance which transcends differences in investors' attitudes toward risk.

## Risk Preference

Whether the performance pattern of a given fund rates high or low should depend on whether individual investors choose it in preference to the pattern demonstrated by other funds. During the last few years we have witnessed the rapid development of a theory of rational choice among portfolios.[2] The theory is too complex to be reviewed here in detail, but certain fragments of it provide the basis for a concept of fund-management performance.

It is interesting to note that when one talks about the historical performance pattern of a fund, he is looking at the past; but when he considers the preferences of individual investors and their choices among funds, he is talking about their appraisal of the future. We shall continue to talk about the performance of funds in terms of historical performance patterns, even though actual investor choices among funds are necessarily based on expectations regarding future performance patterns. The implication is that a good historical performance pattern is one that, if continued into the future, would cause investors to prefer it to others.

Economists sometimes study the investor's choice among possible portfolios in terms of a risk-return diagram (like the one shown in Exhibit 10.2):

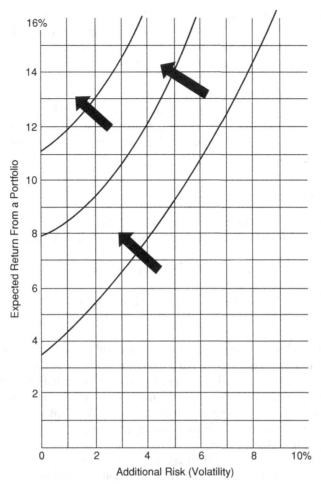

**EXHIBIT 10.2**   Investors' Indifference Curves

■ The vertical axis in the exhibit measures the return that the investor would expect to get, on the average, from a given portfolio. The horizontal axis is some appropriate measure of risk.

(As a technical note for those interested in detail, let me add that it is traditional to measure the respective axes in terms of *expected rate of return*, where the rate is a weighted mean of possible future outcomes, and *standard error*, where standard error is a statistical measure of potential variability around the expected performance. Under certain assumptions regarding the nature of investment uncertainty, expected return and standard error completely characterize a given portfolio. These assumptions seem to fit actual stock-market experience fairly well. When the performance pattern of a mutual fund is clustered closely around the characteristic line, the slope of this line, which is our graphical measure of risk, is statistically an excellent measure of the standard error.)

■ The rate of return is for a standard time period—perhaps a month, quarter, or year—per dollar of the individual investor's initial capital.

■ The curved lines in the diagram are called indifference curves for the reason that the investor is indifferent to portfolio choices lying on a particular indifference curve; that is, he would just as soon have, say, 5 percent more return at $4\frac{1}{2}$ percent more risk as 8 percent more return at $6\frac{1}{2}$ percent more risk, and so on (see the curve at the right of Exhibit 10.2).[3]

■ There is a useful analogy between the investor's relative preference, as shown by indifference curves, and relative heights, as shown by contour lines on a topographical map—that is, lines along which elevation is constant. The arrows in the figure show the direction in which one moves to go from less to more desirable portfolios (or, to complete the topographical analogy, uphill).

## Portfolio Choices

What kinds of portfolio choices are available to the investor? The assets he can include in his portfolio consist of two fundamentally different kinds:

■ Money-fixed claims, such as checking deposits; savings deposits; government, municipal, and corporate bonds.
■ Equity assets, including equity in personal business and partnerships and corporate common stocks.

The investor who holds money-fixed claims is subject to the risk of changes in both the interest rate and price level. Although both risks are real, in American financial history they have been small compared to the risk entailed in owning equities. The relative insignificance of market risk in money-fixed claims is reflected in the narrow range of net returns available in such claims. We shall simplify slightly and represent all assets of this type by a single point on the vertical axis of the risk-return diagram (point B in Exhibit 10.3).

If the investor wants to raise the expected rate of return of his overall portfolio above the rate offered by money-fixed claims, he must undertake some equity risk. On the risk-return diagram in Exhibit 10.3, the investor has available to him the opportunity to invest in shares in a particular balanced or growth fund, Fund A, as well as the opportunity to invest in money-fixed claims, B. If he is free to vary the investment in each outlet more or less continuously, then the locus of portfolio combinations available to him is the straight line—the portfolio-possibility line—joining points A and B. The combination which is best for him will lie at point D along the line which is farthest "uphill" as indicated by the "contour lines" on his indifference map. The preferred combinations for other investors will differ, depending on the precise shape of their indifference curves.

Now consider a second investment, Fund C (top right of Exhibit 10.3). The line BC is the locus of possible portfolios made available to our investor by the existence of this investment. As in the case of locus BA, there will, in general, be a single point, E, along BC, which is the farthest "uphill" for the investor.

The significant fact is that, although the location of the points of optimum balance along lines BC and BA will differ from one investor to another, the optimum point D along line BA will always be superior for a given investor to the optimum point E along line BC. For every possible level of risk an investor might choose, the return on a combined portfolio containing Fund A is greater than the return on a portfolio containing Fund C, which provides the same level of risk. This ensures that, whatever

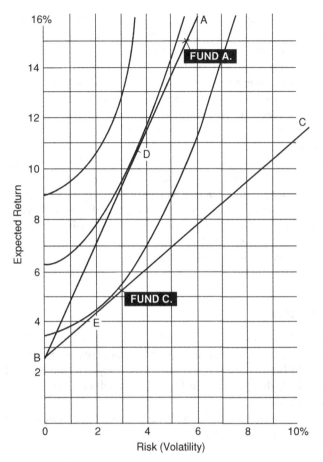

**EXHIBIT 10.3** Risk-Return Diagram for an Investor

the optimum point along line BC may be for a particular investor, the point on BA directly above it (that is, with the same risk) will have a greater expected return. This will be true for every investor who is risk averse, quite independently of the precise shape of his indifference curve.

But if, for every risk-averse investor, line BA is superior to line BC, then, in terms of the portfolio possibilities this line makes available to investors, Fund A is absolutely superior to Fund C. Now it is apparent from Exhibit 10.3 that lines BA and BC differ only in slope. Line BA, which is superior to line BC, slopes upward more sharply, showing that the rate of gain from shifting the investor's portfolio in the direction of greater risk is greater for Fund A than for Fund C. *The steepness of the portfolio-possibility line associated with a given fund is thus a direct measure of the desirability of the fund to the risk-averse investor.* The force of the preceding argument is not diminished by the fact that many investment funds contain money-fixed claims as well as equities.

## Pension and Trust Funds

All very well for mutual funds, you may say. After all, the investor in mutual funds is free to adjust the fraction of his portfolio invested in each one pretty much as he pleases. But what about cases involving pension funds and trust funds, in which the individual beneficiary has no freedom whatever to alter the fraction of his total assets that are managed by the fund? To answer this question, let us consider an illustration: Suppose a man has a certain fraction of his assets invested in a pension fund. Suppose further that the management performance of the pension fund (measured in terms of the slope of the portfolio-possibility line) ranks just equal to the performance of a certain mutual fund. A certain segment of the portfolio-possibility line for the mutual fund will be unavailable to the investor if part of his funds are irrevocably committed to the pension fund, since he is not free to convert all his assets to money-fixed claims. Within the range of the portfolio-possibility line available to him, however, he can achieve the same portfolio behavior with part of his capital committed to the pension fund as he could achieve if he were free to compose the risky portion of his portfolio entirely from the mutual fund in question. If his attitude toward portfolio risk leads him to choose a portfolio in this range, then he will be indifferent as to a choice of a pension fund or a mutual fund with an equal performance ranking. If, on the other hand, his choice lies outside this range, then the pension fund is less useful to him than a mutual fund with a similarly sloped portfolio-possibility line.

### Quantitative Measure

The performance demonstrated by a fund can be measured by the tangent of the slope angle, symbolized by the figure $\alpha$. (For instance, the slope angle for Fund C in Exhibit 10.3 would be the difference between the slope of line BC and a horizontal line going through B; the slope angle for Fund A, which is larger, is the difference between BA and a horizontal.)

The formula for tangent $\alpha$ follows directly from the geometry of Exhibit 10.3. As detailed in Appendix 10.1, it is:

$$\text{tangent } \alpha = \frac{\mu - \mu^*}{\sigma}$$

where $\mu$ equals the expected fund rate of return at a particular market rate of return, $\mu^*$ is measured from a horizontal line through a point that would represent a fund consisting only of fixed-income securities, and $\sigma$ is the symbol for volatility (which can serve as an approximate measure of investment risk as plotted on the horizontal axis of Exhibit 10.3).

## RATING MANAGEMENT

We are now ready to begin with the practical application of the concepts previously described. We will see how performance ratings can be read directly from the characteristic line.

### Relative Ranking

In order to plot a fund, and the associated portfolio-possibility line, on a risk-return chart of the type discussed in the last section, one needs both an expected rate of return and an appropriate measure of risk. A measure of risk is provided by the slope of the characteristic line. The characteristic line also enables management to estimate the expected rate of return. In order to obtain a value for the expected rate of return for the fund, however, it is necessary to assume a rate-of-return value for the market. Depending on the choice of market rate of return, expected return for the fund—hence the slope of the opportunity locus—will vary. The effect of changing the assumed market rate is illustrated in Exhibits 10.4 and 10.5 as follows:

- Exhibit 10.4 portrays a sample of characteristic lines for 20 actual managed funds based on rate-of-return data for the years 1953 through 1962. By making specific assumptions about the market rate of return, the characteristic lines for these funds can be transformed into points on the risk-return charts shown in Parts A and B of Exhibit 10.5. (The term "volatility" on the horizontal axes of these charts, as indicated before, refers to the amount of risk in the fund due to fluctuations in the general market.)
- Part A of Exhibit 10.5 was plotted by assuming a market return of 10 percent. (The characteristic line for each fund is inspected to determine its pattern of return when the market's return is 10 percent, and this pattern is converted to a point reflecting risk and return.) Given this assumption, the funds in question can easily be ranked visually; by drawing straight lines from Point Q to these points, one can obtain the portfolio-possibility lines for the funds in question. The problem is, of course, that the market-return assumption is arbitrary and other returns depend on it.
- Part B results when a market rate of return of 30 percent is assumed instead. Although the risk values for the individual funds are unchanged, the expected rates of return are affected, and a new set of portfolio-possibility lines results.

Inspection shows that the ranking of the funds is unchanged in Parts A and B of Exhibit 10.5. For example, the highest- and lowest-ranking funds in Part A are, respectively, the highest- and lowest-ranking funds in Part B, despite the fact that the two diagrams are based on widely differing assumptions about the expected rate of return for the general market. This illustrates what is actually a quite general result: although the absolute position of funds on a risk-return chart (and their corresponding portfolio-possibility lines) may vary with the level of market rate of return assumed, *the ranking of funds with respect to each other does not.*

## Numerical Measure

What is desired, therefore, is a number that will measure the relative ranking of a fund—preferably without being affected by changes in the absolute level of rate of return of the kind illustrated by Parts A and B of Exhibit 10.5. It happens that there is a number that has these properties: It is the level of rate of return for the general market at which the fund in question will produce the same return as that produced by a fund consisting solely of riskless investment. As Exhibit 10.6 shows, its value can be read directly from the characteristic line:

A horizontal line is drawn so as to intersect the vertical axis at a point representing the rate of return available on money-fixed claims. In Exhibit 10.6 the horizontal line is drawn at 4 percent. (The choice of rate within the range of $3\frac{1}{2}$ percent to

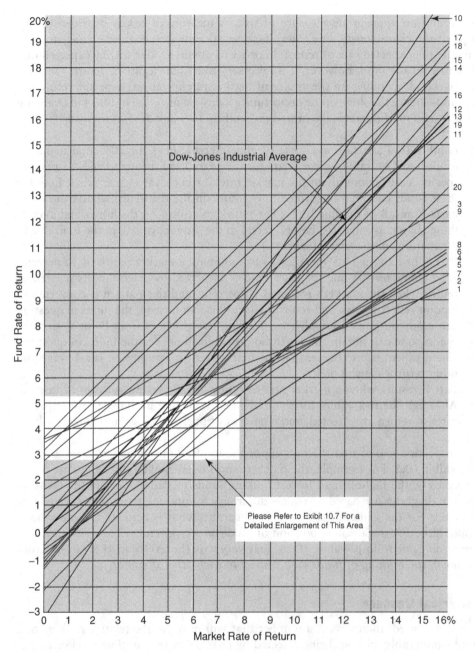

**EXHIBIT 10.4**  Comparison of 20 Managed Funds

5 percent is somewhat arbitrary, but not especially critical as regards its effect on performance ratings.) The point at which the horizontal line intersects the characteristic line determines the rating of the fund, which is read off the horizontal axis as a percentage. The lower this percentage, the higher the rating of the pension, trust, or mutual fund. For those interested in a formal proof that the number just defined

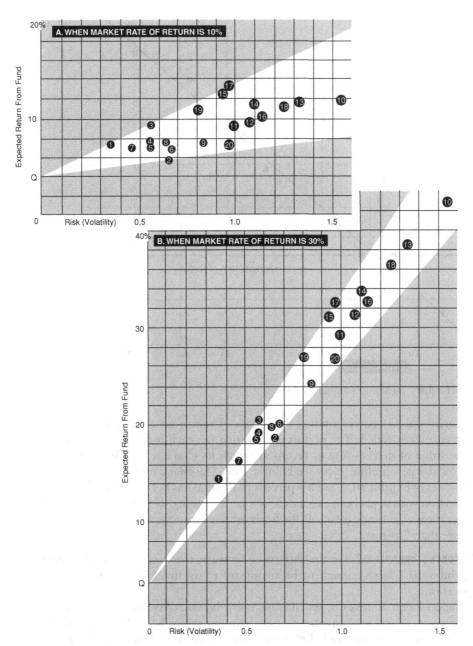

**EXHIBIT 10.5** Fund Rankings under Different Market Conditions

will have the special properties desired, Appendix 10.1 sets forth the steps in the reasoning.

In order to demonstrate the practical significance of the rating technique, let us refer back to Exhibit 10.4. Each of the performance ratings of the 20 funds whose characteristic lines are shown in this chart could be read directly from the figure

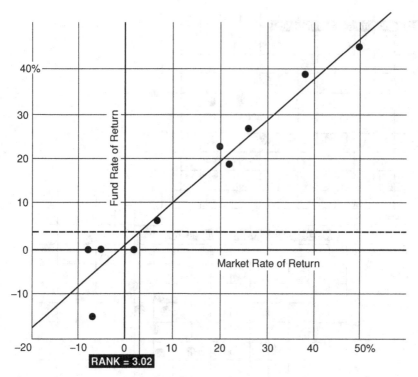

**EXHIBIT 10.6**    Ranking Number of a Fund

if a horizontal line corresponding to the rate of return on a riskless portfolio (here 4 percent) were added. The performance rating for each fund could be determined by the value of market rate of return at which its characteristic line intersects the horizontal 4 percent line. Now see Exhibit 10.7. The characteristic lines are the same as the ones in Exhibit 10.4, but a 4 percent horizontal has been added, and the area of intersection with it has been expanded for ease in reading. Note that the performance ratings for the 20 funds (read off the horizontal axis) range from less than 1 percent to more than 7 percent.

**Differences Important?**    Is the difference between the best and worst rated fund in Exhibit 10.7 large enough to be significant to an investor? Let us consider an illustration:

Suppose that an investor specifies his portfolio volatility should be equal to one. The amount of "riskless" investment or borrowing which he undertakes will depend on the volatility of the fund. Let us say that Fund XYZ has a volatility of two. Since the desired portfolio volatility is one, then the portfolio must be blended of equal parts (in terms of dollars invested) of the fund and riskless investment. If, for example, the beneficiary's capital is initially worth $10,000, then, since a 1 percent reduction in the market rate of return will be accompanied on the average by a 2 percent reduction in the rate of return on $5,000 invested in the fund, the effective reduction in *portfolio* rate of return is 1 percent since:

$$\frac{.02 \times \$5,000}{\$10,000} = .01$$

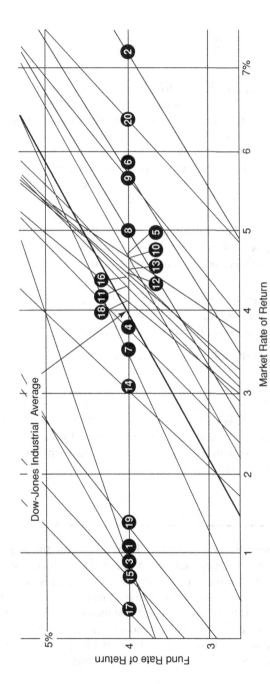

**EXHIBIT 10.7** Performance of Funds

Now assume that the fund in question has a volatility of three-quarters. If the investor's desired portfolio volatility is one, he must invest an amount exceeding his own capital. If his capital is again $10,000, and he borrows $3,333 and invests that sum in Fund XYZ, then a one-percent reduction in the market rate of return will be accompanied on the average by a .0075 percent reduction in the rate of return on $13,333 invested in the fund. The effective reduction in *portfolio* rate of return is then 1 percent because:

$$\frac{.0075 \times \$13,333}{\$10,000} = .01$$

In both cases the portfolios have a volatility equal to one—the value specified—but the differing fund volatilities necessitate quite different investment strategies.

Is the significance of rating differences for a sample of funds influenced by market conditions? It is to a certain extent. We have already seen that one cannot employ characteristic-line data to obtain an expected rate of return for a fund without first assuming a value for the market rate of return. It is consequently not possible to make categorical statements about the spread in expected portfolio performance between the best and worst managed funds which results when an investor specifies a certain level of portfolio volatility. It is nevertheless possible to get a rough idea of the significance of the spread in performance ratings observed in a sample by making different assumptions about the market. If we take the extreme cases in the sample of 20 funds already described, for instance, we find these differences in investment return:

| Expected market rate of return | 10% | 30% |
| Return of highest-ranked fund | 13.6% | 33.4% |
| Return of lowest-ranked fund | 6.6% | 26.6% |

These figures suggest the following conclusions about differences in ratings:

1. In the range of normal market rate of return, the difference in portfolio rate of return between funds ranked high and low is substantial.
2. The difference seems relatively less important, the higher the performance of the general market is. Hence the consequences of rating differences for portfolio performance will be relatively more significant in a normal market than during the bull market of recent history.

## CONCLUSION

In this article we have seen that there is a good way of cutting through the confusion of facts and figures in the marketplace to compare the performance of individual trust, pension, and mutual funds. The new method described is surely not a perfect answer to the needs of fund managers and investment analysts, for it requires the making of certain assumptions about fund performance with which not everyone will completely agree (e.g., the desirability of a fund's holding to a consistent investment policy). But the method goes at least part of the way, I believe, to providing answers that have long eluded executives in the investment business.

We have seen that, consistent with any specified level of the market rate of return, there is associated with each fund a range of combinations of expected portfolio return and risk. The slope of the portfolio-possibility line measures the rate at which the individual investor increases the expected rate of return of his portfolio as his burden of portfolio risk increases. A comparison of slopes among funds provides a means of rating funds which transcends variations in individual investors' attitudes toward risk. Although the slopes vary just as the market rate of return varies, it can be proved that the ranking of the funds represented remains unchanged. The relative rankings can be read directly from the characteristic lines of funds to be compared.

Differences in ranking based on the characteristic lines can be quite significant for individual investors, even though they take varying attitudes toward risk. Also, the differences are independent of market fluctuations. Because the ranking measure has these properties, it provides a useful basis for reviewing the performance of fund management.

## APPENDIX 10.1

Exhibit 10.8 shows the characteristic line for a typical fund. For each possible value of the market rate of return, the characteristic line predicts the corresponding rate of return for the fund pictures. The slope of the characteristic line is measured by tangent $B$; the vertical intercept is $h$. For the particular market rate of return $D$, the expected fund rate of return is $\mu$. A horizontal line drawn a distance $\mu^*$ above the horizontal axis depicts the behavior of a fund consisting solely of fixed income securities. The

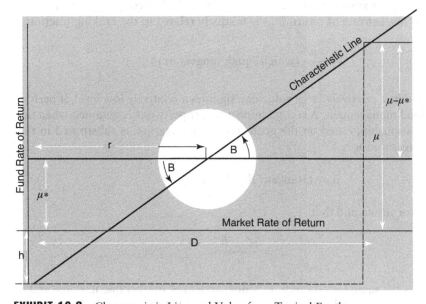

**EXHIBIT 10.8**   Characteristic Line and Value for a Typical Fund

ranking measure $r$ is determined by the intersection of the characteristic line and the horizontal line at height $\mu^*$.

The question is whether the ranking measure $r$ has the properties specified; that is, whether it will—

- Rank funds in the order of their respective values of tangent $\alpha$ (the slope of the opportunity locus as discussed earlier in the article);
- Have the same value for a given fund, independently of fluctuations in the market rate of return.

A moment's reflection shows that no number can have both properties simultaneously unless the general result alluded to in the main text holds true; that is, unless the *relative* ranking of funds—in terms of the slope of the portfolio-possibility line—is unaffected by fluctuations in the general market. Inasmuch as the proof demonstrates that the number in question does indeed have both properties, the general result follows.

From the geometry of the diagram, we have for the volatility:

$$\sigma = \text{tangent } B = \frac{\mu - \mu^*}{D - r}$$

Solving for $r$, we obtain:

$$r = D - \left(\frac{\mu - \mu^*}{\sigma}\right)$$

The expression in parentheses is the ranking measure discussed in the section on portfolio-possibility lines (see "Performance Measure," p. 74), with the volatility, $\sigma$, serving as the approximate measure of investment risk. We conclude that, for any given level of market rate of return $D$, $r$ is uniquely related to the ranking fraction.

$$\frac{\mu - \mu^*}{\sigma} \text{ (which equals tangent } \alpha)$$

We note that a relatively large value of $r$ signifies a relatively low level of performance for fund management. A second important property of $r$ is obtained when the following relationship, based on the geometry of the diagram, is substituted in the previous expression for $r$:

$$\mu = D \text{ tangent } B + h = D \alpha + h$$

Substituting for $\mu$, we find that:

$$r = \frac{\mu^* - h}{\sigma}$$

Now $\mu^*$ is the same for all funds and independent of market fluctuations; and $h$ and $\sigma$ are the intercept and slope, respectively, of the characteristic line. It is clear in this formulation that $r$ is independent of $D$, the market rate of return. Hence $r$ tends to have the same value independently of fluctuations in the general market.

*You pays your money and you takes your choice.*

—*Punch,* Vol. X, p. 16. 1846

## Notes

1. In discussing the cumulative performance of investment funds between January 1, 1953, and September 30, 1958, the report says "... the interpretation of the net result is to be made against the background of the movements in security market prices during this period...general fund performance and comparisons among funds of different types might be quite different in other time periods...," *A Study of Mutual Funds* (Washington, D.C.: Government Printing Office, 1962), p. 308.
2. See, for example, H. M. Markowitz, *Portfolio Selection: Efficient Diversification of Investments* (New York: John Wiley & Sons, 1959); and D. E. Farrar, *The Investment Decision Under Uncertainty* (Englewood Cliffs: Prentice-Hall, Inc., 1962).
3. For elegant mathematical proof of the validity of indifference curves, see James Tobin, "Liquidity Performance as Behavior Towards Risk," *Review of Economic Studies,* February 1958, p. 65; a subsequently written, unpublished manuscript by the author carries the discussion further.

# CHAPTER 11

# Can Mutual Funds Outguess the Market?

## A Report on the Performance of 57 Funds and their Sensitivity to Market Fluctuations

**A**re mutual fund managers successfully anticipating major turns in the stock market? There is a widely held belief that they are. Whether investment managers themselves actually share this belief is hard to say. At one time or another in promoting their services, however, a number of mutual funds have used the claim that they can anticipate major stock market movements.

We have devised a statistical test of mutual funds' historical success in anticipating major turns in the stock market. Applying this test to the performance record of 57 open-end mutual funds, we find no evidence to support the belief that mutual fund managers can outguess the market.

## DEBATED RESPONSIBILITIES

The question we have studied has an important bearing on the responsibilities that investment managers can properly be asked to assume. For instance, today almost everyone agrees that the market was dangerously high in early 1929 and that stocks were a bargain in the 1950s. On hindsight, laymen are tempted to think that these extremes should have been "obvious" to fund managers at the time, and that they should have sold or bought common stocks accordingly. In actuality, of course, fund managers did *not* always sell in 1929 and buy in the 1950s.

What position should the fund manager take to protect himself against accusations that he should have anticipated market movements in this way? More broadly, what does the shareholder have a right to expect from the fund manager? Is the fund manager speculating if he attempts to anticipate major market movements? Or is he negligent if he fails to try? It seems to us that the answers to these questions depend in part on whether or not investment managers actually have the *ability* to anticipate major turns in the stock market.

Because a mutual fund's performance in each succeeding year is readily measured, widely published, and easily compared with that of other mutual funds, managers in this industry are perhaps particularly sensitive to the effect on their funds' performance of a market decline or market rise during the year. We believe that our findings may have significance not only for mutual fund managers, but also for pension, trust, and endowment fund managers—despite the fact that their objectives vary widely. If it is generally true that investment managers cannot outguess the market, then it may be necessary to revise certain conceptions about the responsibilities of investment management across the board.

## ANALYTICAL APPROACH

It is well known that there is a definite tendency for the prices of most common stocks to move up and down together. Because this tendency exists, it is meaningful to talk about fluctuations in the "market." It is also well known that some common stocks are more volatile (i.e., sensitive to market fluctuations) than others.

Thus, when we talk about investment managers outguessing the market, we mean anticipating whether the general stock market is going to rise or fall and adjusting the composition of their portfolios accordingly. That is, if they think the market is going to fall, they shift the composition of the portfolios they manage from more to less volatile securities (including bonds). If they think the market is going to rise, they shift in the opposite direction. The result of such shifts is a change in effective *portfolio* volatility. (A simple graphical measure of portfolio volatility was developed by one of the authors in a previous *Harvard Business Review* (*HBR*) article,[1] and is reviewed in some detail later in this article.)

In order to test whether or not a mutual fund manager has actually outguessed the market, we ask, in effect: *Is there evidence that the volatility of the fund was higher in years when the market did well than in years when the market did badly?* This is the question that was applied to the 57 funds we studied. Of course, we did not know that *all* of them were trying to outguess the market, but that does not matter. Unquestionably, some of them were trying to do this and thought they had the ability.

### Performance Data Used

Data for the mutual funds in our sample were obtained from *Investment Companies 1963,* by Arthur Wiesenberger Company.[2] For open-end investment companies, Wiesenberger employs the following formula to compute rate of return: "To asset value per share at the end of the period, adjusted to reflect reinvestment of all capital gains distributions, add dividends per share paid during the period from investment income, similarly adjusted; divide the total by the starting per share asset value."[3]

The resulting rate-of-return figure is only approximate, since it disregards subtleties relating to (1) the timing within the period of dividend distributions and (2) the relative after-tax value to the shareholder of market appreciation, on the one hand, and of dividend-interest income, on the other. We feel, however, that the measure is probably adequate for our purpose, even though these effects are disregarded.

## The Characteristic Line

If, year by year, the rate of return for a managed fund is plotted against the rate of return, similarly defined, for a suitable market average—such as the Dow-Jones Industrial Average or the Standard & Poor's 500-Stock Index—the result is the kind of patterns shown in Exhibit 11.1. A line fitting the pattern is called the characteristic line. If the line has the same slope for years in which the market goes up as for years in which the market goes down, the slope of the line is constant; the line is straight. When this is so, a single number—the tangent of the slope angle of the line—is sufficient to characterize the sensitivity of the fund in question to market fluctuations, and we can talk meaningfully about "the" volatility of the line.

The fund shown in Part A of Exhibit 11.1 has kept a constant volatility over the years included in the sample. For such funds, the degree of scatter around the characteristic line is a measure of how well diversified the fund is. The more nearly perfect the diversification of the fund, the less scatter around the characteristic line, because the more accurately the fund reflects the stocks in the market average.

## Outguessing the Market

What happens, however, if a fund management tries continually to outguess the market by oscillating between two characteristic lines, one of which has a high volatility and the other, a low volatility?

Part B of Exhibit 11.1 illustrates the extreme case in which management is able to outguess the market at every turn. Whenever management has elected the highly volatile composition demonstrated by characteristic line C-D, the market has risen; whenever management has elected the low-volatility line A-B, the market has fallen. It is clear in this case that the characteristic line is no longer straight.

If, on the other hand, fund management guesses wrong as often as it guesses right, then we have the kind of picture shown as Part C of Exhibit 11.1. Here the fund's performance traces out the undesirable points H, G, F, and E as frequently as it traces out the desirable points A, B, C, and D. The result is considerable scatter in the characteristic-line pattern, *but no curvature.*

Probably no fund management would claim to be able to anticipate the market perfectly. Let us assume, however, that management has some prediction powers. Then, the better the market performs, the more likely management is to have anticipated good performance and to have increased fund volatility appropriately; and the larger, on the average, the chosen volatility is likely to be. The result will be a gradual transition of fund volatility from a flat slope at the extreme left of the characteristic-line diagram to a steep slope at the extreme right, with the slope varying more or less continuously in between, producing a smoothly curved characteristic line pattern with a certain amount of scatter resulting from management's bad predictions (see Part D of Exhibit 11.1) rather than the kinked pattern associated with the policy illustrated in Exhibit 11.1B.

The key to our test for successful anticipation is simple: the only way in which fund management can translate ability to outguess the market into a benefit to the shareholder is to vary the fund volatility systematically in such a fashion that the resulting characteristic line is concave upward, as in Exhibit 11.1D. If fund management has correctly anticipated the market more often than not, then the characteristic line will no longer be straight. (And we can add, for the more mathematically inclined reader, that whether the characteristic line is smoothly curved or kinked, a

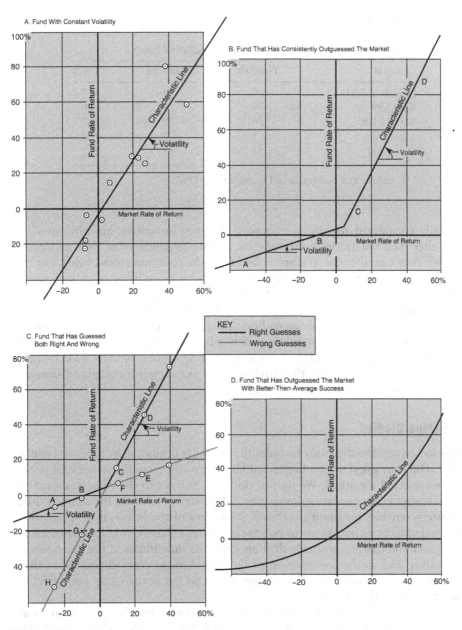

**EXHIBIT 11.1** Illustrative Characteristic Lines

least-squares statistical fit of a characteristic line to the performance data for the fund will be improved by inclusion of a quadratic term in the fitting formula.)

## Choice of Funds

If the management of a balanced fund elects to change the fund's volatility, it can shift the relative proportions of debt and equity, or change the average volatility of the equity portion, or both. However, stock funds and growth funds, which are

**EXHIBIT 11.2**   Breakdown of Sample by Size and Type of Fund

| Market value of assets* | Number of funds | | |
|---|---|---|---|
| | Growth | Balanced | Total |
| Less than $20 | 7 | 10 | 17 |
| $20–$99 | 7 | 13 | 20 |
| $100–$500 | 10 | 7 | 17 |
| More than $7,500 | 1 | 2 | 3 |
| Total | 25 | 32 | 57 |

* In millions of dollars as of December 31, 1962.

commonly considered to consist primarily of equity securities, are obviously not free to alter their volatilities by shifting the relative proportions of debt and equity (although they can alter the average volatility of the common stocks held). For this reason, it is sometimes argued that a balanced fund is more likely to make frequent changes in fund volatility. To allow for this possibility, we divided our sample in roughly equal proportions between balanced and growth funds.

In addition, it is sometimes argued that smaller funds will have less difficulty in changing their portfolio composition quickly when a change in volatility is desired. To account for this, we included in our sample of 57 mutual funds a wide range of fund sizes. Exhibit 11.2 shows the distribution of our sample among fund sizes and between balanced funds and growth funds.

## Time Period Studied

The period covered in the study includes the ten years beginning in 1953 and ending in 1962. One may ask if our findings would have been different if another time period had been selected for study. We do not think so. Subject to the various sources of random scatter in characteristic-line patterns discussed previously, the characteristic-line pattern remains invariant over time, regardless of the behavior of the market, unless and until basic management policies or abilities change. (In fact, management policies and abilities are probably drifting slowly as individuals in the management team mature and as the composition of the management team changes, but these effects are usually small, compared to the effects on the year-to-year rate of return caused by market fluctuations.)

As mentioned earlier, if management is right more often than wrong in its attempts to outguess the market, the characteristic-line pattern will be curved. The degree of curvature depends on how heavily management bets on its expectations—that is, the degree to which management changes fund volatility when its expectations regarding the market change. So long as management policy continues roughly constant in this regard, the degree of curvature manifested in the characteristic line will remain unchanged.

The only criterion for the time period selected for a curvature study is that during the period, the market should have exhibited wide and frequent swings both upward and downward, so that the characteristic-line data are not confined to a segment in the middle of the pattern which, because of its shortness, is indistinguishable from a straight line.

The period 1953–1962 contains one year in which the Dow-Jones Industrials demonstrated a rate of return of 50 percent, and three years in which the return was negative by substantial amounts. We feel that this is a suitable period for our study because it is long enough to cover a variety of ups and downs in the general market, short enough to avoid serious problems resulting from the gradual drift of fund policies over time, and recent enough to reflect modern mutual fund management practices and policies. The fact that the market was generally rising throughout the period has no effect on the characteristic line, and hence in no way invalidates our findings.

We have used yearly data because we feel that even the smaller mutual funds would be reluctant to make the changes in portfolio composition necessary to change fund volatility much more often than once a year. Based as it is on yearly data, however, the study cannot detect any success that fund managements may have had with more frequent changes in volatility.

## Findings

What does the study show? It shows no statistical evidence that the investment managers of any of the 57 funds have successfully outguessed the market. More precisely, we find no evidence of curvature of the characteristic lines of any of the funds.

Here are some of the more technical aspects of our study:

- In order to test for the presence of curvature, we used the methods mentioned earlier. (A least-squares regression technique was employed to fit characteristic-line data for the 57 open-end mutual funds in our sample. That is, for each of the funds we calculated the constants for the equation which "best" describes the performance data of the mutual fund for the Standard & Poor's Composite Price Index as a quadratic function of the performance.)
- Exhibit 11.3 summarizes our results. The value of the F statistic, plotted along the horizontal axis, is a measure of the degree of curvature of the fund (and is normalized to allow for variations in the amount of random scatter observed). The vertical axis shows the number of funds which had F values equal to the F value given on the horizontal axis. As the magnitude of an F value increases, the higher the probability that the amount of curvature seen for the fund is real, i.e., is greater than we would expect by random chance. The vertical dotted line marks the F value (5.6) corresponding to the amount of apparent curvature which even those funds that have no real curvature would display one time in twenty. A fund should show an F value greater than 5.6 in order to be considered to have real curvature.

In our sample of 57 managed funds, only one displayed even an F value of 5.6. This fund's curve and also the actual data points are given in Exhibit 11.4.

In other words, our findings show that for the mutual funds in our sample, at least, it is safe to assume that their characteristic lines are straight. Actual funds tend to resemble the fund in Exhibit 11.1A rather than the funds in Exhibit 11.1B and 11.1D. Our results suggest that an investor in mutual funds is completely dependent on fluctuations in the general market. This is not to say that a skillful fund management cannot provide the investor with a rate of return that is higher in both bad times and good than the return provided by the market averages, but it does suggest that the

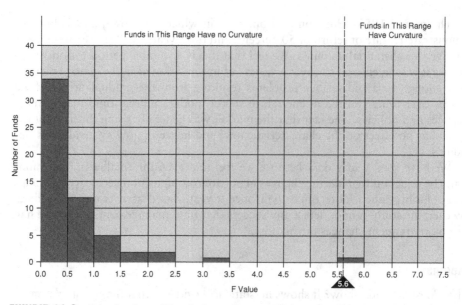

**EXHIBIT 11.3**   Distribution of Funds According to F Value

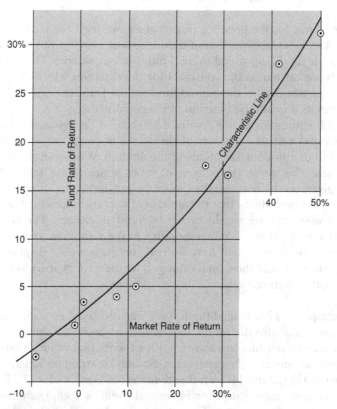

**EXHIBIT 11.4**   Characteristic Line of the Fund That Has the
Greatest F Value

improvement in rate of return will be due to the fund manager's ability to identify underpriced industries and companies, rather than to any ability to outguess turns in the level of the market as a whole.

The fact that only one of the 57 mutual funds in our sample has a characteristic line suggesting curvature indicates that perhaps no investor—professional or amateur—can outguess the market. This finding has clear significance for the man in the street managing his own portfolio, for the man with fiduciary responsibility for a private estate, for the president of a manufacturing company responsible for its pension fund, and for a college treasurer managing an endowment. It means that probably the best assumption they can make is that investment managers have no ability to outguess the market and should not try to. It also means they should not hold fund managers responsible for failing to foresee changes in market climate.

> *Profits on the exchange are the treasures of goblins. At one time they may be carbuncle stones, then coals, then diamonds, then flint-stones, then morning dew, then tears.*
> —Joseph de la Vega, *Confusion de Confusiones* (1688)

## Notes

1. Jack L. Treynor, "How to Rate Management of Investment Funds," Harvard Business Review (HBR), January–February 1965, p. 63.
2. Port Washington, New York, Kennikat Press, Inc., 1963.
3. Ibid., p. 99.

# CHAPTER 12

# The Future of Performance Measurement

*A fund "performs" well for several years, then "performs" badly for several years—while managed the same way by the same people.*

*All fund managers researching the same group of securities perform well in some years and badly in others—even though they are primarily buying from and selling to each other.*

**B**oth phenomena are commonplace, and both would manifest themselves whether managers traded or not. They reflect market factors, rather than factors specific to individual securities. That's why they don't depend on the manager's level of skill in his selection decisions or on which manager is buying and which is selling.

It is now widely accepted that even highly diversified portfolios are sensitive to market-wide factors, and that these factors explain more of investment results than managers' efforts at active management. Isolating the consequences of managers' efforts—in other words, measuring performance, as distinct from results—requires a model of how market-wide factors impact investment results.

Capital asset pricing theory argues that the market portfolio provides a natural standard against which to measure an actual portfolio's performance; in the absence of research advantage, an investor's return will be highest for a given level of risk when he holds the market portfolio. But Richard Roll has pointed out that one can't observe the market portfolio—only arbitrary indexes that may be poor proxies for it. When we measure "market risk" using these proxies, we may seriously overestimate market sensitivities for some securities, hence for some portfolios, while underestimating for others.

By subtracting faulty estimates of "market" effect from investment results, Roll argues, we may attribute too much to the contribution of one manager, while attributing too little to another. Since market effects are so potent compared with the manager's contribution, these attribution errors can be large enough to be very serious.

Roll's concern would disappear if there were only one market-wide factor affecting securities prices and returns. In that case, all portfolios containing very large numbers of securities in very small amounts—including the true market portfolio—would correlate so highly that any one could serve to explain market effect in any other. But both practitioners and academics seem to find evidence of a number of market-wide factors.

Although the factors specific to individual securities will "diversify away" in such portfolios, we cannot assume the same for market-wide factors. Worse still, different portfolios (such as the S & P 500 and the Wilshire 5000) may emphasize different market factors, so that one index may outperform another in some periods and underperform in others. Because we have no way of knowing how the true market portfolio weights each market-wide factor, we cannot know which index is the better market proxy.

But all is not lost. We can still estimate the sensitivities of a particular portfolio to market-wide factors, observe the returns attributable to these factors and compute the respective market effects (i.e., the factor returns times the respective portfolio sensitivities). Then we can estimate the manager's contribution by summing the several market effects and subtracting the sum from his investment result.

Because we don't know how well market-wide factors correlate with the true (but unobservable) market portfolio, we don't know how much of the return due to any one factor is risk premium and how much is surprise. The same necessarily holds for the effect on the portfolio of all the factors combined. But the residual portfolio return we impute to the manager's contribution will be the same. It doesn't even matter which set of market factors we use, so long as it captures all market-wide phenomena that affect portfolio returns significantly.

Selection entails departing from a high level of diversification to take advantage of forces specific to the individual security; timing entails varying the portfolio's sensitivity to market-wide factors. Instead of trying to measure the portfolio manager's departures from an unobservable market portfolio, we measure his departures from a "diversified" portfolio with the same sensitivity to market-wide factors—the additional risk he incurs in selection. We can also measure his conscious or unconscious departures from maintaining constant sensitivities to these factors—the additional risk he incurs by market timing. If he succeeds in his efforts at selection or timing, we can then weigh his success against the extra risk incurred in these departures.

What we cannot do is reward or penalize a manager for his portfolio's relative emphasis on the respective market factors. That would be tantamount to setting up one set of factor weights as ideal—asserting, in effect, that we have somehow come into possession of the knowledge that Roll says we cannot have. But this is just as well, since clients with more than one manager rarely want the individual manager's portfolio to proxy the market.

The practical consequence of Roll's insight will be more discriminating performance measurement—and portfolio management—not less.

# Four

# Economics

If labor and capital are substitutes, then a given amount of capital can provide any number of jobs. And if, for some reason, demand is fixed, then adding capital will reduce the requisite amount of labor. In such a world, unemployment can be caused by an excess of capital. But if labor and capital are complements, then the number of jobs is limited by the number of machines. When there are more workers than machines, it doesn't take exotic theories of demand failure to explain unemployment.

Instead, chronic unemployment can be caused by chronic failures to save and invest. Given the misery and humiliation that the chronically unemployed experience, is it any surprise when countries with more workers than machines are ravaged by social unrest, crime, terrorism, and guerilla war?

But if unemployment is the result of failures to save and invest, then the misery and humiliation are the result of failed economic policies. The discipline of economics has probably had its Ptolemy, its Archimedes. But it obviously isn't making the kind of contribution to humankind's problems that the physical sciences are making. Will it take another 2,000 years for economists to achieve that kind of mastery?

There's no shortage of brilliant minds in economics. Why hasn't academic research moved more rapidly? Thorsten Veblen, who should know, explains why "the first requisite for constructive work in modern science . . . is a skeptical frame of mind."* But academics derive their authority from their erudition. Any challenge to the old ideas is a threat to their authority. Francis Bacon organized the Royal Society to encourage skeptical people who asked impertinent questions—people like Isaac Newton and Charles Darwin. Without the Royal Society there would have been no industrial revolution.

Undoubtedly there will be great scientists stepping up to transform radically the way we think about economics. There will be Newtons and Darwins. Are they waiting for another Francis Bacon?

J.L.T.

---

*Quoted in *Money, the Financial System and the Economy* by George G. Kaufman, Rand McNally, (1973).

# CHAPTER 13

# Unemployment and Inflation

The Phillips Curve attempts to reduce to numbers the intuitively appealing idea that the inflation rate depends loosely on the level of unemployment. It expresses this kind of tradeoff: If we are willing to tolerate high rates of price inflation, we can enjoy low levels of unemployment; if we are willing to tolerate high levels of unemployment, we can enjoy low rates of price inflation. Because a principal task of policy makers is avoiding both high unemployment and runaway inflation, it is hardly surprising that, despite its fairly recent invention, the curve has become a cornerstone of modern demand management.

A swelling chorus of critics of the Phillips Curve asserts, however, that there is no historical evidence of a stable relationship between unemployment and inflation or that, if such a relationship ever existed, it exists no more. They cite the current stagflation—a very high level of inflation coupled with rising unemployment—as evidence. Some go so far as to assert that, without the Phillips Curve, the whole edifice of modern macroeconomics will come tumbling down, depriving policy makers of both their tools and their credentials. Of the problems encountered with it, one critic has written:

> *Elaborate mathematical formulas were drawn from the most advanced computer circuits of the age to determine the necessary 'trade-off' among employment, growth and rising prices. To reduce inflation x per cent would require the loss of y jobs and a change of z per cent in the rate of growth . . . . [Such a* posteriori *analysis] certainly cannot tell us what is likely to happen when historical conditions change . . . . Most of our current debate rests on an analysis of the American economy which, if it was once accurate, is now mistaken in fundamental ways . . . . It will be necessary to reorganize economic life itself—to remodel institutions and relationships that have become fundamentally defective and are now incapable of advancing the interests of America and its people . . . . to initiate drastic changes in the relationship between the United States government, its people, and the institutions of the economy.*[1]

On the other hand, if the Phillips Curve is indeed dead, it doesn't necessarily mean that there is no relationship between unemployment and inflation. It may merely mean that Professor Phillips posited the wrong relationship.

Copyright © CFA Institute. Reprinted from the *Financial Analysts Journal* with permission. May–June 1975. Jack Treynor thanks Fischer Black, Robert Ferguson, Douglas Love, Charles Upton, and Roman Weil for their suggestions and contributions.

If there is a relationship between unemployment and inflation, it presumably reflects the greater power of labor to bid up money wages when fewer unemployed workers are competing with each other for jobs. If this greater power is being exercised in a racing inflation, in which both employers and workers know that prices will continue to rise, will labor's power to bargain for higher wages be directed merely toward keeping up with rising prices? Or will labor demand—and employers concede—wage increases exceeding the rate of price inflation? If so, then the current rate of increase in prices will merely be the standard against which still more rapid wage increases will be negotiated.[2] A higher rate of increase in wages, however, will quickly translate itself into a higher rate of increase in prices.[3] And this higher rate of inflation will then become the new standard. According to this hypothesis, the level of unemployment should be expected to govern, not the inflation rate, but the rate at which the inflation rate is increasing or decreasing.

The difference in concept between the new hypothesis and the Phillips Curve hypothesis is precisely the difference between the speed of a car and its acceleration (or deceleration). If we hit the brake while traveling 60 miles per hour, several seconds will elapse during which our forward speed is still great, even though our acceleration—our change in speed from second to second—is negative. We have all been in anxious situations where we wished that hitting the brake would bring our car to an instant halt. The brake controls the rate at which speed declines, however, rather than speed itself. There is nothing that we can do in these situations but maintain pressure on the brake and wait for its effect to accumulate over enough time to stop the car. The faster the initial speed, the more time it takes.

So it is—according to the new hypothesis—with stagflation. If sufficiently high levels of unemployment brake the inflation rate, we can easily have (as we have now) a high level of unemployment and at the same time be suffering from a high rate of inflation. This is a far cry from the Phillips Curve hypothesis, however, according to which a high level of unemployment translates immediately into a low level of inflation. Thus the two hypotheses are sufficiently different that, if one fits the real world, the other probably won't. In particular, if actual data don't support the relationship between the level of unemployment and the speed of inflation—the Phillips Curve—we cannot safely conclude that there is no relationship between the level of unemployment and the acceleration (or deceleration) in the inflation rate.

In terms of period analysis, we can express the new relationship as follows.[4] Let $w_t$ and $p_t$ represent respectively the levels at time t of money wages and prices, $\Delta w / w$ and $\Delta p / p$ their rates of change for the period beginning at time t, and m the level of unemployment. Then the new hypothesis can be expressed in terms of two equations. The first asserts that the rate of change of money wages depends on some function $Q(m)$ of the level of unemployment in the current period (the first term on the right-hand side) and on the rate of change of prices (the second term) in the last period:

$$\frac{\Delta w_t}{w_t} = Q(m_t) + \frac{\Delta p_{t-1}}{p_{t-1}} \tag{13.1}$$

The second equation asserts that across-the-board changes in the level of wages are promptly mirrored in proportionate across-the-board changes in prices:

$$\frac{\Delta p_t}{p_t} = \frac{\Delta w_t}{w_t} \tag{13.2}$$

(The writer confesses that, in the privacy of his own study, he sometimes refers to the first term in the first equation—the influence of the current level of unemployment—as "demand-pull" inflation and the second—the influence of the current rate of price change—as "cost-push." He freely admits, however, that his is not the conventional, textbook distinction between demand-pull and cost-push inflation.)

Substituting the second equation in the first, we have:

$$\frac{\Delta w_t}{w_t} - \frac{\Delta w_t - 1}{w_t - 1} = Q(m_t)$$

If we now define the inflation rate f equal to

$$\frac{\Delta p}{p} = \frac{\Delta w}{w} \text{ and transpose, we have:}$$

$$f_t - f_{t-1} = Q(m_t)$$
$$\Delta f_t = Q(m_t) \tag{13.3}$$

This equation derived directly from the first two, says that the current unemployment rate (m) determines the change $\Delta f$ in the inflation rate from this period to next period—rather than the current inflation rate f (the Phillips Curve relationship).

**EXHIBIT 13.1**   Phillips Curve Data: 1953–1972

|        | f      | $\Delta f_t$ | $\Delta f_{t+1}$ | m    |
|--------|--------|--------------|------------------|------|
| 1953   | 0.8%   |              |                  | 2.9  |
| 54     | −0.5   | −1.3         | 0.8              | 5.6  |
| 55     | 0.3    | 0.8          | 2.3              | 4.4  |
| 56     | 2.6    | 2.3          | 0.5              | 4.1  |
| 57     | 3.1    | 0.5          | −1.2             | 4.3  |
| 58     | 1.9    | −1.2         | −0.4             | 6.8  |
| 59     | 1.5    | −0.4         | −0.1             | 5.5  |
| 1960   | 1.4    | −0.1         | −0.7             | 5.5  |
| 61     | 0.7    | −0.7         | 0.6              | 6.7  |
| 62     | 1.3    | 0.6          | 0.1              | 5.6  |
| 63     | 1.4    | 0.1          | −0.2             | 5.6  |
| 64     | 1.2    | −0.2         | 0.6              | 5.2  |
| 65     | 1.8    | 0.6          | 1.9              | 4.5  |
| 66     | 3.7    | 1.9          | −0.9             | 3.8  |
| 67     | 2.8    | −0.9         | 2.0              | 3.8  |
| 68     | 4.8    | 2.0          | 1.0              | 3.6  |
| 69     | 5.8    | 1.0          | −0.1             | 3.5  |
| 1970   | 5.7    | −0.1         | −2.2             | 5.0  |
| 71     | 3.5    | −2.2         | 0.0              | 5.9  |
| 72     | 3.5    | 0.0          |                  | 5.6  |

Source: Bureau of Labor Statistics, U.S. Department of Commerce

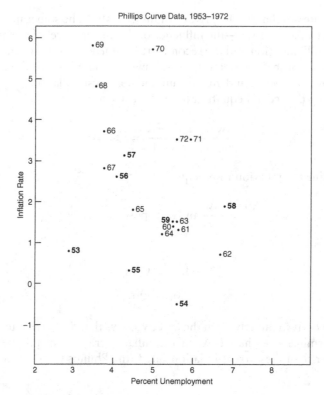

Phillips Curve Data, 1953–1972

**EXHIBIT 13.2** Old Hypothesis

Which, if either, of these relationships is supported by the actual data? Exhibit 13.2 plots the inflation rate against the unemployment rate for the postwar years. Each dot in Exhibit 13.2 represents one year's experience with unemployment and inflation. The distance of the dot from the bottom of the chart measures the inflation rate (scaled along the vertical axis), and its distance from the left-hand side of the chart measures the unemployment rate (scaled along the horizontal axis). If there were truly such a thing as a Phillips Curve relationship, the dots for the various postwar years would fall into a well defined pattern. Instead, they appear to be scattered randomly, like darts on a dart board. Exhibit 13.2 suggests that the Phillips Curve relationship if it exists, is relatively weak.

In Exhibit 13.3 we have plotted instead the *rate of change* of the inflation rate against the level of unemployment for the same time period. As before, each dot represents one year's experience, with its distance from the left-hand side of the graph measuring the level of unemployment. Now, however, the dot's distance from the bottom of the graph measures the rate of change in inflation (i.e., the acceleration or deceleration in the inflation rate) rather than the inflation rate.

We can make several observations about Exhibit 13.3. (1) There is strong evidence that unemployment is associated with the rate of change in the inflation rate, rather than (as in Exhibit 13.2) the inflation rate itself. (2) Economists have long debated whether a little inflation is a good thing. Taken together, Exhibits 13.2 and 13.3

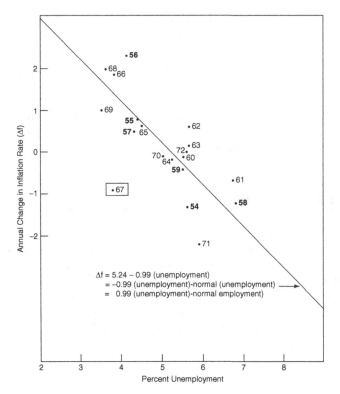

**EXHIBIT 13.3** New Hypothesis

suggest that any level of unemployment below that corresponding to a zero rate of change in inflation will in time result in an unbounded increase in the inflation rate. Although our economy can run equally well at a variety of price levels (assuming that the banking system maintains the same real money stock), it is far from clear that it can run equally well at widely differing inflation rates. Whereas any inflation rate, maintained at a constant level, does nothing to reduce unemployment, a little acceleration in the inflation rate is ultimately intolerable. (The critical level of unemployment, at which the inflation rate may be expected to hold steady, appears to be slightly over five percent.) Thus there is no such thing, strictly speaking, as a tradeoff between unemployment and inflation. Although different definitions of the variables or a different time sample would doubtless lead to a different regression line, the slope of the line in Exhibit 13.3 (which ignores the data point for 1967) is so close to minus one that it suggests the following rule: To reduce inflation by one percent, we must endure unemployment one percent in excess of "normal" (i.e., in excess of five percent) for one year.

Conversely, there is no such thing as "licking" inflation: No matter how low the current level, if this year's unemployment falls much below five percent, next year's inflation rate will be higher, and by an amount that is (within broad limits) predictable. (3) For all practical purposes, we may as well define five percent unemployment as "normal" unemployment; the traditional four percent is meaningless.

(4) It is tempting to attribute the failure of the dots in Exhibit 13.3 to fall on a smooth curve (or, indeed, on a straight line) partly to the changing definition of full employment. Nevertheless, the pattern displayed in Exhibit 13.3 is quite stable over time. When the postwar period is divided into three nonoverlapping subperiods (represented respectively by boldface, lightface and italic dates), the resulting patterns fall virtually on top of one another, suggesting that roughly the same relationship between unemployment and the rate of change in inflation held in all three subperiods. Viewed in terms of the new curve, there is no evidence that the economy has changed in some fundamental way; quite the contrary.

## INFLATION AND STOCK PRICES

The data plotted in Exhibit 13.3 suggest that the relationship between unemployment and the time rate of change in inflation can be approximated by a downward sloping straight line. The data in the chart are, of course, too sketchy to be conclusive. But if the relationship is, in fact, a straight line, then it has the following algebraic expression, where $n_t^*$ is the "neutral" level of employment at which inflation is neither accelerating nor decelerating, $n_t$ is the actual level of employment at time t, $\Delta f_t$ is the rate at which inflation is accelerating or decelerating at time t, and b is the coefficient relating one to the other:

$$\Delta f_t = b(n_t - n_t^*) \qquad (13.4)$$

When the level of employment departs from the neutral level, inflation accelerates (algebraically speaking) at a rate proportional to the amount by which it departs. When b is defined, as we have defined it here, in terms of employment, rather than unemployment, its sign is positive. Thus, for example, positive departures of employment from the neutral level are viewed as inducing positive acceleration in the inflation rate. (Our language often suggests that there is causation running from the level of employment to the rate at which inflation accelerates. The evidence does not prove causation, however—merely association.[5])

If we now sum $\Delta f_t$ from time zero to time T we have:

$$f_T - f_0 = \sum_{t=0}^{T} \Delta f_t = b \sum (n_t - n_t^*) \qquad (13.5)$$

The sum in the right-hand member of Equation 13.5 represents the employment lost in going from the initial inflation rate to the normal rate.

Now suppose (as is frequently supposed in econometric industry studies) that a company's earning power is linearly related to the national level of employment—that the level of national employment is linearly related to the national level of demand, which is linearly related to demand for the company's output, which is linearly related to its earning power. In making this supposition, we focus on the influence of national demand to the exclusion of other influences that might cause the company's share of national demand to change. We can write this kind of relationship as follows, where c and d are merely constants suitable for expressing the linear relationship (d in particular being the sensitivity of the company's earning power to the level of national employment):

$$\text{profitability}_t = c + dn_t \tag{13.6}$$

The present value (PV) of the company is given by an expression like the following, where the $a_t$ are discount factors appropriate to cash earnings for the year t:

$$PV = \sum a_t \text{profitability} \tag{13.7}$$

Substituting our expression for the linear dependence of profitability in year t on employment in year t, we have:

$$PV = \sum a_t \, (c + dn_t)$$
$$= \sum a_t \, (c + dn_t^*) + \sum a_t d \, (n_t - n_t^*)$$
$$= \sum a_t \, (c + dn_t^*) + \frac{1}{b} \sum a_t d \Delta f_t \tag{13.8}$$

In this form, the equation for the present value of the company is expressed as the sum of two terms. The first term is essentially a "steady state" contribution to the present value of the firm and the second is a "transient" contribution. Since $a_t$ exceeds $a_{t+1}$ for all t, the farther out into the future the correction of any current inflationary excess is deferred, the smaller is the loss in present value associated with the transient term.

Suppose, on the other hand, that, whatever the nation accepts as the normal level of inflation ($f^*$), it will undertake policies such that the current level ($f_0$) tends to return to the normal level within a few years. Then the discounting effect will be relatively less important for the transient term, and we can rewrite the present value of the firm as follows.

$$PV = \sum a_t (c + dn_t^*) + \frac{ad}{b} \sum \Delta f_t$$
$$= \sum a_t (c + dn_t^*) + \frac{ad}{b} \, (f^* \cdots f_0) \tag{13.9}$$

The first, "steady state," term is independent of national policies that might cause employment and demand to diverge from the norm, depending as it does only on the normal employment rate. The second, "transient," term depends only on (1) the inflation rate considered normal for the country in question and (2) the current inflation rate. Its value is independent of how the national economy goes from its present state to the normal state.

Although, in evaluating specific common stocks, one will probably not be willing to treat differences in the discount factor over even the few years typically required for an economy to return to normal employment as being equal, as Equation 13.9

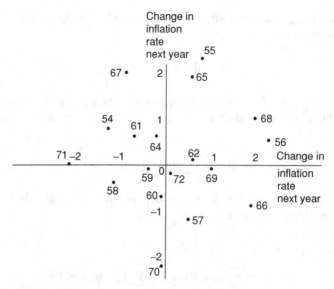

**EXHIBIT 13.4**   Is Next Year's Change in Inflation Rate
Related to This Year's?

treats them, it nevertheless explains why common stock prices are depressed in times
of rapid inflation[6] and (to the extent that high nominal interest rates are associated,
as Irving Fisher alleged, with high inflation rates) why low stock prices are associated
with high nominal interest rates.

## Notes

1. Richard Goodwin, "Awaiting the Copernican Question," *The New Yorker*, January 6,
   1975, p. 38ff.
2. Strictly speaking, it is not the current rate of price inflation, but rather the expected future
   rate, that will provide the negotiating standard. Charles Upton points out, however, that
   in the postwar period, at least, changes in the rate of price inflation approximate a random
   walk (see Figure 13.4). Hence the current rate is hardly an unreasonable surrogate for the
   expected future rate.
3. Roman Weil points out that monetarists will be unwilling to admit that a uniform (percentage), across-the-board increase in wages will induce an across-the-board increase in
   prices. We not only assume that it will, but that any time lags entailed are so short that,
   for our immediate purposes, we can ignore them (see Equation 13.2).
4. The author is indebted to Robert Ferguson of Baker, Weeks & Co., Inc., for this version
   of the proof, which he considers vastly superior to his own. Douglas A. Love has offered
   a similar version.
5. Fischer Black wrote the author: "I think of [unemployment and inflation] as jointly caused.
   When the economy heats up, unemployment goes down, and inflation accelerates. When
   the economy cools off, unemployment goes up, and inflation decelerates. I don't know
   what the mechanism is, and neither do you."
6. As James H. Lorie and others have pointed out, another explanation is certainly the
   overstatement of income for tax purposes and consequent distortion of taxes. As he has
   also pointed out, the vulgar explanation—that stock prices have to fall for stocks to remain
   competitive with bonds when (nominal) bond yields rise—is insupportable.

# CHAPTER 14

# What Professor Galbraith Neglected to Tell His Television Audience

*There are only two ways to keep a modern economy running—the market mechanism and force. But it takes wealth to use the market mechanism. When a country runs out of wealth, it has only two options—rely entirely on force to keep its economy running, or return to the stone age.*

*There is a limit to how far a country can go in raising taxes on earned income before workers riot in the streets. Beyond that point, the burden of government spending falls on capital, rather than labor. When that burden gets too heavy, private enterprise won't replenish the country's capital stock. It is then only a matter of time until private wealth is exhausted and the country is reduced to relying on force—i.e., on a totalitarian government— to keep its economy running.*

1. Modern societies have enormously complex economies, requiring great concentrations of capital and a high degree of specialization of labor.
2. To keep their economies running, these societies depend on the extensive cooperation of people.
3. There are only two known ways to elicit the necessary cooperation:
   a. the market mechanism and
   b. force.

   As regards the guidance of their own behavior, most people prefer the application of the market mechanism to the application of force. So-called "free societies" are those that make maximum use of the market mechanism and minimum use of force.

4. It follows from (3) that in modern societies there are two repositories of power:
   a. command over the market mechanism and
   b. control over the means of force.

In stable societies, the latter is in the hands of government. Command over the market mechanism lies in the hands of people with wealth. A man with one dollar in his pocket has the power to command a Coke, Hershey bar or Big Mac. But he cannot command the cooperation needed to run a steel plant or railroad. This requires large concentrations of wealth—in corporate, if not in individual hands.

5. In totalitarian countries, power—instead of being balanced between those people who control the means of force and those who command the market mechanism—is concentrated in one group of people who control both. Countries in which the former people have taken command of the market mechanism are called communist. Countries in which the latter people have taken control of the means of force are called fascist. After the take-over, however, it is difficult to tell one from the other.

## II

1. Working people have certain expectations about their real income—after taxes, of course. When after-tax real income falls far enough below their expectations, they begin to riot in the streets. When a government is reluctant to lower after-tax real income, its power to increase taxes is confined to the country's privately owned capital stock.
2. The higher are workers' expectations regarding their after-tax income, the larger is the share of the tax burden that must be borne by the capital stock. This problem is frequently referred to in the press as the "problem of rising expectations."
3. Unfortunately, power to tax the capital stock is also limited: When the tax burden on the capital stock exceeds its underlying value, it pays the owners to walk away, leaving the capital stock unmaintained and unprotected. (Anyone who thinks taxes cannot have this effect has not seen the South Bronx lately.)
4. New additions to the privately owned capital stock naturally bear their share of the tax burden. The larger that share looms in relation to the underlying economic value of such additions, the less willing people will be to add to the capital stock.
5. Ultimately, the old capital stock becomes worthless. But all wealth derives from claims on stocks of capital with economic value. In the absence of continuing additions to the privately owned capital stock, a country ultimately runs out of wealth.
6. When a country runs out of wealth, the market mechanism ceases to function. The country then has two choices. It can:
   a. abandon the high degree of specialization of labor and concentrated capital stock essential to a modern economy and return to a stone age economy—with a drastic decline in real income—or
   b. rely exclusively on force to keep its modern economy operating.
7. So far, no modern country that has run out of wealth has elected to return to the stone age; in every case the election has been for a totalitarian society. In the wake of profligate military expenditures, Russia ran out of wealth in 1917; for very different reasons, Germany ran out in 1933. India very nearly reached this point in the years following the oil crisis of 1973.

## III

1. There are a number of signposts along the road to exhaustion of a country's wealth. If its tax system is such that the burden falls unequally on different industries, capital additions will cease in some industries before they cease in others. If the government wants to maintain employment in the former, it is obliged to step in and run them, making the necessary capital additions itself. This is called "nationalization."

2. One way to stimulate privately financed additions to the capital stock is to lower the real rate of interest. Hence another signpost is a persistent downtrend in the real rate. If the real rate of interest is artificially depressed in order to encourage private capital formation, on the average and over time returns on all forms of investment will be abnormally low.

3. The famous American economist Irving Fisher discovered the relationship between the real interest rate, the nominal interest rate and inflation. According to the Fisher Equation, there are two ways to lower the real rate:

   a. lower the nominal rate or

   b. raise the inflation rate.

   Because there are limits to how far a central bank can go in lowering the nominal interest rate, another signpost along the road is inflation.

4. Another way to stimulate private investment, say the neo-Keynesians, is to raise levels of output and employment by increasing government consumption without an offsetting increase in taxation. They argue that the addition to government debt resulting from such "deficit spending" is not harmful, since we taxpayers owe it to each other. Harmful or not, regular recourse to deficit spending is another signpost.

5. It should already be clear, however, that the government debt that accumulates in the course of deficit spending is not merely something we owe to each other. The burden tends to fall on the capital stock, rather than on earned income. It may very well be true that deficit spending stimulates consumption; whether, in view of the discouraging effect of additions to the government debt, it stimulates capital formation is far less clear.

6. Before taxes or subsidies, earned income will reflect the real wage, which is governed in turn by what economists call "the marginal product of labor"—the extra output that employing one more worker will produce. Because it is governed by the marginally efficient capital stock, the real wage rises or falls, depending whether the capital stock is growing faster or slower than employment.

7. Another way to raise the income of workers is by government transfer payments—financed, of course, by taxing capital. The regular, habitual, chronic use of such payments to subsidize the real income of workers is called socialism. Because the burden of supporting these payments falls on new capital as well as old, discouraging new capital formation, it also retards increases in the real wage. In socialist countries, the political party that promises the biggest immediate increase in real income usually gets elected. Because they tend to increase real income now at the expense of increases later, socialist countries often have very low rates of private investment and slow growth in real income (two more signposts), England being the classic example.

8. Because they discourage capital formation, socialist countries tend to run out of wealth. But a country doesn't have to embrace socialism to run out of wealth. Any government policies that discourage private capital formation can lead it down the same road. With or without socialism, the destination is a totalitarian form of government. No wonder Professor Hayek called it "The Road to Serfdom."

# CHAPTER 15

# The Financial Objective in the Widely Held Corporation

In the widely held corporation, the split between ownership and control is often virtually complete. Should those in control of the corporation share that traditional financial objective of those who own it—the maximization of share value?

Chester Barnard has argued that a corporation owes its existence to the consent of a number of factions. When a customer ceases to buy or the worker refuses to work, for example, the result is usually a crisis for management. Edward Banfield calls the ability of the executive to elicit cooperation "power," or "influence," and views executive action in terms of trading in power. Banfield's remarks about management's exercise of power apply *a fortiori* to financial power. The key to management's power to spend is the willingness of its creditors to continue lending. Management has unused financial power whenever the corporation's creditors consider that existing loans have not exhausted their security.

Since, in a rational market, the aggregate value of the corporate common stock equals the economic value of the corporation less the outstanding claims of creditors, the untapped borrowing power of the corporation—hence management's power to spend—is measured by the aggregate market value of the common stock. It is doubtful whether other factions with a financial stake in the corporation will be best served by a policy of merely "satisficing" with respect to the shareholder. Those who regard share value maximization as irrelevant or immoral are forgetting that the stockholder is not merely the beneficiary of the corporation's financial success, but also the referee who determines management's financial power.

The split between ownership and control in the widely held corporation is often virtually complete, with ownership vested in a large and diverse population of stockholders and control wielded by a small group of professional managers. For this kind of corporation, it is no longer realistic to regard management as the hired hand of the owner.[1] Management will have its own interests, which may diverge significantly from the owners'. In particular, some argue, those in control of the corporation may no longer share that traditional financial objective of those who own it—the maximization of share value.

---

Professor Gordon Donaldson of the Harvard Business School has argued that the interest of management "quite naturally relates to the specifics of near-term movements in cash inflow and outflow, with all their inevitable irregularities from one period to another." The administration of cash flows, chiefly through mundane business operations, rarely involves the corporate shareholder. As Donaldson sees it, the stockholder's contribution is limited to providing management with continuity in office and, when needed, new equity capital. Furthermore, "for the large and mature corporation, the second of these may not be a vital consideration. Many such companies do not give serious consideration to stock issues as a source of cash for growth, finding that internally generated funds, net of the customary dividends, very adequately supply the needed growth in the equity base." In other words, management asks of ownership only to be left alone to do its job free of "harassments from individual champions of the stockholder interest" and free of the threat of "raids that would unseat existing management."[2]

If the stockholder's contribution to the corporation is largely passive, why then should management take seriously the objective of maximizing the per share value of the common stock? According to Edward S. Mason (former Dean of the Graduate School of Public Administration, Harvard University), "If ownership is completely divorced from control, it becomes hard to see why stockholders are entitled to more than an interest payment, plus a premium for risks that are substantially smaller for large than for small firms. If there are no legally enforceable responsibilities of management . . . to owners . . . it becomes doubtful whether over time these responsibilities will be recognized." He quotes Lord Keynes, who pointed out that when "the stockholders are almost entirely disassociated from management . . . the direct personal interest of the latter in the making of great profit becomes quite secondary. When this stage is reached, the general stability and reputation of the institution are more considered by the management than the maximum profit for the stockholders."[3]

Professor Robert N. Anthony of the Harvard Business School describes a management point of view toward financial objectives in the widely held corporation that is probably not far from typical: "Many companies formed to achieve some specific short-run objective (e.g., a real estate syndicate, a stock promotion) undoubtedly fit the profit maximization pattern. So do speculators in both securities and commodities. So do various types of fly-by-night operators and get-rich-quick artists. But I know of no study of general business practice that supports the profit maximization premise. . . . Although we find leaders of the business community stressing the importance of a *satisfactory* profit, we also find them discussing business responsibilities, the need for a fair division of income among the parties involved in the business and other subjects that are *incompatible with the profit maximization goal.*" Anthony concludes that profit maximization is not only too difficult to achieve, but also immoral.[4]

In this writer's view, any management—no matter how powerful and independent—that flouts the financial objective of maximizing share value does so at its peril.

## MANAGEMENT ENDS

Chester Barnard has argued that a corporation owes its continued existence to the consent of any number of factions—the customer, the stockholder, the banker, the supplier, the worker, the voter.[5] When one or more of these factions suspends cooperation, the result is usually a crisis for the corporation—and for its management. Consider what happens, for example, when a customer ceases to buy or the worker refuses to work.

Edward Banfield calls the ability of the executive to elicit cooperation "power," or "influence," and views executive action in terms of exercising, and trading in, power. The executive "may have a sizable inventory [of power] and many accounts receivable." The goodwill of the customer constitutes a stock of corporate power, as does the confidence of the banker. "This power is like capital; [the executive] can either 'consume' it or 'invest' it." But, "it goes without saying," Banfield continues, "that if he is to stay in business very long [he] . . . must like any trader maintain his capital and support himself while doing so."

The executive must, in other words, "employ the incentives at his disposal so as to (a) secure the cooperation he needs to accomplish his immediate purposes and (b) replenish the supply of incentives (and if possible increase it) so that he can accomplish other purposes on future occasions . . . . On any particular occasion [he] . . . might indulge himself in the luxury of 'consuming' rather than 'investing' influence, i.e., of using it for present purposes without regard to its replenishment, but if he consumed it for very long he would be out of business."[6]

Since it will usually be hard to determine whether management seeks power for its own sake, to fulfill a social responsibility to the community, or out of practical recognition of the vital need for continued cooperation from the factions on which the corporation depends, the morality of management's drive to develop and maintain its stock of power is necessarily ambiguous.

## MANAGEMENT MEANS

Banfield's remarks about management's exercise of power apply *a fortiori* to financial power, since the corporation has a financial relationship with each of the factions on which its continued existence depends. The customer wants a high-quality product at a competitive price. The worker wants decent working conditions at the highest possible wage. The concerns of the stockholder, banker and supplier are obviously financial. No matter how much the worker likes management, he will stop working soon after the payroll stops. No matter how much the customer likes the corporation's product, he will stop buying when the price ceases to be competitive. When the corporation ceases to fulfill its financial obligations, the stock of goodwill residing in the several factions is exhausted fairly quickly.

In most cases, the financial claims of the several factions must be met with cash, or cash equivalents, and they must be met when they fall due. Otherwise the various factions lose confidence in the corporation and withdraw their support. Cash is truly the lifeblood of the corporation; without it, the corporation sickens and dies very quickly. Although the power to distribute cash at a point in time is only one of the forms the stock of corporate power takes, it is an important form.

*The financial objective of the corporation is to conserve, and when possible enhance, the corporation's power to distribute cash.*

## FINANCIAL POWER

The corporation's financial power cannot be measured by toting up its cash balances. The amount of cash and near cash on hand in excess of the cash inventory required for operating purposes may understate or overstate the corporation's power to distribute cash. It will understate if the corporation has unused borrowing power and overstate if the corporation has liabilities that rely in part on the cash in question for security. (As a practical matter, a corporation is unlikely to have simultaneously a large inventory of "surplus" cash and large debts unless it has a seasonal cash need.)

A corporation can put its creditors, hence its financial power, in jeopardy while maintaining a cash flow from operations entirely adequate to service its debt obligations. For example, a commodity processing company that neglects to hedge its position in the commodities market—either long or short—may find the security for its creditors jeopardized by a sudden fluctuation in the market, even though its processing margins, hence its operating cash flows, are virtually unaffected.

Prospects for future cash flows from operations will have a certain present value, but if this value—together with the value of the company's other assets—is not sufficient to cover its liabilities, creditors are no longer fully protected. The fact that cash flows from operations may ultimately return to creditors the dollar value of their claims does not constitute full compensation, since creditors must incur in the interim equity risk that results in an irreplaceable loss in the present value of their claims.

On the other hand, a rapidly growing company may be absorbing more cash into plant and working capital than it can currently generate from operations. If rapid expansion promises to be profitable, the company can usually find creditors—very often the original creditors—willing to step in and provide additional funds. Inability to generate the cash needed to service outstanding debt without further borrowing is not in itself a disaster—either for management or for creditors.

The willingness of the corporation's creditors to continue lending is in fact the key to the corporation's power to distribute cash. The corporation has unused power whenever creditors consider that existing loans have not exhausted their security.[7]

Although most creditors will insist on some margin of safety, the rough measure of the borrowing power of the corporation at a point in time is the amount by which the gross market value of the corporation exceeds its existing liabilities. Whatever increases the margin tends to increase the amount of cash the corporation can generate at a point in time, hence the financial power of the corporation. Whatever reduces the margin tends to reduce the financial power of the corporation.

*Under most circumstances of practical interest, the financial objective in the widely held corporation is to conserve, and when possible increase, the margin between the gross market value of the corporation and its liabilities.*

## STOCKS, NOT FLOWS

Our interpretation of the corporate financial objective would be of largely academic interest were it not for the fact that, in a rational market, the aggregate value of the corporate common stock equals the gross market value of the corporation less the outstanding claims of creditors. It follows immediately that, except for some margin of safety for the creditors, the untapped borrowing power of the corporation—hence management's financial power—is measured by the market value of the outstanding common stock.

Financial power will fluctuate from day to day with fluctuations in the value of the common stock.[8] Uncertainty surrounding these fluctuations, rather than uncertainty surrounding the flow of cash from operations, is the fundamental financial risk for management. If corporate managements are really preoccupied with "near-term movements in cash inflow and outflow" and their "irregularities from one period to another," they are wasting a lot of valuable time.

## SHARE VALUE MAXIMIZATION IS MANAGEMENT'S OBJECTIVE

The financial objective is, of course, only one among a number of corporate objectives and, as such, is not necessarily controlling in any specific decision. Even when the financial objective is subordinated to other corporate objectives, however, management will be well advised to measure the cost of a decision in terms of financial power. This means, in terms of our interpretation, measuring its effect on the value of the corporate common shares.[9]

The other parties with a stake in the corporation—the worker, the customer, the supplier, the banker and certainly management itself—are hardly likely to be preoccupied with stockholder interests. Yet it is doubtful whether any of these parties will be best served by a policy of merely "satisficing" with respect to the value of corporate shares. Those who criticize the goal of share value maximization are forgetting that stockholders are not merely the beneficiaries of a corporation's financial success, but also the referees who determine management's financial power.

## Notes

1. See Berle and Means, *The Modern Corporation and Private Property* (New York: The Macmillan Company, 1933).
2. G. Donaldson, *Corporate Debt Capacity* (Boston, MA: Division of Research, Graduate School of Business Administration, Harvard University, 1961).
3. E.S. Mason, *The Corporation in Modern Society* (Cambridge, MA: Harvard University Press, 1959).
4. R.N. Anthony, "The Trouble with Profit Maximization," *Harvard Business Review*, 1960.
5. C. Barnard, *Executive Action*, 30th Anniversary Ed. (Cambridge, MA: Harvard University Press, 1968).
6. E. Banfield, *Political Influence* (New York: The Free Press, 1963).
7. It is sometimes supposed that creditors look primarily to the liquidation value of corporate assets for security. Secured lenders are obviously interested in the liquidation value of those corporate assets on which they have a lien. But liquidation value is a limited measure of corporate borrowing power, for several reasons. Investments in research and market development, for example, are likely to have little or no value in liquidation. In some cases, even plant and equipment are so specialized that they have little value apart from the current operation. Even when assets can be assigned a market value, it is likely to fluctuate as widely or more widely than the value of the corporation itself, since the assets depend for their true value on the same economic uncertainties underlying the aggregate corporate earning power.

8. Some will argue that because market value fluctuates constantly, no meaning can be attached to it. Nothing could be further from the truth. In a celebrated 1965 paper, Professor Paul Samuelson argued that "properly anticipated prices fluctuate randomly." If temporary vicissitudes of buying and selling pressures were the primary cause of fluctuations, share prices would not exhibit their familiar random walk.

9. This leads naturally to present value techniques as the appropriate means of evaluation and to the conclusion that the proper discount rates to use are the rates the capital markets will use. If a discount rate is adjusted for risk, therefore, it is risk to investors that is relevant. It follows that the decision maker's personal utility function has no relevance in the choice of the discount rate.

# CHAPTER 16

# The Real Cost of Inflation

It is frequently argued—notably in the editorial pages of *The New York Times*—that, whereas inflation is a nuisance, unemployment is an evil so serious that the social costs of using employment to bring down the inflation rate exceed any possible social benefits. A constant inflation, with everyone's expectations adjusted to it, causes no ill effects. If the cost of curing inflation is able-bodied workers jobless, lost output and families on the dole, then the price is very high; surely we are better off learning to live with inflation than incurring costs like these to cure it.

What this argument overlooks is the fact that money, like everything else, can be priced out of use. And money is vital to a modern exchange economy. As Samuelson has said, the alternative—barter—is absurdly cumbersome and complex. The more advanced our economy becomes, the more specialized and roundabout, the less tolerable barter is as a substitute for money exchange.

Mundell and, more recently, Miller and Upton have pointed out that the price of money is not the real interest rate, but the nominal rate. To the extent that inflation is accompanied by high nominal interest rates, it raises the price of holding money.

The current queues in commercial banking offices are not caused by too many depositors. They are caused by the same old depositors banking more often, in an attempt to reduce their average money balances. At current levels of inflation, many are now spending upwards of a working week a year standing in tellers' queues. The real costs are enormous, and they are only the tip of the iceberg. Businesses are altering production patterns in ways that incur more real startup and inventory carrying costs—merely to economize on the use of money.

When inflation rates climb to 10 percent or more, we are already well along the road back to barter.

# CHAPTER 17

# The Fiscal Burden

As Poland is teaching us, there are limits to how far a country can go in reducing the after-tax real income of labor. Beyond this point, government spending must be financed entirely by taxes on capital.

If the government is having difficulty increasing taxes on labor now, it may not be reasonable to assume it can raise those taxes later. Thus, unless investors are absurdly myopic, they will look beyond current corporate taxes to the ultimate burden, depressing security prices by the present value of this burden. The value of plant yet to be built will also be depressed, because it will have to bear its share of the burden *pro rata* with existing plant.

The result is a powerful inhibition on plant formation that can be mitigated only by raising the inflation rate and lowering the real interest rate—two policy options that the U.S. and Britain resorted to in the 1970s. Now, however, both countries are experimenting with a different set of policy options involving tight money and high real rates. One consequence is that, in order to induce full employment levels of plant formation, these countries must now maintain higher inflation rates than before. Long interest rates, which are the sum of expected real rates and expected inflation rates, are consequently much higher than previously.

Government spending is financed in part by promises to pay. The burden of those promises in present value terms is the same whether repaid sooner, with less interest, or later, with more. The timing of repayment is linked, of course, to the timing of taxes. Lower taxes now mean lower levels of repayment now and higher levels of repayment later, hence higher taxes later. Indeed, the arithmetic of compound interest works out in such a way that the present value of the burden imposed by government is independent of current taxing policy.

"On the Quality of Municipal Bonds" in the May–June [1982] issue of *Financial Analysts Journal* (Chapter 4 in this book) points out that, because a municipality must maintain after-tax wages at competitive levels, any increase in the municipal burden is borne by capital, rather than labor.[1] That article argues that a rational real estate market will adjust aggregate value subject to the municipality's taxing power downward, dollar for dollar, for increases in the present value of this burden.

Is there any useful analogy in this respect between a municipality and a country? Of course, labor can't leave a country as readily as it can leave a city, hence the pressure cities feel to compete with other labor markets is absent. On the other hand, although

---

countries don't normally have to compete with each other on after-tax (real) wages, they do have to compete with their own past: Governments that fail to maintain their after-tax real wage roughly constant run into severe political problems. The basic problem in Poland, for example, is not underemployment, or even inflation. It is the fact that, through failure to maintain and expand its capital stock, the country has permitted the real wage to fall too far, too fast. But note that Poland's real wage is still far above that of Bangladesh, Zaire, and other underdeveloped countries.[2]

The U.S. government also has no power to tax owner-occupied single family dwellings, and only limited power to tax real estate, since much of that capital is unincorporated or tax-sheltered. Through the corporate income tax, however, it can tax corporate capital. And, since there are limits to how much of any country's fiscal burden wage earners can be asked to bear, that portion of the country's capital subject to taxation by the central government must bear the rest of that burden.

The following argument suggests that the effect of this burden on corporate equity values is roughly analogous to the effect of the municipality's burden on the value of its taxable real estate. It also suggests, in analogy with the result for municipalities, that the effect on taxable assets is independent of how taxes are distributed as between present and future.

## THE FISCAL BURDEN

In purely formal analogy with the municipal finance article, we can let:

$\tilde{u}$ = the stream of combined costs (i.e., operating costs plus transfer payments) necessary to operate the government, net of wage and other taxes that reduce personal income;

$\tilde{d}$ = the stream of payments required to service debt;

$\tilde{e}$ = the stream of gross rents on corporate capital;

$\tilde{t}$ = the stream of corporate taxes; and

$V(\ )$ = the present value of the cash stream indicated in parentheses.

The tildes remind us that these symbols represent cash flow streams.

Sooner or later, the government must levy enough taxes to meet its obligations, so we have:

$$\sum \tilde{t} = \tilde{u} + \tilde{d} \tag{17.1}$$

Using the "no free lunch" property of asset markets employed in the municipal finance article, we have:

$$\sum V(\tilde{t}) = V(\tilde{u} + \tilde{d}) \tag{17.2}$$

hence we can write the after-tax value of corporations as:

$$\sum V(\tilde{e} - \tilde{t}) = \sum V(\tilde{e}) - \sum V(\tilde{t}),$$
$$= V\left(\sum \tilde{e}\right) - V(\tilde{u} + \tilde{d}) \tag{17.3}$$

The second term is the present value of the fiscal burden. This burden includes, not only future spending, but also that portion of past spending manifested in government debt still outstanding.

This result says that:

1. The aggregate market value of corporations is their economic value, less the present value of the fiscal burden.
2. By itself, a change in corporate tax policy has no impact on the net (aggregate) value of corporate equities. What does affect that value is a change in wage taxes. Thus, for example, if a country lowers corporate taxes and wage taxes simultaneously, the market value of corporate securities will fall, rather than rise: Reducing wage taxes increases the burden on corporations, while lowering corporate taxes has no effect on their present value.
3. Taking the level of promises outstanding as given, the effect of the burden on the aggregate value of corporate securities is determined by the prospective level of government spending—not the level of (corporate) taxing.

We have noted that there are two elements in the fiscal burden borne by corporate earnings—(1) that portion of future government spending not borne by other sources of tax revenue and (2) government promises already made. Even if we make the heroic assumption that current levels of government spending are an indication of future levels, the current level of corporate taxes is deficient as a measure of the first element. In the first place, it is too low by the amount of the deficit. In the second place, it is too high by the amount of interest charges, which are related to the second element, rather than the first. On the other hand, a large part of the second element comprises promises that don't bear explicit interest charges—future payments to Social Security, veterans' benefits, government employees' pensions, and the like. Even if the current budget were not in deficit, therefore, the magnitude of the two burden elements would be seriously understated by the level of current taxes.

## Consolidated Financial Statements of the U.S. Government

In 1976, the United States Treasury began publishing Consolidated Financial Statements for the United States Government (the so-called "CFS"). Then Secretary of the Treasury William Simon described the purpose of these statements: "Events of the last few years, particularly the rising and seemingly uncontrollable Federal deficits and the financial crises in major cities and states, point to the need for a new perspective— one that looks at a government as a total financial entity and describes its financial condition in plain language and plain accounting." The initial statements covered the years 1974 and 1975; more recent published statements cover the years through 1980.[3]

In their balance sheets, authors of the CFS have made a special effort to provide a comprehensive overview of all government programs, including in particular those entailing promises of future payment that bear no explicit interest charges (see Exhibit 17.1). In 1980, the present value of these programs, as reckoned by the U.S. Treasury, was $2,205.5 billion. Interest-bearing borrowing from the public amounted to $708.9 billion, on which the government incurred interest charges of $59.9 billion.

**EXHIBIT 17.1** U.S. Government Promises to Pay (billions of dollars)

| | Sept. 1980 | Sept. 1979 | Sept. 1978 | Sept. 1977 | Sept. 1976 | June 1975 | June 1974 |
|---|---|---|---|---|---|---|---|
| Liabilities | | | | | | | |
| Borrowing from public | $ 708.9 | $ 639.4 | $ 606.7 | $ 548.6 | $ 494.8 | $ 396.9 | $ 346.1 |
| Retirement and Disability | | | | | | | |
| Military | $ 348.9 | $ 303.9 | $ 147.4 | $ 128.9 | $ 119.3 | $ 96.6 | $ 80.4 |
| Civilian | 430.3 | 368.7 | 173.6 | 155.5 | 140.6 | 118.0 | 108.0 |
| Veterans' compensation | 174.6 | 153.0 | 143.9 | 116.7 | 113.4 | 117.3 | 111.0 |
| Federal employees' compensation* | 10.0 | 8.7 | 8.2 | 7.4 | — | — | — |
| Social Security | 1,241.7 | 1,061.9 | 928.0 | 802.6 | 630.8 | 499.5 | 416.0 |
| | $2,205.5 | $1,896.2 | $1,401.1 | $1,211.1 | $1,004.1 | $ 831.4 | $ 715.4 |
| | $2,914.4 | $2,535.6 | $2,007.8 | $1,759.7 | $1,498.9 | $1,228.3 | $1,061.5 |

*Not recorded (not incurred?) in 1974, 1975, 1976.

**EXHIBIT 17.2**  U.S. Government Operating Expenses (billions of dollars)

| | Sept. 1980 | Sept. 1979 | Sept. 1978 | Sept. 1977 | Sept. 1976 | June 1975 | June 1974 |
|---|---|---|---|---|---|---|---|
| Expenses (including transfer payments) | $730.0 | $652.2 | $570.7 | $470.3 | $436.6 | $385.2 | $371.1 |
| less: | | | | | | | |
| Interest | 59.9 | 48.3 | 48.7 | 41.9 | 37.1 | 23.3* | 21.5* |
| Depreciation | 23.6 | 20.6 | 19.4 | 12.1 | 8.9 | 7.7 | 11.1 |
| | $646.5 | $583.3 | $502.6 | $416.3 | $390.6 | $354.2 | $338.5 |
| Revenues | $587.6 | $529.4 | $480.3 | $417.5 | $348.8 | $321.3 | $275.9 |
| less: | | | | | | | |
| Interest | 13.9 | 10.7 | 21.8 | 18.7 | 16.3 | —* | —* |
| | $573.7 | $518.7 | $458.5 | $398.8 | $332.5 | $321.3 | $275.9 |
| Adjusted Deficit | $ 72.8 | $ 64.6 | $ 44.1 | $ 17.5 | $ 58.1 | $ 32.9 | $ 62.6 |
| Corporate Tax | 63.9 | 68.4 | 70.5 | 54.3 | 39.7 | 37.5 | 40.7 |
| Operating (i.e., flow) Burden | $136.7 | $133.0 | $114.6 | $ 71.8 | $ 97.8 | $ 70.4 | $103.3 |

*Net of interest revenue.

These interest charges contribute to the sum of corporate taxes and the deficit, causing that sum to overstate the current costs of operating the government (net of other taxes). (See Exhibit 17.2.) The following calculation corrects for this double-counting in estimating those costs for 1980:

Expenses (including transfer payments)

|  |  |  |
|---|---|---|
| | | $730.0 (billion) |
| Less: | | |
| Interest | 59.9 | |
| Depreciation | 23.6 | |
| | | $646.5 |
| Revenues | | $587.6 |
| Less: | | |
| Interest | 13.9 | |
| | | $573.7 |
| Adjusted Deficit | | $ 72.8 |
| Corporate Tax | | 63.9 |
| Operating (i.e., flow) Burden | | $136.7(billion) |

This figure includes transfer payments but is net of tax revenues from other sources.

The interest of $59.9 billion was on interest-bearing debt of $708.9 billion, as noted. Capitalizing the operating cost figure at the same ratio, we have a (very) rough estimate of the present value equivalent of the burden imposed by operating costs continuing at this rate:

$$708.9/59.9 \ (136.7) = \$1,617.8 \ (billion)$$

Using this result, we can make a horseback estimate of the total burden:

| | |
|---|---|
| Interest-Bearing Debt | $ 708.9(billion) |
| Non-Interest-Bearing Promises | 2,205.5 |
| Capitalized Net Operating Costs | 1,617.8 |
| Total Burden | $4,532.2(billion) |

Anyone who thinks this number is accurate should read then Comptroller General Elmer Staats' cautionary comments on the 1974–75 CFS. Pointing out that the reports were not audited, he cautioned users that "many assets are carried at no value or outdated cost figures that are virtually meaningless . . . . Among other aspects requiring further study was making sure that the amounts shown from pension liabilities are a fair presentation of actual liabilities."

But the problem is even worse than that envisioned by Elmer Staats, because our burden estimate employs the Treasury's numbers in a way not specifically intended by the authors of the CFS. Are current outlays an accurate indication of the level of future outlays, as assumed in our calculation? Probably not. Should the government's current assets be subtracted in reckoning the burden? Its fixed assets? We have focused on the government's liabilities and ignored its assets. A possible defense for doing so is that our definition of the burden embraces flows as well as stocks; any revenue-generating assets reduce that portion of the flow element in the burden contributed by the deficit. This defense is obviously less valid, however, for, say, resource-rich government lands not in current production. Finally, is there double-counting in reflecting in the burden both outstanding pension obligations and current period pension contributions? We assume not.[4]

## IMPLICATIONS FOR INVESTMENT

Many observers have accused the market of being irrationally low in relation to earnings.[5] Yet it is a tenet of rational expectations that present prices impound, not only the present, but also the predictable future. If future earnings are expected to be lower than current earnings, share prices low in relation to current earnings are not necessarily irrational. Current levels could be quite rational if corporate taxes were expected to increase in the future.

Compared with our estimate of the fiscal burden, the market value of corporate securities is merely the tip of an iceberg. Most of the iceberg is owned by claimants against the federal government, which in turn has claims against private capital through its power to tax corporations (i.e., what we have called the fiscal burden). The visible tip of the iceberg represents that portion of the economic value of private capital actually available to investors. Of course, the market value of corporate equities fluctuates from day to day; as a representative value for the aggregate shares, a figure of $1,000 billion may nevertheless serve to put the burden into perspective.

One important aspect of the burden is that new private investment bears the burden *pro rata* with old private investment. The larger is the fraction of the total iceberg under water, the less there is available to those who provide the capital for new private investment. When the fiscal burden becomes a significant fraction of the total iceberg, investors can be persuaded to continue private capital formation only if real interest rates are low enough that their share of the iceberg's present value exceeds the cost of their investment.[6]

## THE BURDEN RATIO

In nominal dollar terms, the fiscal burden has roughly doubled since 1974 (see Exhibit 17.1). Some portion of the burden is essentially real, while some portion is essentially nominal. Simplifying heroically, let existing government obligations net of present levels of taxation on wages be represented by perpetuities with rates "y" per annum for nominally denominated obligations and "x" per annum for obligations that are essentially real; let "z" per annum measure the level of economic rents on corporate capital. Then we can define the "government burden" as the sum of the present value of government's real obligations and the present value of government's nominal obligations. We have:

$$\text{PV of Burden} = x/r + y/i \qquad (17.4)$$

where r and i are the real and nominal interest rates, respectively. Writing the present value of the economic rents on corporate capital as z/r, we can define the burden ratio by:

$$\text{Burden Ratio} = \frac{x/r + y/i}{z/r}$$

$$= x/z + y/z(r/i)$$

$$= x/z + y/z \left( \frac{1}{1 + w/r} \right)$$

(17.5)

where w is the inflation rate.

The burden ratio measures in present value terms the fraction of the economic value of corporate capital preempted by government promises that can, as a practical matter, be met only by taxing that capital. The problem with a high burden ratio is that it is distributed, not merely across existing corporate plant, but also across any new plant corporations may choose to build. Consciously or unconsciously, therefore, corporations will consider the burden ratio before deciding to incur the cost of new plant.

## INTEREST RATES

Unlike municipalities (returning for a moment to our municipal model), countries have central banks, which afford them some degree of control over nominal interest rates (in the short run) and inflation (in the longer run). In Equation (17.5), the only variables subject to any degree of central bank control are the inflation rate (w) and the real rate (r). Equation (17.5) suggests that high levels of inflation and low levels of real interest rates reduce the burden ratio.

Since maintaining full employment levels of private capital formation is a political imperative of the highest order, it is perhaps not surprising that governments tend to maintain real rates low and inflation rates high when burden ratios are high. Thus the fiscal burden is a basic cause of inflation: Government spending, which increases the fiscal burden dollar for dollar, is inflationary whether monetized or not. Furthermore, since the burden ratio doesn't go away even if government reduces current levels of spending, expectations of future inflation rates and real rates—hence long, as well as short, nominal rates—will be affected. These considerations suggest one possible explanation for the low levels of real rates often observed in times of inflation.

During the decade of the 1970s, the United States (and England) piled up massive fiscal burdens. As these burdens accumulated, inflation rates rose and real rates fell, mitigating the inhibiting effect of fiscal burdens on private capital formation. Now, however, we have for the first time in many years a monetary policy that fosters high real rates—i.e., higher nominal short rates at any given level of inflation. This shift means that inflation alone must now bear what low real rates and high inflation rates formerly bore jointly.

The higher the level of real rates, the higher inflation rates must be in order to bear that burden. This brings us to a curious paradox: For any given average level of private investment over a whole cycle, the average level of inflation must be higher under a monetary policy of high real rates than under a policy of low real rates. The long-run prospect is consequently for both higher real rates and higher inflation rates. And since long nominal rates are the sum of expected inflation and expected real rates, long interest rates are likely to continue high until—for whatever reason—the new monetary policy is abandoned.

## CONCLUSION

At this writing, the inflation rate has fallen farther and faster than many expected. Short interest rates have also begun to fall. These developments have led many to expect a drop in the long interest rate. But short-run policy, while it can reduce or even eliminate inflation, is merely dealing with a symptom.

The argument presented here has suggested that the inflation rate, like the real interest rate, is an instrument of public policy (albeit a less manageable one). The expectations of future inflation impounded in long interest rates are consequently a symptom of an underlying problem that will call forth the use of that instrument. That problem is the fiscal burden.

The fiscal burden is currently so big that a few years of fiscal restraint won't make it go away; conversely, a few years of deficits won't make much difference. On the other hand, ignoring the problem—the fiscal burden—and focusing on the symptom—inflation—is a dangerously narrow policy objective. The objective is not a low inflation rate, but a low rate at full employment. Despite their short-run success with inflation, current tight money policies will actually increase the future burden ratio, since they (1) discourage capital formation and (2) increase the deficit. An even larger burden ratio will make it difficult indeed to maintain full employment at low inflation rates.

## APPENDIX 17.1

### The Tax Burden: Municipalities

Let small letters represent future (generally uncertain) cash flows; let the tilde over a small letter represent a stream of cash flows over time; and let V() represent the present value of the (vector) argument inside the parentheses. Then, for any constants $\alpha$ and $\beta$, the "no free lunch" (NFL) property can be expressed as:

$$V(\alpha\tilde{x}+\beta\tilde{y}) = \alpha V(\tilde{x})+\beta V(\tilde{y})$$

The NFL property is applied to cities characterized by the following assumptions.

### Assumptions

The following definitions are used:

$\tilde{t}_i$ = the (in general, uncertain) stream of future taxes on the ith parcel of real property,

$\tilde{y}_i$ = the future stream of gross rents to be generated by the ith parcel,

$\tilde{u}$ = the future stream of out-of-pocket expenditures required to operate the city (excluding debt service) and

$\tilde{d}$ = the future stream of payments required to service the city's outstanding debt (interest and principal).

Note that $\tilde{t}$, $\tilde{y}$, $\tilde{u}$ and $\tilde{d}$ are all vectors, with individual components corresponding to future points in time.

Investors in the real estate market value property net of taxes; hence, for the *i*th parcel we have:

$$V_i = V(\tilde{y}_i - \tilde{t}_i) \qquad (17.6)$$

We also assume that if the city remains solvent, sooner or later it must levy enough taxes to meet its obligations, so:

$$\sum_i \tilde{t}_i = \tilde{u} + \tilde{d} \qquad (17.7)$$

This assumption merely says that future tax revenues will be absorbed in one of two ways—meeting operating expenses or servicing debt—and that ultimately (which is to say, in present value terms), the stream of tax revenues must be large enough to cover both.

Any refinancing of municipal obligations replacing $\tilde{d}$ by, say, $\tilde{d}^1$ has the property that:

$$V(\tilde{d}^1) \ge V(\tilde{d}) \qquad (17.8)$$

In other words, refinancing will not reduce the present value of the city's debt burden. ($V(d)$ should, of course, be reckoned net of the cash flow consequences of any assets owned by the city.)

Lenders to the city will balk when or before:

$$V(\tilde{d}) \ge V(\Sigma_i \tilde{y}_i - \tilde{u}) \qquad (17.9)$$

The argument on the right-hand side is the city's aggregate cash flow before capital transactions (including debt service). The present value of this cash flow measures the gross value of the city as security for lenders. The left-hand side is, of course, the market value of the city's outstanding debt. Assumption 17.9 says merely that lenders will balk when the value of the outstanding debt threatens to exceed the value of their underlying security.

Finally, the taxpayer will abandon property i when:

$$V(\tilde{y}_i - \tilde{t}_i) \le 0 \qquad (17.10)$$

which is to say, when taxes on his property are heavy enough to drive its market value to zero or below.

## Proof

Applying the NFL property to (1), we have for the market value of the ith parcel:

$$V_i = V(\tilde{y}_i - \tilde{t}_i) = V(\tilde{y}_i) - V(\tilde{t}_i) \tag{17.11}$$

Summing over the city's taxable property, we have:

$$\sum_i V_i = \sum_i V(\tilde{y}_i) - \sum_i V(\tilde{t}_i) \tag{17.12}$$

Applying the NFL property to (7), we have:

$$\sum_i V_i = V\left(\sum_i \tilde{y}_i\right) - V\left(\sum_i \tilde{t}_i\right) \tag{17.13}$$

Substituting from (2) and applying the NFL property again, we have:

$$\sum_i V_i = V\left(\sum_i \tilde{y}_i\right) - V(\tilde{u} + \tilde{d})$$
$$= V(-\tilde{u} + \sum_i \tilde{y}_i) - V(\tilde{d}) \tag{17.14}$$

The left-hand member $\Sigma_i V_i$ is the aggregate market value of the city's real estate. As noted in Equation 17.9, the term $V(-\tilde{u} = \Sigma_i\tilde{y}_i)$ is the value of the city as security—the net cash stream generated from operations of the city taken as a whole, with private and public activities lumped together. The term $V(\tilde{d})$ is the value of the city's outstanding debt, which under assumption Equation 17.8 cannot be reduced by refinancing. It follows from Equation 17.9 that the city's borrowing power is exhausted when the former approaches the latter. But Equation 17.14 says that, when these terms are equal, the aggregate value of the city's real property will be zero. The measure of the city's remaining borrowing power is the aggregate market value of its real estate.

On the other hand, Equation 17.10 says that taxpayer i will abandon his property when:

$$V_i = V(\tilde{y}_i - \tilde{t}_i) \le 0$$

Equation 17.14 is, of course, a statement about aggregates, whereas Equation 17.10 is a statement about the individual real estate parcel. The text notes that a city is taxing inefficiently unless it distributes the burden in such a way that the market value of all taxable property is driven to zero at the same time. When the above equation is satisfied for every property, however, we have:

$$\sum_i V_i = 0$$

hence the right-hand member of Equation 17.14 must be zero. At this point—wholesale property abandonment—the city exhausts its power to borrow. In this sense, the city exhausts its power to tax and to borrow at the same time.

## CONSOLIDATED FINANCIAL STATEMENTS

The financial statements below are reproduced, with the permission of the Department of the Treasury, from the government's 1980 report. Copies of the entire report and future reports may be obtained from the Special Reporting Branch, Bureau of Government Financial Operations, Department of the Treasury, Treasury Annex No. One, GAO Building, Room 1806, Washington, D.C. 20226.

### United States Government Consolidated Statement of Financial Position as of September 30, 1980 and 1979

Assets (In billions)

(What the Government owns—resources that are available to pay liabilities or to provide public services in the future)

|  | 1980 | 1979 |
|---|---|---|
| *Cash and monetary reserves* | | |
| Operating cash in the Treasury | $21.0 | 24.2 |
| International monetary reserves | | |
| (*Note 2*) | 16.8 | 15.2 |
| Other cash | 16.6 | 10.5 |
| | 54.4 | 49.9 |
| *Receivables (net of allowances)* | | |
| Accounts receivable | 11.0 | 9.2 |
| Accrued taxes receivable (*Note 3*) | 26.0 | 26.7 |
| Loans receivable (*Note 4*) | 159.7 | 138.8 |
| Advances and prepayments | 10.6 | 3.4 |
| | 207.3 | 178.1 |
| *Inventories (at cost) (Note 5)* | | |
| Goods for sale | 21.0 | 15.4 |
| Work in process | 1.1 | 1.0 |
| Raw materials | 3.6 | 3.6 |
| Materials and supplies for | | |
| Government use | 47.9 | 40.5 |
| Stockpiled materials and | | |
| commodities | 14.5 | 14.1 |
| | 88.1 | 74.6 |
| *Property and equipment (at cost)* | | |
| Land (*Note 6*) | 12.1 | 9.3 |
| Buildings, structures, and facilities (*Note 7*) | 122.0 | 112.3 |
| Military hardware (*Note 8*) | 189.5 | 158.8 |
| Equipment (*Note 8*) | 57.3 | 54.4 |
| Construction in progress | 28.3 | 25.5 |
| Other | 2.5 | 1.6 |
| | 411.7 | 361.9 |

Accumulated depreciation
(*Note 9*)........................................................ (204.0)   (180.4)

         207.7    181.5

Deferred charges and other assets    32.5     28.0

    Total................................................... $590.0   $512.1

## United States Government Consolidated Statement of Financial Position as of September 30, 1980 and 1979

Liabilities (In billions)

*(What the Government owes—liabilities incurred in the past that will require cash or other resources in the future)*

| | 1980 | 1979 |
|---|---|---|
| Accounts payable............................. | $81.6 | $77.7 |
| Unearned revenue............................ | 17.5 | 14.8 |
| Borrowing from the public (*Note 10*)............ | 708.9 | 639.4 |
| Accrued pension, retirement, and disability plans (*Note 11*) | | |
|   Military personnel...................... | 348.9 | 303.9 |
|   Civilian employees..................... | 430.3 | 368.7 |
|   Social security............................ | 1,241.7 | 1,061.9 |
|   Veterans compensation................ | 174.6 | 153.0 |
|   Federal employees compensation | 10.0 | 8.7 |
| | 2,205.5 | 1,896.2 |
| Loss reserves for guarantee and insurance programs (*Note 12*)............. | 8.7 | 2.3 |
| Other liabilities............................... | 59.7 | 51.4 |
|   Total................................................. | 3,081.9 | 2,681.8 |

### Accumulated Position

| | | |
|---|---|---|
| Accumulated position beginning of period...... | (2,169.7) | (1,898.9) |
| Prior period adjustment (*Note 13*)................. | — | (14.0) |
| Restated accumulated position beginning of period...................... | (2,169.7) | (1,912.9) |
| Current period results..................... | (142.4) | (122.8) |

| | | |
|---|---:|---:|
| Current noncash provision for social security (*Note 14*)......................................... | (179.8) | (134.0) |
| Accumulated position end of period................ | (2,491.9) | (2,169.7) |
| Total.......................................... | $590.0 | $512.1 |

## United States Government Consolidated Statement of Operations for the Years Ended September 30, 1980 and 1979

(In billions)

| | 1980 | 1979 |
|---|---:|---:|
| **Revenues** | | |
| Levied under the Government's sovereign power | | |
|   Individual income taxes............................... | $244.1 | $217.8 |
|   Corporate income taxes............................... | 63.9 | 68.4 |
|   Social insurance taxes and contributions............. | 160.7 | 141.6 |
|   Excise taxes.......................................... | 24.3 | 18.7 |
|   Estate and gift taxes................................. | 6.4 | 5.4 |
|   Customs duties........................................ | 7.2 | 7.4 |
|   Miscellaneous......................................... | 15.1 | 11.3 |
| | 521.7 | 470.6 |
| Earned through Government business-type operations | | |
|   Sale of goods and services........................... | 19.9 | 17.5 |
|   Interest.............................................. | 13.9 | 10.7 |
|   Other................................................. | 32.1 | 30.6 |
| | 65.9 | 58.8 |
| Total.......................................... | 587.6 | 529.4 |
| **Expenses by function (see also summary of expenses by object and agency)** | | |
|   Administration of justice............................ | 3.6 | 4.0 |
|   Agriculture........................................... | 3.7 | 4.0 |
|   Commerce and housing credit........................... | 6.9 | 2.1 |
|   Community and regional development..................... | 8.0 | 9.4 |
|   Education, training, employment, and social services.. | 27.5 | 26.4 |
|   Energy................................................ | 7.8 | 9.3 |
|   General government.................................... | 12.2 | 11.6 |
|   General purpose fiscal assistance..................... | 17.7 | 17.4 |
|   General science, space, and technology................ | 5.2 | 5.2 |
|   Health................................................ | 61.6 | 56.7 |

| Income security (*Note 11*) | | |
|---|---|---|
| Military personnel | 56.1 | 104.1 |
| Civilian employees | 75.9 | 25.7 |
| Social insurance | 127.5 | 115.8 |
| Veterans compensation | 31.8 | 20.3 |
| Other | 52.4 | 37.0 |
| Interest | 59.9 | 48.3 |
| International affairs | 19.5 | 16.8 |
| National defense | 110.1 | 99.8 |
| Natural resources and environment | 15.1 | 14.2 |
| Transportation | 19.0 | 16.1 |
| Veterans benefits and services | 8.5 | 8.0 |
| Total | 730.0 | 652.2 |
| Current period results | $(142.4) | $(122.8) |

## Notes

1. See Jack L. Treynor, "On the Quality of Municipal Bonds," *Financial Analysts Journal*, May/June 1982. The appendix to this article reproduces the argument from the municipal bond paper.
2. An indication that taxation of wage earners is reaching a practical limit in our own country is, of course, the growth in the subterranean economy. See Peter M. Gutmann, "The Subterranean Economy," *Financial Analysts Journal*, November/December 1977.
3. This continuing effort, which every thoughtful investor can applaud, is an outgrowth of a 1973 article in *Fortune* magazine by Carol Loomis ("An Annual Report for the U.S. Government") and the subsequent preparation by Arthur Andersen and Co., at its own initiative and expense, of pilot statements for 1973.
4. To make later years consistent with CFS reporting of earlier years, only net interest expense is shown in Exhibit 17.1. More importantly, depreciation is removed from total expenses; having chosen for our purposes to ignore assets in reckoning the net fiscal burden, we can hardly include depreciation on those assets as an expense.

   Although the CFS appear to treat pension and retirement plans consistently as between the balance sheet (present value of future obligations, actuarially adjusted) and the income statement (primarily additions to the present value resulting from current operations), the income statements report Social Security on a cash basis (current programs, net of receipts), while the balance sheets report the present value of the next 75 years' net payments, hence are on an accrual basis. *In principle*, the double-counting in our use of the CFS data, although certainly significant, is confined to the appreciation that occurs between the time that a Social Security obligation is picked up in the balance sheet figure on a present value basis and the time it is subsequently paid. *In fact*, according to Schedule VII of the CFS, Social Security accruals have regularly exceeded benefits paid. A second source of downward bias in our estimate of the burden lies in the fact that the CFS simply omit many pension programs for which there were no satisfactory data.

5. See, for example, Franco Modigliani and Richard Cohn, "Inflation, Rational Valuation and the Market," *Financial Analysts Journal*, March/April 1979.

6. See Jack L. Treynor, "What Professor Galbraith Failed to Say on TV," *Financial Analysts Journal*, March/April 1978.

7. Reproduced from Jack L. Treynor, "On the Quality of Municipal Bonds," *Financial Analysts Journal*, May/June 1982.

# CHAPTER 18

# A Modest Proposal

In controversies relating to tax policy, "fairness" is the rallying cry of those who argue for shifting the tax burden from labor to capital. By arguing for a reduction in the worker's tax burden, advocates of fairness are presumably trying to increase the worker's after-tax income. But after-tax income depends on the worker's pretax wage as well as on his taxes. And his pretax wage depends on the plant—lift trucks, lathes, packaging machinery, electric generators, oil refineries, tankships, locomotives, and so forth—he has to work with. If economic history teaches only one lesson, it is that when capital investment fails to create new jobs faster than the work force is growing, a country's real wage stagnates (as in the United States) or declines (as in Russia).

The fairness argument ignores not only the importance of capital investment to pretax wages, but also the impact of the tax burden on capital investment. Absent capital controls, investors channel their funds to projects that offer the greatest rewards after taxes. Projects that aren't competitive on this basis don't get undertaken. When a country raises taxes on capital, it reduces the number of projects that can compete successfully for investment funds.

It isn't obvious how the two countervailing considerations—the tax burden on labor and labor's pretax wage—should be balanced to labor's maximum benefit. But the conventional concept of fairness ignores one consideration in favor of the other. An enlightened concept would focus, not on labor's tax burden, but on its aftertax wage.

The only problem with such a concept of fairness is that putting it to work requires some calculation. Lest this requirement discourage policy makers from using the new concept, we have made the calculation ourselves. (The calculation and the standard textbook assumptions behind it are set out below.) The results can be stated very simply: The way to maximize the after-tax wage is to allocate the entire tax burden to labor.

The level of taxation on capital that is fairest to labor is zero. The present level of taxation on capital is indeed grossly unfair, but it is too high—not too low.

Now, about that modest proposal. . . .

## THE CALCULATION: MAXIMIZING LABOR'S AFTER-TAX WAGE

Calculating the division of the tax burden between labor and capital that maximizes labor's after-tax wage depends on how labor and capital combine to produce society's output of goods and services. To find this out, most readers would probably turn to economists. If they seek the answer in their college economics textbooks, however, they are likely to experience some frustration. Although these books discuss combining labor with land, most omit any discussion of combining labor with capital. But labor is far more productive when coupled with a computer, an engine lathe, a lift truck—or a college degree![1]

Textbooks' neglect of the importance of capital investment is all the more remarkable, given the evidence. As one of our best economic textbooks Samuelson's *Economics*, Ninth Edition, admits, although "only one in twenty-five Americans lives on a farm today, compared with one in four as recently as 1929," GNP per capita grew almost sixfold in that period.[2] Clearly, something other than land was improving labor's productivity in this period. That something was capital investment.

As we noted, the fairness argument for taxing capital assumes labor's pretax income will be unaffected by how the tax burden is distributed between labor and capital. But if the real wage depends on investment, and investment depends on the after-tax return to investors, then this assumption breaks down. The optimal distribution of the tax burden is not the one that minimizes labor's taxes, but the one that maximizes labor's after-tax income.

What does our textbook author think of this argument?

*Workers are supposed to applaud the thrift of capitalists because the fruits of that thrift in more and better capital goods will cause labor productivity to rise.*[3]

Noting that other writers have referred to this idea as the "filter down theory of economic progress," he continues:

*Why give the extra income to the capitalist for him to save it and for him to get the future interest fruits on his savings?*[4]

The book then offers some suggestions for eliminating the need for investors, including having the state perform the saving function. Obviously the author doesn't feel kindly toward *investors*. But why is he slighting *investment*? After pages of discussing a production function combining labor with land, the author gives capital two sentences (Samuelson p. 541, p. 3). In his chapter on the economics of agriculture, the author cites the contribution of "the tractor, the combine, the cotton picker, irrigation . . ." as examples of how *technology* has increased the productivity of farm labor. Even here, he refuses to concede the vital role of *investment* in putting these innovations to work.

In the author's words, land is "God-given"! The amount of land available for production is not affected by how it is taxed. Perhaps he also views technology as "God-given." But capital is not "God-given." In an earlier chapter, he reveals a strong positive association between a household's level of income and its propensity to save (i.e., the fraction of household income that is saved rather than consumed.[5]) If saving is logically antecedent to investing, then the households that invest are going to be the high-income households. If we reject the book's suggestion that saving and investment be performed by the state, then there will be no investment without "capitalists"—high-income households with a high propensity to save. Perhaps the reason the author slights the importance of *investing* is that he couldn't concede it without also conceding the importance of *investors*.

The book's author evidently despairs of taxing investors without taxing investment. Perhaps he considered and rejected such proposals as taxing American investors and relying on foreign investors to supply the needed investment funds (a scheme that generates revenue only until all the wealth belongs to foreign, rather than American, investors) or taxing consumption, such as Britain and Germany do. A consumption tax has many appealing features, but shifting the tax burden from workers to investors is not one of them; as we've noted, low-income households consume a larger fraction of their income than high-income households.

## How Labor and Capital Combine

Despite the textbooks, capital investment *is* important to labor's productivity. But is it so important that labor's after-tax wage would go down if the tax burden on capital went up? To answer this question, we have used a favorite of the economics textbooks—the so-called Cobb-Douglas production function—but with capital substituted for land. If we use k for the amount of plant in a country and n for the number of people employed, then the function stipulates that real output y is equal to

$$y = Ak^{\gamma}n^{1-\gamma}, \quad 0 < \gamma < 1$$

where A is some constant.[6]

The Cobb-Douglas function will look strange and arbitrary to anyone who hasn't seen it before. Actually, its behavior checks out pretty well with our intuition about how a production function ought to behave. First, doubling *both* labor and capital doubles output. This is because their respective exponents sum to one.

Second, the marginal productivity of labor (the real wage) increases as the amount of plant increases. Compute the increase in y for a unit increase in n:[7]

$$\frac{dy}{dn} = (1 - \gamma)k^{\gamma}n^{-\gamma}$$

and consider how it changes with a unit increase in k:

$$\frac{\partial}{\partial k}\left(\frac{\partial y}{\partial n}\right) = \frac{\partial^2 y}{\partial k \partial n} = \gamma(1 - \gamma)k^{\gamma-1}n^{-\gamma}$$

This number is always positive, since k, n, $\gamma$ and $1 - \gamma$ are always positive. We have

$$0 < \gamma < 1$$

hence

$$0 < 1 - \gamma < 1$$

Third, if we hold plant input constant and increase labor input, the marginal productivity of labor falls. The value of

$$\frac{\partial}{\partial n}\left(\frac{\partial y}{\partial n}\right) = \frac{\partial^2 y}{\partial n^2} = -\gamma(1-\gamma)k^\gamma n^{-\gamma-1}$$

is always negative.

We use the Cobb-Douglas function to get an expression for the marginal productivity of capital (the return on investment). Then we ask, if the level of investment adjusts to maintain a market-determined after-tax return, how will changes in the tax burden on capital affect that level? How will changes in that level affect labor's *pretax* wage?[8] And, finally, assuming the tax burden on labor and capital together is given and fixed, what allocation of that burden between labor and capital is most beneficial to labor?

Let the total tax burden be T, the portion imposed on capital be T′, and the internationally determined after-tax hurdle rate on investment projects be $\rho$. Then the level of domestic investment k at which the after-tax return just satisfies that hurdle rate can be found from $\partial y/\partial n - T'/k$, which equals:

$$(1-\gamma)\left(\frac{n}{k}\right)^\gamma - \frac{T'}{k} = \rho$$

Because the after-tax return depends on k as well as T, this equation constrains the possible combinations of the two variables. Subject to this constraint, we seek to find the value of T′, the portion of the total tax burden T borne by capital, that maximizes labor's after-tax wage. We are given $\gamma$, T and $\rho$. We assume a value for n (e.g., the level of employment considered socially optimal). Our objective is to maximize the after-tax real wage M:

$$M = \gamma n^\gamma k^{1-\gamma} - \frac{(T-T')}{n}$$

subject to the above constraint. Along the locus of (T′, k) combinations satisfying this constraint, T′ is a single-valued function of k:

$$T' = k\left[(1-\gamma)\left(\frac{n}{k}\right)^\gamma - \rho\right]$$

Let us eliminate T′ from the maximand M:

$$M = \gamma\left(\frac{n}{k}\right)^{\gamma-1} - \frac{T-T'}{n}$$

We have:

$$M = \gamma\left(\frac{n}{k}\right)^{\gamma-1} - \frac{T}{n} + \frac{k}{n}\cdot\left[(1-\gamma)\left(\frac{n}{k}\right)^\gamma - \rho\right]$$

$$= \gamma\left(\frac{n}{k}\right)^{\gamma-1} - \frac{T}{n} + (1-\gamma)\cdot\left(\frac{n}{k}\right)^{\gamma-1} - \left(\frac{\rho}{n}\right)k$$

$$= \left(\frac{n}{k}\right)^{\gamma-1} - \left(\frac{\rho}{n}\right)k - \frac{T}{n}$$

Seeking an extremum of M with respect to k, we differentiate and set the derivative equal to zero:

$$\frac{dM}{dk} = (\gamma - 1)\left(\frac{n}{k}\right)^{\gamma-2}\left(-\frac{n}{k^2}\right) - \frac{\rho}{n} = 0$$

$$n^{\gamma-1}k^{-\gamma} = \frac{\rho}{n(1-\gamma)}$$

$$\frac{k}{n} = \left(\frac{1-\gamma}{\rho}\right)^{\frac{1}{\gamma}}$$

The corresponding value of T' is

$$T' = n\left(\frac{1-\gamma}{\rho}\right)^{\frac{1}{\gamma}} \cdot \left[(1-\gamma)\left(\frac{\rho}{1-\gamma}\right) - \rho\right] = 0$$

Is T' = 0 a maximum or a minimum? We compute the second derivative of M with respect to k:

$$\frac{dM}{dk} = (1-\gamma)n^{\gamma-1}k^{-\gamma} - \frac{\rho}{n}$$

$$\frac{d^2M}{dk^2} = -(1-\gamma)(\gamma)n^{\gamma-1}k^{-\gamma-1}$$

This expression is always negative. Our maximand has one and only one extremum, and that extremum is a maximum.

Although T' is a single-valued function of k, k is not always a single-valued function of T'. If policy makers set T' equal to zero, will the private sector be constrained to invest the amount that maximizes M?

When T' = 0, our constraint equation becomes

$$(1-\gamma)\left(\frac{n}{k}\right)^{\gamma} = \rho$$

$$\frac{n}{k} = \left(\frac{\rho}{1-\gamma}\right)^{\frac{1}{\gamma}}$$

and we have

$$\frac{k}{n} = \left(\frac{1-\gamma}{\rho}\right)^{\frac{1}{\gamma}}$$

We have seen that this is the ratio of k—the level of investment—to n—the specified level of employment—that maximizes M.

The allocation of the tax burden between labor and capital that maximizes labor's after-tax real wage is the one that puts the entire burden on labor. This is true independently of the values of $\gamma$, $\rho$ and n. In particular, *any* policy choice with regard to the level of unemployment, n, will lead to the same result.

The level of taxation on capital that is "fairest"—or the most beneficial—to labor is zero. The present level is too high.

## Notes

1. To avoid circumlocution, we shall talk about the effects of combining labor with plant. But, of course, much of the investment capital that enhances our productivity is not plant that one can "kick" (as Colyer Crum puts it), but rather tacts and skills acquired in the course of our formal (and informal) education. This human capital presumably explains most of the difference between the wage of an unskilled worker—a ditch digger or hod carrier—and that of a brain surgeon, movie director or factory manager. Progressive income taxes are really taxes on this kind of capital, rather than on labor. "The most valuable of all capital is that invested in human beings" (Alfred Marshall, *Principles of Economics*)
2. P. A. Samuelson, *Economics*, Ninth Edition (p. 406 and p. 4).
3. *Ibid.*, p. 550.
4. *Ibid.*
5. *Ibid.*, p. 209.
6. A word about the units in which output, y, capital input, k, and labor input, n, are measured. It is convenient to measure output and capital input in the same units. Then the marginal productivity of capital is a proper rate of return. It doesn't, however, make sense to measure labor inputs in the units chosen for output and capital input. Instead, we are free to choose the labor unit so that the constant coefficient in the Cobb-Douglas model equals one. The Cobb-Douglas model is obviously a steady-state model. It suppresses dynamic effects of changes in population or technology. In such a model, the distinction between stocks and flows gets tricky. The inputs are perhaps best thought of as stocks and the output as a flow.
7. Henceforth we drop the constant A. See endnote 6.
8. Assume competition in the respective markets driven labor's wage to the marginal productivity of labor and the return to plant investment to the marginal productivity of capital. Then we can use $\partial y \neq \partial k$ for the (pretax) return to capital. Given the fact that multiplying capital and labor inputs by the same factor increases output by that factor, Euler's Theorem assures us that:

$$n\frac{\partial y}{\partial n} + k\frac{\partial y}{\partial k} = y$$

Thus:

Aggregate Labor Income + Aggregate Return to Capital = Total Output

Part of total output will be diverted to government. Barring a chronic deficit, the diversion will be financed from taxes.

# CHAPTER 19

# A More Modest Proposal

**A**fter reading my editorial ("A Modest Proposal") in the January/ February 1992 issue of *FAJ*, Richard Roll conferred with Stephen Ross and called me to point out an error in my math. Robert Ferguson also picked up the math error, which was due to my having done the proof two ways and then combined the introduction of the Cobb-Douglas production function from one way with the proof from the other. (As Bob Ferguson and I discovered, I had assigned the exponent gamma to labor when I did the proof one way and to capital when I did it the other.)

Dick Roll and Steve Ross also suspected there was no need to restrict the proof to the Cobb-Douglas function. I hope they will feel that the following proof is indeed simpler and more general.

## THE PROOF

A production function specifies the output of goods and services that results from various combinations of labor and capital inputs. We take the desired level of employment as given, and focus on how output F varies with a changing level of capital input k. Define $\phi$ as the fraction of a given total tax burden T borne by labor. Define $\rho$ as the after-tax return required by the international capital markets.

We have argued that the allocation of the tax burden fairest to labor is not the one that minimizes labor's tax, but the one that maximizes labor's after-tax wage. The pretax wage depends on the level of investment.

As seen by labor, the policy problem is eliciting the level of investment k that maximizes its after-tax income M. (Since the level of employment is taken as fixed, maximizing after-tax income also maximizes the after-tax wage.) Labor's after-tax income is total output F less the total tax burden T (i.e., the total after-tax income to be shared by capital and labor) less the after-tax income required by capital, $\rho k$. We have:

$$M = F - T - \rho k \qquad (19.1)$$

This expression displays the two ways in which the level of capital investment k affects labor's aftertax income—through total output F and through the after-tax return to capital $\rho k$. An increase in k will increase total output. But it will also increase the portion of total output diverted to capital. The level of k that maximizes this expression is found by setting the rate of change of M with respect to k equal to zero. We have:

$$\frac{dM}{dk} = \frac{dF}{dk} - \rho = 0 \tag{19.2}$$

Labor can use this equation to calculate the level of investment that is best for labor.

What tax policy will persuade capital to invest the amount that is optimal for labor? To answer this question, we need to look at the investment from capital's point of view. To be attractive, the after-tax return must equal the required rate of return $\rho$. The *before-tax* return is dF/dk. The tax burden per dollar invested is $[(1 - \phi)T]/k$. Thus the after-tax return is:

$$\frac{dF}{dk} - \frac{(1 - \phi)T}{k}$$

The level of the capital input k is related to capital's share of the tax burden: The higher the burden, the lower the after-tax return. Raising capital's share of the tax burden reduces the number of investment projects that can meet the after-tax return on capital required by international capital markets. The level of investment k falls until the after-tax return just equals $\rho$:

$$\frac{dF}{dk} - \frac{(1 - \phi)T}{k} = \rho \tag{19.3}$$

By varying $\phi$, policy makers can vary the amount of capital that will be provided. By substituting from Equation 19.3:

$$\frac{dF}{dk} - \rho = 0, \quad \frac{dF}{dk} = \rho$$

we get the particular tax policy that is best for labor. We have:

$$\rho - \frac{(1 - \phi)T}{k} = \rho, \quad (1 - \phi)T = 0 \tag{19.4}$$

And, unless T is zero,

$$1 - \phi = 0, \quad \phi = 1$$

Labor's after-tax income, hence its after-tax wage, is greatest when labor bears the whole tax burden and capital bears none.

## THE QUADRENNIAL MARKET CYCLE

Since the William McKinley election of 1900, a definite up, down, and up again stock market pattern has accompanied each U.S. President's term. The initial "honeymoon market" can be very short, measured in days or weeks, as it was with Woodrow

Wilson (twice), Franklin D. Roosevelt (two out of four terms), Richard M. Nixon (twice) and Jimmy Carter. The longest initial market lifts of the century occurred at the beginning of Ronald Reagan's second term (second honeymoon?) and the beginning of George Bush's [Sr.] term (the market dropped only beginning in mid-July 1990, with the invasion of Kuwait by Iraq).

During each presidency, and for a variety of reasons, equity prices recede from the honeymoon highs and give up part or all of their prior gains. The unfortunate Herbert Hoover stands out as the only president who saw the stock market register an absolute decline during each of his four years. But he saw the quadrennial pattern during his term, as the market rallied in his final months.

The "pendulum pattern" can be explained, too simply perhaps, as initial enthusiasm for a new president, a subsequent period of disillusionment, followed by a rally from the previous low, either because a popular president seems likely to be returned for another four years in office or an unpopular one is in the process of being turned out to do other things.

Dick Roll had felt that any production function of practical interest would have diminishing returns to scale when one holds the labor input fixed and varies the capital input. I happen to agree. As explained in the original article, this means the function F has a negative second partial derivative with respect to capital k. Returning to my expression for the first derivative (Equation 19.2), we have:

$$\frac{d^2M}{dk^2} = \frac{d^2F}{dk^2} < 0$$

## Redistribution

At the level of aggregates contemplated here, there are two kinds of redistribution issues. Let's consider first a tax on capital (for example) in excess of the total tax burden, with the difference going to labor—in other words, a *negative tax* on labor. Nothing in my proof precludes a negative tax burden—for either labor or capital. If this kind of redistribution at the aggregate level is good for labor (or capital) it will show up in the results. But it doesn't. The results say that, at the level of aggregates, this kind of redistribution is never good for labor.

Second, because we take the level of the total tax burden as given, we have suppressed the question of how much the government should spend and who should benefit. But suppose the government justifies some part of what it spends as helping labor. Under the optimal distribution of the tax burden, every penny spent to help labor will be paid by labor. Government can no longer claim that such spending redistributes wealth from capital to labor. The only remaining justification is that a dollar spent by government is more beneficial to labor than a dollar spent by labor: "Big Daddy knows best."

This argument holds unless part of the tax burden is borne by capital. But then labor, as we have shown, is worse off than if it had borne the full burden itself.

# CHAPTER 20

# Real Growth, Government Spending, and Private Investment

**M**uch recent political debate has implicitly been about where our country should be along the tradeoff between unemployment and inflation. The word "growth" came up often in the debate. Yet exchanging unemployment for inflation, or inflation for unemployment, is not growth. Real growth is about improving the tradeoff—less unemployment at any given level of inflation, or less inflation at any given level of unemployment.

There is only one way to improve the tradeoff between real prices and employment—add plant. And the way to add plant is to invest. Real growth occurs only when private-sector decision makers are willing to make the necessary plant additions. The proper focus of the political debate about government spending is its impact on their decisions.

## ISN'T IT TIME TO GET THE COUNTRY MOVING AGAIN?

Real growth is not measured by jobs and output. The reason relates to the real wage, or its inverse—the real price level. An efficiently managed economy uses its most efficient plant to produce any given level of output. The *least* efficient plant in use at any given level must recover in the price of its product the labor expended in production. At the same time, all plant producing the same product is compelled by market forces to charge the same price. So the level of real prices—prices measured in hours of labor effort—is determined by the prices necessary for the least efficient plant still in use to break even.

Still higher levels of employment and output require more plant. In the absence of new plant, old unused plant—by definition plant less efficient than that already in use—must be pressed into use. But it takes a higher real price for that less efficient plant—plant that uses more hours of labor to produce a unit of product—to recover its labor cost. Thus it takes higher real prices—lower real wages—to elicit higher levels of output and employment. (See Exhibit 20.1.)

At any point in time, policy-makers can reduce unemployment if they are willing to accept a lower real wage. Or they can raise the real wage if they are willing to

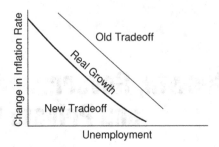

**EXHIBIT 20.1**   The Inflation-Unemployment
Tradeoff

accept more unemployment. But such tradeoffs don't represent real growth. Real growth is a matter of improving the tradeoff—more employment and output at any given real wage, or higher real wages at any given level of employment and output.

Fortunately, there is no secret about what it takes to improve the tradeoff. Because new plant is never more costly to operate (per unit of output) than old plant, it affects this tradeoff in a particularly simple way: At any given price level, output will be the sum of the old output for that price level plus the output of all the new plant. (See Exhibit 20.2.) At any given price level, the jobs created by the new plant represent pure gain in the level of employment. Thus additions to the capital stock make it possible to increase jobs and output without raising real prices and lowering real wages, or to increase real wages without reducing jobs and output.

If the work force is adding people, while nobody is adding plant, policy-makers have to choose between letting unemployment increase and letting the real wage fall. When the work force is growing, some investment will be required just to keep the real wage from falling. Only when investment exceeds this level will the real wage actually rise. It follows that societies with rapidly growing work forces will find it hard to maintain, much less increase, real wages. Consider, for example, the contrasting economic experiences of Japan and the United States, illustrated in Exhibit 20.3 Japan's real-wage performance was impressive—especially compared with U.S. experience. But U.S. employment performance was impressive—especially compared with Japan's.

## WHAT DOES GOVERNMENT SPENDING HAVE TO DO WITH PRIVATE INVESTMENT?

To answer this question, we appeal to J. B. Williams' Conservation of Value axiom. According to this axiom, the value of the sum of (or difference between) future cash

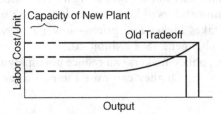

**EXHIBIT 20.2**   Adding New Plant

**EXHIBIT 20.3** Japanese and U.S. Economies

|  | '65 | '90 | Ratio |
|---|---|---|---|
| *Japan*: Manufacturing Employment | 91.8 | 104.1 | 1.13 |
| Real Wage | 0.53 | 1.09 | 2.06 |
| U.S.: Non-Agricultural Employment | 62.3 | 113.1 | 1.82 |
| Real Wage | 0.93 | 1.00 | 1.08 |

flow streams is the sum of (or difference between) their respective current values. Consider, for example, the following government cash flows:

$$\text{Taxes on Capital} + \text{Taxes on Labor} = \text{Government Spending}$$
$$-\text{Borrowing} + \text{Repayment} \quad (20.1)$$

If Equation 20.1 holds for the government's instantaneous flows at every point in time, then it must also hold for the corresponding future cash flow *streams*. But then Conservation of Value applies. Letting V[.] represent the present value of the cash flow stream denoted within the brackets, we have:

$$V\,[\text{Taxes on Capital}] + V\,[\text{Taxes on Labor}] = V\,[\text{Government Spending}]$$
$$+V\,[\text{Existing Debt}] \quad (20.2)$$

(If borrowing and repayment transactions have roughly zero present values, then the only borrowing with net present value impact on this equation is currently outstanding debt.)

In similar fashion, consider the following equation for a corporation's cash flows:

$$\text{Cash Flow from Operations} + \text{Receipts from Investors} = \text{Tax Payments}$$
$$+ \text{Disbursements to Investors} \quad (20.3)$$

If this holds for the corporation's instantaneous cash flows at every point in time, then it must also hold for the corresponding future cash flow streams. But then Conservation of Value applies. We have:

$$V\,[\text{Disbursements to Investors} - \text{Receipts from Investors}]$$
$$= V\,[\text{Cash Flow from Operations}] - V\,[\text{Tax Payments}] \quad (20.4)$$

To keep our argument simple, we consider a country in which all productive assets are owned in corporate form, and that has only one level of government; in the country we consider, corporations pay all the taxes levied on capital. If Equation 20.4 holds for every corporation, it also holds for the private sector as a whole. Solving for the term corresponding to future taxes on capital in Equation 20.1 and substituting in Equation 20.4, we have:

$$V \text{ [Disbursements to Investors } - \text{ Receipts from Investors]}$$

$$= V \text{ [Cash Flow from Operations]} - V \text{ [Government Spending]}$$

$$-V \text{ [Existing Government Debt]} + V \text{ [Taxes on Labor]} \tag{20.5}$$

Government debt reduces the value of investors' claims on private capital just as if it were corporate (i.e., private) debt. So does any future government spending not defrayed by taxes on labor. To say anything useful about the impact of fiscal policy on investment decisions in the private sector, then, we need to be able to make "rational" forecasts of future taxes on labor.

The key to such forecasts lies in two recent pieces in this space entitled "A Modest Proposal" and "A More Modest Proposal."[1] There we argued that a worker's well-being depends not on his tax burden, but on his after-tax wage. We found that, when the volume of investing is taken into account, the worker's after-tax wage is highest when he bears the full burden of government spending, and capital bears none.[2]

Workers have the preponderance of votes in any democratic society. Governments don't last long that don't benefit workers. But economics is perverse, and only those who have studied economics know that. Today, most politicians who reach national prominence have studied some economics. They deal with the problem by giving the voters the best policies the voters can stand.

We can thus draw the following conclusions:

1. Because a higher tax on labor would be better for labor, the current tax on labor is always the highest that is politically feasible.
2. Because the current tax on labor is the highest that is politically feasible, any current deficit is not going to be repaid by increasing the tax on labor; it is going to be repaid by taxing capital. The debt that results from government deficits is not, as some economists argue, something we owe to ourselves: It is owed by capital to the owners of the debt.
3. The operating deficit is that portion of government spending that capital will pay later, with interest, rather than now. But what influences investors is the *present value* of the burden on them. Changing the tax on capital changes the timing of the burden, but not its present value. Thus the burden on capital is not measured by the tax on capital.[3]

Incremental government debt reduces the value of private claims dollar for dollar. When the net value of private claims—the lefthand side of Equation 20.3—goes to zero, the government has exhausted its power to tax capital. Beyond this point, any value created by new private investment is preempted by taxation. But long before this point, new investment—which investors can justify only if its value exceeds their cost—has already ceased.

## DOES GOVERNMENT SPENDING CREATE JOBS?

Perhaps the most commonly offered justification for government spending is that it boosts demand, creating jobs for workers, who then consume more, creating still more jobs. To judge whether government spending can stimulate real growth, however, we have to examine the effect of that spending on investment. Does that spending encourage investment, or discourage it?

The answer isn't obvious. Government spending that isn't defrayed by taxes on labor will have to be paid, sooner or later, by taxes on capital, including new capital. The value of new investment to the investor will be reduced by such taxes. Thus it's at least plausible that investment could be discouraged by government spending.

The combined effect of one dollar of government spending on the first, second, and later stages of resulting income creation is called the Keynesian multiplier. If government spending inhibits private investment, then any stimulus depends on the difference between two multiplier effects—the multiplier effect of government spending and the multiplier effect of private investment. As every modern economics textbook explains, the Keynesian multiplier of government spending and private investment is the same. Thus any net stimulus from government spending depends critically on how big the resulting loss in private investment is. If, for example, a dollar of government spending reduces private investment by one dollar, then the net effect of the two kinds of stimulus is zero.

A net stimulus of zero would, of course, be unfortunate. To the extent that government spending adds to the government debt, it reduces the value of future investments as well as current investments. The long-term effect on the tradeoff between unemployment and inflation—on real growth—would be entirely adverse.

## GOVERNMENT SPENDING VERSUS PRIVATE INVESTMENT

The evidence, in Exhibit 20.4, shows a strong negative association between changes in government spending and changes in private investment. Could this association reflect a tendency by government to increase spending whenever private investment lags? No, because it takes government a couple of years to change its spending rate. Could this association reflect some kind of natural limit on the sum of government spending and private investment? Perhaps, although it isn't obvious what, in the absence of capital controls, this limit would be.

The more comprehensive sum of consumption, government spending, and private investment rose from 1962, when it constituted 97.1 percent of gross domestic product, to 1986, when it represented 103 percent of gross domestic product. (The increase is due mainly to consumption, which rose from 63.8 percent in 1962 to 68.6 percent in 1991.)

This evidence suggests there is no constraint on the sum of government spending and private investment, at least in the later years of the sample period.

Dividing the period into two subsamples, one with sums below the median value for the period and the other with sums above the median value, reveals the same strong negative association between government spending and private investment observed for the entire period. Because of the time trends in consumption, the subsample with the higher sums is drawn mainly from the more recent, hence more relevant, years in the sample period. For this subsample, one dollar of incremental government spending reduces private investment by about one dollar.

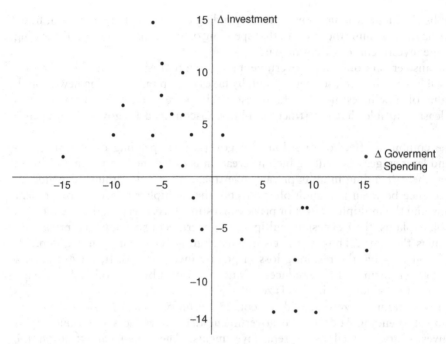

**EXHIBIT 20.4**   Government Spending and Private Investment in the United States, 1962–1990

## WHAT ABOUT ECONOMIC INSTABILITY?

Modern episodes of underemployment have been occasioned by central banks' struggles with inflation. In a recent *Wall Street Journal* piece ("The Bogus Jobs Problem," August 28, 1992), Herbert Stein makes the important point that the United States has coped heroically with a rapidly expanding work force, and argues that economic instability, not jobs, is the problem. But jobs and instability are related. The wag who said every recession since World War II was made in Washington was right. The motive in every case was inflation, or fear of inflation. But recessions aren't the only way to restrain inflation. The other way is to keep the real wage rising by creating new jobs faster than they are being absorbed by a growing work force.

The object of all bargaining for increased money wages is an increased real wage. If one worker can secure a higher money wage, the impact on prices will be minuscule, and he will gain a higher real wage. But when *all* workers secure a higher money wage, the impact on prices is so big that their objective—higher real wages—is defeated. The evidence, in Exhibit 20.5, shows almost no association between (percentage) changes in the money wage and changes in the real wage. Wage earners are acting out a giant fallacy of composition, in which money-wage increases merely result in price increases.

Excessive striving for money-wage increases leads to inflation, which leads to recessions to control the inflation. By giving workers what they really want, real-wage increases slow inflation, and hence reduce the need for recessions. The evidence, in Exhibit 20.6, shows a negative association between changes in the real

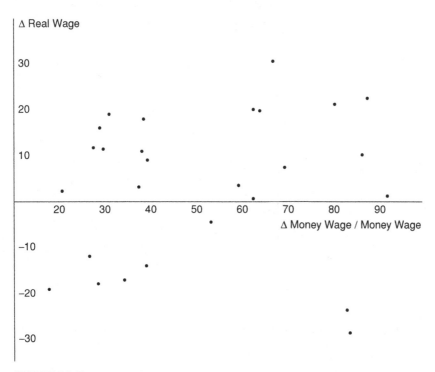

**EXHIBIT 20.5**   U.S. Real Wages versus Money Wages, 1962–1990

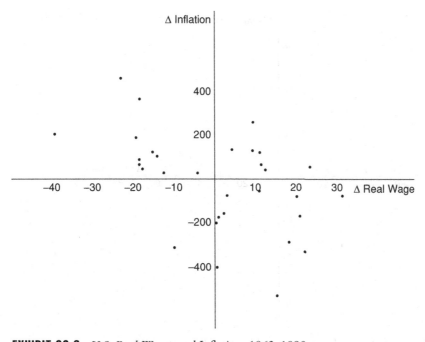

**EXHIBIT 20.6**   U.S. Real Wages and Inflation, 1962–1990

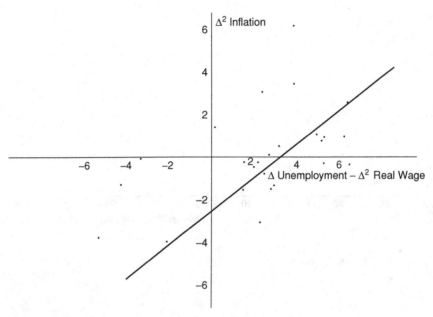

**EXHIBIT 20.7**   Predicting Inflation from Changes in Unemployment and Real Wages

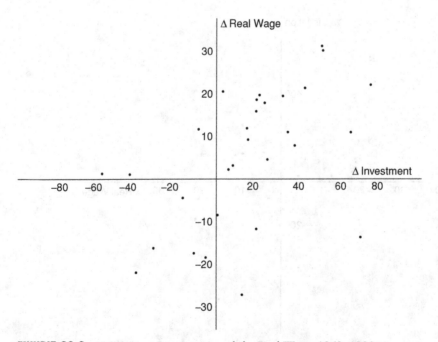

**EXHIBIT 20.8**   U.S. Private Investment and the Real Wage, 1962–1990

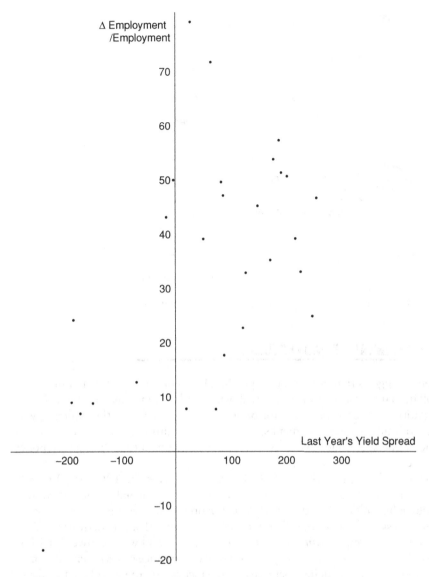

**EXHIBIT 20.9** U.S. Monetary Policy and Job Growth, 1963–1990

wage and changes in the inflation rate. (To be sure, the association becomes stronger when a second explanatory variable—unemployment—is added. Exhibit 20.7 shows the success of *first* differences in unemployment coupled with *second* differences in the real wage in predicting *second* differences in the inflation rate.) Real-wage increases reduce the necessity for periodic recessions, as well as being desirable for their own sake. And, as Exhibit 20.8 shows, private investment increases the real wage.

Gross Capital Formation/GDP

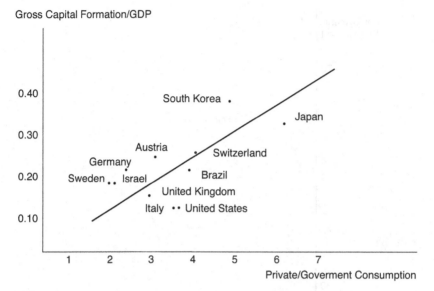

**EXHIBIT 20.10**   Goverment Consumption and Capital Formation

## ISN'T THE ALTERNATIVE INEFFECTUAL?

The evidence suggests that government spending has reduced investment almost dollar for dollar, that investment raises the real wage, and that increases in the real wage reduce inflation, hence the necessity for periodic recessions. Given the evidence, why would anybody advocate government spending as the solution to our economic problems? One of the spending advocates' favorite arguments is that "monetary policy hasn't worked."

The U.S. evidence, in Exhibit 20.9, suggests that, over the 1963–1990 period, monetary policy has been very powerful. Except in very unusual economic circumstances, which haven't prevailed since the great depression, government spending has never been necessary to achieve full employment. The moral seems reasonably clear. The one thing governments *can* do to increase jobs, raise real wages, lower inflation, and reduce the frequency and severity of recessions is—reduce government spending.

The importance of reducing spending is underscored by the final bit of evidence in Figure 20.10, showing the impact of various countries' spending policies. Gross capital formation per unit of gross domestic product is a measure of a country's rate of real economic growth. The ratio of private to government spending is an inverse measure of the importance accorded government in the country's economy. The association in Exhibit 20.10 is obviously strong. But the United States is currently at the wrong end of the chart, with Sweden, Israel, and Italy for neighbors.

## APPENDIX 20.1

The deficit can always be reduced by increasing the tax on capital. But the tax on capital isn't a meaningful measure of anything. Consider, for example, the textbook relation "saving equals investment." It needs some amplification when applied to an open economy with open capital markets and a government sector:

1. America's investing may be foreign or domestic.
2. Domestic investment may be financed by foreign investors or Americans.
3. Saving is net of taxes and the government deficit.

Let us restate, introducing the necessary amplifications:

$$\text{After-tax Saving} = \text{Government Deficit} + \text{Investing}$$

(We depart from textbook usage by employing *investing* for what is done by Americans and *investment* for what is done in America. Obviously, it's what is done in America that governs jobs and real wages.)

Adding taxes to both sides restores real meaning to the relation:

$$\text{Pretax Saving} = \text{Government Spending} + \text{Investing by Domestic Investors}$$

Observing that

$$\text{Trade Balance} = \text{Investing} - \text{Investment}$$

and substituting, we have

$$\text{National Income} = \text{Consumption} + \text{Government} + \text{Investment} + \text{Trade Balance}$$

To increase investment, reduce consumption, government spending, or the trade balance (i.e., reduce the trade surplus or increase the deficit). If we reject increasing the trade deficit, then there are only two ways to increase investment—reduce government spending or reduce consumption.

Taxes on income that would otherwise be spent reduce consumption. Although propensity to consume on income to labor is high, we've argued that higher taxes on labor aren't politically feasible. And increasing the tax on capital will have little, if any, effect on consumption, because changing the current tax on capital doesn't change its present value.

## Notes

1. See the January/February 1992 and March/April 1992 issues of *Financial Analysts Journal*, respectively.
2. We asked, what allocation of a fixed tax burden between capital and labor is fairest to labor? We acceded to tradition by ignoring entirely the question of fairness to investors. But we amended the traditional concept in a way we feel will serve labor better. Instead of focusing narrowly on labor's tax burden, we focused on the difference between labor's real income and its tax burden. We assumed (1) a given government burden; (2) a production function with declining returns to proportion and both first and second derivatives of real output with respect to the capital input; (3) a required after-tax rate of return imposed by the international capital markets; and (4) a closed labor market and an open capital market.

Believing that, in the long run, only a full-employment solution is going to be acceptable, we took the labor input as fixed.

3. The current addition to the burden on investment is government spending less taxes on labor. This burden is divided between old investment already in place and new investment. Financing the burden with debt reduces the burden on old capital that will be obsolete before the debt is paid off. To that extent, debt financing increases the burden on new investment, making it harder to attract capital. The way to increase investment is not to lower current taxes on capital, but to reduce the burden.

# CHAPTER 21

# Securities Law and Public Policy

In a closed capital market, the aggregate wealth of investors equals the value of the economy's real assets (less their share of the government burden). Most of these assets—engine lathes, electric generating plants, diesel locomotives, real estate—are highly illiquid, no more liquid, probably, than used cars or secondhand watches, and for similar reasons: The seller knows far more than the buyer about whether the asset has been abused, undermaintained, and so on.

The average citizen is far from rich. One practical consequence is that his unexpected cash needs loom large in relation to his wealth. If he held his wealth in the form of direct claims on the economy's real assets, he would have to incur prohibitive liquidation costs to meet his cash needs. Thus he can't afford to own such assets directly. Broadly speaking, countries solve this problem in three ways.

(1) The state owns the productive assets. The saver holds his wealth in the form of claims on the state. Claims on the state can, of course, be vastly more liquid than direct claims on the country's productive assets.

(2) Ownership of real assets is concentrated in a few rich families. Their unexpected cash needs will be larger than those of the average family, but not much larger. Because their needs loom small in relation to their wealth, they can meet these needs while still devoting the bulk of their portfolios to real assets.

(3) Financial institutions and markets make claims on real assets liquid enough that the average family can use them to meet their unexpected cash needs without excessive penalty.

Two kinds of institution can transform claims on real assets into something the average citizen can afford to own. *Banks* can diversify across the cash needs of their claimants; their liquidation problem is confined to the *difference* between deposits and withdrawals. *Corporations* can diversify across a variety of real assets, thereby minimizing the potential advantage of information on a single asset to those who trade ownership claims on the corporation's portfolio.

But widespread ownership of real assets requires something more than these admittedly important institutions. It requires securities markets. Corporate shares that are traded in dealer markets are vastly more liquid than shares that aren't. Dealers play a critical role in making ownership (albeit indirect) of the economy's real assets feasible for the average family.

---

The first way to solve the ownership problem concentrates all economic power in the state; we call it communism. The second way concentrates all economic power in a small group of people who use that power to cultivate a mutually beneficial partnership with the state; we call it fascism. The third way is what we call democratic capitalism.

But the third way requires active, liquid securities markets—and such markets require healthy dealers. If a dealer accumulates a large position by accommodating trades that are motivated by information entering consensus price before the dealer can lay the position off, such trades can damage the dealer, perhaps fatally. That's a valid reason for discouraging trading on so-called "inside" information, quite apart from whether such trading entails misappropriation of corporate property or wire fraud.

Similarly, market manipulation (which, in dealer markets, is manipulation of dealer prices) may harm dealers by misleading them about the true location of equilibrium prices. That's a legitimate reason for discouraging market manipulation.

Our securities laws, however, are vague not merely about the purpose of proscriptions against the use of inside information and market manipulation, but about what is being proscribed. Because dealers play a critical role in democratic capitalism, their health is a proper concern of public policy. We shouldn't be shy about recognizing that concern in our securities laws.

# CHAPTER 22

# Shirtsleeves to Shirtsleeves in Three Generations

**B**ecause it justifies and supports our activities as researchers, investment advisers, traders, consultants, and regulators, the level of investment in society is an appropriate concern for investment professionals. As "A Modest Proposal" explained, the working man should also care greatly about the investment level, because it determines his real wage.[1] There is an important link, however, between the *level* of wealth in society and the *distribution* of wealth. Because poor people consume a larger fraction of their income than rich people do, an unequal distribution of wealth leads to more saving, hence more investment.

Alas, the distribution of wealth is a bone of contention. A common notion is that "them that has, gits," that it's hard to become rich unless you are rich to begin with. According to one influential critic of the American system, "Personal savings behavior ... has little or nothing to do with the process [that generates a highly skewed distribution of wealth]" ... "once a duke always a duke."[2] The critic argues that if we could somehow spread wealth around more evenly, we could break the vicious circle of concentration begetting concentration. But he cautions: "A once-in-a-lifetime wealth tax ... is too infrequent to place much of a constraint on an individual's wealth ... [if] society ... wants to prevent individuals from having massive net worths and the economic power that goes with large fortunes."[3] In this view, the concentration of wealth is evidence of "market failure"—failure of the free market system to achieve what "society" allegedly wants.

To the extent the critic's ideas are widely shared, one would expect the poor to feel both limited responsibility for their condition and limited respect for the rich. Democratic governments' attempts to placate these feelings are costly.

1. Governments only redistribute wealth downward.
2. But poorer households save less than rich households. So redistribution reduces saving.
3. As we will show, redistribution by governments has no permanent effect. So governments redouble their efforts, again with no permanent effect, except to reduce aggregate saving, aggregate wealth, and the real wage.

---

The great Swiss-Italian economist Vilfredo Pareto discovered that, far from providing evidence of "market failures," actual wealth distributions for countries with widely differing emphases on redistribution had the same shape. This note offers an explanation for the observed similarity. It also argues that:

1. There is *no* link between initial endowments and the ultimate distribution of wealth.
2. Contrary to the critic, "personal savings behavior" has *everything* to do with the ultimate distribution.
3. The distribution of wealth can *never* be used to document "market failures" relating to earned income.

## WEALTH DISTRIBUTION

Market failures, if they exist, have their direct effect, not on the highly efficient market for investment assets, but on *earned income*. To cite the distribution of wealth as evidence of market failures is to assume that it reflects the distribution of earned income—if not in the short run, then in the long run.

Alas, when we turn to studies of the evidence on *income* distribution, we find a frequent error (which, by the way, our critic avoids)—the use of combined income, rather than earned income.[4] It is well known that future earned income is a form of capital. Appropriately discounted to the present, its value can be commensurate with that of investment assets. Conversely, investment assets will generate future income that can be commensurate with earned income. Combined income—earned income plus investment income—and combined wealth—the value of investment assets plus the capitalized value of future earned income—are the same thing to a constant factor.

Thus the distinction between the distribution of combined income and the distribution of combined wealth is an empty distinction; the many studies of income distribution that focus on combined income are really studies of *wealth* distribution. But, as we shall see, long-run wealth distribution tells us nothing about the distribution of earned income. So studies that don't distinguish between earned income and investment income can tell us nothing about market failures.

## CHANGES IN WEALTH

Attempts to explain the distribution of wealth have been dominated from the beginning by the idea of *diffusion*: From an initial wealth level, a household either gets richer or poorer, arriving at a new wealth level from which it then gets richer or poorer, etc. After sufficient time, some households have migrated to extremes of wealth and poverty, while most have ended up somewhere near the middle. Researchers have puzzled over the fact that the resulting distributions of wealth aren't normal, or even log-normal.

It seems to us these researchers may have given random wealth changes too much emphasis. Consider the physicist's problem of predicting the pressure gas will exert on a closed container. This pressure, which is the result of collisions of molecules of gas with the container's walls, depends on the molecules' velocity. The molecules are also colliding with each other. Under certain circumstances, the latter collisions diffuse velocity. But it doesn't take models of this diffusion process to explain pressure on the container, because that pressure averages across the velocities of thousands of molecules.

Now back to wealth. At a moment in time, the thousands of households at a given wealth level are experiencing a range of fortune, with a few households at a given wealth level going broke and a tiny handful striking it rich. But these events will have a negligible effect on the average experience. Suppose (1) all wealth levels experience the same average market rate of return and (2) average consumption is a linear function of the level of wealth. As regards (1), even severe critics of the free enterprise system admit that capital markets are remarkably efficient. As regards (2), the evidence supports the assumption that on average, consumption is a linearly increasing function of wealth.[5]

Under our assumptions, the difference between return to combined wealth and consumption causes households to move from one wealth level to another. As households move to new wealth levels, they adopt the consumption behavior characteristic of those new levels, which then leads to further transitions. Averaged across the whole population, these transitions from one wealth level to another are continuous in the sense that, over sufficiently short time periods, households move up or down only to adjacent wealth levels.

We ask: Given the transition behavior at each wealth level, for what distribution of wealth will this game of musical chairs give us back the same distribution we started with? Because it lacks this special property, any other initial distribution of wealth will revert in time to the ultimate distribution. This is why earned income, one-time wealth transfers by government and initial endowments of investment assets can have no long-run effect.

The key to our derivation of this distribution is the rate at which aggregate wealth (hence the number of households) at a given wealth level is changing. To spare readers who don't like limit arguments, the derivation of this rate is relegated to the appendix. To spare readers who don't like mathematics, the application of this rate is also relegated to Appendix 22.1.

Exhibit 22.1 displays the combined wealth distribution for the United States in 1962, using data provided by Professor Lester Thurow of MIT.[6] As we explain in the appendix, our so-called "exponential" model is the result of a number of simplifications. The appendix describes its predictions: "As the . . . fraction [of households above] . . . [the wealth] cutoff goes down, the . . . fraction [of the aggregate wealth owned by households below . . . the cutoff] goes up exponentially." We have plotted Professor Thurow's data on semilog graph paper, with wealth below the cutoff on the log axis (and households above the cutoff on the Cartesian axis). These points will plot in a straight line if, despite the simplifications, our exponential model correctly explains the distribution of wealth. Exhibit 22.1 suggests that, except for the point corresponding to the lowest wealth category, it does.

Our mathematical result has two terms—an exponential term and a linear term. In our simplified exponential model we have discarded the linear term, which is dominated at high wealth levels by the exponential term. But it may be more important at low wealth levels. As the lower plot in Exhibit 22.1 shows, when plotted on semilog graph paper, this linear term makes a contribution to our mathematical result that is convex upwards. If the scale of this convexity in the term our model discards were

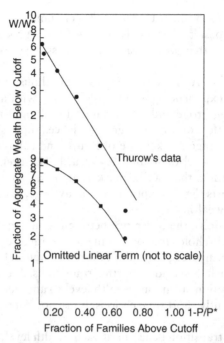

**EXHIBIT 22.1**   A Distribution of Wealth in the U.S., 1962.

big enough, it could conceivably explain the departure of Lester Thurow's data from the predictions of the model.

## APPENDIX 22.1

We make no distinction between young consumers and old consumers or between consumers relying on earned income and consumers relying on investment assets. Suppose we specify the distribution of wealth by a density function, p(w), describing the fraction of the nation's households with level of wealth w.

Then the aggregate wealth at that level is:

$$w \, p \, (w)$$

If the market rate of return is r and consumption of representative households at that level obeys C(w), then aggregate wealth grows or shrinks at the rate:

$$[rw - C\,(w)]\, p\,(w, t)$$

As aggregate wealth grows or shrinks, however, individual households may be moving into different wealth levels. If we consider a small wealth increment, then the rate at which the aggregate wealth in that increment is changing is the *difference* between the rates at which wealth is arriving on one side of the increment and leaving on the other. We show later that, as we make the increment in wealth per household smaller, the limiting value of this difference is:

$$\frac{\partial}{\partial w} \{ [rw - C(w)] \, p(w, t) \} / \frac{dp}{dw}$$

By the "ultimate" distribution of wealth we mean the "steady-state" distribution for which the density of households at each wealth level isn't changing. But when the number of households isn't changing, the aggregate wealth at each level isn't changing either. Thus the numerator of the above expression must be zero for every wealth level—every value of w. We have:

$$\frac{\partial}{\partial w} \{ [rw - C(w)] \, p(w) \} = 0$$

What shall we assume about the relation C(w) between the level of household wealth and consumption? The evidence, cited in many textbooks, is that consumption rises less than proportionately as household wealth increases. (Under our assumption of a single market rate of return, income proxies for wealth, and *vice versa*.) We model this relation by:

$$C(w) = a + bw,$$

$$0 < b < r, a > 0$$

Substituting this relation in the condition for the steady-state wealth distribution we get:

$$\frac{d}{dw}[(rw - a - bw)p(w)] = 0$$

Differentiating, we have:

$$(r - b) \, p(w) + (r - b) \, w \frac{dp}{dw} - \frac{adp}{dw} = 0$$

$$-\frac{dp}{p} = \frac{(r - b) \, dw}{(r - b) \, w - a}$$

which is an exact differential. Letting u represent saving:

$$u = (r - b) \, w - a$$

we have

$$du/dw = r - b, \, dw = du/r - b$$

With these substitutions, the equation becomes:

$$-dp/p = du/u$$

Taking the respective integrals, we have:

$$\ln 1/p = \ln u + \ln k = \ln ku$$
$$p = 1/ku$$

ln k being a constant of integration.

The evidence on the distribution of wealth is awkward to discuss in terms of density functions. It is more conveniently expressed in terms of cumulative functions—specifically, running sums of households up to a given level of household wealth and running sums of *wealth* up to a given level of household wealth.

For cumulative households up to a given level w of household wealth, P(w), we have:

$$P(w) = \int p(w)\,dw$$

We saw that:

$$p(u) = \frac{1}{ku}$$

Recalling that:

$$dw = \frac{du}{r - b'}$$

we have:

$$P(u) = \frac{1}{k(r-b)} \int \frac{du}{u} = \frac{1}{k(r-b)} \ln u$$
$$u = exp\left[k(r-b)P\right]$$

For cumulative wealth W(w), we have:

$$W(w) = \int wp(w)\,dw$$

Our definition of u in terms of w implies, conversely, that w can be expressed:

$$w = \frac{u + a}{r - b}$$

We have:

$$W(u) = \int \frac{(u+a)}{ku} \frac{du}{(r-b)^2}$$

$$= \frac{1}{k(r-b)^2} \int \left(1 + \frac{a}{u}\right) du$$

$$= \frac{u + a \ln u}{k(r-b)^2}$$

Substituting for u and ln u we have:

$$W(P) = \frac{exp\,[k(r-b)\,P] + ak(r-b)\,P}{k(r-b)^2} = \frac{exp\,[k(r-b)\,P]}{k(r-b)^2} + \frac{aP}{r-b}$$

P measures the number of households below some given wealth level and W measures the aggregate wealth of those households. For large P, the first term dominates; aggregate wealth rises exponentially with the number of households below the cutoff level.

In using indefinite integrals to represent what in principle should be definite integrals with lower as well as upper limits, we are effectively discarding the lower limits. If we had included the lower limits, we would have had to recognize that the integrand below the "crossover" point between saving and dissaving is different from the integrand above the crossover point. We think these complications have only a modest impact on our result.

Can we convert our result relating *absolute* wealth to *absolute* households to *percentage* terms?

$$W(P) = \frac{exp\,[k(r-b)\,P]}{k(r-b)^2} + \left(\frac{a}{r-b}\right) P$$

Suppose we ignore the second term. Let P* and W* represent 100 percent of households. Then:

$$W^* = \frac{exp\,[k(r-b)\,P^*]}{k(r-b)^2}$$

$$W/W^* = exp\,[k(r-b)(P - P^*)]$$

$$W/W^* = exp\left[k(r-b)\left(\frac{P}{P^*} - 1\right) P^*\right]$$

$$W/W^* = \left[\ell^{k(b-r)P^*}\right]^{1-P/P^*}$$

This result says that the fraction of the aggregate wealth owned by households below a given wealth cutoff varies with the fraction of households above that cutoff. As the latter fraction goes down, the wealth fraction goes up exponentially (the expression in brackets is less than one, since b − r < 0.) The only difference between one country's wealth distribution and another's is the expression:

$$k(b-r)P^*$$

Nothing relating to the distribution of earned income, redistribution by government or initial wealth endowments enters into this expression. On the other hand, this expression has no effect on the *shape* of the distribution, which is consequently the same for all countries.

## RATE OF WEALTH CHANGES

The results in this paper are based on an expression for the rate at which aggregate wealth, hence households, at a given wealth level is changing. Here we derive that expression. We begin with the definition of the density p(w) of households at a given wealth level w:

$$p(w_1) = \lim_{w1 \to w0} \frac{W(w_1) - W(w_0)}{P(w_1) - P(w_0)}$$

Differentiating both members, we get:

$$\frac{dp}{dt}(w_0) = \lim \frac{\frac{dW}{dt}(w_1) - \frac{dW(w_0)}{dt}}{P(w_1) - P(w_0)}$$

But we have:

$$\frac{dW}{dt}(w) = [rw - C(w)]\,p(w)$$

So the derivative becomes:

$$\frac{dW}{dt}(w_0) = \lim_{w_1 \to w_0} \frac{[rw_1 - C(w_1)]\,p(w_1) - [rw_2 - C(w_2)]\,p(w_2)}{P(w_1) - P(w_0)}$$

$$= \frac{\partial}{\partial p}\{[rw - C(w)]\,p(w)\}$$

Thanks to l'Hospital's Theorem, we can rewrite this expression:

$$\frac{dp}{dt}(w) = \frac{\frac{\partial}{\partial w}[rw - C(w)]\,p(w)}{\frac{dp}{dw}}$$

### Notes

1. J. L. Treynor, "A Modest Proposal," *Financial Analysts Journal*, January/February 1992, and "A More Modest Proposal," *Financial Analysts Journal*, May/June 1992.
2. L. C. Thurow, *The Zero-Sum Society* (New York: Basic Books, 1980), pp. 176, 196.

3. L. C. Thurow, *The Impact of Taxes on the American Economy* (New York: Praeger, 1971), p. 130.
4. *Ibid.*, p. 124.
5. See P. A. Samuelson, *Economics*, Ninth Edition (New York: McGraw Hill, 1973), p. 209 or R. Dornbusch and S. Fischer, *Macroeconomics* (New York: McGraw Hill, 1978), p. 57.
6. Thurow, *The Impact of Taxes on the American Economy, op.cit.*, p. 6.

# CHAPTER 23

# Is Training a Good Investment?

**A**s citizens, we need to understand the social consequences of training, whether undertaken by business or by government. As investors, however, we also need to understand the economic consequences. One consequence when business undertakes a training program is its cost. Another consequence, one that we must consider no matter who pays for the program, is the program's effect on the employer's subsequent operating cash flow. The long-term consequences can be good or bad, irrespective of the initial cost. If the long-term consequences are bad, they can sometimes be offset, but they can rarely be undone. In these important respects, investments in training resemble investments in plant. Just as it behooves outside investors to understand the economics of plant, it also behooves them to understand the economics of training.

## THE UNSKILLED WAGE

Skills are a set of potentially valuable reflexes or habits. Training is the process that confers these habits on uneducated people—people unable to acquire them without outside help. The economic value of an education—as opposed to the psychic rewards—lies in the ability it confers to acquire new skills without outside help. If uneducated people had this ability, no skills would be scarce.

Advances in technology are making the educated person's task harder. You must know more these days to be an airline pilot, brain surgeon, or securities lawyer than you did 40 years ago. Either you have to learn faster, or you have to study longer. At the same time, advances in technology are making the uneducated worker's job easier. You need *less* skill to drive a tractor than a team of oxen, to type with a word processor than with a Smith-Corona, to calculate on a Casio than on a Frieden.

It was never easy for the uneducated worker to vault from one group to the other. The real problem with technological progress is not that it increases the demands on educated people, but that it reduces the demands that make skilled workers scarce.

Whether we are talking about a pianist with a concert grand, a typist with a word processor, or a machinist with an engine lathe, "skill" refers to a worker's effectiveness with a tool or machine. At every point in time, an industry has either more skilled workers than machines or more machines than skilled workers. If the industry has more skilled workers than machines, then others with the same skills are not using those skills. If the worker using his skills is being paid a skill premium, the others will be willing to do his work for a smaller skill premium. In this way, the wage will quickly be bid down to what others with scarce skills—including those with no skills—can command.

The notion of scarcity is the key to the meaning of the egregious misnomer "unskilled wage": The unskilled wage is the wage of every worker whose skills, no matter how numerous and subtle, are not scarce.

## THE PLANT-LABOR BALANCE

The price theorist will quickly point out that the relevant number of machines is not a physical quantity but an economic quantity: Obsolete machines do not count. But which machines are obsolete? The answer is unambiguous for industries that make their output decisions competitively: Use the "unskilled wage" to compute variable costs of producing for the plant capacity in the industry, and rank all the plant by this cost. At any given level of output, one plant will have the highest operating cost—the plant that would be idled first if the given level of output were lower. This is the "marginal" plant at that level of output. If the industry makes its decisions competitively about how much to produce from its given stock of plant, then it will push output to the point where the cost of using the marginal capacity equals price (see Exhibit 23.1). Plant with operating cost higher than the marginal plant's is obsolete.

Now, suppose that, at the "unskilled" wage, plant that would otherwise be profitable to operate is idled by a scarcity of skilled labor. Its owners will be better off hiring skilled labor away from a plant that is operating, even if they have to pay a higher wage to do so (Exhibit 23.2). The owners will bid up the wages of the scarce workers until no plant remains that is both profitable to operate and idle—that is, until the demand for these workers no longer exceeds the supply. (It is time to refine our definition of scarcity: Workers are scarce when demand exceeds supply at the "unskilled" wage.)

The level of output a scarce labor supply and the industry's plant capacity can produce will elicit a product price from the demand curve facing the industry. That

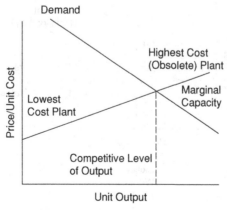

**EXHIBIT 23.1** Price and Output with No Scarcity of Requisite Skills

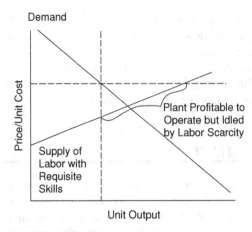

**EXHIBIT 23.2**   Disequilibrium When Scarce Skills Are Paid the Unskilled Wage

level of output will also correspond to a (fictitious) marginal cost for the industry when labor hours are costed out at the "unskilled" wage. The wage rate must increase by the ratio of that demand price to the fictitious cost based on the unskilled wage. We call the equilibrium-producing increase in the hourly wage the *skill premium* (see Exhibit 23.3).

Every active plant will have to pay this premium *per hour of scarce labor employed*, but a less efficient plant will pay a larger premium *per unit of output produced* than another plant. When labor in the industry is being paid this premium, the competitive industry's *de facto* supply curve is its cost curve based on the unskilled wage rate scaled up at every possible level of output by the ratio of demand price to fictitious marginal cost (i.e., cost evaluated at the unskilled wage).

If, for example, product cost based on the unskilled wage is half the demand-based price, then the skill premium is equal to the unskilled wage; the skilled wage is

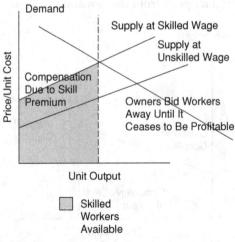

**EXHIBIT 23.3**   How the Skilled Wage Is Determined

twice the unskilled wage; and at every point, a cost curve consistent with a competitive equilibrium—the *de facto* industry supply curve—is twice as high as the cost curve the industry would have if its labor were not scarce.

## THE CONSEQUENCES OF TRAINING

We are now in a position to say something about *training*, which increases the number of workers with certain skills: Other things equal, training reduces the skill premium (see Exhibit 23.4). It may, of course, put more people to work in jobs requiring scarce skills, but it always reduces the skill premium paid for those jobs. If training creates more people with the requisite skills than there are jobs requiring those skills, the skill premium goes to zero. Whereas the people who received the training are then worth no more than before, the people who formerly enjoyed the skill premium enjoy it no longer.

If the workers in an industry are not scarce, training others will not create jobs. When the employed workers are scarce, training others will lower the employed workers' wage—ultimately to the "unskilled" level, at which point the training has not increased anybody's value. At that point, there will be more jobs in the industry than previously, but the previously scarce workers will not be happy. And, unless the new workers were previously unemployed, they will not be happy either.

## CAPACITY ADDITIONS AND TRAINING

Labor scarcity raises an industry's costs, but it also raises its product price. Thus, scarcity can be either good or bad for investors. For industries in which aggregate dollar rent to the owners of plant is higher when skilled labor is scarce, training is bad, not only for the scarce workers but also for the owners. It will not pay the owners of these industries to invest in training (see Exhibit 23.5). The two diagrams shown in the exhibit suggest that, for many industries, there will be a breakeven

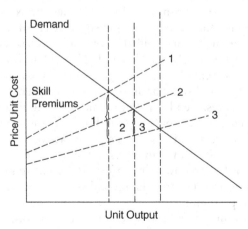

**EXHIBIT 23.4** Effect of Training on the Skill Premium

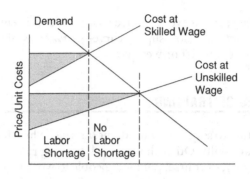

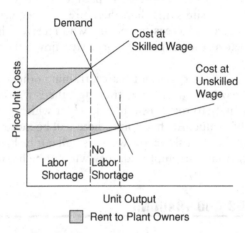

**EXHIBIT 23.5**   Effect of Labor Scarcity, Different Demand Slopes

level of demand elasticity above which scarcity is bad and training is good and below which scarcity is good and training is bad.

A much harder question is whether, when industries require skilled labor, plant additions enhance or reduce investment value. Consider, for example, the plant additions depicted in Exhibit 23.6. Initially (top panel), there is little or no scarcity rent on plant and no skill premium, because skilled labor is just sufficient to produce the level of output that equilibrates supply and demand. Then, plant is added in two stages. The first-stage additions (center panel) add greatly to the scarcity rents accruing to the employer, but the second-stage additions (bottom panel) create a skilled-labor shortage. Equilibrium is restored by a skill premium so big that little or no scarcity rent remains for the employer. From the shareholder's point of view, the first-stage plant investment was successful, the second-stage disastrous.

In this example, the effect of training is not simple. Because there is no labor shortage and hence no skill premium until after the second-stage capacity additions, training initially has no effect. After the second-stage additions, however, training can eliminate the skill premium.

Absent barriers to migration from one employer to another (company unions, geographic location, language, etc.), training must be viewed as increasing the availability of skilled labor, not to the *company* that provides the training, but rather to

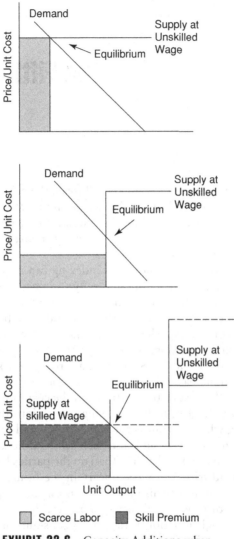

**EXHIBIT 23.6** Capacity Additions when Skilled Labor Is Scarce

an *industry.* The more companies an industry contains, the less willing they will be to train. (Trust-busters take note!)

## SUMMARY

Training is an investment, with initial costs and long-term consequences. To know whether the long-term consequences are good or bad, shareholders must consider each case on its specifics. The important specifics, however, are the same as those to consider for investments in plant: the elasticity of demand, the shape of the supply curve, and the availability of skilled labor.

# CHAPTER 24

# The Fifth Horseman

**A**lthough the pain of the recent recession is still fresh, the pain of the great inflation of the 1970s is receding into history. We are beginning to hear old arguments—arguments that became unfashionable during and after the great inflation—that inflation is not a problem if all contracts are properly indexed to allow for it or if inflation is constant and predictable.

Inflation creates problems no amount of indexing can overcome, and investors need to understand these problems. One has only to imagine an economy without money—in which, for example, a shoemaker with a toothache must barter with a dentist who needs a pair of shoes. Finding the other side of a barter transaction can be uncertain and time consuming. That societies have preferred using even primitive moneys over barter is not surprising. But money can be so expensive to use that it is scarcely better than no money at all. Society's main reason for keeping the inflation rate low is that inflation increases the costs of using money.

Two such costs are the cost of transacting and the cost of holding.

*Cost of transacting.* Relative to barter, using money introduces a second transaction: Between selling what the transactor wants to sell and buying what he wants to buy, the transactor must buy money and then sell it. If he knows less about the value of the money he is buying and selling than do the parties he is transacting with, he can lose on the round trip. The more uncertain the future value of the money, the more the transactor can lose. This uncertainty is one of the problems with using seashells or cigarettes—or foreign currency—as money.

The notion that a high inflation rate can be constant and predictable is not supported by the evidence. Exhibit 24.1 plots *absolute* changes in the inflation rate against the level of the inflation rate preceding the changes. The U.S. experience has been that large *changes* in the inflation rate are more likely when the inflation rate is already high. But changes in the inflation rate are mostly surprise. So higher inflation rates lead to bigger inflation surprises—bigger surprises about the future value of money and bigger transaction risks for those using money.

*Cost of holding.* Money-market assets obey the following rule:

$$\text{Pecuniary return} + \text{Convenience yield} = \text{Real return} + \text{Inflation}$$

The pecuniary return on assets less liquid than money compensates transactors for foregoing money's convenience yield. At a point in time, a wide range of pecuniary

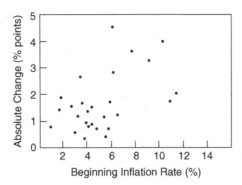

**EXHIBIT 24.1** Beginning of Year Inflation
Rates versus Annual Absolute Changes,
1964–1992

returns and convenience yields may be available, but the sum will be the same for every money-market asset.

The sum of convenience yield and pecuniary return goes up with increases in the transactions demand for money and down with increases in the supply. The pecuniary return is readily observable, whereas convenience yield is not. So it is handy to measure the sum by the pecuniary return on assets with minimal convenience yield; we call this sum the *short interest rate*. And because the sum is gross of inflation, we call it *nominal*.

Subject to certain lags and frictions, central banks can control this rate by controlling the money stock. But suppose they seek to stabilize the "real" short rate—the short interest rate with the spot inflation rate subtracted. Then, when the inflation rate changes, they must change the money stock so the convenience yield on money—hence the pecuniary return on less-liquid assets—once again produces the desired real rate of return.

During the time lag between selling one thing and buying another, the transactor who uses money to facilitate these transactions gives up the pecuniary return on less-liquid assets. True, the foregone pecuniary return is only nominal (i.e., unadjusted for inflation), but the convenience yield on money is also only nominal. So the opportunity cost of holding money is measured by the pecuniary return foregone. Even if a central bank is merely trying to maintain a constant real return, rising inflation will result in a higher pecuniary return on less-liquid assets, hence a higher opportunity cost to holding money.

When the cost of using money rises, more and more transactors will be driven back to barter. The awkwardness of barter will slow the pace of transactions, hence the level of output and employment, even if real rate relationships are unchanged. When all transactors are reduced to barter, business conditions will bear a remarkable resemblance to a depression.

Adam Smith celebrated the efficiencies afforded by division of labor, by specialization. Barter is the enemy of specialization. At any given level of employment, greater specialization means more transactions and greater difficulty in finding the other side of *each* transaction among a greater variety of increasingly narrow specialists.

The more advanced—the more specialized—an economy, the more it depends on money and the more vulnerable it is to the consequences of inflation. If, over time, modern economies become more specialized, the demands on central bankers will become steadily more stringent.

Archaeologists seek reasons for the demise of ancient cities in the four horsemen of the apocalypse—war, famine, pestilence, and disease. But Jane Jacobs tells us a key measure of cities' success is diversity.[1] For cities, progress means increasing diversity, hence increasing specialization. Any city will collapse if increasing diversity outruns the sophistication of its monetary system.

Is inflation the fifth horseman of the apocalypse?

## Note

1. Jane Jacobs, *The Economy of Cities*, (New York: Random House, 1969): 50. She states, "Cities are places where adding new work to older work proceeds vigorously. Indeed, any settlement where this happens becomes a city. Because of this process, city economies are more complicated and diverse than the economies of villages, towns, and farms, as well as being larger . . . Obviously, cities have more different kinds of divisions of labor than villages, towns, and farms do."

# CHAPTER 25

# A Theory of Inflation

*Inflation entails a loop running from prices to wages and back again from wages to prices. Change in inflation rates result from two types of intervention in that otherwise closed loop. Inflation surprise intervenes when the labor productivity of the marginal plant, hence the real wage, turns out different from what negotiators expected when they fixed the money wage. The second kind of intervention is quite predictable. Although changes in tradables prices affect money wages, changes in money wages do not affect tradables prices. The practical result is that the tradables inflation rate affects the home goods inflation rate, but not vice versa. In small, open economies, the predictable tradables effect is more important. In large, closed economies, the effect of real wage surprise on home goods price is more important. In the many countries somewhere between the extremes, both inflation mechanisms are too important to ignore.*

## INTRODUCTION

In this paper, Section 1: Inflation Surprise in the Closed Economy describes an inflation mechanism for the closed economy, Section 2: Inflation Trends in the Open Economy describes a mechanism for the open economy, and Section 3: Open Economies in a Closed World uses both mechanisms to explain inflation in some economies that are neither wholly closed nor wholly open.

Section 1 focuses on the United States and Japan. Evidence in Section 2 suggests that the U.S. and Japan are the worst possible cases for studying inflation behavior in open economies. Because of its simplicity, however, we think the closed economy model is a good place to start.

Perhaps there are some wholly open economies (Lichtenstein? Monaco?). Certainly, there are none in our small sample. Accordingly, Sections 2 and 3 deal instead with countries that are less than wholly closed. To avoid circumlocution in those sections, we call such countries "open."

By this standard, of course, the United States and Japan are open. But the inflation model in Section 1 is for an idealized economy that is wholly closed. Readers may agree with us that the United States and Japan are nevertheless the best tests for this model.

---

## SECTION 1: INFLATION SURPRISE IN THE CLOSED ECONOMY

In some degree, large or small, with some sign, positive or negative, inflation will always be present in a closed economy for which the following hold:

1. The objective of wage negotiators is a certain *real* wage.
2. But wage contracts are expressed in terms of a *money* wage.
3. The real wage is determined in the aggregate, not by negotiators, but by the (real) marginal product of labor.

These considerations suggest that if wage negotiators try to influence the real wage by influencing the money wage, arguing for unusually large increases, for example, when labor markets are tight, they will experience endless frustration and disappointment, year after year.

Day-to-day changes in NYSE stock prices are random, even though some investors think they can profit from stale information. Similarly, is the level of real wages unaffected by the degree of ease or tightness in the labor market? A simple test is how inflation and inflation changes behave when wage negotiators are not striving for a result they cannot achieve collectively—when they are not committing a fallacy of composition. Samuelson defines a fallacy of composition as "a fallacy in which what is true of a part is, on that account, alone, alleged to be necessarily true of the whole" and proceeds to give some helpful examples; "If all farmers work hard ... [and produce] a bumper crop, total farm income may fall . . ." (Paul A. Samuelson, *Economics* p. 14. McGraw Hill 1973.)

Suppose that, instead of attempting to influence the real wage, negotiators content themselves with trying to predict it. (There would then be no immediate link to unemployment or to the relative strength of the negotiators' bargaining positions.) Specifically, suppose they proceed by

- Predicting the real wage,
- Predicting the price level, and
- Computing the money wage that is consistent with their predictions.

We can focus on the essence of this "rational" inflation process if we break time up into discrete intervals, and assume all wage contracts are renegotiated at the beginning of each interval, based on

1. The same intentions regarding the real wage, and
2. The same expectations about money prices.

Letting

$$W = \text{money wage}$$
$$P = \text{money prices}$$
$$w = \text{real wage}$$

we have the "real wage" identity

$$w \equiv \frac{W}{P}$$

$$dw \equiv \frac{P\,dw - W\,dP}{P^2}$$

Using the calculus formula for the total differential of a quotient and dividing by the original identity, we have what we will call our *basic identity*.

$$\frac{dw}{w} \equiv \frac{P\,dW - W\,dP}{P\,W} = \frac{dW}{W} - \frac{dP}{P}$$

which expresses the real wage identity in terms of rates of change.

It is clear from our basic identity that, when real wages are not changing, the rate of price inflation equals the rate of wage inflation. And if, when real wages are not changing, negotiators set the rate of change in money wages equal to last period's rate of change in money prices, then next period's price inflation will equal last period's price inflation. But what happens when real wages are changing?

Once negotiators have fixed the money wage by negotiation, the actual level of money prices will depend on the real wage. If the actual real wage turns out to be different from the expected real wage, negotiators will be surprised by the effect on money prices and the inflation rate.

In other words, in order to arrive at a money wage, negotiators have to make some assumption about the future real wage. But when the actual real wage turns out to be different, they are already locked into that money wage. The only variable in the identity that can reconcile that money wage with the actual real wage is the level of money prices. But if this level is different from what negotiators anticipated, so is the inflation rate.

As noted, wage negotiators do not know what either money prices or real wages will be for the period they are negotiating. Fortunately, the expectations operator is a linear operator. This means that the expectation of a sum is the sum of the expectations. So we can write

$$E\left[\frac{dw}{w}\right] \equiv E\left[\frac{dW}{W}\right] - E\left[\frac{dP}{P}\right]$$

But negotiators have fixed the *actual* money wage for the period. Substituting the actual money wage for the expected money wage and transposing we have

$$\frac{dW}{W} \equiv E\left[\frac{dw}{w}\right] + E\left[\frac{dP}{P}\right]$$

The actual inflation rate must satisfy our basic identity with the money wage previously fixed by negotiation and real wage negotiators can neither predict nor control. Substituting our expression for the money wage into the identity

$$\frac{dP}{P} \equiv \frac{dW}{W} - \frac{dw}{w}$$

we have

$$\frac{dP}{P} \equiv E\left[\frac{dP}{P}\right] + E\left[\frac{dw}{w}\right] - \frac{dw}{w}$$

$$\frac{dP}{P} - E\left[\frac{dP}{P}\right] \equiv -\left\{\frac{dw}{w} - E\left[\frac{dw}{w}\right]\right\}$$

In this quite general result, a real phenomenon—surprise in the rate of change in the real wage—drives a monetary phenomenon—surprise in the rate of change in the money price level.

The model asserts that

1. Surprises in the rate of inflation will be simultaneous with surprises in the real wage.
2. The effect on price inflation will be the same, whether the real wage surprise is due to an oil crisis, a currency change, or an employment surprise.
3. On average, a 1 percent surprise in the real wage will produce a 1 percent surprise in the inflation rate in the opposite direction, irrespective of the time dimension.[1]

This line of reasoning suggests that changes in the inflation rate can occur without any change in negotiators' relative bargaining positions, without any shifts from ease to tightness, or vice versa, in the labor market and without imputing to negotiators some mistaken notion that they can influence the real wage.

But are real wage changes

1. Big enough to explain changes in inflation?
2. Correlated with inflation changes?
3. Too predictable to explain inflation surprise?

## Real Wage Surprise

Alas, it is not enough for a change in employment to generate change in the real wage. It has to generate real wage *surprise*. Because they are driven by demographics, for example, work force changes should be predictable. Is it nevertheless possible for the resulting changes in the real wage to be unpredictable?

The key to such questions is the economy's production function. It may take years to produce a capital good—four years for an oil refinery, six years for a fossil fuel electric generating plant, and so forth. How does the economy respond to sudden changes in current demand?

The economy has a stock of plant capacity. Over time, additions to that stock accumulate and, with them, a cumulative number of jobs $N(t)$ and a cumulative quantity of output $Y(t)$. At any real time $t$, $N(t)$ and $Y(t)$ are given, reflecting the history of capital investment and technology, and including three categories of plant: operating, idle, and scrapped.

At any given level of current demand, employers strive to use their newer, more efficient plant, idling the older, less efficient plant.[2] When plant built before time $\tau$ is idled, employment $n$ and output $y$ are, respectively,[3]

$$n = N(t) - N(\tau)$$
$$y = Y(t) - Y(\tau)$$

To vary output and employment at time $t$, policy makers vary $\tau$. But different values of $\tau$ correspond to different vintages of marginal plant—hence different productivities for the marginal worker and different real wages. Other things equal, the higher are output and employment, the earlier is $\tau$, the older is the marginal plant, and the lower is the resulting real wage.[4]

When employment $n$ increases suddenly, how fast does output rate $y$ increase? Holding $t$ fixed and varying $\tau$, we have

$$\Delta_n \approx \frac{\partial n}{\partial \tau}\Delta\tau = -\frac{dN}{d\tau}\Delta\tau$$

$$\Delta_y \approx \frac{\partial y}{\partial \tau}\Delta\tau = -\frac{dY}{d\tau}\Delta\tau$$

At time $t$ the rate of change of output $y$ with respect to labor input $n$ is

$$\frac{\Delta y}{\Delta n} = \frac{-\left(dY/d\tau\right)\Delta\tau}{-\left(dN/d\tau\right)\Delta\tau} = \frac{dY/d\tau}{dN/d\tau} = \frac{dY}{dN}$$

where $dY/dN$ is the labor productivity of plant built at time $\tau$. We see that the marginal productivity of labor, hence the real wage, at time $t$ depends on this ratio.[5]

When $\tau$ changes, $dY/dN$ changes. So this number is the key to real wage surprise. When one undertakes to forecast the real wage, one has to answer three questions:

1. What is tomorrow's employment level?
2. How big a change in $\tau$ will it take to produce the new employment level? Consider the circumstances at time $\tau$. Presumably, technology was advancing whether we were investing in it or not. But if not, then small changes in the *current* level of employment will correspond to big changes in $\tau$, hence big changes in technology and big changes in the real wage. Such fallow investment periods correspond to "flat spots" on the $N(t)$ and $Y(t)$ curves—regions where jobs and output did not change when $\tau$ was changing. When a current decision to change the level of employment requires policy makers to traverse such a flat spot, the requisite change in $\tau$, hence in technology and in the real wage, is abnormally big. But today's marginal plant is often 20–40 years old. Unless the precise location of these flat spots is still known, even predictable changes in $n$ can cause big surprises in $\tau$, hence in the real wage.
3. What is the productivity $dY/dN$ of marginal plant corresponding to tomorrow's $\tau$? Between today and tomorrow $\tau$ may not change at all. Or it may change suddenly if demand changes suddenly. (War? Financial panic?)

Although our theory of inflation is about surprise, we are obliged to use data on changes (or changes in rates of change, etc.). The difficulties posed by these three questions suggests there is plenty of uncertainty in real wage changes. But we cannot plausibly argue the changes we observe are entirely surprise.

## Testing the Model

We have argued that the actual money wage is related to negotiators' expectations by

$$\frac{dW}{W} = E\left[\frac{dw}{w}\right] + E\left[\frac{dP}{P}\right]$$

It is not obvious how negotiators form their expectations for the real wage. But they know they do not control money prices, and they find the macroeconomics mysterious. So, extrapolation has to be tempting. And, given that changes in the rate of price inflation are nearly random, last year's actual is an obvious basis for this year's expectation. This suggests a way to estimate the change in the real wage negotiators expect. Transposing and incorporating the extrapolation we have

$$E\left[\frac{dw}{w}\right] = \frac{dW}{W} - B\left[\frac{dP}{P}\right]$$

where both right-hand terms are observable and B[ ] is the backshift operator.

But what if instead negotiators base their real wage expectation on extrapolation? Then, we would have *two* bases for our estimate of their real wage expectation. If our assumptions about extrapolation are valid, however, each should give the same estimate. Exhibit 25.1 tests the correlation between the two estimates.

If we combine the estimate that extrapolates price with our basic identity, we obtain

$$\frac{dP}{P} - B\left[\frac{dP}{P}\right] = -\left\{\frac{dw}{w} - E\left[\frac{dW}{W}\right]\right\}$$

If we combine the estimate that extrapolates the real wage with our basic identity, we obtain

$$\frac{dP}{P} - B\left[\frac{dP}{P}\right] = -\left\{\frac{dw}{w} - B\left[\frac{dW}{W}\right]\right\}$$

The first extrapolation suggests that changes in the inflation rate result from real wage surprise. The second suggests a way to predict changes in the inflation rate, using first differences to proxy real wage surprise. We think the second is both more heroic and more useful than the first.

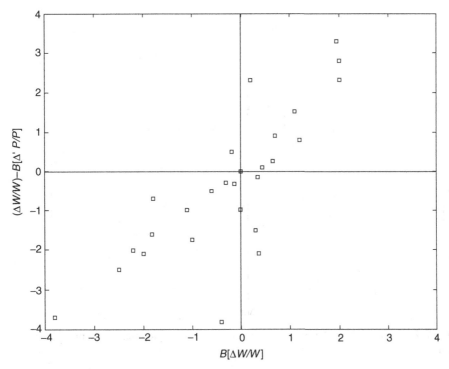

**EXHIBIT 25.1**   United States, 1972–1999: The Correlation between the Two Estimates

The remaining figures make extensive use of some new symbols:

$f$ = work force,
$m$ = percentage unemployment = $(f - n)/f$,
$\Delta m$ = change in percentage unemployment,
$\omega$ = inflation rate = $(\Delta P)/(P\Delta t)$,
$\Delta\omega$ = first difference in inflation rate $\omega$ ,
$\Delta^2\omega$ = second difference in inflation rate $\omega$ ,
$\Delta w$ = first difference in real wage $\mu r$,
$\Delta w/w$ = fractional change in real wage,
$\Delta[dw/w]$ = first difference of $\Delta w/w$,
$\Delta^2[\Delta w/w]$ = second difference of $\Delta w/w$.

All data are annual.[6]

Appendix A explores the relation between employment and unemployment. Exhibits 25.2 and 25.3 show the power of unemployment to explain inflation change. The original Phillips curve plotted the inflation rate against the unemployment level. Because this paper is concerned with changes in inflation rates, Exhibit 25.2 displays first differences of these two variables for the United States (Appendix B discusses implications of our model for these curves.)

According to our model, a 1 percent real wage disappointment will raise the inflation rate 1 percent. But the model is about surprise. Some of the change in the

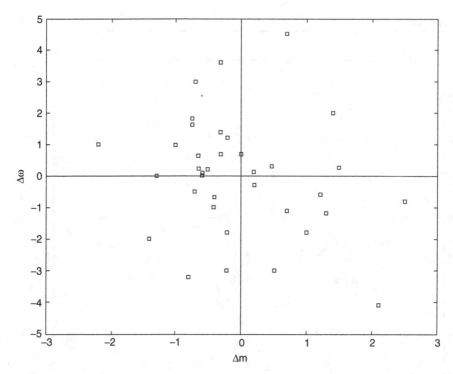

**EXHIBIT 25.2**  United States, 1958–1995: The Power of Unemployment to Explain Inflation

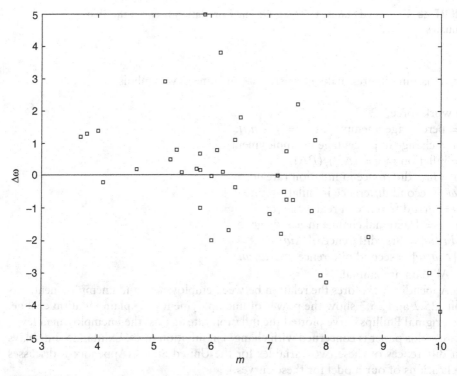

**EXHIBIT 25.3**  United States, 1958–1995: The Power of Unemployment to Explain Inflation Change

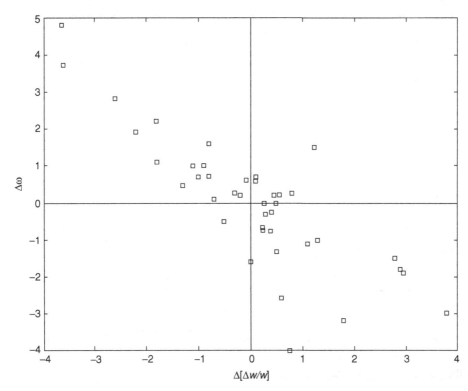

**EXHIBIT 25.4** United States, 1959–1995: Using the Real Wage to Explain Inflation (First Differences)

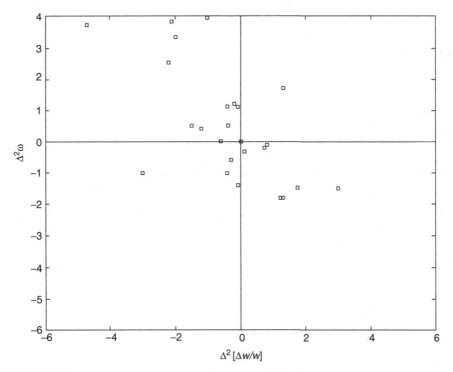

**EXHIBIT 25.5** United States, 1973–1999: Second Differences

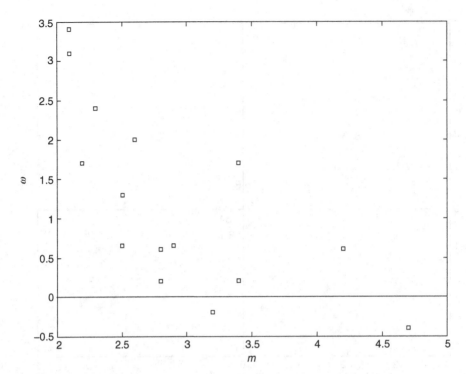

**EXHIBIT 25.6**  Japan, 1985–1999: Phillips I

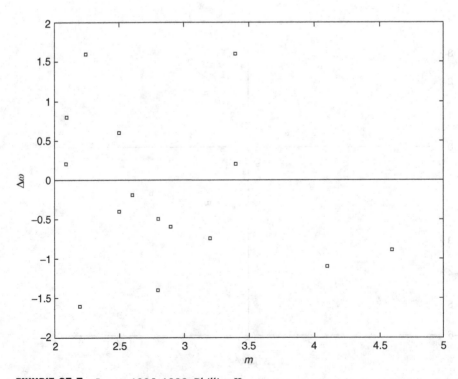

**EXHIBIT 25.7**  Japan, 1985–1999: Phillips II

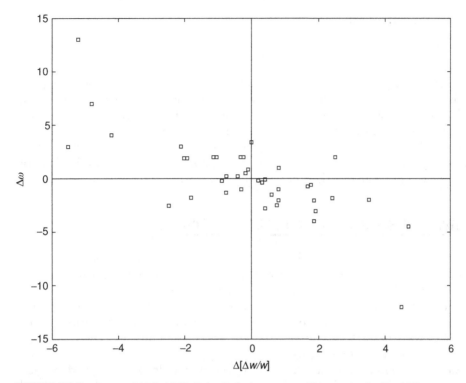

**EXHIBIT 25.8**   Japan, 1985–1999: Price Inflation versus Changes in the Real Wage
Trend

real wage is surprise. Some is predictable. The surprising changes are our explanatory
variable; the predictable changes are merely noise (see Appendix C). Because we
cannot separate the former from the latter, we have an errors-in-variables problem.
As in all such problems, our estimate of the coefficient is biased downward. Exhibit
25.4 shows the power of the real wage to explain change in the inflation rate in the
United States. But it also suggests that not all real wage change is surprise, and that
the real wage does not explain everything. Exhibit 25.5 plots second differences of
these variables.

Exhibits 25.6 and 25.7 show Philips Curve data for Japan. Exhibit 25.8 plots the
change in price inflation for Japan against change in the real wage trend. The reader
is cautioned against extrapolating from the data for the United States and Japan. The
evidence in Section 2 suggests that they are much less open than most countries, and
that an entirely different inflation mechanism is operating in such countries.


## Stagflation

Stagflation is the simultaneous occurrence of high unemployment and high inflation. It is a puzzle if one thinks labor scarcity is the key to inflation. But the puzzle
disappears when one focuses on the real wage. We saw that

$$\tau = N^{-1}\left[N(t) - n\right]$$

Since the current real wage depends only on $\tau$, it depends only on

$$N(t) - n$$

Stagflation results when investment fails to create new, high productivity jobs, measured by $N(t)$, fast enough to keep up with employment $n$. Most productive work involves a partnership between man and machine (truck and driver, lathe and operator). It is quite true that, when output increases suddenly, workers get scarcer. But machines also get scarcer. The model in this section suggests that inflation is caused by a disappointing real wage—that is, by a disappointing marginal productivity of labor, due to "too many workers chasing too few jobs."

## SECTION 2: INFLATION TRENDS IN THE OPEN ECONOMY

When economists talk about inflation, what they have in mind is not mere price change, but rather *momentum* in price change. Momentum—the tendency for past price change to beget future price change—is a home goods phenomenon.

Barbers in Seville cannot meet the demands of shaggy New Yorkers. Haircuts are textbooks' favorite example of a home good (or service, as in this case). When the money wage in the United States rises, the price of haircuts rises, along with the money prices of other home goods.

Steel is different. Manufacturers in Detroit can (and do) use steel made in Germany, Japan, and Korea. So the price of steel reconciles global supply with global demand (Detroit, Milan, Stuttgart, and Coventry). Steel is a tradable good (a "tradable").

When the money wage in the United States rises, wages in Pittsburgh, Bethlehem, and Gary also rise. But, unless and until either the global price of steel rises or the value of the dollar falls, the price of steel in the United States does not budge.

Economists' favorite examples of tradables are commodities—copper, pig iron, newsprint, petroleum, pulp, soy beans, sugar, and wheat. But today, automobiles and brown goods (radios, TVs, etc.) are also tradable goods.

With appropriate allowances for differences in transportation and other distribution costs, the price of tradables is everywhere the same. The local price is merely the global price translated into the country's local currency. Changes in local demand change the local price, hence local output, only when they change the global price. A country's home goods, on the other hand, do not have to compete with other countries' home goods. So there is no global price. Changes in local demand can be met only by changes in local output, induced by changes in local price.

The so-called "Australian model" contemplates a country so small that certain of its demand changes have no effect on global prices—hence no effect on local tradables prices and no effect on local tradables output. The late, great MIT economist, Rudiger Dornbusch, described it this way: "The country is assumed to be a price taker in the world market for importables and exportables alike . . . The distinction between importables and exportables becomes immaterial for most questions . . . With no need to distinguish . . . we can aggregate them into a composite commodity called tradable goods . . . [which] are then distinguished from non-traded goods or home goods."[7]

**EXHIBIT 25.9**   Exports (in $ billions)

| Year | World | United States | Ratio |
|------|-------|---------------|-------|
| 1972 | 4004 | 492 | 12.3 |
| 1973 | 5560 | 708 | 12.7 |
| 1974 | 8173 | 994 | 12.2 |
| 1975 | 8507 | 1089 | 12.8 |
| 1976 | 9602 | 1168 | 12.2 |
| 1977 | 10,881 | 1232 | 11.3 |
| 1978 | 12,596 | 1458 | 11.6 |
| 1979 | 16,300 | 1864 | 11.4 |
| 1980 | 19,459 | 2256 | 11.6 |
| 1981 | 19,497 | 2387 | 12.2 |
| 1982 | 18,006 | 2164 | 12.0 |
| 1983 | 17,568 | 2056 | 11.7 |
| 1984 | 18,642 | 2240 | 12.0 |
| 1985 | 18,878 | 2188 | 11.6 |
| 1986 | 20,580 | 2272 | 11.0 |
| 1987 | 24,312 | 2541 | 10.5 |
| 1988 | 27,795 | 3224 | 11.6 |
| 1989 | 30,241 | 3638 | 12.0 |
| 1990 | 34,386 | 3936 | 11.4 |
| 1991 | 35,303 | 4217 | 11.9 |
| 1992 | 37,577 | 4482 | 11.9 |
| 1993 | 37,616 | 4648 | 12.4 |
| 1994 | 42,818 | 5126 | 12.0 |
| 1995 | 51,232 | 5847 | 11.4 |
| 1996 | 53,436 | 6251 | 11.7 |
| 1997 | 55,300 | 6887 | 12.5 |
| 1998 | 54,360 | 6821 | 12.5 |
| 1999 | 56,358 | 7021 | 12.5 |
| 2000 | 63,405 | 7811 | 12.3 |
| 2001 | 61,148 | 7308 | 12.0 |
| 1/11.9 = 8.4 times | | 3572/30 = 11.9 | |

But can we apply the distinction to the United States—the world's largest economy? Is U.S. tradables demand so big that it dominates world tradables demand? Alas, we do not have data on tradables demand—either for individual countries or for the world as a whole.

It is easy to approximate the fraction of a country's GDP devoted to commerce with other countries. Although exports may not equal imports, their average gives us a rough measure. But we do not think this is the appropriate measure of the country's *openness*—of the relative importance of tradables. If local demand absorbs the entire output of a local tradables industry, it will contribute nothing to the host country's exports, while absorbing purchasing power that might otherwise be devoted to the country's imports. Are Harley-Davidsons more popular in the United States than Yamahas? Are Yamahas more popular in Japan than Harley-Davidsons? Are Fiats more popular in Italy than Toyotas? Toyotas more popular in Japan than Fiats? Then, exports (or imports) are going to underestimate the importance of tradables to the overall price level of these countries.

Here's a simple way to get a very rough sense of the relative importance of U.S. tradables to world tradables—hence, of the likely impact of U.S. demand on global prices: Assume that the ratio of tradables consumption to imports or exports is the same for the United States as it is for the world. Then, the ratio of U.S. tradables consumption to world tradables consumption equals the ratio of U.S. imports (exports) to world imports (exports).

Because it is less affected by year-to-year fluctuations in U.S. prosperity, the export ratio is more stable. As Exhibit 25.9 shows, over the last 30 years it has varied from 10.5 to 12.8 percent, with an average value of 11.9 percent.

If, when the U.S. demand increases, home goods and tradables demand increase in the same proportion, then on average the percentage increase in home goods demand is $8.4 = 1/0.119$ times the percentage increase in global tradables demand. In understanding U.S. inflation, we think the difference between tradables and home goods should be treated as a difference in kind. And if that is true for the United States—the biggest economy in the world—it is surely true for every other country.

So fluctuations in the local money wage are going to have modest effects on global tradables prices, even if they have big effects on local home goods prices. So the closed loop connecting wage changes to prices and price changes to wages, which is so important for the home goods inflation model of Section 1, does not hold (or holds very weakly) for tradables. Whereas in a wholly closed economy, inflationary momentum continues until disturbed (e.g. by real wage surprise), in a wholly open economy, there is no home goods mechanism. We argue next that an economy that is neither wholly open nor wholly closed will exhibit inflation momentum, but the effect of a local disturbance will die out over time. And the more open the economy, the faster the disturbance will die out.

## The Theory

Define

$x$    real quantity of home goods
$z$    real quantity of tradables
$H$    money price of home goods
$T$    money price of tradables
$G$    money value of the open economy's real output of home goods ($x$) and
          tradables ($z$)

What do wage negotiators in an open economy look at, in order to judge what is happening to the price level? Consider first the money value of the gross domestic product:

$$G = xH + zT$$

Its total differential is

$$x\Delta H + z\Delta T + H\Delta x + T\Delta z$$

The first two terms reflect changes in money prices. We have argued that rational wage negotiators will allow only for inflation, focusing on the first two terms, and ignoring the last two, which reflect changes in the physical volume of output. We define $G$ as that part of the change in $G$ due to price-level changes:

$$\Delta G = x\Delta H + x\Delta T$$

Inflation rates are fractional changes. Dividing by gross domestic product, we have a measure of the percentage, or fractional, impact of price changes on money GDP:

$$\frac{\Delta G}{G} = \frac{x\Delta H}{G} + \frac{z\Delta T}{G}$$

$$= \frac{xH}{G}\left(\frac{\Delta H}{H}\right) + \frac{zT}{G}\left(\frac{\Delta T}{T}\right)$$

It follows from the definition of $G$ that

$$\frac{xH + zT}{G} = 1$$

$$\frac{zT}{G} = 1 - \frac{xH}{G}$$

Letting

$$C = \frac{xH}{G}$$

$$1 - C = \frac{zT}{G}$$

(C for "closed") we can write

$$\frac{\Delta G}{G} = C\left(\frac{\Delta H}{H}\right) + (1 - C)\left(\frac{\Delta T}{T}\right)$$

The measure of home goods inflation $\Delta H/H$ reflects both the real wage effects discussed in Section 1 and the effects of change in the hourly wage. In the absence of real wage surprise, the money price of home goods will change as fast (expressed as a percentage, or fractional change) as the money wage is changing. We have

$$H = Wh$$

$$\frac{dH}{dW} = h_0 = \frac{H}{W}$$

$$\frac{dH}{H} = \frac{dW}{W}$$

Substituting for the home goods inflation rate d$H$/$H$ the contemporaneous money wage inflation rate d$W$/$W$, we have

$$\frac{\Delta G}{G} = C\left(\frac{\Delta W}{W}\right) + (1 - C)\frac{\Delta T}{T}$$

where $C$ is the fraction of the market basket's value consisting of home goods and $(1 - C)$ is the fraction consisting of tradables.

Finally, assume that wage negotiators set next period's money wage $W$ so that the resulting rate of wage inflation equals last period's rate of price inflation in $G$. We have

$$\left(\frac{\Delta W}{W}\right)_{t+1} = \frac{\Delta G}{G_t}$$

With this substitution, the expression for the total differential becomes

$$\left(\frac{\Delta W}{W}\right)_{t+1} = C\left(\frac{\Delta W}{W}\right)_t + (1 - C)\left(\frac{\Delta T}{T}\right)_t$$

For the *change* in the inflation rate, we have

$$\left(\frac{\Delta W}{W}\right)_{t+1} - \frac{\Delta W}{W_t} = (C - 1)\left(\frac{\Delta W}{W}\right)_t + (1 - C)\left(\frac{\Delta T}{T}\right)_t$$

$$= (1 - C)\left\{\left(\frac{\Delta T}{T}\right)_t - \left(\frac{\Delta W}{W}\right)_t\right\}$$

Absent surprise, the local rate will move toward the global rate, traversing in each period a fraction of the remaining difference. We think this version of the total differential is the one best suited to estimating *predictable* change in countries' inflation rates. It is the one we use in the country regressions discussed below.

## SECTION 3: OPEN ECONOMIES IN A CLOSED WORLD

In the closed economy, there is one inflation rate and one source of surprise. In the open economy, there are two inflation rates and three sources of surprise. In the absence of any surprise since time zero, the momentum in the home goods inflation rate $X$ damps toward the tradables rate—which is to say, toward the global rate $Z$.[8]

Fortunately, the dynamics of *global* inflation are relatively simple. The reason is that the global economy is a closed economy. There is only one kind of surprise. And there is no damping because, for the global economy, there are no tradables: Without tradables, there can be no tradables inflation rate to complicate the feedback loop between money wages and global money prices. For this reason, the model of Section 1 applies exactly to the global economy: The global inflation rate $Z$ changes when, and only when, there are surprises in the real global price level (or equivalently, the real global wage level).

## Real Wage Surprise

Surprise also affects the local inflation rate. The three sources are:

1. Home goods prices, which are driven by local demand and supply. (A mysterious occupational disease wipes out a country's population of barbers. The real price of haircuts skyrockets.)
2. Currency values. Changes alter local money prices of tradables. We argue below that currency changes will tend to be a surprise. A one-time currency change will kick off inflation momentum in the money wages-home goods loop, subject to the usual damping in subsequent periods. Because the *global* inflation rate will not be affected, after the currency change, the local *tradables* inflation rate will not be affected either. So, in future periods, the only surviving momentum from the currency change will be in money *home goods* prices (and money wages). (Mozambique attempts to solve its trade deficit with a 50 percent devaluation of the meticai. Hunters respond with a sharp increase in money wage demands, which then raise the money price of bush meat, accelerating the already rapid home goods inflation. But, once repriced to reflect the new value of the meticai, the inflation rate for Land Rovers is essentially unchanged.)
3. Global prices, which have two quite different effects. Because they change the global inflation rate, they also change the local tradables rate. But they also create surprise in the tradables portion of the worker's market basket. Negotiators' money-wage response kicks off momentum in the home goods loop. Like all home goods momentum, the latter effect damps out over time. But, because the global economy is closed, the momentum in global prices, hence in local tradables prices, does not damp out over time. Instead, it changes only when there are further global surprises. (An oil crisis creates global surprise and raises the *global* inflation rate. Local workers respond to the increase in local oil prices by increasing their wage demands, which then raise the money price of haircuts. So the *home goods* inflation rate also increases.)

## HOW INFLATION RATES CHANGE

A flow chart is the easiest way to see how the two inflation rates are affected by the three kinds of surprise.

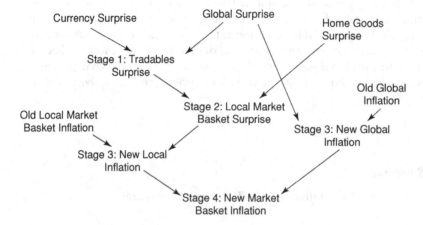

The stage numbers in the flow chart refer to combinations of

1. Global surprise and currency surprise
2. Tradables surprise and home goods surprise
3. Surprise and old inflation rate (global and local)
4. Local inflation rate and global inflation rate

The home goods-tradables combination discussed in Section 2 is an example of Stages 2 and 4. It considered the price $G$ of a "basket" of two goods with prices $H$ and $T$ and the respective quantities $x$ and $z$. We had

$$G = xH + zT$$
$$dG = x\,dH + z\,dT$$
$$= xH\left(\frac{dH}{H}\right) + zT\left(\frac{dT}{T}\right)$$
$$\frac{dG}{G} = \left(\frac{xH}{G}\right)\left(\frac{dH}{G}\right) + \left(\frac{zT}{G}\right)\left(\frac{dT}{T}\right)$$

The fractional change in the value of the basket was the sum of the fractional changes in the individual prices, weighted by the value of the corresponding terms (Stage 4). But the same weights apply to the impact on market basket surprise of home goods surprise $\Delta h/h$ and tradables surprise, when we express these surprises as fractional changes in the respective prices (Stage 2).

Section 1 provided an example of the sort of combination contemplated in Stage 1. It expressed changes in the quotient $P = G/W$ in terms of a difference

$$\frac{\Delta p}{p} = \frac{\Delta G}{G} - \frac{\Delta W}{W}$$

involving fractional changes. Now we have another quotient.

$$\text{Local tradables price} = \frac{\text{Global price}}{\text{Currency value}}$$

Can we express the variables in this quotient as fractional changes? We can express local tradables surprise as price change divided by initial price—that is, as a fractional change. We can do the same with global inflation surprise $\Delta Z$. And, if we define $\Delta V$ as the *ratio* of the change in currency value to its initial value, then we can write

$$\left\{\begin{array}{l}\text{Fractional}\\\text{tradables}\\\text{price}\\\text{surprise}\end{array}\right\} = \left\{\begin{array}{l}\text{Fractional}\\\text{global}\\\text{price}\\\text{surprise}\end{array}\right\} - \left\{\begin{array}{l}\text{Fractional}\\\text{currency}\\\text{surprise}\end{array}\right\}$$

$$= \Delta Z - \Delta V^9$$

Finally, the closed-economy inflation model in Section 1 addresses the combination in Stage 3:

New inflation = Old inflation rate + real price surprise

(expressed as a fractional change ($\Delta h/h$)).

Using the appropriate rule for each combination we have[10]

$$\Delta Z - \Delta V$$

$$C\left(\frac{\Delta h}{h}\right) + (1 - C)(\Delta Z - \Delta V)$$

$$X + C\left(\frac{\Delta h}{h}\right) + (1 - C)(\Delta Z - \Delta V)$$

$$C\left[X + C\left(\frac{\Delta h}{h}\right) + (1 - C)(\Delta Z - \Delta V)\right]$$
$$+ (1 - C)(Z + \Delta V)$$

Consolidating terms, we have

$$CX + (1 - C)Z + C^2\left(\frac{\Delta h}{h}\right)$$

$$+ \left(1 - C^2\right)\Delta Z - C(1 - C)\Delta V$$

This is the new market basket inflation rate, expressed in terms of the old market basket rate $X$, the old global rate $Z$, and the three sources of surprise.

When we compute the first difference of a time series, convention dictates that we assign to values in the new series the later of the corresponding dates. For example, we have

$$Z_{t+1} - Z_t = \Delta Z_{t+1}$$

We write the effect on $Z$ of all the global surprises between time $t$ and time $t + 1$ as

$$Z_t + \Delta Z_{t+1}$$

On the other hand, all three sources of surprise can affect the local market basket inflation rate $X$ between time $t$ and time $t + 1$. Observing the same convention, we write our expression for the new market basket rate

$$X_{t+1} = C X_t + (1 - C) Z_t + C^2 \left( \frac{\Delta h_{t+1}}{h_t} \right)$$
$$+ \left(1 - C^2\right) \Delta Z_{t+1} - C (1 - C) \Delta V_{t+1}$$

We have for the corresponding change in the local rate

$$X_{t+1} = (1 - C)(Z_t - X_t) + C^2 \left( \frac{\Delta h_{t+1}}{h_t} \right)$$
$$+ \left(1 - C^2\right) \Delta Z_{t+1} - C (1 - C) \Delta V_{t+1}$$

In Box-Jenkins terms, the inflation model for the open economy is stationary, first-order autoregressive with no moving average component (because $\Delta H$, $\Delta Z$ and $\Delta V$ are all current surprises). The right-hand side displays the four elements in the year-to-year change in an open economy's inflation rate:

1. Regression of home goods momentum toward global momentum
2. "Home goods" surprise
3. Global surprise
4. Currency surprise

## TESTING THE MODEL

Ideally, we would like to test an open-economy inflation model that includes as explanatory variables global surprise, currency surprise, and home goods surprise. Alas, we do not have price data for the portion of the worker's market basket that is home goods. What we *can* measure is the CPI and the worker's money wage, hence the *combined* effect of home goods, currency, and global surprise on his real wage. So we can apply the model of Section 1.

On the other hand, we can incorporate the momentum effects of Section 2 if we can identify a suitable proxy for a "global" inflation rate. Although the IMF actually supplies such an index, we choose instead to use their index for "industrial" countries. Our thinking is that we want to give heavier emphasis to countries' most important potential trading partners.

But even with this crude data we can address two questions:

1. Does our proxy for surprise in the worker's market basket help explain change in the local inflation rate?
2. Does the local rate tend to regress toward the global rate?

The first is important for any economy that is not wholly open. The second is important for any economy that is not wholly closed. For the many real economies that are neither wholly open nor wholly closed, both questions are often important.

The regression model we propose has a constant term, a term for market basket, hence real wage, surprise, and a term for the difference between the home goods inflation rate and the global rate. Our dependent variable $\Delta X$ is change in (i.e., first difference of) the local inflation rate. Our proxy for real wage surprise is the first difference of the fractional change in the real wage. Our proxy for the "global" inflation rate is the IMF's CPI index for 23 industrial countries. Our time sample is 1968–1997.

The twelve countries in our sample, Australia, Netherlands, Canada, Spain, France, Sri Lanka, Italy, Sweden, Japan, the United Kingdom, Korea, and the United States, are the only countries that provided wage data to the IMF for our whole sample period. Exhibit 25.10) suggests that this limited sample nevertheless spans a broad range of inflation behavior.

It is quite possible that France is not the only country for which our inflation model flops—that is, it just happened to be the only flop that supplied "wage" data for our entire time sample. (France calls the crucial IMF time series "labor cost," rather than "wage." Maybe the series is not intended to proxy the money wage.)

## CONCLUSIONS

Sections 1 and 2 describe two radically different inflation mechanisms. Our evidence suggests that, in some countries, one mechanism or the other dominates. Unfortunately, most central bankers are home grown. When one kind of country (big, relatively closed, "hard currency") gives policy advice to the other kind (small, relatively open, "soft currency"), there is potential for frustration, misunderstanding, and failure. We think a formal model general enough to comprehend both experiences (Section 3) can make these dialogues more productive.

Do we now know the truth about inflation? Physicists are fond of saying that all physics is false. Surely, all economics is false in the physicists' sense, and this paper is no exception. The writer hopes some researchers will tackle the task of demonstrating the falsity of the ideas in this paper. If they do, Karl Popper would surely approve.

**EXHIBIT 25.10**   Inflation Behavior in the Open Economy 1968–1997

| | | Coefficients of Explanatory Variables | |
|---|---|---|---|
| Country | Probability of Null Hypothesis | Global-Local | $\Delta^2$ Real Wage |
| United States | 0.000 | 0.072 | −1.060 |
| Japan | 0.000 | 0.122 | −1.460 |
| Korea | 0.000 | 0.589 | −0.476 |
| Sweden | 0.000 | 0.710 | −0.204 |
| United Kingdom | 0.006 | 0.636 | −0.403 |
| Canada | 0.007 | 0.586 | −0.287 |
| Spain | 0.016 | 0.315 | −0.236 |
| Sri Lanka | 0.029 | 0.537 | −0.079 |
| Australia | 0.031 | 0.365 | −0.234 |
| Netherlands | 0.044 | 0.158 | −0.274 |
| Italy | 0.046 | 0.438 | −0.076 |
| France | 0.145 | 0.430 | −0.125 |

## APPENDIX 25.1 DEVISING MEANINGFUL TESTS

If the size of the work force were constant, changes in employment and unemployment would be perfect complements; one series would explain inflation exactly as well as the other. Even if labor shortages actually had nothing to do with inflation, unemployment could have impressive explanatory power. Exhibit 25.11 shows the strong association between unemployment and employment for the United States.

Is there nevertheless a test that can distinguish between the "labor" model and the "machine" model? Of the two variables that determine unemployment—the level of employment and the size of the work force—the first reflects the degree of ease or shortage in both labor and machines. But the second has no direct effect on the demand for machines. So if the second—the size of the work force—explains inflation, then our model is wrong.

Assume $f$ is the work force, $n$ the level of employment, and $m$ the unemployment expressed as a fraction of the work force.
Then, we have

$$m = \frac{f-n}{f} = 1 - \frac{n}{f}$$
$$\Delta m = -\left(\frac{f\Delta n - n\Delta f}{f^2}\right)$$
$$= \frac{n}{f}\left(\frac{\Delta f}{f} - \frac{\Delta n}{n}\right)$$
$$\frac{\Delta m}{1-m} = \left(\frac{\Delta f}{f} - \frac{\Delta n}{n}\right)$$

The expression $(1 - m)$ is always positive and usually close to one. If unemployment $(m)$ drives inflation, both the work force $(f)$ and the level of employment $(n)$

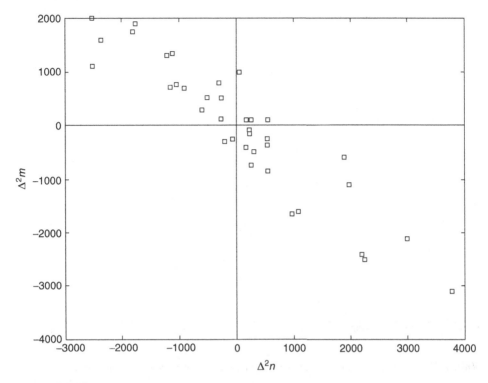

**EXHIBIT 25.11**   United States, 1959–1999: Unemployment versus Employment

should have indirect effects on inflation through the unemployment variable. How much effect each has on inflation would depend on how much effect each has on unemployment.

If labor scarcity is the key to inflation, then work force increases should tend to lower the inflation rate. If, on the other hand, it is really employment rather than unemployment that is driving inflation, then work force changes should have no effect on inflation. So, in this naive view, work force data should provide a simple test.

But the U.S. evidence is very disappointing. Exhibit 25.12 shows the (astonishing to us) lack of association between the work force and unemployment, expressed in second differences. How do we explain this, given the *functional* dependence of unemployment on the work force expressed in our identities? There are only two ways *f* could have no influence on *m*:

1. No excursion in *f*. As one would expect of an instrument of policy, *n* displays more excursion than *f* does. But *f* is not lacking in excursion.
2. Influence of *n* on *m* offsets the influence of *f* on *m*.

Given that *f* is driven by demographics and *n* is driven by economics, an accidental offset is improbable on its face. That fact that *f* has, on average, been completely

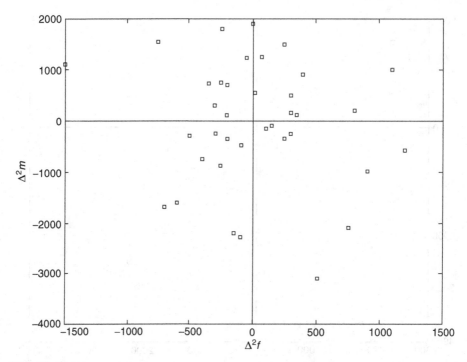

**EXHIBIT 25.12**    United States, 1958–1995: Unemployment versus the Workforce

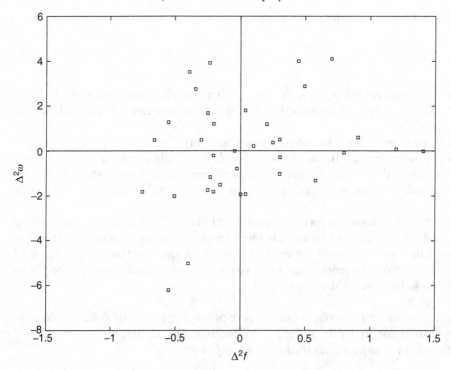

**EXHIBIT 25.13**    United States, 1959–1995: Inflation versus the Workforce (Second Differences)

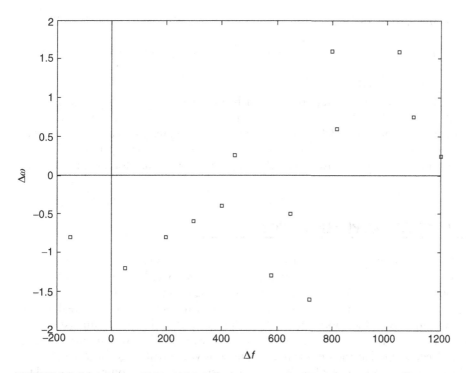

**EXHIBIT 25.14**   Japan, 1958–1995: Inflation versus the Workforce (First Differences)

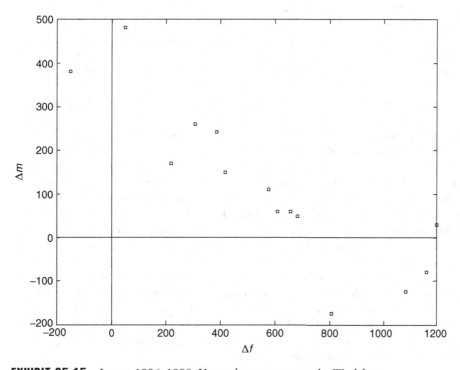

**EXHIBIT 25.15**   Japan, 1986–1999: Unemployment versus the Workforce

offset by *n* has to be the result of deliberate policy on the part of the Fed. Evidently *m* changes, not when *f* changes, but only when the Fed *wants m* to change. Apparently, believing that the key to inflation is *un*employment, the Fed deliberately offsets work force changes with changes in the level of employment. It is hard to avoid the conclusion that the Fed thinks *m* is critical in controlling inflation.

Suppose, however, the key to inflation is employment, rather than unemployment. Because the Fed offsets them with employment increases, work force increases should be *in*flationary, not *de*flationary. Exhibit 25.13 regresses inflation against the work force (second differences in both variables). The association is weakly (but insignificantly) positive. Contrast the U.S. experience with that for Japan (Exhibits 25.14 and 25.15).

## APPENDIX 25.2 THE PHILLIPS CURVES

Our model has implications for both versions of the Phillips Curve. Macroeconomic considerations determine what workers actually get: A lower level of unemployment corresponds to a higher level of demand, employment, and output. But higher real marginal costs (labor hours per unit of output) and real prices mean lower real wages (units of output per labor hour). So this year's real wage will be less than last year's. Suppose negotiators abandon their notions about what a job is worth and, instead, take last year's actual as their guide in choosing this year's real wage target; then they will be surprised. And the result will be an increase in price inflation proportional to the disappointment in real wage growth.

But if unemployment, hence the real wage, then holds constant at the new level, next year's real wage will equal last year's. The actual growth—zero—will accord with what negotiators expected. In the absence of real wage surprise, the rate of price inflation will not change. And any other fixed level of unemployment will have its own rate of inflation. This is the original Phillips model, with the level of unemployment determining the inflation rate (Phillips, 1958).

Now let us return to our original assumption that negotiators determine what they think jobs are worth in real terms. Consider a constant low level of unemployment with high marginal labor costs and real prices, and low real wages. If negotiators ignore the macroeconomic considerations year after year, then they will always come to the same conclusion about what jobs are worth—hence how much real wages need to grow from last year's actual—and experience the same surprise. But we have seen that the surprise in the rate of price inflation depends on the surprise in real wage growth (with a minus sign; it actually depends on the *disappointment*). Year after year, inflation will accelerate. This result is consistent with those inflation models in which the level of unemployment determines the time rate of change in the inflation rate (Friedman, 1977).

Presumably there is some level of unemployment, hence level of real wages, at which they accord with negotiators' conclusions about what jobs are worth. In the absence of a difference, negotiators do not expect change in real wages in the next period—and they are not surprised. So, at this level of unemployment, there is also no surprise in the rate of price inflation. This level is, of course, the NAIRU (non-accelerating inflation rate of unemployment).

## Which Phillips Model?

Alas, our model is moot on the question which Phillips model applies. What do negotiators actually do with their expected change in the real wage? Do they use it to build a new expectation from scratch, using last period's actual? Or do they interpret "expected change" as "change in expectations"? The Phillips I negotiators take the former route. They observe *last period's actual* real wage, and estimate the change. But the Phillips II negotiators take the "expected change" and apply it to *last period's expectation.*

It is easy to demonstrate that Phillips I and Phillips II are equally defensible, if the expectation and backshift operators commute. We have

$$E\left[\Delta w\right] = E\left[(1 = B)\,w\right] = \left[E - EB\right]w$$
$$= \left[E - BE\right]w = \Delta\left[Ew\right]$$

$$\uparrow \qquad\qquad\qquad\qquad \uparrow$$
$$\text{Phillips I} \qquad\qquad\qquad \text{Phillips II}$$

But do E[ ] and B[ ] commute? The expectation held at time $t$ is of the wage at $t + 1$. But, applied to the current wage, the expectation operator E[ ] gives us last period's expectation of this period's backshift actual.

On the other hand, the operator B[ ] refers to last period's number. Applied to an expectation, it refers to the previous period's expectation of last period's actual. But this is what BE[ ] means. Applied instead to the wage, the backshift operator refers to last period's actual. So EB[ ] also means the previous period's expectation of last period's wage.

Wage negotiators really can exchange BE[ ] for EB[ ]!

## APPENDIX 25.3

Our model of the relation between real wage surprise and inflation surprise has a coefficient of one. The evidence in Figure 25.4 suggests a coefficient of 0.6. The difference is too big to be explained by estimation error. We think the discrepancy arises out of:

1. Our practice of using change as a surrogate for surprise.
2. The creation by the Fed of employment changes that offset the effect of work force changes on unemployment. One result is that unemployment changes are uncorrelated with work force changes. Another is that employment changes reflect work force, as well as policy, changes. (*Appendix 25.1 explains why Fed intervention causes work force (f) and unemployment (m) changes to be uncorrelated with each other.*)

3. The reflection in work force changes of certain demographic effects that are highly predictable, making these changes poor surrogates for surprise.

But if changes in $f$ are mostly predictable, changes in $m$, reflecting Fed policy, are mostly surprise: The Fed's judgments are subject to error. Each period it corrects for the net difference between last period's judgment and this period's judgment. But implicitly last period's judgment was also a judgment about this period's judgment. So the period-to-period change is always surprise; the Fed's current steering input is usually dominated by the current surprise. As an explanatory variable, unemployment does not have the errors-in-variables problem employment has.

Is unemployment merely a convenient proxy for those changes in employment, hence those changes in the real wage, that are surprise?

## APPENDIX 25.4: ESTIMATING OPENNESS

What the closed-form model in Section 2 is clearly not is the best way to estimate the economy's degree of openness. There are two problems, either of which would probably be fatal.

**Regression Bias** We noted, however, that the true values satisfy

$$\frac{xH}{P} + \frac{zT}{P} = 1$$

So the bias in the sum of our estimates for

$$C = \frac{xH}{P}$$

**EXHIBIT 25.16** Estimates of Inflation Change Based on Momentum Model of Section 2 1968–1997

| Country | Coefficient | Standard Error | P |
|---|---|---|---|
| Sweden | 0.730 | 0.185 | 0.001 |
| Canada | 0.687 | 0.223 | 0.005 |
| United Kingdom | 0.665 | 0.214 | 0.004 |
| Korea | 0.636 | 0.204 | 0.004 |
| Sri Lanka | 0.526 | 0.182 | 0.007 |
| Australia | 0.411 | 0.173 | 0.025 |
| France | 0.403 | 0.213 | 0.069 |
| Italy | 0.390 | .0158 | 0.021 |
| Spain | 0.272 | 0.120 | 0.031 |
| Japan | 0.260 | 0.222 | 0.252 |
| Netherlands | 0.205 | 0.148 | 0.179 |
| United States | 0.017 | 0.342 | 0.961 |

**EXHIBIT 25.17** 1997 Data*

| Country | Imports | Exports | Surplus/(Deficit) | Coefficients from Table 2 |
|---|---|---|---|---|
| Sweden | 35.7 | 42.5 | 6.8 | 0.730 |
| Canada | 37.8 | 39.5 | 1.7 | 0.687 |
| United Kingdom | 28.5 | 28.5 | — | 0.665 |
| Korea | 33.5 | 34.6 | 1.1 | 0.636 |
| Sri Lanka | 43.6 | 36.5 | 7.1 | 0.526 |
| Australia | 20.1 | 20.5 | 0.4 | 0.411 |
| France | 22.7 | 26.0 | 3.3 | 0.403 |
| Italy | 22.4 | 26.5 | 4.1 | 0.390 |
| Spain | 27.2 | 28.4 | 1.2 | 0.272 |
| Japan | 10.2 | 11.4 | 1.2 | 0.260 |
| Netherlands | 53.8 | 60.6 | 6.8 | 0.205 |
| United States | 12.6 | 11.3 | 1.3 | 0.017 |

*As a percentage of GDP.

and

$$1 - C = \frac{zT}{P}$$

is equal to the amount by which it differs from one. This holds for every country.

The second problem relates to the frequency of wage negotiations. We have used annual data. But we cannot be certain that wages are renegotiated annually. If a country's effective frequency is 3 years, for example, then the true measure of openness is the cube of the number in the exhibit. We would like to think the ranking in the exhibit is meaningful, but it is possible that the effective negotiation frequency is different for different countries.

Exhibit 25.16 displays regression estimates for a fairly wide range of countries. The statistical significance of our measure suggests that, for the more open countries, at least, the effect of global inflation is too important to ignore. Our "openness" number for the Netherlands is suspiciously low, however, ranking it between Japan and the United States. (See Exhibit 25.17.)

## Nomenclature

| | |
|---|---|
| $W$ | money wage |
| $P$ | money price level |
| $p$ | real price level |
| $w$ | real wage |
| $E[\ ]$ | last period's expectation of this period's actual |
| $t$ | real time |
| $N(t)$ | jobs represented by the accumulated stock of capital |
| $Y(t)$ | real output represented by the accumulated stock of capital |
| $\tau$ | the point in real time at which the marginal capacity was built |
| $n$ | employment |
| $y$ | output |

$\Delta$ [ ]    the first time difference
B[ ]    last period's value
$H$    money price of home goods
$T$    money price of tradables
$x$    output of home goods
$z$    output of tradables
$h$    real price of home goods
$C$    ratio of home goods output to total output
$X$    local inflation rate
$Z$    global, hence tradables, inflation rate
$X_0$    wage inflation rate at time zero
$Z_0$    global inflation rate at time zero
$\Delta Z$    (fractional) global surprise
$V$    (fractional) currency surprise
$\Delta h$    (fractional) surprise in real home goods prices
$\Delta X$    change in local inflation rate
$f$    work force
$m$    percentage unemployment = $(f - n)/f$
$\omega$    inflation rate
$M$    money value of gross domestic product

## Notes

1. Some people think falling wages are *deflationary*. They surely have in mind what we have termed the real-wage identity $w = W/P$. They are arguing that, if money prices do not change, then real and money wages must move up and down together. Are these the same people who argue that raising the minimum wage will raise the real wage? In these people's solar system, everything revolves around money prices. In our solar system, everything revolves around real wages (or equivalently, real prices). Whether this Copernican turn is justified depends, of course, on the evidence.

2. The only efficiency considered in this paper is *labor* efficiency. (Fuel efficiency is more important than labor efficiency, for example, for airliners.) If the only efficiency contemplated is labor efficiency, then the sole purpose of technology is to improve the labor productivity of plant. We also assume that newer technology is never used to improve the productivity of an old plant.

3. $N(t)$ and $Y(t)$ have to be measured from some arbitrary time datum. But the values of $n$ and $y$ do not depend on the choice of datum, as long as it precedes $\tau$.

4. Why are not idle machines scrapped? Because they represent an option on the real price of output (with a strike price equal to their unit labor cost of producing). Idle machines are not scrapped until their option value falls below their scrap value.

5. We can express $\tau$ in terms of employment $n$. We have

$$N(t) = N(t) - n$$

$$\tau = N^{-1} \{N(t) - n\}$$

Substituting in our expression for $y$ we have

$$y = Y(t) - Y\{N^{-1}[N(t) - n]\}$$

This production function expresses a closed economy's output $y$ at time $t$ as a function of its employment level $n$ and its investment history, as contained in the monotonic, hence invertible functions $(Y(\Delta))$ and $(N\Delta)$.

6. With one exception, all the data used in this paper came from the *International Monetary Fund's International Financial Statistics Yearbook*. To lengthen our time sample for unemployment data, we used the *Bureau of Labor Statistics Handbook*.

7. *Open Economy Macroeconomics*, Basic Books, 1980, p. 97.

8. If it were actually true that

$$X_t = C^t (X_0 - Z_0) + Z_0$$

then we would also have

$$
\begin{aligned}
X_{t+1} &= C\left[C^t (X_0 - Z_0) + Z_0\right] + (1 - C)\, Z_0 \\
&= C^{t+1} (X_0 - Z_0) + C Z_0 - C Z_0 + Z_0 \\
X_{t+1} &= C^{t+1} (X_0 - Z_0) + Z_0
\end{aligned}
$$

If the hypothetical relation held for time $t$, it would also hold for time $t + 1$. In fact, Section 2 demonstrated that we have for the first period

$$
\begin{aligned}
X_1 &= C X_0 + (1 - C)\, Z_0 \\
&= C (X_0 - Z_0) + Z_0
\end{aligned}
$$

But if this result holds for $t = 1$, it holds for $t = 2$; if it holds for $t = 2$, it holds for $t = 3$. Mathematical induction shows that, relative to the old local rate $X_0$, the old global inflation rate $Z_0$ becomes steadily more important with time.

9. In order to peg the value of its currency in the forward market, a central bank has to offset speculators' positions with a position of its own. When the speculators are right about the next move in the currency value, they win and the central bank loses. So central banks will strive to make their currency changes unpredictable. But wage negotiators will be just as surprised by these changes as currency speculators.

10. Surprises also change the value of the home goods and tradables terms in the worker's market basket; if their *relative* value changes, C changes. We suppress this second-order effect.

## References

Alogoskoufis, G.S. (1992). "Momentary Accommodation, Exchange Rate Regimes and Inflation Persistence." *Economic Journal* 102, 461–480.

Atesoglu, H.S. (1998). "Inflation and Real Income." *Journal of Post Keynesian Economics* 20, 487–492.

Cameron, N., Hum, D., and Simpson, W. (1996). "Stylized Facts and Stylized Illusions: Inflation and Productivity Revisited." *Canadian Journal of Economics* 29, 152–162.

Deravi, K., Gregorwicz, P., and Hegji, C.R. (1995). "Exchange Rates and the Inflation Rate." *Quarterly Journal of Business & Economics* 34, 42–54.

Fair, R.C. (1999). "Does the NAIRU Have The Right Dynamics?" *American Economic Review* 89, 58–62.

Friedman, M. (1997). "Inflation and Unemployment." Nobel lecture. *Journal of Political Economy* 85, 457–72.

Ghali, K.H. (1999). "Wage Growth and the Inflation Process: A Multivariate Cointegration Analysis." *Journal of Money, Credit & Banking* 31, 417–431.

Gordon, R.J. (1998). "Foundations of the Goldilocks Economy: Supply Shocks and the Time-Varying NAIRU." *Brookings Papers on Economic Activity* 2, 297–346.

Horvath, J., Kandil, M., and Sharma, S.C. (1998). "On the European Monetary System: The Spillover Effects of German Shocks and Disinflation." *Applied Economics* 30, 1585–1593.

Marini, G., and Scaramozzino, P. (1992). "Expected Inflation and Output Variability in Flexible Price and Contracting Models." *Oxford Economics Papers* 44, 232–241.

Mehra, Y.P. (1991). "Wage Growth and the Inflation Process: An Empirical Note." *American Economic Review* 81, 931–937.

Novaes, A.D. (1993). "Revisiting the Inertial Inflation Hypothesis for Brazil." *Journal of Development Economics* 42, 89–110.

Phillips, A.W. (1958). "The Relation between Unemployment and the Rate of Change of Money Wage Rates in the United Kingdom, 1861–1957." *Economica* 25, 283–299.

Rabin, A. (1987). "A Reexamination of The Acceleration of Worldwide Inflation in the Early 1970s." *Journal of Macroeconomics* 9, 275–285.

Rahman, M., Mustafa, M., and Swindle, B. (1999). "Causal Flow from Business Fluctuations to U.S. Inflation: An Empirical Revisit." *Journal for Business and Economic Studies* 5, 37–45.

Rassekh, F., and Wilbratte, B. (1990). "The Effect of Import Price Changes on Domestic Inflation: An Empirical Test of the Ratchet Effect." *Journal of Money, Credit Banking* 22, 263–267.

Ratti, R.A. (1985). "The Effects of Inflation Surprises and Uncertainty on Real Wages." *Review of Economics and Statistics* 67, 309–314.

Samuelson, P.A. (1973). *Economics*, 9th edn. McGraw Hill, p. 14.

Siklos, P.L. (1988). "Output-Inflation Trade-Offs: Some New Evidence from Postwar U.S. Quarterly Data." *Journal of Macroeconomics* 10, 249–260.

Surrey, M.J.C. (1989). "Money, Commodity Prices and Inflation: Some Simple Tests." *Oxford Bulletin of Economics & Statistics* 51, 219–238.

Throop, A. W. (1988). "An Evaluation of Alternative Measures of Expected Inflation." *Federal Reserve Bank of San Francisco Economics Review* 3, 27–43.

Wisley, T.O. (1992). "The Phillips Curve and Differing Inflation Expectations." *Quarterly Review of Economics & Finance* 32, 116–122.

# CHAPTER 26

# How to Regulate a Monopoly

**R**egulators worry about how investors look at public utilities. Investors worry about how regulators look at public utilities. Both have a big stake in making the investment implications of regulation as intuitive and transparent as possible. Here is one investor's view of the solution.

First, a quick review of the economics: The price at which customers will just absorb a given level of output falls as the output rate rises. Adding output will lower the price not merely on the added output but on *all* output. But then the net gain, allowing for both the increased units and the price sacrifice on all units (the "marginal revenue" curve), is below the price (also called "average revenue") curve.

In general, a producer will have a number of plants, some with a higher variable unit cost of producing than others. As the producer activates less-efficient capacity, the variable unit cost of the marginal capacity ("marginal cost") rises. The producer's average cost will always trail the marginal cost.

These four quantities—average revenue (price), marginal revenue, marginal cost, and average cost—are the key to the issues in regulating a monopoly's output decisions.

## THE REGULATION PROBLEM

In industries where the individual company's output is small enough, an increase in unit output is more important to a company than the adverse impact on price. Even though in such industries the effect of each company's adverse price impact is suffered by all, companies will tend to push output to the point at which marginal cost equals price. Economists (possibly betraying more sympathy for customers than for shareholders) call such industries "perfectly competive."

The traditional approach to protecting the monopolist's customer has been rate regulation—fixing the monopolist's *price* to achieve a certain desired return on investment. But ROI measures focus on average, rather than marginal, cost. So, the model for traditional rate regulation is not perfect competition but, rather, one in which output expands until *average* cost equals price. If average cost trails marginal cost as output rises, the output level at which average cost equals price is even higher than the output level at which *marginal* cost equals price.

---

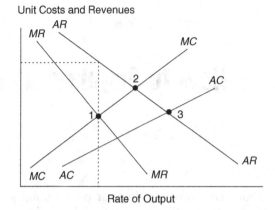

**EXHIBIT 26.1** Costs and Revenues as Unit Rate of Output Increases

If the objective is Pareto optimality (a situation in which one cannot, through reallocation, make someone better off without making someone else worse off), the concern is an equilibrium in which both consumer and producer are free to experiment. But in that case, the concern is not *plant* decisions because decisions to proceed with capacity additions are essentially irreversible. Regulators concerned with Pareto optimality will consequently focus on *output* decisions, which take existing plant capacity as given.

Exhibit 26.1 shows how various unit costs and revenues (measured on the vertical axis) behave as the unit rate of output (on the horizontal axis) increases. The figure shows the two falling revenue curves, with marginal revenue, MR, below average revenue, AR—that is, price). It also shows the two rising cost curves, with average cost, AC, trailing marginal cost, MC. Exhibit 26.1 displays the three equilibriums at issue in the regulation problem:

1. The monopolist's equilibrium (marginal revenue equals marginal cost)
2. The perfect competitor's equilibrium (average revenue equals marginal cost)
3. The regulator's equilibrium (average revenue equals average cost)

The dotted line shows how the monopolist's equilibrium, which focuses on marginal revenue rather than price per se, also affects price. On the one hand (not surprisingly), the monopolist's equilibrium produces the highest price ("average revenue") as well as the lowest output rate. On the other hand, the Pareto-optimal regulator produces the highest output and the lowest price.

## A NEW APPROACH

The traditional approach to regulation has been to set a monopoly's price so that its rate of return is comparable to that of normal companies. Therefore, utility commissions hear testimony on

- Which companies (or industries) are comparable,
- What their return on investment is, and
- What the regulated monopoly's return on investment is.

Because all three questions are closer to metaphysics than economics, they provide fertile ground for controversy—endless, unresolved, and unresolvable controversy.

Fortunately, monopolies can be regulated with a minimum of metaphysics by replacing *rate* regulation with *output* regulation. Under output regulation, the regulatory body requires the monopolist to increase the monopoly's output rate until the price dictated by customers just covers the marginal cost. Every time customers demand shifts, the monopolist must search anew for the level of output that equates marginal cost with price. (Unregulated businesses search for this level all the time.) The price the customer is willing to pay is directly observable, hence requires no negotiation. The task of the regulatory commission reduces to

- Estimating "productivities" for plants that might be marginal in the future (i.e., plants with productivities slightly better or worse than the currently marginal plant's),
- Assuring that the monopolist does, in fact, converge quickly to the competitive level of output when demand shifts,
- Observing current prices of production factors, and
- Recording the sales prices experienced by the monopolist.

As for costs of production, exaggerating unit variable costs is obviously in the monopolist's interests. Regulators must thus have full and continuous access to the monopolist's records. Even then, cost estimates will probably be matters for negotiation.

The cost estimation should be relatively easy, however, because estimation includes no depreciation or fixed-cost allocations; it is merely a matter of observing current productivity, current wage rates, and current raw-material prices. In addition, because the only data required are current data, measurement problems created by accumulating inflation virtually disappear.

Output regulation, because it corresponds to Equilibrium 2 rather than Equilibrium 3, produces higher prices and lower outputs than conventional rate regulation. But plant decisions and financing decisions can be left entirely to the discretion of the monopolist (and the monopoly's shareholders). Under output regulation, the monopolist is not compensated for disappointing demand. Shareholders bear this risk, just as they do in unregulated industries. In this approach, the character of their claim is more like that of a stock and less like that of a bond.

# CHAPTER 27

# Man's Most Important Invention

**W**hat is man's most important invention? Some people vote for the wheel. Others vote for the body of techniques that give man mastery over fire. The writer would vote for neither.

In the writer's opinion, man's most important invention is money. Money is the key to the successful operation of an exchange economy. Only an exchange economy permits extensive division of labor and the rapid advance in skills and knowledge that goes with it. If man had invented money, but not the wheel or fire, the specialization made possible by money would assure discovery of the latter in short order.

Without money, an economy is reduced to barter. A shoemaker in a barter economy who needs bread must find a baker who needs shoes. Specialization cannot progress very far in a barter economy before this kind of exchange becomes impossibly clumsy and time-consuming.

The barter problem is solved by the introduction of an intermediate good that can serve as a temporary store of value. It is then no longer necessary for the shoemaker who needs bread to find the baker who needs shoes, or vice versa.

The only hitch is that not all goods are equally well suited to play the role of the intermediate good. To see this, one need only consider what would happen if we used as money warehouse receipts on used taxi cabs. The shoemaker selling shoes for warehouse receipts might be more concerned with the quality of the underlying taxi cabs than his customer was with the quality of the shoes. An exchange system based on taxi-cab money could be even clumsier and more time-consuming than barter.

When the monetary system breaks down, barter reemerges and division of labor declines. Current threats to impose protectionism, which directly attacks division of labor, and price controls, which lead to rationing, which leads to barter, are sobering developments: If we don't cure our monetary system of the sickness behind these symptoms, we may deprive ourselves of the benefits of man's most important invention.

---

# CHAPTER 28

# Will the Phillips Curve Cause World WW III?

This chapter begins with an absurdly simple observation: In industry, labor and capital—workers and machines—are complements, not substitutes. Our textbooks are surely right that various proportions of land and farm labor can produce the same output. But in industry, where specialization, hence money, hence inflation are important, the proportions are fixed for each kind of machine.

A truck is not more productive with four hands on the steering wheel than with two. A truck driver is not more productive with two trucks than with one. And so it goes with power looms, engine lathes, drill presses, and the like. How many workers does it take to man a rolling mill, an oil refinery, a fossil-fuel electric generating plant? Adding workers beyond the required number will not increase the output of such plants.

Confusion, possibly encouraged by the unfortunate example in the textbooks, has obscured the two key points of this chapter:

1. When a country's demand level fluctuates, workers and machines get more and less scarce together. The effects of the two scarcities on inflation are confounded.
2. When, on the other hand, a country's labor force shrinks, causing labor to become more scarce, machines become less scarce.

The first point means that it is hard for central bankers to deduce from the history of demand fluctuations which scarcity is causing inflation. The second point means that when a country's labor force is shrinking, it's critical for its central bankers to know whether inflation is caused by a scarcity of workers or a scarcity of machines. If the former, it should tighten; if the latter, it should ease.

## CAUSE OF INFLATION

In a recent paper[1] the author argued that inflation is caused by a shortage of machines: Wage negotiators understand that they don't control the real wage. Instead, when they negotiate a money wage for the next period, they base it on assumptions about

---

Reprinted from the *Journal of Investment Management*, Vol. 5, No. 3 (2007).

what the real wage and the level of money prices will be, using the identity

$$\text{money wage} \equiv \text{real wages} \times \text{money prices}$$

In the event, if the real wage is different from what negotiators expected when they fixed the money wage, something has to give. That something (transposing the identity) is money prices:

$$\text{money prices} \equiv \frac{\text{money wage}}{\text{real wage}}$$

When money prices are different from what wage negotiators expected, so is the inflation rate. But negotiators use last period's inflation rate for the next period's negotiation. So every time the actual real wage is different from what negotiators expected, the inflation rate changes.

The marginal productivity of labor is the labor productivity of the marginal machine. Every time the identity of the marginal machine changes, the real wage changes. For example, when next period's marginal machine is older and less efficient, the real wage falls. If wage negotiators expected a higher real wage, money prices (and the inflation rate) rise.

## U.S. EXPERIENCE IN THE 1930s

On one hand, it is easy to see mistakes with the benefit of hindsight. On the other, it is important to learn as much from hindsight as we can.

**EXHIBIT 28.1**   How Central Bank Policy Led to the Great Depression

| Year | Acceptances | Inflation | Real Rate |
|------|-------------|-----------|-----------|
| 1922 | 3.51% | −0.59% | 4.10% |
| 1923 | 4.09% | 2.88% | 1.11% |
| 1924 | 2.98% | — | 2.98% |
| 1925 | 3.29% | 3.43% | −0.18% |
| 1926 | 3.59% | −2.23% | 5.82% |
| 1927 | 3.45% | −1.14% | 4.59% |
| 1928 | 4.09% | −1.16% | 5.25% |
| 1929 | 5.03% | — | 5.03% |
| 1930 | 2.48% | −7.02% | 9.50% |
| 1931 | 1.57% | −10.06% | 11.63% |
| 1932 | 1.28% | −9.79% | 11.07% |
| 1933 | 0.63% | 2.32% | −1.69% |
| 1934 | 0.25% | 3.03% | −2.78% |
| 1935 | 0.13% | 1.47% | −1.34% |
| 1936 | 0.16% | 2.17% | −2.01% |
| 1937 | 0.43% | 0.71% | −0.28% |
| 1938 | 0.44% | −1.41% | 1.85% |
| 1939 | 0.44% | −0.71% | 1.15% |
| 1940 | 0.44% | 1.44% | −1.00% |

## Will the Phillips Curve Cause World War III? - United States

| Year | m Unemployment Rate | P** Price level | W** Wage level | w** Real wage level | Δw/w Fractional change in real wage | ω Inflation rate | Δω Change in inflation rate |
|---|---|---|---|---|---|---|---|
| 1984 | No figure available | 682 | 743 | 1.089 | 0.00% | 4.30% | * |
| 1985 | 7.20% | 706 | 771 | 1.092 | 0.37% | 3.60% | -0.70% |
| 1986 | 7.00% | 719 | 787 | 1.095 | 0.27% | 1.90% | -1.70% |
| 1987 | 6.20% | 746 | 801 | 1.074 | -1.92% | 3.70% | 1.80% |
| 1988 | 5.50% | 776 | 823 | 1.061 | -1.21% | 4.00% | 0.30% |
| 1989 | 5.30% | 814 | 848 | 1.042 | -1.79% | 4.80% | 0.80% |
| 1990 | 5.60% | 857 | 875 | 1.021 | -2.02% | 5.40% | 0.60% |
| 1991 | 6.80% | 894 | 904 | 1.011 | -0.98% | 4.20% | -1.20% |
| 1992 | 7.50% | 921 | 926 | 1.005 | -0.59% | 3.00% | -1.20% |
| 1993 | 6.80% | 948 | 949 | 1.001 | -0.40% | 3.00% | 0.00% |
| 1994 | 6.10% | 973 | 975 | 1.002 | 0.10% | 2.60% | -0.40% |
| 1995* | 5.60% | 1000 | 1000 | 1.000 | -0.20% | 2.80% | 0.20% |
| 1996 | 5.40% | 1029 | 1032 | 1.003 | 0.30% | 2.90% | 0.10% |
| 1997 | 5.00% | 1053 | 1064 | 1.010 | 0.70% | 2.30% | -0.60% |
| 1998 | 4.60% | 1070 | 1091 | 1.020 | 1.00% | 1.60% | -0.70% |
| 1999 | 4.20% | 1093 | 1124 | 1.028 | 0.78% | 2.20% | 0.60% |
| 2000 | 4.00% | 1130 | 1162 | 1.028 | 0.00% | 3.40% | 1.20% |
| 2001 | 4.70% | 1162 | 1200 | 1.032 | 0.39% | 2.80% | -0.60% |
| 2002 | 5.80% | 1045 | 1068 | 1.022 | 1.84% | 1.60% | -1.20% |
| 2003 | 6.00% | 1068 | 1099 | 1.029 | 0.67% | 2.30% | 0.70% |
| 2004 | 5.50% | 1097 | 1127 | 1.027 | -0.19% | 2.70% | 0.40% |
| 2005 | 5.10% | 1134 | 1157 | 1.020 | -0.66% | 3.40% | 0.70% |

*Numbers have been indexed to 1995 for P, W and w

**EXHIBIT 28.2** Inflation History for the US. (The Table, Phillips Curve and Fractional Change in Real Wage in the US).

## Will the Phillips Curve Cause World War III? - Japan

| Year | m Unemployment Rate | P** Price level | W** Wage level | w** Real wage level | Δw/w Fractional change in real wage | ω Inflation in rate | Δω Change in inflation rate |
|---|---|---|---|---|---|---|---|
| 1984 | 0 | 857 | 740 | 0.864 | 1.10% | 2.30% | 0.40% |
| 1985 | 2.60% | 874 | 764 | 0.874 | 1.20% | 2.00% | -0.30% |
| 1986 | 2.80% | 880 | 786 | 0.893 | 2.20% | 0.60% | -1.40% |
| 1987 | 2.80% | 881 | 802 | 0.910 | 1.90% | 0.10% | -0.50% |
| 1988 | 2.50% | 887 | 830 | 0.936 | 2.80% | 0.70% | 0.60% |
| 1989 | 2.30% | 907 | 856 | 0.944 | 0.90% | 2.30% | 1.60% |
| 1990 | 2.10% | 935 | 889 | 0.951 | 0.70% | 3.10% | 0.80% |
| 1991 | 2.10% | 965 | 919 | 0.952 | 0.20% | 3.20% | 0.10% |
| 1992 | 2.20% | 982 | 939 | 0.956 | 0.40% | 1.70% | -1.50% |
| 1993 | 2.50% | 994 | 957 | 0.963 | 0.70% | 1.30% | -0.40% |
| 1994 | 2.90% | 1001 | 979 | 0.978 | 1.60% | 0.70% | -0.60% |
| 1995** | 3.20% | 1000 | 1000 | 1.000 | 2.20% | -0.10% | -0.80% |
| 1996 | 3.40% | 1001 | 1019 | 1.018 | 1.80% | 0.10% | 0.20% |
| 1997 | 3.40% | 1019 | 1034 | 1.015 | -0.32% | 1.70% | 1.60% |
| 1998 | 4.10% | 1025 | 1031 | 1.006 | -0.90% | 0.70% | -1.00% |
| 1999 | 4.70% | 1022 | 1036 | 1.014 | 0.80% | -0.30% | -1.00% |
| 2000 | 4.70% | 1015 | 1046 | 1.031 | 1.70% | -0.70% | -0.40% |
| 2001 | 5.00% | 1008 | 1047 | 1.039 | 0.80% | -0.70% | 0.00% |
| 2001* | 5.00% | 993 | 994 | 1.001 | 0.80% | -0.73% | 0.00% |
| 2002* | 5.40% | 984 | 977 | 0.993 | -0.80% | -0.92% | 1.90% |
| 2003* | 5.30% | 981 | 978 | 0.997 | 0.40% | -0.25% | 0.67% |
| 2004* | 4.70% | 981 | 977 | 0.996 | -0.10% | -0.01% | 0.24% |
| 2005* | 0 | 980 | 992 | 1.012 | 1.60% | -0.29% | -0.28% |

**Numbers have been indexed to 1995 for P, W and w.

* New Formula for the results

**EXHIBIT 28.3** Inflation History for Japan. (The Table, Phillips Curve and Fractional Change in Real Wage in Japan).

Based on the Consumer Price Index, the U.S. inflation rate was negative from 1926 on. But judging from the rates on bankers' acceptances, the Fed made no adjustment in velocity, hence in its nominal rate. The result was real short interest rates averaging around 5 percent for four consecutive years. When demand finally collapsed, the CPI fell about 25 percent between 1929 and 1933 (Dornbusch and Fischer). Needless to say, the Fed completely lost control of the real rate, which was never less than 9 percent in that period. See Exhibit 28.1.

Today, no central bank would knowingly steer its economy into negative inflation rates.

## JAPAN'S PROBLEM

Because in industry machines and workers are complements, when a country's work force is shrinking, it will retire its oldest, least efficient plant. As labor gets scarcer, machines will get less scarce. If whether inflation rises or falls depends on the scarcity of workers, the central bank should tighten. If whether inflation rises or falls depends on the scarcity of machines, it should ease. When their work force is shrinking, it's critical for central bankers to know which inflation theory is right—Professor Phillips' or the author's. Exhibit 28.2 demonstrates that there is little to choose between the forecasting performance of the two models for the United States, which wasn't experiencing a shrinking labor force. Exhibit 28.3 suggests a significant difference in performance for Japan, which was.

Japan was the first major country to have a shrinking labor force; its central bankers went with the Phillips curve and expected inflation. Accordingly, they raised their overnight rate 400 basis points (Exhibit 28.4).

If the central bankers relied on Exhibit 28.3 for their policy decisions, we can forgive them for tightening when they should have eased. By the time they could reverse their policy, it was too late. The result was a classic liquidity trap, with negative inflation rates. Even though the central bankers retained control of the nominal overnight rate (which reflects the scarcity of money), they lost control of the real rate.[2]

**EXHIBIT 28.4**  When Japan Anticipated a Shrinking Workforce

| Year | $\omega^*$ | $i^*$ | $r^*$ | $\Delta$GDP | $\Delta^2$ GDP | Workforce |
|------|------|------|-------|------|-------|-----------|
| 1990 | 3.1 | 7.24 | 4.14 | 5.3 | | |
| 1991 | 3.2 | 7.46 | 4.26 | 3.0 | −2.3 | 65,050 |
| 1992 | 1.7 | 4.58 | 2.88 | 0.9 | −2.1 | 65,780 |
| 1993 | 1.3 | 3.06 | 1.76 | 0.5 | −4.0 | 66,150 |
| 1994 | 0.7 | 2.20 | 1.50 | 1.0 | 0.6 | 66,450 |
| 1995 | −0.1 | 1.21 | 1.31 | 1.6 | 0.6 | 66,660 |
| 1996 | 0.1 | 0.47 | 0.46 | 3.3 | 1.7 | 67,110 |
| 1997 | 1.7 | 0.48 | −1.22 | 1.9 | −1.4 | 67,870 |
| 1998 | 0.7 | 0.37 | 0.33 | −1.1 | −3.0 | 67,930 |
| 1999 | −0.3 | 0.06 | 0.36 | 0.8 | 1.9 | 67,790 |
| 2000 | −0.7 | 0.11 | 0.81 | 1.5 | 0.7 | 67,660 |
| 2001 | −0.7 | 0.06 | 0.76 | 0.1 | −1.4 | 67,520 |

$^*\omega$ = inflation rate; $i$ = nominal overnight rate; $r$ = real overnight rate.

**EXHIBIT 28.5**   Fertility Rates (2000–2005)

| | |
|---|---|
| France | 1.9 |
| Germany | 1.3 |
| Italy | 1.3 |
| Spain | 1.3 |

## JAPAN'S EXPERIENCE IN THE 1990s

Japan didn't fail to understand the lesson of the U.S. experience with the Depression. To suggest otherwise is unfair to a smart, sophisticated group of central bankers. Indeed, other central bankers would have made the same mistake. And, unless they learn the proper lesson from the Japanese experience, they *will* make the same mistake when confronted with Japan's circumstance.

In the event, the workforce failed to grow, just as Japan's central bankers expected. As Japan continued to invest, machines became more plentiful. As the least efficient machines were retired, the labor productivity of the marginal machine, hence the real wage, rose. With the money wage fixed by negotiation, money prices fell. Between 1990 and 2001, Japan's CPI inflation rate fell almost 400 basis points (Exhibit 28.4).

## SHRINKING WORK FORCES IN EUROPE

The Japanese experience suggests that when your labor force is shrinking, you cannot rely on the Phillips Curve. But central bankers wouldn't be human if they weren't reluctant to abandon an old friend. The problem today is European fertility rates, which are now far below the 2.1 rate necessary to maintain the current size of their populations (Exhibit 28.5). When the first of the smaller cohorts grow up and reach the workforce, it too will begin to shrink. As Exhibit 28.6 shows, work forces in the major countries have already leveled off. Will European central bankers repeat Japan's mistake?[3]

A workforce begins to shrink when there are fewer young people entering than old people leaving. Some young people will enter after graduate school, some after college, some after high school and some after dropping out. Perhaps a reasonable age to focus on is high-school graduation—the cohort aged 15 to 19.

Looking at the cohort groupings for the major European countries, we see that

1. The drop in fertility rates has affected the people already in the workforce only slightly.

**EXHIBIT 28.6**   Recent Work Force Trends (in millions)

| Country | 1999 | 2000 | 2001 | 2002 | 2003 | 2004 |
|---|---|---|---|---|---|---|
| France | | 26.2 | 26.4 | 26.7 | 27.3 | 27.5 |
| Germany | 39.9 | 39.7 | 40.0 | 40.0 | 40.2 | |
| Italy | 23.4 | 23.7 | 23.9 | 24.1 | 24.2 | |
| Spain | 16.4 | 16.8 | 17.8 | 18.3 | 18.8 | |
| TOTAL | | 106.4 | 108.1 | 109.1 | 110.5 | |

**EXHIBIT 28.7**   According to David Foote, the Younger Cohorts are Smaller

| Country | Age 10–14 (in thousands) | Age 15–19 (in thousands) | Age 20–24 (in thousands) | Age 55–59 (in thousands) |
|---------|--------------------------|--------------------------|--------------------------|--------------------------|
| France  | 3680                     | 3826                     | 3908                     | 4152                     |
| Germany | 4242                     | 4810                     | 4741                     | 4702                     |
| Italy   | 2763                     | 2797                     | 3066                     | 3773                     |
| Spain   | 1934                     | 2085                     | 2580                     | 2336                     |
| TOTAL   | 12,619                   | 13,518                   | 14,295                   | 14,963                   |

2. The drop is probably noticeable in the 15-or 16-year-olds, and substantial in the younger cohorts.
3. The timing seems to be different for different countries (Exhibit 28.7).

But there is still time. Demographer David Foot estimates that for Canada the first year of the lower fertility rate was 1990. The babies born in 1990 won't begin to reach the Canadian labor force until 2008. Is Europe's timetable similar?

Liquidity traps are aptly named, because they are hard to get out of. Central bankers can learn from Japan's experience, but how fast? Speed is more important for Europe than it was for Japan. Japan extricated itself by devaluing the yen against its important trading partners. But the major European countries will not be able to devalue against each other. And neither Japan nor the United States can afford to oblige the Europeans by increasing the value of its currency—Japan because its inflation rate is already too low, and the United States because its trade deficit is already too high.

## ESCAPING FROM A LIQUIDITY TRAP

Historians are in wide agreement that World War II was instrumental in restoring prosperity. "At the end of the Depression decade…one in seven workers remained unemployed. By war's end, unemployment was negligible."[4] Civilians will of course resist the idea of using war to solve another stubborn, widespread demand failure. Leaders of democratic countries understand the problem. West Pointer General Brehon B. Somervell, who rose in World War II to become one of our highest ranking officers, acknowledged the problem with civilians: "only in a small percentage of instances do they have enough hate."[5]

The White House also recognized the problem. On the eve of the 1940 presidential election, it used a radio address to the nation to promise: "Your boys are not going to be sent into any foreign war."[6]

## CONCLUSION

For some readers the author's distinction between "substitutes" and "complements" may seem academic. But the distinction isn't academic for central bankers.

If labor and capital are substitutes, than a scarcity of labor will also be a scarcity of capital. If a country's workforce is shrinking, its plant is also getting scarcer. But if they are complements, then a scarcity of one results in a surplus of the other. In particular, a shrinking workforce results in a surplus of machines. Should it ease or tighten? The central bank needs to know which scarcity causes inflation.

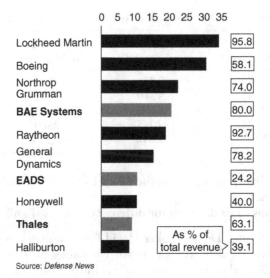

Source: *Defense News*

**EXHIBIT 28.8** The Big Guns: Defense Revenues, 2004 (in $ Billions)

Skeptical readers may question whether the author is capable of an objective comparison of the two inflation theories. But the Japanese experience raises questions about the Phillips Curve. And the situation in Europe suggests that we need to resolve those questions now.

Anyone who takes the author's argument seriously will do his bit to bring it to the attention of the appropriate central bankers. Still there is a significant chance that, despite our concerted efforts, we will fail—especially when one considers that some central bankers probably think labor and capital are substitutes. In an effort to conclude this chapter on a constructive note, the author offers the following list (Exhibit 28.8), recently published by the *London Economist*, April 15, 2006 of the world's most successful munitions manufacturers.

## Notes

1. "A Theory of Inflation", *Journal of Investment Management*, Vol. 1, No. 1.
2. As Merton Miller and Charles Upton pointed out, the opportunity cost of holding money is the (short) nominal interest rate—not the real rate. Thus when a central bank changes the scarcity of money (as reflected, for example, in the appropriate measure of velocity), it changes the nominal rate. Alas, there is no velocity so low that the nominal rate will be less than zero. So when the inflation is negative, the real rate can't be less than inflation's absolute value.
3. Labor and capital aren't substitutes in Europe either: Agriculture has become a trivial part of these countries' GDP (2004?): France 2.8%, Germany 1.1%, Italy 2.3%, Spain 3.6%
4. Kennedy, David M. *Freedom from Fear: American People in Depression and War*, Oxford Press (1999), p. 857.
5. Ibid., p. 655.
6. Ibid., p. 463.

# Trading

Aside from "technical" motives (motives based on price patterns), there are only two motives to trade: value and information. The value investor thinks price has drifted away from true value. The information investor thinks he knows something other investors don't.

If you are trading on value, you aren't the only one. Which of the investors trading on value will get the trade? If you are trading on information, you aren't the only one. How many investors will trade on the information before you do? How many after? Beyond the dealer is your counterparty, who buys when you sell and sells when you buy. What do you think your counterparty's motive for trading is?

J.L.T.

# CHAPTER 29

# What Kind of Security Analysis Contributes to Performance?

**W**hich is the more important in security analysis—a solid, well rounded, thorough approach that makes sure that no obvious stone is left unturned, or a brilliant approach? Obvious ideas are much more likely to be fully discounted, hence unlikely to offer any further profit opportunity. On the other hand, since they have already been discounted, no future price action in response to these ideas remains to embarrass the investor who overlooks them.

Elsewhere the writer has argued that the mere absence of analytical errors in the evaluation of a security is of little value in identifying profit opportunities, because the law of large numbers tends to reduce to a negligible level the combined effect of other investors' errors—unless there is a systematic tendency for investors generally to commit the same error. But this suggests that profitable investment ideas are likely to be ideas that diverge boldly from the consensus. On the other hand, investment based on a brilliantly unorthodox investment idea that turns out to be wrong does a portfolio no more harm than investment based on failure to recognize a sound idea that has already been discounted, because neither has any subsequent effect on price.

In the field of investment management, at least, brilliance is to be preferred to soundness every time.

# CHAPTER 30

# The Only Game in Town

It has been pointed out by Colyer Crum and others that financial institutions are dominated by organizational goals other than investment performance. George Goodman argued in his book *The Money Game* that the securities business is an emotional business with a high degree of entertainment value for at least some of the participants. If Crum and Goodman are right, people presumably participate in the stock market because, like parlor games and sports, it offers the opportunity to win more dramatically and more concretely than is possible in ordinary workaday life.

On the other hand, academic studies (in particular the studies of Professor Michael Jensen of the University of Rochester) of professionally managed portfolios have shown not only that professional investors as a group fail to perform better than amateurs, but that it is even difficult to find individual portfolios which have achieved performance significantly better than neutral. On the basis of this kind of evidence it would appear that if participants in the stock market play to get the experience of winning, then the securities business is a very poor game indeed. Why does anybody choose to play the stock market game?

Another closely related question is why we observe wide swings in the enthusiasm with which people play the stock market game. The turnover rate on the New York Stock Exchange in 1968 was roughly twice what it was as recently as 1962. Every time one investor benefits from a trade, after all, another loses. If enthusiasm for the game is influenced by past successes or failures one would expect that, aggregated across the entire investing population, the level of enthusiasm as manifested in trading volume (or better yet, in turnover volume) would be very stable.

And, finally, why is it that among professional portfolio managers yesterday's heroes are so often today's goats?

The answer to all three questions lies, I believe, in a widespread confusion between market gains (and losses) and trading gains (and losses). It is, of course, possible to diversify a portfolio so completely that essentially the only investment risk remaining is market risk—that is, uncertainty regarding whether the market as a whole will move up or down. If the market moves up then investors in general will benefit from the market movement whether they are trading securities or merely holding what they have. But if they are trading while the market moves up, they are very likely to attribute the increase in their wealth to their trading activity rather than to the fact

---

that the market has moved up. This is what I mean by confusion of trading gains with market gains.

The effect of the confusion is particularly noticeable in portfolios that are unusually sensitive to market movements. Portfolios invested in small, growing, highly levered companies, for example, are often so sensitive to market movements that a 10 percent rise (or fall) in the general market level will cause a 20 percent rise (or fall) in the value of the portfolio. When one manages this kind of portfolio it is very easy to convince oneself (and others) that one is a trading genius when the market is going up, and this is precisely what happened to a number of widely publicized mutual fund portfolios in the period between 1957 and 1965. On balance the market rose sharply in this period and the value of portfolios that were especially sensitive to changes in market level rose much more sharply. But their gains were market gains, not trading gains. Because these funds were trading actively during this period, however, their gains were attributed to trading, and many other portfolio managers who had previously traded less actively began to emulate them.

The result was that beginning around 1964 and 1965 many types of equity portfolios that had previously traded very little suddenly perked up and began to trade very actively. A review of trading volume figures for individual investors will show that they behaved very similarly. If people confused market gains with trading gains it is easy to understand why they continued to play the stock market game even though their trading performance rarely departed from neutral.

## THE MARKET MAKER: KEY TO THE STOCK MARKET GAME

Investors persist in trading despite their dismal long-run trading record partly because they are seduced by the argument that because prices are as likely to go up as down (or as likely to go down as up), trading based on purely random selection rules will produce neutral performance; therefore, trading based on any germ of an idea, any clue or hunch, will result in a performance better than neutral. Apparently this idea is alluring; nonetheless, it is wrong.

The key to understanding the fallacy is the market maker. The market maker is the exchange specialist in the case of listed securities and the over-the-counter dealer in the case of unlisted securities. The role of the market maker is, of course, to provide liquidity by stepping in and transacting whenever equal and opposite orders fail to arrive in the market at the same time. In order to perform this function the market maker stands ready to transact with anyone who comes to the market.

One can discuss the economics of market making in terms of three kinds of transactors who confront the market maker: transactors possessing special information; "liquidity-motivated" transactors who have no special information but merely want to convert securities into cash or cash into securities; and transactors acting on information that they believe has not yet been fully discounted in the market price but which in fact has.

The market maker always loses to transactors in the first category. A wide spread between the market maker's bid and asked prices will discourage transactors from trading on any special information that implies only a small change in equilibrium price; but because these transactors have the option of not trading with the market maker in such circumstances, he will never gain from them—unless of course they have misappraised their special information. It is evident that transactors with special information are playing a "heads I win, tails you lose" game with the market maker.

On the other hand, the market maker always gains in his transactions with liquidity-motivated transactors. The essence of market-making, viewed as a business, is that in order for the market maker to survive and prosper, his gains from liquidity-motivated transactors must exceed his losses to information-motivated transactors. To the market maker, the two kinds of transactors are largely indistinguishable. The spread he sets between his bid and asked price affects both: The larger the spread, the less money he loses to information-motivated transactors and the more he makes from liquidity-motivated transactors (assuming that a wider spread doesn't discourage the latter transactions).

Unfortunately, the liquidity of a market is inversely related to the spread. The smallest spread a market maker can maintain and still survive is inversely related to the average rate of flow of new information affecting the value of the asset in question, and directly related to the volume of liquidity-motivated transactions. This is where the third kind of transactor comes in: From the market maker's point of view, his effect is identical to the liquidity-motivated transactor's. The market maker naturally welcomes the cooperation of wire houses and information services like the *Wall Street Journal* that broadcast information already fully discounted since many investors are easily persuaded to transact based on that information, hence enable the market maker to maintain substantially smaller spreads than would be possible without their trading activity.

## THE MARKET CONSENSUS

It is well known that market makers of all kinds make surprisingly little use of fundamental information. Instead, they observe the relative pressure of buy and sell orders and attempt to find a price that equilibrates these pressures. The resulting market price at any point in time is not merely a consensus of the transactors in the market place, it is also a consensus of their mistakes. Under the heading of mistakes we may include errors in computation, errors of judgment, factual oversights, and errors in the logic of analysis. Unless these errors are in some sense systematic across the population of investors—or, to put it the other way around, to the extent that the commission of these errors is more or less statistically independent one investor from another—market price is virtually unaffected by these errors. This is a consequence of the law of large numbers: Because the number of individual transactors is large and because their mistakes of judgment and estimation are likely to be independent, one transactor from another, the net effect of their mistakes on the equilibrium price is likely to be miniscule.

If, instead of seeking out the market price that equilibrates buying and selling pressures based on these appraisals, the market maker imposed his own judgment of what a security was worth, he would be risking an error of his own of the same order of magnitude as the errors committed by other investors. It is not surprising in this light that market makers generally have so little use for fundamental considerations in their work. This observation also points up the futility of trying to trade profitably by making unusually conscientious, thorough, or sophisticated security analyses. The ultimate in sophisticated analysis is not likely to improve on the accuracy of the market consensus.

When the role of the market maker is as described here, the market maker can be viewed as a conduit through which money flows from liquidity-motivated transactors to transactors with special information. This result follows directly from the original observation that in order to stay in business, the market maker must earn more from liquidity-motivated transactors than he loses to transactors with special information. Every time one transacts against the market maker, he incurs a "spread cost" in addition to any explicit brokerage commission. The size of the effective spread on listed stocks is hidden because oscillations between "bid" and "asked" are camouflaged by the constant fluctuations in the equilibrium value of the stock. If trading volume is small, and insiders' profits are large, the spread cost incurred in transacting is necessarily large, however. Whereas it is indeed true that the transactor is as likely to gain as lose from fluctuations in equilibrium value, what he loses in trading against the spread must be large enough to provide insiders with their profits, and hopefully leave something for the market maker besides. This is why trading on hunches or rumors is more likely to degrade performance than improve it.

## COPPERING THE PUBLIC

The question is sometimes asked, if trading by the general public is so futile then why isn't trading against the public consistently profitable? The answer lies in the special manner, just described, in which the public loses. If all trading took place between those who get information early and those who get it late, then one could make money by trading against those who get it late. But if our picture is accurate, those who get information early make their profits from the market makers, who in turn make *their* profits from those who trade without genuinely new information. If the public traded directly against insiders, one could deduce which way insiders were trading by observing which way the public was trading (as, for example, with odd-lot information). It is true that the public loses quite consistently on its trading (as opposed to investing—as we noted, it is entirely possible to remain invested without trading), but it loses because it is trading against the market maker's spread. The public would lose just as much if at every point in time the direction of its trading were the reverse of what it actually is; hence, there is no value in coppering the public.

This argument exaggerates the "spread" problem for those listed stocks that have an active auction market. How active the auction markets for NYSE stocks are can be judged, however, from the fact that in recent years Exchange members were transacting for their own accounts on one side or the other of two out of three transactions.

# CHAPTER 31

# What the Courts Ought to Know about Prudence

Two ideas in modern capital theory have important implications for the concept of the prudent fiduciary. According to the first—the efficient markets hypothesis—it is virtually impossible to trade profitably on public information. There will be little or no relationship between what is known about a security and its future price movement; future price movement depends entirely on what is not yet known. If what is known bears no relation to future price changes in individual securities, then an investor cannot avoid portfolio losses by acting on what is known; although reasons for sharp price drops are often obvious after the drop, they are rarely obvious beforehand.

The second important idea is that, in a diversified portfolio, market risk is much more important than "unique" risk. In a diversified portfolio, the weighted average of the market sensitivities of the individual securities held is the main determinant of how fast the value of the portfolio can change. In the individual security, sensitivity to market fluctuations typically explains only a fraction of observed changes in security price. But because the so-called unique returns (the portion of return for individual securities not explained by market fluctuations) tend to be statistically independent, one security from another, the law of averages operates powerfully to diminish the combined impact of the unique returns, provided the absolute level of unique risk contributed by any one security or industry is sufficiently limited.

There are consequently two dimensions to prudence:

1. Maintaining an average level of market sensitivity across the holdings of the portfolio that is in line with the risk objectives of the beneficiary.
2. Avoiding undue exposure to a handful of securities, or to one or a few closely related industries, recognizing that, the higher the (relative) level of a given source of unique risk, other things equal, the less of it in market-value terms a prudently diversified portfolio will hold.

Retrospective judgments about the prudence with which a portfolio was managed ought to be based on the level of exposure, rather than the fact that a drop in value occurred. A small exposure, coupled with a very large price drop, can seriously impair the value of a portfolio. A sharp drop in the value of a portfolio is never conclusive proof that the manager was taking undue risk—particularly if the drop was accompanied by a sharp drop in the general level of the market (see below). It has to be recognized that the objective of prudence is making sharp drops in portfolio value *improbable*, rather than *impossible*.

As noted, it is only the average level of market sensitivity for the portfolio that matters; it is not imprudent to hold high-market-sensitivity common stocks in a low-risk portfolio, provided the other holdings in the portfolio bring the average down into line with portfolio objectives. Furthermore, unless a portfolio is concentrated in one company, it is not in general possible to say whether a particular holding violates the diversification criterion without looking at other companies and industries in the portfolio. Hence both criteria relating to prudence are *portfolio* criteria, not criteria for individual securities.

Application of traditional prudence criteria on a security-by-security basis restricts a portfolio to securities in a narrow range of market sensitivity, with relatively low levels of unique risk. The mere fact that there is a limited number of such companies strongly militates against the possibility of good performance. Further, if the portfolio has to compete for the same securities with a large number of other portfolios similarly constrained, then one will expect to find the prices of those securities driven up, the expected returns driven down, and performance of such portfolios suffering accordingly.

The ultimate purpose of requiring fiduciaries to act prudently is to protect the beneficiary. The beneficiary would be equally well protected, and far better served, if the traditional prudence criteria were discarded in favor of modern criteria.

# CHAPTER 32

# De Facto Market Makers

At the heart of the notion of liquidity is a tradeoff between price and time. At one extreme are those transactors willing to transact at someone else's price for the privilege of transacting quickly. At the other are professional market makers who transact at times of someone else's choosing, while specifying the price.

Depending on their reasons for transacting, investors will choose very different transaction strategies along the spectrum between these extremes.

Consider in particular the investor who performs a ground-up analysis of a company, arriving at a comprehensive estimate of its investment value. If the current price is sufficiently below his estimate to cover transactions costs, he buys; if sufficiently above, he sells (or, institutional constraints permitting, sells short). In effect, he is transacting at prices of his own choosing, but at times of others' choosing. Thus, although his situation is very different from (and, in some ways, inferior to) that of the exchange specialist, block positioner, or OTC dealer, the investor whose transactions are motivated by this kind of research positions himself at virtually the same point along the price-time spectrum as the *de jure* market maker.

The investors who play the role of *de facto* market makers are in fact essential to the *de jure* market makers: Without the former, the latter would be unable to lay off large positions acquired in the normal course of their market making business.

The *de facto* market maker is much more vulnerable than the *de jure* market maker, who often gets out from under simply because he lays off his positions quickly. It is the former's spread, however, that the *de jure* market maker must reckon with when he wants to lay off his position.

It is sometimes said that whether or not an institution should be trading in a given security depends on the quality of the market for that security (i.e., the size of the spread). The question, however, is not whether to trade, but how to trade. If spreads are wide enough *de facto* as well as *de jure* market making can be attractive.

---

# CHAPTER 33

# The Power of a Few
# Knowledgeable Investors

**A**re a few knowledgeable investors sufficient to drive the price of a security to the point where it fully discounts a new investment insight? If they are, it is presumably because they will continue adding to their positions until the discrepancy between the price of the security and its worth based on the new insight has disappeared.

Although a new insight may have very important implications for the price of a stock, it never eliminates the possibility that other unanticipated insights will impinge on the price before the knowledgeable investor can realize his price advantage. No matter how sure an investor is of his insight, the position necessary to realize this advantage also exposes him to additional risk. Even though the rational investor will take larger positions when he perceives a larger price advantage, his positions will always be limited by the need to limit the portfolio impact of this risk.

The price advantage perceived by the investor with the insight is the difference between the original value of the insight and the accumulated price response to date. The advantage perceived by the investor without the insight is the (to him, unwarranted) accumulated price response. When both kinds of investors limit their positions, a small price rise (say) is sufficient to induce the many investors without the new insight to sell small amounts equaling in the aggregate the large amounts that the few investors with the insight want to buy.

On the other hand, the price will not discount the insight fully until everybody has it. (When everybody has the insight, they must be persuaded to hold no more of the security than they wanted to hold before anybody had the insight. This is only possible if no price advantage remains—i.e., if the insight is fully discounted in the price.)

A small number of knowledgeable investors may be sufficient to drive the price to its ultimate value if they take unlimited positions, but they won't be sufficient if they limit their positions in order to limit their risk.

---

# CHAPTER 34

# Four Rules for Successful Trading

An editorial in the March/April 1973 issue of this journal criticized the Prudent Man rule, arguing that prudence applies to portfolios, rather than individual securities, and that the criteria for prudently managed portfolios are (1) adequate diversification and (2) a level of market risk suitable for the client. A portfolio manager should be concerned, however, not merely with what he holds, but how he trades. What good is a portfolio whose holdings meet the criteria for prudence if the portfolio manager burdens it with heavy trading losses?

Apart from temporary runs of bad luck, trading losses are not the consequence of purchases that subsequently fall in price or sales that subsequently rise; even when purchased in total ignorance, securities are as likely to go up as down, and securities sold as likely to go down as up. The unsuccessful portfolio manager is not one who buys overpriced stocks and sells underpriced stocks, but rather one who incurs the cost of buying and selling unnecessarily.

How many people are trading in the same direction he is, for the same reason? Can he really justify paying a premium for quick execution? Does he have some basis for believing his insight is not already impounded in the consensus? If he has detected an error in conventional thinking, does he have some assurance that it isn't counterbalanced in the consensus by other, offsetting errors? Has he measured the batting average of his information source?

The more confident he is, the larger his positions and the larger his trades. The larger his trades, the smaller on average the number of names in his portfolio at any given time and the higher his turnover and his trading costs. (And, of course, the smaller the number of names in general, the less well diversified the portfolio.) Thus the premier rule of successful trading is not to have unwarranted confidence in one's investment ideas.

The second rule for successful trading is to keep an eye on transactions costs. The cost of a transaction depends on:

1. Size of the trade (hence on the degree of confidence)
2. Typical spread for the security traded (hence on the kind of security and market)
3. Speed of execution
4. Commission cost

---

A key element here is dealer spread. Because spreads vary from stock to stock, it is desirable to know the level of spread cost that characterizes a security before one trades it. (Since every investment ultimately entails two transactions, the full dealer bid-asked spread will usually be an appropriate estimate of this element of the round-trip transaction cost.)

The problem with the small company, for example, is not that it is risky—the editorial on prudence tried to make this clear—but that it is expensive to trade. Other things equal, the larger the company:

1. The more company developments that occasion trading opportunities, hence the greater the transaction frequency
2. The less the impact on price of any given development
3. The smaller the specific risk

The net effect of all three tendencies is that, more often than not, the volume of trading will be smaller for a small company than for a large company, although less than proportionately. Thus, if dealer spread—measured as a percentage of price—varies with specific risk and inversely with volume (see "The Only Game in Town," March/April 1971) it will tend to be larger for small companies than large ones.

The third rule is to measure the cost of one's own executions. Because spreads vary widely from one security to another, the cost of a specific execution becomes meaningful only when judged against the characteristic spread of the security traded. Although influences unrelated to the quality of execution loom large in the price history of the individual trade, these influences become less important when averaged across a large number of executions.

When the portfolio manager has measured the forecasting value of his ideas on one hand and the cost of trading on the other he is ready to apply the fourth (and most obvious) rule—to determine for each trading opportunity whether the first is large enough to justify incurring the second.

# CHAPTER 35

# Index Funds and Active Portfolio Management

**S**ome observers view index funds as a threat to active investment management and to the research function in particular. The following line of argument supports a rather different view.

Most actively managed portfolios hold some assets because the portfolio manager believes they offer abnormal return—return beyond that required to justify their current prices. In taking a position on these assets, the manager exposes the portfolio, not only to their expected abnormal return, but also to the specific risk surrounding this expectation. Because, on one hand, abnormal returns don't continue indefinitely and because, on the other, the undesirable specific risk does, these positions tend to be temporary—hence the designation *active* for portfolios comprised solely of such positions.

Since they offer no expectation of abnormal return, however, there is no justification for incurring specific risk in a portfolio whose holdings are relatively permanent. Accordingly, such entirely *passive* portfolios as one encounters in practice tend to be fairly well diversified.

Most traditional portfolios contain an active part and a passive part. Most purchases are based on expectations of abnormal return, and enter the active part. But once the market comes around to the investor's point of view, or the investor comes around to the market's point of view, that expectation disappears. Rarely, however, does the investor sell an asset as soon as this "point of reconciliation" is reached. Assets held beyond this point comprise the passive part of his portfolio.

Consider, for example, two portfolios drawn from the same universe of qualified assets, and managed on the basis of the same stream of purchase recommendations. One turns over 200 percent a year; the other, 100 percent a year. Unless the manager of the first portfolio is selling active assets before they reach their point of reconciliation, we can deduce that the average purchase reaches that point in less than six months. By selling them at this point, he spares his client most of the specific risk that assets held beyond their point of reconciliation would otherwise impose.

There is, of course, one problem with selling securities when they reach their point of reconciliation: The portfolio manager must know when that point is reached.

---

The second manager, buying the same securities for the same reasons, holds them an average of one year. On average, his securities spend at least six months in the passive part of his portfolio before they are traded. For this manager, an accurate estimate of the point of reconciliation is much less critical. On the other hand, unless the securities comprising the passive part of his total portfolio are well diversified, the second manager is imposing specific risk on his clients for which there is no compensating expectation of abnormal return.

If the first manager holds an average of 10 securities, then, under our assumptions, the second will hold an average of 20, of which 10 will be passive. Despite some early academic arguments to the contrary, a passive portfolio consisting of 10 securities is likely to fall far short of the diversification that a well managed index fund can achieve.

Trading costs are roughly the same for both managers. In the first case, the active manager sells from the active part of his portfolio; in the second, from the passive part of his portfolio. In the second case of course, he will also incur the trading and other costs incurred in managing an index fund. But, unless the passive part of his portfolio is very large compared with the active part, those costs will be small. (On the other hand, if the passive part *is* very large compared to the active part, it may be nearly as well diversified as an index fund.)

The real threat posed by index funds is to the passive, rather than the active, part of traditionally managed portfolios. The availability of index funds confronts the portfolio manager with a tradeoff between the extra effort required to know which of his purchases have reached their point of reconciliation, on one hand, and the extra risk burden imposed by not knowing, on the other.

It is often said that portfolio managers are less skillful at selling than at buying. With the advent of index funds, skill in selling has suddenly become a lot more important.

# CHAPTER 36

# Opportunities and Hazards in Investigative Research

The widely held company typically features a range of products, multiple markets, many plants and thousands of employees. Despite their constant appeals for more information about such companies, what investors really want is a distillation. But a distillation requires judgment, and judgment requires a model.

Investment models are based on investors' perceptions of reality, and although reality is changing continually, investors' perceptions of it tend to change occasionally and discretely. Thus, if new information is to challenge old models, it must be too compelling to ignore; otherwise it will be rejected. Broadly speaking, therefore, there are only three circumstances in which information will affect security prices: (1) if the information fits comfortably into currently held models; (2) if the information challenges old models but is so important and so self-evidently correct that investors are compelled to accept it; or (3) if, although not important in and of itself, when placed in the perspective of a new model in conjunction with an accumulation of previously rejected information, it persuades investors to discard their old model.

Since in nearly efficient markets public information quickly ceases to offer a profit opportunity, the kinds of information that fit Cases 1 and 2 above will be of potential value to the investor only if non-public, as well as material. Such information will more than likely be inside information—not a promising subject for serious investment research.

Case 3 information would seem to offer investors the best likelihood of a legitimate return on investment research. To benefit from it, however, an investor must recognize a new model that explains accumulating information better than the old model. To do so, he must break free from the vicious circle by which the old model accepts only information that reinforces its validity, making more and more likely the rejection of new information that challenges it. Recognition of a new model is truly creative, in the same way that fresh perceptions in art or music are creative.

On the other hand, because the rate at which Case 3 information alters the market consensus—hence price—is limited by the rate at which investors can be persuaded to abandon an old model for a new one, the investment opportunity offered by such information does not cease when the information becomes public. Case 3 information could be the last bastion of investigative research.

---

Unless he is careful, however, the analyst using Case 3 information may find himself accused of using inside information. In the series of previously rejected information items, there will always be one that will appear in the perspective of the new model to be the clinching evidence for abandoning the old. The courts are likely to view this item as material—even though immaterial of and by itself and immaterial in the context of the old model.

Unfortunately, the analyst will rarely be able to identify this "material" information in advance; the piece critical to his discovery may not be the piece that seems critical in hindsight. Obliged to act before his analysts persuades the consensus to adopt his new model, his only certainty is that, the more persuasive his analysis, the harder it will be for a court to detach itself from the new perspective in order to judge his information in light of the old.

Investigation can hasten the analyst's discovery of a new model. Paradoxically, however, an investigation that burdens him with nonpublic information may delay his opportunity to utilize that model. He can be indifferent to how the courts construe the materiality of his information only if he defers action until all his information is public.

# CHAPTER 37

# What Does It Take to Win the Trading Game?

**A** transactor naturally assumes that his counterpart—the transactor on the other side—is drawn randomly from the population of investors. In fact, the latter transactor is drawn from that much smaller group of investors who have a reason to transact. The latter's reason for trading represents an element in the former's trading cost that dwarfs commissions and transfer taxes.

Generally speaking, there are two fundamentally different motives for trading. One is information that the transactor believes will change the outlook for a company, hence the price of its shares. The other is value—a perceived discrepancy between market price and what the transactor thinks the shares are worth.

Concerned with the incremental impact of his information on price, the information-based transactor has little interest in value. On the other hand, because his information becomes worthless when fully discounted, he is always in a hurry. To secure a timely transaction, he will often be willing to pay the price of the value-based transactor on the other side.

Because he sets the price at which the transaction takes place, the value-based transactor can exact a premium for assuming the risk of getting bagged. He is, in effect, determining the spread between the price at which one can sell quickly and the price at which one can buy quickly. The spread will expand until, at equilibrium, the discrepancy between a stock's price and its value is just sufficient to compensate the value-based transactor for his risk.

Decisions to research are tantamount to judgments that the market spread on a security is not in equilibrium, given the volume of information affecting price. A decision to *analyze* a company implies that a discrepancy between share price and value will outweigh the cost of getting bagged; a decision to *investigate* implies that information differentials will outweigh the spread cost incurred in trading on them. Without specifying whether one is contemplating investigation or analysis, it is impossible to say whether a large spread—the usual measure of market efficiency—is attractive or unattractive.

The recent performance of investment institutions suggests that the original assumption of "stock pickers"—that research information was so robust that it would overcome any sloppiness in playing the game—clearly isn't true anymore (if, indeed,

---

it ever was). If any manager is to excel today, he needs to know what the active management game is.

The active/passive, core/non-core approach to institutional investing has given us an important clue: By holding a *passive* portfolio, one can invest without trading; *active* investing is really a trading game. While passive investing can be profitable for everybody, a trading game has to have a loser for every winner. It should be obvious that the losers aren't passive investors—who, after all, can assure themselves of getting the market return. They must be other active investors.

One indication of how much we know about winning the trading game is that we don't even know how to lose. The conventional notion about how active traders lose—that they buy stocks before they go down, and sell before they go up—is demonstrably false. Losers' research would have to be good indeed to enable them to time their trades so catastrophically. In the total absence of research, price in the wake of a purchase is as likely to go up as down. Inept research results in lack of correlation between trades and subsequent changes in value, not negative correlation.

What, then, is the key to losing at the active management game? According to the academic view of market efficiency, securities markets are so efficient that they discount instantaneously everything that is known, and discount it correctly. Apart from the paltry costs of commissions, transfer taxes, and so forth, investors cannot degrade their performance by trading against such a market. Nor can the academic view resolve a second performance puzzle: Why do paper portfolios consistently turn in spectacular performances, even after adjusting for the visible costs of trading and after adjusting for risk—while actual portfolios strain to beat the market averages?

To be sure, the academic view of market efficiency is a far cry from that of the typical institutional investor. Although fully aware that the markets are highly competitive, this investor would hold that academics have an incomplete and seriously misleading view of how markets actually operate. He considers that security prices over the short run may fluctuate irrationally in response to trading pressures fostered by greed and fear. But, if security prices are governed by the excesses he envisions, why do actual portfolios find it so hard to win?

## A THIRD VIEW

I believe in a third view of market efficiency, which holds that the securities market will not always be either quick or accurate in processing new information. On the other hand, it is not easy to transform the resulting opportunities to trade profitably against the market consensus into superior portfolio performance. Unless the active investor understands what really goes on in the trading game, he can easily convert even superior research information into the kind of performance that will drive his clients to the poorhouse.

## WHY PROFIT OPPORTUNITIES EXIST

In arguing for perfectly efficient markets, academics often claim that even a few investors possessing new information will quickly drive the price of an affected security to a level commensurate with that information, since they will continue trading until the price discrepancy created by the new information disappears. Rational investors will not behave this way, however. No matter how valuable their new information, no matter how great its potential impact on price, other information to which they are not privy can change the price of the security.

The value of securities is constantly bombarded by new information relating to competition, customers, distribution channels, manufacturing costs, research and development, changes in market position, and so forth; that information can work against even the most thorough investor as readily as it can work for him. For example, an investor may be bullish on a common stock because he knows the company in question has perfected a new manufacturing process that will sharply reduce costs. He may not know, however, that a competitor is about to launch a technically advanced product that will sweep his company's product off the market. Thus he may be entirely correct in his assessment of the significance and timing of developments in manufacturing technology, yet still lose money.

The rational investor will limit the position he takes on the basis of new information. This limits his impact on price. In a world of such investors, information becomes fully impounded in price only when all investors in the market have received and acted on it. The speed with which price reacts to new information is thus limited by the speed with which that information propagates through the population of investors.

This brings us to another problem—the belief that the market consensus values information properly once it has propagated. According to the law of large numbers, although individual investors will err in assessing investment information, their errors will tend to average out across a population of thousands of institutions or millions of individuals. The implicit assumption is that the errors of individual investors are independent, one investor from another: If I estimate high, likely as not you will estimate low. But today's market includes hundreds of institutional investors with enormous aggregate market impact listening to the same industry analyses, reading the same periodicals. How often will their assessment errors violate the independence assumption? If the answer is "often," then the market consensus will err in assessing information, and by significant amounts.

In sum, although the market is highly competitive, market efficiency as such should not prevent active investors from outperforming the market, by capitalizing on either inefficiencies in the propagation of information or inefficiencies in valuation. Then why aren't more active investors consistently successful? The answer lies in the cost of trading.

## THE PRICE OF EXECUTING

A transactor naturally assumes that his counterpart—the transactor on the other side—is drawn randomly from the population of investors. This illusion is heightened by dealers and block positioners, who present a bland facade that tends to hide the motives of individual transactors. In fact, the transactor on the other side is drawn, not from the general population of investors, but from that much smaller number of investors who have a reason to transact.

His reason for trading represents an element in trading cost that dwarfs commissions and transfer taxes. In general, active investors will be able to demonstrate that their research is valuable—gross of the cost of trading with such investors. Net of this cost, they will find it hard to outperform a passive portfolio consistently. And investors who transact without good research will incur this cost of trading without any offsetting benefits: Indeed, this is precisely how the unsuccessful investor fails.

This hidden cost of trading explains why paper portfolios perform better than real portfolios. In a paper portfolio, trading decisions execute whether or not a transactor on the other side has a motive for transacting. The successful "executions" in the paper portfolio that fail to execute in the actual portfolio are precisely those trades for which the transactor on the other side had no such motive. The superior performance of paper portfolios can be traced directly to those costless trades that, in an actual portfolio, would not have executed.

## THE COST OF TRADING

Suppose that the gross return for each trade in the paper portfolio is the same, whether or not the trade executed in the actual portfolio. In theory, then, the difference in performance between trades that executed and trades that did not is the trading cost that is present in the former and absent in the latter; this represents the price one must pay to transact. In practice, of course, we are talking about the difference in return per dollar traded between the trades in the paper portfolio that didn't execute in the actual portfolio and the trades that did.

If we know the return per dollar invested in the actual portfolio and the return per dollar invested in the paper portfolio—including both trades that executed in the actual portfolio and trades that didn't—we can derive the cost of trading as follows:

$$\frac{xp - r}{x(1 - x)T}$$

where T equals the turnover rate on the paper portfolio, x equals the turnover rate on the actual portfolio (expressed as a fraction of T), p equals the return per dollar invested in the paper portfolio and r equals the return per dollar invested in the actual portfolio. (See Appendix 37.1 for a proof of this equation.)

This formula gives some indication of the magnitude of the problem. Suppose, for example, the turnover rate for the paper portfolio is 100 percent per year, the fraction of trades that execute in the actual portfolio is 0.5, the return from trading on the paper portfolio is 5 percent and the risk-adjusted return on the actual portfolio is zero. According to the formula, the cost of trading (expressed as noted, not per dollar invested, but per dollar traded) is 10 percent.

In practice, of course, the investor would need a more refined equation to make decisions surrounding actual executions, since both the fraction of paper trades that execute in the actual portfolio and the cost of trading will depend on the investor's trading strategy. The above formula merely measures averages; every trading strategy has its own cost and its own probability of success.

## SUCCESS IN TRADING

To succeed at the trading game, the active investor needs to understand the motives of the transactor on the other side. Generally speaking, transactors have two

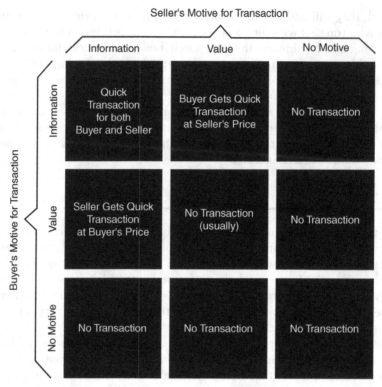

**EXHIBIT 37.1**   Trading Array

fundamentally different motives. One of these is information—not (presumably) the kind of overwhelmingly material information that gets him in trouble with Exchange Act strictures against the use of inside information, but nevertheless specific information that will change the outlook for a company, hence the market price of its shares. The other motive for transacting is value—a perceived discrepancy between market price and what the investor thinks a security is worth based on publicly available information.

The information-based investor has remarkably little interest in value; he is interested in the incremental impact his information will have on the price of a security—not the absolute price that results. On the other hand, because his information becomes worthless when fully discounted in price, the information-based transactor is always in a hurry. The value-based transactor has little interest in time. He is prepared to wait until price provides sufficient "cushion" on one side or the other of his value estimate (depending on whether he is a buyer or seller). Our trading array illustrates how these two kinds of transactors interact. (See Exhibit 37.1)

Transactions between two value-based investors will never occur unless one of them is seriously in error, since neither will trade in the absence of a discrepancy between price and value, and such discrepancy cannot simultaneously be to the advantage of both buyer and seller. Transactions between an information-based buyer and an information-based seller will occur only when their respective information has contrary implications for price and neither transactor is aware of the other's information. In that case, the transaction will execute quickly, and at a price that each transactor will consider a bargain.

On average, however, both transactors will be disappointed—and by an amount equal (ignoring brokerage commissions, transfer taxes, and dealer spreads) to the research-based expectation of the transactor on the other side. If one defines the cost of trading as the difference between what a transactor expects based on unbiased research and what he gets, then the principal element in the average cost of trading is the gross research advantage motivating the transactor on the other side.

This holds equally true for transactions between an information-based buyer and a value-based seller (or vice versa). The information-based buyer will want to transact before his information gets impounded in price, but the value-based transactor will be unwilling to sell unless the price exceeds his estimate of the security's value. If the information-based buyer is willing to pay the price, he will get a quick transaction, but he will be paying a price concession for it. He is likely to be disappointed to the extent that the concession absorbs the price impact of his information.

On the other hand, the value-based seller will ultimately be disappointed if the information possessed by the buyer subsequently changes the value of the shares. Getting bagged is the principal business risk of the value-based transactor. But because he sets the price at which the transaction takes place, he can exact a premium for assuming this risk. The value-based transactor is, in effect, making the market in the security; he determines the spread between the price at which one can sell quickly and the price at which one can buy quickly.

This spread will vary with the likelihood of large price moves in a security. If a company has volatile sales, a high degree of cost or capital structure levering, and a low degree of product diversification, the risk of getting bagged trading in its shares will be great. In equilibrium, the spread on the stock will expand until, on average, the discrepancy between its price and its value is just sufficient to compensate the value-based transactor for this risk. If the spread on the stock expands beyond this point, value-based transactors will be attracted to the stock, driving the spread back toward equilibrium. Conversely, if the spread shrinks, value-based transactors in the stock will withdraw. In equilibrium, therefore, the cost of trading on information will be closely related to the cost of trading on value.

## IMPLICATIONS FOR RESEARCH

Our view of the trading game suggests that, for every security, there are two equilibria of interest to the active investor—one governing value and one governing spread. A judgment about the first kind of equilibrium lies behind every decision to trade, but a judgment about the second should lie behind every decision to research. In making a judgment about the second kind of equilibrium, the investor must consider whether investigation can uncover information differentials that outweigh the spread cost incurred in trading on them, or whether analysis can identify discrepancies between price and value that outweigh the expected cost of getting bagged.

In effect, decisions to research must always be based on the relation between spread and the potential impact of information on a security's price. For an institution that considers itself capable of doing both value-oriented and information-oriented research (i.e., both analysis and investigation), this is the critical assessment in deciding which kind of research to do. For institutions limited to one kind of research or the other, this assessment is critical in deciding whether the security in question represents a promising opportunity for their kind of research.

Aside from legal and other constraints on the fraction of the shares of a company outstanding that one institution can hold, large value-oriented institutions that seek out actively traded securities with small spreads are obviously not doing themselves any good, because their gross gain on a transaction varies directly with the spread (hence with the degree of inefficiency) in a security. Conversely, small agile institutions that emphasize information are not doing themselves any good when they seek out securities with inefficient markets, because for them spread is the measure of the cost of transacting. Other things equal, large spreads work to the advantage of value-based transactors, because the variation of price about value will be wide, and to the detriment of information-based transactors, because the price impact of their information may be absorbed in the cost of trading against the spread.

## IMPLICATIONS FOR PORTFOLIO MANAGERS

Good research inputs are worthless to the portfolio manager unless he can (1) persuade someone to transact with him and (2) do so at a price that doesn't offset the value of his research inputs (or worse). A critical judgment for him is how much investment advantage his counterpart on the other side is bringing to the transaction. In addition to trying to negotiate the best possible price for himself, therefore, he must try to estimate the value of the other's research advantage and try to conceal the value of his own research advantage.

Although couched in terms of the price of the security being transacted, the negotiation on price really centers on the value of the respective managers' research advantages. The bids and offers in the negotiating process convey information about the advantages, very much in the fashion of bidding in contract bridge, or betting in poker. Perhaps more than any other game, active management resembles Five Card Stud: In the long run, the "cards" research deals the portfolio manager may matter less than his judgment about when to raise and when to fold.

## CONCLUSION

Our image of the transactor on the other side is one of the proverbial little old lady in tennis shoes—no particular motive for transacting, or at least none that we should be concerned about. For most transactions—and virtually all transactions of institutional size—this image is false. The transactor on the other side is typically someone in touch with the best research advice on Wall Street, someone with an avaricious streak a mile wide—indeed, someone very much like ourselves. When he has a motive for transacting, whether information or value-based, transacting will be expensive, but when he has no motive, there will be no transaction. The active manager can truly say with Pogo, "We have met the enemy, and he is us."

## APPENDIX 37.1: THE COST OF TRADING

Let g equal the gross return on dollars traded and c the cost of inducing a trade. Then the return on investment in the paper portfolio is:

$$p = (g - xc)T$$

The return on investment in the actual portfolio is:

$$r = (g - c)xT$$

Everything in these two equations is measurable except c and g.
    Multiplying out these two equations, we have:

$$p = gT - xcT$$
$$r = gxT - xcT$$

Multiplying the first by x and subtracting the second, we have:

$$xp = gxT - x^2cT$$
$$-r = -gxT + xcT$$
$$xp - r = x - x^2(cT)$$

We solve for c, the cost of trading:

$$c = \frac{xp - r}{x(1 - x)T}$$

# CHAPTER 38

# In Defense of Technical Analysis

*Many investors occasionally receive what they believe to be nonpublic information about a security. Others feel that by applying superior analytical skills to public information, they are able to arrive at valuable insights that are not generally appreciated. In either case, there is a substantial opportunity for profit if the investor is correct. The investor must be correct on two counts. First, the estimate of the worth of the information must be reasonably accurate in terms of its impact on the price of the stock, and second, the investor must make a realistic assessment of the likelihood that the market already has received the information or insight in question. This paper is concerned only with the latter problem. The probability distribution of the date on which the market receives information already in the hands of the investor is calculated for a simple model of information propagation. It is then shown how this probability distribution can be brought to bear on the management of a portfolio.*

Suppose an event occurs which has an impact on the business prospects of a single company. Any investor who is informed of this event will revise the estimate of the value of the company's stock and hence its return/risk characteristics. Assuming the investor felt he or she owned a suitable amount of the stock just before receiving the information, the investor's reassessment of its return/risk characteristics in relation to those of other securities will lead him or her to conclude that he or she owns too little or too much now. As a result, the investor will either purchase or sell shares. Since the investor can accomplish this only by enticing other investors who have not received the information to act in a complementary manner, which requires a contrary reassessment of the stock's return/risk characteristics (but not value) on their part, the impact on the stock's price will have to be a change in the direction of the first investor's reassessed value. But only when all investors have received the information will the stock's price reach the revised value.[1] Furthermore, the price change produced by the spread of this information will be a unique return in the Treynor-Black sense[*][†] since no other company's prospects are involved.[2]

---

If events of this sort were few and far between, then a plot of the cumulative daily unique return of a stock corresponding to a particular event might look like Exhibit 38.1A. Implicit in that drawing is the assumption that it takes several days for information to propagate throughout the investment community. In a market where information spreads more rapidly, Exhibit 38.1B would be more accurate. And in a highly efficient market, Figure 1C would be the case.[3] In terms of daily unique returns, these patterns translate to the patterns in Exhibit 38.2, A–C, respectively.

Suppose the market is efficient.[4] Then the patterns in Exhibits 38.1C and 38.2C are the relevant ones, and a stock's price changes from its initial value to its revised value the same day information is introduced to the investment community. But this date may be sometime after the event which the information refers to. As a result, some few privileged investors may obtain the information prior to its introduction to the investment community. Thinking of the market as a single monolithic entity, then if the investor receives the information before the market does and takes an appropriate position, he or she can expect a profit on the day the market receives

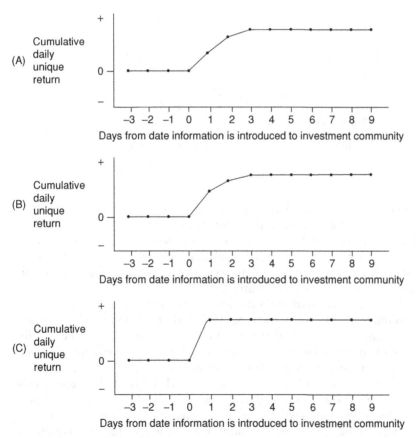

**EXHIBIT 38.1**   Behavior of Market Price when Information Spreads Slowly

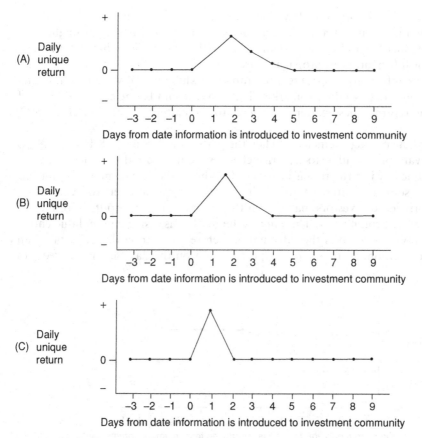

**EXHIBIT 38.2** Behavior of Returns when Information Spreads Slowly

the information. If, on the other hand, the investor takes his or her position and it turns out that the market received the information first, then no profit will be forthcoming and he or she will lose by the amount of his transaction cost and suffer an additional opportunity loss. If the investor takes no position, then he or she suffers an opportunity loss if the market has yet to receive the information and suffers no loss if the market already has the information.

Suppose that the typical time from the date of an event, $t_E$, to the date its occurrence is communicated to the market, $t_M$, is very short compared to the typical time between events. Suppose also that the same is true of the time it takes for the investor to learn of an event. Then there is a simple solution to this dilemma. *Assume* that whenever the investor receives information about a security, at $t_I$, he or she plots its past unique returns $(X_{-\infty}, \cdots, X_{t_I})$. If the market already has received the information, there will be a tell-tale relatively recent spike of the proper size, as in Exhibit 38.2C. Any other spikes will be old. In this case, the investor will know that this information is valueless and will not establish a position. If there is no relatively recent spike of the proper size, the investor will know that he or she received the information first and will establish an appropriate position.

The above procedure provides the investor with the probability that $t_M$ exceeds $t_I$ given the security's past unique returns, $P(t_M > t_I | (X_{-\infty}, \cdots, X_{t_I})$. It is this probability that makes possible an intelligent decision concerning the establishment of a position. And under the assumption that $(t_M - t_E)$ and $(t_I - t_E)$ are typically very short compared with the time between events, $(t_{Ei} - t_{Ei-1})$, the investor will obtain either 0 or 1 for this probability. But if the time between events typically is not long compared with $(t_M - t_E)$ and $(t_I - t_E)$, then it will not generally be clear when the market received the information. A plot of past unique returns will have many recent spikes corresponding to other events and a particular day's spike may correspond to more than one event. Assume the situation with respect to the event under consideration is as shown in Exhibit 38.3A and that the impact of other events is as shown in Exhibit 38.3B. The net result will be the pattern shown in Exhibit 38.3C. As can be seen, no obvious evidence of the spike in Exhibit 38.3A remains, and $P(t_M > t_I | X_{-\infty}, \cdots, X_{t_I})$ is no longer easy to obtain. In fact, the unique returns in Exhibit 38.3C for several dates other than $t_M$ are closer to the right size than the one for $t_M$.

One way of attacking this problem is to use knowledge of the process by which information reaches the market and the investor to suggest which dates are the most likely ones. If certain dates are much more likely a priori candidates for $t_M$ than

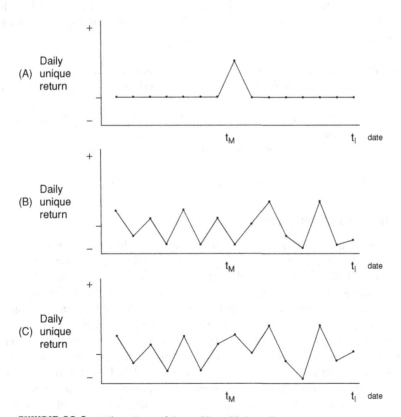

**EXHIBIT 38.3**   When Several Days Have Unique Returns

others, then this should partially offset the fact that some of these other dates have unique returns more commensurate with the information. Suppose, for example, that it is known that information concerning an event always reaches the market within six days and always reaches the investor within eight days. Then in examining past unique returns, the investor can ignore all but the most recent eight days, even if some earlier days have precisely the right size unique return and none of the most recent eight days does.

In the above example, the investor had knowledge of both $t_I$ and the process by which information reached the market, and provided information about $t_M$. Generally, such knowledge will permit the investor to calculate the probability of $t_M$ given $t_I$, $P(t_m|t_I)$. If the investor also has knowledge of the process by which the unique returns caused by events other than the one under consideration are generated, he or she can then calculate the probability of a particular past history of unique returns given $t_M$ and $t_I$, $P(X_{-\infty}, \cdots, X_{t_I}/t_M t_I)$. Combining this with $P(t_M|t_I)$, the investor can obtain the probability of $t_M$ given $(X_{-\infty}, \cdots, X_{t_I})$ and $t_I$, $P(t_M|(X_{-\infty}, \cdots, X_{t_I} t_I))$. This enables him or her to calculate $P(t_M > t_I|(X_{-\infty}, \cdots, X_{t_I} t_I))$, which is what the investor requires to make his or her decision about establishing a position.

A more detailed and formal discussion of these issues follows.

## A Recapitulation of the Problem

Consider an investor who receives what he or she believes to be nonpublic information about a security at time $t_I$. To use this information effectively, the investor must be concerned with:

1. The value of the information in terms of its impact on the price of the stock.
2. The process by which information is transmitted to the market and to the investor.
3. The probability that the market will receive (or has received) the information at a particular time, $t_M$.
4. A portfolio strategy which permits capitalizing on the information.

Each of these four issues is examined in turn in the remainder of the paper.

## The Value of the Information

Probably the simplest way to characterize the value of the information is to think of it as a specific dollar amount. A more sophisticated and more realistic view is to think of the amount as jointly determined by the communication under consideration and other events, which have occurred or will occur at various times, that have a direct or indirect impact on the security.[5] In this case, the value of the information will be a function of time, and the size of its impact on the price of the stock will depend on the specific date, $t_M$, on which the market receives the information. This paper takes a simple approach. The effect of the information is assumed to be a change in the price of the security by a multiplicative factor of $e^V$, where $V$ is defined to be the value of the information. Roughly speaking, the information is assumed to change the price of the stock in the period ended at $t_M$ by 100 percent. In what follows, $V$ is assumed known. Incorporating a probabilistic specification is straightforward.

## The Propagation of Information

The process by which information is assumed to be transmitted to the market and to the investor is represented schematically in Exhibit 38.4. In that figure, there are four nodes labeled $S_1$, $S_2$, $S_3$, and $S_4$. Each node represents a state of nature. Specifically:

$S_1 = $ the state in which neither the market or the investor have received the information;

$S_2 = $ the state in which the investor has received the information but the market has not;

$S_3 = $ the state in which the market has received the information but the investor has not; and

$S_4 = $ the state in which both the market and the investor have received the information.

At the time the event occurs, $t_E$, the system is in state $S_1$. In each succeeding period, it may transition to any of the other three states. Suppose that the process by which a transition occurs is akin to flipping two biased coins, one for the investor and one for the market, where each double flip represents one period and tails denotes receipt of the information. Let $\gamma$ denote the probability of tails for the market's coin and $\alpha$ denote the probability of tails for the investor's coin.

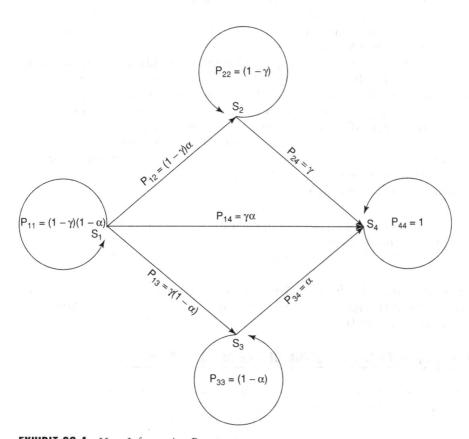

**EXHIBIT 38.4**  How Information Propogates

**EXHIBIT 38.5**  Transition Probabilities

| | | To | | | |
|---|---|---|---|---|---|
| | | $S_1$ | $S_2$ | $S_3$ | $S_4$ |
| | $S_1$ | $(1-\gamma)(1-\alpha)$ | $(1-\gamma)\alpha$ | $\gamma(1-\alpha)$ | $\gamma\alpha$ |
| | $S_2$ | 0 | $(1-\gamma)$ | 0 | $\gamma$ |
| From | $S_3$ | 0 | 0 | $(1-\alpha)$ | $\alpha$ |
| | $S_4$ | 0 | 0 | 0 | 1 |

Then:

$\gamma =$ the probability that the market will receive the information in the next period if it does not have it now; and

$\alpha =$ the probability that the investor will receive the information in the next period if he does not have it now.

After the event occurs, the system may remain in state $S_1$ for some time. The probability, $P_{11}$, that it will be in state $S_1$ in the next period if it is now is $(1-\gamma)(1-\alpha)$. The probability, $P_{12}$, that it will transition to state $S_2$ in the next period if it is in state $S_1$ now is $(1-\gamma)\alpha$. Denoting:

$P_{ij} =$ the probability that the system will be in state $S_j$ in the next period if it is in state $S_i$ now.

Then a similar calculation for each possible transition yields the results shown in Exhibit 38.5. In Exhibit 38.4, the circular arrows enclosing probabilities denote transitions corresponding to remaining in the same state for one more period. The straight arrows between states, with their probabilities, denote transitions from one state to another. All possible transitions and their respective probabilities are shown. This is a Markov process whose transition matrix is Exhibit 38.5.

Once the investor has been communicated with, he or she will want to calculate the probability distribution of $t_M$. In doing so, the investor should make use of the information about $t_M$ contained in

1. The date he or she received the communication.
2. The communication itself.
3. The security's past unique returns.

In the mathematical development that follows, information about $t_M$ contained in the communication is ignored. Its incorporation into the analysis is straightforward and is discussed briefly later.

## THE PROBABILITY DISTRIBUTION OF THE MARKET DATE

Letting $X_t$ represent the security's unique return (in continuous form) for the period ended at time $t$, the probability of interest is

$$P\left(t_M | X_{-\infty}, \cdots, X_{t_I} t_I\right) \tag{38.1}$$

Using Bayes theorem[6], this can be written as

$$P\left(t_M | X_{-\infty}, \cdots, X_{t_I} t_I\right) = \frac{P(t_M | t_I) P(X_{-\infty}, \cdots, X_{t_I} | t_M t_I)}{\sum_{t_M = -\infty}^{\infty} P(t_M | t_I) P(X_{-\infty}, \cdots, X_{t_I} | t_M t_I)} \tag{38.2}$$

In this paper, it is assumed that the unique return associated with all events other than the one under consideration has a normal distribution with mean zero and variance $\sigma^2$. This eliminates the need for the investor to have total knowledge of events. Thus,

$$P(X_{-\infty}, \cdots, X_{t_I} | t_M t_I) = \prod_{i=-\infty}^{t_I} \left[ \frac{e^{-X_i^2 / 2\sigma^2}}{\sqrt{2\pi}\sigma} \right], \quad t_M > t_I \tag{38.3}$$

and

$$P(X_{-\infty}, \cdots, X_{t_I} | t_M t_I) = \prod_{i=-\infty}^{t_I} \left[ \frac{e^{-(X_i - \delta_i t_M V)^2 / 2\sigma^2}}{\sqrt{2\pi}\sigma} \right], \quad t_M \leq t_I \tag{38.4}$$

The expression on the right-hand side of (38.4) can be rewritten as

$$e^{-(X_{t_M} - V)^2 / 2\sigma^2} e^{X_{t_M}^2 / 2\sigma^2} \prod_{i=-\infty}^{t_I} \left[ \frac{e^{-X_i^2 / 2\sigma^2}}{\sqrt{2\pi}\sigma} \right]$$

But

$$-(X_{t_M} - V)^2 + X_{t_M}^2 = -X_{t_M}^2 + 2V X_{t_M} - V^2 + X_{t_M}^2$$
$$= 2V X_{t_M} - V^2$$

and (38.4) becomes

$$P(X_{-\infty}, \cdots, X_{t_I} | t_M t_I) = e^{-V^2 / 2\sigma^2} e^{V X_{t_M} / \sigma^2} \prod_{i=-\infty}^{t_I} \left[ \frac{e^{-X_i^2 / 2\sigma^2}}{\sqrt{2\pi}\sigma} \right], \quad t_M \leq t_I \tag{38.5}$$

The calculation of $P(t_M | t_I)$ requires three steps. The first step consists of using Bayes theorem to obtain $P(t_E | t_I)$ starting with a prior on $t_E$, $P(t_E)$, and the structure in Exhibit 38.4. The second step consists of using the structure in to obtain $P(t_M | t_I t_E)$. The last step consists of combining the distributions obtained in the first two steps using

$$P(t_M | t_I) = \sum_{t_E} P(t_E | t_I) P(t_M | t_I t_E) \tag{38.6}$$

In this paper, $t_E$ is assumed to have the following distribution.

$$P(t_E) = \left( \frac{1}{\delta} \right) \quad t_E = \left( T_0 - \frac{\delta}{2} + 1 \right), \cdots, \left( T_0 + \frac{\delta}{2} \right) \tag{38.7}$$

If the communication contains information about $t_M$, it will usually be in the form of specific information about $t_E$. This can be incorporated into the analysis by choosing an appropriate prior for $t_E$. Suppose, for example, that the communication consists of the statement that a particular event occurred during a specific week but does not include the exact date. Then by choosing $T_0$ and $\delta$ correctly, a uniform prior with positive weight for only the days of that week could be constructed. More generally, the prior should take whatever form is necessary to reflect adequately the nature of the information about $t_M$ contained in the communication.

Using Bayes theorem,

$$P(t_E|t_I) = \frac{P(t_E)P(t_I|t_E)}{\sum_{t_E=T_0-(\delta/2)+1}^{t_I-1} P(t_E)P(t_I|t_E)} \tag{38.8}$$

The structure in Exhibit 38.4 implies that

$$P(t_I|t_E) = \alpha(1-\alpha)^{t_I-1-t_E}, \quad t_I > t_E \tag{38.9}$$

Substituting Equations 38.7 and 38.9 in Equation 38.8 results in

$$P(t_E|t_I) = \frac{(\alpha/\delta)(1-\alpha)^{t_I-1-t_E}}{\sum_{t_E=T_0-(\delta/2)+1}^{t_I-1} (\alpha/\delta)(1-\alpha)^{t_I-1-t_E}}$$

$$= \frac{\alpha(1-\alpha)^{t_I-1-t_E}}{\alpha \sum_{i=0}^{t_I-T_0-2+(\delta/2)} (1-\alpha)^i}$$

$$P(t_E|t_I) = \frac{\alpha(1-\alpha)^{t_I-1-t_E}}{[1-(1-\alpha)^{t_I-T_0-1+(\delta/2)}]} \tag{38.10}$$

By choosing $T_0$ properly, the investor can be sure that $(t_I - t_0 - 1)$ is bounded. In this case,

$$\lim_{\delta \to \infty} P(t_E|t_I) = \alpha(1-\alpha)^{t_I-1-t_E}, \quad t_E < t_I \tag{38.11}$$

Because the structure of Exhibit 38.4 implies independence between $t_M$ and $t_I$ except through $t_E$,

$$P(t_M|t_I t_E) = P(t_M|t_E) \tag{38.12}$$

$$P(t_M|t_I t_E) = \gamma(1-\gamma)^{t_M-1-t_E} \tag{38.13}$$

Substituting Equations 38.11 and 38.13 in Equation 38.6,

$$P(t_M|t_I) = \sum_{t_E=-\infty}^{t_{MI}-1} \alpha(1-\alpha)^{t_I-1-t_E}\gamma(1-\gamma)^{t_M-1-t_E}$$

$$t_{MI} = \min(t_M, t_E) \tag{38.14}$$

When $t_M \le t_I$ Equation 38.14 is

$$P(t_M|t_I) = \sum_{t_E=-\infty}^{t_M-1} \gamma\alpha(1-\alpha)^{t_I-M_I}[(1-\gamma)(1-\alpha)]^{t_M-1-t_E}$$

$$= \gamma\alpha(1-\alpha)^{t_I-t_M} \sum_{i=0}^{\infty}[(1-\gamma)(1-\alpha)]^i$$

$$P(t_M|t_I) = \frac{\gamma\alpha(1-\alpha)^{t_I-t_M})}{[1-(1-\gamma)(1-\alpha)]}, \quad t_M \le t_I \tag{38.15}$$

When $t_M > t_I$, Equation 38.14 is

$$P(t_M|t_I) = \sum_{t_E=-\infty}^{t_I-1} \gamma\alpha(1-\gamma)^{t_M-t_I}[(1-\gamma)(1-\alpha)]^{t_I-1-t_E}$$

$$= \gamma\alpha(1-\gamma)^{t_M-t_I} \sum_{i=0}^{\infty}[(1-\gamma)(1-\alpha)]^i$$

$$P(t_M|t_I) = \frac{\gamma\alpha(1-\gamma)^{t_M-t_I}}{[1-(1-\gamma)(1-\alpha)]}, \quad t_M > t_I \tag{38.16}$$

Equation 38.2 can be evaluated using Equations 38.4, 38.5, 38.15, and 38.16. The denominator of Equation 38.2 is found as follows

$$\sum_{t_M=-\infty}^{\infty} P(t_M|t_I)P(X_{-\infty},...,X_{t_I}|t_Mt_I)$$

$$= \sum_{t_M=-\infty}^{t_I} P(t_M|t_I)P(X_{-\infty},...,X_{t_I}|t_Mt_I)$$

$$+ \sum_{t_M=t_I+1}^{\infty} P(t_M|t_I)P(X_{-\infty},...,X_{t_I}|t_Mt_I) \tag{38.17}$$

The first sum on the right-hand side of Equation 38.17 is

$$\sum_{t_M=-\infty}^{t_I} \frac{\gamma\alpha(1-\alpha)^{t_I-t_M}}{[1-(1-\gamma)(1-\alpha)]} e^{-V^2/2\sigma^2} e^{VX_{t_M}/\sigma^2} \left[\prod_{i=-\infty}^{t_I} \frac{e^{-X_i^2/2\sigma^2}}{\sqrt{2\pi}\sigma}\right]$$

$$= \frac{\gamma\alpha e^{-V^2/2\sigma^2}}{[(1-1-\gamma)(1-\alpha)]} \left[\prod_{i=-\infty}^{t_I} \frac{e^{-X_i^2/2\sigma^2}}{\sqrt{2\pi}\sigma}\right] \sum_{t_M=-\infty}^{t_I} (1-\alpha)^{t_I-t_M} e^{VX_{t_M}/\sigma^2}$$

$$\tag{38.18}$$

The second sum on the right-hand side of Equation 38.17 is

$$\sum_{t_M=t_I+1}^{\infty} \frac{\gamma\alpha(1-\gamma)^{t_M-t_I}}{[1-(1-\gamma)(1-\alpha)]} \left[\prod_{i=-\infty}^{t_I} \frac{e^{-X_i^2/2\sigma^2}}{\sqrt{2\pi}\sigma}\right] \tag{38.19}$$

$$= \frac{\alpha(1-\gamma)}{[1-(1-\gamma)(1-\alpha)]} \left[\prod_{i=-\infty}^{t_I} \frac{e^{-X_i^2/2\sigma^2}}{\sqrt{2\pi}\sigma}\right] \tag{38.20}$$

For the case $t_M \leq t_I$, the numerator of Equation 38.2 is a single term from the sum in Equation 38.18

$$\frac{\gamma \alpha e^{-V^2/2\sigma^2}}{[1 - (1-\gamma)(1-\alpha)]} \left[ \prod_{i=-\infty}^{t_I} \frac{e^{-X_i^2/2\sigma^2}}{\sqrt{2\pi}\sigma} \right] (1-\alpha)^{t_I - t_M} e^{VX_{t_M}/\sigma^2} \qquad (38.21)$$

Thus,

$$P(t_M | X_{-\infty}, ..., X_{t_I} t_I)$$
$$= \frac{\gamma e^{-V^2/2\sigma^2}(1-\alpha)^{t_I - t_M} e^{VX_{t_M}/\sigma^2}}{(1-\gamma) + \gamma e^{-V^2/2\sigma^2} \sum_{j=-\infty}^{t_I} (1-\alpha)^{t_I - j} e^{VX_j/\sigma^2}}, \quad t_M \leq t_I \qquad (38.22)$$

For the case $t_M > t_I$, the numerator of Equation 38.2 is a single term from the sum in Equation 38.19, and

$$P(t_M | X_{-\infty}, ..., X_{t_I} t_I)$$
$$= \frac{\gamma (1-\alpha)^{t_M - t_I}}{(1-\gamma) + \gamma e^{-V^2/2\sigma^2} \sum_{j=-\infty}^{t_I} (1-\alpha)^{t_I - j} e^{VX_j/\sigma^2}}, \quad t_M > t_I \qquad (38.23)$$

Two immediate consequences of Equations 38.22 and 38.23 are

$$P(t_M \leq t_I | X_{-\infty}, ..., X_{t_I} t_I)$$
$$= \frac{\gamma e^{-V^2/2\sigma^2} \sum_{j=-\infty}^{t_I} (1-\alpha)^{t_I - j} e^{VX_j/\sigma^2}}{(1-\gamma) + \gamma e^{-V^2/2\sigma^2} \sum_{j=-\infty}^{t_I} (1-\alpha)^{t_I - j} e^{VX_j/\sigma^2}} \qquad (38.24)$$

and

$$P(t_M > t_I | X_{-\infty}, ..., X_{t_I} t_I)$$
$$= \frac{(1-\gamma)}{(1-\gamma) + \gamma e^{-V^2/2\sigma^2} \sum_{j=-\infty}^{t_I} (1-\alpha)^{t_I - j} e VX_{j/\sigma^2}} \qquad (38.25)$$

Equation 38.25 provides the investor with the information needed to make an intelligent decision about establishing a position in the security.

To see how Equation 38.25 can be used, suppose that $\gamma$ and a $\alpha$ both are 0.5 per day. This means that for both the investor and the market, the probability is 0.5 that they will receive the information tomorrow if they did not receive it today. Also, assume that the value of the information is about 2.0 percent of the price of the stock, so that $V = 0.02$. Finally, suppose that the security's standard deviation of daily unique return is about 1.0 percent, so that $\sigma = 0.01$.

Exhibit 38.6 contains a hypothetical record of past unique returns, $X_j$, for the security. Each return is a draw from a normal distribution with mean 0.0 and standard deviation 0.01. Thus, none of these past unique returns reflects the impact of the information, and the market date lies in the future.

An examination of Exhibit 38.6 suggests that the market date could well have been in the past. Two days prior to the investor date, a daily unique return of almost 1.0 percent was experienced. This is suggestive of an unusual event. The same can be said of the unique returns experienced three and ten days prior to the investor date.

Exhibit 38.7 contains an evaluation of Equation 38.25. Note how rapidly the contribution of the terms in the sum in the denominator declines. Although only 30 terms are included, it is clear that no significant accuracy has been lost. This behavior reflects the rapid decline of the powers of the fraction $(1 - \alpha)$. Thus, it is typical.

For this hypothetical, but realistic example, the probability that the market has not yet received the information is about 70 percent. This implies a probability of 30 percent that the market has received the information. Statistically, the case is remarkably clear cut. An intuitive analysis of Exhibit 38.6 on the other hand, is unrewarding. The usefulness of the technique is evident.

A more sophisticated investment strategy is presented in the next section. Two additional consequences of Equations 38.22 and 38.23, which will be needed there, are

$$P(t_I < t_M \leq t_I + H | X_{-\infty}, \ldots, X_{t_I} t_I)$$

$$= \sum_{t_M=t_I+1}^{t_I+H} \frac{\gamma(1-\gamma)^{t_M-t_I}}{(1-\gamma) + \gamma e^{-V^2/2\sigma^2} \sum_{j=-\infty}^{t_I} (1-\alpha)^{t_I-j} e^{VX_{j/\sigma^2}}}$$

$$P(t_I < t_M \leq t_I + H | X_{-\infty}, \ldots, X_{t_I} t_I)$$

$$= \frac{(1-\gamma)\left[1-(1-\gamma)^H\right]}{(1-\gamma) + \gamma e^{-V^2/2\sigma^2} \sum_{j=-\infty}^{t_I} (1-\alpha)^{t_I-j} e^{VX_{j/\sigma^2}}} \qquad (38.26)$$

**EXHIBIT 38.6**  Hypothetical Unique Returns

| $(t_j - j)$ | $X_j$ | $(t_I - j)$ | $X_j$ |
|---|---|---|---|
| 0 | −0.0107 | 15 | −0.0146 |
| 1 | 0.0022 | 16 | −0.0120 |
| 2 | 0.0092 | 17 | 0.0079 |
| 3 | 0.0083 | 18 | 0.0077 |
| 4 | −0.0206 | 19 | −0.0133 |
| 5 | −0.0018 | 20 | −0.0060 |
| 6 | −0.0110 | 21 | 0.0006 |
| 7 | 0.0035 | 22 | 0.0049 |
| 8 | −0.0106 | 23 | −0.0105 |
| 9 | −0.0070 | 24 | −0.0063 |
| 10 | 0.0098 | 25 | 0.0024 |
| 11 | 0.0028 | 26 | −0.0073 |
| 12 | −0.0101 | 27 | −0.0031 |
| 13 | 0.0229 | 28 | −0.0057 |
| 14 | −0.0043 | 29 | −0.0090 |

and

$$P(t_M > t_I + H | X_{-\infty}, \ldots, X_{t_I} t_I)$$

$$= \sum_{t_M = t_I + H + 1}^{\infty} \frac{\gamma(1 - \gamma)^{t_M - t_I}}{(1 - \gamma) + \gamma e^{-V^2/2\sigma^2} \sum_{j=-\infty}^{t_I} (1 - \alpha)^{t_I - j} e^{V X_j / \sigma^2}}$$

$$P(t_M > t_I + H | X \ldots, X_{t_I} t_I)$$

$$= \frac{(1 - \gamma)^{H+1}}{(1 - \gamma) + \gamma e^{-V^2/2\sigma^2} \sum_{j=-\infty}^{t_I} (1 - \alpha)^{t_I - j} e^{V X_j / \sigma^2}} \qquad (38.27)$$

**EXHIBIT 38.7**  Computation of the Probability That the Market Date is Later Than the Investor Date

| $(t_I - j)$ | $(1 - \alpha)^{t_I - j}$ | $\frac{V X_j}{\sigma^2}$ | $e^{V X_j / \sigma^2}$ | $(1 - \alpha)^{t_I - j} e^{V X_j / \sigma^2}$ | Cumulative Sum |
|---|---|---|---|---|---|
| 0 | 1.0000000000 | −2.140 | 0.1177 | 0.1176548430 | 0.1176548430 |
| 1 | 0.5000000000 | 0.440 | 1.5527 | 0.7763536093 | 0.8940084523 |
| 2 | 0.2500000000 | 1.840 | 6.2965 | 1.5741345650 | 2.4681430180 |
| 3 | 0.1250000000 | 1.660 | 5.2593 | 0.6574138556 | 3.1255568730 |
| 4 | 0.0625000000 | −4.120 | 0.1624 | 0.0010152822 | 3.1265721550 |
| 5 | 0.0312500000 | −0.360 | 0.6977 | 0.0218023852 | 3.1483745400 |
| 6 | 0.0156250000 | −2.200 | 0.1108 | 0.0017312993 | 3.1501058400 |
| 7 | 0.0078125000 | 0.700 | 2.0138 | 0.0157324430 | 3.1658382830 |
| 8 | 0.0039062500 | −2.120 | 0.1200 | 0.0004688735 | 3.1663071560 |
| 9 | 0.0019531250 | −1.400 | 0.2466 | 0.0004816347 | 3.1667887910 |
| 10 | 0.0009765625 | 1.960 | 7.0993 | 0.0069329366 | 3.1737217280 |
| 11 | 0.0004882813 | 0.560 | 1.7507 | 0.0008548206 | 3.1745765480 |
| 12 | 0.0002441406 | −2.020 | 0.1327 | 0.0000323866 | 3.1746080350 |
| 13 | 0.0001220703 | 4.580 | 97.5144 | 0.0119036126 | 3.1865125470 |
| 14 | 0.0000610352 | −0.860 | 0.4232 | 0.0000258278 | 3.1865383750 |
| 15 | 0.0000305176 | −2.920 | 0.0539 | 0.0000016459 | 3.1865400210 |
| 16 | 0.0000152588 | −2.400 | 0.0907 | 0.0000013842 | 3.1865414050 |
| 17 | 0.0000076294 | 1.580 | 4.8550 | 0.0000370404 | 3.1865784460 |
| 18 | 0.0000038147 | 1.540 | 4.6646 | 0.0000177940 | 3.1865962400 |
| 19 | 0.0000019073 | −2.660 | 0.0699 | 0.0000001334 | 3.1865963730 |
| 20 | 0.0000009537 | −1.200 | 0.3012 | 0.0000002872 | 3.1865966600 |
| 21 | 0.0000004768 | 0.120 | 1.1275 | 0.0000005376 | 3.1865971980 |
| 22 | 0.0000002384 | 0.980 | 2.6645 | 0.0000006353 | 3.1865978330 |
| 23 | 0.0000001192 | −2.100 | 0.1225 | 0.0000000146 | 3.1865978480 |
| 24 | 0.0000000596 | −1.260 | 0.2837 | 0.0000000169 | 3.1865978650 |
| 25 | 0.0000000298 | 0.480 | 1.6161 | 0.0000000482 | 3.1865979130 |
| 26 | 0.0000000149 | −1.460 | 0.2322 | 0.0000000035 | 3.1865979160 |
| 27 | 0.0000000075 | −0.620 | 0.5379 | 0.0000000040 | 3.1865979200 |
| 28 | 0.0000000037 | −1.140 | 0.3198 | 0.0000000012 | 3.1865979220 |
| 29 | 0.0000000019 | −1.800 | 0.1653 | 0.0000000003 | 3.1865979220 |

$$P(t_M > t_I / X_{-\infty}, \ldots, X_{t_I} t_I) = \frac{(1 - 0.5)}{(1 - 0.5) + (0.5)(0.1353352832)(3.1865979220)}$$

$$P(t_M > t_I / X_{-\infty}, \ldots, X_{t_I} t_I) = 0.699$$

## Capitalizing on the Probability Distribution of the Market Date

In selecting a portfolio strategy which permits the investor to capitalize on the information received, it is important to remember that the impact of the information on the price of the security is in the nature of a unique return in the Treynor-Black sense. If the investor uses the Treynor-Black approach to portfolio construction, he or she will be interested in that portion of the probability distribution of unique return associated with the communication. In what follows, it is assumed that the investor either purchases or sells short the security at time $t_I$ and liquidates the position $H$ time units later at time $t_I + H$. The investor is assumed to be a Treynor-Black investor whose investment horizon is $H$ time units in the future. Denoting that portion of the unique return associated with the communication by $r$,

$$P\left(r = 0 | X_{-\infty}, \cdots, X_{t_I} t_I\right) = P\left(t_M \le t_I | X_{-\infty}, \cdots, X_{t_I} t_I\right)$$
$$+ P\left(t_M > t_I + H | X_{-\infty}, \cdots, X_{t_I} t_I\right) \quad (38.28)$$

and

$$P\left(r = \frac{V}{H} | X_{-\infty}, \cdots, X_{t_I} t_I\right) = P\left(t_I < t_M \le t_I + H | X_{-\infty}, \cdots, X_{t_I} t_I\right) \quad (38.29)$$

The mean of $r$ is

$$\mu_r = P\left(r = \frac{V}{H} | X_{-\infty}, \cdots, X_{t_I} t_I\right)\left(\frac{V}{H}\right) \quad (38.30)$$

The variance of $r$ is

$$\sigma_r^2 = \varepsilon\left(r^2\right) - \mu_r^2,$$

$$= P\left(r = \frac{V}{H} | X_{-\infty}, \cdots, X_{t_I} t_I\right)\left(\frac{V}{H}\right)^2$$

$$- \left[P\left(r = \frac{V}{H} | X_{-\infty}, \cdots, X_{t_I} t_I\right)\right]^2 \left(\frac{V}{H}\right)^2$$

$$= \left(\frac{V}{H}\right)^2 P\left(r = \frac{V}{H} | X_{-\infty}, \cdots, X_{t_I} t_I\right)$$

$$\times \left[1 - P\left(r = \frac{V}{H} | X_{-\infty}, \cdots, X_{t_I} t_I\right)\right]$$

$$\sigma_r^2 = \left(\frac{V}{H}\right)^2 P\left(r = \frac{V}{H} | X_{-\infty}, \cdots, X_{t_I} t_I\right)$$

$$\cdot P\left(r = 0 | X_{-\infty}, \cdots, X_{t_I} t_I\right) \quad (38.31)$$

Equations 38.28, 38.29, 38.30, and 38.31 are easily evaluated using Equations 38.24, 38.26, and 38.27. In Treynor-Black terminology, 38.30 is the appraisal premium associated with the communication and 38.31 is its associated appraisal variance. This portion of the unique return over the interval from $t_I$ to $(t_I + H)$ is proportional to a point binomial random variable.

Denoting the remaining portion of the unique return over the interval from $t_I$ to $(t_I + H)$ by $R$,

$$R = \frac{1}{H} \sum_{j=t_I+1}^{t_I+H} Y_j \tag{38.32}$$

By assumption,

$$P\left(Y_{t_I+1}, \cdots, Y_{t_I+H}\right) = \prod_{i=t_I+1}^{t_I+H} \left[\frac{e^{-Y_i^2/2\sigma^2}}{\sqrt{2\pi}\sigma}\right] \tag{38.33}$$

Since $R$ is a weighted sum of independent normal variables, it also has a normal distribution with mean and variance given by

$$\mu_R = 0.0$$

and

$$\sigma_R^2 = \frac{\sigma^2}{H} \tag{38.34}$$

Thus,

$$P(R) = \frac{e^{\left(-R^2/2\sigma^2/H\right)}}{\sqrt{2\pi}\sigma/\sqrt{H}} \tag{38.35}$$

The total unique return, $\rho$, over the interval from $t_I$ to $(t_I + H)$ is simply

$$\rho = R + r \tag{38.36}$$

where $R$ and $r$ are independent. The joint probability distribution of $R$ and $r$ is

$$P\left(R, r | X_{-\infty}, \cdots, X_{t_I} t_I\right) = P(R)\, P\left(r | X_{-\infty}, \cdots, X_{t_I} t_I\right) \tag{38.37}$$

Since $r$ is proportional to a point binomial and $R$ is normal, the probability distribution for $\rho$ is

$$P\left(\rho | X_{-\infty}, \cdots, X_{t_I} t_I\right) = P\left(r = 0 | X_{-\infty}, \cdots, X_{t_I} t_I\right) P(R = \rho)$$

$$+ P\left(r = \frac{V}{H} | X_{-\infty}, \cdots, X_{t_I} t_I\right) P\left(R = \rho - \frac{V}{H}\right) \tag{38.38}$$

Equation 38.38 shows that $\rho$ has a bimodal distribution with one mode at 0.0 and the other at $(V/H)$. This distribution is the weighted sum of two normal distributions with identical variances $(\sigma^2/H)$ and means of 0.0 and $(V/H)$. Furthermore, since all the variables involved are independent and all returns are expressed in continuous form,

$$\mu_\rho = \mu_R + \mu_r = \mu_r \tag{38.39}$$

and

$$\sigma_\rho^2 = \sigma_R^2 + \sigma_r^2 \tag{38.40}$$

The investor's appraisal premium is given by Equations 38.39, the appraisal variance by Equations 38.40, and the appraisal ratio, $\gamma_\rho^2$ by

$$\gamma_\rho^2 = \frac{\mu_\rho^2}{\sigma_\rho^2} \tag{38.41}$$

$$\gamma_\rho^2 = \frac{\mu_r^2}{\sigma_R^2 + \sigma_r^2} \tag{38.42}$$

Making all the appropriate substitutions,

$$\mu_\rho = \mu_r = \frac{\left(\frac{V}{H}\right)(-\alpha)\left[1-(1-\gamma)^H\right]}{(1-\gamma)+\gamma e^{-V^2/2\sigma^2}\sum_{j=-\infty}^{t_l}(1-\alpha)^{t_l-j}e^{VX_j/\sigma^2}} \tag{38.43}$$

$$\sigma_\rho^2 = \sigma^2/H + (V/H)^2$$

$$(1-\gamma)\left[1-(1-\gamma)^H\right]$$

$$\cdot\frac{\left[(1-\gamma)^{H+1}+\gamma e^{-V^2/2\sigma^2}\sum_{j=-\infty}^{t_l}(1-\alpha)^{t_l-j}e^{VX_j/\sigma^2}\right]}{\left[(1-\gamma)+\gamma e^{-V^2/2\sigma^2}\sum_{j=-\infty}^{t_l}(1-\alpha)^{t_l-j}e^{VX_j/\sigma^2}\right]^2} \tag{38.44}$$

$$P\left(\rho|X_{-\infty},\cdots X_{t_l}t_l\right)$$

$$=\left[\frac{(1-\gamma)^{H+1}+\gamma e^{-V^2/2\sigma^2}\sum_{j=-\infty}^{t_l}(1-\alpha)^{t_l-j}e^{VX_j/\sigma^2}}{(1-\gamma)+\gamma e^{-V^2/2\sigma^2}\sum_{j=-\infty}^{t_l}(1-\alpha)^{t_l-j}e^{VX_j/\sigma^2}}\right]\frac{e^{-\rho^2/2(\sigma^2/H)}}{\sqrt{2\pi}\left(\sigma/\sqrt{H}\right)}$$

$$+\left[\frac{(1-\gamma)\left[1-(1-\gamma)^H\right]}{(1-\gamma)+\gamma e^{-V^2/2\sigma^2}\sum_{j=-\infty}^{t_l}(1-\alpha)^{t_l-j}e^{VX_j/\sigma^2}}\right]\frac{e^{-(\rho-V/H)^2/2(\sigma^2/H)}}{\sqrt{2\pi}\left(\sigma/\sqrt{H}\right)} \tag{38.45}$$

## CONCLUSIONS

Adherents of technical analysis claim that unusual profit can be achieved using only past security prices. Most academics believe that the securities markets are efficient enough to make this impossible. This paper has shown that past prices, when combined with other valuable information, can indeed be helpful in achieving unusual profit. However, it is the nonprice information that creates the opportunity. The past prices serve only to permit its efficient exploitation.

### Notes

1. Investors are assumed to have homogeneous beliefs when they have identical information. This assumption is not necessary, but makes the exposition easier.
2. The argument can be generalized to information other than that pertaining to a single company.
3. The propagation of information can be likened to the spread of a disease. This view leads to a characteristic pattern of cumulative unique return where the rapidity of approach to the new equilibrium price depends on a single parameter in much the same fashion that a nuclear decay rate can be expressed in terms of a half-life. This parameter can be used as a definition of market efficiency.
4. A reasonable assumption in light of the evidence.
5. Suppose the investor is told that a company has just received a contract from the government. For the moment, the investor would have to guess about its size. Suppose a few days later this investor hears that the government has just let a $100 million contract for the same product this company makes. Now the investor knows the size. The value of the information in the first communication could be viewed as dependent on the second communication, or vice versa.
6. Bayes theorem ordinarily is written as

$$P(A_k|B) = \frac{P(A_k)P(B|A_k)}{\sum_i P(A_i)P(B|A_i)} \tag{a}$$

Associating $A_i$ with $t_M$, $B$ with a particular sequence of past unique returns $(X_{-\infty}, ..., X_{t_I})$, and $C$ with a particular $t_I$, Expression (1) can be written as $P(A_k|BC)$ and Equation (2) can be written as

$$P(A_k|BC) = \frac{P(A_k|C)P(B|A_kC)}{\sum_i P(A_i|C)P(B|A_iC)} \tag{b}$$

Equation (b) is exactly the same as (a) except for the additional conditioning variable $C$. To see that version (b) is valid, first note that a fundamental theorem of probability is

$$P(ABC) = P(A)P(B|A)P(C|AB) \tag{c}$$

Since the order of these events is immaterial,

$$P(ABC) = P(C)P(B|C)P(A|BC)$$

and

$$P(ABC) = P(C)P(A|C)P(B|AC) \tag{d}$$

Setting the two right-hand sides of (d) equal and solving for P(A | BC) gives

$$P(A|BC) = \frac{P(A|C)P(B|AC)}{P(B|C)} \tag{e}$$

Rewriting $A$ as $A_k$, (e) becomes

$$P(A_k|BC) = \frac{P(A_k|C)P(B|A_kC)}{P(B|C)} \tag{f}$$

The evaluation of P(B | C) proceeds as follows:

$$P(BC) = \sum_i P(A_i BC)$$
$$P(C)P(B|C) = \sum_i P(C)P(A_i|C)P(B|A_iC)$$
$$P(B|C) = \sum_i P(A_i|C)P(B|A_iC) \tag{g}$$

Thus

$$P(A_{k|BC}) = \frac{P(A_k|C)P(B|A_kC)}{\sum_i P(A_i|C)P(B|A_iC)}$$

and Equation (2) is valid.

## References

*Robert Ferguson. "Active Portfolio Management—How to Beat the Index Funds." *Financial Analysts Journal* 31 (May/June 1975) 63–72.

†Jack L. Treynor and Fischer Black. "How to Use Security Analysis to Improve Portfolio Selection." *Journal of Business* 46 (January 1973) 66–86.

# CHAPTER 39

# The Economics of the Dealer Function

*A dealer facilitates market liquidity by intermediating between transactors to whom time is important in exchange for charging buyers a higher price than he pays sellers. A value-based investor may also fulfill this function, but at a larger bid-asked spread than that imposed by the dealer. Relative to the value-based investor, the dealer has limited capital, hence limited ability to absorb risk; he will thus limit the position—long or short—he is willing to take.*

*When the dealer's position reaches a maximum, he will lay off to the only other transactor motivated by price—the value-based investor. The dealer's price is tied to the value-based investor's price at these layoff points. As the value-based investor shifts his prices in response to new information, the dealer's interior prices shift along with his layoff prices.*

*An investor should realize that, when he trades with the crowd, he is trading at the value-based investor's spread, which may be many times the size of the explicit dealer's spread. More generally, the actions of the crowd— whether it is buying or selling, and in what volume—will determine whether the price of trading quickly is high or low, hence whether the value of his information justifies trading.*

**A** market-maker may be defined as someone who accommodates transactors to whom time is important in return for the privilege of charging buyers a higher price than he pays sellers. By this definition, both dealers and value-based investors (VBTs) are market makers. Yet their roles differ in several important respects—

- In amount of capital, hence ability to absorb losses;
- In length of holding, hence exposure to getting bagged;
- In the spreads (i.e., the difference in bid and asked price imposed on simultaneous purchases and sales).

In particular, the VBT's spread is larger than the dealer's spread; we call them, respectively, the "outside" and "inside" spread. In the absence of dealers, transactors in a hurry would buy and sell at prices that differ by the full outside, or VBT, spread— even if purchase and sale took place only seconds apart. By intermediating between hurried buyers and hurried sellers, a dealer enables them to benefit from each other's trading, even if the trades aren't simultaneous.

Dealers are thus valuable to transactors in a hurry, because they greatly reduce the spreads encountered by those transactors. By doing so, they also greatly improve the liquidity of the markets in which they deal. Alas for the dealer and for market liquidity, a seller is not always followed by a buyer. Indeed, even if the arrival of buyers and sellers is random, a seller may be followed by a long run of sellers (or a buyer by a long run of buyers), with the result that the dealer builds up a large position.

Compared with the VBT, the dealer has very limited capital with which to absorb an adverse move in the value of the asset. Furthermore, the dealer's spread is too modest to compensate him for getting bagged. The dealer consequently sets limits on the position—long or short—he is willing to take. When his position reaches a limit, he lays off to the only other transactor in the market who is motivated by price—the value-based investor. (Strictly speaking, when his position grows uncomfortably short, he "buys in"; to avoid circumlocution, we shall use the term "lay off" algebraically.) In effect, the value-based investor is the market-maker of last resort. Exhibit 39.1 combines these elements in a diagram.

In the problem we address, the value-based investor's bid and asked price and the standard size of orders coming to the dealer for accommodation are givens. We also take as given the maximum position—long or short—the dealer is willing to assume. We ask two questions:

- How will the dealer's mean price—the mean of his bid and asked—vary with his position?
- How big will the dealer's spread be? What detemines it?

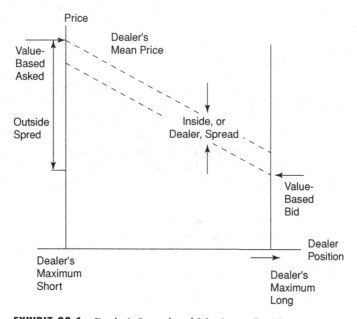

**EXHIBIT 39.1** Dealer's Spread and Maximum Position

We shall assume that VBT's get new information as soon as the dealer's customers. Otherwise, of course, accumulations in the dealer's position will not be unaffected by the arrival of new information.

When information reaches the VBT, his bid and asked prices shift to reflect it. Because the dealer's price is tied to the VBT bid and ask at his layoff points, his prices move along with the VBT prices. In general, therefore, dealer prices are responding to two different forces—changes in the VBT's estimate of value and changes in the dealer's position.

## DETERMINING THE DEALER'S SPREAD

Dealers have salaries, telephone bills, and other costs, just like any businessman. Unless these costs have a significant variable component, however, a dealer's dominant variable cost will be the cost of laying off. If, in dealing, price is related to variable cost, then the price the dealer exacts for his services—the dealer's spread—will be related to the cost of laying off—the outside spread.

In the limiting case of perfect competition among dealers, the revenues the dealer receives from his accommodations will equal the costs of laying off. Because the outside spread will typically be many times the dealer's spread, however, revenues will equal costs only if layoffs are far less frequent than accommodations. More precisely, the ratio of the two spreads must equal the inverse ratio of the respective transaction frequencies. To obtain this ratio, we need to know the frequency of transactions.

### The Frequency of Layoffs

Perhaps the simplest way to think about this problem is in terms of accommodation trades of a fixed size. Such trades cause the dealer's position to jump from one inventory position to an adjacent position. The continuum of dealer positions is thus reduced to a number of discrete positions, like beads spaced evenly along a string. Purchases and sales arrive in random order (but equal frequency), so moves up or down the string occur in random order. This is illustrated in Exhibit 39.2.

At the ends of the string are beads corresponding to the dealer's maximum tolerable positions. We call them the "layoff positions." (We assume the dealer is willing to adjust his layoff positions so they are separated by a whole number of standard accommodations.) When the dealer's position reaches either extreme, the next transaction may move it back toward a neutral position or forward beyond the dealer's maximum. In the latter case the dealer either buys in (paying an asking price

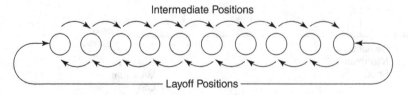

**EXHIBIT 39.2** Dealer's String of Transactions

above his own asking price) or lays off (realizing a bid price below his own bid). Thus every share (every unit) laid off represents a loss to the dealer.

If there are no fixed costs of laying off that can be spread over the units laid off, it behooves the dealer to lay off only the units (long or short) acquired in accommodating the current trade. After such a layoff, his position is restored to the layoff position, from which subsequent accommodations will sometimes move him back toward the neutral position at no additional layoff cost.

To define this process algebraically, let X be the dealer's position, $X^*$ the dealer's maximum position, S the standard accommodation and G(X) the frequency with which the dealer finds himself in that position in the steady state. Then, for interior positions, we can write:

$$G(X) = 0.5\,G(X - S) + 0.5\,G(X + S)$$

reflecting the fact that buy and sell accommodations are equally likely. In other words, the frequency with which the position X occurs depends on the frequency with which the adjacent positions occur, times the probability (0.5 in each case) of moves from those positions toward the X position, rather than away from it.

We can rewrite this relation as follows:

$$0.5G(X) - 0.5G(X - S) = 0.5G(X + S) - 0.5G(X)$$

Now its meaning is clearer: The rate of change of G(X) is everywhere the same. Only a straight-line function of X satisfies this condition. Furthermore, the symmetry between buy and sell orders dictates that this function be symmetric with respect to positive and negative values of X. The only straight-line function that satisfies this condition is a horizontal line: G(X) is a constant; the probability of each position is the same.

If layoffs are the same size as a standard accommodation then, when a dealer reaches his layoff position, his next accommodating transaction is equally likely to (1) move him one position closer to neutrality or (2) force him to lay off, in which case the net effect is to return him to the layoff position. If $X^*$ is the upper layoff position, then in the steady state we have:

$$G(X^*) = 0.5\,G(X^*) + 0.5\,G(X^* - S),$$

$$G(X^*) = G(X^* - S) = G(X)$$

A similar result holds for the lower layoff position.

If all possible positions, including layoff positions, occur with the same frequency, then layoff positions occur with a frequency equal to the standard accommodation divided by twice the dealer's layoff position, times two, because there are two layoff positions. But layoff positions actually lead to layoffs only half the time. Thus layoffs occur with a frequency equal to the standard accommodation divided by twice the dealer's layoff position:

$$\text{Layoff Frequency} = S/2X^*$$

The spread, $p_a - p_b$, that enables the dealer to break even is:

$$p_a - p_b = S/2X^*(P_a - P_b)$$

where $P_a - P_b$ is the outside, or VBT's spread. If the dealer charges more than this, he's covering at least some of his other costs. Not surprisingly, the competitive inside spread is proportional to the outside spread. But it also increases with the size of the standard accommodation and varies inversely with the maximum position the dealer is willing to take.

## DETERMINING THE DEALER'S MEAN PRICE

Now, what about *price*—the mean of the dealer's bid and asked? The dealer's current price should relate in a rational way to what the price is expected to be in the future. Otherwise, his current price will create profit opportunities across time for those who trade with him.

At positions between his layoff positions, the dealer should set price according to the price he expects to be setting one trade later. The next trade will, of course, move his position up or down with equal probability. If the price the dealer would set in those positions is known, then the price he sets in his current position must be the probability-weighted average of those two prices; otherwise he will create easy profits for those trading against him.

Let the prices for the three positions $X - S$, $X$ and $X + S$ be $p(X - S)$, $p(X)$ and $p(X + S)$, respectively. Because the adjacent positions are equally likely, we have:

$$2p(X) = p(X - S) + p(X + S)$$

This is clearly another straight-line function of position:

$$p(X) - p(X - S) = p(X + S) - p(X)$$

The positions immediately beyond the respective layoff positions have known prices corresponding to the prices at which value-based investors will accommodate the dealer. The straight-line price function must satisfy those prices. If we let S be the standard transaction quantity, then we have:

$$p(X^* + S) = P_{BID} = P_b$$

$$p(-X^* - S) = P_{ASK} = P_a$$

and
$$p(X) = \frac{P_a + P_b}{2} - \left(\frac{P_a - P_b}{X^* + S}\right)\frac{X}{2}$$

The ratio $(P_a - P_b)/(X^* + S)$ measures the sensitivity of the dealer's mean price to changes in his position. It depends on both (1) the outside spread, reflecting the risk character of the asset, and (2) the dealer's willingness to take a position.

What these results show is that it is expensive to buy when everyone else is in a hurry to buy and expensive to sell when everyone else is in a hurry to sell.

We have begged the question of how big a position the dealer should tolerate. The answer probably has something to do with whether value-based investors, who help determine the dealer's mean price, get new information as quickly as information-based investors. It probably also has something to do with the risk character of the dealer's other assets, and with the size of his capital. Rich people make the best dealers.

## Pricing Large Blocks

In the real world, of course, the individual accommodation trades brought to the dealer will vary in size. This raises the question: How should the dealer price trades larger than the standard trade? In particular, should he price the trade on the basis of the average position incurred in accommodating a trade, or the final position? If the average, then the cost of large trades is the same as the cost of small trades. If the final, the effective cost is much higher.

If large trades are frequent, then they will affect the probabilities we have assumed for transitions from one dealer position to another. If such trades are sufficiently infrequent that we can safely ignore their effects on the probabilities, then we can treat the occasional large trade as a string of standard trades.

Consider, for example, the cost of a large round trip as depicted in Exhibit 39.3. If the dealer's purchase and sale prices are based on his average position, then the cost of the round trip is the shaded area in the figure. This implies a cost per share equal to the area divided by the number of shares traded or the inside spread. If, however, the dealer's prices are based on his final positions (i.e., after the customer's purchase is completed and after the customer's sale is completed), then the round-trip cost of trading is depicted by the shaded area in Exhibit 39.4.

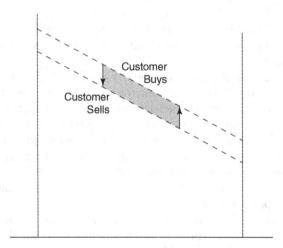

**EXHIBIT 39.3**  Cost of Large Round Trip, Based on Dealer's Average Position

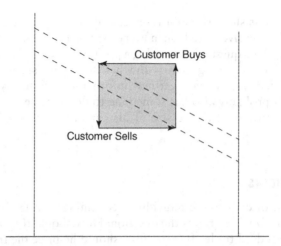

**EXHIBIT 39.4**   Cost of Large Round Trip, Based on
Dealer's Final Positions

Unfortunately for the customer, the key to rational pricing behavior on the part of the dealer in this situation is our earlier comment that "the dealer should set price according to the price he expects to be setting one trade later." *This* price is determined by the dealer's final position when the trade is completed—not his average position during the trade. Although the *next* trade is equally likely to be in the same direction or the opposite direction, he knows that the *current* trade is equivalent to an unbroken run of standard-sized trades in the same direction.

A dealer will price a large block on the basis of his final position (rather than an average of his intermediate positions) because, in contrast to the assumptions underlying the standard accommodation model, he knows that his position will not fluctuate randomly around the intermediate positions. Instead, it will fluctuate randomly around the final position. The prices corresponding to that position should thus apply to the whole block. This, of course, implies that the size effects in prices are not reversible: The customer doesn't get back when he sells the block what he paid when he bought it.

What about the cost of trading a series of smaller blocks—in other words, of trading so the dealer doesn't know how big the whole series is until the last trade? In this case, the customer can get intermediate prices for intermediate trades, paying the final price only for the final trade. Of course, if the smaller blocks are big enough to push the dealer to his maximum, then nothing has been gained, because the outside spread price would have governed if the entire block had been handled as a single trade. In the meantime, too, the customer runs the risk that the information motivating his trade will get impounded in the price (i.e., the mean of the VBT's bid and ask) before he completes his trade.

In sum, (1) a large block will move the dealer's position, hence his price, in a direction that will increase the price of the trade, unless (2) the dealer's position is already at the maximum limit to which the block would otherwise move him, in which case (3) the size of the block has no effect on the dealer's price.

## VALUATION ERRORS IN VBTs' ESTIMATES

So far we have assumed that VBTs estimate the value of the asset in question correctly. This implies that they agree, in which case the cumulative probability distribution of their assessments is the Z-shaped distribution given in Exhibit 39.5. Actual bid and asked prices, set one-half the outside spread below and above the assessment, will have their own cumulative probability distributions, which will also be Z-shaped, echoing the shape of the assessment distribution.

If the assessments of value-based traders are in error, however, they will be dispersed around a central assessment, and their cumulative probability distribution will no longer be Z-shaped. It will instead be S-shaped, as in Exhibit 39.6, with gradually rounded corners and long, tapering tails. As before, the distributions of value-based traders' bid and asked prices will echo the assessment distribution. They too will now be S-shaped rather than Z-shaped, with rounded corners and long, tapering tails.

The bid and asked distributions will still be set one-half the outside spread to the left and right, respectively, of the distribution of value assessments. But something curious has happened: The distance between the upper tail of the bid distribution and the lower tail of the asked distribution has narrowed. Error in value-based traders' assessments has reduced the dealer's cost of laying off.

Strictly speaking, if the error distributions have infinitely long tails, the dealer's cost of laying off has been eliminated. What really matters to the dealer are the prices that elicit the necessary volume of bids and offers from the tails. It should be clear that, as the average (e.g., standard) error in value-based traders' assessments increases, the cost of laying off in the required volume declines.

Many investment professionals assert that their work in assessing security values not only serves their clients, but also makes security markets more efficient. It is certainly true that, without value-based investors, dealers would have no one to lay off to. But now we see that, if competition among dealers is sufficiently brisk,

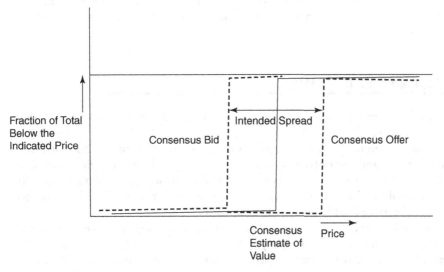

**EXHIBIT 39.5** Cumulative Distribution of Value-Based Estimates of Value, When Estimates Are Correct

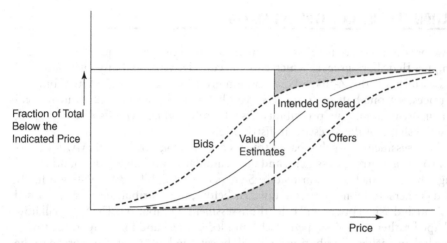

**EXHIBIT 39.6**   Cumulative Distribution of Value-Based Estimates of Value, When Estimates Are in Error
*Shared areas represent negative layoff price (and buy-in cost) for the dealer.

any reduction of outside spread resulting from value-based investors' errors will be passed along to the inside spread, thereby improving market efficiency. In this case, of course, dealers will be indifferent between less error on average in value-based investors' assessments and more; it is their customers who are the ultimate beneficiaries of larger assessment errors.

If, on the other hand, dealers are not subject to the pressures of competition, then the savings they realize from an increase in the average size of value-based traders' assessment errors will not be passed on to their customers in the form of smaller inside spreads. Markets will not be more efficient. And dealers will no longer be indifferent between less error and more—which is to say, between higher standards of investment analysis and lower ones.

## THE ECONOMICS OF INVESTING

What are the lessons for the reader who wants to be a successful investor, rather than a successful dealer?

First, in reckoning the cost of any trade, there are two spreads to consider—the inside spread and the outside spread. The latter, which is what the dealer pays to trade at a time of his choosing, is also what the investor pays to trade with the crowd. Normally invisible to the investor, it is often an order of magnitude or two bigger than the more readily visible inside spread.

Second, when an investor comes to the market with insights not yet impounded in the price, what he pays for speed depends on what the crowd, often motivated by different information, is paying for speed. In particular, it depends on whether the information-motivated crowd is eager to buy or eager to sell. If he is buying when the crowd is selling, for example, he is in effect market-making to the crowd. He is receiving, rather than paying, some or all of the outside spread. And if it turns out that the information motivating the crowd was not yet in the price, he will get bagged along with those other investors who make it their business to accommodate information-motivated investors—namely, value-based investors.

Third, and more generally, what the information-motivated crowd is doing—whether it is buying or selling, and in what volume—determines the current price of trading fast. The investor needs to know this price in order to judge whether the time value of his own insight is high enough to make the price worth paying. If it is, he trades. If it isn't, he doesn't trade.

Fourth, because orders motivated by liquidity tend to arrive as a random mixture of buys and sells, whereas orders motivated by information don't, the latter are much more likely to push the dealer to the extreme of laying off to or buying in from the value-based investor. These considerations are important for the value-based investor attempting to set his spread so that gains from liquidity trading will be large enough to offset losses on information trading.

Fifth, because liquidity-motivated trading is by definition uncorrelaled with information-motivated trading, hence with trading by the crowd, its expected cost is the inside spread. But the cost of "pseudo" information-motivated trading is the outside spread. The volume of "pseudo" trading is critical to the viability of the value-based investor.

Finally, the functions of a trading desk should be to

(a) Estimate the inside spread on all securities of interest to investors;
(b) Estimate the outside spread;
(c) Maintain running estimates of outside bid and ask on all securities of current trading interest: the price of trading quickly is the difference between the price of the trade and the mean of the outside bid and ask;
(d) Obtain from research estimates of the time value of current recommendations and
(e) Match (c) and (d).

## APPENDIX 39.1

Our argument for each position occurring with the same frequency is highly heuristic, to say the least. When the dealer's possible positions are reduced to a limited number of discrete states, the basic structure of the problem is that of a Markov process. It is well known that the steady-state probabilities of such a process are related to the transition probabilities by the requirement that the product of the vector of

**EXHIBIT 39.7**  Matrix Equation

$$\begin{pmatrix} 1 \\ 1 \\ 1 \\ 1 \\ 1 \end{pmatrix} \begin{pmatrix} 0.5 & 0.5 & & & \\ 0.5 & 0 & 0.5 & & \\ & 0.5 & 0 & 0.5 & \\ & & 0.5 & 0 & 0.5 \\ & & & 0.5 & 0.5 \end{pmatrix} = \begin{pmatrix} 1 \\ 1 \\ 1 \\ 1 \\ 1 \end{pmatrix}$$

steady-state probabilities and the matrix of transition probabilities be the same vector of steady-state probabilities.

We can thus test our heuristic conclusion that the dealer's position frequencies are all equal by testing the truth of the matrix equation given in Exhibit 39.7. Inspection confirms that the equation is satisfied.

# CHAPTER 40

# Market Manipulation

In sentencing Michael Milken to 10 years in prison, Judge Kimba Wood admitted she was unable to find him guilty of using either inside information or market manipulation. Otherwise, his sentence would have been harsher.

Few of us would like to be found guilty of market manipulation (especially by Judge Wood!). Clearly our first step in avoiding culpability is to find out what it is. Yet chances are most of us don't know. Our ignorance is the result, not of a cavalier disregard for securities law, but rather of the law's failure to provide a clear definition.[1]

Layman's intuition suggests that market manipulation is trading that creates artificial discrepancies between price and value, the intention being to profit from these discrepancies. In securities markets, however, discrepancies between price and value are common. For example, anxious investors, who want to trade quickly, rely on bargain hunters who exploit differences between trading prices and equilibrium prices.

In actual practice, the relation between trade price and equilibrium price is complicated by the presence of dealers. Bargain hunters require substantial bargains—in the form of discounts on or premiums to equilibrium price—in order to be willing to trade. An anxious buyer and an anxious seller could theoretically accommodate each other at equilibrium price—thus avoiding trading at prices that provide profits for bargain hunters—but only if their trades arrived in the market simultaneously. Dealers provide a conduit that enables anxious buyers and sellers to trade with each other, even when their trades are not simultaneous.

The dealer takes the other side of each anxious trade, accumulating a position that fluctuates with the arrival of anxious buys and sells. When his position gets too large for his risk tolerance, he lays off to bargain-hunting buyers or buys in from bargain-hunting sellers. Because they occur at the dealer's initiative, these trades take place at bargain-hunters' bargain prices—in other words, at prices far from equilibrium.

The dealer adjusts the prices at which he accommodates his own anxious customers to reflect the likelihood of an expensive layoff or buy-in (i.e., to reflect his position). When the dealer is uncomfortably long, he sets his accommodation prices close to the bargain hunter's bid. When the dealer is uncomfortably short, he sets his accommodation prices close to the bargain hunter's offer. Because the spread between

---

the bargain hunter's bid and ask is large, the dealer's prices to his anxious customers can vary over a wide range—from the bargain hunter's bid to the bargain hunter's offer—even when equilibrium price isn't changing.

If follows that, by changing his position, anxious trading with the dealer can alter his prices. In order for such trading to be market manipulation, however, it must be profitable. Reflection shows that round-trips with the dealer can be profitable for the investor (and unprofitable for the dealer) *only* if the dealer's price changes lag his position changes. But the dealer can avoid such losses merely by basing his trade prices on his position after, rather than before, each trade. It seems fair to assume that Darwinian selection among dealers will produce markets in which this kind of manipulation will be unprofitable to investors.

What, then, is market manipulation? A possible answer is suggested by the following observations. In setting trade prices with their anxious customers, dealers are influenced by the prices at which they can lay off to or buy in from bargain hunters. In order to consider these prices a bargain, the bargain hunter must have some estimate of equilibrium value. Such an estimate is *implicit* in every bargain-hunter's price (although not equal to that price, as there would be no bargain if it were).[2] But the dealer will give more weight to prices that represent genuine bets by the bargain hunter. In particular, the dealer will give greatest weight to the prices at which trades with bargain hunters actually execute.

But suppose an executed trade doesn't represent a genuine bet, reflecting the bargain hunter's best estimate of equilibrium value. When the bargain hunter's bid or offer executes, he can immediately initiate an offsetting anxious trade with the dealer. As noted, the dealer's price to his anxious customers will be close to the price at which he estimates he will be able to lay off to or buy in from bargain hunters. Thus the price differential experienced by the bargain-hunting wash trader will be small. And because the dealer executes anxious trades quickly, the time elapsed between the two trades will be short. The wash trader's cost of trading and his financial exposure will both be modest.

In this scenario, the bargain hunter's first trade influences the dealer's opinion of value. His second, offsetting, trade doesn't. A wash trade of this sort is thus a dandy way to manipulate the dealer. It does so by manipulating the dealer's opinion of value, however, rather than the dealer's position.

## Notes

1. According to an article in the December 1991 issue of the *Harvard Law Review* (discussed in the March 6, 1992 issue of the *Wall Street Journal*), the Securities Exchange Act prohibits market manipulation but does not define it. The authors (University of Chicago law Professor Daniel R. Fischel and Lexecon Inc. Vice President David J. Ross) conclude that "only dishonest intent to move stock prices can be called manipulation."

2. By being willing to trade at the dealer's prices, aren't anxious investors also conveying information about equilibrium value? Richard Brealey has pointed out that unlike bargain hunters, who trade on time-consuming estimates of a security's absolute value, most anxious investors are trading on the incremental value of their information.

# CHAPTER 41

# Types and Motivations of Market Participants

*The most meaningful measure of performance for active portfolios is not total return but the increment in return that results from trading. A crucial element in this equation is "invisible" transaction costs—those related to exchanging perceived price advantages for perceived time advantages (or vice versa).*

I believe in active securities management. My only complaint is that some active managers seem to have a narrow understanding of the game. This is particularly true of what I call the invisible costs of trading. Managers rarely mention them when discussing trading costs, and conventional measures of trading costs omit the invisible costs.

A view of trading that excludes these costs leads to the conclusion that bad performance is the result of bad research, but this is impossible. The purpose of research is to forecast price movements. Worthless research makes worthless forecasts. A worthless forecast is equally likely to be followed by a price increase or decrease. Worthless research leads to unnecessary risk and unnecessary trading, but in terms of its average contribution to return, gross of trading costs, bad research cannot be worse than no research.

Most of the return in a diversified portfolio is the broad impact of economic and market news on the asset categories in the portfolio. This impact is the same whether the assets within these categories are traded or merely held.

For long-term, average experience in diversified portfolios, we have the following crude equation:

$$\text{Return from trading} = \text{Research} - \text{Trading costs}$$

in which the return from trading is often negative but the research term never is. In such portfolios, consistent underperformance cannot be explained by bad research. The culprit must be trading costs, but the visible trading costs—commissions plus dealer spread—are too modest for listed stocks to explain any significant underperformance.

---

## KEY ELEMENTS IN INVESTMENT PERFORMANCE

The explanation for negative returns lies in two facts:

- Trading is a zero-sum game (before dealer spread and commissions). Every trade will have one winner and one loser (relative, of course, to not trading).
- In its motivation, the great majority of securities trading is adversarial.

Broadly speaking, active investors contemplate two kinds of price movement: changes in equilibrium price, and changes in the discrepancy between trade price and equilibrium price. The difference in trade prices between any two points in time is always some combination of these two. All active investing is motivated by forecasts, implicit or explicit, of one kind or the other.

Information traders, for example, believe they know something other investors do not know. This information is not yet reflected in equilibrium price, but it will be when knowledge spreads to enough other investors. The information traders are betting on a change in equilibrium price. They rely on research to dig up information with potential market impact that is not widely known—that is, they rely on investigation.

Value traders, on the other hand, believe they have identified a discrepancy between trade price and equilibrium value. They believe that such discrepancies are only temporary. They are betting that, given market pressures toward equilibration, the observed discrepancy is more likely to diminish than increase. They rely on research to provide an estimate of equilibrium value they can compare with trade price—that is, they rely on analysis of facts and figures in the public domain.

The distinction between information and value traders, shown schematically in Exhibit 41.1 and Exhibit 41.2, cuts across the distinction between buyers and sellers. Information traders can be motivated by either good news (in which case they are

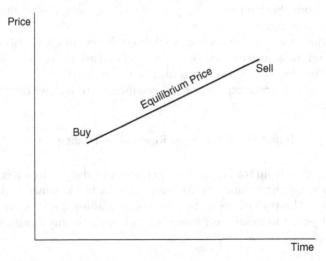

**EXHIBIT 41.1**   How Information Traders See Trading
Opportunities

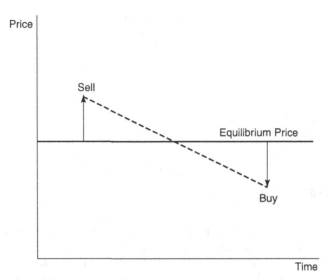

**EXHIBIT 41.2**  How Value Traders See Trading Opportunities

buyers) or bad news (in which case they are sellers). Value traders can be motivated by a trade price above what they think a security is worth (in which case they are sellers) or by a trade price below what they think a security is worth (in which case they are buyers).

To the layperson, a bargain price is a price below true (equilibrium) value. Value traders, however, can be motivated by a trade price either above or below their perceptions of equilibrium. Both price discrepancies represent potentially profitable trading opportunities—bargains. In this symmetrical sense of the word, we refer to value traders as bargain hunters.

## TRADING, AS WELL AS HOLDING, RISKS

We have noted that information traders are betting on a change in equilibrium price, whereas value traders are betting on a change in the discrepancy between trade price and equilibrium price. Both incur risks, however. Even if value traders have estimated equilibrium price correctly and identified a true bargain, equilibrium price may change before they can close out their positions. Even if information traders have uncovered information that correctly anticipates a change in equilibrium price, they may be forced to buy and sell (or sell and buy) at trade prices different from equilibrium.

The key question for active investors is whether these risks are merely random risks. If so, then information traders are probably justified in focusing on the potential change in equilibrium price, and the value traders are probably justified in focusing on departures of trade price from their estimates of equilibrium.

Are active investors as likely to gain as lose from these risks? Consider information traders. To justify ignoring discrepancies between the prices they trade at and equilibrium prices at the times of their trades, they need to be able to assume

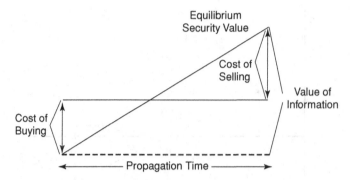

**EXHIBIT 41.3**   Trading on Good News

that these discrepancies are random. For information traders to transact with value traders on the other side, however, value traders must be motivated by a perceived discrepancy between trade price and equilibrium price that offers them a bargain. The discrepancy cannot be good for value traders on the other side without being bad for information traders. The trade-price discrepancies that information traders ignore in their focus on potential changes in equilibrium price are not random.

Or consider value traders. To justify ignoring the possibility of changes in equilibrium price between the trade that opens their positions and the trade that closes them, they need to be able to assume that these changes are random—as likely to help as hurt them. For them to transact with information traders on the other side, however, the latter must be motivated by the expectation of a change in equilibrium value. The change cannot be good for information traders on the other side without being bad for the value traders.

If trading risks are not random, then viewing value trading as searching for bargains or information trading as scooping the consensus is dangerously oversimple. Most trades will not execute unless genuine research motivation exists on both sides. Indeed, one would expect the average active trade to be one in which the transactors break even before brokerage commission and dealer spread. Exhibit 41.3 illustrates such a trade: The information trader loses on the cost of buying and then selling what he gains from the increase in equilibrium value (compare with Exhibit 41.1). The value trader loses on the change in equilibrium value (i.e., on getting bagged) what he gains by trading at prices different from equilibrium (compare with Figure Exhibit 41.2).

## INVISIBLE TRADING COSTS DEFINED

The oversimple view leads to a conception of active investing as a game that can be won but not lost. Curiously, this view accords nicely with the old academic notion of efficient markets: If information gets into the consensus instantly, value traders have nothing to worry about. If trade price never departs from consensus price, information traders have nothing to worry about.

If, contrary to the old academic view, securities markets are not perfectly efficient, then today's consensus price is no longer an unbiased estimate of the future consensus price and today's trade price is no longer a good proxy for today's consensus price.

The value trader can get bagged, and the information trader can pay an exorbitant price for trading quickly.

In fact, markets are not perfectly efficient. Departures from perfect efficiency are unavoidable, because without them, the party on the other side of the transaction would have no motive to transact. Because these departures provide the necassary motivation, they are transaction costs.

These costs are orders of magnitude larger than the ostensible transaction costs— brokerage commissions and market impact. We call them invisible costs of trading, because value traders will not know what information made their bargains possible until it bags them. Information traders will not know how much their trade prices departed from consensus prices until the trading pressure generated by their information abates. It is hard to understand how active investors can consistently lose big if their only costs are brokerge commissions and market impact, but it is easy to understand when invisible trading costs are considered.

## EXCHANGING PRICE FOR TIME

These two modes of active investing require different kinds of research and different kinds of trading. Value traders are interested in trading only if a perceived price discrepancy becomes large enough to make it worthwhile. Because they use publicly available, consensus-type information, they are under no pressure to trade quickly. Time is unimportant compared with price. Information traders want to trade before their nonpublicly known or nonconsensus information gets into the consensus and hence into price. Price is unimportant compared with time.

Because information traders are highly unlikely to arrive in the market at precisely the same time, they are rarely able to accommodate each other's trades. Unless one or both errs in estimated equilibrium value, a trade price cannot simultaneously be a bargain (in the symmetrical sense noted) to both a value-motivated buyer and a value-motivated seller. A trade will not occur, however, unless both sides are motivated. Thus, the transaction of greatest practical interest has an anxious information trader on one side and a bargain-hunting value trader on the other.

Adversarial transactions in individual securities typically involve the exchange of time for price. One transactor is making a price sacrifice to trade at a time of his choosing; the other is forgoing the time initiative in the transaction to trade at a price of his choosing.

In every completed transaction, one party would have fared better by not trading. No information is so important that its worth cannot be exceeded by the cost of trading quickly. No price bargain is so big that it cannot be exceeded by the value of new information adverse to the bargain hunter. On every trade, time is worth either more than it costs or less. If the former, the transactor buying time (the information trader) will win and the transactor selling time (the value trader) will lose. If the latter, the transactor selling time will win and the transactor buying time will lose. The active investors who lose consistently are those who buy time for more than it is worth or sell time for less than it is worth. Although couched in specific security transactions, what active investors are really buying and selling is time.

By "time," of course, we mean the right to transact quickly. What information traders, eager to trade before their information gets impounded in price, are willing to pay for this right detrmines its worth. What they actually pay is the bargain—the difference between trade price and equilibrium price—demanded by bargain-hunting value traders. To know what time costs, one must have a good estimate of equilibrium price with which to compare trade price.

## ACTIVE INVESTING IS A GAME OF ODDS

In practice, value traders know (or think they know) the cost of time, because they can compare trade price with their estimate of consensus price, but they do not know what time is worth. Because they have new information, information traders know what time is worth, but because they are in too much of a hurry to estimate consensus price, they do not know what time costs.

A problem occurs because active investors' research fails to supply both sides of the worth-cost comparison. In practice, they look to their trading desks to supply the missing side. Value traders hope their trading desks can smoke out the information that is creating the bargain their research identifies. Information traders hope their trading desks can estimate the cost of trading quickly, including the price effects of other investors' anxious trading. Of course, even a sophisticated trading desk is dealing with fragmentary information. Even if active investors are dealing with hard information on one side of the equation, they are dealing with soft information on the other.

The situation is reminiscent of a card game in which you know your cards but not your opponent's. You know your research motive, and the transactor on the other side knows his, but you do not know his research motive and he does not know yours. The outcome depends on the value of your research, the value of the other player's research, and the trade price. Negotiations on trade price are loosely analogous to betting in poker or bidding in contract bridge. Fund managers' contributions to performance derive from their skill in these negotiations—skill in ferreting out information about the other transactors' research motives while concealing information about their own.

Obviously, the task of negotiating securities transactions cannot be conducted in a vacuum. In particular, it is not logical to decide to make a trade and then try to figure out how to execute it. Nor is it logical to give the responsibility for decisions to one party (the fund manager) and the responsibility for executions to another (the trader). Such arrangements are analogous to giving one party in a poker game the responsibility for deciding whether to pass and another party responsibility for deciding how much to bet, or in bridge, giving one player the decision whether to bid the contract and giving another the responsibility for bidding. In these card games, knowing when to play and when not to play is vital. It is also vital in active investing. Like these card games, active investing is a game of odds. Research deals the cards, but it cannot decide when to raise and when to fold.

## HOW WE THINK ABOUT THE NATURE OF THE GAME

Most of the price distortions value traders detect are caused by anxious information traders. If their information is impounded in the price after value traders trade, the latter experience an adverse price move equal to the value of the information. Information traders, however, have no easy way of knowing whether their information is already in the price. So many of the "bargains" value traders perceive are caused by information that will not result in an adverse price movement.

If value traders had their way, they would trade only on those price bargains created by information that was already in the price at the time of their trades. They cannot get bagged by this information.

The media are an obvious clue. The numbers in the body of the following array are probabilities for the four possible joint events that can occur when new information creates an apparent price bargain:

|  | In Price (P) | Not in Price (P′) |  |
|---|---|---|---|
| Story in media (S) | 0.4 | 0.1 | 0.5 |
| No story in media (S′) | 0.2 | 0.3 | 0.5 |
|  | 0.6 | 0.4 |  |

The four possibilities for the apparent price bargain are as follows:

- It can be the result of information already in both the media and the price (i.e., the price change exceeds that justified by the information) (S/P).
- It can be impounded in the price without ever having been acknowledged in the media (S′/P).
- It can be acknowledged in the media without yet being impounded in the price (S/P′).
- It has yet to be either acknowledged by the media or impounded in the price (i.e., *equilibrium* price has not moved but *trade* price has moved) (S′/P′).

The values shown for these joint probabilities are chosen merely to be illustrative. They sum to 1, as they must, because the four joint events are the only ones possible (and are obviously mutually exclusive). The values for the second and third events are small. (Common sense suggests both are unlikely, and the third is perhaps even less likely than the second.)

Is a big story in the media that could generate some anxious information trading? Does the stock appear to be mispriced even when the value implications of the story are taken into account? If the answer to both questions is "yes," then the opportunity for value traders falls in the upper left quadrant of the array.

A story in the media (consistent, of course, with the observed discrepancy) increases the likelihood that the information causing the discrepancy is already in the price. As the joint probability in the upper right suggests, however, the story does not guarantee it: Another story, not in the media, may not yet be in the price.

If no story is in the media, then the information is much less likely to be in the price. The story might have disseminated broadly through the population of investors without ever getting into the media, but this case is unlikely; hence, the low joint probability in the lower left quadrant.

Value traders are not interested in joint probabilities. They want to know whether the information causing the price discrepancy they observe is in the price. If it is, they want to trade. If it is not, the price discrepancy may not be big enough to compensate them for getting bagged. In other words, they want to know the conditional probabilities of the information's being already impounded in the price, given that a story has or has not appeared in the media.

Bayes's theorem tells value investors how to calculate those probabilities. If the story is in the media, the probability that the information is already in the price (PIS) is the joint probability that the story is both in the price and in the media, divided by the sum of the probabilities that the story is in the price as well as the media and that the story is not in the price although in the media. We have

$$PIS = \frac{PS}{PS + P'S} = \frac{0.4}{0.4 + 0.1} = 0.8$$

If the story is not in the media, the probability that the information is already in the price is the joint probability that the story is in the price, although not in the media, divided by the sum of the probabilities in the "no story in media" row—that is, the sum of the respective probabilities that the story is in the price, although not in the media, and that the story is in neither the media nor the price. We have

$$PIS = \frac{PS'}{PS' + P'S'} = \frac{0.2}{0.2 + 0.3} = 0.4$$

If, on the other hand, value traders ignore the media, then the probability that the information is in the price is simply the sum of the joint probabilities in the "in price" column (because these cases exhaust all the ways the information can be in the price). We have

$$0.4 + 0.2 = 0.6$$

The probability of getting bagged is the probability that the information is not in the price, or 1 minus these probabilities ($1 - 0.6 = 0.4$).

The numbers in this matrix are merely illustrative, but they do suggest that value traders can reduce their trading costs by playing the odds. If they ignore the media, for example, their probability of getting bagged is 0.4; their expected cost of getting bagged by the information is 0.4 times the value of the information. If they break even before brokerage commissions and dealer spread, their invisible trading costs just offset the value of their research:

$$\text{Price discrepancy} - 0.4(\text{Bagging information}) = 0$$

If value traders consistently win at the expense of information traders, some of the latter will leave the game even as more value investors are drawn into the game. The bargains required to equilibrate value and information trading will shrink. The adjustment will continue until the two kinds of investors are again breaking even. The reverse will happen if information traders are gaining at the expense of value traders. Thus our example is not chosen idly; it represents the equilibrium bargain in departures of trade price from equilibrium price. If, on average, the price bargains motivating a value trader's trades are worth 20 percent of the consensus value of the stock, then to break even requires

$$0.2 - 0.4(\text{Bagging information}) = 0$$

$$\text{Bagging information} = \frac{0.2}{0.4} = 0.5$$

or 50 percent of the value of the stock.

If our value traders trade only when a story is prominent in the media, then, as we calculated, the story would be in the price of the stock 80 percent of the time, but the value traders would get bagged 20 percent of the time and their gain per trade would be

$$0.2 - (1 - 0.8)(0.5) = 0.2 - 0.1 = 0.1$$

or 10 percent. According to our hypothetical table, media stories occur half the time (i.e., half the times that our active investors identify bargains). Assume their research has been identifying bargains at a rate sufficient to generate turnover of 100 percent a year. Then their new turnover rate will be half that, or 50 percent a year. Their abnormal annual return, before commissions and dealer spread, will be

$$0.5 \times 0.1 = 0.05$$

or 5 percent a year. Assuming round-trip visible trading costs of 2 percent, we have

$$0.5(0.1 - 0.02) = 0.04$$

or 4 percent a year for their net gain from active investing. For their former losses to brokerage and dealer spread, we have

$$1.00 \times 0.02 = 0.02$$

or 2 percent a year. The total improvement is 600 basis points. Because public news stories are, after all, public, no additional research is involved.

For most active investors, 600 basis points is a substantial improvement. Why do value traders not invest this way? For several reasons:

- Out of sight, out of mind. Invisible trading costs are not easily measured, much less seen or visualized.
- Because they trade with dealers, rather than each other, active investors forget that theirs is an adversary game—and a zero-sum game at that—before commissions and dealer spread.
- If the average investor underperforms the market, his trading costs exceed the value of his research. Yet he devoted much time and effort to research. He rarely thinks about the motives of his trading counterpart.
- Lacking a clear picture of the other transactor's trading motive, he sees his task as buying and selling securities, rather than buying and selling time.
- Because he does not see active investing as buying and selling time, he does not realize that his task is comparing what time is worth to what it costs—and that

his research supplies only one side of this comparison. He does not see active investing as a game of odds—about knowing when to trade and when not to trade.

## CONCLUSION

Trades are not executed; they are negotiated. Concluding these negotiations, which will jointly determine which trades are actually made and the price of those trades, is the line function in portfolio management.

Research is a necessary, even critical, input to the negotiating process, but by itself, it can never be sufficient.

Thus, the research function stands in a staff support relationship to the negotiator. The trading desk also stands in a staff support relationship to the negotiator; its main function is not merely to execute but to supply that support.

## QUESTION AND ANSWER SESSION

**Question:**   What do you believe to be the proportion of value traders as opposed to information traders in the market?

**Treynor:**   If no dealers existed, and if you accepted the notion that the paradigmatic trade is one with a value trader on one side and an information trader on the other, then the two populations would have to be almost equal. Of course, dealers do exist, and I have not focused nearly enough attention in this presentation on dealers and their role. They change the necessary equality of value and information traders, because as a previous speaker very correctly said, the real function of dealers is to connect anxious traders, most of them information traders, arriving in the market at different times, that deprives value traders of most of their opportunities to trade with information traders until a second, offsetting information trader arrives. That basically short-circuits the process I described. It permits information buyers to transact with information sellers across time, which then means that, in principle, the only trades the value traders get are those in which the dealers, having accumulated (more or less by random) positions so large that they cannot sleep at night, take the initiative and lay off to value traders at value traders' prices. Those are almost the only trades value traders get.

**Question:**   Many people seem to categorize themselves as value traders, and very few categorize themselves as information traders. Please comment.

**Treynor:**   My hunch is that most retail investors are information traders. They do not have the organization, discipline, or time to be anything else. In fact, a retail institutional split exists between information- and value-motivated traders.

**Question:**   How does your analysis carry over from the stock-picking type of trading to the quantitative investor, the factor-model type of investor who is trying to forecast based on macroeconomic indicators and looking at exposure rather than particular stocks?

**Treynor:**   Basically, those kinds of traders are "timers." Timers, in my lexicon, make macro forecasts or climate forecasts, deduce something about the implications for the vehicle securities, and then trade appropriately. I consider myself a timer because I am much more interested in the top-down problem than any other in active investing. After thinking about it for years, I must conclude that I do not understand the trading aspect of timing at all.

**Question:** You made an implicit assumption about the accuracy of the media. Does the issue of disinformation or just parroting press releases by interested parties change the analysis or add a couple of lines to your matrix?

**Treynor:** I do not know why anybody uses inside information when rumor is so much more profitable. With inside information, you only get a one-way profit, but with rumor, especially false tumor, you get a two-way profit. Of course, it is illegal strictly speaking, but who is going to track down the source of a rumor? We get spurious information, but we also get valid information from which active investors—information investors—draw invalid conclusions and identify the wrong stock to trade. Remember the famous Seaboard Air Line case? Something good happened to airline stocks, and Seaboard Air Line—which was a railroad—boomed. The most common case, however, is trading on valid conclusions drawn from valid information that is already in the price.

**Question:** You often have value investors teamed up with information traders. Does this lead to unnecessary costs, or can it, in fact, have some positive aspects?

**Treynor:** I used to think the answer to this question was very simple. On an institutional level, because speed is important for information traders, the best organization is one with as few points of decision, as little hierarchy, as possible. Speed is of the essence: You win when you trade before information gets into the price; you lose every time you trade after information gets into the price. You do not want the decision maker inhibited by knowing that some guy above him and another guy above him are going to second-guess the decision maker's decision.

On the other hand, as Sydney Cottle used to say so often and so eloquently, value investing is comparison. If you are going to have a broad base for comparison, you need to have discipline. You need to have consistent value structures and organizations that enforce that consistency. Because speed is not important, it does not cost you much to have a hierarchy to review the process on several levels.

# CHAPTER 42

# The Invisible Costs of Trading

## Trading Is An Adversary Game—and a Zero-Sum Game at That

I believe in active securities management. My only complaint is that some active managers seem to have a narrow understanding of what the game is. This is particularly true of what I will call the invisible costs of trading. Managers rarely mention them in discussions of trading cost; conventional measures of that cost omit them.

A view of trading that excludes these costs leads to the conclusion that bad performance is due to bad research. But this is impossible: The purpose of research is to forecast price movements. Worthless research makes worthless forecasts. A worthless forecast is equally likely to be followed by a price increase or a price decrease. Worthless research leads to unnecessary risk and unnecessary trading—but, in terms of its average contribution to return, gross of the visible trading costs, bad research cannot be worse than no research.

Most of the return in a diversified portfolio is the broad impact of economic and market news on the categories of assets held. This impact is the same whether the assets within these categories are traded or merely held. For active portfolios, therefore, the meaningful measure of performance is not total return, but the (algebraic) increment in return due to trading.

For long-term, average experience in diversified portfolios, we have the crude equation:

$$\text{Return from Trading} = \text{Research} - \text{Trading Cost}$$

in which the return from trading is often negative, but the research term never is. In such portfolios, consistent underperformance cannot be explained by bad research. The culprit must be trading cost. But the visible trading costs—commissions plus dealer spread—are too modest for listed stocks to explain any significant underperformance.

## KEY ELEMENTS IN INVESTMENT PERFORMANCE

The explanation for costs of trading lies in two facts:

1. Trading is a zero-sum game (before dealer spread and commissions). For every trade, there will be one winner and one loser (relative, of course, to not trading).
2. In its motivation, the great majority of securities trading is adversarial.

Broadly speaking, active investors contemplate two kinds of price movement:

1. Changes in equilibrium price.
2. Changes in the discrepancy between trade price and equilibrium price.

The difference in trade prices between any two points in time is always some combination of these two kinds of price movement. All active investing is motivated by forecasts, implicit or explicit, of one kind or the other.

The information trader, for example, believes he knows something other investors don't know. It isn't in equilibrium price yet, but it will be when knowledge spreads to enough other investors. The information trader is betting on a change in equilibrium price. He or she relies on research to dig up information with potential market impact that isn't widely known—i.e., on *investigation*.

The value trader, on the other hand, believes he has identified a discrepancy between trade price and equilibrium value. He believes such discrepancies are only temporary. He is betting that, given market pressures toward equilibration, the observed discrepancy is more likely to diminish than increase. He relies on research to provide an estimate of equilibrium value he can compare to trade price—an *analysis* of the facts and figures in the public domain.

The distinction between information and value traders cuts across the distinction between buyers and sellers. Information traders can be motivated by either good news (in which case they are buyers) or bad news (in which case they are sellers). Value traders can be motivated by a trade price above what they think a security is worth (in which case they are sellers) or by a trade price below what they think a security is worth (in which case they are buyers).

To the layperson, a bargain price is a price below true (i.e., equilibrium) value. But value traders can be motivated by either a trade price above their perception of equilibrium or a trade price below it. Both price discrepancies represent potential profitable trading opportunities—i.e., bargains. In this symmetric sense of the word, we shall refer to value traders as *bargain hunters*.

## ACTIVE INVESTING INCURS TRADING, AS WELL AS HOLDING, RISKS

We have noted that the information trader is betting on a change in equilibrium, while the value trader is betting on a change in the discrepancy between trade price and equilibrium price. There are risks for both, however. Even if the value trader has estimated equilibrium price correctly and identified a true bargain, equilibrium price may change before he can close out his position. Even if the information trader has uncovered information that correctly anticipates a change in equilibrium price,

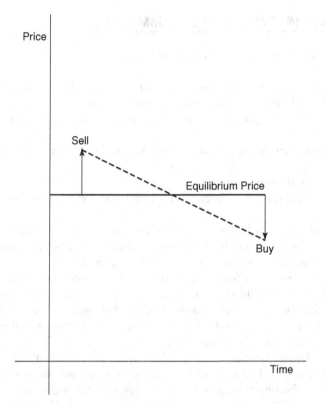

**EXHIBIT 42.1** How the Value Trader Sees Trading Opportunity

he may be forced to buy and sell (or sell and buy) at trade prices different from equilibrium. (See Exhibits 42.1 and 42.2.)

The key question for the active investor is whether these risks are merely random risks. If so, then the information trader is probably justified in focusing on the potential change in equilibrium price. If so, then the value trader is probably justified in focusing on departures of trade price from the estimate of equilibrium. Is the active investor as likely to gain as lose from these risks?

Consider the information trader. In order to justify ignoring discrepancies between the the prices he trades at and equilibrium prices at the times of his trades, he needs to be able to assume that these discrepancies are random. But in order for him to trasacnt with a value trader on the other side, for example, the latter must be motivated—must perceive a discrepancy between trade price and equilibrium that offers a bargain. The discrepancy cannot be good for the value trader on the other side without being bad for the information trader. The trade price discrepancies the information trader is ignoring in his focus on potential changes in equilibrium price are not random.

Or consider the value trader. In order to justify ignoring the possibility of changes in equilibrium price between the trade that opens the position and the trade that closes it, he needs to be able to assume that these changes are random—as likely to help as to hurt. But in order for him to transact with an information trader on the other side, for

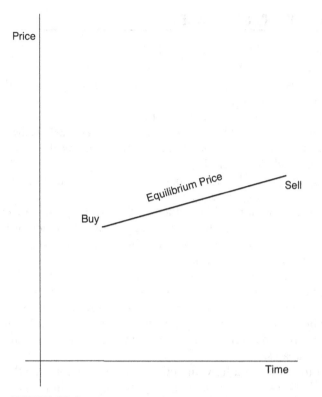

**EXHIBIT 42.2**   How the Information Trader Sees
Trading Opportunity

example, the latter must be motivated—must expect a change in equilibrium value. The change cannot be good for the information trader on the other side without being bad for the value trader.

If trading risks are not random, then it is dangerously oversimple to view value trading as searching for bargains, or information trading as scooping the consensus. (See Exhibit 42.3.)

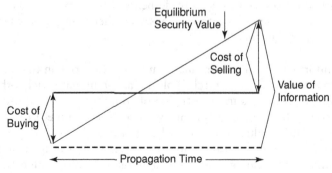

**EXHIBIT 42.3**   Trading on Good News

## INVISIBLE TRADING COSTS DEFINED

The oversimple view leads to a conception of active investing as a game that can be won, but not lost. Curiously, this view accords nicely with the old academic notion of efficient markets; if information gets into the consensus instantly, the value trader has nothing to worry about. If trade price never departs from consensus price, the information trader has nothing to worry about.

But if, contrary to the old academic view, securities markets aren't perfectly efficient, then today's consensus price is no longer an unbiased estimate of the future consensus price. And today's trade price is no longer a good proxy for today's consensus price. The value trader can get bagged, and the information trader can pay an exorbitant price for trading quickly.

In fact, markets are not perfectly efficient. Departures from perfect efficiency are unavoidable, because, without them, the party on the other side of the transaction would have no motive to transact. Because these departures provide the necessary motivation, *they are costs of transacting*.

These costs are orders of magnitude bigger than the ostensible costs of transacting—brokerage commissions and market impact. We call them the invisible costs of trading. Why invisible? The value trader won't know what information made his bargain possible until it bags him. The information trader won't know how much his trade price departed from consensus price until the trading pressure generated by his information abates.

It is hard to understand how an active investor can consistently lose big if the only costs are brokerage commission and market impact. But it's easy to understand when one allows for the invisible costs of trading.

## EXCHANGING PRICE FOR TIME

We have noted that these two modes of active investing call for different kinds of research. They also call for different kinds of trading:

- The value trader is interested in trading only if a perceived price discrepancy gets big enough to make it worth the while. Because he uses publicly available information, he is under no pressure to trade quickly. Time is unimportant compared to price.
- The information trader wants to trade before his nonpublicly known or nonconsensus information gets into the consensus, hence into price. Price is unimportant compared to time.

Because information traders are highly unlikely to arrive in the market at precisely the same time, they are rarely able to accommodate each other's trades. And, unless one or both errs in his estimate of equilibrim value, a trade price cannot simultaneously be a bargain (in the symmetric sense noted) to both a value-motivated buyer and a value-motivated seller. But a trade won't occur unless both sides are motivated. Thus the transaction of greatest practical interest has an anxious information trader on one side and a bargain-hunting value trader on the other.

Adversarial transactions in individual securities typically involve the exchange of time for price: One transactor is making a price sacrifice in order to trade at a time of his choosing; the other is forgoing the time initiative in the transaction in order to trade at a price of his choosing.

In every completed transaction, there is one party who would have been better off not trading. There is no information so important its worth cannot be exceeded by the cost of trading quickly. There is no price bargain so big that it cannot be exceeded by the value of new information adverse to the bargain hunter.

On every trade, time is either worth more than it costs, or less. If the former, the transactor buying time (e.g., the information trader) will win, and the transactor selling time (e.g., the value trader) will lose. If the latter, the transactor selling time will win, and the transactor buying time will lose.

The active investors who lose consistently are those who buy time for more than it is worth or sell time for less than it is worth. Although couched in specific security transactions, what active investors are really buying and selling is time.

By "time," of course, we mean the right to transact quickly. What information traders, anxious to trade before their information gets impounded in price, are willing to pay for this right determines its worth. What they actually pay is the bargain—the difference between trade price and equilibrium price—demanded by bargain-hunting value traders. In order to know what "time" costs, one must have a good estimate of equilibrium price with which to compare trade price.

## ACTIVE INVESTING IS A GAME OF ODDS

In practice, the value trader knows (or thinks he knows) the cost of time, because he can compare trade price with his estimate of consensus price. But he doesn't know what time is worth. Because he has new information, the information trader knows what time is worth, but, because he is in too much of a hurry to estimate consensus price, he doesn't know what time costs.

A problem occurs because the active investor's *research* fails to supply both sides of the worth- versus cost-of comparison. In fact he looks to the *trading desk* to supply the missing side. The value trader hopes his trading desk can smoke out the information that is creating the bargain his research identifies. The information trader hopes his trading desk can estimate the cost of trading quickly, including the price effects of other investors' anxious trading.

But, of course, even a sophisticated trading desk is dealing with fragmentary information. Even if active investors are dealing with hard information on one side of the equation, they are dealing with soft information on the other.

The situation is reminiscent of a card game in which you know your cards but not your opponent's. You know your research motive, and the transactor on the other side knows his. But you don't know his research motive, and he doesn't know yours. The outcome depends on the value of your research, the value of his research, and the trade price.

Negotiations on trade price are loosely analogous to betting in poker, or bidding in contract bridge. The fund manager's contribution to performance derives from skill in these negotiations—skill in ferreting out information about the other transactor's research motive while concealing information about his own.

It should be obvious that the task of negotiating securities transactions cannot be conducted in a vacuum. In particular, it isn't logical to decide to make a trade and then try to figure out how to execute it. Nor is it logical to give the responsibility for decisions to one party (i.e., the fund manager) and the responsibility for executions to another (i.e., the trader).

Such arrangements would be analogous in poker to giving the responsibility for deciding whether or not to pass to one party and the responsibility for deciding how much to bet to another. Or, in bridge, giving the decision whether to bid the contract to one party and the responsibility for bidding to another.

In these card games, knowing when to play and when not to play is vital. It is also vital in active investing. Like these card games, *active investing is a game of odds.* Research deals the cards, but it can't decide when to raise and when to fold.

## HOW WE THINK ABOUT THE NATURE OF THE GAME AFFECTS OUR PERFORMANCE

Consider an example. Most of the price distortions detected by the value trader are caused by anxious information traders. If their information is impounded in the price *after* the value trader trades, he experiences an adverse price move equal to the value of the information. But, as noted, information traders have no easy way of knowing whether their information is already in the price. So many of the so-called bargains perceived by the value trader are caused by information that won't result in an adverse price movement.

If the value trader had his way, he would trade only on those price bargains created by information that is already in the price at the time of his trade, since he can't get bagged by this information.

The media are an obvious clue: Is there a big story in the media that could generate some anxious information trading? Does the stock appear to be mispriced even when the value implications of the story are taken into account? If the answer to both questions is "yes," then the opportunity for the value trader falls in the upper left quadrant in Exhibit 42.4. (The table applies only when the value investor has identified a price discrepancy.)

A story in the media (consistent, of course, with the observed discrepancy) increases the likelihood that the information causing the discrepancy is already in the price. But, as the joint probability in the upper right of Exhibit 42.4 suggests, the story doesn't guarantee it: There may be *another* story, not in the media, that is not yet in the price.

But if there is *no* story in the media, then the information is much less likely to be in the price. The story *might* have disseminated broadly through the population

**EXHIBIT 42.4** Joint Probabilities (bargain price only)

| | In Price (P) | Not in Price (P′) | Probability |
|---|---|---|---|
| Story in Media (S) | 0.4 | 0.1 | 0.5 |
| No Story in | 0.2 | 0.3 | 0.5 |
| Media (S′) | 0.6 | 0.4 | |

of investors without ever getting into the media. But this case is unlikely; hence the low joint probability in the lower left in Exhibit 42.4.

The value trader is not interested in joint probabilities. He wants to know whether the information causing the price discrepancy he observes is in the price. If it is, he wants to trade. If it isn't, the price discrepancy may not be big enough to compensate him for getting bagged. In other words, he wants to know the *conditional* probabilities of the information's being already impounded in the price, given that there is, or is not, a story in the media.

Bayes' theorem tells the value investor how to calculate those probabilities. If the story is in the media, the probability that the information is already in the price is the joint probability that the story is both in the price and the media, divided by the sum of the probabilities in the "story in media" row—i.e., the sum of the respective probabilities that the story is in the price as well as the media and that the story is not in the price although in the media.

We have

$$\text{PIS} = \frac{\text{PS}}{\text{PS} + \text{P'S}} = \frac{0.4}{0.4 + 0.1} = 0.8$$

If the story is not in the media, the probability that the information is already in the price is the joint probability that the story is in the price though not in the media, divided by the sum of the probabilities in the "story not in media" row—in other words, the sum of the respective probabilities that the story is in the price though not in the media and that the story is in neither the media nor the price.

We have

$$\text{PIS}' = \frac{\text{PS}'}{\text{PS}' + \text{P'S}'} = \frac{0.2}{0.2 + 0.3} = 0.4$$

If, on the other hand, the value trader ignores the media, then the probability that the information is in the price is simply the sum of the joint probabilities in the "In Price" column (since these cases exhaust all the ways the information can be in the price).

We have

$$0.4 + 0.2 = 0.6$$

The probability of getting bagged is the probability that the information is not in the price, or one minus these probabilities.

The numbers in our table are merely illustrative, but they do suggest that a value trader can reduce trading cost by playing the odds. If he ignores the media, for example, his probability of getting bagged is one minus 0.6, or 0.4; the expected cost of getting bagged by the information is 0.4 times the value of the information. If he breaks even before brokerage commissions and dealer spread, his invisible trading cost just offsets the value of his research:

$$\text{Price Discrepancy} - 0.4 \, (\text{Bagging Information}) = 0$$

If value traders are consistently winning at the expense of information traders, some of the latter will leave the game even as more value investors are drawn into the game. The bargains required to equilibrate value and information trading will shrink. The adjustment will continue until the two kinds of investors are again "breaking even." The reverse will happen if information traders are gaining at the expense of value traders.

Thus our example is not chosen idly: It represents the equilibrium bargain in departures of trade price from equilibrium price. If on average the price bargains motivating trades are worth 20 percent of the consensus value of the stock, then break-even for a value trader requires

$$0.2 - 0.4 \text{ (Bagging Information)} = 0$$

$$\text{Bagging Information} = 0.2/0.4 = 0.5$$

or 50 percent of the value of the stock.

If our value trader trades only when a story is prominent in the media, then, as we calculated, the story would be in the price of the stock 80 percent of the time, but he would get bagged 20 percent of the time, and his gain per trade would be

$$20\% - (1 - 0.8) \times (50\%) = 20\% - 10\% = 10\%$$

According to our hypothetical table, media stories occur half the time (i.e., half the time that our active investor identifies a bargain). Assume his research has been identifying bargains at a rate sufficient to generate 100 percent per year turnover. Then his new turnover rate will be half that, or 50 percent per year. His abnormal return per year, before commissions and dealer spread, will be

$$50\% \times 10\% = 5\%$$

Assuming round-trip visible costs of trading of 2 percent, we have

$$50\% \times (10\% - 2\%) = 4\%$$

**EXHIBIT 42.5**   Shared Beliefs of Active Managers

---

What you hold is more important than how you trade.

Trading costs are measured by commissions and short-term "market impact" (i.e., visible costs).

Other side of most securities trades is a dealer.

Market inefficiency is measured by what it takes to motivate the dealer.

Research is more important than trading.

Portfolio decisions and the costs of executing are separate problems.

If an active investor loses consistently, it is because of faulty research.

Since, before commissions and dealer spread, trading is as likely to gain as lose, research ideas are pure gravy. The object of the game is to trade on as many as possible.

---

**EXHIBIT 42.6**   Contrasting Beliefs

| Information Managers | Value Managers |
|---|---|
| Departures from equilibrium price are small. | Departures of trade price from equilibrium create bargains. |
| I get my information before it is impounded in price. | New information is impounded quickly. |
| The generation of private information is key to effective research. | Analysis of published financial data is key to effective research. |
| In trading, time is more important than price. | In trading, price is more important than time. |

for his net gain from active investing. For his former losses to brokerage and dealer spread we have

$$100\% \times 2\% = 2\% \text{ per year}$$

The total improvement is 600 basis points. Since public news stories are, after all, public, no additional research is involved.

For most active investors, 600 basis points is a substantial improvement. Why don't value traders invest this way?

Exhibits 42.5 and 42.6 summarize active investors' beliefs about active management. Why do active investors think this way?

- Out of sight, out of mind. The invisible costs of trading are not easily measured, much less seen or visualized.
- Because they trade with dealers, rather than each other, active investors forget that theirs is an adversary game—and a zero-sum game at that—before commissions and dealer spread.
- If the average investor underperforms the market, his trading costs exceed the value of his research. Yet he devotes most of his time and effort to research. He rarely thinks about the motives of his trading counterpart.
- Lacking a clear picture of the other transactor's trading motive, he sees his task as buying and selling securities, rather than buying and selling time.
- Because he doesn't see active investing as buying and selling time, he doesn't realize that his task is comparing what time is worth to what it costs—and that his research supplies only one side of this comparison. He doesn't see active investing as a game of odds—about knowing when to trade and when not to trade.

## CONCLUSIONS

Trades are not executed; they are negotiated. Conducting these negotiations, which will jointly determine which trades are actually made and the price of those trades, is the line function in portfolio management.

Research is a necessary, even critical, input to the negotiating process, but by itself it can never be sufficient.

Thus the research function stands in a staff support relation to the negotiator. The trading desk also stands in a staff support relation to the negotiator; its main function is not merely to execute but to supply that support.

## Notes

1. Reprinted, with permission, from the proceedings of an AIMR conference in Toronto in November 1992 entitled *Execution Techniques, True Trading Costs, and the Microstructure of Markets.*
2. The author gratefully acknowledges the many valuable questions and criticisms raised by James R. Vertin, Chairman, AIMR Council on Education and Research, and Donald L. Tuttle, Senior Vice President, AIMR, He especially appreciates the open-minded consideration of what is still a very controversial stance.

# CHAPTER 43

# Zero Sum

**D**o repeated patterns exist in the way active managers research and execute that, after luck has averaged out across dozens of trades, ultimately make the difference between success and failure? There is a right way to change a tire, make an omelet, or remove an appendix, but if there is a right way to manage securities actively, managers do not agree on what it is. When Crerend and Broom (1974) surveyed active management firms, they found stunning diversity in organization, decision process, and culture.

As Charley Ellis pointed out in his 1971 book *Institutional Investing*, active management tends to be a hectic, high-pressure activity focused on the specifics of the current trade. It does not lend itself to reflection, to focusing on abstract principles. So, because they are not examined, patterns in the way active managers manage tend to become grooves—irrespective of their merits. Isn't it time to begin asking certain basic questions: What *is* the active management game? When we play the game, how do we win, how do we lose?

## WHAT IS THE ACTIVE MANAGEMENT GAME?

Many active investors view active portfolio management as a treasure hunt in which the object is to identify as many investment opportunities as possible and act on them, almost without regard for cost. If the opportunities offer gross gains of 20 percent or more and trading costs are confined to brokerage and dealer spread—say, 2 percent or less—then the "treasure hunt" model is a useful model: The active manager should focus on the opportunities and ignore the cost or delegate cost control to the trading desk.

Some games, however, fit the treasure hunt model badly. A football quarterback, for example, cannot successfully focus on touchdown passes and delegate interceptions. A chess player cannot successfully focus on attacking an opponent's king and delegate defending her own king. A poker player cannot successfully focus on the cards in his hand and delegate speculation about the cards held by the other players. Some chess players and some poker players do focus exclusively on offense, but nearly all who do are failures. Applying the treasure hunt model to games it does not fit is dangerous.

Football, chess, and poker are *adversarial*, not treasure hunting, games, with opponents who have as much to gain from beating you as you have to gain from beating them. Thinking your offense is more important to the outcome than their offense is *hubris*. And if their offense is as important as your offense, then your *defense* is as important as your offense.

I have argued that because predictions based on investment research cannot correlate with actual price changes worse than randomly, "bad research cannot be worse than no research" (1994, p. 71). Substantial, persistent underperformance must be the result, instead, of trading costs that are far larger than mere commissions or dealer spreads. The source of these other (hidden) costs of trading is two facts:

- In its motivation, the great majority of securities trading is adversarial. Institutional trades are likely to be even more adversarial than retail trades.
- Trading (before dealer spread and commissions) is a zero-sum game. Every trade will have one winner and one loser (relative, of course, to not trading).

Can both sides profit from a transaction? If the assets they are exchanging appreciate, then both parties to the transaction profit, but if one asset appreciates more than the other, the transaction reverses the relative performance of the parties to the transaction. One is better off for having transacted; the other is worse off. Their combined gain is what they would have gained without a transaction. So, what one party gains from the transaction, the other loses. For example, in the absence of a transaction, one gains $y_1$ and the other gain $y_2$, for an aggregate gain of $y_1 + y_2$. With a transaction, the transactor who formerly owned asset #1 gains

$$y_2 = y_1 + (y_2 - y_1)$$

and the transactor who formerly owned asset #2 gains

$$y_1 = y_2 + (y_1 - y_2)$$

where the expressions in parentheses are the gains or losses from transacting. Because these expressions sum to zero identically, active management is a zero-sum game.

Whether it is an adversarial game depends on whether transactors are playing to win. If they are using their securities merely as a cash substitute, they are not playing to win and active management is not an adversarial game. Much of today's trading is done by institutional funds that have hundreds or even thousands of claimants, and the liquidity needs are virtually random from claimant to claimant. So, institutions' cash inflows and outflows are sufficiently independent that they largely offset— roughly half will be buying and half will be selling. Institutional trading, therefore, is rarely liquidity motivated; the institutions are playing to win.[1]

In traditional securities transactions, one of the assets exchanged is cash. In these transactions, the gains and losses are confined to the other asset. The asset's new market price will equal the old market price plus the (algebraic) sum of the value increments implied by the traders' motives. Consider the asset with $v$ consensus value (the price to which value traders would agree if they all had the same information):

$$v = V(g_1, g_2, \ldots; u_1, u_2, \ldots)$$

where the $g_i$'s explain why different securities have different values at the same time and the $u_j$'s explain why the same security has different values at different times, with total differential

$$dv = \sum_i \frac{\partial V}{\partial g_i} dg_i + \sum_j \frac{\partial V}{\partial u_j} du_j$$

Corresponding to this consensus value will be a market price, $P'$, defined as

$$P' = V(g_1, g_2, \ldots; u_1, u_2, \ldots) + e$$

where $e$ measures the degree to which trading activity drives actual price $P'$ away from consensus value, with total differential

$$dP' = \sum_i \frac{\partial V}{\partial g_i} dg_i + \sum_j \frac{\partial V}{\partial u_j} du_j + de$$

where information-motivated stock pickers focus on the first term, market timers focus on the second, and value-motivated stock pickers focus on the third (the anticipated change in $e$). That is, the market price's total differential displays the insights that motivate the three kinds of active managers. A given transaction requires two motives—one to buy, one to sell—drawn from these three.

Information traders are betting on a change in the consensus price. They believe they know something other investors do not know and that their information is not yet reflected in the asset's market price but will be when knowledge spreads to enough other investors.

Timers try to anticipate changes in the consensus values of the $u$'s—the macro variables. A stock picker may be an information trader or a value trader. Either may be a buyer or a seller. Either may be trading value stocks or growth stocks (i.e., may be a "value investor" or a "growth investor").

Value traders believe they have identified a discrepancy between trade price (value) and consensus price. They believe such discrepancies are only temporary. They are betting that, given market pressures toward equilibration, the observed discrepancy is more likely to diminish than increase. The difference between *future* consensus price and *future* market price is not, of course, known, but the value trader has a nonzero assessment of the current difference and a corresponding expectation, $de$, of how that difference must change if (on average) the difference is to be zero in the future.

With these observations in mind, we can define an expected change in market price that reflects simultaneously the expectations of information traders, timers, and value traders. The expected change in market price is defined as $P - P'$, where $P$ is the "new" market price implied by the two transactors' trading motives and $P'$ is the old market price obtaining prior to the trade. The impact of each transactor's motive can plausibly be added *provided* no common element exists in the motives—that is, no overlap exists that would lead to double counting. To believe that some portion of the other transactor's motive overlaps your own is tantamount to believing that some portion of your motive is already public; hence, it is already reflected in the "old" price. In that case, you should not be including that portion in your motive. So, the normal relationship between the old and new market prices is

$$P = P' + M_1 + M_2$$

where $M_1$ and $M_2$ are the transactors' motives, measured algebraically.

In order for a transaction to take place, the transactors must have opposite views about what the asset's price change will be after the transaction. If the transactors disagree about the asset's future value, any transaction price between the transactors' expectations will produce opposite views about future price change. Of course, not all these prices will produce equilibrium, in the sense of equal and opposite active positions that the transactors given their expectations, are comfortable with. Exhibit 43.1 displays the effect of trade price and size on the willingness of transactors to trade.

The so-called equilibrium trade is the largest trade acceptable to both buyer and seller. It is also the *only* trade that enables both buyer and seller to be satisfied with their active positions. It is thus the trade toward which both trading desks are striving; it plays a key role in this discussion. Sometimes, the equilibrium trade price equals the new market price; sometimes, it does not. When it does, the return on the equilibrium trade (before the dealer spread and commissions) is zero. So, equality is the breakeven case between winning and losing.

Let $P_1$ and $P_2$ be the transactors' expectations for the new consensus price. Then, if the trade price is $p$, the transactors' expected returns are, respectively, $P_1 - p$ and $P_2 - p$. The trading rules for the respective transactors are

$$\begin{cases} h_1 = H_1(P_1 - p) \\ h_2 = H_2(P_2 - p) \end{cases}$$

where $H_1$ and $H_2$ are factors that differ from one investor to another. Treynor and Black (1973) stipulated that an investor's active holdings be proportional to expected

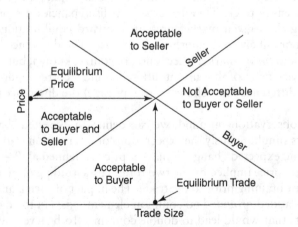

**EXHIBIT 43.1**   Effect of Trade Price and Trade Size on Acceptability of the Trade

residual return and inversely proportional to the return's variance rate, with a factor of proportionality that increases with increasing capital and declines with increasing risk aversion. Transactors can differ in their estimates of the variance, but here, we are averaging across large groups of investors. Accordingly, we combine these differences into a single constant of proportionality for each group. Trading equilibrium requires the two active positions to sum to zero, so we have

$$b_1 + b_2 = 0$$
$$= H_1(P_1 - p) + H_2(P_2 - p)$$

and

$$p = \frac{H_1 P_1 + H_2 P_2}{H_1 + H_2}$$

where $p$ is the equilibrium trade price.

Trade size $x$ here satisfies

$$x = H_1 \left( P_1 - \frac{H_1 P_1 + H_2 P_2}{H_1 + H_2} \right)$$
$$= \frac{H_1 H_2}{H_1 + H_2} (P_1 - P_2)$$

Doubling both $H_1$ and $H_2$ will double the trade size, which is proportional to $P_1 - P_2$.

## HOW WE WIN AND LOSE

Over a sufficiently long holding period, a trader's private information will become public. In that period, however, changes in the market value will often be dominated by information new to both traders. This information generates a game of chance for active traders—it generates most of their *holding risk*.

*Trading risk* arises because it is not in either trader's interest to confide in the other. The parties to a transaction are not going to exchange expectations—not, at least, until the trade is consummated. But if you know nothing about the other transactor's expectation, what should you assume—that the other trader is liquidity motivated or is trading on stale information? Let expectations $E^1$ and $E^2$ be the expectations of the respective transactors. Then,

$$\begin{cases} P_1 = P' + M_1 + E_1(M_2) \\ P_2 = P' + E_2(M_1) + M_2 \end{cases}$$

Note that $E_1(M_2)$ and $E_2(M_1)$ would constitute overlap if they were included in calculating the new consensus price.

Substituting these expected values for $P_1$ and $P_2$ into the expressions for equilibrium trade price and size produces

$$p - P' = \frac{H_1 M_1 + H_2 E_2(M_1) + H_2 M_2 + H_1 E_1(M_2)}{H_1 + H_2}$$

and

$$x = \frac{H_1 H_2}{H_1 + H_2} \{[M_1 - E_2(M_1)] - [M_2 - E_1(M_2)]\}$$

The expression for trade size makes clear that if $E_2(M_1) = M_1$ and $E_1(M_2) = M_2$, the trade size is zero. The mere fact of a trade implies that trading bias—biased expectations of the other party's motive—was present.

Trading bias also, however, has everything to do with the success or failure of the trade. Return on the trade is the difference between the new consensus price $P$ and the trade price $p$:

$$P - p = (P - P') - (p - P')$$

We can express $P - P'$ as

$$P - p' = M_1 + M_2 = \frac{H_1 M_1 + H_2 M_1 + H_1 M_2 + H_2 M_2}{H_1 + H_2}$$

Subtracting $p - P'$ from $P - P'$ produces the return on the trade:

$$P - p = \frac{H_2[M_1 - E_2(M_1)] + H_1[M_2 - E_1(M_2)]}{H_1 + H_2}$$

Return is a weighted average of the two underestimates. Subject to the weights, who wins and who loses, therefore, depends on who makes the bigger estimation error. The weights depend on who is the bigger active trader—that is, who has the bigger $H$ (risk aversion, portfolio size, and so on).

Here are four ways to lose the active management game:

- Have no motive (then, the other party cannot underestimate it).
- Have a motive so visible and obvious that the other party cannot underestimate it.
- Assume the other party has no motive. (You cannot underestimate the other party more badly than that.)
- Make bigger bets on your research than the other party would. Are you managing a bigger portfolio? More aggressively? The game is powerfully tilted against active managers who make big bets. Tactics that succeed for the isolated investor will often fail when the investor is trading in a crowd.

Finally, consider the active manager who bases trades on a computer analysis of the behavior of past prices. One way to maximize return is to maximize (algebraically) the expression

$$M_2 - E_1(M_2)$$

Clearly, maximizing this expression *minimizes the expression for trade size*. Computer algorithms trained on past data to maximize return will tend to seek out trading strategies that cannot be executed in institutional size. But a trade's contribution to portfolio performance depends on the *product* of return and trade size: The latter is as important as the former.

## CONCLUSION

The converse is equally true: An easy way to maximize trade size is to minimize expected return. We have all heard active managers say, "It is strange—our best executions often turn out to be our worst investments." It is not so strange when managers understand the importance of the research motive of the transactor on the other side.

The reason most actively managed portfolios perform close to breakeven is that the substantial gains from their own research are offset by substantial losses to the research of their trading counterparties. Success in active management is more easily achieved by reducing losses caused by the other trader's research than by increasing gains to one's own research—that is, by paying attention to *defense* as well as *offense*.

### Notes

1. We can look at departures from an otherwise passive portfolio as a series of "active" holdings or as a series of trades. Although a trade at a point in time is merely a change in a holding, the benefits of active management are related to *holdings* whereas the costs are related to *trades*. The trading desk concerns itself with the costs incurred at the time of the trade; the research staff concerns itself with its own trading motive but not with the other investor's. Neither trading desk nor research staff addresses the motive on the other side. This way of organizing active management makes sense only if the research motive on the other side is small enough to be ignored (i.e., only if active management is a treasure hunt).

### References

Crerend, William J., and Edward Broom. 1974. "A Taxonomy of Money Management." *Financial Analysts Journal*, vol. 30, no. 3 (May/June):24–27, 30, 23.

Ellis, Charles D. 1971. *Institutional Investing*. Homewood, IL: Dow Jones-Irwin.

Treynor, Jack L. 1994. "The Invisible Costs of Trading." *Journal of Portfolio Management*, vol. 21, no. 1 (Fall):71–78.

Treynor, Jack L., and Fischer Black. 1973. "How to Use Security Analysis to Improve Portfolio Selection." *Journal of Business*, vol. 46, no. 1 (January):66–86.

# CHAPTER 44

# Insider Trading

## Two Comments

### JACK L. TREYNOR

In making investment decisions, we rarely buy unless we see possibilities in a company that aren't yet in the price; we rarely sell unless we have concerns that aren't in the price. We would like to be the owner when good things happen to a stock and to avoid being the owner when bad things happen. But, of course, when we buy, we deprive the previous owners of the benefit from the good things; when we sell, we defer to the new owner the damage from the bad things.

If we assume the previous owner (when we buy) or the subsequent owner (when we sell) is as motivated as we are, then that owner's motive represents a cost we bear only when we trade—i.e., a cost of trading. We might like to eliminate the other person's trading motive by passing laws against acting on that motive. But we don't, because then we'd make our trading motives illegal also.

So, what's the purpose of insider trading laws? The key is the dealer's role as an intermediary between buyer and seller. The buyer's motive hurts the seller, and the seller's motive hurts the buyer—unless one motive or the other gets into the consensus price between the dealer's first transaction and the dealer's second transaction. From the dealer's perspective, "inside" information is information so unambiguous in its implications, so authoritative in its source, that it gets into the security's price too quickly.

Therefore, laws against acting on inside information have two purposes: (1) to protect dealers and (2) to give investors the confidence that they are protected from people who know more than they do. If dealers play an essential role in making securities markets liquid, capitalist societies have a stake in protecting dealers. If people who feel protected from insiders are more likely to invest, capitalist societies have a reason for providing that confidence.

So, capitalist societies are probably healthier with insider trading laws. But those laws don't protect the little guy. Instead, they protect some rich, powerful big guys—dealers.

---

## DEAN LEBARON

Imagine a classroom *filled* with students—some smart, others not, most in between—who are about to take a test. A few of the students are fortunate; they come from privileged economic or social backgrounds that provide them with an advantage in answering the test questions. And a few are unfortunate; their underprivileged economic or social backgrounds are a disadvantage to them. To deal with this disparity, the teacher decides that the advantaged students should stay home on test day.

Is that decision wise? If one purpose of the test is to discover who is bright and who is not, plus measure collective skills of the group, does excluding these students skew the results? I think so.

This analogy fits the rules that exclude insiders from trading except at specified intervals, presumably because they know more than less-informed market participants. If one of the primary jobs of markets is price discovery—accurate price discovery—this exclusion makes no sense. By eliminating insiders, we make markets *less* informed. Market prices no longer reflect the combined knowledge of all participants. We push prices in the direction that less well informed investors would take them. And we may increase volatility from uncertainty.

I favor encouraging insider trading at all times. However, I would require insiders to identify their market orders so that the rest of us can judge, without knowing the details underpinning the actions, whether the trading contains information.

What about protecting dealers? The little anecdotal information I have on dealer returns suggests that this group doesn't need legislative protection. In my classroom analogy, dealers would be equivalent to professional test takers. You could hire them to answer test questions as you would answer them, and they would make no administrative mistakes, such as not using a No. 2 pencil. Not everyone could afford to hire these professionals, and they would add a cost burden, of course, in the market. But they are not adding liquidity; most test takers would not need their services. And dealers are not providing real liquidity, only a temporary accommodation between buyers and sellers. Most market participants don't need that service. Moreover, most examples of the cost of the service suggest that it is uneconomical and could be replaced with other (electronic) systems.

I'm not sure that prohibitions against insider trading have much to do with dealer margins, but anything that contributes to market inefficiency, such as insider trading rules, increases the opportunity for higher dealer margins.

Jack is correct in concluding that insider trading is harmful to markets and most market participants. And the point that dealers are helped indirectly by insider trading rules is correct. Among the dealers' other advantages are their inside knowledge of trading patterns, at least on the NYSE.

I conclude that because insider trading helps price discovery, we should encourage insiders to be active market participants. But how can we do so? First, we should allow insiders to trade all the time with only the requirement that their intentions for trading be flagged as potentially privileged. Second, companies should make continuous public markets—for example, as a specialist function with an open book and in continuous registration for capital raising or share buybacks. Companies should be the most informed insiders and should continuously reveal their pricing ideas by market behavior.

# Accounting

**D**o accountants distinguish with sufficient care between the unknown future and the known past? They appeal to certain conventions to help them cope with change, with surprise, with the always uncertain future. Retail investors will probably continue to accept the accountants' conventions.

But double-entry bookkeeping was invented long before there were any institutional investors. And institutions are beginning to recognize that they have a choice: How many judgments—implicit or explicit—about the future will they delegate to the accountants? How many will they reserve to themselves? Is there a more efficient division of labor?

Thoughtful accountants are offering constructive suggestions.

J.L.T.

# CHAPTER 45

# Financial Reporting—for Whom?

**W**e stand at a critical crossroads in corporate financial accounting; the findings of the Wheat and Trueblood Committees may influence the respective roles of corporate managers, accountants, and investors in the reporting process for many years to come. In an article in the March–April 1972 issue of the *Harvard Business Review,* Professors Walter Frese and Robert Mautz remind us that corporate managers, as well as security analysts and accountants, have an important stake in the findings. Unfortunately, the authors encourage in their article a view of the purpose of accounting that will serve managers very badly: (1) The authors see a fundamental distinction between the "stewardship" conception of financial reporting and reporting aimed at assisting the investor. They observe with astonishment that, "A number of writers now say that the major purpose of financial statements is to enable stockholders, analysts, and others to predict the financial future of the company." (2) Possibly influenced by *The New Industrial State* or *Power Without Property,* the authors view the corporation as a self sufficient entity, responsible only unto itself. "Management has certain prerogatives. . . . One of these is to report on the success of the company as it sees that success . . . not as someone else defines success but success *in terms of its own goals, objectives and actual achievements.*" The accountant then becomes merely the scorekeeper in a game that has no objective beyond a vague notion of winning. (3) The authors see no essential role for determinations of investment value in measuring corporate progress, noting with evident regret that "It is proposed that accounting be taken out of its traditional role of reporter of completed transactions. . . . " "Management would not be judged on its ability to buy cheap and sell dear" and asking, "Once accounting leaves the reporting of actual transactions and undertakes to measure all 'changes of value' what are the limitations?"

In sum: The corporation is a self sufficient entity. Accounting has only to keep score on management's success as measured by "completed transactions" in some way that managers themselves can generally agree is meaningful. What, therefore, do investors and determinations of value have to do with the purposes of financial reporting?

Beginning with the industrial revolution, business enterprise has emphasized capital facilities with lives very much longer than the ordinary span of time between "buying cheap" and "selling dear," whose primary purpose has been to reduce the out-of-pocket costs of producing a salable product. Merely reporting "completed

---

transactions" indicating whether a corporation was "buying cheap and selling dear" failed to provide adequate evidence that investors — whether lenders or new shareholders—would get a positive return on their investment. Indeed, because of the time spans typically involved, no mere reporting of actual or completed transactions could answer that question.

Because of the large amounts of cash required for capital investments, the corporate form of organization, providing for limited liability, became popular as a way to attract equity funds from people other than management; between equity issues, corporations had to manage vicissitudes of cash flow either by stockpiling cash or near-cash or by borrowing. Tax considerations strongly encouraged corporations to rely primarily on borrowing rather than stockpiling (Montgomery Ward being the classic exception). But lenders constrained by the limited liability feature to seek their security in the value of the corporate assets (tangible or intangible; separately or together) consequently take a very serious interest in asset values, as well as completed transactions.

The authors ask, "Whose ideas of 'value' are to be used?" It is obvious from the considerations cited above that as long as corporations continue to be net borrowers rather than net lenders, management has great reason to be concerned about the value investors attach to their enterprise. In view of the transformation wrought by the industrial revolution and its handmaiden, the corporate form of organization, the authors should not be surprised that management is no longer rated on its ability to "buy cheap and sell dear," but rather on its ability to enhance the economic value of corporate assets. And inasmuch as investment values depend entirely on the future, "stockholders, analysts, and others" do indeed require financial statements that enable them to "predict the financial future of the company."

If investors' determinations of value weren't important for corporation management, Professors Frese and Mautz would have no reason to be troubled. What really troubles them is not the importance of these determinations, but the fact that they are influenced by arbitrary accounting decisions. In rejecting the roles of the investor and investment value in appraising the stewardship of corporate management, however, they are throwing out the baby with the bath.

# CHAPTER 46

# The Revenue-Expense View of Accrual Accounting

The Financial Accounting Standards Board's memorandum on the conceptual framework for financial accounting and reporting (December 2, 1976) distinguished two justifications for accrual accounting—the assets-liabilities view and the revenue-expense view: "Advocates of the revenue and expense [approach to accrual accounting argue that a] list of assets [and] liabilities . . . . makes no representation that it reflects the wealth of the enterprise. For that reason they prefer the term 'balance sheet' to 'statement of financial position.'"

According to the discussion memorandum, some proponents of this view contend that the goal of accounting is "to measure the earning power of an enterprise." But what does "earning power" mean? According to them, "in fundamental financial analysis (probably the origin of the term) it means the long-term average ability of an enterprise to produce earnings."

If current accrual decisions must reflect long-term earnings, then the accountant cannot rely solely on current accounting data. He is compelled to make judgments about the future. Thus the current and future earnings figures that result from his accrual decisions are not facts, but estimates. If earning power has to do with "long-term . . . . earnings," then—unlike facts—it cannot be "measured."

What does "matching" mean, if not identification of receipts that an expenditure gives rise to, and vice versa? When an expenditure gives rise to receipts at more than one point in time, the accountant must make a judgment regarding the magnitude of as-yet-unknown receipts to justify capitalizing some portion of the expenditure. More generally, *any* matching of receipts and expenditures across time requires an assessment of the uncertainty and magnitude of future flows, an assessment that represents an implicit investment judgment on the part of the accountant making the accrual.

CHAPTER **47**

# The Trouble with Earnings

The main objective of financial accounting has slowly but surely become providing information for security analysis. Informing the analyst was not always a primary or even a secondary objective of financial accounting, nor were accounting outputs always the primary input for security analysis; but today it is probably realistic to view the activities of the accountant and the security analyst as two parts of a larger process primarily devoted to estimating the value of corporate common stocks.

The earnings concept is the link between these ostensibly complementary activities. Yet there is no genuine communication between analysts and accountants when it comes to the meaning of earnings. The analyst treats earnings as if it were an economic concept. In view of his purpose—attaching economic value to the firm—he can scarcely do otherwise.

The accountant's concept of earnings dates from a time when specialization of labor within the investment industry had scarcely begun, and when, indeed, ownership and management had not begun to separate. The accountant is, of course, the oldest of the professionals in the investment industry, and he continues to regard accounting earnings as his most important product. The accountant defines it as what he gets when he matches costs against revenues, making any necessary allocations of cost to time periods; or as the change in the equity account over the accounting period, before capital transactions. These are not economic definitions of earnings, but merely descriptions of the motions the accountant goes through to arrive at the earnings number.

There is no way to carry on constructive discussion of an undefined concept. One approach the security analyst might take in attempting to establish meaningful communications with the accountant would be to ask him to give an economic definition of earnings. As we shall soon see, however, the accountant has very practical reasons for deferring his definition as long as possible. Accordingly, our tactic will be to narrow the accountant's room for maneuver by supplying a definition of earnings— one that has economic meaning—and then asking whether the security analyst would show much interest in the concept, given our definition.

Professor Lawrence Revsine[1] has suggested defining earnings as an estimate of the change in present value of the firm over the accounting period—a definition that seems to accord closely with Professor Hick's celebrated definition of earnings as the measure of how much value can be withdrawn from the firm over the accounting period without leaving it poorer than it was at the beginning. Unfortunately, it is easy to show that the earnings concept so defined is not well suited to linking the measuring and reporting function of the accountant to the judging and valuation function of the security analyst.

In simplest terms our argument runs as follows. If accounting earnings are construed as an attempt to measure changes in the present value of the firm (or, in the context of per share accounting, changes in the value of the share) then in order to arrive at the change in value the accountant must first arrive at the value. The accountant could save the analyst a great deal of trouble by simply reporting to him the end-of-period value from which change in value over the period was derived.

*If earnings is the difference between the worth of the firm at the beginning and the end of the accounting period, then analysis of a firm's worth logically precedes measurement of earnings, rather than the other way around.*

The present joint process by which the accountant arrives at earnings by estimating or measuring the change in value over the accounting period, and the analyst in turn uses these earnings to estimate value at the end of each period, is in some danger of being logically circular. There is, of course, redundancy in having two different people estimate investment worth at two different stages of the overall process. But the wasted effort is far less important than the fact that, in attempting to estimate the value of the firm, the analyst is using earnings data which in turn depend importantly on accountant's estimates of the value of some of the firm's major assets. If estimation of economic value requires earnings data, and earnings data requires estimates of economic value, how do we get the joint process off the ground? The pragmatic answer of the accountant is: by making arbitrary, mechanical estimates of value in the development of earnings. Unless he thinks that "garbage in, garbage out!" applies only to computers, however, the thinking security analyst is not going to be happy with this answer.

It is sometimes argued that, because market value fluctuates—sometimes wildly—the appropriate book figure can be a more reliable indicator of an asset's "true" or "intrinsic" value, where the latter is believed to be somehow more stable than market value. It is surprising that this notion is still taken seriously by so many in view of the rapidly spreading recognition that, if values don't fluctuate as a random walk, they can't be true economic values.[2] In every kind of market, asset value depends on expectations of future earning power (i.e., economic rents), which are subject to continual and unpredictable change.

The analyst is expected to produce good estimates of economic value from earnings data that are based in turn on bad estimates of economic value. Whether book values are good or bad estimates is, however, beside the point. The point is that an arbitrary, mechanical estimate of value is still an estimate of value. There are many different kinds of markets (e.g., markets for specific productive assets on one hand—industrial real estate, used machine tools, etc.—and markets for claims on firms owning productive assets on the other), but there is only one kind of economic value. Although, through extensive use and familiarity, book values have taken on for many investors a kind of mystical significance completely unrelated to economic reality, for any practical purpose they must either be construed as proxies for economic values or as having no meaning at all. But if book values are interpreted as proxies for economic values, then it is clear that the problem of circularity has not been avoided, but merely obscured.

Security analysis is not strictly circular when the accountant confines himself to estimating the value of such current assets as inventories and receivables in order to estimate the rate of flow of economic earnings (what economists call quasi-rents) attributable to the firm. The security analyst can choose to delegate the task of estimating a change in value (hence the value) of current assets to the accountant, accepting whatever approximating conventions the accountant may invoke in order to simplify his task, if the goal is estimating the market value of other, more important assets.

If the earnings of the firm are due almost entirely to the services of its employees and officers, or to special monopoly powers derived from patents or secret manufacturing processes, the use of accounting earnings by the security analyst may not be circular, simply because in such cases accountants' determinations of asset values have relatively little influence on reported earnings.

But consider, for example, the firm in which the main source of economic rents is assets—bricks and mortar and machinery—that are depreciated over time. The accountant estimates the decline in the value of these assets over the accounting period, in order to report a figure to the analyst, that the analyst extrapolates and then capitalizes to estimate the value of the firm—including the value of the assets being depreciated. Reporting the change in value over the accounting period implies an estimate of the value itself at the beginning and end of the period. The analyst cannot employ a figure based on an accountant's estimate of the change in value of assets, when these assets constitute a major source of investment value in the firm, without introducing into his reasoning a fatal circularity.

At this point, some readers will raise the standard objections to using earnings gross of depreciation for security analysis, arguing that, whereas "cash flow" fluctuates over time in ways unrelated to the firm's economic prospects, the earnings concept tends to smooth out the "spurious" fluctuations. Fluctuations in the reported stream of rents will translate into fluctuations in the investor's estimate of the firm's value only if the investor insists on capitalizing cash flow by applying a constant "P/E" ratio to the current value of the stream without regard for the future pattern. Needless to say, if the analyst insists on being provided with a single number so simply related to market value, then he is delegating away to whoever provides that number most of the real task of security analysis.

## THE PRICE OF RELEVANCE

The security analyst is an interloper from the accountant's point of view. The security analyst is doing something that implicitly or explicitly the accountant was doing before the security analyst came along—namely, judging the worth of a company at certain points in time. The accounting profession has had to recognize the existence of the security analyst because the analyst, by bringing to bear economic and business judgment, has been able to do a more convincing job on the determination of economic worth than the accountant. But the accountant has not accommodated the security analyst by trimming back his own function to exclude that part of the task of determining corporate worth now performed by the analyst. Instead, he continues to encourage use by investors of accounting earnings.

Present accounting practice tends to conceal the dependence of the earnings concept on estimates of worth by substituting accounting ritual for judgment in the determination of asset values. But it is becoming more and more difficult for accountants to convince practical decision makers that earnings figures based on such arbitrary procedures have any relevance; current accounting practices (e.g., current value accounting, introduction of market values into computations of portfolio earnings) are tending to narrow the gap between book and market values. And in removing that gap, accountants are actually moving toward Hicks' definition of earnings whether they like to admit it or not.

It is natural and human for accountants to want to maintain the traditional scope of financial accounting, but in their attempts to bring accounting up to date and satisfy critics' demands for greater relevance, they are bringing steadily closer the day when it will be obvious to everyone in and outside their profession that the earnings concept is not suited to the needs of investors.

## IN CONCLUSION

1. If the roles of the accountant and the security analyst are viewed together as part of a larger process of arriving at estimates of security values, little real progress can be made until we have an economic definition of earnings that is accepted by both accountant and security analyst, and until it can be established that earnings, given this definition, has any role to play in the deliberations of the analyst.
2. On the other hand, virtually all the most heated controversies in financial accounting (for example, the creation of artificial reserves in order to enhance reported future income, the pooling versus purchase controversy, full-cost accounting in the petroleum industry, bank earnings, etc.) revolve around the accounting evaluation of assets (or, equivalently, the creation of reserves against the value of fixed assets) and the impact on accounting earnings. These issues, over which the Accounting Principles Board has labored long and hard, will be seen to be empty issues once it is recognized that *no* number affected by an accountant's determinations of the value of assets contributing significantly to the investment worth of the firm can be useful to the security analyst—regardless of how the accountant's determinations are made. The hot controversies will disappear when the concept of accounting earnings loses its central role in security valuation.
3. It is often suggested that skill in adjusting accounting data is important for the security analyst, and that skillful adjustment requires judgment. But the way to make the conventional earnings figure useful for security analysis is merely to remove the effect of any accounting determinations of worth. Hence in any given case there is only one correct adjustment. Very little skill—and certainly no judgment!—is required to make it.
4. Current methods of security valuation depend on treating earnings as if they were economic rents. Far from being rents, however, accounting earnings are more like estimates of change in the value of the firm over the accounting period—if indeed they have any economic meaning at all. If this is the meaning of accounting earnings, however, then their use in estimating the value of the firm is circular; the analyst will have to face the fact that he actually lacks any defensible basis

for valuation methods based on earnings and start looking for methods with a plausible basis.

5. If accountants want to continue to enjoy a role in the investment management process they should prepare to focus their energies on supplying whatever data a workable theory of security valuation requires, rather than defending the present ritual.

## NOTES

1. Department of Accounting, University of Illinois.
2. Paul Samuelson, "Proof That Properly Anticipated Prices Fluctuate Randomly." *Industrial Management Review,* Spring 1965.

# CHAPTER 48

# The Trueblood Report

The early chapters of the Report of the American Institute of Certified Public Accountants (A.I.C.P.A.) Study Group on the Objectives of Financial Statements (the Trueblood Report) make a number of admirable contributions. They emphasize the importance for financial statements of serving users outside the enterprise, point out that needs of investors and creditors are very similar, and assert that both users have a common need to predict future cash flows. In subsequent chapters, however, the report splits into two parallel and—so it seems to this writer—wholly unreconciled lines of reasoning.

One line of reasoning begins by conceding that "present accounting practices require estimates of the future." These estimates are necessarily based on some accountant's interpretation of the past, even though "in many instances .... the past may not be a good indicator of the future." It concludes that, "Financial statements are more useful if they include but distinguish information that is primarily factual and therefore can be measured objectively from information that is primarily interpretive."

Of the three forms of financial reporting advocated by the report—the Statement of Financial Position, the Statement of Earnings, and the Statement of Financial Activities—only one minimizes the role of accountants' interpretations: "The Statement of Financial Activities should report mainly on factual aspects of enterprise transactions having or expected to have significant cash consequences. The Statement should report data that require minimal judgment and interpretation by the preparer."

The other line of reasoning begins by introducing in new language an old concept of the objective of accounting—measuring the progress of the firm: "The fundamental purpose of accounting is to provide interim measures of enterprise progress" (i.e., earnings). It ends with the conclusion that "earnings as reported in financial statements have come to be, and in all probability will continue to be, the single most important criterion for assessing the enterprise's accomplishments and earning power."

It is hard to understand how the report could come to this conclusion given its definition of earnings: "If one could reduce the future cash flows to a single number at various times through an appropriate discounting process, earnings for the period could be determined by comparing changes in present value." It is the investor who is undertaking to "reduce the future cash flows to a single number through an appropriate discounting process." It makes no sense for him to discount back to present value projections of future "changes in present value." He is interested in making his own determination of the present value of the firm, based on his own projection of the future cash flows, based in turn on his own interpretation of the "objectively measurable, factual" past. Though interested in evidence of the enterprise's ability to generate cash, the investor has little reason to be interested in the accountant's determinations of changes in its present value—even if these determinations are "imprecise, because . . . . based on allocations and similar estimates." Measuring "the enterprise's accomplishments" may be somebody's objective for accounting statements, but it cannot be the investor's.

Despite the profound conceptual difference between a stream of changes in present value and a stream of cash flows, the report attempts to equate them under the rubric of "earning power": "The decision-maker's judgment aims at estimating the enterprise's ability to be better off, to generate more cash . . . . This ability is the enterprise's earning power." The enterprise's "better off-ness," however, is treated by the report as synonymous with its "progress," its "accomplishments"—in short, with the change in present value that the report defines to be "earnings." Thus the report's two definitions of earning power—"ability to be better off" and "ability to generate more cash"—far from being synonymous, are mutually exclusive.

Estimating how "well off" the enterprise is (hence what it has "accomplished") is the job of the investor. When he recognizes that earnings is by the report's own definition an accountant's estimate of the "change in present value of the enterprise's future cash flows," he is likely to begin paying far more attention to the Statement of Financial Activities and far less to the Statement of Earnings.

# CHAPTER 49

# A Hard Look at Traditional Disclosure

For many investors, "fundamental analysis" has come to mean value estimates based on accounting numbers. I think it should mean something else—namely, prediction of future operating cash flow from present facts. As I will try to show, accounting numbers are not facts, but rather guesses about the future. My notion of what fundamental analysis is can be reconciled with the use of accounting numbers *only under certainty.*

One suspects Fr. Luca Pacioli intended the accounting model to be used to determine retrospectively the value of various kinds of claims on completed ventures. If so, investors have made two giant strides *away* from the original application:

1. They have applied it to continuing enterprises, where future and past production and sales have important joint costs.
2. Instead of recognizing that it is an apparatus for estimating the value of claims on the enterprise, they have used its outputs as inputs to a wholly separate and unreconciled apparatus for estimating value. There is a name for this kind of analysis among engineers. They call it plumbing—joining systems together without considering whether they are internally compatible.

Actually, there is a good reason why outside users use accounting numbers this way. Lindsay and Margenau point out in their influential physics text that every variable in physics has two definitions—one that explains how it is measured and one that explains how it is used: "The very idea of symbolism implies .... that a symbol must represent a concept transcending the particular operation which it is used to represent."[1] In other words, every concept in physics has a "how" definition (the particular measurement) and a "why" definition (a concept justifying the measurement). The distinction is brilliantly illustrated by Carl G. Hempel's concept of "hage." Hempel defines hage as the product of a person's height and age.[2] Hage can be defined in the first way, but not in the second, as the concept is of no earthly use whatever.

Accounting numbers also have the first kind of definition, but not the second. To establish their usefulness to investors, one must provide the missing definitions. With these definitions in hand, the outside user can decide whether particular accounting concepts are really relevant to his real-world needs.

---

Thirty years ago, two accounting professors at NYU proposed replacing conventional disclosure with a forecast of the company's future cash flows.[3] The forecast would be updated periodically. Now, of course, a cash flow forecast extending many years into the future contains a lot of numbers. And each update would contain a lot more numbers. A few years of this kind of quarterly disclosure could amount to serious information overload.

A solution to the overload problem is suggested by the following observation. There is an important class of transformations of the cash flow stream that are essentially costless, quick, reversible, and capable of being undertaken at any time at the option of the reporting company's management. These are, of course, changes in cash flow across time in the capital markets, executed at market interest rates. What is preserved in the course of a company's borrowing and lending is, of course, the *present value* of its future cash flow. Indeed, all the useful information about its future cash flows is contained in this single number. The rest is spurious.

If accountants were trying to provide outside users with this information, how would they behave? Suppose, for example, a manufacturing company went into the market for steel and bought some ingots, presumably in an armslength transaction with no particular cleverness on the part of the buyer. There is thus no reason to assume that the present value of the firm's future cash flow stream would be either raised or lowered by the transaction. You would expect an accountant to take great pains to prevent this type of transaction—which, of course, is more nearly the rule than the exception in most firms—from affecting the present value of the cash flow stream.

Indeed, assume the accountant is confronted with a whole cycle of transactions—beginning, say, with the purchase of raw materials and then on to the purchase of labor to convert the raw materials into product, the subsequent sales converting product into accounts receivable and, finally, the transactions converting accounts receivable into cash. If he has any real questions whether specific transactions in this cycle are achieving any change in the present value of the company's cash flow stream, he may prefer to reserve judgment about their impact until he has the whole cycle in hand—at least up to the point of the sale transaction.

Accountants call the present value of the firm's future cash flow stream *equity*. They call the process of preventing transactions that have no present-value impact from altering the firm's equity as reported *accrual accounting*. And the principle of deferring a reckoning of the present-value impact of transactions until a cycle is completed is called by accountants the *realization principle*. The economic content in accrual accounting is an estimate of the essential, irreducible information about the firm's future cash flow stream.

The firm's future cash steam can, of course, be divided into component streams, which also have present values. In particular, the total stream can be divided into component streams with positive present values and component streams with negative present values. The former are called *assets* and the latter *liabilities*.

Let us formalize this view of accrual accounting using some elementary mathematics. If we think of future cash flow streams as vectors, with components corresponding to various points in future time, then we can use the standard rules of vector addition to describe the aggregation and disaggregation of cash flow streams. If, in addition to this vector notation for the cash flows, we introduce a present-value operator on these vectors, we have a convenient way of denoting the present value of any given cash stream. Let us call specific future cash flow streams *accounts* and their present values *balances*.

Using this notation, we divide the firm's future cash flow stream into three components—cash (and near cash), assets other than cash, and liabilities. Then we can write Equation 49.1:

$$e = c + a - 1 \tag{49.1}$$

Mathematicians like to impute to their operators a handy property that makes their calculations more tractable—*linearity*. A linear operator has the following property:

$$V[\alpha x + \beta y] = \alpha V[x] + \beta V[y] \tag{49.2}$$

Present-value operators consistent with the Capital Asset Pricing Model and Arbitrage Pricing Theory are linear operators. If the present-value operator employed in accrual accounting is linear, we have Equation 49.3:

$$V[e] = V[c] + V[a] - V[l] \tag{49.3}$$

Note that Equation 49.1, which is a statement about future cash flows, is an identity. Equation 49.3, which is a statement about the present value of those cash flows, ("balances"), is not. Equation 49.3 depends on the linearity assumption expressed in Equation 49.2. (Equation 49.3 is, of course, a "balance sheet.") Nevertheless, some accountants call this relation between the equity balance, the cash balance, the asset balance, and the liability balance the "accounting identity." The fact that they refer to Equation 49.3 as an identity attests to their eagerness to invoke the linearity assumption for their present-value operator.

Equation 49.3 is, of course, a convenient framework for discussing the familiar accounting concepts of revenues and expenses, since revenues increase the value of this equation and expenses reduce it. If we transpose Equation 49.3 so that the cash balance appears on the left-hand side and the equity balance is transposed to the right, we have Equation 49.4:

$$V[c] = V[l] + V[e] - V[a] \tag{49.4}$$

*Receipts* increase the value of Equation 49.4, while *expenditures* reduce it. If we once again transpose the accounting identity so that all terms are on the right-hand side, we have Equation 49.5:

$$O = V[l] + V[e] - V[c] - V[a] \tag{49.5}$$

This version is convenient for discussing debits and credits. A credit increases the value of this equation, while a debit reduces it. Since the value of Equation 49.5 must be zero both before and after any transaction, we have the important accounting theorem: Debits equal credits.

Apparently accounting concepts *do* have the kind of definitions that establish their relevance to the real world—"why" definitions as well as the "how" definitions provided by accounting textbooks. What the "why" definitions reveal, however, is that these numbers are assertions about the *future*, rather than the past. (Accountants sometimes argue that, because the reported numbers are derived from historical transactions, they are facts, rather than forecasts. But forecasts, just like facts, are based on past observation; indeed, they have no other basis. Thus one cannot use their source to distinguish facts from forecasts. Whether accounting numbers are forecasts or not has to do, not with *how* they are derived, but with *why* they are derived.)

When one considers what accounting numbers mean, one finds it hard to justify their use in investment analysis. Yet the outside user has traditionally tried very hard to justify them. He begins by asking, what numbers do accountants publish? Then he asks himself, what computations can I make with these numbers? What trends, turnover rates, percentages? Finally, how can I make some of these computations sound relevant and plausible?

An alternative is to begin with the outside user's analytical problem—forecasting operating "cash flow." In order to make forecasts that are more than mere extrapolation, he needs laws of motion—relations between past and future observables that hold fairly generally. These relations will define the historical data he needs in order to make his forecasts.[4] When outside users approach their task this way, there is a natural division of labor between their work and the work of the reporting accountant: The outside user makes the forecasts, and the accountant supplies the necessary historical data—the observable facts.

Outside users treat published accounting numbers as if they were facts. But accounting numbers can serve as the facts in this joint process if and only if the future is certain. The accounting model may play other socially useful roles, but its role in the kind of financial disclosure advocated here can be justified only by treating it as a certainty model.

Companies' most important features—products, customers, plant—often change slowly. Yet they can be prosperous today and bankrupt tomorrow. For such companies, the greatest sources of change and surprise are often external to the company. Because they are really forecasts, accounting numbers implicitly combine company specifics with externals entailing large forecasting risk. The result is an unnecessarily low signal-to-noise ratio for the outside user.

Then, too, meaningful comparison across companies or industries requires a common set of forecasts of the externals. The outside user can neither assure himself that accounting numbers for different companies reflect a common set of forecasts nor adjust them until they do, because the externals are implicit, rather than explicit, in accounting numbers.

## Notes

1. Lindsay and Margenau, *Foundations of Physics* (1936), p. 20.
2. Cited in R. Sterling, "Toward a Science of Accounting," *Financial Analysts Journal*, September/October 1975.
3. J. Owen and R. P. Brief, "The Role of the Accountant in Investment Analysis," *Financial Analysts Journal*, January/February 1975.
4. To those who argue that accountants' forecasts are useful because outside users don't know the equations of motion, we merely point out that the accountants generating these forecasts don't know them either.

# CHAPTER 50

# The Trouble with Corporate Disclosure

I t is a safe bet that, when he was inventing double-entry accounting, Luca Pacioli did not have actively traded, publicly owned companies in mind, or security analysts or portfolio managers. What he created was an ingenious theory of value. We should not think less of him for failing to distinguish between macro- and micro-variables, between measurements and forecasts, between the known past and the uncertain future.

Graham and Dodd urged investors to incorporate accounting numbers into their analysis because these numbers were the only ones available. But in so doing, Graham and Dodd stood logic on its head: Instead of letting accountants tell investors how to analyze, they should let the investors tell the accountants what to report.

In other words, the logical way to proceed is as follows:

1. Think through the economics—macro and microeconomics—of the process required to analyze a company's value.
2. Tell the accountants what input numbers this process requires.

To encourage the broadest possible investment comparisons, the process should focus on a single analytical model of investment value containing all the explanatory variables that might be relevant for any company. The variables will be of two types:

1. Variables specific to the company that distinguish it from other companies ("micro" variables), and
2. Variables potentially common (but with widely ranging importance) to all companies ("macro" variables).

The "micro" variables should be measurable facts: capacities and out-of-pocket operating costs for plant, market shares, and the like. All information about the future should be confined to the "macro"-variables. All corporate reporting should be confined to micro-variables. No accounting "principles" are required because the companies are reporting testable facts.

Think of the "micro" numbers as explanatory variables and the future-related "macro" numbers as undetermined coefficients. Then, the value of a company is the

---

Reprinted from the *Journal of Investment Management*, Vol. 1, No. 4, 2003.

price estimated by this model for the undetermined coefficients that best explain the observed market prices of all actively traded companies at that moment.

When we reduce share valuation to a multiple regression problem, we eliminate any timing problems, because we are using the market's macroeconomic expectations—rather than the portfolio manager's, the analyst's or, worst of all, the accountant's. (Can the accountant assign values to inventory, accounts receivable, depreciation reserves without making explicit—or, worse yet, implicit—macroeconomic judgments?)

We can get an inkling of how serious the timing problem is for accountants by asking the following question: Does an earnings time series behave like a time series reflecting levels of rivalry, plant capacities, and the like, or does it behave like a time series of forecasts? Forecasts have distinctive time series properties because forecast changes—their first differences—are random.

**EXHIBIT 50.1**   Percent S&P Earnings Change, Regressed Against Itself, 1 Year Earlier

| Year | S&P | P/E | Ê | ΔÊ/E | Year | S&P | P/E | Ê | ΔÊ/E |
|------|-----|-----|-----|------|------|-----|-----|-----|------|
| 1926 | 1349 | 1088 | 1240 | | 1956 | 4667 | 1369 | 3409 | (59) |
| 1927 | 1766 | 1591 | 1110 | (105) | 1957 | 3999 | 1187 | 3369 | (12) |
| 1928 | 2435 | 1764 | 1380 | 243 | 1958 | 5521 | 1910 | 2891 | (142) |
| 1929 | 2145 | 1332 | 1610 | 167 | 1959 | 5989 | 1767 | 3389 | 172 |
| 1930 | 1534 | 1581 | 970 | (398) | 1960 | 5811 | 1777 | 3270 | (35) |
| 1931 | 812 | 1331 | 610 | (371) | 1961 | 7155 | 2243 | 3190 | (24) |
| 1932 | 689 | 1680 | 410 | (328) | 1962 | 6310 | 1719 | 3671 | 151 |
| 1933 | 1010 | 2295 | 440 | 73 | 1963 | 7502 | 1866 | 4020 | 95 |
| 1934 | 950 | 1939 | 490 | 114 | 1964 | 8475 | 1862 | 4549 | 132 |
| 1935 | 1343 | 1767 | 760 | 551 | 1965 | 9243 | 1781 | 5190 | 141 |
| 1936 | 1718 | 1684 | 1020 | 342 | 1966 | 8033 | 1447 | 5551 | 70 |
| 1937 | 1055 | 934 | 1130 | 111 | 1967 | 9647 | 1810 | 5330 | (40) |
| 1938 | 1321 | 2064 | 640 | (434) | 1968 | 10386 | 1803 | 5760 | 81 |
| 1939 | 1249 | 1388 | 900 | 406 | 1969 | 9206 | 1593 | 5779 | 3 |
| 1940 | 1058 | 1008 | 1050 | 167 | 1970 | 9215 | 1796 | 5131 | (112) |
| 1941 | 869 | 749 | 1160 | 105 | 1971 | 10209 | 1791 | 5700 | 111 |
| 1942 | 977 | 949 | 1030 | (112) | 1972 | 11805 | 1839 | 6419 | 126 |
| 1943 | 1167 | 1241 | 940 | (87) | 1973 | 9755 | 1195 | 8163 | 272 |
| 1944 | 1328 | 1428 | 930 | (11) | 1974 | 6856 | 771 | 8892 | 89 |
| 1945 | 1736 | 1808 | 960 | 32 | 1975 | 9019 | 1133 | 7960 | (105) |
| 1946 | 1530 | 1443 | 1060 | 70 | 1976 | 10746 | 1084 | 9913 | 245 |
| 1947 | 1530 | 950 | 1611 | 520 | 1977 | 9510 | 870 | 10931 | 103 |
| 1948 | 1520 | 664 | 2289 | 421 | 1978 | 9611 | 779 | 12338 | 129 |
| 1949 | 1676 | 722 | 2321 | 14 | 1979 | 10794 | 726 | 14868 | 205 |
| 1950 | 2041 | 719 | 2839 | 223 | 1980 | 13576 | 916 | 1482 | (3) |
| 1951 | 2377 | 974 | 2440 | (141) | 1981 | 12255 | 804 | 1524 | 28 |
| 1952 | 2657 | 1107 | 2400 | (16) | 1982 | 14064 | 1110 | 1267 | (169) |
| 1953 | 2481 | 988 | 2511 | 46 | 1983 | 16493 | 1180 | 1398 | 103 |
| 1954 | 3598 | 1299 | 2770 | 103 | 1984 | 16724 | 1076 | 1554 | 112 |
| 1955 | 4548 | 1256 | 3621 | 307 | 1985 | 21128 | 1149 | 1839 | 183 |

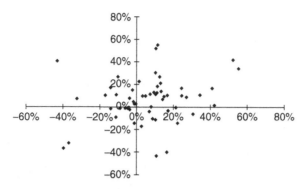

**EXHIBIT 50.2**   Percent S&P Earnings Change, Regressed Against Itself, 1 Year Earlier

The first two columns in Exhibit 50.1 are taken from Ibbotson and Brinson's 1987 book, *Investment Markets* (McGraw-Hill: New York). If the second column (P/E) equals the first (P) divided by the S&P average earnings (E), then, we have

$$\frac{P}{P/E} = P\left(\frac{E}{P}\right) = E$$

Our third column is our estimate $\hat{E}$ of the earnings number consistent with the first two columns. The fourth column displays the fractional changes from year to year in $\hat{E}$. Exhibit 50.2 speaks (loudly) for itself.

Then, I consulted top-ranking accounting experts:

Ray Ball and Ross Watts performed a runs test (for randomness) on the earnings changes of 714 firms.

They found

| | |
|---|---|
| Actual number of runs | 6,522 |
| Random number of runs | 6,524 |

## References

Ball and Watts, "Some Time Series Properties of Accounting Income." *Journal of Finance*, June 1972, p. 670.

Beaver, W. H. "An important implication is that any concept of earnings that is valuation-based is no longer a well-defined concept." *Financial Reporting: An Accounting Revolution*, Prentice-Hall, 1981, p. 102.

Sterling, R. R. "The primary problem of accounting is that our figures do not have empirical referents . . . We must rid ourselves of the belief that accounting cannot be an empirical science." *Toward a Science of Accounting*, Scholars Book Co., 1978, p. 213.

# Investment Value

**A**s Sidney Cottle said, making estimates of investment value is about comparison—between companies in the same industry, between industries in the same economy and between economies. But meaningful comparison requires consistency. If, implicitly or explicitly, we make different assumptions about the future for different assets, our comparisons won't be consistent. Clearly, the first step is to make assumptions about the macroeconomy explicit in our valuation models.

The unknown future will often differ in important ways from the known past. Unfortunately, our language and our thinking often confound the past and the future. Will the future be as congenial to the "good" manager or the "good" company? To be meaningful, estimating investment value shouldn't entail any forecasts—conscious or unconscious—in the particulars we use to distinguish one asset from another.

To minimize the danger, we discuss the particulars under four headings:

1. Productive assets
2. Brand franchise
3. Intellectual property
4. The value of control

Under the fourth heading we consider how the combined value of the first three is divided between the owners and the managers.

Each of the four has its own logic, its own laws of motion. Will parsing out the particulars in this way facilitate Sidney Cottle's comparisons?

J.L.T.

# CHAPTER 51

# Top-Down Economic Forecasts and Securities Selection

**R**esearch organizations are in the midst of a transition from permitting analysts to apply their own security valuation models to imposing a common model. Most organizations adopting common models are adopting relative value models, which acknowledge that a company's investment value depends, not only on the intrinsics of the company, but also on the economic market climate in which it is being valued.

An organization gains little from imposing a common valuation model on all its analysts unless it also imposes a common set of extrinsics, or market climate, variables. Hence many organizations have imposed, along with common models, "top-down" economic forecasts. Since a forecast of extrinsics disagreeing with the market consensus implies an investment opportunity broader than any individual common stock or, indeed, any industry, an organization that bases investment decisions on top-down forecasts is engaged, consciously or unconsciously, in market timing.

If the organization forecasts a more optimistic climate than the consensus forecasts, its selections will be systematically biased toward common stocks sensitive to the forecast. If industry A is more sensitive to the extrinsic variable in question than industry B, divergence between the top-down economic forecast and the market consensus will affect the relative attractiveness of industries A and B. If Company X is more highly levered than Company Y, but both are sensitive to the variable in question, a divergence will affect the relative attractiveness of the respective companies' shares.

The use of top-down economic forecasts will generally confound timing and selection and muddy the responsibility for forecasts of extrinsics on one hand and forecasts of intrinsics on the other. Only one forecast of extrinsics avoids the problem, and that is the market consensus forecast—the forecast implicit in the prices of the securities themselves.

Securities, of course, are often mispriced (hence the use of stock selection). As such, they may, individually, be unreliable guidelines to the consensus forecast. By relying on the law of averages, however, we can use the broad spectrum of security prices to derive all the information about the consensus forecast we need for pure selection decisions.

# CHAPTER 52

# The Value of Control

Sixty years ago, Berle and Means pointed out that the risk-taking function of ownership and the managerial function were separate functions, that in the widely held corporation these functions were performed by different people, and that management could legally use its control to divert a significant portion of the corporation's income to itself. Shareholders will thus value their shares *net* of the present value of these diversions—in Jensen and Meckling's term, they will "price protect."

Takeovers entail a transfer of control, as well as ownership. That takeover premiums—the difference between the value of the shareholders' claim and the takeover price—are currently averaging 40 percent of share value tells us something about the value of control.

In order to avoid depressing its own firm's share price, the takeover management must impose smaller diversions on the target enterprise than did the target management. Management buyouts have an advantage in this respect, because when management is the owner, such diversions are pointless. Investors should be cautious, however, about assuming that diversions to those in control won't resume when a management buyout subsequently goes public.

## WHAT BERLE AND MEANS FORESAW

Much of the current interest in takeovers and leveraged buyouts stems from certain changes in the nature of the widely held corporation envisioned by Berle and Means in their brilliant book, *The Modern Corporation and Private Property.* Writing in 1933, they described the possible consequences of separation between ownership and control:

> *Profits act as the return for the performance of two separate functions ... these two functions of risk and control are, in the main, performed by two different groups of people ... are no profits to go to those who exercise control, and in whose hands the efficient operation of enterprise ultimately rests?*
>
> *If we are to assume that the desire for personal profit is the prime force motivating control, we must conclude that the interests of control are*

*different from, and often radically opposed to, those of ownership... There are numerous ... ways in which at least part of the profits of a corporation can be diverted toward the benefit of those in control.*

*[T]his corporate development has created a new set of relationships... If, by reason of such relationships, the men in control of a corporation can operate it for their own interests, and can divert a portion of the asset fund or income stream to their own uses, such is their privilege... Since the new powers have been acquired on a quasi-contractual basis, the security holders have agreed in advance to any losses which they may suffer by reason of such use.*

Berle and Means were cautious men. What is not apparent from the chosen quotations is the authors' unwillingness to assert that the widely held corporation would turn out this way. They said that either the traditional model, founded in trust law, of corporate assets managed for the exclusive benefit of the shareholder would prevail, or the new model, articulated in these quotations, would prevail.

We now know which model has prevailed. (Some day, even the authors of our corporate finance texts will know.) Today, those "in whose hands the efficient operation of enterprise ultimately rests" are being generously rewarded for performing this function. That Jensen and Meckling, in their famous 1976 paper in the *Journal of Financial Economics* ("Theory of the Firm: Managerial Behavior, Agency Costs, and Ownership Structure") refer to these rewards as *opportunism* tells us which of the two Berle and Means models Jensen and Meckling prefer. They argue that the shareholders will fully discount the cost of these rewards to them; they call this behavior *price protection*. We will use the price protection concept, extending it in ways we hope Jensen and Meckling will approve. But because the model of the widely held corporation they prefer is not the model that has prevailed, we shall avoid using the word *opportunism* for the rewards to control.

## Consequences for Share Value

When a corporation is rewarding those in control, only part of the corporate dividend goes to the shareholder. Part goes to management, or to those in control of management. And part, of course, goes to the government in the form of income taxes. All three represent claims on the gross value of the firm's equity, and so all three are subject to the same investment risk. How does the prospect of a control dividend affect the value of the shareholders' claim?

Let us focus first on the combined claim. And let us express that claim as a dividend yield—as the fraction of the gross equity's current value to be disbursed to the three claimants. We express what the then equity value would be, absent any such disbursements now or later by $V(t)$, with $V(0)$ corresponding to the (known) value now.

Unlike $V(0)$, of course, the values $V(1), V(2), \ldots$, are generally unknown at time 0—i.e., they are risky. That means the dividends at time 1, time 2, and so on are also risky. The value remaining after the dividend at time zero is then:

$$V(0) - pV(0) = (1 - p)V(0) \tag{52.1}$$

which is worth $(1 - p)V(1)$ at time 1. The dividend at time (1) is:

$$p(1 - p)V(1) \tag{52.2}$$

leaving

$$(1 - p)V(1) - p(1 - p)V(1) = (1 - p)(1 - p)V(1) \tag{52.3}$$

which, at time 2, is worth:

$$(1 - p)^2 V(2) \tag{52.4}$$

etc.

What is the value now of this stream of dividends? At times $0, 1, 2, \ldots$, the individual dividends are worth, respectively:

$$pV(0), p(1 - p)V(1), p(1 - p)^2 V(3) \tag{52.5}$$

But at time zero, they are worth, respectively:

$$pV(0), p(1 - p)V(0), p(1 - p)^2 V(0),$$

etc.

The sum of their present values is:

$$pV(0) \sum_{t=0}^{\infty} (1 - p)^t = pV(0) \frac{1}{1 - (1 - p)} = V(0) \tag{52.6}$$

Let us define yields $p_1$, $p_2$, $p_3$ on the remaining value of the gross equity to the shareholders, management and government, respectively. Of course, we have:

$$p_1 + p_2 + p_3 = p \tag{52.7}$$

Consider, for example, the stream of dividends to the shareholder. Since the equity value remaining at time 1 is $(1 - p)V(1)$, the dividend to the shareholder at time 1 is:

$$p_1(1 - p)V(1) \tag{52.8}$$

The equity value at time 2 being $(1 - p)^2 V(2)$, the dividend to the shareholder at time 2 is:

$$p_1(1 - p)^2 V(2) \tag{52.9}$$

But $V(1)$, $V(2)$, $\ldots$, have present values $V(0)$, $V(0)$, $\ldots$. Clearly the stream of dividends flowing to the shareholder has the present value

$$p_1 V(0) \sum_{t=0}^{\infty} (1 - p)^t = \frac{p_1}{p} V(0) \tag{52.10}$$

Similarly, the tax and control dividends have respective present values of

$$\frac{p_2}{p}V(0), \frac{p_3}{p}V(0) \tag{52.11}$$

Lest it cause any confusion, we call attention to our practice of defining yields relative to combined ("gross") present value, rather than to shareholder value alone, as yields are defined conventionally. Of course, one can use either our yields or conventional yields in Equations 52.10 and 52.11, as long as one is consistent.

It follows from Equations 52.7, 52.10, and 52.11 that:

$$V_1 + V_2 + V_3 = \left(\frac{p_1 + p_2 + p_3}{p}\right)V(0) = \frac{p}{p}V(0) = V(0) \tag{52.12}$$

In addition, we know that the shareholder and government yields $p_1$ and $p_2$, respectively, are related by:

$$\frac{p_1}{p_2} = \frac{(1-T)}{T} \tag{52.13}$$

where T is the firm's effective income tax rate. Pretax "income" as defined by accountants and taxing authorities is the stream that would be available to *shareholders* if there were no income taxes. By definition, therefore, diversions to management are not "income" and won't be taxed as such. We also know that the shareholder and control values are related by:

$$\frac{V_1}{V_3} = \frac{p_1}{p_3} \tag{52.14}$$

If we take V as given, we can solve for the value of the respective claims using Equations 52.12, 52.13, and 52.14. Solving for $V_1$, the value of the shareholders' claim, we get:

$$V_1 = \frac{V}{\dfrac{p_3}{p_1} + \dfrac{1}{1-T}} \tag{52.15}$$

We can calculate the elasticity of this value with respect to the shareholder yield. It is:

$$\frac{p_1}{V_1}\frac{\delta V_1}{\delta p_1} = \frac{p_3/p_1}{p_3/p_1 + \dfrac{1}{1-T}} = \frac{1}{1 + \dfrac{p_1/p_3}{1-T}} \tag{52.16}$$

Although the total value is insensitive to the total dividend yield, the shareholder value is sensitive to the shareholder yield, when the control yield is held constant.

## The Economics of Takeovers

Although often cited as the motive for hostile takeovers, synergy is rarely demonstrated. The real motive is to transfer control from the management of the target corporation (the "target management") to the management of the corporation taking over (the "takeover management"). With control of the target firm, the takeover management gets the value of control. But the takeover management doesn't pay for the takeover; the takeover shareholder does. If the price of the takeover—what the shareholder pays—is higher than what the shareholder gets, the transaction will hurt the takeover shareholder. What the shareholder gets is the gross value of the target firm, less the value of control by the takeover management:

Pre-Takeover Price + Value of Target Control − Value of Takeover Control (52.17)

What the shareholder pays is the takeover price. Thus we have, for the net gain to the shareholder:

$$\text{Pre-Takeover Price} + \text{Value of Target Control} - \text{Takeover Price}$$

$$= \text{Value of Target Control} - \text{Value of Takeover Control}$$

$$- \text{Takeover Premium} \qquad\qquad (52.18)$$

Now suppose takeover firms are addicted to takeovers, so that only the identity of the next target firm is news to the takeover shareholder. Then (1) any damage to the takeover shareholder will not, on average, be visible in share price reaction to the news, and (2) the takeover shareholder will price protect against, not merely the imminent takeover, but all future takeovers. To avoid severely depressing the share price of its firm, the takeover management must avoid saddling its shareholders with transactions that cost more than they are worth.

The value of control to the takeover management cannot be less than zero. If takeover managements succeed in keeping the above expression positive, then the value of control to the target management cannot be less than the takeover premium. If the value of control to the takeover management *were* zero, the takeover management would have no motive for the takeover. But, to the extent this number exceeds zero, it increases the requisite value of control by the target management dollar for dollar.

If a takeover firm could buy a target firm for its pretakeover price plus one dollar, control would transfer from the target management to the takeover management, which could then reward itself as generously for control as did the target management without harming its own shareholders. But if the takeover entails a premium—a difference between the target management's old share price and the takeover price—the takeover shareholder suffers, unless the takeover management reduces the reward to control. If takeover firms strive with each succeeding takeover to avoid impoverishing their own shareholders then, because takeover premiums can't be negative, successive takeovers of the same corporate assets can only reduce the reward to control. In this special sense, Jensen is surely right that takeovers lead to improvements in "efficiency." Obviously, the target firms for which the biggest takeover premiums are feasible are those whose managements enjoy the biggest rewards to control.

Obviously, too, the number of times the same enterprise can be taken over without damaging takeover shareholders at some stage is limited.

## THE TAKEOVER PREMIUM

The difference between the takeover price and the value of the shareholders' claim absent any prospect of takeover is called the *takeover premium*. It is in the takeover management's interest to raise control value as high as they can without making their own shareholder worse off than he was before the acquisition. When this rule is just satisfied, the takeover premium will equal the difference between the target's value to the new shareholder and its value to the old. Using our expression for value to the shareholder, we can write this difference:

$$\frac{V}{\frac{p_3^*}{p_1^*} + \frac{1}{1-T}} - \frac{V}{\frac{p_3}{p_1} + \frac{1}{1-T}} = V\frac{\frac{p_3}{p_1} - \frac{p_3^*}{p_1^*}}{\left(\frac{p_3}{p_1} + \frac{1}{1-T}\right)\left(\frac{p_3^*}{p_1^*} + \frac{1}{1-T}\right)} \qquad (52.19)$$

Expressed as a fraction of the pre-takeover market value, the premium is

$$\left(\frac{p_3}{p_1} - \frac{p_3^*}{p_1^*}\right) \Big/ \left(\frac{p_3^*}{p_1^*} + \frac{1}{1-T}\right) \qquad (52.20)$$

In the last takeover boom, premiums in hostile takeovers were averaging around 40 percent of pretakeover market value. How big can the takeover firm's control yield be? Assuming an effective corporate income tax rate of 40 percent, we have:

$$0.4 = \left(\frac{p_3}{p_1} - \frac{p_3^*}{p_1^*}\right) \Big/ \left(\frac{p_3^*}{p_1^*} + \frac{1}{0.60}\right)$$

$$\frac{p_3^*}{p_1^*} = 0.714\frac{p_3}{p_1} - 0.476 \qquad (52.21)$$

When the ratio $p_3/p_1$ for the target firm is less than two-thirds, the value of this expression is negative; target firms with ratios $p_3/p_1$ below two-thirds cannot be acquired without injuring the takeover firm's shareholders. If takeovers are occurring at 40 percent premiums, then this ratio probably exceeds two-thirds, at least in target firms. If you don't want to be acquired when takeover premiums are running 40 percent of pretakeover value, keep your ratio of control yield to shareholder yield below two-thirds.

These calculations ignore any direct tax benefit associated with the purchase transactions (hostile takeovers are commonly accomplished by tender offers).

## THE ARITHMETIC OF LEVERAGED BUYOUTS

The value of control to management of a traditional leveraged buyout is zero, because the managers *are* the shareholders. When no other species of acquisition will satisfy the requirement that the value of control to the new management be less than the value of control to the old management, a leveraged buyout—which minimizes the value of control to the takeover management—may still satisfy it. To the investment banker trying to find a takeover to arrange, a leveraged buyout is consequently the takeover of last resort.

When the leveraged buyout's management subsequently takes the company public, it creates a new opportunity for valuable control. But the new public shareholders will pay a penalty equal to the value of that control if they buy the firm for full value when the firm goes public. Management may be able to focus new shareholders' attention on the profitability of the company's operations as a leveraged buyout—when there was no control yield and no value to control.

On the other hand, the larger the control yield after the leveraged buyout goes public, the easier it is to justify a subsequent takeover. With the right kind of managers, the cycle of takeover, leveraged buyout, going public, can be repeated. Jensen and Meckling should be fascinated by leveraged buyouts because, when used this way, they represent a way of defeating the price protection mechanism.

## CONCLUSION

Surrounding takeovers are some remarkably stubborn mysteries.

1. If takeover prices are fair, then how can pretakeover share prices be efficient?
2. If pretakeover share prices are efficient, why are takeover firms willing to pay such high prices for target firms?
3. If takeover prices regularly exceed the true value of target firms, why aren't the share prices of takeover firms dramatically depressed?
4. Why do takeover managements always insist they aren't going to interfere with the target management if, as they allege, their objective is drastic improvements in the target firm's efficiency?
5. Why do they always interfere?

At the outset, we contrasted the two models of the widely held corporation articulated by Berle and Means. The questions listed above are mysteries only if one persists in interpreting corporate finance in terms of the trust model. Isn't it time to abandon this model?

# CHAPTER 53

# Economic Life versus Physical Life

Accountants sometimes suggest that the division of labor between them and security analysts is particularly clean when it comes to determining the life of capital assets: The accountant is concerned with the physical life of the asset, whereas the analyst is concerned with its economic life. The physical life of the asset ends when the asset wears out; the accountant estimates depreciation (hence earnings) using projections based on the physical lives of antecedent assets. For the analyst, directly concerned with predicting economic rents, the asset's life ends when its ability to continue earning an economic rent ends.

Unfortunately for accountants who defend this division of labor, most productive assets never wear out—or, more precisely, never wear out if properly maintained. Instead, the supply of newer assets with equal or lower out-of-pocket operating costs accumulates until, at the current level of demand, marginal cost is below the out-of-pocket operating cost for the old asset. At this point, the asset becomes uneconomical to operate unless it is undermaintained, thereby saving some portion of its out-of-pocket operating cost. Unfortunately for the asset, if it continues to operate in this economic purgatory for very long, it wears out. Thus in most cases where assets do wear out, economic and physical life are very closely linked, with causation flowing from economic life to physical life.

The accountant dealing with depreciation would like to believe he is dealing with certainties of physical wear and tear. Unfortunately, physical life, being closely linked to economic life, is subject to the same economic uncertainties. The accountant cannot make forecasts of physical life without implicitly making forecasts of the future rents an asset will command. In their joint activities relating to asset life—as in so many other aspects of financial analysis—the roles of the accountant and the securities analyst are hopelessly intertwined.

---

# CHAPTER 54

# The Investment Value of Plant

**P**rice theorists call industries that push output to the point where marginal cost equals price "perfectly competitive." In such industries, there are two relationships between price and output—the *supply curve* resulting from producers' behavior and a *demand curve* describing customers' behavior. There will usually be a unique combination of output and price that satisfies both relationships simultaneously.

It would be a great analytical convenience if output and price could be so neatly determined. Mere convenience is not, however, sufficient reason for assuming that industries actually behave this way, or even that they *ought* to behave this way.

Industries make two kinds of decisions that affect unit volume and price—

(1) Decisions about how much to produce, given their current stock of plant capacity—which of the currently available plant to operate and which to idle ("output" decisions) and
(2) Decisions about plant additions that would alter the stock of available capacity ("plant" decisions).

*Plant* decisions affect price, are visible to competitors and are almost always irreversible. An *output* decision that turns out bad can usually be reversed. Furthermore, producers can "feel" their way to output changes. Thus it wouldn't be surprising if producers made the two kinds of decisions in quite different ways.

Without some assumptions about how an industry makes these two decisions, no meaningful estimate of the investment value of plant is possible. We argue that, absent collusion, perfect competition approximates the way most industries, most of the time, make output decisions. We also argue that any industry that makes its plant decisions this way is unworthy of investor interest.

## A NEW TRACTOR

An example will serve to explain why industries can't be perfectly competitive. As textbook writers have long been fond of farming as the ideal, we begin with one based on wheat farmers.

Suppose, for simplicity, there is an unlimited supply of farmland that, with the same variable cost, can produce a bushel of wheat. And suppose that, just as the

---

textbooks assume, wheat farmers ignore the effect of their decision on price when deciding how much to produce. Then they will increase their output up to the point at which the price of the marginal bushel just covers their variable cost.

If every farmer has the same variable cost, then the marginal bushel's variable cost is the industry's average cost. With price equal to marginal cost equal to average cost, the industry is just breaking even on operating cash flow, with nothing left over for mortgage payments or even for payments on tractors.

Now suppose a superior tractor comes along, which lowers the variable cost of producing a bushel of wheat. Initially, of course, most farmers still use their old tractors. The marginal bushel—whose variable cost determines price—is still being produced the old way. Industry price and output remain unchanged. But farmers who buy the new tractor find that, at the old price, they have a positive operating cash flow; this represents the return on their investment in the new tractor.

Because wheat farmers don't consider the effect of their decisions on price, it is just a matter of time before so many farmers buy the new tractor that the marginal bushel is being produced at the new, lower variable cost. Price falls until it equals the new marginal cost, which once again equals average cost. Operating cash flow falls back to zero and, with it, the return on the investments in the new tractors.

What has happened? As long as the new tractors were *scarce*—as long as there weren't enough to go around—they generated a positive cash flow. When there were enough new tractors to produce all the wheat demanded—when they ceased being scarce—their contribution to cash flow went to zero.

As noted, this contribution to cash flow—the so-called *scarcity rent* or *economic rent*—represents the return to the investment in the new tractor. We now see that, although the tractor's *physical* life may last for a generation, its *economic* life is over when it ceases being scarce.

Whether the new tractor justifies the investment depends on the length of the tractor's economic life. That in turn depends on *how fast the wheat farmers buy new tractors*. The new tractor may be a better investment at a price high enough to discourage most farmers from buying it than at a lower price.

The wheat farmers have a maximum price they can justify paying for a tractor at each level of tractor output. This relationship, together with the relation between the tractor manufacturers' marginal cost and output rate, determines tractor price and output. But now the wheat farmers are no longer ignoring the effect of their decisions on the price of wheat.

The wheat farmers are still making output decisions competitively, but they are not making plant decisions—their tractor purchase decisions—competitively. If they made their plant decisions competitively, most of them would end up bankrupt. No investor in his right mind would be interested in supplying capital to such an industry. We conclude that the industries of interest to securities investors are not usefully described by the economist's ideal of perfect competition.

## THE HIGH-COST PRODUCER

Most modern industries are oligopolistic—characterized by having only a few producers. In the United States, there have rarely been more than three or four manufacturers of aspirin, spark plugs, cornflakes, facial tissue, ketchup, and so forth.

Suppose that, contrary to the perfectly competitive model, an oligopolistic industry takes price effects into account in setting its output level. By doing so, the industry may be able to make more money by producing less. In the absence of collusion between producers, the decision about how much capacity to withhold from production falls to the high-cost producer. To understand how far short of the perfectly competitive level this industry's output will fall, we need to understand this producer's point of view.

The high-cost producer gains nothing from using marginal plant, because its variable cost equals the industry's price. Indeed, by *not* using this plant, the producer can raise the industry's price slightly, thereby raising the price of every unit it *does* manufacture. But consider the highest-cost capacity the producer is still using. Its variable cost is *almost* as high as the industry price. Furthermore, by shutting it down, the producer can raise the industry price received on its remaining output. Clearly, this argument can be repeated until the rent on the marginal plant is high enough or the remaining output is small enough that further production cuts don't pay.

This point determines the level of *industry* output rational for the high-cost producer. The higher the output of *low*-cost producers, the less *high*-cost producers will choose to produce. Because low-cost producers have bigger unit margins than high-cost producers, they have more to lose from cutting their own output. But they also lose less from increases in their own output. Because increases in their output will be accompanied by decreases in output by high-cost producers, *industry* output will be dampened and price will not fall by as much as it would in a purely competitive system.

These considerations suggest that an industry with a handful of producers (in contrast to an industry comprised of thousands of wheat farmers) will take price into account in its output decisions, and hence decide to produce at less than perfectly competitive levels of output. But they also suggest that the critical decision maker is the high-cost producer. How will it make the output decision? Let:

$q^*$ = perfectly competitive level of industry output,
$q'$ = combined output of all but the high-cost producer,
$q$ = level of *industry* output that is best for the high-cost producer,
$D(\cdot)$ = industry demand curve (i.e., the price corresponding to output) and
$S(\cdot)$ = industry marginal cost curve.

By definition, the perfectly competitive level of industry output, $q^*$, satisfies:

$$D(q^*) = S(q^*)$$

More generally, the level of industry output best for the high-cost producer is that at which its gain from an extra unit of output just offsets the loss from the effect of the production increase on price. The potential gain is the difference between the industry price $D(q)$ and the high-cost producer's marginal cost. But the high-cost producer's marginal cost is the *industry's* marginal cost $S(q)$. So the difference is:

$$D(q) - S(q)$$

The effect on industry price of producing an incremental unit is dD/dq. The loss on the high-cost producer's output q − q′ is:

$$\frac{dD}{dq}(q - q')$$

At the level of output best for the high-cost producer, the incremental loss just offsets the incremental gain:

$$D(q) - S(q) + \frac{dD}{dq}(q - q') = 0$$

We can expand D(q) and S(q) in a Taylor series around the perfectly competitive level of industry output q*:

$$D(q) = D(q^*) + \frac{dD}{dq}(q - q^*)$$

$$S(q) = S(q^*) + \frac{dS}{dq}(q - q^*)$$

Substituting in our equation for the best level, we have:

$$\frac{dD}{dq}(q - q^*) - \frac{dS}{dq}(q - q^*) = \frac{dD}{dq}(q - q') = 0$$

$$\left(2\frac{dD}{dq} - \frac{dS}{dq}\right)q = \left(\frac{dD}{dq} - \frac{dS}{dq}\right)q^* + \frac{dD}{dq}q$$

$$q = \frac{(q' + q^*)\dfrac{dD}{dq} - q^*\dfrac{dS}{dq}}{2\dfrac{dD}{dq} - \dfrac{dS}{dq}}$$

$$\frac{q}{q^*} = \frac{\left(1 + \dfrac{q'}{q^*}\right)\dfrac{dD}{dq} - \dfrac{dS}{dq}}{2\dfrac{dD}{dq} - \dfrac{dS}{dq}}$$

The ratio q/q* measures how closely the industry approaches the ideal of perfect competition—specifically, the fraction of the ideal output level achieved by the output level best for the high-cost producer. As the output of the high-cost producer q − q′ declines, q′ approaches q* and the ratio approaches one.

The worst case for competition is the case where the high-cost producer constitutes the sole producer, a monopolist. Then q′ equals zero. The ratio q/q* ranges from ½, when the demand curve's slope is shallow and the cost curve's slope is steep, to 1, when the demand curve's slope is shallow and the cost curve's slope is steep.

Industries where brand recognition is important will often have three or four dominant firms, with no firm less than 50 percent bigger than its next smaller competitor (the "PIMS" rule). Consider a three-firm industry in which, as often happens, the smallest firm is also the high-cost firm. Let $x$ be the output of the largest of the three firms, expressed as a fraction of the industry's output. If the smallest firm is as large as possible consistent with the PIMS rule, we have:

$$x + \frac{2}{3}x + \left(\frac{2}{3}\right)^2 x = 1$$

$$9x + 6x + 4x = 9$$

$$x = \frac{9}{19}, \frac{2}{3}x = \frac{6}{19}, \left(\frac{2}{3}\right)^2 x = \frac{4}{19}$$

We have:

$$q' = \frac{9}{19} + \frac{6}{19} = \frac{15}{19}$$

$$\frac{q}{q^*} = \frac{\dfrac{34}{19}\dfrac{dD}{dq} - \dfrac{dS}{dq}}{\dfrac{38}{19}\dfrac{dD}{dq} - \dfrac{dS}{dq}}$$

Industry output will range between about 89 percent (34/38) and 100 percent of the perfectly competitive level.

Examples like these suggest that, in the absence of collusion, and given three or more firms, most industries will push their *output* decisions close to the perfectly competitive level. We think this is a useful assumption for investors.

## HOW PLANT ADDITIONS AFFECT THE SUPPLY CURVE

We have noted that, when an industry pushes its output to the point where marginal cost equals the price dictated by demand at that level of output, the industry's marginal cost curve becomes a supply curve. How does the addition of new capacity affect this curve?

With the passage of time, technology usually either advances or stands still, as what we knew yesterday is a subset of what we know today. Technological improvement of plant manifests itself in reductions in the variable cost of producing a unit of output. In some industries—notably the electric-generating industry and the airline industry—the effort at improvement focuses on fuel. In most industries, however, it focuses on labor cost.

As we have seen, the economic rent enjoyed by a given unit of plant is the difference between its variable cost and the variable cost of the marginal plant. Over time, the identity of the marginal plant changes (as in the case of the wheat farmers). Every time marginal cost—the variable cost of producing one unit on the marginal plant—falls by one dollar, the economic rent (per unit produced) on plant still in production falls by one dollar.

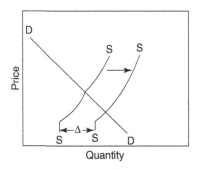

**EXHIBIT 54.1** Addition of New Plant

Shifts in demand will change the identity of the marginal plant, hence these rents. But shifts in demand are hard to predict. What is easy to predict (over the time required to build new plant) is the effect of capacity additions. Per unit of capacity, new plant may cost more or less than old plant. But, as noted, because of technological improvements, its variable cost of producing never goes up. This fact has an important practical consequence: New capacity enters the supply curve at the extreme lower left. Instead of changing the *shape* of the supply curve, new capacity merely nudges the curve to the right (see Exhibit 54.1).

Suppose we know the old supply curve, $S(q)$, specifying the industry's marginal cost—the variable cost of producing a unit of output on the marginal plant—as a function of the industry's output rate. Now the industry adds new capacity in amount $\Delta$. We can derive the new supply curve by observing that, at any given price, the new output will be the output from the old plant plus the output from the new capacity. Because the new capacity will produce output $\Delta$, the price required to elicit a specified output q after the capacity addition is the price required to elicit the difference $q - \Delta$ from the old capacity. But this is the price given by the old supply curve.

Let the old curve be $S(q)$. Then the new curve is $S(q-\Delta)$:

$$S_{new}(q) = S_{old}(q - \Delta)$$

The new supply curve is the old curve, shifted right by the amount $\Delta$. Given the same old demand curve, this shift is likely to change the identity of the marginal plant and, with it, marginal cost. But note that the change in marginal cost doesn't depend on the *efficiency* of the new plant. Its efficiency won't affect the industry's marginal cost until it becomes the marginal plant. In short, its *capacity* affects marginal cost at the beginning of its economic life; its efficiency affects marginal cost at the end.

Now suppose an industry adds capacity at a roughly constant rate $\lambda$. Then the capacity $\Delta$ added over an interval $\tau$ is $\lambda\tau$. Given the supply curve $S(q)$ at the beginning of this interval, the supply curve at the end can be approximated by:

$$S(q - \Delta) = S(q - \lambda\tau)$$

It is sometimes useful to represent the supply curve as a function of both output rate q and the real time t. Then we have:

$$S(q, \tau) = S(q - \lambda\tau, 0)$$

More generally:

$$S(q, \ t_2) = S(q - \lambda t_2 + \lambda t_1, t_1)$$

## ECONOMIC LIFE OF PLANT

If an industry adds capacity at an average rate $\lambda$, when will the plant it is adding now be obsolete? Let the plant's variable cost of producing one unit of output be c. When it is the marginal plant, industry price will be C. If the industry demand function is D(q), then output q at that time will satisfy:

$$D(q) = c$$

But when today's new plant is just obsolete, industry output will equal the capacity of all the plant added subsequently. On one hand, none of that plant is yet obsolete; on the other, all the capacity that preceded today's new plant is obsolete.

Let the economic life of today's new plant be t. Then industry output when it is just obsolete is:

$$q = \lambda t$$

Substituting, we have:

$$D(q) = D(\lambda t) = c$$

The economic life t of today's new plant depends only on the demand function D(q), the industry's expected rate of capacity addition $\lambda$, and the new plant's variable unit cost c. Because demand functions are monotonic, the value of t that satisfies this equation will be unique.

It is often convenient to express economic life in terms of the *inverse* demand function—in other words, the quantity demanded at a given price. We denote this by $Q_D(p)$. This definition implies, of course, that:

$$Q_D[D(q)] = q$$
$$D[Q_D(p)] = p$$

Using the inverse demand function, we can write a closed-form expression for economic life t:

$$q = t = Q_D(c)$$
$$t = 1/\lambda \ Q_D(c)$$

What about the economic life of *old* plant? The industry's output level when old plant is just obsolete is obviously the capacity added since that plant was new. Let the capacity added between then and now be Q. Then we have:

$$Q + \lambda t = Q_D(c)$$

$$\lambda t = Q_D(c) - Q$$

$$t = \frac{Q_D(c) - Q}{\lambda}$$

where c is now the old plant's variable unit cost. If the rate of capacity addition in the future is expected to be roughly what it was in the relevant past, then the remaining life t satisfies:

$$\lambda(\tau + t) = Q_D(c)$$

$$\tau + t = 1/\lambda \; Q_D(c)$$

$$t = 1/\lambda \; Q_D(c) - \tau$$

where $\tau$ is the present age of the old plant.

## THE VALUE OF FUTURE ECONOMIC RENTS

We have observed that, at any point in the plant's economic life, its rent is the difference between the plant's variable unit cost of producing and the industry's marginal cost (i.e., the variable unit cost of producing on the industry's marginal plant.) As we have seen, capacity additions to the industry tend to push its marginal cost down until, finally, no difference—no economic rent—remains.

The typical pattern of rents over the life of plant is roughly a right triangle, with a "base" equal to the plant's economic life and an "altitude" equal to its rent when new. The plant's aggregate rent over its life (without present-value adjustments) is the area of this triangle.

The pattern of rents for *old* plant also tends to be a right triangle, but with both the base and altitude diminished. For example, when half a plant's economic life remains, its current rent will tend to equal roughly half its initial rent. Accordingly, its future aggregate rent will tend to be one-quarter its future aggregate rent when new. So a new plant will tend to realize three-quarters of its future aggregate rent in the first half of its economic life. And, because of compounding effects, *more* than three-quarters of the new plant's present value will tend to be generated during the first half of its economic life (see Exhibit 54.2).

A more sophisticated model of plant value assumes that marginal cost falls exponentially with time (so that the fractional reduction in each year is the same). Assume the fractional reduction is $\mu$ per annum and the initial marginal cost is M. Then, if the plant's own variable unit cost is C, its economic life ends T years hence, when:

$$Me^{-\mu T} = C$$

$$T = \frac{\ln M - \ln C}{\mu}$$

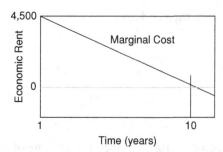

**EXHIBIT 54.2**   Economic Rent Over
Plant's Lifetime

Its rent at time t is the difference between marginal cost $Me^{\mu t}$ and C, or:

$$Me^{\mu t} - C$$

Discounted at rate r, the plant's present value is:

$$\int_0^T e^{-rt}(Me^{-\mu t} - C)dt = \frac{1}{r+\mu}(M - e^{-rT}C) - \frac{C}{r}(1 - e^{-rT})$$

The second term is the present value of the annuity comprising the plant's own variable cost. The first term is the contribution to the plant's present value of marginal cost.

But we know that

$$e^{-rt} = \left(e^{-\mu T}\right)^{\frac{t}{\mu}} = \left(\frac{C}{M}\right)^{\frac{t}{\mu}}$$

Rewriting our present-value expression as:

$$\frac{M}{r+\mu}\left(1 - \frac{C^{-rT}}{M^e}\right) - \frac{M}{r}\left(\frac{C}{M} - \frac{C^{-n}}{M^e}\right)$$

we have

$$\frac{M}{r+\mu}\left[1 - \left(\frac{C}{M}\right)^{\frac{r+\mu}{r}}\right] - \frac{M}{r}\left[\frac{C}{M} - \left(\frac{C}{M}\right)^{\frac{r+\mu}{r}}\right]$$

In using this expression for the value of plant, M is the sum of the plant's variable cost and current rent.

We have calculated the present value of plant with a 20-year economic life, initial rent of $10 million, and variable unit cost of $10 million, using the straight-line or triangle method and the exponential decay (in marginal cost, not rent) method, assuming a discount rate of 10 percent. The present values are $56.7 million and $51.7 million, respectively.

## PHYSICAL VERSUS ECONOMIC LIFE

By now, the reader has probably sensed a conflict between the right-triangle model and a more traditional model of the time pattern of rents over the life of plant. In the traditional model, rents continue at roughly the same rate until the plant wears out. The time pattern is rectangular, rather than triangular.

The difference has investment implications. The rectangular model implies that, present-value effects aside, the value of plant is proportional to its remaining life. The triangular model implies that the value of plant varies with the square of its remaining life (see Exhibit 54.3). In the traditional rectangular model, physical life determines economic life. In the triangular model, however, economic life determines physical life.

Junkyards are full of worn-out plant. Does this mean that physical life determines economic life—that the traditional, rectangular model is the correct model for the time pattern of rents over the life of plant?

Consider plant that is just obsolete, plant whose variable unit cost is just above the industry's marginal cost. Suppose also that its variable unit cost includes a substantial element of maintenance cost, so that suspending maintenance cost would make the obsolete plant competitive once again. It may then behoove its owner to suspend maintenance and keep the otherwise obsolete plant in production.

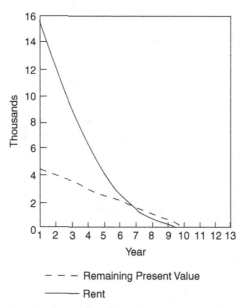

**EXHIBIT 54.3**  How Economic Rent and Remaining Present Value Decline with Time

But when plant is operated without the necessary maintenance, it wears out. (And the owner forgoes the option of operating the plant in the future, if demand and price improve.) So the reprieve is merely temporary, and the worn-out plant ends up in the junkyard. Economic life has determined physical life, however, rather than the other way around.

## MARGINAL COST DECAYS WITH TIME

The value of plant depends on economic rents, hence on the level of the industry's marginal cost, at each point during the plant's life. The right-triangle model illustrates the importance of the rate at which marginal cost is falling: This rate directly affects both economic life and the level of economic rents in the interim. If the reader is already convinced that the faster the industry adds capacity, the steeper the demand curve, the steeper the supply curve, the faster marginal cost will fall, he can skip this section.

At each point, the marginal plant is the oldest still operating. This means that, until a plant is obsolete, the plant governing marginal cost is plant already in the industry's supply curve. If we want to predict future economic rents for a plant, it isn't necessary to know the efficiency of any plant other than what is already in the supply curve.

We have seen that the relevant portion of future supply curves is given by

$$S(q, t) = S(q - \lambda t, o)$$

where t is measured from the present moment, and $\lambda$ is, as before, the expected rate of capacity addition, and $S(q, o)$ is the current supply curve. The output level q at time t is determined by equality between supply and demand:

$$D(q) = S(q, t) = S(q - \lambda t, o)$$

Price, hence marginal cost, at time t is then determined by $D(q)$.

We ask, how fast will marginal cost, hence economic rents, fall? Differentiate the equation with respect to t:

$$\frac{dD}{dq}\frac{dq}{dt} = \frac{\partial S}{\partial t}\frac{dq}{dt} - \lambda$$

and solve for dq/dt:

$$\frac{dq}{dt} = -\frac{\lambda\frac{\partial S}{\partial q}}{\frac{dD}{dq} - \frac{\partial S}{\partial q}} = \frac{\lambda}{1 - (dD/dq)/(\partial S/\partial q)}$$

Marginal cost falls with time at rate:

$$-\frac{dD}{dq}\frac{dq}{dt} = \frac{\lambda\dfrac{dD}{dq}\dfrac{\partial S}{\partial q}}{\dfrac{dD}{dq} - \dfrac{\partial S}{\partial q}} = \frac{\lambda}{[1/(\partial S/\partial q)] - [1/(dD/dq)]}$$

If the demand and supply curves slope steeply, and the expected rate of capacity addition $\lambda$ is large, then marginal cost will fall rapidly with time, and so will economic rents. The slope of the supply curve is directly observable. The slope of the demand curve can be estimated if its elasticity is known. From the definition of the elasticity $h_D$ we have:

$$h_d = -\frac{q\,dD}{D\,dq}$$

$$\frac{dD}{dq} = -\left(\frac{D}{q}\right)h_d$$

Exhibit 54.4 lists demand elasticities for some representative products.

**EXHIBIT 54.4**  Demand Elasticities

| | |
|---|---|
| Air Travel (coach) | 1.07 |
| Apples | 1.27 |
| Bar Steel | 1.30 |
| Beef | 0.65 |
| Butter | 0.62 |
| Cabbage | 0.25 |
| Chicken | 0.65 |
| Copper (long term) | 0.90 |
| Cold Rolled Steel | 1.49 |
| Corn | 0.63 |
| Cream | 0.69 |
| Cucumbers | 0.70 |
| Eggs | 0.43 |
| Hot Rolled Steel | 0.54 |
| Lettuce | 2.58 |
| Milk | 0.49 |
| Onions | 0.44 |
| Oranges | 0.62 |
| Peaches | 1.49 |
| Peanuts | 0.38 |
| Peas | 2.83 |
| Plate Steel | 1.81 |
| Pork | 0.45 |
| Potatoes | 0.27 |
| Structural Steel | 1.99 |
| Tomatoes | 2.22 |
| Wool | 0.33 |

*Source:* W. Adams, *The Structure of American Industry*, 5th ed. (New York: MacMillan, 1977).

## TECHNOLOGY AND THE SUPPLY CURVE

So far, we have taken an industry's supply curve as given. But what shapes the supply curve? What makes it steep or gradual, convex or concave?

We have noted that advances in plant technology are manifested in reductions in the variable unit cost of producing. For a given rate of capacity addition, more rapid technological advance—more rapid reduction in the variable unit cost of producing on new plant—will result in a steeper supply curve. For a given rate of technological advance, more rapid capacity addition will result in a less steep supply curve.

Once plant is built, its efficiency—its variable unit cost of producing—is locked in. Of course, it behooves its builder to avail himself of the best technology available at the time of construction. Points high up correspond to old, high-cost technology; points low down correspond to recent, relatively low-cost technology.

These observations suggest that each point on an industry's supply curve has a variable unit cost of producing fixed by the technology available when the plant was built. The capacity in the supply curve with that cost depends on the rate at which the industry was investing at that time. We can formalize these ideas by introducing a *technology function*, $T(c)$, expressing the time $T$ when new plant technology achieved a unit variable cost of production $c$, and an investment function, $I(t)$, expressing the cumulative capacity added up to time $t$. The technology function captures the history of technological progress in the industry; the investment function captures the history of its capacity additions.

How is the supply curve related to the two dimensions of its history captured by the technology function and the investment function? When the industry's product price is $p$, the unit variable cost of producing on its marginal plant is also $p$. When we substitute price $p$ for the unit variable cost $c$ in the industry's technology function $T(c)$, it tells us when such plant was built. At that price $p$, all plant added prior to $T(p)$ is obsolete. Thus the industry's output at time $t$ is the capacity $I(t)$ accumulated up to that time, less the portion of that capacity that is obsolete at price $p$, or:

$$Q_s(p,\, t) = I(t) - I[T(p)]$$

where $Q_s$ is the inverse supply function—the rate of output elicited by product price $p$ at time $t$.

Earlier we saw that the rate at which an industry's marginal cost, hence its economic rent, falls depends on the slope of its supply curve. What does the slope of the supply curve depend on? Differentiate the new equation with respect to price $p$:

$$\frac{\partial Q_s}{\partial p} = -\frac{dI}{dt}\frac{dT}{dp}$$

A steeply sloping supply curve corresponds to a small value for this expression, hence to rapidly changing technology (a small value of $dT/dp$) and a low rate of investment $dI/dt$.

# CHAPTER 55

# Growth Companies

Monitoring companies' sales forces, advertising, and new product development—and worrying about competitors' sales forces, advertising, and new product development—demands a degree of involvement in day-to-day detail that few of us feel we can justify in our roles as outside investors. How much do we need to know? The traditional answer assumes that what we need to know is confined to accounting numbers—to normalized current earnings, earnings trend, and so forth. The only way to appraise the adequacy of this answer is to get behind the numbers and consider certain business realities.

## THE CONCEPT OF BRAND FRANCHISE

Strolling down the aisles of a supermarket, one sees two prices for most packaged goods—or two clusters of prices, with prices within the clusters differing by pennies. For many products, the spread between the two prices is large, often one-third of the higher price (see Exhibit 55.1). Multiplied by unit sales, *marketing spread* often contributes more to operating cash flow than does the company's plant.

Marketing spread reflects a curious fact about consumer behavior: Consumers who are anxious and insecure about choosing the "right" brand make one brand their standard of comparison. Judging all other brands by how closely they resemble the standard, these consumers are indifferent between paying one price for their standard and a different, substantially lower price for any other brand. Sometimes, they buy their standard and pay the higher price. At other times, they buy the other brand and pay the lower price. The consumers who are loyal to a particular brand in this special sense constitute that brand's *franchise*.

## COMPETITORS AND PRODUCERS

A manufacturer cannot interview customers as they come to their purchase decisions and charge different prices depending on how customers feel about its brand. In broad principle, the manufacturer must choose which price to charge. At the lower price, it can sell to any customer in the market, including those who regard its brand

**EXHIBIT 55.1**   Product Price Spreads

|  | | Price | | |
| Product | Size | National Brand | Brand X | Differential |
| --- | --- | --- | --- | --- |
| Concentrated laundry detergent | 20 pounds | $15.75 | $7.75 | 49% |
| Bleach | 1 gallon | 1.19 | 0.82 | 69 |
| Dishwashing liquid | 32 ounces | 2.59 | 1.69 | 65 |
| Facial tissue | 175 count | 1.23 | 0.83 | 67 |
| Corn flakes | 18 ounces | 1.75 | 1.59 | 91 |
| Sweetened corn flakes | 20 ounces | 3.09 | 2.49 | 81 |
| Raisin bran | 20 ounces | 3.15 | 2.49 | 73 |
| Sweetened oat cereal | 15 ounces | 2.79 | 2.09 | 75 |
| Aluminum foil | 75 feet | 1.93 | 1.53 | 79 |
| Paper towels | 201 feet | 1.93 | 1.53 | 79 |
| Tonic water | 1 liter | 0.99 | 0.59 | 60 |
| Club soda | 1 liter | 0.99 | 0.59 | 60 |
| Diapers | 44 count | 10.99 | 7.69 | 72 |
| Petroleum jelly | 13 ounces | 3.47 | 2.57 | 74 |
| Baby oil | 20 ounces | 4.29 | 2.99 | 70 |
| Swabs | 300 count | 2.35 | 1.49 | 63 |
| Bathroom tissue | 165 feet | 1.49 | 0.79 | 53 |
| Average | — | — | — | 69 |

as the standard, and use all the plant capacity that is economic to use at that price. At a higher price, the manufacturer can sell only to its franchise, idling the capacity that franchise is not big enough to absorb.

The marketing spread between the two price levels presents manufacturers with a choice between two fundamentally different strategies. If its franchise is small enough, a manufacturer will make more money selling at the lower price rather than restricting output to the amount of its franchise. If its franchise is large enough, the manufacturer can restrict output to what the customers in that franchise (who are willing to pay the higher price) can absorb. Because this strategy restricts output, it will pay to cultivate the franchise—to sell, to promote, to advertise, and to develop new products. If franchise expansion is the strategy chosen, the manufacturer is called a *competitor.*

Pricing a product at the bottom of the marketing spread rather than the top will eliminate all value from any franchise the manufacturer may have. Accordingly, the manufacturer will not advertise its brand, and new product development will be minimal, defensive, and imitative. If low price is the selected strategy, the manufacturer is called a *producer.*

In some industries, the marketing spread is negligible or zero. In such industries, franchise is worth nothing. Accordingly, nobody in the industry spends money on advertising or new product development. Such products are called commodities. In commodity industries, plant value is all-important.

Certain other industries have no plant. Value derives entirely from brand franchise. (Consulting firms, engineering firms, and advertising agencies do not talk about the value of their franchise. Instead, they talk about "reputation.") The bulk of industries have both marketing spread (and its concomitant, valuable market franchise) and valuable plant.

Not all companies in such industries are competitors, however; some are merely producers.

Although competitors and producers have different costs and different prices, they both supply the same market. A sale by competitors displaces a sale by producers and *vice versa*. Thus, the determinants of marketing spread have nothing to do with scarcity, or market equilibrium, or price theory.

Different products with different markets will have different marketing spreads. Product spreads will evolve over time as the degree of customer anxiety about the choice between brands evolves. Changing the spread is not the object of marketing; neither is increasing industry sales. The object of almost all marketing effort is capturing or defending franchise.

## MARKETING PEACE VERSUS MARKETING WAR

Customers for a given product change their allegiances and drift from one competitor's brand franchise to another's. If a firm wants to maintain its franchise, it has to replace the lost customers. Maintenance requires wooing new customers via expenditures on selling, promotion, advertising, and other kinds of marketing. Competitors with large franchises will endeavor to defend them; competitors with small franchises will endeavor to enlarge them.

The level of marketing effort required to maintain a given franchise depends on competitors' levels of effort—on the industry's *level of rivalry*. At a low level of rivalry, the cost of maintaining a franchise will be a fraction of the benefits it provides, but at a sufficiently high level, maintenance costs can absorb all the benefits.

In principle, the dividing line between marketing war and marketing peace is easy to state: In peace, the gross benefits of brand franchise exceed the costs of defending it; in war, the costs of defending brand franchise exceed its gross benefits.[1]

A crude way to estimate the costs of defending or extending franchise is to assume that at any given level of rivalry for the industry, the costs of maintaining franchise will be proportional to the size of the franchise. This assumption is really two assumptions:

- The rate at which a franchise loses customers to the competition is proportional to its size.
- The rate at which marketing effort can seduce customers away from the competition is proportional to the effort.

The first assumption is plausible; the second is probably only a rough approximation to a complicated reality. These assumptions are almost certainly overly simple: They make no allowance for economies of scale in marketing.

It is convenient to measure franchise, $z$, in dollar terms as the product of unit sales and marketing spread. Change in franchise, $\Delta z$, depends on the initial size of the franchise, $z$, and the competitor's level of marketing effort, $u$:

$$\Delta z = Au - Bz$$

When the competitor's effort, $u^*$, is such that its franchise gains just offset its losses, we have

$$\Delta z = 0 = Au^* - Bz$$

$$Au^* = Bz$$

$$u^* = (B/A)z$$

Thus, $(B/A)z$ represents the maintenance level of marketing effort. The value of franchise is the present value of the net flowback—the benefit of $z$ less the cost of maintaining it; that is,

$$z - (B/A)z = z(1 - B/A)$$

Adding across all competitors in a market, we have

$$\Sigma \Delta z = A\Sigma u - B\Sigma z = 0$$

The right-hand term ($B\Sigma z$) is the industry's total attrition (for the year, say)—all the customers who abandon their previous brands. Which brands will be the beneficiaries? The left-hand term ($A\Sigma u$) reflects our assumption that the fickle customers will be allocated among competitors in proportion to the competitors' marketing efforts. Suppressing differences in $A$ from competitor to competitor, we can solve for the coefficient in the expression for the maintenance level of effort.

$$B/A = \Sigma u / \Sigma z$$

Substituting in the expression for the next flowback, we have

$$z\left[1 - \frac{\Sigma u}{\Sigma z}\right]$$

In most industries, the level of rivalry, $\Sigma u$, will fluctuate, but when it exceeds $\Sigma z$, franchise ceases being an asset and becomes a liability; the industry has crossed the line between marketing peace and marketing war.

A plausible model for competitors' behavior in times of marketing peace is Rapoport and Chammah's Tit for Tat:[2] If one competitor raises its level of effort significantly beyond the maintenance level, other competitors raise theirs until the offending competitor is no longer experiencing any franchise gain—that is, until its new level of effort has once again become its maintenance level. Now, the competitor is making less money and has the same franchise as before.

But under Tit for Tat, if the competitor lowers its level of effort, its competitors will lower theirs. In this way, competitors in a market enforce a reasonable degree of stability in marketing peace. Investors may be tempted to assume that (1) current franchise shares are a basis for unbiased forecasts of future franchise shares and (2) the current level of marketing rivalry is an unbiased forecast of the future level. The truth of both assumptions depends on whether all the competitors in the industry really want peace. If they do not, then Tit for Tat, which ignores differences in resources among players and the constraints resources impose, is no longer the appropriate model.

Marketing wars are fought with dollars rather than bullets. The game is outlasting the competitor: The winner is the competitor who is still spending when his competition has run out of spending power. From the point of view of existing shareholders, however, a marketing war is the worst time for a publicly owned competitor to sell new shares: The competitor's future is in doubt, and its cash flow is depressed. Instead, the cash required to fight a marketing war comes from borrowing. The winner keeps the level of rivalry high until the loser either abandons its franchise or exhausts its borrowing power.

Once the loser exhausts its borrowing power, it cannot defend its franchise. Lending on the value of the franchise presumes that franchise can be defended. The only safe assumption for a lender is that in marketing war, the level of rivalry will remain high until the most vulnerable borrower has abandoned its franchise.

In marketing, as in the military, transitions from (relative) peace to all-out war are often sudden and unpredictable, and these transitions are at least as unpredictable for lenders as they are for the competing firms. This situation poses a problem for a lender that is relying on the value of a borrower's market franchise as security: When marketing war breaks out, the value of the lender's security may disappear overnight.

Only one determined competitor is enough to start a war, and anything that reduces a company's borrowing power makes war more attractive to its competitors. Normally, a rough upper limit on a company's borrowing power is suggested by the difference between the gross value of its operations and its liabilities. The portion of the value of its operations stemming from franchise, however, is not valid security for a lender. How much a competitor can borrow, hence how much it can spend, to defend its *franchise* depends on the value of its *plant*, less outstanding lenders' claims—a number we call *plant equity*.

## ECONOMIC GOODWILL AND GROWTH

We have argued that goodwill gains in marketing investment come from taking valuable franchise away from a competitor—an endeavor that surely increases the risk of reprisal, escalation, and ultimately, marketing war. Judging these risks and determining which are worth taking are principal tasks of a company's management. Part of the task is concealing from competitors which risks management is prepared to take—that is, which marketing investments management is willing to make. If management is concealing its plans for marketing investment from the competition, then it is surely concealing them from outside investors as well.

The spoils in the battle for franchise are zero-sum: What one competitor gains, another must lose. For the industry as a whole, marketing effort is pure loss. Public knowledge that one competitor has ambitious growth plans can only lower the investment value of the industry. Taken together, these considerations suggest that the existing shareholders will find it hard to persuade new shareholders to pay up for any putative goodwill on future marketing investment. If so, the existing shareholders can get the goodwill gains only if the company avoids issuing new shares. Combined with lenders' reluctance to accept brand franchise as security for lending, the practical result is a serious constraint on a competitor's capacity to spend money on marketing; such investments have an opportunity cost not measured by their cost of capital.

## PAYBACK IN MARKETING

The sooner a marketing project pays back, the sooner the resources invested in the project are available for other marketing projects. The resources preempted by a marketing project are proportional to the *product* of the initial investment and the time to payback: A $5 million project with a ten-year payback has the same opportunity cost as a $10 million project with a five-year payback. Payback is more important in franchise decisions than it is in plant decisions. (Present value is obviously important in both.)

In peacetime, additional franchise means additional operating cash flow. As that flow accumulates, plant equity increases. In time, therefore, plant equity drawn down to acquire franchise will rebuild. In the interim, however, the company has both more franchise to defend and less plant equity to defend it with, thus leaving it vulnerable to marketing war.

In a marketing war, the difference between winning and losing may turn on how much the firm can borrow and spend to immediate effect. If, for example, war breaks out when an expensive project is only 10 percent short of fruition, the project contributes nothing to winning, and its accumulated cost reduces dollar for dollar the firm's capacity for selling efforts that could make an immediate contribution.

In this regard, one species of marketing effort—new product development—deserves special mention. Many new products take years to develop. In some industries, the product must be maintainable (with ample stores of replacement parts, fully trained tech reps, etc.), as well as manufacturable, before it can be marketed. Until it begins contributing to operating cash flow, it makes no contribution to plant equity—the portion of the company equity a rational lender would be willing to lend against. In the meantime, expenditures on developing the new product reduce plant equity dollar for dollar, with the drain accumulating up to (and maybe beyond) the point at which the new product can be marketed. For the company in question, this is the point of maximum vulnerability.

A new product can be a great competitive weapon. If a competitor knows the company has a new product in the pipeline, it may be strongy tempted to declare war when most of the development effort is already expended but before the product is ready for marketing. It clearly behooves companies to keep secret their new product development, but to conceal it from their competitors, they must also conceal it from their shareholders. Such development reduces not only their plant equity but also their market value. In this respect, new product development differs from most other species of marketing effort—advertising, for example—that are highly visible and contribute to high price-earnings ratios.

## CONCLUSION

Is current marketing effort an investment in future cash flows? If it is not, then every year, competition in an industry begins all over again with results depending only on current marketing efforts. Is this the way competition really works? Suppose a cigarette manufacturer spends as much on Old Golds next year as Philip Morris spends on Marlboros. Suppose an automobile manufacturer spends as much on Packard as the competition spends on Mercedes. Suppose a shaving cream manufacturer spends as much on Burma Shave as the competition spends on Foamy. Would the manufacturers of Marlboros, Mercedes, and Foamy be starting from scratch in their respective competitions with Old Golds, Packard, and Burma Shave? Or would they benefit from customer loyalties built up by years of past effort? We do not know the other entrenched competitors' answers to these questions, but we do know Gillette's: "We do not sell product. We capture customers."

The sales force captures shelf space, retail outlets, and so forth in order to capture customers. Advertising captures customers. New product development captures customers. Until captured customers defect, they contribute to future, as well as current, operating cash flow.

Without some understanding of the dynamics of competition, outside investors are reduced to extrapolation. If outsiders extrapolate operating cash flow when a company is improving its operating results by liquidating brand franchise, then they cannot afford not to know more than they know. If outsiders extrapolate operating cash flow when a company is adding brand franchise so rapidly that it risks a marketing war, then they cannot afford not to know more than they know.

Fischer Black argued that, in reporting earnings, accountants are attempting to report a number proportional to value. If the earnings number is proportional to value, then it must have the same time-series properties as value. If value fluctuates randomly, then earnings must fluctuate randomly. The evidence suggests that, except for certain celebrated anomalies, both prices and earnings do exhibit random walk behavior.[3]

Suppose that, in reporting earnings, accountants are reporting a number proportional to that particular portion of value we have called plant equity. (After all, accountants include plant in their determination of book value but omit such investments in franchise as advertising and research and development.) Then, growth companies will violate Black's rule, because

- Investments in franchise will reduce reported earnings;
- Franchise will contribute to plant equity, and hence reported earnings, only when and as it generates cash;
- Firms with valuable franchises will have high price-book ratios; and
- Such companies will exhibit earnings growth, even if their franchises are not growing.

Apparently, the traditional features of growth companies are incidental consequences of the way reporting companies account (or fail to account) for brand franchise. If we define a growth company as one that *derives a significant part of its investment value from brand franchise*, then we can focus and simplify our thinking about this important subject.

## Notes

1. Al Reis and Jack Trout, in *Marketing Warfare* (New York: McGraw-Hill, 1986), term the struggle between the Haves and the Have-nots "marketing warfare." Actually, most of this

struggle is simply the thrust and parry of day-to-day marketing—promotions, sales, and advertising campaigns—with franchise shares changing gradually. Occasionally, however, the struggle between competitors erupts into a stark, life-or-death contest that results in sudden, drastic rearrangements of franchise. We prefer to reserve the term "marketing war" for the second kind of struggle.

2. Anatol Rapoport and Albert M. Chammah, *Prisoner's Dilemma* (Ann Arbor: University of Michigan Press, 1965).

3. See I.M.D. Little, "Higgledy Piggledy Growth," The Bulletin of the Oxford University Institute of Statistics, vol. 24, no. 4 (November 1962); A.C. Rayner and I.M.D. Little, *Higgledy Piggledy Growth Again* (Oxford: Basil Blackwell, 1966); and John Lintner and Robert Glauber, "Higgledy Piggledy Growth in America," Seminar on the Analysis of Security Prices, University of Chicago, May 1967.

# CHAPTER 56

# Bulls, Bears, and Market Bubbles

*According to some finance scholars, a securities market that does not exhibit a random walk cannot be rational. They point out that for a rational investor, changes in his or her expectations are entirely a surprise. The same is true for the consensus when investors share the same expectation. In real markets, however, investors disagree, and the equilibrium level reflects their wealth, as well as their expectations. When, for example, news raises the market level, the market rewards the bulls and penalizes the bears, leaving the bulls with more wealth, hence greater market impact, and the bears with less. The wealth shift causes an additional change in the equilibrium level and a further wealth shift. If investors' disagreement is large enough, the second change in equilibrium price can be bigger than the first and the third bigger than the second. Rational behavior by individual investors can cause a market bubble.*

**S**ome finance scholars dismiss market bubbles as accidental strings of random, unrelated market-level changes. Others attribute bubbles to human failures to behave rationally. My view is that bubbles, if they exist, are not necessarily either accidental or irrational.

## ARE BUBBLES ACCIDENTAL?

Consider the 71 trading days from November 1, 1996, to February 14, 1997: Suppose that 13 percent of the 15.75 percent rise in the Dow Jones Industrial Average during that period was a surprise. If the annual standard deviation of return for a year of 250 trading days is 20 percent, then the 71-day standard deviation is

$$0.20\sqrt{\frac{71}{250}} = 10.66$$

By this standard, the period was not so unusual that market bubbles would be needed to explain it.

---

What is meant by a bubble? If a bubble is some self-reinforcing, self-perpetuating mechanism that prevents successive security price changes from being random, then an up-day in the market would be more likely to be followed by another up-day than by a down-day. To be sure, a certain amount of upward drift in stock prices is expected. The famous (but controversial) Ibbotson-Sinquefield 9 percent, for example, translates into

$$\frac{0.09}{250} = 0.00036$$

per day.[1]

To put this daily drift into perspective, I calculated the daily standard deviation:

$$\frac{0.20}{\sqrt{250}} = \frac{0.20}{15.81} = 0.0126$$

The expected upward drift is

$$\frac{0.00036}{0.0126} = 0.0286$$

of a standard deviation. Normal distribution tables suggest bubble-free markets will exhibit 51 percent up-days and 49 percent down-days. If the market is a true random walk, the number of up-days and the number of down-days should be nearly equal.

This observation suggests a way to distinguish between a market-level change resulting from a few big days and a market-level change caused by a bubble. Bubbles should be distinguished by a disproportionate number of up-days (in the case of bull markets) or down-days (in the case of bear markets). Suppose a value of $+1$ is arbitrarily assigned to up-days in a sample and $-1$ to down-days (and zero to flat-days). Then the average of the algebraic sum over a time sample should indicate whether a bubble was present.

Were there too many up-days in the sample period? If I assigned values this way, the daily average for the sample period would have been

$$0.51(1) + 0.49(-1) = 0.02 \text{ (theoretical mean)}$$

Based on the Ibbotson-Sinquefield statistics, however, the daily variance would have been

$$0.51(1)^2 + 0.49(-1)^2 - 0.02^2 = 0.51 + 0.49 - 0.0004$$

$$= 0.9996 \text{ (theoretical variance)}$$

for a daily standard deviation of 0.9998 and a standard deviation for the 71-day sample average of

$$\frac{0.9998}{\sqrt{71}} = 0.1187$$

assuming independence. During the sample period, there were 15 up-days for every 8 down-days. Measured in standard deviations, the resulting one-day sample average of 0.296 is

$$\frac{0.296}{0.119} = 2.49$$

a 2.5-sigma event, with a right-tail probability of $0.5000 - 0.4974 = 0.0026$.

The 15 percent return from November 1 to February 14 was not all that improbable, but maybe the way it happened was—*if* day-to-day changes were random. Of course, the brief time sample doesn't prove anything. But perhaps it will open the minds of readers schooled in the random-walk model to the possibility of market bubbles.

## ARE BUBBLES IRRATIONAL?

The key to the idea that efficient markets should fluctuate randomly is a theorem in *Applied Statistical Decision Theory*, a book on Bayesian statistics by Howard Raiffa and Robert Schlaifer (Harvard Business School, 1961). The theorem supposes a forecaster who makes repeated forecasts of a quantifiable but uncertain future event as new information is received. Each forecast will have an expectation; as the forecasts change, the forecaster's expectation will change.

What does the expectation implicit in the current forecast say about the next forecast? The theorem says that the forecaster's *current* expectation of the expectation implicit in the next forecast of the event is the expectation implicit in the current forecast of the event. But then the forecaster's current expectation of the *change* between the expectations implicit in the current forecast and the next forecast is zero. Whatever the *actual* change turns out to be, it will be entirely a surprise. The forecaster's expectation of the event will fluctuate randomly.

If the market level is based on this forecaster's expectation, it too will fluctuate randomly. If instead, the market level is based on the expectations of many such investors, will it still fluctuate randomly? The textbook answer is *yes*. My answer is *no*. The market level depends not merely on investors' expectations but also on their wealth (and on how aggressively they bet their wealth on their expectations). If active investors hold two views about the future of the market, then today's equilibrium level will reflect both views. But the weight accorded the two views will not necessarily be the same. In particular, if more wealth is represented by one view than by the other, then other things being equal, the equilibrium market level will be closer to the former view than to the latter.

A change in market level will change the distribution of wealth. But a different wealth distribution can result in a different equilibrium—even with the old expectations. It is not obvious that, if the market level is temporarily perturbed, equilibrium forces will return it to its original level. If not, then the mere presence of heterogeneous expectations sets the stage for market bubbles, in which the equilibrium level is no longer uniquely defined and market-level changes are no longer random.

If the perturbation drives the market level up slightly, for example, the bulls will gain at the expense of the bears. Because of the wealth shift, the market will accord

**EXHIBIT 56.1**   Market Bubble Cycle

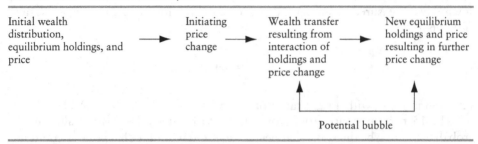

greater weight to the bulls than formerly and less weight to the bears. So, now the equilibrium market level has risen.

In the real world, changes in equilibrium price, wealth shifts, and consequent trading are all going on simultaneously. To keep the analysis simple, however, I broke the cycle down into discrete steps that are shown in Exhibit 56.1.

A price change caused by new information is an obvious way to get the cycle started, and information that reaches some active investors sooner than others creates both trading and wealth transfers. But even information that reaches all active investors simultaneously generates wealth shifts, hence trading, when their expectations are heterogeneous. This analysis is based entirely on such instantly propagated information (IPI).

A crucial question for market bubbles is the size of the price change at the end of the cycle: Is it bigger or smaller than the price change at the beginning? If smaller, then successive repetitions of the cycle will converge to a particular wealth distribution and equilibrium price, but if the price change at the end of one cycle is bigger than the price change at the beginning, then the stage is set for a market bubble.

The appendix raises this question for two polar models of a securities market. In the simpler model, in addition to the active investors—the bulls and bears—is a third group: passive investors who have no opinion about the future level of the market, of whom there are just enough to own the market exactly once.[2] In this case, the positions of the bulls and bears have to be offsetting; when the market level changes, what one active group gains, the other loses.

In the more complex model, there are no passive investors. Instead, the market is entirely owned by the bulls and the bears. (The bears have a long "passive" position as well as a short "active" position.)

As Appendix 56.1 demonstrates, the potential for a bubble is very sensitive to the degree of disagreement between bulls and bears. Perhaps a large disagreement is more likely when investors are contemplating a threat of war, a presidential election, or an economic turning point.

Bubbles can end in any of three quite different ways. I have assumed expectations are fixed to demonstrate that the equilibrium market level can change—and keep on changing—without any change in expectations. But in real markets, expectations change continually. News reaching bulls and bears improves both expectations; for example, it raises the equilibrium price, shifting wealth from the bears to the bulls and changing the weights affecting the equilibrium price. So, news can begin a market bubble, and adverse news can end it.

If the disagreement among active investors is about a specific future event, the resulting bubble will end when the outcome of the disputed event becomes obvious. A bubble also can end when the losing active investors go broke. When either the bulls' or the bears' wealth equals zero, the following occurs:

- All the wealth of the losing active investors has been conveyed to the winners. The metaphorical battle between the bulls and the bears has ended in unconditional surrender.
- The equilibrium price equals the expectation of the winners.
- The expectations that matter are no longer heterogeneous; hence, there is no pressure for further changes in equilibrium price (absent changes in expectations).

Most bubbles are consequently short lived, with only modest impact on the time-series character of market indexes. Instead, the indexes are probably dominated by the impact of new information.

Which of these two models you prefer may depend in part on whether you think any investors are truly neutral in their opinions about the market. If you think not, you may want to ask yourself two simple questions:

- The last time the market dropped 20 percent, was I fully invested?
- After the drop, did I say, "Everybody knew the market was too high"?

If you answered "yes" to both questions, then the market has at least one neutral investor.

## APPENDIX 56.1

Market bets depend on three distinct considerations: the investor's perception of potential reward and potential risk, his or her aggregate wealth, and how aggressively the investor bets it. With regard to the first consideration, reward and risk, optimal dollar holdings are proportional to expected excess return—specifically, to the difference between the investor's expectation and the current market level—and inversely proportional to the variance surrounding that expectation. Bulls and bears often differ with regard to their expectations and their aggregate wealth.

If bulls and bears are drawn randomly from the same population, as regards forecast error and aggressiveness, then if the two groups are sufficiently populous, the average values of these parameters will be about the same.

Let $K$ equal the ratio of aggressiveness to forecast error variance for the population. Let the bulls and bears hold respective positions, $h_1$ and $h_2$, proportional to both the difference between the current market level, $p$, and their respective expectations, $P_1$ and $P_2$, and their respective wealth, $W_1$ and $W_2$. For the first model

$$h_1 = W_1(P_1 - p)K$$
$$h_2 = W_2(P_2 - p)K$$
$$h_1 + h_2 = 0$$

Solving for the equilibrium market level,

$$p = \frac{W_1 P_1 + W_2 P_2}{W_1 + W_2}$$

and for position $h_1$,

$$h_1 = W_1 \left( P_1 - \frac{W_1 P_1 + W_2 P_2}{W_1 + W_2} \right) K$$

$$= W_1 \left( \frac{W_1 P_1 + W_2 P_1 - W_1 P_1 - W_2 P_2}{W_1 + W_2} \right) K$$

$$= \frac{W_1 W_2}{W_1 + W_2} (P_1 - P_2) K$$

$$= -h_2$$

Assume new information propagates so quickly that it creates no information asymmetries. Such information generates no wealth transfer if investors' expectations are homogeneous, but what happens if, as in the present case, they are not?

If the IPI alters both expectations by an amount $\Delta$, then it has no effect on the difference $P_1 - P_2$. Absent a wealth transfer, the new equilibrium price, $p'$, would be

$$p' = \frac{W_1 (P_1 + \Delta) + W_2 (P_2 + \Delta)}{W_1 + W_2}$$

$$= p + \Delta$$

and the new holdings would be

$$h_1' = \left( \frac{W_1 W_2}{W_1 + W_2} \right) (P_1 + \Delta - P_2 - \Delta) K$$

$$= \left( \frac{W_1 W_2}{W_1 + W_2} \right) (P_1 - P_2) K$$

$$= h_1$$

and

$$h_2' = h_2$$

But information will actually transfer wealth from the bears to the bulls (or vice versa) in an amount proportional to their active positions, $h_1$ and $h_2$. The bulls' new wealth is

$$W_1 + h_1 \Delta$$

and the bears' is

$$W_2 + h_2 \Delta = W_2 - h_1 \Delta$$

The wealth shift changes the desired holdings. For $h_1'$

$$h_1' = \frac{(W_1 + h_1\Delta)(W_2 - h_1\Delta)}{W_1 + W_2}(P_1 - P_2)K$$

$$= -h_2'$$

$$= h_1 + \left(\frac{W_2 - W_1}{W_2 + W_1}\right)h_1\Delta(P_1 - P_2)K$$

Therefore,

$$\frac{h_1' - h_1}{h_1} = \left(\frac{P_1 - P_2}{W_1 + W_2}\right)(W_2 - W_1)\Delta K$$

So, IPIs lead to trading, even though buyer and seller get their information at exactly the same time. Turnover in their portfolios is *least*, however, when $W_1$ equals $W_2$.

**When Expectations Are No Longer Changing.**  The wealth shift induced by the IPI also leads to further price changes. For the initial shift,

$$h_1\Delta = \frac{W_1 W_2}{W_1 + W_2}(P_1 - P_2)K\Delta$$

$$= -\frac{W_1 W_2}{W_1 + W_2}(P_2 - P_1)K\Delta$$

$$= -h_2\Delta$$

Adjusting the old wealth measures for this shift results in new ones, $W_1'$ and $W_2'$:

$$W_1' = \frac{W_1^2 + W_1 W_2 (1 + P_1 K\Delta - P_2 K\Delta)}{W_1 + W_2}$$

$$W_2' = \frac{W_2^2 + W_1 W_2 (1 + P_2 K\Delta - P_1 K\Delta)}{W_1 + W_2}$$

The new equilibrium price level, $p'$, is

$$p' = \frac{\left[W_1^2 + W_1 W_2 (1 + P_1 K\Delta - P_2 K\Delta)\right]P_1}{W_1^2 + 2W_1 W_2 + W_2^2}$$

$$+ \frac{\left[W_2^2 + W_1 W_2 (1 + P_2 K\Delta - P_1 K\Delta)\right]P_2}{W_1^2 + 2W_1 W_2 + W_2^2}$$

$$= \frac{W_1^2 P_1 + W_2^2 P_2 + W_1 W_2 \left[P_1 + P_2 + (P_1 - P_2)^2 K\Delta\right]}{(W_1 + W_2)^2}$$

How does $p'$ compare with the original equilibrium price level, $p$? The latter can be rewritten so that

$$p = \frac{W_1^2 P_1 + W_2^2 P_2 + W_1 W_2 (P_1 + P_2)}{(W_1 + W_2)^2}$$

The difference is

$$\frac{W_1 W_2}{(W_1 + W_2)^2} (P_1 - P_2)^2 K\Delta = W_1 W_2 \left(\frac{P_1 - P_2}{W_1 + W_2}\right)^2 K\Delta$$

Note that doubling the initial wealth of both bulls and bears leaves the ratio $(p' - p)/\Delta$ unchanged. Defining total active wealth, $W$, by $W = W_1 + W_2$ results in

$$\frac{p' - p}{\Delta} = W_1 (W - W_1) \left(\frac{P_1 - P_2}{W}\right)^2 K$$

When this ratio is less than 1, the market is stable in the weak sense that, unless expectations change, price will ultimately return to its original equilibrium. When the right-hand side exceeds 1, there is a self-reinforcing process that, over time, results in a "bubble"—an accumulating series of changes in both market level and wealth distribution.

Why isn't the bubble explosive? Apparently, one or both steps in the repeating cycle require time. It is one thing for investors to calculate the likely impact of news on equilibrium price and make appropriate adjustments. It is quite another to feel their way toward a changed equilibrium when they cannot identify the source of the change. It is at least plausible that the main source of time lag between successive repetitions of the cycle is in the effect of a wealth shift on price—rather than in the effect of a price change on wealth.

For an IPI to generate trading, the bulls and the bears must disagree; to produce a market bubble in this three-sector model, with its "passive" investors, the disagreement must exceed a certain threshold. When $W_1 = W_2 = W/2$, the expression $W_1(W - W_1)$ reaches its maximum:

$$\frac{W}{2} \left(W - \frac{W}{2}\right) = \left(\frac{W}{2}\right)^2$$

Where trading is *least*, $(p' - p)/\Delta$ is *greatest*. (Note that "trading" *changes sign* at this point: Active positions that were increasing start to decrease.) At the maximum value of the ratio,

$$\frac{p' - p}{\Delta} = \left(\frac{W}{2}\right)^2 \left(\frac{P_1 - P_2}{W}\right)^2 K$$

$$= \left(\frac{P_1 - P_2}{2}\right)^2 K$$

With the first model, a bull market can occur only if the difference of opinion is big enough that the maximum value exceeds 1. The condition is

$$\frac{p' - p}{\Delta} = \frac{(P_1 - P_2)^2}{4} K > 1$$

$$(P_1 - P_2)^2 > \frac{4}{K}$$

**A Two-Sector Market.** One can readily conceive of a market in which every investor subscribes to one or the other of two opinions. In such a market, the bulls and bears have "passive" positions, as well as the "active" positions reflecting their respective opinions. When the market level changes, the value of all four positions is affected. (For example, when the market goes up, the value of the bears' passive position increases.) But both investors' willingness to take active positions goes up when their overall wealth goes up (and down when their overall wealth goes down). The new system of equations governing equilibrium reflects all four positions and the fact that positions now sum to the market rather than to zero. That is,

$$h_1 = W_1 (P_1 - p) K + \left(\frac{W_1}{W_1 + W_2}\right) h$$

$$h_2 = W_2 (P_1 - p) K + \left(\frac{W_2}{W_1 + W_2}\right) h$$

$$h_1 + h_2 = h$$

The new equilibrium equation is

$$K[W_1 (P_1 - p) + W_2 (P_2 - p)] + h = h$$

$$W_1 P_1 + W_2 P_2 = (W_1 + W_2) p$$

$$p = \frac{W_1 P_1 + W_2 P_2}{W_1 + W_2}$$

Equilibrium price is the same as before; substituting results in

$$p_1 - p = \frac{W_1 P_1 + W_2 P_1 - W_1 P_1 - W_2 P_2}{W_1 + W_2}$$

$$= \left(\frac{W_2}{W_1 + W_2}\right)(P_1 - P_2)$$

So,

$$h_1 = \frac{W_1 W_2}{W_1 + W_2} K (P_1 - P_2) + \left(\frac{W_1}{W_1 + W_2}\right) h$$

$$= \left(\frac{W_1}{W_1 + W_2}\right)[W_2 K (P_1 - P_2) + h]$$

Similarly,

$$P_2 - p = \frac{W_1 P_2 + W_2 P_2 - W_1 P_1 - W_2 P_2}{W_1 + W_2}$$

$$= \left(\frac{W_1}{W_1 + W_2}\right)(P_2 - P_1)$$

Hence,

$$h_2 = \left(\frac{W_1 W_2}{W_1 + W_2}\right) K(P_2 - P_1) + \left(\frac{W_2}{W_1 + W_2}\right) h$$

$$= \left(\frac{W_2}{W_1 + W_2}\right) [W_1 K(P_2 - P_1) + h]$$

Clearly,

$$h_1 + h_2 = h$$

Again, if an IPI did not shift wealth, it would have changed equilibrium price by its impact, $\Delta$, on $P_1$ and $P_2$ and would have left $h_1$ and $h_2$ unchanged. But consider the impact of an IPI with value $\Delta$ on wealth in this two-sector model:

$$W_1' = W_1 + h_1 \Delta$$

$$= W_1 + \left(\frac{W_1 W_2}{W_1 + W_2}\right) K(P_1 - P_2)\Delta + \left(\frac{W_1}{W_1 + W_2}\right) h\Delta$$

$$W_2' = W_2 + h_2 \Delta$$

$$= W_2 + \left(\frac{W_1 W_2}{W_1 + W_2}\right) K(P_2 - P_2)\Delta + \left(\frac{W_2}{W_1 + W_2}\right) h\Delta$$

The new price, $p'$, is

$$p' = \frac{(W_1 P_1 + W_2 P_2)(W_1 + W_2)}{(W_1 + W_2)^2}$$

$$+ \frac{W_1 W_2 K \Delta (P_1 - P_2)^2 + h\Delta (W_1 P_1 + W_2 P_2)}{(W_1 + W_2)^2}$$

But for the old equilibrium price, $p$,

$$p = \frac{(W_1 P_1 + W_2 P_2)(W_1 + W_2)}{(W_1 + W_2)^2}$$

So, the difference is

$$p' - p = \frac{W_1 W_2 K (P_1 - P_2)^2 \Delta + h(W_1 P_1 + W_2 P_2)\Delta}{(W_1 + W_2)^2}$$

and for the ratio of the difference to the original price change,

$$\frac{p' - p}{\Delta} = W_1 W_2 K \left( \frac{P_1 - P_2}{W} \right)^2 + h \left( \frac{W_1 P_1 + W_2 P_2}{W_1 + W_2} \right) \frac{1}{W}$$

Now, $h$ is the total (net) investor position and $W = W_1 + W_2$ is the original (net) value of the position. So, the ratio $W/h$ equals the original equilibrium price. But that price was

$$\frac{W_1 P_1 + W_2 P_2}{W_1 + W_2}$$

So,

$$h \left( \frac{W_1 P_1 + W_2 P_2}{W_1 + W_2} \right) \frac{1}{W} = 1$$

Substituting, the $\Delta$ price ratio yields

$$\frac{p' - p}{\Delta} = W_1 (W - W_1) K \left( \frac{P_1 - P_2}{W} \right)^2 + 1$$

The first term (which was the ratio's value for the three-sector model) is always positive, so in a two-sector market, the potential for bubbles is present any time there is disagreement. Evidently, the absence of passive investors in this model makes the market more susceptible to bubbles.

## Notes

1. In 1976, Roger Ibbotson and Rex Sinquefield published in the *Journal of Business* the first of their famous statistical reviews of U.S. stock and bond market performance ("Stocks, Bonds, Bills, and Inflation"). From the end of 1925 to the end of 1974, the geometric mean return on the S&P 500 Composite Index, including dividends, was 9.4 percent. In 1983, the authors published the second in a series of books, reporting returns from the end of 1925 to the end of 1981. The return over the longer time sample was 9.1 percent. When they published in 1986, the return from the end of 1925 to the end of 1985 was 9.8 percent. These numbers are the basis for the "famous" Ibbotson-Sinquefield 9 percent. But of course, as their time sample continues to lengthen, both the mean and the standard deviations (21.9 percent from the end of 1925 to the end of 1980, for example) bounce around. The authors would be the first to point out to the investors who made their 9 percent famous that even a 70-year sample (1925–1995) is too short to make stable estimates of the mean.

2. Then the bulls' position, as well as the bears', are in forward contracts. Their wealth is in the bank.

# CHAPTER 57

# The Canonical Market Bubble

**A**lthough the financial press has been using the word "bubble" recently, they almost never define it. So each of us is free to have his own definition. Perhaps we could agree that a bubble is a change in the general market level too big to be explained by any new information.

My own view also entails a feedback process, in which market-level changes lead to changes in investors' behavior, which lead to further market level changes, *und so weiter*. In modern security markets there are two kinds of feedback processes that don't require new information:

1. Those changing investors' opinions,
2. Those changing investors' wealth.

When such processes change investors' opinions they are an appropriate subject for experts in behavioral finance. But they aren't rational. When instead, feedback processes change investors' *wealth*, they can be rational, even without new information.

The equilibrium level of the market is an average of investors' opinions, weighted by how heavily they bet their opinions. Our first "bubbles" paper argued that the equilibrium level will be very different, depending whether the wealth belongs to the optimists (the bulls") or the pessimists (the "bears").

As the market level changes, wealth shifts from investors who bet wrong on the change to investors who bet right. But the equilibrium level depends on the distribution of wealth. The old paper showed how this process can feed back on itself, leading to further level changes and further wealth shifts. This is a feedback process that doesn't require either the bulls or the bears to change their opinion—hence to behave irrationally—in order to generate a bubble.

The old paper assumed there were only two opinions. We think a more realistic assumption is that opinions will be distributed, with most of the investors clustered in the middle and relatively few in the tails. Can we generate a bubble in a market where opinions are continuously distributed—but still rational, in the sense of being unaffected by the feedback process?

The first element in our distributed model is the same betting rule we used in the previous paper (a detailed discussion can be found in J. Peter Williamson's textbook[1]). The rule tells the investor how to allocate his risk-taking across a set of mutually independent risks (such as those in Bill Sharpe's Diagonal Model). In particular, it tells him how much market risk to take. Investors bet on their opinions proportional to their wealth, proportional to the degree of disagreement between their appraisal x and the market level p, and inversely proportional to the variance ($\sigma^2$) of their appraisal errors. If, as the market level changes, active investors are steadfast in their appraisals, then they will bet a fraction of their wealth equal to

$$\left( \frac{x - p}{\sigma^2} \right)$$

Averaged across a big securities market, investors with different opinions may be equally bold, but not equally numerous or equally rich. Instead, the wealth associated with different opinions will be different. The second element in our distributed model is a function f (x, p) specifying for each possible market level p the wealth associated with a particular opinion x. As with our two-opinion model, wealth transfers will occur when the market level p changes. Although it reflects these past wealth transfers, this expression for the wealth distribution is obviously path-independent. How likely is it that a bubble that alters investors' opinions would have this path-independence property?

The third element in our model is the notion of market equilibrium. The sum of all the active bets on market-level change must be zero. For every market level p we must have

$$\int_0^\infty f(x, p) \left( \frac{x - p}{\sigma^2} \right) dx = 0$$

where $f(x, p) \left( \frac{x - p}{\sigma^2} \right)$ is the bet of investors with opinion x.

## THE SIZE OF WEALTH CHANGES

When the market level changes the investors with appraisal x gain or lose in proportion to their bet. We have

$$\frac{df}{dp} = \left( \frac{x - p}{\sigma^2} \right) f(x, p)$$

This is a differential equation in p. The solution is

$$\frac{df}{f} = \left( \frac{x - p}{\sigma^2} \right) dp$$

$$\ln f = \frac{1}{\sigma^2} \left( xp - \frac{p^2}{2} \right) - \frac{K}{2\sigma^2}$$

K any constant of integration, hence

$$\ln f = -\frac{1}{2\sigma^2}(p^2 - 2xp + K)$$

$$f(x, p) = e^{-\frac{1}{2\sigma^2}(p^2 - 2xp + K)}$$

We explore certain properties of a special case of this solution in Appendix 57.1. First, however, we ask why bubbles occur in some market environments but not in others.

## THE PRECONDITION FOR MARKET BUBBLES

Assume all appraisals have the same error variance. Then, if individual investors incur their errors independently, the variance of their appraisals around equilibrium price should be an unbiased sample of that common variance. But each investor has to make an intuitive judgment about the size of his own errors. And it's possible, not merely for investors to misjudge, but for most to misjudge in the same direction.

Active investors observe a market price p, assume a value $\sigma^2$ for the variance of their appraisal errors, and then bet accordingly. The result of these bets is

1. An equilibrium price $\hat{p}$, and
2. The *actual* variance $\hat{\sigma}^2$ of their appraisals.

The condition for equilibrium price is:

$$\int \left(\frac{x - \hat{p}}{\sigma^2}\right) f(x, p)dx = 0$$

$$\int xf(x, p)dx = \hat{p} \int f(x, p)dx$$

$$\hat{p} = \frac{\int xf(x, p)dx}{\int f(x, p)dx} = \int xf(x, p)dx$$

if f(x, p) is a frequency function with $\int f(x, p)dx = 1$.

We have prices on both sides of this equation. The *perceived* price p determines how investors bet. And *equilibrium* price $\hat{p}$ depends on these bets. We can take advantage of the dual role of price to ask: When perceived price changes, how much does equilibrium price change? When is the latter change bigger than the former? We have

$$\frac{\partial \hat{p}}{\partial p} = \int x \frac{\partial f}{\partial p}dx$$

Using our differential equation in f (x, p) we have

$$\frac{\partial \hat{p}}{\partial p} = \int x \left(\frac{x - p}{\sigma^2}\right) f(x, p)dx = \frac{1}{\sigma^2}\left[(\hat{\sigma}^2 + \hat{p}^2) - p\hat{p}\right] \approx \frac{\hat{\sigma}^2}{\sigma^2}$$

for small departures of observed price from equilibrium. If active investors are over-confident about their appraisal errors, then we have

$$\sigma^2 < \hat{\sigma}^2$$

and

$$\frac{\partial \hat{p}}{\partial p} > 1$$

In order for investors to disagree, someone must be wrong. In a two-opinion market, the degree of disagreement tells both groups something about the possible size of their error (their *hubris*). Because it also determines the size of the wealth transfers when the market level changes, a big disagreement is the precondition for a bubble.

In a distributed market, the ratio of the error variances plays the same role. On one hand, it's a measure of investors' *hubris* regarding their errors. On the other, it governs the size of active investors' positions, hence the size of the wealth transfers when the market level changes. So it's the key to whether a given change in value will elicit a still bigger value change in the same direction.

Hubris in individual investors is not uncommon. But what could cause a *systematic* bias in investor's judgments about the size of their errors? Unlike their active positions, investors' passive positions are necessarily long the market: If they don't distinguish between their active positions and their passive positions, they will confuse their trading gains with their holding gains. So any exogenous increase in the market level can produce the necessary overconfidence. (If this is the *only* source of hubris, however, then bear bubbles will be rare.)

This model doesn't require investors to change their opinions. The model *does* require them to disagree. Unless one insists that mere disagreement is *ipso facto* irrational, this model is consistent with *rational behavior*. But in this model

1. The equilibrium corresponding to a given set of investor expectations is not unique: The same expectations—and even the same initial wealth endowments—can ultimately result in many different equilibrium market levels.
2. Prof. Samuelson's famous 1965 paper offers "Proof that Properly Anticipated Prices Fluctuate Randomly." In a bubble, changes in the market level can be non-random, even if expectations are rational.

## PASSIVE INVESTORS

The distribution of investors' opinions about the market level is almost certainly bell shaped. If they tend to be steadfast in their opinions during the progress of a bull bubble, then, as the distribution of wealth moves upward—toward more optimistic appraisals—the market level is moving away from the hump of the *opinion* distribution and toward its upper tail—toward opinions that are both

1. More extreme, and
2. Less populated.

In the absence of a bubble, wealth accrues to investors who guess right. So investors who guess right tend to end up with more economic clout than investors who guess wrong. But in a bubble the wealth, hence the clout, ends up with the investors who merely hold the most extreme opinions. Can we be comfortable with the economic signals provided by a bubble?

## IN A BUBBLE, WHO BUYS? WHO SELLS?

We turn now to a different question: If investment opinions are continuously distributed, where in the distribution is the boundary between those who are buying and those who are selling? (Presumably, this boundary shifts as the distribution of wealth shifts.) The key to the answer is the expression for an active investor's optimal holding. Changes in the market level affect his holding in two different ways:

1. Degree of disagreement. If an investor is steadfast in his view of the proper market level, the size of his disagreement changes every time the market level changes. If his disagreement is small enough, the *relative* change will be big. But if his disagreement is big enough, the *relative* change will be small.
2. Wealth. If the active investor's disagreement is small enough, his wealth change will be small. But if his disagreement is big enough, his wealth change will be big.

If, as before, the position h of the active investor with opinion x is

$$h = f(x, p)\left(\frac{x - p}{\sigma^2}\right)$$

then, when the market level $p$ changes, he trades an amount

$$\frac{\partial h}{\partial p} = \left(\frac{x - p}{\sigma^2}\right)\frac{\partial f}{\partial p} - \frac{f(x, p)}{\sigma^2}$$

But we had for the wealth effect of the change

$$\frac{\partial f}{\partial p} = \left(\frac{x - p}{\sigma^2}\right) f$$

Substituting for $\frac{\partial f}{\partial p}$ we have

$$\frac{\partial h}{\partial p} = \left(\frac{x - p}{\sigma^2}\right)^2 f - \frac{f}{\sigma^2}$$

This expression is zero when we have

$$\left(\frac{x-p}{\sigma^2}\right)^2 = \frac{1}{\sigma^2}$$

$$x - p = \pm\sigma$$

$$x = p \pm \sigma$$

The market level divides the optimists from the pessimists. But, curiously, it doesn't divide the buyers from the sellers. Instead, buyers and sellers divide into *three* groups, with opinions in the following ranges:

$$x < p - \sigma$$
$$p - \sigma < x < p + \sigma$$
$$x > p + \sigma$$

We see that it takes not one critical opinion level to separate the buyers from the sellers, but two.[2]

We see that the effect of a market level change on extreme investors is dominated by its impact on their wealth, whereas the effect on moderate investors is dominated by its impact on their degree of disagreement. When, for example, the market level rises, the extreme bull responds to his increasing wealth by lengthening his position. The extreme bear responds to his declining wealth by reducing his short position. Both respond by buying. The moderate bull responds to the reduction in his disagreement with the market level by shortening his long position. The moderate bear responds to the increase in his disagreement by increasing his short position Both respond by selling.

## APPENDIX 57.1

### The Rewards and Penalties of a Bubble

The "constant" of integration K in our solution is any expression that doesn't depend on p. When we set it equal to $x^2$, we have

$$\ln f = -\frac{1}{2}\left(\frac{p-x}{\sigma}\right)^2$$

$$f(x, p) = e^{-\frac{1}{2}\left(\frac{p-x}{\sigma}\right)^2} \tag{57.1}$$

We call this special case of our canonical bubble the "Normal" model.

In a distribution of investment opinion, more people make small errors than big errors. But what really matters for equilibrium price is not the *number of people* associated with an opinion but rather the *amount of wealth*. In the special case of a "Normal" bubble, the dispersion of the wealth with respect to opinions is obviously constant over time as the bubble evolves. During the bubble, wealth f(x, p) is distributed according to

$$f(x, p_2) = e^{-\frac{1}{2}\left(\frac{x-p_2}{\sigma}\right)^2} \tag{57.2}$$

If we assume that, before the bubble, wealth was distributed randomly, $f(x, p_1)$ is also *the frequency distribution of active investors*—which never changes as the bubble proceeds. Before the bubble, wealth and opinions are identically distributed by

$$f(x, p_1) = e^{-\frac{1}{2}\left(\frac{x-p_1}{\sigma}\right)^2} \tag{57.3}$$

We have

$$\left(\frac{x-p_1}{\sigma}\right)^2 = -2\ln f(x, p_1)$$

Consider the difference between

$$(x-p_2)^2 = x^2 - 2xp_2 + p_2^2$$

and

$$(x-p_1)^2 = x^2 - 2xp_1 + p_1^2$$

which is

$$(x-p_2)^2 - (x-p_1)^2 = p_2^2 - 2x(p_2 - p_1) - p_1^2 = (p_2 - p_1)(p_2 + p_1 - 2x)$$

So we can express the distribution of wealth during the bubble by

$$(x-p_2)^2 = -2\sigma^2 \ln f(x, p) + (p_2 - p_1)(p_2 + p_1 - 2x)$$

Now we can see how it relates to the original distribution f(x, p₁) of opinion. We have

$$f(x, p_2) = e^{\ln f(x, p_1) - \frac{(p_2 - p_1)(p_2 + p_1 - 2x)}{2\sigma^2}}$$

$$= f(x, p_1)e^{\frac{\left(x - \frac{p_2 + p_1}{2}\right)(p_2 - p_1)}{\sigma^2}}$$

So the wealth *ratio for an active investor with opinion x* is

$$e^{\frac{\left(x - \frac{p_1 + p_2}{2}\right)(p_2 - p_1)}{\sigma^2}}$$

This expression says that whether an active investor gained or lost from a bubble that proceeded from price level p₁ to price level p₂ depends on whether his appraisal was above or below the average of the beginning and ending price levels

$$\frac{(p_1 + p_2)}{2}$$

and on the change in price level $p_2 - p_1$. It also says that, for a given appraisal variance $\sigma^2$, the ratio of ending to beginning wealth varies exponentially with the product of these two factors.

## Notes

1. *Investments*, Praeger, 1970.
2. In the previous section, we assumed that all investors had the same error variances and then explained the consequences of *bias* in their collective judgment about that variance. Here the relevant variance is the individual investor's opinion. This is a number that can differ from
   1. The average *opinion*, and
   2. The *true* average value.
   But all we can observe is (2).

# CHAPTER 58

# The Investment Value of Brand Franchise

*Brand loyalty manifests itself in consumers' willingness to pay a higher price for the brand they prefer. Some manufacturers choose to limit their output, sell only to customers loyal to their brand (their franchise), and charge the higher price. Others choose to charge a lower price rather than limit their output. Because franchises can contribute as much, or more, to future cash flows as their plants contribute, companies in the first group support their franchises by large investments in advertising, introducing new versions of their products, and so on. Accountants, however, are reluctant to capitalize the expenditures that support franchises, which causes gaps between market value and book value. If the fixed marketing costs can be identified, however, analysts can estimate the investment value of the franchise and the manufacturer's efficiency in defending it.*

Economists have a lot to say about the value of plant, property, and equipment, but they are silent on an element of investment value that, for some companies, is even more important—brand franchise. Investors cannot afford to ignore the value of a brand franchise for a company's future cash flows. Economists, by indiscriminately invoking the Law of One Price, treat all industries as commodity industries, in which brand franchise has no value. As a result of the strategic choices companies make, however, consumers experience the reality—the Law of Two Prices—on the shelves of their friendly retailers every day. The neglect by economists of the reality of franchise pricing results in a wholly unnecessary mystique regarding these high prices—unnecessary because the marketing and economic aspects of brand franchises are easily linked.

Accounting principles exacerbate the problem of valuing brand franchises. Churchill once said that the United States and Britain were two nations separated by a common language. Investment analysts and marketing strategists are two groups of professionals separated by the language of accounting, which calls *investments* in brand franchises (e.g., research and development, advertising) "expenses." The

Copyright © CFA Institute. Reprinted from the *Financial Analysts Journal* with permission. March–April 1999.
I would like to thank Thomas K. Philips and Barr Rosenberg for pointing out a logical flaw in the original draft of this article.

neglect by accountants of the implications brand franchises have for future cash flows results in high price-to-book ratios and high price-to-earnings ratios.

This article describes an approach analysts can use, if the fixed costs of supporting a brand franchise can be identified, to estimating the investment value of a manufacturer's franchise and the manufacturer's efficiency in defending it. The valuation model has elements recognizable to the marketing strategist—such as franchise, marketing effort, and level of rivalry—as well as elements recognizable to the investment analyst—such as cash flow, present value, and return on investment. But the model can hardly be called "traditional." The traditional approach to estimating value has been to ask what data public companies provide and then to let those data define the valuation methods. This article defines what data analysts and investors need to value a company's investment in its brand franchise and explains how to use the data.

A valuation model cannot be formulated, of course, with total disregard for the kind of data the model requires. The data required for a satisfactory model should have the following characteristics:

- The data should be verifiable, at least in principle. When data are verifiable, "objectivity" ceases to be an issue. The data should not be opinions about the future. Opinions cannot be verified.
- Data specific to a particular asset should reflect the specifics of the asset—not the interaction of the asset with general economic conditions or someone's opinion about future prosperity. A simple test for the specificity of the data is whether the data would be the same in a different economic or market climate.
- The data should not depend on arbitrary decisions by anybody—not the U.S. SEC, not the Financial Accounting Standards Board, and certainly not the reporting company.

## BRANCH FRANCHISE POWER

The key to the value of brand franchises lies in consumer anxiety. The Law of One Price asserts that, in the absence of transportation and distribution costs, roughly simultaneous transactions in a given good or service will have the same price. The law assumes, however, that the parties to the transaction have what lawyers call a "meeting of the minds." In actual transactions, the parties have their own mental images of what is being transacted, and these two images are rarely the same.

For example, in many markets, the seller knows more than the buyer. This information asymmetry is typical of the markets for used cars and second-hand watches, and even more characteristic of markets for consumables—headache remedies, toothpaste, corn flakes, ketchup, soup, and so on. In consumables, the manufacturer knows what raw materials, what equipment, and what workers were used in the product's manufacture. In most cases, all the consumers can see at the point of purchase is an opaque container.

The result is anxiety in the mind of the consumer, which often has its origins in the way the product is manufactured over its life cycle. Exhibit 58.1 summarizes the differences between a fledgling and a mature industry. When an industry is new, the very definition of the product is fluid and demand is low. So, using general-purpose

**EXHIBIT 58.1**   Life-Cycle Characteristics

| Fledgling Industry | Mature Industry |
| --- | --- |
| Product concept evolving rapidly | Product concept stabilized |
| Size of market uncertain | Market established |
| Process-centered manufacturing | Product-centered manufacturing |
| Fluid supplier relationships | Stable supplier relationships |
| Quality hard to control | Quality easy to control |
| Consumer disappointments common | Consumer disappointments rare |

rather than dedicated machine shops, foundries, and heat-treating facilities makes economic sense (what Buffa [1984] called "process-focused" production). Quality at this stage is inevitably uneven and almost impossible to control. But it is precisely at this point in the life cycle of the product that consumers are having their first experiences with the product and forming first impressions that will be as lasting as their first impressions of people.

Later, when the role of the product is well defined and potential demand is clearer, manufacturers build production facilities dedicated to the new product (what Buffa called "product-focused production"). Day in and day out, the same people perform the same steps in the manufacturing process. The source of quality problems is identified. Learning takes place, and as production problems are solved, knowledge about solutions circulates throughout the industry.

Consumers, however, cannot forget the pain of the early disappointments. They are still anxious, which is what gives the power to brand names. Indeed, brands can continue to be important long after the industry has solved its quality problems. The day consumers do conquer the last of their anxieties is the day the industry becomes a commodity industry. Fresh milk is an example. When pasteurization was new, the reputation of the dairy (e.g., Borden, Beatrice, Hood) was important. Today, nobody worries about milk quality, and dairy brands with their premium prices have largely disappeared.

Marketing is most important in the middle of the cycle, when brand identities have been established in consumers' minds but consumers are still worried about quality: "Almost as good as a Xerox." "Not exactly like Hertz." Marketing experts have known for years that consumers deal with their anxiety about transactions by focusing on the manufacturer's brand. In a process not unlike falling in love, consumers replace their generalized ideal of what a product should be with the highly particularized image of a specific brand. If they prefer Fords, then every way in which a Chevy differs from a Ford makes the Chevy less desirable. Their preferred brands become the standards by which all other similar products are judged. Consumers are not unwilling to buy the others, but they are willing to pay more for their ideal brands. Of course, which competing product is the ideal differs for different consumers. Each brand, Chevy and Ford, has its own group of loyal customers—its *brand franchise*.

## MARKETING AND THE BRAND FRANCHISE

Ideally, a manufacturer would price each sale transaction according to whether the buyer was in its franchise or not, but this approach is usually impractical. In practice, the manufacturer that chooses the lower price can sell everything that it can economically make at that lower price (in economics, can realize the full value of the scarcity rents on its plant capacity) and, of course, because sales are not restricted to its franchise, the manufacturer who chooses to sell at the lower price is free not to engage in product innovation, advertising, or promotion. The manufacturer that chooses the higher price is restricting its branded output, irrespective of how much capacity the manufacturer has, to the size of its franchise market. Therefore, this manufacturer does whatever it can to increase its franchise—product innovation, advertising, and promotion. The manufacturer uses a higher-priced marketing effort to increase (or defend) its share of the franchise in its industry.

When consumers choose to buy at the lower price, they are not affecting total supply or total demand. So, their choice is not affecting the scarcity of production capacity or the scarcity rents on that capacity. Because the choice merely shifts consumers from one brand to another or to unbranded competitive products, it has nothing to do with scarcity or market equilibrium—hence, nothing to do with price theory. So, the task of analyzing the value of a franchise has little in common with the task of analyzing the value of plant, property, and equipment.

The costs of marketing often include a significant fixed element.[1] When the size of that element is not known (i.e., when firms do not report their fixed costs separately for manufacturing and for marketing), pricing that investment is a challenge. But analysts can estimate the costs. This discussion of how to value a brand franchise considers three issues that brand franchise raises for investors:

- The estimation problem in the case where fixed costs are either known or small enough to ignore,
- The economics of brand franchise when fixed costs are important, and
- The impact of brand franchise on monopoly power, with particular attention to fixed costs, sunk costs, and ease of entry.

## The Estimation Problem

Customers are fickle. An industry may appear to have stable and unchanging franchise shares, but it is actually in constant flux. The competitors' franchise shares are like swimming holes in a river; water is constantly flowing in and flowing out, although the overall level of each hole may change little. To maintain its franchise, a manufacturer must take customers away from its competitors as fast as they are taking away customers from the manufacturer.

To begin estimating the costs of supporting a brand franchise, assume that, net of any fixed marketing costs in the industry, a competitor can romance away twice as many potential customers if it spends twice as much and vice versa. If a manufacturer's franchise is measured by its gross cash "flow-back," $z$ (franchise share multiplied by brand premium) and its marketing effort net of fixed marketing costs is defined as $v$ (both variables at annual rates), then one-period changes in gross flow-back, $\Delta z$, satisfy the equation

$$\Delta z = \alpha v - \beta z \tag{58.1}$$

where $\alpha$ and $\beta$ are coefficients that express the sensitivity of change in franchise to, respectively, marketing effort and initial franchise size.

At every point in time, gains and losses in franchise share sum to zero; that is,

$$\sum \Delta z = 0 \tag{58.2}$$

so, if we assume that $\beta$, unlike $\alpha$, is the same for all competitors, then

$$0 = \sum \alpha v - \beta \sum z \tag{58.3}$$

with the result that

$$\beta = \frac{\sum \alpha v}{\sum z} \tag{58.4}$$

Obviously, $\beta$, even if it is the same for all competitors at a point in time, can vary across time.

But the efficiency with which competitors transform dollars of marketing effort into change in franchise (gross of the $\beta$-related losses) is in a certain sense *relative* to the other competitors. So, then, an appropriately weighted *average* of the individual efficiencies should be constant across time—even if individual efficiencies or associated weights are changing. Let that average be $\alpha$. Then, without any loss of generality, we can write

$$\Sigma \alpha v = \hat{\alpha} \Sigma v \tag{58.5}$$

and assert that $\hat{\alpha}$ is constant across time.

The basic model then becomes

$$\Delta z = \alpha v - \hat{\alpha} \left( \frac{\sum v}{\sum z} z \right) \tag{58.6}$$

where the expression in parentheses, like $v$, is observable. The unknown coefficient $\alpha$ is not necessarily constant across time for the same competitor.

Consider regression estimates of the undetermined coefficients $\alpha$ and $\alpha$: In the cross-section, large $v$'s are likely to be associated with large $z$'s and, therefore, with large values of $(\Sigma v / \Sigma z) z$. So, the two independent variables are highly correlated. Standard errors of estimate will be correspondingly large. We can minimize this problem by recasting the regression in the form

$$\frac{\Delta z}{z} = \alpha \left( \frac{v}{z} \right) - \hat{\alpha} \left( \frac{\sum v}{\sum z} \right) \tag{58.7}$$

Now, consider a single-variable regression of $\Delta z/z$ on $\Sigma v \, \Sigma z$: The suppressed explanatory variable $v/z$ is plausibly uncorrelated with $\Sigma v \, \Sigma z$, both across competitors and across time. We use the resulting estimate of $\alpha$ to compute values of $\alpha$ for each data point (i.e., for each competitor at each point in time).

We can use this result to distinguish, competitor by competitor and period by period, between level of marketing effort and efficiency. A small gain in franchise share achieved with high efficiency may represent a better job of marketing management than a large gain achieved with an exorbitant effort. We can make this useful distinction, however, only when fixed costs are little known or unimportant.

## The Economic Impact of Fixed Costs

The fixed costs of product development and advertising represent the competitor's admission ticket to the variable-cost game.[2] We can measure competitors' total marketing efforts by the cash outflow $u$ and their total fixed marketing costs (assuming the costs can be measured) by $F$ (all variable annual rates). Then, the variable-cost portion of a company's marketing effort is $u - F$. In industries where fixed advertising and development costs are important, change in franchise is

$$\Delta z = \alpha(u - F) - \beta z \qquad (58.8)$$

The value of $z$ to investors is reduced by the marketing effort required to maintain the company's market share. The maintenance value of $u$ (the value at which franchise gains just offset franchise losses) can be termed $u^*$; substituting $u^*$ for $u$ in the expression for franchise change produces

$$\alpha(u^* - F) - \beta z = 0$$
$$\frac{u^* - F}{z} = \frac{\beta}{\alpha}$$

and

$$u^* = \left(\frac{\beta}{\alpha}\right) z + F \qquad (58.9)$$

Net flow-back from the investment is gross flow-back minus the maintenance level of effort, or

$$z - u^* = z - \left[\frac{\beta}{\alpha} z + F\right]$$
$$= z\left(1 - \frac{\beta}{\alpha}\right) - F \qquad (58.10)$$

For the industry as a whole, we have

$$\Sigma \Delta z = \alpha \Sigma u - \alpha \Sigma F - \beta \Sigma z = 0 \qquad (58.11)$$

hence,

$$\alpha \Sigma (u - F) = \beta \Sigma z \qquad (58.12a)$$

and

$$\frac{\beta}{\alpha} = \frac{\Sigma(u - F)}{\Sigma z} \tag{58.12b}$$

Substituting in the expression for net flow-back produces

$$z - u^* = z\left[1 - \frac{\Sigma(u - F)}{\Sigma z}\right] - F \tag{58.13}$$

Recall that our first criterion for a satisfactory model was that the data be verifiable. One variable in the formula for measuring franchise value should probably be treated as a forecast rather than as a verifiable fact—and, indeed, a forecast that depends on events outside the industry. That variable is $\Sigma z$—the industry's total franchise, measured in gross cash flow. It depends on overall industry sales, which usually depend on prosperity beyond the industry. When investors forecast this number, they are "timing" the industry. The way to avoid such timing is to use the forecast that best explains the current market prices of companies in the industry. (The *current* value of $\Sigma z$ is observable but probably not relevant.)

The other variables in the formula are verifiable. They are specific to the firm and its industry, and they are not influenced by anybody's forecasts or anybody's arbitrary rules:

$$\frac{\Delta z}{z} = \alpha\left(\frac{v}{z}\right) - \hat{\alpha}\left(\frac{\Sigma v}{\Sigma z}\right) \tag{58.14}$$

Maintenance level $v^*$ of $v$ is defined by

$$0 = \alpha\left(\frac{v^*}{z}\right) - \hat{\alpha}\left(\frac{\Sigma v}{\Sigma z}\right) \tag{58.15}$$

so

$$v^* = z\left(\frac{\hat{\alpha}}{\alpha}\right)\left(\frac{\Sigma v}{\Sigma z}\right) \tag{58.16}$$

Then, net flow-back is

$$z - v^* = z\left[1 - \left(\frac{\hat{\alpha}}{\alpha}\right)\left(\frac{\Sigma v}{\Sigma z}\right)\right] \tag{58.17}$$

In this result, fixed costs are not explicit. When we introduced fixed costs, we defined $v$ as equal to $u - F$ and $v^*$ as equal to $u^* - F$ if, on average, all competitors have the same fixed costs. On the other hand, Equations 58.13 through 58.19 assume away differences in marketing efficiency—that is, assume $\alpha = \alpha$ for different competitors.

The present value of a franchise share $z$ discounted at market rate $\rho$ is

$$\frac{z}{\rho}\left[1 - \frac{\Sigma_{(u-F)}}{\Sigma z}\right] - \frac{F}{\rho} \qquad (58.18)$$

For an established competitor, the incremental rate of return is

$$\frac{\partial(z - u^*)}{\partial u} = \frac{\partial(z - u^*)}{\partial z}\frac{\partial z}{\partial u}$$

$$= \alpha\left[1 - \frac{\Sigma(u - F)}{\Sigma z}\right] < \alpha \qquad (58.19)$$

The rate of return goes up with the gross flow-back from the *industry's* franchise, goes down with the level of rivalry, $\Sigma u$, and goes up with the number of competitors.

## Brand Franchise and Monopoly Power

In a marketing war, the level of rivalry is so high that net flow-back becomes negative. The bigger the franchise share, the bigger the rate of loss. Marketing wars are basically wars of attrition intended to exhaust competitors' borrowing power. For example, if Competitor A has the same size franchise as Competitor B (and the same marketing efficiency) but more untapped borrowing power, B will run out of steam sooner than A; A will win the war. If, on the other hand, A and B have equal untapped borrowing power but A's franchise (hence, its rate of loss) is bigger, then B will win the war. To win such a war, a company must have a higher ratio of borrowing power to franchise than its competitors have. Because the purpose of a marketing war is to force a competitor to abandon its franchise, no rational lender will rely on franchise value as the security for a loan. So, borrowing power depends on the value of the plant (less liabilities).[3] A marketing war ends when a competitor either exhausts its borrowing power or, seeing that its cause is hopeless, abandons defense of its franchise. Either way, a marketing war shifts franchise share toward the competitor with the highest ratio of borrowing power to franchise. And because marketing wars benefit those competitors, they can be more aggressive in marketing peace. When rivalry escalates, high-ratio competitors lead the way, with low-ratio competitors following willy-nilly.

But there is no point entering an industry if you aren't sufficiently well capitalized to defend your entry. Companies do not have to compete for franchise in order to enter an industry, but when they enter the battle for brand franchise, they incur the maintenance-level costs of their marketing efforts. So, maintenance cost (see Equation 58.9),

$$u^* = z\frac{\Sigma(u - F)}{\Sigma z} + F \qquad (58.20a)$$

can be used as the measure of ease for entrants that expect to compete for franchises. We can rewrite this expression as

$$u^* = F\left(1 - \frac{nz}{\Sigma z}\right) + z\frac{\Sigma u}{\Sigma z} \qquad (58.20b)$$

Differentiating with respect to $n$ produces

$$\frac{\partial u^*}{\partial n} = -\frac{Fz}{\Sigma z} \qquad (58.21)$$

Because $F$, $z$, and $\Sigma z$ are all positive, entry of a competitor always lowers maintenance cost for existing competitors. We conclude that what established competitors should fear is not entry but, rather, entry of financially strong competitors.

Lawyers often assume that higher fixed costs will make entry more difficult. Does it pay established competitors to increase the industry's fixed marketing costs—for example, by increasing the frequency of new-product introductions? Differentiating the maintenance cost expression with respect to $F$ produces

$$\frac{\partial u^*}{\partial F} = 1 - \frac{nz}{\Sigma z} \qquad (58.22)$$

A new competitor's maintenance level of $u$ will fall with increasing $F$ if its franchise satisfies

$$z > \frac{\Sigma z}{n} = \text{Average } z \qquad (58.23)$$

So, acquiring competing companies, if they are large, evidently pays. (Consider the extreme case of Company Q acquiring a company of negligible size: Company Q's $z$ does not increase, but its $n$ falls by 1.) Calculating

$$\frac{\partial}{\partial n}\left(\frac{\Sigma z}{n}\right) = -\frac{\Sigma z}{n^2} \qquad (58.24)$$

shows that when a company is acquired (i.e., when $n$ falls by 1), the industry average increases by $\Sigma z/n^2$. So, the rule is: Never acquire a company with franchise $z$ such that $z < \Sigma z/(n^2)$. Large established firms benefit by encouraging new firms, not merely because entry reduces their maintenance costs, but because it lowers the threshold for acquisition targets. (Small companies who would prefer to be priced as potential takeover targets will also favor entry.)

## THE TWO MEANINGS OF "COMPETITION"

When economists talk about competition, their ideal is an industry that pushes output up to the point where marginal cost equals price. Unless demand is perfectly price elastic, however, increments in output will lower equilibrium price—penalizing all output and causing marginal revenue to be less than price. So, it usually pays an industry not to produce up to the perfectly competitive level.

The owner of the industry's marginal capacity, however, is concerned only with the price penalty on its own output. If this manufacturer is small—if it has limited capacity—the price penalty will be less important to it than if it is big. The manufacturer will push output closer to the point at which the unit cost of producing on the marginal capacity equals the price—that is, behaving more like the economist's ideal. So, the economist worries when, as a result of business combinations or barriers preventing new entrants from starting small, an industry is divided up among a few large firms.

The word "competition" has a different meaning for marketing strategists than for economists or accountants. They use it to refer to the battle for brand franchise. In industries where such franchises are valuable, companies often spend hundreds of millions of dollars a year in the battle. (As in "competitive sports," one company's franchise gain is another's loss.) When the level of rivalry is high enough, however, it takes more money than the brand itself can generate. At that point, competitors turn to their other financial resources—scarcity rents on their plant capacity. But the only plant capacity with high scarcity rents is capacity with a low variable unit cost of producing, which, of course, is why the valuable franchises end up in the hands of low-cost producers.

"Low" and "high" as they apply to cost, however, are relative. How does the high-production-cost type survive in such an industry? By not competing for franchise share. Instead, their output is distributed as off-brand, generic, or house brand products. So, such industries have two types of companies—*competitors* who battle for franchise share and *producers* who do not—and two kinds of entry.

The producer type is critical to the industry's willingness to use its high-cost capacity. Because producer types own that capacity, they decide whether or not to use it, even though the decision affects selling prices for all the companies in the industry, including the competitor types.

If the industry has important fixed costs that are the same for small companies as for large companies, small-scale attempts at entry will fail.[4] If marketing expenditures entail significant fixed costs—space in national media, creative spots for ads good enough to justify the space, development of new products good enough to justify the ads—it does not pay a company to have a franchise unless it is a big franchise. (Introductions of new brands into such an industry may be few and far between.) A big marketing effort is needed to defend a big franchise. And if the industry requires low-cost capacity to defend a franchise, it takes a lot of low-cost capacity to defend a big franchise. In such industries, low production costs and big franchises tend to go together.

When competitor types are large, they have a big stake in industry pricing. When competitors are low cost, they have a big stake in output. Will they, nevertheless, withhold some of their production? If a competitor produces less than its own franchise demands, the competition benefits at the expense of the competitor, which weakens the competitor's ability to defend its franchise. (Because marginal producers will increase their output when a low-cost competitor reduces its output, the net reduction in industry output a competitor can achieve is never more than half its gross reduction.)

Entry into the battle for franchise is obviously daunting. But for a producer type, entry requires only some plant with a high unit variable cost of producing and, hence, a low second-hand value. Some industries have fixed costs of production, but even those costs are usually small compared with the fixed costs of marketing. So, in an industry with high fixed marketing costs, producer types tend to be small compared with competitor types.

## IMPLICATIONS FOR ANTITRUST

When high fixed costs in an industry are associated with marketing rather than production, they put pressure on competitor types to become as large as possible, which discourages entry into the battle for franchise and produces industries in which the low-cost companies are large and the high-cost companies are small—which is to say, industries in which the companies that own the marginal capacity have little incentive not to use it.

High fixed costs may have discouraged entry and competitive pricing in the commodity industries—the railroads, steel companies, and oil companies—that preoccupied trust busters in the 1890s. Trying to extrapolate that experience to the kind of modern industries discussed here may lead to confusion between the two meanings of "competition" with consequences that are disappointing or even perverse.

## APPENDIX 58.1

### Sunk Costs versus Fixed Costs

Antitrust lawyers have recently discovered the concept of sunk costs. The lawyers' discovery attests to their recognition of industries in which marketing, as well as production, is important—in which competitor types as well as producer types are important.

A sunk cost is an investment that is certain to be worthless if you change your mind. Examples are

- Leasehold improvements,
- Creative costs of a discarded advertising program,
- Investment in a discarded brand, and
- Abandoned new-product development programs.

Sunk costs differ from simply making risky investments. If you make an investment in a liquid security and change your mind, although you have no guarantee that you can recover the cost (so, the investment is risky), you do have a chance to recover it. If the buyer's expectations are sufficiently rosy, you can sell the investment and recover the cost. Sunk costs are gone with no possibility of recovery.

One kind of investment has social value; the original investor is merely the first of what may ultimately be several owners. The sunk cost has value only to the original investor.

By this test, investment in capital goods—in productive capacity—is rarely a sunk cost. In particular, if the original buyer fails, the plant still has potential value to other buyers. (To be sure, most capital goods are not as liquid as securities. They raise the same kind of uncertainties in a potential buyer's mind that a used car raises.)

By the same test, investment in a brand franchise is almost always a sunk cost:

- It has no social value. Instead, it merely transfers franchise from one competitor to another.
- If the owner abandons the brand, or an acquiring firm replaces it with its own brand, all prior investment in that brand becomes worthless.

These considerations suggest that if sunk costs pose a special problem for new entrants, it is the costs of marketing, rather than the costs of production, that pose the problem.

## Notes

1. Classic examples of fixed marketing costs are the creative costs of an advertising campaign—costs that must be incurred before a single TV spot or page in *Newsweek* has run. Costs of developing a new product may also be considered part of marketing costs. Development costs must be incurred before the sales force can sell the product, before advertising can promote it, and so on. Typically, these fixed costs must be incurred in order for the "variable" costs of marketing to have any value, and the fixed costs are independent of the scale of the marketing program—specifically, of sales volume, the size of the sales force, the size of the media buy, and so on. A car maker can choose to economize on its manufacturing fixed costs—rearranging the chrome, for example, when a competitor introduces a genuinely new model. But this choice is not rigidly dictated by the size of its franchise or the scale of its marketing effort. And the car maker is deferring, rather than actually reducing, its costs. For long-range planning or investment analysis, representative or long-term averages of fixed marketing costs are appropriate.
2. The cost of product development is a marketing cost. Does the competitor develop its new products (or product improvements) in a corner of the factory? Do the key professionals wear laboratory smocks rather than the power suits favored by the company's salesforce? If so, should we conclude that product development is a cost of production rather than marketing? No, because what matters (in analyzing production, as well as marketing) is the *purpose* for which the competitor incurs the costs.

   When we distinguish between *competitors*, who care about the size of their brand franchise, and *producers*, who do not, we find that product development, like advertising, is a cost producers choose not to incur. So, we know what the purpose of product development is.
3. The value of the plant derives from its economic, or scarcity, rent. This rent is the difference between the unit variable cost of producing in that plant and (in a competitive industry) marginal cost—the unit cost of producing in the marginal plant. On the one hand, per unit of capacity, the higher the unit variable cost of producing in the plant, the lower the rent on the plant. On the other hand, the risk regarding the future rent depends only on the unit cost for the industry's marginal plant (i.e., on uncertainty about which plant will be marginal). So, the *absolute* risk is the same for all plants irrespective of the absolute rent. And when industry demand expectations change, competitors' borrowing power does not change proportionately. Still, a useful generalization is possible: Other things being equal, the competitors with low-cost plants cope more effectively with both marketing wars and marketing peace.

4. Keep in mind that lawyers make an important distinction between fixed costs and sunk costs (see Appendix 58.1).

## References

Axelrod, Robert. 1984. *The Evolution of Cooperation*. New York: Basic Books.

Buffa, Elwood S. 1984. *Meeting the Competitive Challenge*. Homewood, IL: Dow Jones-Irwin.

Oxenfeldt, Alfred R. 1962. *Models of Markets*. New York: Columbia University Press.

Porter, Michael E. 1976. *Interbrand Choice, Strategy and Bilateral Market Power*. Cambridge, MA: Harvard University Press.

——1985. *Competitive Advantage*. New York: Free Press.

Reis, Al, and Jack Trout. 1981. *Positioning: The Battle for Your Mind*. New York: McGraw-Hill.

——1986. *Marketing Warfare*. New York: McGraw-Hill.

Spence, A. Michael. 1974. *Market Signaling*. Cambridge, MA: Harvard University Press.

Srivastava, Rajendra K., Tasadduq A. Shervani, and Liam Fahey. 1998. "Market-Based Assets and Shareholder Value: A Framework for Analysis." *Journal of Marketing*, vol. 62, no. 1 (January):2–18.

Yip, George S. 1982. *Barriers to Entry*. Lexington, MA: Lexington Books.

# CHAPTER 59

# The Investment Value of an Idea

The first step in appraising investment value is translating what we know today about an asset into implications for its future. And the way an idea evolves is fundamentally different from the way either a plant or a brand franchise evolves. The cash flow of each of the three "asset classes" has its own time pattern.

For example, every capital good—lift truck, engine lathe, backhoe, power loom—embodies a solution to a particular problem. From the date of its manufacture until it arrives at the scrap yard, a capital good embodies the same solution—the same idea (or set of ideas). As soon as a better solution becomes available, manufacturers will stop making the old capital good. But the examples already in service will continue for many years, even after the solution they embody becomes the marginal solution—even after they cease to be scarce and, hence, to contribute to their user's investment value.

But what about the value of the *idea* embodied in the capital good? Does it belong to the user or the manufacturer? Consider what happens when the buyer drives a new car—a capital good—away from the dealer. If its secondhand value exceeds what he paid for it, then at least the part of the value of the innovations embodied in the car belongs to the new owner. But if, as folklore suggests, the price goes down, then the new owner has paid at least full value for those innovations. Does the same thing happen to new tankships? New airliners? If so, then the *ideas* from which a new model derives its value belong to the seller (i.e., the manufacturer).

## WHY IDEAS ARE RISKY

The value of the idea to the manufacturer ends with the arrival of an idea that solves the same problem better, faster, or cheaper. More often than not, it will be spawned by a different technology, developed by a different company.[1] But the better idea does not actually "arrive" when the metaphorical bulb lights up in the inventor's head. The challenger does not displace the current champion until the challenger's development is complete.

Consider fusion. Like fission, it produces no carbon dioxide and, hence, no global warming. But unlike fission, it is allegedly safe (no Three Mile Islands or Chernobyls) and clean (no radioactive waste to store under Yucca Mountain). Twenty years ago,

---

scientists estimated that fusion was ten years away from completing its development. Today, scientists are still estimating that fusion is ten years away from completing its development. Until then, manufacture of fossil-fuel generating plants will continue. And the implications for global warming are dire. As they raise the standards of living for their vast populations, China and India are rapidly increasing energy consumption.

Ideas with potential investment value go through four stages:

1. *Research.* Does the idea have enough economic potential to warrant the investment to make it practical? If so, it enters Stage 2.
2. *Development.* Although George Stephenson's steam locomotive was patented in 1815, the Stockton and Darlington Railway in England did not begin operations until 1830. Although Rudolf Diesel's version of the internal combustion engine was invented in 1893, it did not begin to replace the steam locomotive until the late 1920s.
3. *Application.*
4. *Death*, which occurs suddenly when a better idea is fully developed. When manufacturers stopped making (and railroads stopped buying) steam locomotives, the value of Stephenson's idea ended.[2]

A sword of Damocles hangs over every valuable idea. The probability that the sword will fall in any given future year is, of course, an investment judgment. (Do ideas change faster in the fields of biotechnology and software than they do in certain gray-belt industries?) This article spells out ways in which the consensus judgment regarding the mortality rate enters into the market price of the idea—and into its systematic risk.

## WHEN WILL THE NEW REPLACE THE OLD?

Fusion, monoclonal antibodies, and fuel cells are ideas with huge economic promise. When will they be fully developed? Nobody knows. They represent a risk to current, fully developed technologies, but the risk they pose is actuarial.

We can express this ignorance with a number—a probability that development will be completed in a given year. Because the completion of the rival's development is the death knell for the established technology, the two events have the same probability. For the old technology, it is a mortality rate.

Consider the present value of the current technology's rent in Year 10: If the challenger's development is completed in Year 9, then that rent contributes nothing to the present value. But, of course, we do not now know when the challenger will arrive. So, we reduce the Year 9 value of Year 10's rent by the factor

$$1 - \gamma$$

where $\gamma$ is the mortality rate (the probability that the challenger completes commercial development in any given year). The Year 9 value will not contribute to the Year 8 value, however, if the challenger's development is completed in Year 8, and so on. Therefore, the *expected* value of the reigning champion one year hence is its *market*

**EXHIBIT 59.1** Accuracy of Approximation for Small Values of $\gamma$

| $\gamma$ | $e^{-\gamma}$ | $1-\gamma$ |
|---|---|---|
| 0.10 | 0.9048 | 0.90 |
| 0.15 | 0.8607 | 0.85 |
| 0.20 | 0.8187 | 0.80 |
| 0.25 | 0.7788 | 0.75 |
| 0.30 | 0.7408 | 0.70 |

value—call it $v$—discounted by the probability that the challenger *does not* complete development:

Exhibit 59.1 demonstrates a useful approximation for small values of $\gamma$.

Let $\rho$ be the market discount rate for such ideas. If the expected value of the champion one year hence can be approximated by

$$(1 - \gamma)v \approx e^{-\gamma}v$$

then its market value now is

$$e^{-\rho}(1 - \gamma)v \approx e^{-(\rho+\gamma)}v$$

If the economic rent enjoyed by the champion is $f$ a year, its value now is

$$v = f \int_0^{\infty} e^{-(\rho+\gamma)t}\, dt$$

$$= \frac{-fe^{-(\rho+\gamma)t}}{\rho + \gamma} \Big|_0^{\infty}$$

$$= \frac{-f}{\rho + \gamma}(0 - 1)$$

$$= \frac{f}{\rho + \gamma}$$

so the practical effect of adding the mortality rate to the market discount rate is to increase the rate at which future scarcity rents are discounted back to the present.

Consider the case in which the market discount rate is 10 percent and the mortality rate for the current champion is 10 percent. Exhibit 59.2 shows the present value of a dollar of future economic reward, discounted at 20 percent over the intervening years. As the reader can see, it hardly matters whether we impose an arbitrary cutoff at Year 32—or, for that matter, at Year 16. The chance that the current champion will survive every future challenge is slim indeed. But we allow for that consideration when we "discount" for both appropriate capital-market discount rate $\rho$ and mortality rate $\gamma$.

**EXHIBIT 59.2**   Value of $1.00 of Economic Reward
(market discount rate = 10 percent, mortality rate =
10 percent, discount of 20 percent)

| No. of Years Hence | Discount Factor |
| --- | --- |
| 1 | $0.8187 |
| 2 | 0.6703 |
| 4 | 0.4493 |
| 8 | 0.4493 |
| 16 | 0.0408 |
| 32 | 0.0017 |

## GROWTH COMPANIES

In their important 1961 paper, Merton Miller and Franco Modigliani argued that mere growth does not create any incremental value for investors unless the added assets are worth more than they cost. But Miller and Modigliani were probably thinking about conventional investment assets.

Unless a challenger successfully completes its development in the interim, the expected value of the idea next year will be roughly the same as the value this year. So the investor's expected reward is simply this year's economic rent on the idea and the investor's rate of return is

$$\frac{f}{v} = \frac{\rho + \gamma}{f} f$$
$$= \rho + \gamma$$

But this return is bigger than the return on conventional assets with the same market discount rate.

The explanation is simple: This return is the rate of return on the idea until it is successfully challenged. In hindsight, a company that derives its value from ideas that have survived previous challenges will appear to have a very exciting track record. Until its ideas are overtaken by better ideas, such a company will outperform normal companies. Are ideas the only legitimate source of the growth in "growth" companies?

## SYSTEMATIC RISK

Valuable ideas apparently contain an extra element of *specific* risk. But what about their *systematic* risk? Adding the mortality rate to the market discount rate increases the sensitivity of the discounted value to short-term prospects for the economy. To simplify the math, assume the following:

1. There are no rents from the idea in hard times.
2. Development of potential competitors continues.

**EXHIBIT 59.3** Idea's Present Value in Hard Times of Various Durations ($\rho = 0.10$)

| $\gamma$ | 1 Year | 2 Years | 4 Years | 8 Years |
|---|---|---|---|---|
| A. Discount factors | | | | |
| 0.10 | 0.82 | 0.67 | 0.45 | 0.20 |
| 0.15 | 0.78 | 0.61 | 0.37 | 0.14 |
| 0.20 | 0.74 | 0.55 | 0.30 | 0.09 |
| 0.25 | 0.70 | 0.50 | 0.25 | 0.06 |
| 0.30 | 0.67 | 0.45 | 0.20 | 0.04 |
| B. Discount factors: Benefit stream of $1.00 a year | | | | |
| $0.10 | $4.10 | $3.35 | $2.25 | $1.00 |
| 0.15 | 3.12 | 2.44 | 1.48 | 0.56 |
| 0.20 | 2.47 | 1.83 | 1.00 | 0.30 |
| 0.25 | 2.00 | 1.43 | 0.71 | 0.17 |
| 0.30 | 1.68 | 1.13 | 0.50 | 0.10 |

So the idea's present value depends on how long hard times are expected to last. Under these circumstances, Panel A of Exhibit 59.3 shows the discount factors for a range of values for $\gamma$. Panel B provides the corresponding values of a benefit stream of $1.00 a year when it is subjected to discounts for both (1) an undelayed benefit stream subject to the indicated $\rho$ and $\gamma$ and (2) a delayed the benefit stream the indicated number of years.

As the reader can see, the investment value of an idea can be very sensitive to the immediate prospects for prosperity. The short term is more important in valuing ideas than it is in valuing plant.

More generally, let $t$ be the number of bad years the consensus expects. Then, for the present value of an economic rent of $1.00 a year, we have

$$v = \frac{e^{-(\rho+r)t}}{\rho + \gamma}$$

and

$$\frac{dv}{dt} = -(\rho + \gamma)v$$

and for the effect of a change in consensus $t$ on the idea's rate of return,

$$\left(\frac{1}{v}\right)\left(\frac{dv}{dt}\right) = -(\rho + \gamma)$$

But expectations regarding a change in the market's estimate of $t$ affect most asset values to some degree. And when unforeseen events change these expectations, the result is *systematic risk*.[3] So $\gamma$, which measures the idea's *specific* risk, also has a big impact on its systematic risk. Because a portfolio of ostensibly unrelated ideas will have a large element of systematic risk that cannot be diversified, lenders will want to be able to reach other assets.

To summarize:

- The risk of sudden death can be incorporated into estimates of investment value by simply adding the appropriate mortality rate to the market discount rate.
- Ideas for which the Damocletian sword has not yet fallen will reward investors with rates of return higher than the market rate. Shares of their corporate owners will behave like growth stocks.
- An idea will exhibit more systematic risk than conventional investment assets with the same value. Because it cannot be diversified away, this risk places special burdens on the owner's capacity for risk bearing.

## WEALTH BORROWERS AND WEALTH LENDERS

Obviously, one household's liability is another household's asset. Only slightly less obvious is that one household's ownership of government debt is some other hapless household's future tax liability. When the balance sheets of all the households in society are summed, the lendings and borrowings cancel, leaving only the real assets. It follows that the total wealth available to bear the risk in these assets is identically equal to their total value.

The function of wealth is to bear society's investment risks. The other contributors to a business enterprise—workers, suppliers, bankers, and so on—will not contribute until they are satisfied that the business's equity is big enough to insulate them from risks they are not paid to bear. If an asset has sufficiently small value in relation to its risk, society will require the bearer of its risk to have other sources of wealth—assets whose value is larger in relation to their risk.

The equity in a levered corporation is an indication of the value available to protect lenders from the risk in its assets. The high degree of leverage in real estate suggests that the value in buildings is large in relation to their risk. It frees up the remainder of the value to bear other risks. But most real estate is mortgaged, and most publicly owned corporations are levered. The implication is that some other asset must exist whose risk is larger in relation to its value. If corporate and real estate assets are lenders of risk-bearing wealth (i.e., wealth *lenders*), where are the wealth *borrowers*?

## ENTREPRENEURIAL RISK

A study released in January 1967 titled "Technological Innovation: Its Environment and Management," often referred to by the short name "The Connor Report" (named for John Thomas Connor, who was U.S. Secretary of Commerce from January 1965 to January 1967), sought to identify the new ideas in the first half of the Twentieth century that had created the most jobs (Connor 1967). It found that "the most important inventions come from independent inventors—that is, from somebody's garage or basement. "The Connor Report" listed 31 such inventions, including Xerography, the Polaroid camera, power steering, the automatic transmission, Kodachrome, the vacuum tube, air conditioning, rockets, streptomycin, penicillin, and the helicopter.

John Heaton and Deborah Lucas (2000) estimated the value of new ideas currently in development at approximately $10 trillion. This number may seem big in comparison with the value of stocks, but there are, of course, a lot of garages and basements—many attached to houses with mortgages. What is special about what Heaton and Lucas called "entrepreneurial risk" is the high ratio of risk to value. Ideas have a higher ratio of risk to value than conventional assets—plant and brand franchises—with the same market discount rate.

Households have assets with a lot of value in relation to their risk—value that is potentially available to lenders—as long as they do not incorporate. But without the limitation on liability conferred by incorporation, proprietors are cautious about their spending, preferring to develop an idea in the basement or the garage.

Realizing the economic potential of an idea may require manufacturing facilities, raw-materials, work-in-progress and finished-goods inventories, accounts receivable—in other words, a lot of relatively conventional, low risk-to-reward assets. When a venture has accumulated enough of the low risk-to-reward assets to reduce its overall risk-to-reward ratio sufficiently, it is at last ready for incorporation—which obviously has to precede its IPO.

## Notes

1. Can the owner of the currently valuable technology invent its successor? Baldwin-Lima-Hamilton Corporation made great steam locomotives. How did they fare with diesels? Curtis-Wright Corporation's turbo-compound radials powered the fastest piston-engine airliner. How did Curtis-Wright fare with jet engines? How did IBM fare with operating system software? Bell Labs with printed circuits? Professor Lynn Stout of the UCLA Law School has pointed out a serious *agency problem* that works against the owner of today's solution providing tomorrow's solution: The human capital of the corporation's staff is invested in the old technology. To speed the arrival of the new technology may not be in their interest, even if it is in their employer's interest.
2. Steam continued in active service until 1960 in certain Class I railroads.
3. When the systematic risk increases, $\rho$ increases—and we are off to the races.

## References

Connor, John T. 1967. "Technological Innovation: Its Environment and Management." Washington, DC: U.S. Government Printing Office.

Heaton, John C., and Deborah Lucas. 2000. "Portfolio Choice and Asset Prices: The Importance of Entrepreneurial Risk." *Journal of Finance*, vol. 55, no. 3 (June):1163–1198.

Miller, Merton H., and Franco Modigliani. 1961. "Dividend Policy, Growth, and the Valuation of Shares." *Journal of Business*, vol. 34, no. 4 (October):411–433.

# Active Management

Is active management just buying on good news and selling on bad news? Or is there more to it than that? Are there principles in active management that, in the long run, determine who wins and who loses?

J.L.T.

# CHAPTER 60

# How to Use Security Analysis to Improve Portfolio Selection

I t has been argued convincingly in a series of papers on the Capital Asset Pricing Model that, in the absence of insight generating expectations different from the market consensus, the investor should hold a replica of the market portfolio.[1] A number of empirical papers have demonstrated that portfolios of more than 50–100 randomly selected securities tend to correlate very highly with the market portfolio, so that, as a practical matter, replicas are relatively easy to obtain. If the investor has no special insights, therefore, he has no need of the elaborate balancing algorithms of Markowitz and Sharpe.[2] On the other hand if he has special insights, he will get little, if any, help from the portfolio-balancing literature on how to translate these insights into the expected returns, variances, and covariances the algorithms require as inputs.

What was needed, it seemed to us, was exploration of the link between conventional subjective, judgmental, work of the security analyst, on one hand—-rough cut and not very quantitative—and the essentially objective, statistical approach to portfolio selection of Markowitz and his successors, on the other.

The void between these two bodies of ideas was made manifest by our inability to answer to our own satisfaction the following kinds of questions: Where practical, is it desirable to so balance a portfolio between long positions in securities considered underpriced and short positions in securities considered overpriced that market risk is completely eliminated (i.e., hedged)? Or should one strive to diversify a portfolio so completely that only market risk remains? As this implies, in the highly diversified portfolio market sensitivity in individual securities seems to contribute directly to market sensitivity in the overall portfolio, whereas other sources of return variability in individual securities seem to average out. Does this mean that the latter sources of variability are unimportant in portfolio selection? When balancing risk against expected return in selction of individual securities, what risk and what return are relevant? Will increasing the number of securities analyzed improve the diversification of the optimal portfolio? Is any measure of the contribution of security analysis to portfolio performance invariant with respect to both levering and turnover? How do analysts' opinions enter in security selection? Is there any simple way to characterize the quality of security analysis that will tell us when one analyst can be expected to make a greater contribution to a portfolio than another? What role, if any, does confidence in an analyst's forecasts have in portfolio selection? This paper offers answers to these questions.

The paper has a normative flavor. We offer no apologies for this. In some cases, institutional practice and, in some cases, law are shortsighted; in all cases they reflect what is by anybody's standard an old-fashioned idea of what the investment management business is all about. If we tried to develop a body of theory that reflected some of the constraints imposed institutionally and legally, it would inevitably be a theory with a very short life expectancy. Our model is based on an idealized world in which there are no restrictions on borrowing, or on selling securities short; in which the interest rate on loans is equal to the interest rate on short-term assets such as savings accounts; and in which there are no taxes. We expect that the major conclusions derived from the model will largely be valid, however, even with the constraints and frictions of the real world. Those that are not valid can usually be modified to fit the constraints that actually exist.

Certain recent research has suggested that professional investment managers really have not been very successful,[3] but we make the assumption that security analysis, properly used, can improve portfolio performance. This paper is dircted toward finding a way to make the best possible use of the information provided by security analysts.

The basic fact from which we build is one that a number of writers have recognized—namely, that there is a high degree of co-movement among security prices. Perhaps the simplest model of covariability among securities is Sharpe's Diagonal Model. As Sharpe sees it, "The major characteristic of the Diagonal Model is the assumption that the returns of various securities are related only through common relationships with some basic underlying factor. . . . This model has two virtues: it is one of the simplest which can be constructed without assuming away the existence of interrelationships among securities and there is considerable evidence that it can capture a large part of such interrelationships."[4] This paper takes Sharpe's Diagonal Model as its starting point; we accept without change the form of the Diagonal Model and most of Sharpe's assumptions.

Use of the Diagonal Model for portfolio selection implies departure from equilibrium in the sense of all investors having the same information (and appraising it similarly)—as, for example, is assumed in some versions of the Capital Asset Pricing Model. The viewpoint in this paper is that of an individual investor who is attempting to trade profitably on the difference between his expectations and those of a monolithic market so large in relation to his own trading that market prices are unaffected by it. Throughout, we ignore the costs of buying and selling. This makes it possible for us to treat the portfolio-selection problem as a single-period problem (implicitly assuming a one-period utility function as given), in the tradition of Markowitz, Sharpe, et al. We believe that these costs are often substantial and, if incorporated into this analysis, would modify certain of our results substantially.

## DEFINITIONS

Following Lintner, we define the excess return on a security for a given time interval as the actual return on the security less the interest paid on short-term risk-free assets over that interval.

A regression of the excess return on a security against the market's excess return gives two regression factors. The first is the market sensitivity, or "beta," of the security; and, except for sample error, the second should be zero. We define the explained return on the security over a given time interval to be its market sensitivity times the market's excess return over the interval.

We define the independent return to be the excess return minus the explained return. The independent return, because of the properties of regression, is statistically independent of the market's excess return. Our model assumes that the "independent" returns of different securities are almost, but not quite, statistically independent. The "risk premium" on the $i$th security is equal to the security's market sensitivity times the market's expected excess return. Symbols for these concepts are defined as:

$$r = \text{riskless rate of return}$$
$$x_i = \text{return on the } i\text{th security}$$
$$y_i = \text{excess return on the } i\text{th security}$$
$$y_m = \text{excess return on the market}$$
$$b_i = \text{market senstivity of the } i\text{th security}$$
$$b_i y_m = \text{explained, or systematic, return on } i\text{th security}$$
$$z_i = \text{independent return on } i\text{th security}$$

Let $E[\ ]$ and var $[\ ]$ represent the expectation and variance, respectively, of the variable in brackets. Then define

$$\bar{z}_i = E[z_i]$$
$$\bar{y}_m = E[y_m]$$

We call the first the "appraisal premium" for the $i$th security, and the second, the "market premium." We have

$$\sigma_i^2 = \text{var}[z_i - \bar{z}_i]$$
$$\sigma_m^2 = \text{var}[y_m - \bar{y}_m]$$

and

$$b_i E[y_m] = \text{market premium on the } i\text{th security}$$

If one defines the "explained error" in a security's return as the explained return minus the risk premium, and the "residual error" as the independent return minus the appraisal premium, the structure of the model described above can be summarized in the following way:

Actual return
    Riskless rate, $r \Delta t$
Excess return
    Explained return
        Market premium, $b_i \bar{y}_m$
        Explained error, $b_i(y_m - \bar{y}_m)$
    Independent return
        Appraisal premium, $\bar{z}_i$
        Residual error, $z_i - \bar{z}_i$

We can arrange this structure to group together the components of the total return as follows:

Actual return
    Expected return
        Riskless rate, $r\Delta t$
        Market premium, $b_i \overline{y}_m$
        Appraisal premium, $\overline{z}_i$
    Actual minus expected return
        Explained error, $b_i(y_m - \overline{y}_m)$
        Residual error, $\overline{z}_i - z_i$

Using our definitions we can write the one-period return on the $i$th security as

$$x_i = r\Delta t + y_i = r + b_i y_m + z_i \tag{60.1}$$

Sharpe's Diagonal Model stipulates that

$$E\left[(z_i - \overline{z}_i)(z_j - \overline{z}_j)\right] = 0,\; E\left[(z_i - \overline{z}_i)(y_m - \overline{y}_m)\right] = 0 \tag{60.2}$$

for all $i, j$. As noted above, these relationships can hold only approximately.

The return on a security over a future interval is uncertain. This paper shares with Markowitz the mean-variance approach, implying normal return distributions. There is fairly conclusive evidence that the distribution is not normal, but that its behavior is similar to that of a normal distribution, so the model assumes a normal distribution as an approximation to the actual distribution. The qualitative results of the model should not be affected by this approximation, but the quantitative results should be modified somewhat to reflect the actual distribution.

However one defines "risk" in terms of the probability distribution of portfolio return, the distribution, being approximately normal, is virtually determined by its mean and variance. But under the assumptions noted here (finite variances and independence) the mean and variance of portfolio return depend only on the means and variances of independent return for specific securities and on the explained return (and, of course, on the portfolio weights). On the other hand, risk in the specific security is significant to the investor only as it affects portfolio risk. Hence it is tempting to identify risk in the $i$th security with the elements in the security that contribute to portfolio variance—the variance of the independent return $\sigma_i^2$ ("specific risk") and the variance of explained return $b_i^2 \sigma_m^2$ ("market risks"). In what follows, we will occasionally yield to this temptation.

Let the fraction of the investor's capital devoted to the $i$th security be $h_i$. Using symbols defined above, the one-period return on his portfolio is

$$\sum_{i=1}^{n} h_i x_i - r\Delta t \left(\sum_{i=1}^{n} h_i - 1\right) = \sum_{i=1}^{n} h_i (y_i + r\Delta t) - r\Delta t \left(\sum_{i=1}^{n} h_i - 1\right)$$

$$= r\Delta t + \sum_{i=1}^{n} h_i y_i \tag{60.3}$$

We note that, although there are three sources of return on the individual security—the riskless return, the explained return, and the independent return—only two of these are at stake in portfolio selection. Henceforth we shall ignore the first term in Equation 60.3.

Understanding the way in which portfolio mean and variance are influenced by selection decisions requires expansion of security return into all its elements. Excess return on the portfolio, expressed in terms of the individual securities held, is

$$\sum_{i=1}^{n} h_i b_i \, y_m + \sum_{i=1}^{n} h_i z_i \tag{60.4}$$

Evidently we have only $n$ degrees of freedom—the portfolio weights $h_i$, with i = 1, ..., n—in selecting among $n + 1$ sources of return. Since the market asset can always be freely bought or sold to acquire an explicit position $h_m$ in the market asset, when we take this into account we have for the excess portfolio return the expression

$$\left( h_m + \sum_{i=1}^{n} h_i b_i \right) y_m + \sum_{i=1}^{n} h_i z_i \tag{60.5}$$

It is obvious that availability of the market asset makes it possible to achieve any desired exposure to market risk, approximately independently of any decisions regarding desired exposure to independent returns on individual securities. In effect, we then have $n + 1$ mutually independent securities, where

$$h_{n+1} = h_m + \sum_{i=1}^{n} h_i b_i, \; \mu_i = E(z_i), i = 1, \ldots, n, \mu_{n+1} = E[y_m] \tag{60.6}$$

If we apply these conventions and run our summations from 1 to $n + 1$, we have for the mean and variance of the portfolio return, respectively,

$$\mu_p = \sum_{i=1}^{n+1} h_i \mu_i, \sigma_p^2 = \sum_{i=1}^{n+1} h_i^2 \sigma_i^2 \tag{60.7}$$

We take as our objective minimizing $\sigma_p^2$ while holding $\mu_p$ fixed. We form the LaGrangian

$$\sum_{i=1}^{n+1} h_i^2 \sigma_i^2 - 2\lambda \left( \sum_{i=1}^{n+1} h_i \mu_i - \mu_p \right) \tag{60.8}$$

introducing the undetermined multiplier $\lambda$, differentiate with respect to $h_i$, and set the result equal to zero:

$$2 h_i \sigma_i^2 - 2\lambda \mu_i = 0 \tag{60.9}$$

Solving for $h_i$ we have

$$h_i = \lambda \mu_i / \sigma_i^2 \tag{60.10}$$

Substituting this result in Equation 60.7 we have

$$\mu_p = \lambda \sum_{i=1}^{n+1} \mu_i^2 / \sigma_i^2, \, \sigma_p^2 = \lambda^2 \sum_{i=1}^{n+1} \mu_i^2 / \sigma_i^2 \tag{60.11}$$

We see from Equation 60.11 that the value of the multiplier $\lambda$ is given by

$$\lambda = \sigma_p^2 / \mu_p \tag{60.12}$$

The optimum position $h_i$ in the $i$th security ($i = 1, \ldots, n$) is given by Equation 60.13

$$h_i = \frac{\mu_i}{\mu_p} \frac{\sigma_p^2}{\sigma_i^2}, \, i = 1, \ldots, n \tag{60.13}$$

In order to obtain an expression for the optimal position $h_m$ in the market portfolio, we recall that

$$\mu_{n+1} = E[y_m] = \mu_m$$
$$\sigma_{n+1}^2 = \text{var}[y_m] = \sigma_m^2$$

and substitute these expressions together with the definitions of $h_{n+1}$ from Equation 60.5 in Equation 60.11 to obtain

$$\sum_{i=1}^{n} h_i b_i + h_m = \lambda \mu_m / \sigma_m^2 \tag{60.14}$$

Multiplying both members of Equation 60.10 by $b_i$ and summing we have

$$\sum_{i=1}^{n} h_i b_i = \lambda \sum_{i=1}^{n} b_i \mu_i / \sigma_i^2 \tag{60.15}$$

which can be substituted in Equation 60.14 to give

$$h_m = \lambda \left( \mu_m / \sigma_m^2 - \sum_{i=1}^{n} \mu_i / \sigma_m^2 \right) \tag{60.16}$$

It was apparent in Equation 60.5 that market risk enters the portfolio both in the form of an explicit investment in the market portfolio and implicitly in the selection of individual securities, the returns from which covary with the market. Equation 60.13 says "take positions in securities $1, \ldots, n$ purely on the basis of expected independent return and variance." The resulting exposure to market risk is disregarded.

Equation 60.16 provides us with an expression for the optimal investment in an explicit market portfolio. This investment is designed to complement the market position accumulated in the course of taking positions in individual securities solely with regard to their independent returns. Under the assumptions of the Diagonal Model, position in the market follows the same rule as position in individual securities; but because market position is accumulated as a by-product of positions in individual securities, explicit investment in the market as a whole is limited to making up the difference between the optimal market position and the by-product accumulation (which may, of course, be negative, requiring an explicit position in the market that is short, rather than long).

Equation 60.16 suggests that the optimal portfolio can usefully be thought of as two portfolios: (1) a portfolio assembled purely with regard for the means and variances of independent returns of specific securities and possessing an aggregate exposure to market risk quite incidental to this regard; and (2) an approximation to the market portfolio. Positions in the first portfolio are zero when appraisal premiums are zero. Since the special information on which expected independent returns are based typically propagates rapidly, becoming fully discounted by the market and eliminating the justification for positions based on this information, the first portfolio will tend to experience a significant amount of trading. Accordingly, we call it the "active portfolio."

It is clear from Equation 60.10 that changes in the investor's attitude toward risk bearing ($\lambda$), or in his market expectations ($\mu_m$), or in the degree of market risk ($\sigma_m^2$)—which, as we shall see, depends on how well he can forecast the market—have no effect on the proportions of the active portfolio.

The Capital Asset Pricing Model suggests that any premium for risk bearing will be associated with market, rather than specific risk. If investors in the aggregate are risk averse, then an investment in the market asset—explicit or implicit—offers a premium. We call this particular source of market premium "risk premium"—as opposed to "market premium" deriving from the investor's attempts to forecast fluctuations in the general market level. When all the appraisal premiums are zero, the optimal portfolio is therefore the market portfolio—even if investor has no power to forecast the market. We shall call a portfolio devoid of specific risk "perfectly diversified." In other words, in our usage "perfect diversification" does not mean the absence of risk, nor does it mean an optimally balanced portfolio, except in the case of zero appraisal premiums.

In general, a given security may play two different roles simultaneously: (1) A temporary position based entirely on expected independent return (appraisal premium) and appraisal risk. As price fluctuates and the investor's information changes, the optimum position changes. (2) A position resulting purely from the fact that the security in question constitutes part of the market portfolio. The latter position changes as market expectations change but is virtually independent of expectations regarding independent return on the security. Hence we call the approximation to the market portfolio employed to achieve the desired level of systematic risk the "passive portfolio." The literal interpretation of Equation 60.16 is that a desired explicit market position $h_m$ would be achieved by adding positions in individual securities in the proportions in which they are represented in the market as a whole. For example, let the fraction of the market as a whole comprised by the $i$th security be $h_{mi}$. Then an explicit market position $h_m$ can be achieved by taking positions $h_m h_{mi}$ in the individual securities. These positions are, of course, in addition to positions taken with regard to specific return. Overall positions are then given by combining positions desired for fulfilling the two functions of bearing appraisal and market risk:

$$h_i = \lambda h_{mi} \left( \mu_m/\sigma_m^2 - \sum_{i=1}^{n} b_i \mu_i/\sigma_i^2 \right) + \mu, \sigma_i^2 \qquad (60.17)$$

This is the result one would get by solving the Markowitz formulation, under the assumptions of the Diagonal Model, in the absence of constraints. But it is not a solution of much practical interest, because approximations to the market portfolio add very little additional specific risk while being vastly cheaper to acquire than an exact pro rata replica of the market.

A practical interpretation of Equation 60.16 is that portfolio selection can be thought of as a three-stage process, in which the first stage is selection of an active portfolio to maximize the appraisal ratio, the second is blending the active portfolio with a suitable replica of the market portfolio and the third entails scaling positions in the combined portfolio up or down through lending or borrowing while preserving their proportions. Because the investor's attitude toward risk bearing comes into play at the third stage, and only at the third stage, a second-stage definition of "goodness" that disregards differences in attitude toward risk bearing from one investor to another is possible.[5]

## THE SHARPE AND APPRAISAL RATIOS

From Equation 60.10 we have, for the optimal holdings, $h_i = \lambda \mu_i/\sigma_i^2$, where, for the optimal second-stage portfolio, we have

$$\mu_p = \lambda \sum_{i=1}^{n+1} \mu_i^2/\sigma_i^2$$

$$\sigma_p^2 = \lambda^2 \sum_{i=1}^{n+1} \mu_i^2/\sigma_i^2 \qquad (60.18)$$

How good is the resulting portfolio? A relationship between expected excess return and variance of return is obtained by forming

$$\frac{\mu_p^2}{\sigma_p^2} = \frac{\lambda^2 \left( \sum\limits_{i=1}^{n+1} \mu_i^2/\sigma_i^2 \right)^2}{\lambda^2 \sum\limits_{i=1}^{n+1} \mu_i^2/\sigma_i^2} = \sum_{i=1}^{n+1} \mu_i^2/\sigma_i^2 \qquad (60.19)$$

The resulting ratio is essentially the square of a measure of goodness proposed by William Sharpe[6]; we shall call it the Sharpe ratio. It is obviously independent of scale. The right-hand expression readily partitions into two terms, one of which depends only on market forecasting and the other of which depends only on forecasting independent returns for specific securities:

$$\frac{\mu_p^2}{\sigma_p^2} = \mu_{n+1}^2/\sigma_{n+1}^2 + \sum_{i=1}^{n} \mu_i^2/\sigma_i^2$$

It is easily shown by writing out the numerator and denominator, and then simplifying as in Equation 60.19, that the second term of Equation 60.19 is the ratio of appraisal premium, squared, to appraisal variance. This number is obviously invariant with respect to changes in the holdings in the active portfolio by a scale factor, hence of shifts in emphasis between the active and passive portfolios. It measures how far one has to depart from perfect diversification to obtain a given level of expected independent return. Because it summarizes the potential contribution of security appraisal to the portfolio, we call it the appraisal ratio.

Consider, for example, two portfolio managers with the same information about specific securities and the same skill in balancing exposure to specific returns. One can generate a larger appraisal premium than the other simply by taking large positions in specific securities (relative to the market). Hence appraisal premium (as, for example, measured by the Jensen performance measure)[7] is not invariant with respect to such arbitrary changes in portfolio balance. The fact that the appraisal ratio *is* invariant with respect to such changes commends it as a measure of a portfolio manager's skill in gathering and using information specific to individual securities. If, in addition to the same information specific to individual securities, two portfolio managers have the same market expectations, then their scale of exposure to specific returns (relative to their market exposure) should, of course, also be the same, as implied by Equation 60.16. But in performance measurement, it is not safe to assume that the optimal balance will be struck by every portfolio manager. (How well he adheres to the optimal balance between market and specific risk is certainly one aspect of performance. But it is an aspect quite distinct from how well he uses security analysis.)

The appraisal ratio has much to recommend it as a measure of potential fund performance, although it does not directly measure the utility of the overall portfolio to investors. If "aggressiveness" refers to the amount of market risk borne by a diversified fund, and "activity" refers to the amount of trading undertaken in optimizing the active portfolio, then the second stage (at which the active portfolio is balanced against the passive portfolio) determines the degree of activity in the risky portion of the fund, and the third stage (at which the active portion is mixed or levered to obtain the balance between expected return and risk which meets the investor's personal objectives) determines the aggressiveness of the overall fund.

What happens to the degree of portfolio diversification as (1) the number of securities considered is increased? (2) the number of securities considered is kept constant while the contribution to the appraisal ratio of the average security is increased? Does the former improve the degree of diversification while the latter degrades it? We demonstrate below that the degree of diversification in an optimally balanced portfolio depends on these factors only as they influence the appraisal ratio. (It also depends on market ratio, but the latter is obviously independent of both the contribution to the appraisal ratio of the average security and the number of securities considered.) We also demonstrate that the higher the appraisal ratio (for a given market ratio) the less well diversified the resulting portfolio will be. In short, the more attractive incurring specific risk is relative to incurring market risk, the less well diversified an optimally balanced portfolio will be. Indeed, it is easily shown that at optimal balance we have

$$\frac{\text{appraisal premium}}{\text{market premium}} = \frac{\text{appraisal variance}}{\text{market variance}} = \frac{\text{appraisal ratio}}{\text{market ratio}} \qquad (60.20)$$

where market ratio is defined, analogously with appraisal ratio, as

$$\text{market ratio} = \frac{(\text{market premium})^2}{\text{market variance}} \qquad (60.21)$$

The demonstration below actually applies to optimal (relative) holdings of any two assets whose specific returns are statistically independent. In particular, the "assets" consisting of the market, on one hand, and a weighted combination of independent returns, on the other, are statistically independent for any set of weights, including the optimal set. On the one hand, we have the contribution to the optimally balanced portfolio of market return, $y_m$, with expectation $\mu_m$ and variance $\sigma_m^2$. On the other hand, we have the contribution from optimally balanced returns $z, \ldots, z_n$,

$$\sum_{i=1}^{n} h_i z_i$$

with expectation $\mu_a$ defined by

$$\mu_a = \sum_{i=1}^{n} h_i \mu_i$$

and variance $\sigma_a^2$ defined by

$$\sigma_a^2 = \sum_{i=1}^{n} h_i^2 \sigma_i^2$$

This contribution is, of course, the essential part of the active portfolio, since the contribution of market risk to the overall portfolio is independent of the market risk in the active portfolio (see Equation 60.16). It is also statistically independent of the market portfolio, since we have

$$E\left[ y_m \sum_{i=1}^{n} h_i z_i \right] = \sum_{i=1}^{n} h_i E[z_i y_m] = 0$$

Let optimal holdings for the market and active portfolios, respectively, be represented by $h_m$ and $h_a$. Then from Equation 60.10 we have

$$\frac{h_a}{h_m} = \frac{\mu_n/\sigma_a^2}{\mu_m/\sigma_m^2}$$

$$\frac{h_a\mu_a}{h_m\mu_m} = \frac{\mu_a^2/\sigma_a^2}{\mu_m^2/\sigma_m^2} \tag{60.22}$$

which demonstrates the equality between the first and third fractions in Equation 60.20. Squaring and then multiplying both sides by $(\mu_n^2/\sigma_n^2)/(\mu_a^2/\sigma_n^2)$ we have

$$\frac{h_a^2\sigma_a^2}{h_m^2\sigma_m^2} = \frac{\mu_a^2/\sigma_a^2}{\mu_m^2/\sigma_m^2} \tag{60.23}$$

which demonstrates the equality between the second and third fractions of Equation 60.20. In an optimally balanced portfolio, total portfolio variance is given by

$$\sigma_p^2 = \sum_{i=0}^{n} h_i^2\sigma_i^2 = \sum_{i=0}^{n} \left(\lambda\frac{\mu_i}{\sigma_i^2}\right)^2 \sigma_i^2$$

$$= \lambda^2 \sum_{i=0}^{n} \frac{\mu_i^2}{\sigma_i^2} = \lambda^2 \frac{\mu_0^2}{\sigma_0^2} + \sum_{i=1}^{n} \frac{\mu_i^2}{\sigma_i^2} \tag{60.24}$$

where the first term is the contribution of market variance and the second is the contribution of the combined variance of the independent returns (i.e., the unique variance). Partitioning total variance into these two terms enables us to write the coefficient of determination $\rho^2$ expressing the fraction of total variance accounted for by systematic, or market, effect as

$$p_p^2 = \frac{\lambda^2 \dfrac{\mu_0^2}{\sigma_0^2}}{\lambda^2 \dfrac{\mu_0^2}{\sigma_0^2} + \lambda^2 \displaystyle\sum_{i=1}^{n} \dfrac{\mu_i^2}{\sigma_i^2}} = \frac{1}{1 + \dfrac{\displaystyle\sum_{i=1}^{n} \dfrac{\mu_i^2}{\sigma_i^2}}{\dfrac{\mu_0^2}{\sigma_0^2}}} = \frac{1}{1 + \dfrac{\text{appraisal ratio}}{\text{market ratio}}} \tag{60.25}$$

In this form it is clear that any improvement in the quality of security analysis, or in the number of securities analyzed at a given level of quality, can only cause an optimally balanced portfolio to become less well diversified.

Consider again the expression for appraisal ratio

$$\text{appraisal ratio} = \sum_{i=1}^{n} \frac{\mu_i^2}{\sigma_i^2} \tag{60.26}$$

On the average, half the securities analyzed will be overpriced and half under-priced. Thus if short selling is permitted, on the average half the positions in an ideal active portfolio will be long positions and half short. Since the degree of market risk will generally be distributed among securities randomly with respect to the sign of the current price discrepancy, hence the sign of positions in the active portfolio,[8] the expected level of market risk in an ideal active portfolio is zero. In the ideal case, therefore, the second-stage blending between active and passive portfolios is particularly simple: All the appraisal risk is in the active portfolio, and all the market risk is in the passive portfolio. When short selling is not permitted, however, the expected level of market risk in the active portfolio is the average level for the universe from which active securities are selected. Half the terms in Equation 60.26 are suppressed, thus on average reducing the appraisal ratio by half.

## DERIVING FORECASTS OF INDEPENDENT RETURNS FROM SECURITY ANALYSIS

How are the appraisal premiums and variances for individual securities generated by the security analysis process? There are doubtless many ways of answering this question. The one that follows, which assumes a bivariate normal for the joint distribution of the analyst's opinion and the subsequent independent return, is certainly one of the simplest.

Presumably the analyst begins by appraising the security in question. We have shown that the composition of the active portfolio should be independent of expectations regarding the level of the market as a whole. It follows that, in order to be useful in selection of the active portfolio, the analyst's findings should be expressed in such a way that they are invariant with respect to his overall market expectations. Perhaps the easiest way for the analyst to generate opinions with the desired invariance property (under the independence assumptions of the Diagonal Model) is to estimate the value of the security (i.e., what the equilibrium price would be if all investors had his information) consistent with the consensus macroeconomic forecast implicit in the general level of security prices obtaining at the time of the estimate. The value an analyst assigns to a security may be either greater or less than its present price. (Some analysts may be unwilling to assign a value to the security; they may be more comfortable giving a "buy" price and "sell" price, and we can take the point halfway between as their estimated value.)

The analyst then compares his appraisal with the current market price of the security. It is not important how discrepancies between the analyst's estimate and the market price are expressed. The important thing is that there be a significant correlation between the discrepancies and the subsequent actual returns. A portfolio manager can show good results consistently only if his analysts as a group are able to identify discrepancies that are significantly related to the subsequent actual independent return. If data are available for a series of time intervals, one can regress independent returns on various securities for various time intervals against the discrepancies for those time intervals in order to determine the relation between the discrepancies and the actual returns.

The familiar two-variable regression model can be used to relate the expected independent return for the $i$th security to the analyst's current estimate $e_i$ of the discrepancy between market value and his own appraisal as follows:

$$\bar{z}_i = f_i(e_i + g_i) \tag{60.27}$$

It is possible for an analyst to be persistently bullish or bearish about the independent returns for his stocks. Or the analyst may be free from bias, but consistently overstate (or understate) independent returns, regardless of sign. The term $g_i$ corrects for any persistent upward or downward bias in the analyst's estimate, and the factor $f_i$ corrects for any tendency on the part of the analyst to be too "excitable"; that is, to estimate too high when his appraisal exceeds the current market value and too low when current market value exceeds his appraisal. The same factor can also serve to provide the necessary adjustment when the analyst is not "excitable" enough.

The expression $f_i(e_i + g_i)$ translates an estimate $e_i$ expressed as a percentage of current market value into $\mu_i$. It is worth noting that a forecast of the independent return necessarily implies something about the expected rate at which the market price will adjust to eliminate the alleged discrepancy. Thus the forecast of independent return contains the time dimension, whereas the analyst's estimate of the discrepancy between his appraisal and the current market price does not.

The expected independent rate of return $z_i$ and the estimated discrepancy $e_i$ are assumed to be distributed according to a bivariate normal distribution. The analyst's confidence that he rather than the market is right may vary from one point in time to another; nevertheless, in what follows, the parameters of the distribution are assumed to be stationary. (Since we are discussing an individual security, we drop the subscript.) The variables $z$ and $e$ are characterized by variances, or their respective square roots $s_z$ and $s_e$. A third parameter is necessary to complete the specification of this distribution, namely the correlation coefficient $p$ between the variables $z$ and $e$. In composing the active portfolio we are interested in the conditional distribution of $z$ given $e$, or $z|e$. Unless an analyst is able to anticipate *all* the events affecting the price, hence the return, on a security, some portion of the independent return variance remains unexplained by his forecasts.

In terms of the parameters characterizing the joint normal distribution of $e$ and $z$, Equation 60.27 can be rewritten

$$z = \rho \left( \frac{S_z}{S_e} \right) (e + g) \tag{60.28}$$

Regressing $z$ against $e$, we get estimates of the slope coefficient $\rho(S_z/S_e)$ and the constant term $(\rho S_z/S_e)g$. It is important to look at the significance of the regression factors found. Normally data covering a number of intervals will be needed to show that any of the regression factors is significantly different from zero. Some of the deviations of the regression coefficients from zero will be due to sample error rather than an actual relation between analysts' estimates and independent returns.

We are also interested in the residual variance (i.e., that part of the total variance in the independent returns on a security not explained by the analyst's estimate). The amount of a security that should be held in the active portfolio depends not only on the independent return expected on the security but also on the residual variance of the independent return around its expected value. The variance $\sigma^2$ of forecast errors between $\bar{z}$ and actual $z$ is

$$\sigma^2 = \text{var}[z|e] = (1 - \rho^2)s_z^2 \tag{60.29}$$

We saw in Equation 60.26 that the value of the appraisal ratio for an optimally diversified portfolio depends only on the value of the ratio $\bar{z}^2/\sigma_z^2$ for individual securities. Given the analyst's current appraisal $(e)$, the conditional value of this ratio is

$$\frac{\bar{z}^2}{\sigma^2} = \frac{\rho^2}{1 - \rho^2} \frac{(e + g)^2}{s_e^2} \tag{60.30}$$

The right-hand factor in Equation 60.30 is, of course, merely the square of the analyst's estimate, corrected for bias and normalized to unit variance. The current contribution of the security in question to the appraisal ratio of the active portfolio also depends on the analyst's ability to forecast fluctuations in independent return successfully $(\rho)$.

To say that one analyst is "better" than another implies something about the expected value of the contributions of their respective securities to an active portfolio averaged over a series of holding periods and without specific reference to the forecasts obtaining at the beginning of each holding period. At the beginning of each holding period, expectations of independent returns are formed as described above. We continue to denote these expectations by a bar over the appropriate symbol: $\bar{z}$. But now consider a longer-run expectation, based purely on the joint distribution of estimated and actual return, denoting the latter kind of expectations by $E[...]$: We note that, since the expected value over time of $(e + g)$ is zero (with $g$ correcting for any bias in $e$), the expected value of $(e + g)^2$ is given by

$$E[(e + g)^2] = \text{var}[e] = s_e^2 \tag{60.31}$$

Thus if the expectation of Equation 60.30 is taken with respect to the distribution of the analyst's forecasts, we have

$$E\left[\frac{\bar{z}^2}{2}\right] = \frac{\rho^2}{1 - \rho^2} \tag{60.32}$$

In the absence of prior knowledge concerning the analyst's current forecast, therefore, the potential contribution of the security in question to the optimum active portfolio depends solely on $\rho$. The larger $\rho$ is, the more the security contributes to the optimal active portfolio. The expression in Equation 60.32 can be thought of as the ratio of the variance in residual price changes explained by the analyst's estimates to the variance left unexplained.

In any forecasting problem, there are three kinds of variables: (1) the dependent variable (in this case, independent return); (2) one or more independent explanatory variables (in this case, the analyst's opinion, etc.); and (3) the expected value, or maximum-likelihood forecast of the dependent variable, based on knowledge of the independent variables. In the case considered in this section, the explanatory variable was the difference between the analyst's estimate of value and current price.

When $(e)$ is treated as the discrepancy between current price and appraised value, then, however long a discrepancy has been outstanding, the fraction expected to be resolved in the next holding period is the same (or, equivalently, the probability of complete resolution in the next period is the same). The fraction to be resolved (or the probability of resolution) is independent of the scale of the discrepancy. No allowance is made for the possibility that the rate of resolution may depend in part on the kind of insight leading to identification of the discrepancy or on the source of the insight.

For any or all these reasons, the portfolio manager may prefer to supply his own approach to formulating forecasts of independent return. If $(e)$ is interpreted as representing the explanatory variable upon which the forecast is based—whether derived by fundamental, technical, or other means—the regression model in which $(e)$ appears Equation (60.27)—is reduced to the less ambitious role of relating the explanatory variable, forecast, and actual return, without linking the forecasting process directly to the determinations of the security analyst. The price of this decision is, of course, that the process by which the explanatory variable is generated then becomes a black box, determination of whose contents is outside the scope of the model presented here.

The fact that $(e)$ is susceptible of the more general interpretation means, however, that the results regarding the role of the coefficient of determination $\rho^2$ in portfolio selection are not limited to the model presented here, in which price discrepancy is itself the explanatory variable, but are in fact as general as the application to the forecasting problem of the regression model itself.

All the preceding comments on forecasting the independent return apply to forecasting the market return $y_m$.

## SUMMARY

1. It is useful in balancing portfolios to distinguish between two sources of risk: market, or systematic risk on the one hand, and appraisal, or insurable risk on the other. In general it is not correct to assume that optimal balancing leads either to negligible levels of appraisal risk or to negligible levels of market risk.
2. Without any loss in generality, any portfolio can be thought of as having three parts: a riskless part, a highly diversified part (that is, virtually devoid of specific risk), and an active part which in general has in it both specific risk and market risk. The amount of market risk in the active portfolio is unimportant, as long as one has the option of increasing or reducing market risk via the passive portfolio. The overall portfolio can usually be improved by taking a long or short position in the market as a whole.
3. The rate at which a portfolio earns riskless interest is independent of how the portfolio is invested or whether or not the portfolio is levered and depends only on the current market value of the investor's equity.
4. The rate at which the portfolio earns risk premium depends only on the total amount of market risk undertaken and is independent of the size of the investor's equity and of the composition of his active portfolio.

5. Optimal selection in the active portfolio depends only on appraisal risk and appraisal premiums and not at all on market risk or market premium; nor on investor objectives as regards the relative importance to him of expected return versus risk; nor on the investment manager's expectations regarding the general market. Two managers with radically different expectations regarding the general market but the same specific information regarding individual securities will select active portfolios with the same relative proportions. (Here, as elsewhere in this paper, we ignore possible differences in the tax objective, liquidity considerations, etc.)

6. The appraisal ratio depends only on (a) the quality of security analysis and (b) how efficiently the active portfolio is balanced. It is independent of the relative emphasis between active and passive portfolios and of the degree to which the risky portfolio is levered or mixed with debt. It is also independent of the market premium. Obviously, it is not necessary for a professionally managed fund to be optimal in terms of all three stages in order to be socially (or economically) successful: An individual investor may choose to perform the third-stage balancing himself, with the appropriate amount of personal borrowing or lending. He may even perform the second-stage balancing himself, determining the appropriate emphasis between a brokerage acount or "go-go" fund on the one hand and a virtually passive old-line mutual fund or living trust on the other. On the other hand, any attempt to compare the skill with which professional investment managers select securities (i.e., performs the first-stage balancing) using historical rates of return must be designed invariant with respect to second- and third-stage balancing policies.

7. The security analyst's potential contribution to overall portfolio performance over time depends only on how well his forecasts of future independent returns correlate with actual independent returns, and not on the magnitude of these returns.

## APPENDIX 60.1

In his paper, "Simplified Model for Portfolio Analysis,"[10] William Sharpe proposes the following model of the return from a risky security:

$$R_i = A_i + B_i I + C_i$$
$$I = A_{n+1} + C_{n+1} \tag{60.33}$$

where $A_{n+1}$ and the $A_i$ are constants, and $C_{n+1}$ and the $C_i$ are random variables with expected values of zero and variances $Q_i$ and $Q_{n+1}$, respectively. Sharpe postulates that the covariances between $C_i$ and $C_j$ are zero for all values of $i$ and $j$ ($i \neq j$).

As Sharpe sees it "the major characteristic of the Diagonal Model is the assumption that the returns of various securities are related only through common relationships with some basic underlying factor. . . . This model has two virtues: it is one of the simplest which can be constructed without assuming away the existence of interrelationships among securities and there is considerable evidence that it can capture a large part of such interrelationships."[11] Regarding the way the model is intended to be used. Sharpe says, "The Diagonal Model requires the following predictions from a security analyst: (1) the values of $A_i$, $B_i$, and $Q_i$ for each of $n$ securities, (2) values of $A_{n+1}$ and $Q_{n+1}$ for the Index."[12] In order to give the best possible results, the analyst's estimates of the $A_i$ should be free from bias, consistent from one security to the next, and reflect both the analyst's current appraisal of the securities and his knowledge of current market prices. It is, of course, also necessary that he have a rational basis for estimating the $Q_i$. If there is indeed a significant degree of comovement among securities, then his estimates must recognize this fact.

In the equations which follow, $r$ is the risk-free interest rate. Let $E[\ ]$ represent the expectation of the random variable in the brackets, $\mathrm{var}[\ ]$ the variance, and $\mathrm{cov}[\ ]$ the covariance of the two variables within the brackets. If Sharpe's market index $I (= A_{n+1} + C_{n+1})$ can be identified with the return on market as a whole, then, according to the Sharpe-Lintner-Treynor theory, expected return on the $i$th security in equilibrium must satisfy

$$E[R_i - r] = k \, \mathrm{cov}[R_i, I]$$
$$= k \, \mathrm{cov}[A_i + B_i(A_{n+1} + C_{n+1}) + C_i, A_{n+1} + C_{n+1}]$$

Eliminating constant terms and terms in $C_i$, which by definition have zero covariance with $I$, we have

$$E[R_i] = B_i k \, \mathrm{var}\, C_{n+1} = B_i k Q_{n+1}$$

In equilibrium, therefore, we have

$$E[R_i] = r + B_i k Q_{n+1} \tag{60.34}$$

On the other hand, the Sharpe Diagonal Model stipulates that

$$E[R_i] = A_i + B_i A_{n+1}$$

The only way both equations can hold for all values of $B_i$ is if

$$A_i = r$$
$$A_{n+1} = k Q_{n+1} \tag{60.35}$$

It is clear that, in a dynamic equilibrium in which all investors evaluate new information simultaneously. $A_i$ is the riskless rate and $A_{n+1} B_i$ is the expected excess return on the $i$th security.

Once we abandon the assumption that all investors have the same information, it is no longer true that expected excess return on the $i$th security is proportional to $B_i$. It is apparent that the values of $A_i, i = 1, \ldots, n$, $A_{n+1}$ leading to a given set of expectations of the $R_i$ are not uniquely determined by specifying expected returns for a set of securities. A set of values that implies that half the universe of securities are overpriced relative to the current market and half are underpriced, that is, the set for which

$$\sum_1 M_i(A_i - r) = 0 \tag{60.36}$$

we call market neutral.

In order to eliminate the ambiguity, we shall assume henceforth the $A_i$ are implicitly defined to be market neutral. Then $A_i$ is the sum of the pure rate and expectation of a disequilibrium price movement, and $A_{n+1}$ is the expected excess return on the market. In the case in which an investor has special information on the $i$th security, $A_i$ will differ from the equilibrium value by an amount that we will call the appraisal premium, in deference to the source of the premium:

$$\text{appraisal premium} = A_i - r$$

$$A_i = \text{appraisal premium} + \text{riskless rate} \tag{60.37}$$

We can now summarize our interpretations of the symbols in Sharpe's Diagonal Model (modified slightly as noted above):

1. $A_i$ = the sum of the risk-free rate and the appraisal premium on the $i$th security.
2. $A_{n+1}$ = the investor's expectation of excess return for the market as a whole. If he is not trying to outguess the overall market, it is the premium offered to investors generally for bearing market, or systematic, risk.
3. $B_i$ = the volatility of the $i$th security—that is, its degree of sensitivity to market fluctuations.
4. $C_{n+1}$ = the difference between actual return on the market and expected return on the market. Its variance is $Q_{n+1}$. If an analyst has no power to forecast market fluctuations, $Q_{n+1}$ is the variance of the market return.
5. $C_i$ = the difference between actual return on the $i$th security and the return explained by the actual market return (plus the prime interest rate). Its variance is $Q_i$. If an analyst has no power to forecast the independent return, $Q_i$ is the residual variance of return of the $i$th security regressed against the market.

Now consider again Sharpe's expression for return on the $i$th security: $R_i = A_i + B_i(A_{n+1} + C_{n+1}) + C_i$. Can we define $I = A_{n+1} + C_{n+1}$ in terms of the $R_i$? If not, then $I$ is not truly an "index" in the sense of return on a market average. Let $M_i$ be the total market value of the $i$th security. Then define

$$I = A_{n+1} + C_{n+1} + \sum M_i(R_i - r) \tag{60.38}$$

When the so-called market index $I$ is defined in this way, one of the assumptions in Sharpe's model no longer holds exactly. Forming the sums of each term in Equation (60.33) over the whole set of securities, weighted by respective market values, and rearranging, we have

$$\sum M_i(R_i - A_i) = (A_{n+1} + C_{n+1})M_i B_i + \sum M_i C_i \tag{60.39}$$

Substituting from Equation (60.38) and invoking Equation (60.36) we have

$$(A_{n+1} + C_{n+1})(\sum M - \sum MB) = \sum MC$$

This expression can hold in general only if

$$\begin{cases} \sum_i M_i C_i = 0 \\[2mm] \dfrac{\sum_i M_i B_i}{\sum_i M_i} = 1 \end{cases} \tag{60.40}$$

The second equation merely requires that the weights sum to 100 percent. The first, however, is a constraint on the independence of the $C_i$. The constraint conflicts slightly with Sharpe's own model, which postulated $E[C_i C_j] = 0$ for all $i \neq j$, and $E[C_i C_{n+1}] = 0$ for all $i$. The conflict arises from a confusion—possibly unintended or possibly intended—in the Diagonal Model between an underlying explanatory variable to which all securities are sensitive in greater or lesser degree, and a Market Index such as $I = \sum_i M_i(R_i - r)$.

## Notes

1. William F. Sharpe, "Capital Asset Prices: A Theory of Market Equilibrium under Conditions of Risk," *Journal of Finance* 19, no. 3 (September 1964): 425–42: John Lintner, "The Valuation of Risk Assets and the Selection of Risky Investments in Stock Portfolios and Capital Budgets," *Review of Economics and Statistics* 57, no. 1 (February 1954): 13–37; and Jack L. Treynor's paper, "Toward a Theory of the Market Values of Risky Assets" (unpublished, 1962).
2. Harry Markowitz., *Portfolio Selection: Efficient Diversification of Investments* (New York: John Wiley & Sons, 1959; New Haven, Conn.: Yale University Press, 1970); and William Sharpe "A Simplifed Model for Portfolio Analysis," *Management Science* 9 (January 1963):277–293.
3. Michael Jensen, "The Performance of Mutual Funds in the Period 1945–1964," *Journal of Finance* 23 (May 1968): 389–416.
4. See Sharpe, n. 2.
5. See, for example, William Sharpe, "Mutual Fund Performance," *Journal of Business* 39 (January 1966): 119–138.
6. Ibid.
7. See n. 3.
8. See Equation (60.27).
9. See, for example, Harald Cramer, *The Elements of Probability Theory* (Princeton, N.J.: Princeton University Press, 1946), pp. 141 and 142.
10. See Sharpe, n. 2.
11. Ibid.
12. Ibid.

# CHAPTER 61

# Why Clients Fail

**W**hen a client imposes his investment enthusiasms on his portfolio manager, he is often being his own worst enemy. In particular, it is often difficult for him to realize that what he considers the reasonable, obvious, and common-sense investment idea is the one most likely to be impounded in security prices so quickly that it will be impossible to trade profitably on it. There are two statements about the investment business that every client should paste on his mirror, where he can see them every morning: (1) For the reason just given, most of what is knowable about securities and their intrinsic values is not worth knowing, and (2) most of what is worth knowing (i.e., what will have impact on future security price changes) is unknowable. Most price change is pure surprise, even to the most sophisticated observer. Thus failure to anticipate price changes is not necessarily a mistake. The time investment professionals now spend absorbing investment information that has already been discounted and apologizing for "mistakes" that were avoidable only with the benefit of hindsight could otherwise be spent making useful contributions to the client's future portfolio performance.

A related tendency among clients who are businessmen is to select fund managers in their own image—to select men who attach great value to a rounded consideration of the obvious, and little, if any, value to seeking out neglected subtleties. Although, for the reasons just given, the off-beat investment idea is more likely to be productive in terms of investment success than the safe, reasonable, roundly considered idea, such clients often prefer fund managers preoccupied with the latter.

Clients often betray their own ideas about the proper approach to fund management in interviews with prospective fund managers. Unfortunately for the client, fund managers who alter their management style to conform in hopes of securing the client's business are likely to do less well managing according to someone else's style than managing according to their own.

And many clients behave contrary to their own best interest in the setting of investment goals. Some clients seem to operate on the assumption that a fund manager who will promise 20 percent is better than a fund manager who will promise 15, who in turn is better than a fund manager who will promise only 10; or on the assumption that, if a fund manager can be coerced into accepting an objective of 15 percent, he is likely to deliver a better actual performance than if his investment objective were 10.

In such cases, a performance objective expressed in terms of rate of return is merely a euphemism for the level of investment risk the fund manager is compelled to assume.

But the most serious problem with investment clients is their tendency to involve themselves with the professional's day-to-day thinking. In this respect, professional investors still have a long way to go. Doctors and lawyers, for example, do not suffer foolish questions from their clients gladly. They consider that their task requires special talents and special training and that, unless the client has these special qualifications, he shouldn't presume to involve himself in the thinking processes of the professional. Most investment clients, on the other hand, feel entitled to ask the manager of their funds why he bought this or didn't buy that, or what he thinks about problems in the Middle East and how they will affect stock prices.

Although the involvement of the client in the thinking of the professional investor has a long tradition, one might expect that, as institutional clients become more important and individual clients less important, this involvement would diminish. Many institutional clients are sophisticated people with broad knowledge of the investment business. The problem is getting worse, rather than better, however, as the balance of power between the investment professional and his client shifts toward the client.

It is hardly surprising that much of contemporary research is consequently aimed at impressing the client rather than improving the performance of his portfolio. In a hard-dollar research environment, the consequences would be more serious. Whereas, in the traditional soft-dollar environment many fund managers can afford more research than they have time to digest, in a hard-dollar environment the two kinds of research compete for the same research dollar.

The key to success in investing, like the key to success in science, is discovery. It is commonplace among scientists that in order to discover one must ask the right questions. When the investment professional subordinates his questions to the client's questions, he is abdicating his most important responsibility: discovering the neglected subtleties that lead to investment success.

# CHAPTER 62

# Long-Term Investing

*When one talks about market efficiency, it is important to distinguish be-*
*tween ideas whose implications are obvious and consequently travel quickly*
*and ideas that require reflection, judgment, and special expertise for their*
*evaluation and consequently travel slowly. The second kind of idea—rather*
*than the obvious, hence quickly discounted insight relating to "long-term"*
*business developments—is the only meaningful basis for "long-term invest-*
*ing."*

> *If the market is inefficient, it will not be inefficient with respect to the first*
> *kind of idea, since by definition the first kind is unlikely to be misevaluated*
> *by the great mass of investors. If there is any market inefficiency, hence*
> *any investment opportunity, it will arise with the second kind of investment*
> *idea—the kind that travels slowly. On the other hand, many investors argue*
> *that research devoted to identifying the second kind is impractical because*
> *the market consensus, based as it is on the opinions of investors lacking the*
> *special expertise required, will never respond to it.*

> *Whether the great mass of investors is capable of responding to an in-*
> *vestment idea, however, is irrelevant. An analyst's opinion of a security's*
> *value is the price at which, risk-adjusted, the return on that security is com-*
> *petitive with the return on other securities in the market. If an analyst's idea*
> *correctly reveals a security as undervalued, it reveals a security that, at its*
> *present price, offers a superior long-term return—whether or not the market*
> *consensus ever responds to the idea. The mere inclusion of securities based*
> *on such ideas will assure superior performance.*

The investor who would attempt to improve his portfolio performance through
unconventional, innovative research is currently being challenged on three fronts:
(1) The efficient marketers say he will be unable to find any ideas that haven't been
properly discounted by the market. (2) Lord Keynes says that even if he finds these
ideas his portfolio will be viewed as "eccentric" and "rash" by conventionally minded
clients and professional peers. (3) The investment philistine says that even if he stands
by his ideas he won't be rewarded because actual price movements are governed by
conventional thinking, which is immune to these ideas.

---

Successful response to the first challenge lies in distinguishing between two kinds of investment ideas: (a) those whose implications are straightforward and obvious, take relatively little special expertise to evaluate, and consequently travel quickly (e.g., "hot stocks"); and (b) those that require reflection, judgment, and special expertise, for their evaluation, and consequently travel slowly. (In practice, of course, actual investment ideas lie along a continuous spectrum between these two polar extremes, but we can avoid some circumlocution by focusing on the extremes.) Pursuit of the second kind of idea—rather than the obvious, hence quickly discounted, insight relating to "long-term" economic or business developments—is, of course, the only meaningful definition for "long-term investing."

If the market is inefficient, it is not going to be inefficient with respect to the first kind of idea since, by definition, this kind is unlikely to be misevaluated by the great mass of investors. If investors disagree on the value of a security even when they have the same information, their differences in opinion must be due to errors in analysis of the second kind of idea. If these investors err independently, then a kind of law of averages operates on the resulting error in the market consensus. If enough independent opinions bear on the determination of the consensus price, the law of large numbers effect will be very powerful, and the error implicit in the consensus will be small compared to errors made on the average by the individual investors contributing to the consensus.

Under what circumstances, then, will investors' errors in appraising information available to all lead to investment opportunities for some? As the key to the averaging process underlying an accurate consensus is the assumption of independence, if all—or even a substantial fraction—of these investors make the same error, the independence assumption is violated and the consensus can diverge significantly from true value. The market then ceases to be efficient in the sense of pricing available information correctly. I see nothing in the arguments of Professor Eugene Fama or the other efficient markets advocates to suggest that large groups of investors may not make the same error in appraising the kind of abstract ideas that take special expertise to understand and evaluate, and that consequently travel relatively slowly.

According to Fama, "disagreement among investors about the implications of given information does not in itself imply market inefficiency unless there are investors who can consistently make better evaluations of available information than are implicit in market prices." Fama's statement can best be revised to read: "Disagreement among investors *due to independent errors in analysis* does not necessarily lead to market inefficiency." If the independence assumption is violated in practice, every violation represents a potential opportunity for fundamental analysis.

The assertion that the great bulk of practicing investors find long-term investing impractical was set forth almost 40 years ago by Lord Keynes:

> *Most of these persons are in fact largely concerned not with most superior long term forecasts of the probable yield of an investment over its whole life, but with foreseeing changes in the conventional basis of evaluation a short time ahead of the general public. They are concerned not with what an investment is really worth to a man who buys it for keeps, but with what the market will evaluate it at under the influence of mass psychology three months or a year hence.*

Obviously, if an investor is concerned with how the "mass psychology" appraisal of an investment will change over the next three months, he is concerned with the propagation of ideas that can be apprehended with very little analysis and that consequently travel fast.

On the other hand, the investment opportunity offered by market inefficiency is most likely to arise with investment ideas that propagate slowly, or hardly at all. Keynes went on to explain why practical investors are not interested in such ideas:

> It is the long term investor, he who most promotes the public interest, who will in practice come in for the most criticism, wherever investment funds are managed by committees or boards or banks. For it is in the essence of his behavior that he should be eccentric, unconventional and rash in the eyes of average opinion. If he is successful, that will only confirm the general belief in his rashness; and if in the short run he is unsuccessful, which is very likely, he will not receive much mercy. Worldly wisdom teaches that it is better for reputation to fail conventionally than to succeed unconventionally.

Thus Keynes not only described accurately the way most professional investors still behave; he also supplied their reasons for so behaving. He was careful never to say, however, that the long-term investor who sticks by his guns will not be rewarded.

But is the price of unconventional thinking as high as Keynes alleges? Modern portfolio theory says that an individual security can be assessed only in the context of the overall portfolio: As long as the overall portfolio has a reasonable level of market sensitivity and is reasonably well diversified, the beneficiary has nothing to fear from unconventional holdings—and still less to fear from conventional holdings bought for unconventional reasons. There is, of course, marketing advantage in holding securities enjoying wide popular esteem but, as investors as a class become more sophisticated, they are less likely to be challenged on specific holdings.

There is, finally, a school of thought that asserts that research directed toward improving our analytical tools is automatically impractical because it does not describe the behavior of a market consensus based on opinions of investors unfamiliar with these tools. This line of argument puts a premium on investment ideas that have broad appeal or are readily persuasive, while rejecting the ideas that capture abstract economic truths in terms too recondite to appeal to the mass of investors.

The investment philistine who asserts that it is impossible to benefit from superior approaches to investment analysis if the market consensus is not based on these approaches misunderstands what appraisal of a security means: An analyst's opinion of the value of a security is an estimate of the price at which, risk-adjusted, the return on the security is competitive with the returns on other securities available in the market. A superior method for identifying undervalued securities is therefore tantamount to a method of identifying securities that at their present prices offer superior long-term returns. The mere inclusion of such securities in a portfolio will guarantee a superior investment performance.

## THE RETURNS TO LONG-TERM INVESTING

Suppose that an investor identifies a stock for which the market persistently underestimates actual earnings. A standard stock valuation model such as the Gordon-Shapiro

**EXHIBIT 62.1**  A Rough Basis for Estimating Return

| g | assume $\rho = 10\%$ | |
|---|---|---|
| | $\lambda$ | $\rho' - \rho$ |
| 0 | 0.5 | 10% |
| 5% | 0.5 | 5% |
| 0 | 0.67 | 5% |
| 5% | 0.67 | 2.5% |

$g$ = rate of growth in earnings and dividends
$\lambda$ = ratio of market-consensus estimate of magnitude
of future earnings to true magnitude
$\rho' - \rho$ = abnormal rate of return that will be realized
by holding stock indefinitely, even if market continues
to underestimate true earnings

model formalizes this idea. For simplicity, the model assumes that (1) the future dividend payout ratio will be constant over time and (2) the percentage rate "g" at which earnings (hence, given (1), dividends) grow will be constant over time. The value of the stock equals the present worth of the growing stream of dividends, discounted at rate "$\rho$" (i.e., the "cost of capital").

Let the ratio "$\lambda$" of the consensus forecast of earnings at any point in time to true earnings (which, assuming the consensus correctly anticipates the constant payout rate, will also be the ratio of the consensus forecast of dividends to true dividends) also be constant over time. Then true earnings, true dividends, the consensus forecast of earnings, and the consensus forecast of dividends will all grow at the same rate g. If $\lambda$ equals one (i.e., if the consensus correctly anticipates future earnings), return (dividends and appreciation combined) to the shareholder "$\rho'$" will equal $\rho$, the cost of capital. If $\lambda$ is less than one (i.e., if the consensus consistently underestimates future earnings), the return to the shareholder $\rho'$ will exceed the equilibrium market return. The difference, $\rho' - \rho$, is the shareholder's reward for being right when the consensus is wrong. If the consensus continues to be wrong indefinitely his reward will continue indefinitely.

Exhibit 62.1 provides a rough basis for estimating how big the return differential $(\rho' - \rho)$ from holding undervalued stocks will be under the assumption that the general mass of investors never come around to forecasting earnings correctly (see Appendix 62.1). It should be noted that these are returns *per annum*. The trading rate required to realize these returns is obviously very low.

To the threefold challenge, a threefold reply is offered: (1) The efficient marketer's assertion that *no* improperly or inadequately discounted ideas exist is both unproved and unlikely. (2) Keynes' suggestion that unconventional investing is impractical is no longer valid in the age of modern portfolio theory. (3) The investment philistine who says good ideas that can't persuade the great mass of investors have no investment value is simply wrong.

The skeptical reader can ask himself the following question: If a portfolio manager consistently exhibited the kind of abnormal returns suggested in Exhibit 62.1, while maintaining reasonable levels of market sensitivity and diversification, how long would it be before his investment record began to outweigh, in the eyes of his clients, the unconventionality of his portfolio holdings?

## APPENDIX 62.1

### I. The Return Differential from Holding Undervalued Stocks

Let "E(t)" be earnings of the firm at time "t," "b" be the dividend payout ratio, "$\rho$" the market discount rate (the cost of capital) and "g" the projected growth rate. If, for the sake of argument, we define "correct" pricing of the company in terms of the well known Gordon-Shapiro formula, we have for the intrinsic value "v,"

$$v = \frac{bE(t)}{\rho - g}$$

If the internal return on reinvested funds is "$\tau$," we have

$$E(t) = \tau (1 - b) \int_0^1 E(\tau) \, d\tau = g \int_0^t E(\tau) \, d\tau = E_0 e^{gt}$$

If priced correctly, we have for price as a function of time

$$v(t) = \frac{bE_0 e^{gt}}{\rho - g}$$

If underpriced by factor $\lambda$, we have

$$v(t) = \frac{\lambda bE_0 e^{gt}}{\rho - g}$$

Differentiating, we obtain the rate of price appreciation

$$\frac{dv}{dt} = \lambda bE_0 \frac{g}{\rho - g} e^{gt}$$

From previous considerations we know that the dividend is given by

$$bE_0 e^{gt}$$

For the price change and dividend together we have

$$bE_0 e^{gt} \frac{\lambda g + \rho - g}{\rho - g}$$

$$\text{rate of return} = \frac{\text{price change} + \text{dividend}}{\text{price}}$$

$$= \frac{\lambda g + \rho - g}{\lambda}$$

$$= (\rho - g) \left( \frac{1}{\lambda} - 1 \right)$$

This is the return differential realized by holding a stock underpriced by a factor $\lambda$. Since $1/\lambda$ is always positive, we have $\rho' - \rho > 0$.

## II. How Would the Price of a Mispriced Security Have to Behave in the Future to Prevent the Long-Run Holder from Realizing an Extraordinary Return?

The equilibrium return is "$\rho$." If we replace "$\lambda$" in the previous model by "$\lambda(t)$," we can state this condition as:

$$\frac{d}{dt}\left[\lambda(t)\frac{bE_0 e^{gt}}{\rho - g}\right] + bE_0 e^{gt} = \rho\lambda(t)\frac{bE_0 e^{gt}}{\rho - g}$$

The left-hand side is the return from a mispriced security in the more general case in which the value of $\lambda$ is changing over time. The right-hand side is the normal return on the actual (mispriced) market price. We ask: How must $\lambda$ change over time if the investor is to realize only a normal return on the mispriced security? Carrying out the indicated differentiation, we have

$$\lambda(t)bE_0\frac{g}{\rho - g}e^{gt} + \frac{d\lambda}{dt}\frac{bE_0 e^{gt}}{\rho - g} + bE_0 e^{gt} = \rho\lambda\frac{(t)bE_0 e^{gt}}{\rho - g}$$

This can be simplified as follows:

$$\lambda(t)g\frac{d\lambda}{dt} + (\rho - g) = \rho\lambda(t)$$

$$(g - \rho)\lambda(t) + \frac{d\lambda}{dt} = g - \rho$$

The solution to this differential equation is:

$$\lambda(t) = \lambda_0 e^t \rho^{-gn} + 1$$

**EXHIBIT 62.2**  How Fast the Stock Price Must Fall

| | $\lambda(0) = 0.5$ implies $\lambda_n = -0.5$ | | | |
| --- | --- | --- | --- | --- |
| | $\rho - g = 5\%$ | | $\rho - g = 10\%$ | |
| | $(\rho - g)t$ | $\lambda(t)$ | $(\rho - g)t$ | $\lambda(t)$ |
| $t = 0$ | 0 | 0.5 | 0 | 0.5 |
| 1 | 0.05 | 0.474 | 0.10 | 0.448 |
| 2 | 0.10 | 0.448 | 0.20 | 0.390 |
| 4 | 0.20 | 0.390 | 0.40 | 0.254 |
| 8 | 0.40 | 0.254 | 0.80 | negative |
| 16 | 0.80 | negative | | |

When t = 0, we have

$$\lambda(0) = \lambda_0 + 1$$

Hence, if $\lambda(0) < 1$, we have $\lambda_0 = \lambda(0) - 1 < 0$. Since the exponent $\rho - g > 0$, $\lambda$ must fall faster and faster to prevent investors from realizing an extraordinary return on an underpriced stock. In a few years it has fallen as far as it can—in other words, to zero (see Exhibit 62.2).

# CHAPTER 63

# The Institutional Shortfall

In his recent article "The Loser's Game" (*Financial Analysts Journal*, July–August 1975), Charles Ellis introduced a phrase that will probably get a lot of use over the next few years. The phrase—"institutional shortfall"—refers to the failure of institutional equity portfolios to outperform the market indices. Some academics see the shortfall as evidence that securities research is worthless.

The shortfall—if indeed it exists—is consistent with a very different interpretation. Consider, for example, an institution that turns its portfolio 50 percent per year. If its annual return exhibits a one percent shortfall in relation to the market average, risk-adjusted, then this institution is experiencing a round-trip trading disadvantage—the difference between the cost of trading and the value of research—equal to two percent of the dollar value traded. Thus if research is indeed worthless, the maximum cost of trading for this institution is two percent round-trip, or one percent one way—including commissions.

In order to reconcile the assumed figures with a more realistic trading cost, it is necessary to impute a positive value to research. If, for example, one assumes that the round-trip cost of trading is 10 percent, the net round-trip trading disadvantage is 10 percent minus the value of research (let us call the latter x).[1] We have:

$$0.50(0.10 - x) = 0.01, x = 0.08$$

In order for the institution's shortfall to be as low as one percent, the average value of research must be at least eight percent of the dollar value of each round-trip turn. If, as is traditional, research motivates the institution's purchases, but not its sales, then virtually the full burden of justifying the round-trip cost of trading falls on the purchase decision. Under these assumptions, research ideas worth less than 10 percent of the price of the stock will not justify a purchase.

By the same token, if an equity portfolio has broken even (risk-adjusted), the average value of the research ideas on which it actually traded was at least this high.

## Note

1. Some years ago (in a very different market climate), Charles Ellis assumed—purely for the sake of argument—that the *one-way* cost of trading was 10 percent. See "Portfolio Operations," *Financial Analysts Journal* (September–October 1971), p. 40.

# CHAPTER 64

# Persuasion and Long-Term Investing

A recent article in this journal distinguished between "long-term" ideas—ideas requiring reflection, judgment, and special expertise for their evaluation—and "short-term" ideas—the obvious, hence quickly discounted, ideas that are self-evident to the great mass of investors.[1] Long-term ideas lead to a style of investing that another article called "de facto market making": Long-term ideas will influence the value that the long-term investor assigns to securities, hence the price he will bid for securities he doesn't own on one hand, or ask for securities he does own on the other.[2] But they will not hurry him into taking the initiative in attempting to change his positions.

The distinction between the two kinds of ideas would seem to have implications for the role of persuasion in transmitting these ideas from investor to investor. At one extreme, the long-term idea cannot be communicated from one investor to another and persuasion will be of no avail. At the other, the conventional idea whose implications are obvious should not require any persuasion for one investor to communicate it to another.

Where, then, does a useful role for persuasion lie? If it lies anywhere, it lies in the middle ground between the obvious investment ideas and the recondite—in the ground occupied by those ideas that become "obvious" after a little persuasion. But how is an investor to react to persuasion? If he is a short-term investor, he will eschew ideas that require too much persuasion; whereas if he is a long-term investor, he will eschew ideas that require too little.

One thing seems clear: If an idea is sufficiently long-term that the investor who is able to grasp it is in no hurry to trade on it then, almost by definition, the idea is unsuited to ordinary modes of persuasion. In particular, if it takes a broker to persuade the client of the merit of an investment idea, the idea is not strictly long-term. One is probably safe in concluding that such long-term investment ideas as an investor is able to identify are likely to come out of his own shop if not, indeed, out of his own head.

## Notes

1. Jack L. Treynor, "Long-Term Investing," *Financial Analysts Journal* (May–June 1976), pp. 56–59.
2. Jack L. Treynor, "*De Facto* Market Makers," *Financial Analysts Journal* (September–October 1975), p. 6.

CHAPTER **65**

# Is "Reasonable Knowledge" Enough?

My March–April 1973 editorial on prudence asserted that "there are ... two dimensions to prudence: (1) maintaining an average level of market sensitivity across the holdings of a portfolio that is in line with the risk objectives of the beneficiary; and (2) avoiding undue exposure to a handful of securities...." There is a certain elegance to the modern capital theoretic view on prudence expressed by these two dimensions. On the other hand, one is left with an uneasy feeling that a portfolio could satisfy both dimensions and still serve its beneficiary very badly.

Suppose the portfolio trades actively: Market spreads—the difference between bid and asked prices—are significant. To the cost of trading against these spreads one must, of course, add commission costs. Unless the research ideas on which trades are based have some genuine value, on average trading will reduce the value of the portfolio by the sum of these two costs—even if it is well diversified and maintains a "prudent" level of market risk.

The two dimensions are sufficient if the portfolio manager is enjoined from trading. But such an injunction would, of course, mean the end of active portfolio management and the end of investment research directed toward investment decisions by fiduciaries. Thus analysts have a stake in finding a way to extend the new concept of prudence in a way that permits it to govern active, as well as passive, portfolios.

Perhaps it is for this reason that some have thought to add to its two dimensions the requirement that the portfolio manager maintain "reasonable knowledge" about the individual securities in his portfolio. This writer has problems, however, with the notion of reasonable knowledge. In order to prevent portfolio managers from squandering their clients' assets, the criterion must prevent the portfolio manager from trading when the value of his investment information fails to have a reasonable chance of exceeding the cost of trading. If reasonable knowledge means knowing what other investors know, then it falls short of this standard, because what other investors know is already impounded in price, hence offers no potential return to offset that cost.

It appears that there is an aspect to prudence in managing an active portfolio—"trading prudence"—that goes beyond the two dimensions of holding prudence described in the earlier editorial, and that a reasonable knowledge requirement does not come to grips with this aspect.

# CHAPTER 66

# How Technical Should Investment Management Be?

**W**e are all aware that technical ideas borrowed from the sciences have been creeping into investment management. To some professional investors, terms like *regression coefficient, correlation coefficient, residual variance* and *standard error* are now almost as familiar as *turning point, short interest, current ratio* and *normalized earnings*. Others feel, however, that the new ideas are wholly unnecessary and, indeed, used mostly to put the listener on the defensive, or to give the speaker an aura of erudition and technical expertise that merely serves to conceal a lack of genuine insight into the investment problem. How technical should investment management be?

In his article, "Stock Market Outlook: No Metamorphosis" (*Financial Analysts Journal*, September–October 1977), Arthur Zeikel suggested that market prices are based on the consensus extrapolation, hence that opportunities for active management lie in identifying situations where the underlying logic will defy extrapolation and disappoint the market consensus. In this view, extrapolation of a five-year earnings trend will often be a good way to estimate the market consensus, but rarely, if ever, a good way to detect a trading opportunity.

Charley Ellis, in "The Loser's Game" (*Financial Analysts Journal*, July–August 1975), argued that investment analysis as practiced in the 1970s was no longer sophisticated enough to win the active management game. Perhaps Zeikel's theory of extrapolation explains why: Investors still using extrapolation to predict future trends are unlikely to improve upon a market consensus that is itself based on extrapolation.

Surely this message has sunk in. Yet investors continue to play the extrapolation game. Maybe they feel that, while extrapolation is relatively easy for them, investigation into the underlying logic of change is hard—often too hard.

Man uses mechanical devices to accomplish physical tasks that his unassisted body could not perform. Technique, which is nothing more nor less than canned intelligence, allows man to solve problems too hard for his unassisted intellect. Unless we investors become more intelligent (which seems unlikely) more extensive use of technique is our only alternative to extrapolation (i.e., to the "loser's game").

On the other hand, there is no point burdening ourselves with technique that is unnecessarily complicated and abstract. How technical should active investment management be? With apologies to Abraham Lincoln, just technical enough to get the job done.

# CHAPTER 67

# If You Can Forecast the Market, You Don't Need Anything Else

**C**learly, any investor who bought and sold the market at its turning points would outperform (by a vast margin) anyone who based his investment decisions on analysis of individual securities. Should active investors give up on security selection and join the market timers?

Unfortunately, nobody can call market turning points with anything approaching certainty. Many market timers once regarded as spectacularly successful are no longer in business. Apparently their earlier successes reflected a healthy degree of luck, which, unlike skill, cannot be replicated.

Over time, a market timer's level of prediction accuracy may be so low that a fundamental analyst with an ability to predict individual securities prices will outperform him. Our title obviously requires refinement to remain meaningful. Perhaps we should say. "A given level of prediction accuracy is worth more to portfolio performance if it pertains to market, rather than specific, return"—where the latter refers, of course, to the return on a specific security with market effect removed.

The value to portfolio performance of a given level of accuracy in predicting specific return depends in part on the degree of correlation between that return and specific returns of other securities. The higher the correlation, the less the value, since correlation reduces the investor's ability to diversify away that portion of specific return that he is unable to predict. On the other hand, market return is by definition uncorrelated with the specific returns of individual securities. Thus the contribution to portfolio performance of a given level of accuracy in predicting overall market return will not suffer from correlation problems. In the absence of correlation between specific returns, however, Sharpe's famous Diagonal Model will hold. One consequence of that model is that a given level of prediction accuracy for the market as a whole will be worth only as much as the same level of prediction accuracy for the specific return of one security.

If you can forecast market returns perfectly, you don't need anything else. But it is equally true that if you can forecast the specific return for a single security perfectly—diversification being pointless—you don't need anything else. The assertion of our title holds true only if you can forecast the market perfectly. If you can't, the assertion is empty.

---

# CHAPTER 68

# Market Efficiency and the Bean Jar Experiment

**M**arket efficiency is a premise, not a conclusion.[1] The finance literature offers no proof of market efficiency; indeed, the only rationale offered in that literature is inconsistent with risk aversion. The rationale asserts that investors aware of a discrepancy between price and value will expand their positions until the discrepancy disappears. The problem is that, as those positions expand, portfolio risk increases faster than portfolio return. Beyond a certain point, further expansion is irrational if the investors in question are risk-averse.

The standard rationale has another problem. It assumes that those investors who know the true value of a security expand their positions when that value exceeds the market price, while those investors with a mistaken estimate of value don't. But the latter also perceive a discrepancy between price and their estimate of value. In effect, the rationale assumes that those investors who are right know they are right, while those investors who are wrong know they are wrong—an unlikely state of affairs.

Where does the accuracy of market prices come from, if not from a few determined investors who know they are right? It comes from the faulty opinions of a large number of investors who err independently. If their errors are wholly independent, the standard error in equilibrium price declines with roughly the square root of the number of investors.

But what assurance do we have that investors' errors are really independent? Are errors *ever* independent across the population of investors? Who is to say whether GM or AT&T is correctly priced or mispriced? Fortunately, the mechanism whereby a large number of error-prone judgments are pooled to achieve a more accurate "consensus" is not confined to finance, or even economics.

## THE BEAN JAR

The mechanism is present even in traditional "bean jar" contests, where observers are asked to guess the number of beans filling a jar. How accurate is the mean of the guesses? How much more accurate than the average guess? Do shared errors creep into the guesses, hence into the mean?

Results of bean jar experiments conducted in the author's investment classes indicate that the mean estimate has been close to the true value. In the first experiment, the jar held 810 beans; the mean estimate was 841, and only two of 46 guesses were closer to the true value. In the second experiment, the jar held 850 beans, and the mean estimate was 871; only one of 56 guesses was closer to the true value.

These results suggest that, in situations where the subjects have not been schooled in a "correct" approach, the bulk of the individual errors will be independent, rather than shared. Apparently it doesn't take knowledge of beans, jars, or packing factors for a group of students to make an accurate estimate of the number of beans in a jar. All it takes is independence.

In a second set of bean jar experiments, the observers were cautioned to allow (after recording their original guesses) for first, air space at the top of the bean jar and, second, the fact that the jar, being plastic rather than glass, had thinner walls than a conventional jar, hence more capacity for the same external dimensions. The means of the guesses after the first and second "warnings" were 952.6 and 979.2, corresponding respectively to errors of 102.6 and 129.2. Although the cautions weren't intended to be misleading, they seem to have caused some shared error to creep into the estimates.

## PUBLISHED RESEARCH AND MARKET PRICES

Shared errors may be as common in appraising companies as in appraising bean jars. There is one class of shared errors that is particularly important to asset prices—the shared errors created by published research. When a piece of investment research is published, some investors will be persuaded by it and some (including those who haven't read it, or abstracts of it) won't. The accuracy of value estimates based on this research will presumably be higher than the average accuracy of the individual estimates it replaces. If other things were equal, this effect would increase the accuracy of the mean estimate, hence the price.

But other things aren't equal. Publication of an estimate may replace many independent estimates with a single estimate. Any error in the published estimate will be reflected in the estimates of all the investors persuaded by it. The impact of any published research will thus depend on both its accuracy and its persuasiveness.

Consider the case of a totally persuasive piece of research, one that reaches and persuades every investor. Any error implicit in this research will be fully reflected in equilibrium price. Suppose the publishing analyst (who is, after all, only human) makes an error equivalent to 10 percent of a security's true value. Suppose, further, that he is five times more accurate than the average investor in his audience. And suppose, finally, that before he published, the investors in his audience had 10,000 independent opinions. If their opinions had roughly equal weights, then the error in the stock's price after publication of the research will be 20 times as large as the error before publication.[2] In general, the more persuasive a published opinion is, the more damage it does to market efficiency.

The number of investors persuaded by a piece of research increases with time elapsed since its publication up to an asymptotic limit that may take several months (or less) to reach. The accuracy of market price first rises following publication of research, then begins to fall. It keeps on falling until persuasion has gone as far as it can go. The calculations presented in Appendix 68.1 suggest that the point of minimum error is likely to be reached before a published opinion has propagated very far.

## TRADING ON INFORMATION

These considerations suggest one approach for investing in published research: Wait until propagation is complete, or almost complete, and then copper it. (Has frequency of reference to the research in brokers' letters and periodicals died down? Has that influential Wall Street analyst known to many of us as Zachary Zilch finally adopted the key arguments in the research?)

In order to profit from fully propagated research, one must of course know the sign of the (net) error in the research; this is tantamount to knowing which way the research moved the price. Unfortunately, many other pieces of information arriving in the interim will also have moved the price, and in combination they may be more important than any error in the research. The induction task facing the investor is substantial.[3]

As Appendix 68.1 explains, the accuracy of a mean estimate depends critically on the degree of shared (i.e., systematic) error present. Absent shared error, the standard error of the mean will be the average individual standard error divided by the square root of the number of individual errors. As that number increases, the standard error of the mean falls. If the number is large enough, the mean error approaches zero. The practical implication is clear: Analyzing dimensions of value on which other investors form their independent opinions is a "futile and unnecessary endeavor."[4]

To put it the other way around, unless the analyst has reason to think shared error is present, the market price will always be his best source of information on value. Specifically, if a company's value is significantly sensitive to 100 attributes and the analyst can identify shared errors in two, his estimating advantage in these two will usually be overwhelmed by his disadvantage in the other 98. If shared errors are rare, or at least hard to identify, then the analyst is better off estimating the incremental impact of the shared errors he can identify, rather than attempting to estimate the overall value of the company.

## CONCLUSION

Stocks, like people, are concrete: They have histories and personalities, unique strengths and weaknesses. We all like to believe we can judge people, and some of us like to believe we can judge stocks. But attributes are abstractions. Many of us are diffident about our ability to evaluate abstractions, deferring instead to experts. For this reason, shared error (i.e., the expert's error) will be far more common in investors' assessment of attributes than in their assessment of stocks. But this means that investment opportunity in attributes will arise more often than investment opportunity in stocks.

Stocks often have common attributes; a shared error present in one such attribute represents an investment opportunity with respect to every stock whose value depends on it. And, if we weight our investment in these stocks appropriately, we can minimize our exposure to their other attributes.

Some students of political science have argued that democracies are more successful electing the right officials than electing the right policies. If so, the reason is not hard to find: Voters defer to experts in their choice of policies, but not in their choice of men. Shared error is consequently less of a problem in the latter than in the former.

## APPENDIX 68.1

### Published Research and Shared Error

In general, published research will have two dimensions—(1) its relative accuracy, or how much it reduces the error of the average investor who is persuaded by it, and (2) its persuasiveness, or what fraction of the investor population abandons their previous view in deference to the published view.

Let the average of the untutored investors' standard valuation errors be $\sigma_1$ and the standard error of the published research be $\sigma_2$. Let the number of investors be n and the number persuaded by the published view at a point in time be m. Then the error variance of the equilibrium price is:

$$\frac{1}{n^2}\left[(n-m)^2\frac{\sigma_1^2}{n-m}+m^2\sigma_2^2\right]$$

assuming the untutored opinions are independent of each other and of the published opinion. (The standard error in the consensus of persuaded investors is of course $\sigma_2$, and the standard error in the consensus of unpersuaded investors is $\sigma_1/\sqrt{n-m}$.)

Differentiating the expression for the error variance of the equilibrium price with respect to m, we have:

$$\frac{1}{n^2}\left(-\sigma_1^2+2\sigma_2^2 m\right)$$

The second derivative is

$$2\left(\frac{\sigma_2}{n}\right)^2 > 0$$

Thus the error in the price reaches its minimum when

$$m=\frac{1}{2}\left(\frac{\sigma_1}{\sigma_2}\right)^2$$

As still more investors are persuaded to the published view, accuracy declines. The obvious thing about this expression is that it doesn't depend on n. This fact permits us to compute the sort of results presented in Exhibit 68.1. As the number of investors persuaded increases up to n, the error variance increases up to $\sigma_2^2$. The lowest the variance ever gets is:

$$\frac{\sigma_1^2}{n}\left[1-\frac{1}{n}\left(\frac{\sigma_1}{\sigma_2}\right)^2\right]$$

**EXHIBIT 68.1** Number of Persuaded Investors at Which Error in Price is Minimal

| Relative Accuracy $(\sigma_1/\sigma_2)$ | Number of Investors |
|---|---|
| 2 | 2 |
| 10 | 50 |
| 100 | 5,000 |

## Measuring Standard Error

Assume the individual investor takes a position, $k_i$, proportional to the discrepancy between a security's price, p, and his perception of its value, $v_i$, so that:

$$k_i = w_i \left( \frac{v_i - p}{\sigma_1^2} \right)$$

where $w_i$ is the investor's factor of proportionality.

Market equilibrium requires that all active positions—all departures from the market portfolio—must sum to zero. We therefore have:

$$\sum_i k_i = \sum_i \frac{w_i}{\sigma_i^2} (v_i - p) = 0$$

$$p = \frac{\sum_i \left( \frac{w_i}{\sigma_i^2} \right) v_i}{\sum_i \frac{w_i}{\sigma_i^2}}$$

Let:

$$W_i = \frac{w_i/\sigma_i^2}{\sum_i w_i/\sigma_i^2}$$

Then we have:

$$p = \sum W_i v_i$$

$$\sum W_i = 1$$

Clearly, price p is a weighted mean of individual investors' opinions.

Now consider the true value of the security, P. The error, $e_p$, in the price is:

$$e_p = p - P$$

$$= \sum W_i v_i - P$$

$$= \sum W_i v_i - \Sigma W_i P$$

If we define the individual investor's error, $e_i$, as follows

$$e_i = v_i - P$$

we have:

$$e_p = \sum W_i e_i$$

If we assume individual investors' errors are mutually independent, then the variance of the error in the price is:

$$\sigma_p^2 = E(e_p^2)$$

$$= E_i\left[\sum_i (W_i e_i)^2\right]$$

$$= \sum_i W_i^2 E(e_i^2)$$

$$= \sum_i W_i^2 \sigma_i^2$$

assuming $E(e_i)$ equals zero for all i.

To simplify, replace the individual investor's error variance $\sigma_i^2$ with a representative variance $\sigma^2$, and his weight $W_i$ with an average weight $W$. Then:

$$\sigma_p^2 = \text{variance}(e_p)$$

$$= E(e_p^2)$$

$$= \sigma^2 \sum W^2$$

if we assume $E(e_i) = 0$, hence $E(e_p) = \Sigma W_i E(e_i) = 0$. But we know that:

$$\sum W = \sum W_i = 1$$

If there are N investors, we have:

$$\sum W = NW = 1$$
$$W = \frac{1}{N}$$

whence,

$$W^2 = \frac{1}{N^2}$$
$$\sum_i W^2 = N\left(\frac{1}{N^2}\right) = \frac{1}{N}$$

We thus have:

$$\text{variance}(e_p) = \sigma^2 \sum W^2 = \frac{\sigma^2}{N}$$

Thus the standard error $\sigma_p$ is:

$$\sigma_p = \sqrt{\text{variance}(e_p)}$$

$$= \sqrt{\frac{\sigma^2}{N}}$$

$$= \frac{\sigma}{\sqrt{N}}$$

## Notes

1. Readers interested in this subject are referred to F. Black, "Noise," *Journal of Finance*, July 1986, pp. 529–543.
2. When individual investors bet against the market price, they are in effect betting that the price reflects a shared error. (Betting against the market assumes we are exempt from an error other investors share.) On the other hand, when academics assert that markets are efficient, they are effectively asserting that shared errors are nonexistent, or at least rare.
3. In fact, it is reminiscent of, but more difficult than, the problem addressed in J. Treynor and R. Ferguson, "In Defense of Technical Analysis," *Journal of Finance*, July 1985, pp. 757–773.
4. J.H. Langbein and R.A. Posner, "The Revolution in Trust Investment Law," *American Bar Association Journal* 62, pp. 764–768. The authors' actual words (regarding the general concept of market efficiency) were: "Trustees who ignore the new learning and who underperform the market will be hard pressed to justify their adherence to an investment strategy of demonstrated riskiness, costliness and futility."

# CHAPTER 69

# Information-Based Investing

**J**ohn Maynard Keynes likened active investing to a newspaper contest in which the object is to select the girl who will be chosen most beautiful by the other contestants.[1] He seemed to be saying that, while value is in the eye of the beholder, true value is in the eye of the consensus.

Was Keynes describing value-based investing?[2] If so, then the consensus, which determines price, is always right.[3] But if the consensus is always right, how can the contestant ever win? Unless one is prepared to believe that Keynes intended his simile to demonstrate the total futility of active investing, one must assume he was talking about information-based, rather than value-based, investing.

Keynes' contestant is apparently privileged to review investment ideas before the consensus reacts; his task is to identify those ideas that will be popular enough to change the consensus. Or perhaps some investors' final reactions will differ from their initial reactions, in which case the information-based investor can succeed by reacting initially the way these investors will react finally. Either way, he must somehow determine how other investors will react before they know themselves.

To win this game, information-based investors must be quick. Or the consensus must be slow. The performance of information-based investors who devote their efforts to trying to be quick would probably improve if they shifted their emphasis to ideas likely to catch on slowly with the consensus.

This is not the impossible task it may at first appear. In the first place, the information-based investor needs to be quicker than the consensus only in the case of ideas he chooses to invest in. In the long run, half the remaining ideas will favor his existing positions and half will hurt him; the resulting price changes will increase the risk in his existing positions—no small consideration—but leave his expected return undiminished. Thus the information-based investor doesn't have to beat the consensus on every idea that comes along.

In the second place, one can dismiss most new ideas fairly readily. One simply has to ask how well the following adjectives fit the idea in question:

- Practical
- Reasonable
- Plausible
- Sensible
- Sound

---

If these adjectives describe the idea, it is certain to be popular with the consensus. Investors will assimilate it quickly, leaving the information-based investor little opportunity to establish his position first. They will assimilate the idea quickly because it fits comfortably into their established way of looking at the world.

Ideas widely and quickly accepted for this reason are called *facts*. Facts are rarely a useful basis for information investing.[4]

Fortunately for the information-based investor, not all new ideas are facts. When investors are confronted with ideas that clash with their existing world view, they tend to reject such ideas out of hand. Such ideas are called *theories*.[5]

The businessman is deeply skeptical about theories. He makes largely irreversible commitments of resources to projects that fail if even one of his key assumptions turns out false. So it is important to him that each such assumption be highly plausible. The businessman has the additional problem of convincing lenders, shareholders *et al.*, that his proposals are sound. Only proposals premised on what those people regard as fact can do that.

Even though the investor is making largely reversible commitments to projects that will succeed if the consensus is wrong about even one thing he is right about, he too is often partial to facts. For one thing, in the court of investor opinion, old theories are less likely to survive the challenge of new ideas than are old facts. When two ideas clash, the more "factual"—the one more easily reconciled with investors' other beliefs—wins. Then, too, if "factual" ideas turn out badly, the investor can scarcely be criticized for thinking what everyone else thought. There is comfort in investing in ideas with a high probability of survival, and comfort in investing in ideas other people like.

But neither popularity nor a high probability of survival contributes to investment performance. The more factual information is, the more likely it is to be fully impounded in price before the investor can trade on it. Thus the riskiest kind of information-based trading is that based on new facts: Given the speed with which facts propagate, betting that facts aren't fully impounded in price when they reach us is a bad bet.

The obvious vehicle for the information-based investor is theory—ideas most investors don't trust. Because most investors don't trust theories, they are impounded in consensus price only when emerging facts subsequently support them. If a theory is "proved" right by the arrival of corroborating facts, the great mass of formerly skeptical investors will finally be persuaded: The price movement accompanying their mass conversion will be substantial.

If the theory proves wrong, any adverse price movement will be small, because few investors liked the theory in the first place. By contrast, when a fact turns out to be wrong, most investors are compelled to change their opinion, and there is a big adverse price move.

**EXHIBIT 69.1**   Fact, Theory, and Subsequent Price Moves

| Idea | Right | Wrong |
|------|-------|-------|
| Fact | No Price Move | Big Adverse Move |
| Theory | Big Price Move | No Adverse Move |

**EXHIBIT 69.2**  Impact of Price Move and Trading Cost on Portfolio Performance

|  | When Idea is | |
|---|---|---|
|  | Right | Wrong |
| *Equilibrium Price* | | |
| Fact | 0 | — |
| Theory | + | 0 |
| *Trading Cost* | | |
| Fact | — | — |
| Theory | — | — |
| *Combined* | | |
| Fact | — | — — |
| Theory | + — | — |

Furthermore, the information-based investor who trades on theories can trade slowly, avoiding the high price of trading quickly. That portion of trading cost represented by spread tends to be much larger when the investor trades in a crowd.[6] When the investor trades on new facts, he is by definition trading on information most investors have received only recently. He is thus likely to find himself paying a lot to trade. When, instead, the investor trades on a new theory, he trades almost alone.

Exhibit 69.1 displays the differences between the potential price moves in facts and theories. Exhibit 69.2 summarizes the combined effect on portfolio performance of equilibrium price moves and trading costs.

By the simple expedient of restricting his bets to ideas the consensus doesn't like—in other words, theories—the information-based trader can maximize his chances for positive investment performance. If he turns out to be wrong, he loses little (apart from certain modest trading costs), because the consensus, hence price, doesn't change. If he turns out to be right, he stands to reap substantial gains.

This is not to say the information-based investor should bet on every new theory. The consensus will be right about most of the ideas it doesn't like, and the investor who bets on them will incur commissions and other modest trading costs unnecessarily. That the consensus doesn't like an idea is a necessary, but not a sufficient, reason for betting on it: The investor must also satisfy himself that he likes the idea.

## CONCLUSION

Most new ideas are facts. It would consequently be surprising if most information-based investing were not based on facts. But trying to beat the consensus to the punch on the basis of new facts is likely to be unproductive or worse (unless the facts in question are inside information). Unless an information-based institution distinguishes between fact and theory, its investment performance is going to be unimpressive.

Our minds don't work reliably at the rarified altitudes inhabited by theory. So when we think about theory, it's easy to be wrong. But it costs little to be wrong unless other investors agree with us. Thus the cost of being wrong about theories is small, while the rewards of being right are large. So far as this writer can see, there is nothing in the nature of market efficiency that guarantees the failure of information-based investing.

## Notes

1. J. M. Keynes, *The General Theory of Employment, Interest, and Money* (New York: Harcourt, Brace & World, 1964), p. 156.
2. W. Crerend and E. Broome ("A Taxonomy of Money Management," *Financial Analysts Journal*, May–June 1974) pointed out that stock selection is performed by two radically different kinds of organizations—"bottom up" and "top down." Subsequently, I argued (in "What Does It Take to Win the Trading Game?" *Financial Analysts Journal*, January–February 1981) that bottom-up organizations base their selection decisions on new information, whereas top-down organizations base their decisions on comparisons of price and value. I also argued that the radical difference in organizations is justified by the intrinsic differences in the decision process between the two kinds of firms.
3. This is not my view of value investing. See "Market Efficiency and the Bean Jar Experiment," *Financial Analysts Journal*, May–June 1987.
4. For a statistical test based on recent price history that estimates whether a new fact is already in price, see Treynor and R. Ferguson, "In Defense of Technical Analysis," *Journal of Finance*, July 1985.
5. The distinction between fact and theory is obviously relative, rather than absolute. How people judge new ideas depends on their existing belief system, rather than any notion of absolute truth. In 1491, the idea that the earth was flat was a fact. The idea of a round earth was a theory. In Western culture, at least, the idea that the earth is round is now a fact. But the reality hasn't changed.
6. See Treynor, "The Economics of the Dealer Function," *Financial Analysts Journal*, November–December 1987.

# CHAPTER 70

# The 10 Most Important Questions to Ask in Selecting a Money Manager

Sooner or later, successful businessmen find themselves sitting on boards of endowed institutions—private universities and colleges, hospitals, and charitable foundations. Many of these boards have finance committees or investment committees that either get directly involved in the money manager selection process or hire and supervise those members of the institution's staff who do.

The 10 questions discussed below are among the questions most frequently asked in the selection process. As such, they constitute a checklist for the busy board member anxious to ensure that the right questions are asked, even if the actual asking is delegated to someone else.

1. *Does the money manager present his ideas smoothly and without hesitation?*

   The answer to this question tells you something about the quality of the money manager's ideas—specifically, whether they are old or new. A nonstop presentation, a steadfast gaze, an absence of pauses or glitches are important clues. If a money manager has made the same presentation dozens or even hundreds of times before, his ideas are old and probably already incorporated in security prices. Trading on such ideas cannot help your portfolio's performance, but can easily hurt it.

2. *Is the money manager clear and confident about his ideas?*

   It's one thing to have a clear vision of the investment future; it's another to be right. One of the saddest truths about human nature is man's inability to think about more than one idea at a time. The more clearly we see an old idea, the harder it is to give fair consideration to a conflicting new one. Can your money manager change and grow? Can he learn? The clarity of his vision is an important clue.

3. *Do his ideas have common-sense appeal?*

   Common-sense appeal means appeal to a broad audience. Security prices move when the great mass of investors react. The problem with common-sense ideas is that the great mass of investors has already reacted to them.

4. *Are you comfortable with the money manager's answers?*

   There are two polar answers to every question—an answer that leads to further questions and further answers, and an answer that maximizes comfort. The former answer leads to deeper understanding precisely because it is uncomfortable. The comfortable answer closes off further inquiry. Does your money manager have a restless, questing mind? Asking yourself this question is a simple way to find out.

5. *Does the money manager exhibit detailed knowledge of a broad range of companies and industries?*

Money managers aren't superhuman. They have limited time to absorb new ideas and limited time to think. Fortunately, facts are the easiest thing for most investors to understand and absorb, hence are far more likley to be correctly reflected in securities prices than are abstract ideas. Does the walking encyclopedia have time to think about the kind of insight that could still help your portfolio? If you are not sure about the answer, then this is an important question for you.

6. *Does the money manager react decisively to new developments?*

The investment significance of newsworthy developments is in the price of a security before one can trade—particularly in institutional size. One of the most valuable things a money manager can do—and help his clients do—is stand fast rather than yield to strong feelings of greed or fear elicited by current events.

7. *Does the money manager have a large asset base?*

Because no one has ever successfully established correlation between past performance and future performance, clients tend to select money managers on the basis of their ideas. A large asset base means that the money manager is investing on the basis of ideas with broad popular appeal. The problem with such ideas has already been noted.

8. *Does the money manager live baronially—with expensive clubs; houses and cars; and travel by the QE II, the Concorde, or the Orient Express?*

How well a money manager manages his own money is an important test of how well he will manage your money. How he lives is the tip-off: If he is able to achieve a high rate of return on his own portfolio, small sacrifices now mean big rewards later. If he is living sumptuously now, it is entirely possible, if not likely, that the return on his own portfolio is low.

9. *Are his offices impressive?*

Although there are important exceptions, most money managers rent, rather than own, their offices. Thus an office suitable for an oil sheik implies a big rent, hence a big fixed cost for the money manager. If the money manager has the assets, hence the management fees, to support such an office, no problem. But if he is just starting out, that fixed cost puts the manager under pressure to attract the requisite assets quickly; marketing becomes a high priority. Is a money manager highly motivated? A visit to his office is a good way to find out.

10. *Is the money manager impressively capitalized?*

A depositor looks to a bank's assets to determine the safety of his deposit (if it isn't entirely insured). But the assets of a money manager are not the assets of the client.

The money management business is not capital-intensive. A money manager doesn't need much capital to do his job well. But it does cost a lot to fund the kind of marketing program that can produce a rapid asset build-up. Unless a money manager is more interested in building his asset base than in building his performance record, he doesn't need a silent partner.

As the Bible says, "No man can serve two masters." Where did the money manager's capital come from? In particular, did it come from someone in an adversarial relation to the money manager's clients? Charley Ellis has pointed out that investing is a loser's game for money managers. With so many losing inadvertently, a manager who loses on purpose is going to be hard to spot.

The author is a money manager. If the reader suspects the author of having modest capital and assets under management, few clients and simple offices, the reader is correct. The author also concedes that his presentations lack professional polish, his investment convictions occasionally waver, and his ideas have limited appeal; maybe he should have called this piece, "Sour Grapes."

# Pensions

**E**ven the claimants on a fully-funded, fixed-benefit pension plan can be in jeopardy if the assets in the pension portfolio are risky. If the risky investments succeed, the claimants won't be better off. But if the risky investments fail, the pension claimants will be worse off. They share in any losses, but the pension sponsor gets all the gains.

Are pension sponsors playing a heads-I-win, tails-you-lose game with their pension claimants? Have claimants unwillingly granted a valuable option to their pension sponsor—a *pension put* that grows more valuable when the risk of the pension assets increases?

Because the pension sponsor shares in the losses, his equity will suffer. But if other companies' pension plans own his stock, they too will suffer. Will his pension plan suffer because it owns their stock? Etc., etc. If the pension portfolios of such corporations own each other's stock is there a *pension multiplier*?

J.L.T.

# CHAPTER 71

# Risk and Reward in Corporate Pension Funds

T he two key questions in pension planning are, "How much should the corporation contribute?" and "How much risk should the pension portfolio take?" The answer to the first is closely related to the second. One of the participants in the CFA pension study asked the following question:

If the company says, "We are much more concerned with safety than ... with reducing costs" would you invest ... precisely the way you would where the company says, "... our objective is to reduce ... [expense] to the absolute minimum?"[1]

The failure of the participants to answer "Yes" to this question suggests that reducing the level of corporate contributions is an important consideration in setting risk policy for many corporate pension plans. Indeed, corporations have become performance-conscious in their drive to reduce pension costs. The result, in many cases, has been a heavier investment in stocks and a shift, within stocks, from "blue chips" to "high fliers." The rising level of risk in corporate pensions increases the possibility of losses.

In some cases, losses have prevented workers from getting their pension benefits. In such cases it is clear that the workers were taking some risk. As another participant in the CFA study says,

> All actuarial work is based on the assumption that the employer will con-
> tinue to exist.... If the whole operation doesn't last long enough for ...
> young employees to go all the way through to retirement then the plan is
> not going to be actuarially sound at all.... The agonizing truth [will] emerge
> progressively.[2]

It is at least possible that part of the risk in such cases is being borne by the corporation (i.e., by its shareholders) and that part of the benefit will go to pensioners.

The author is deeply indebted to William Dreher, of the actuarial firm William Dreher and Associates, Robert Ferguson, of Baker, Weeks, and Glenelg Caterer, formerly Director of Research for Lionel D. Edie and Co., for their comments. In particular, most of the important points in the footnotes were raised by William Dreher.

But it is certain that the pensioners are bearing some of the risk, while the corporation is getting some of the benefits.

Consider a bank which invests depositors' funds in risky assets. Unless the bank's capital is large enough to serve as an adequate buffer, the depositors will bear part of the risk. Because the investment decisions are delegated to the banker, however, depositors may never know how much risk they were taking unless the decisions turn out badly. And because they won't know how much risk they were taking if the decisions turn out well, they are unlikely in the latter event to get their share of the reward.

These banking practices have led in the past to impoverished and deeply unhappy depositors (and to some very rich bankers). Unfortunately, there is a close analogy between these discredited banking practices and certain corporate pension practices: If a corporation invests the pension fund in risky investments and they succeed, the corporation will profit; if the investments fail, substantial losses may be borne by the pension beneficiaries.

Over the years the financial community has gradually evolved institutions and laws for avoiding the kind of inequity that can arise when one group of people is in a position to take risks with money belonging to another group. Running through these laws and institutions is a common thread—a clear separation between the respective roles of the equity holder on one hand, with his large risks and hope of large gain, and the lender on the other hand, who is shielded from the primary investment risk in the enterprise.

The separation is enforced by giving the latter the legal power to protect himself when a decline in the value of the underlying asset threatens the value of his claim (e.g., a Chapter X bankruptcy proceeding against a corporation, or a declaration of insolvency by a bank examiner, who in effect represents the depositors). Any deliberate action on the part of the intermediary that conceals from a claimant the degree of risk in his claim is regarded as fraudulent, hence a crime against society, as well as grounds for a recovery action by the claimant.

This principle is being ignored in corporate pension practice today. In most cases, there is no clear division between those who bear investment risk and those who don't. Ultimately many pension beneficiaries are going to wake up to find that investment losses have deprived them of their main source of support in retirement. The result will be thousands—possibly millions—of tragedies at the level of the individual family and a general breakdown of society's confidence in the modern corporation's ability to meet its obligations with integrity. The door has been left wide open to an abuse that nearly wrecked our banking system in the nineteenth century, and can easily wreck our corporate pension system in the twentieth.

Broadly speaking, there are three ways to eliminate the abuse:

1. Restrict corporate pension portfolios to riskless assets. In this case, it is clear that what the corporation puts in determines what the beneficiaries get out. The beneficiaries are vulnerable to inflation in excess of expectations obtaining at the time the level of contributions was negotiated.
2. Make the workers the owners of the pension portfolio. Then they get the gains as well as the losses. The level of portfolio risk is up to them, or to a portfolio manager hired by, and responsible to, them.[3] The corporation's responsibility ends

with its contributions, which (in this case, as in the first) are the true measure of the cost of the pension program to the corporation.

3. Permit the corporations to invest pension funds in risky assets, but make certain that the corporation bears the risk, essentially by making the pension beneficiaries creditors of the corporation.[4] The corporation owns the pension fund, and uses it to help meet pension obligations as they fall due. Corporate contributions to the fund merely represent a shifting of corporate assets from one form to another and, as such, bear only an incidental relation to the true current costs to the corporation of its pension program.

Current corporate pension practice rarely fits the first of these three proposals because corporate pension assets are commonly invested at least in part in risky securities. It certainly doesn't fit the second when labor contracts specify the level of ultimate pension obligations rather than corporate contributions, with the corporations pursuing investment policies designed to minimize the contributions.

But current practice does not fit the third proposal either because in many (probably most) cases pension claims are not contractually enforceable. As previously noted, whether a pension beneficiary obtains the benefits specified in his labor contract depends largely on the vicissitudes of the pension portfolio. If a high risk policy taken in hopes of reducing pension contributions fails and leads to portfolio losses, the hapless pension beneficiary may be the loser.

The third proposal is clearly closest to current corporate pension practice. But of the three it is also the one that invites abuse.

If pension assets are risky, are the beneficiaries automatically in jeopardy? Not necessarily. Again we appeal to the analogy between pension beneficiaries and bank depositors. Loan defaults occur, and the rate of default is sensitive to economic and market conditions generally, so that even a highly diversified loan portfolio is risky.

Yet in a properly run bank, depositor's claims can truly be said to be virtually riskless—even in the absence of a Federal Deposit Insurance Corporation. The reason is, of course, that a well-run bank maintains equity capital sufficiently large in relation to its deposits to absorb any losses incurred in the loan portfolio.

In similar fashion, the corporation can encourage risk taking in its pension portfolio without jeopardizing the beneficiaries as long as:

1. Pension beneficiaries are considered to have a claim on the general credit of the corporation in the event that assets in the pension portfolio prove inadequate;
2. The going-concern value of the corporation is adequate to meet the contingent claims.

Whether the second condition is satisfied is most easily determined in terms of what we may call the *augmented corporate balance sheet* (see Exhibit 71.1). On the left-hand side we have the assets of the corporation—measured, however, at market rather than book value and augmented by the current market value of the pension portfolio.[5] On the right-hand side of the balance sheet we have the usual claims of corporate creditors, but augmented by the present value of the pension obligations as computed below. In the augmented balance sheet the residual equity available to corporate shareholders is the margin of protection for the pension beneficiaries. (The

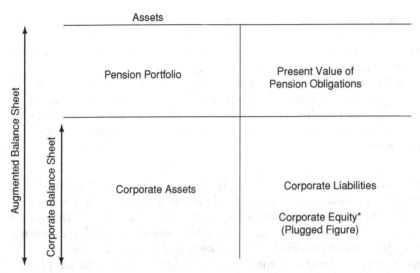

Assets

Pension Portfolio | Present Value of Pension Obligations

Corporate Assets | Corporate Liabilities

Corporate Equity* (Plugged Figure)

Augmented Balance Sheet

Corporate Balance Sheet

* Because equity is a residual, it will generally be different for the augmented and original corporate balance sheets.

**EXHIBIT 71.1**   Augmented Balance Sheet
(All Assets Current Market Value)

introduction of the pension assets on the left side and the present value of pension claims on the right will generally change the residual equity.)

The key to interpreting the augmented balance sheet is the present value of the pension claims.[6] The rate at which future obligations are discounted back to the present is critical. The appropriate discount rate is the riskless interest rate; if one considers that the corporation has no obligation to protect pension beneficiaries against inflation, then the appropriate discount rate is the rate on government obligations of comparable maturity. If, on the other hand, one considers that the current statement of future pension obligations is really a statement expressed in current dollars of future obligations, the real value of which is understood to be fixed, then the appropriate discount rate is the riskless interest rate with inflationary expectations removed—a rate commonly estimated at roughly 3 percent.[7]

The present value that results from discounting at the appropriate rate is an estimate of the market value of the assets on which the beneficiaries must have a claim if they are not to be subjected to investment risk: If the assets available exceed the present value of future pension claims only when the latter are discounted at a higher rate, the expected proceeds from the assets will fail to meet the claims unless the assets are invested aggressively, with the attendant possibility of loss.[8]

Pension beneficiaries can assure the maintenance of an adequate margin only if they have the power to force a corporate reorganization whenever the margin is threatened. Unlike conventional corporate creditors, pension beneficiaries are not in a position to force the corporation to go along with reorganization by suspending their willingness to lend; since the conventional creditor is better able to act, it may be desirable to put him in a position where in order to protect himself he must also protect the pension beneficiary.[9] If pension beneficiaries' claims were treated as prior to the claims of other corporate creditors then, of course, the other creditors would quickly begin to think about the soundness of their loans in terms of the augmented, rather than the conventional, balance sheet.

If all corporations with risky pension assets adopted these two proposals, there would be several important consequences:

1. In reckoning the residual value of a corporation's common shares, the security analysts would be well advised to include both for the present value of corporate pension obligations reckoned as described above and the value of the pension portfolio.

2. In the perspective of the augmented balance sheet as noted above, the corporate "contribution" to the pension fund merely exchanges one asset for another, leaving the true corporate equity unchanged. It does not widen the pension beneficiary's margin of protection, nor is it in any true economic sense a cost to the corporation. The true pension cost incurred in an accounting period is the present value (reckoned as above) of the additional pension obligations incurred in the period.[10] The only practical effect of the corporate contribution is to enlarge that portion of the assets in the augmented balance sheet which by their nature can be invested in riskless assets or, if invested in risky assets, diversified. Only to the extent that the fund manager exploits these possibilities will the pension beneficiary in a plan that is "fully funded" in this special sense be more secure as a result of the contribution.[11]

In terms of the point of view presented in this paper, what are the implications for ethical corporate policy? The main one is that the corporation that invests pension funds in risky assets, on one hand, while refusing to give beneficiaries the status of corporate creditors on the other, is serving notice that it refuses to protect its beneficiaries against the kind of abuse described at the beginning of this article.[12] In particular, any corporation that is insolvent in the sense of the augmented corporate balance sheet is imposing risks on the beneficiaries for which they are unlikely to get fully rewarded.

In technical terms, the right to skim off any value in the pension fund in excess of pension claims if the fund prospers, while burdening beneficiaries with the losses if the fund fails to meet the claims, constitutes a call. In the case of corporate pension funds the call is conferred on the corporate shareholders by the pension beneficiaries, often without the latters' assent or knowledge. The value of any call depends on the riskiness of the assets subject to call, increasing as the risk increases. The effect of increasing the riskiness of the pension assets is to increase the value of the call against the pension beneficiaries, thereby reducing the true value of their claims and increasing the value of the corporate shares.

When a corporation refuses to give pension beneficiaries creditor status (option 3), such a transfer takes place every time the general level of investment of risk in the pension portfolio is increased.

If the corporation finds option 3 unacceptable, but nevertheless intends to compensate the beneficiaries fully for the risks they take, it can simply turn the contributions over to an elected representative of the beneficiaries (option 2). Or it can retain control of the assets but limit pension investments to high-grade bonds (option 1).

## Notes

1. *Pension Fund Investment Management*, CFA Research Foundation, Richard D. Irwin, Inc., Homewood, Illinois, 1969.
2. *Op. cit.*
3. As a practical matter it is highly inefficient and probably dangerous to parcel out pension assets among the individual workers. A device that effectively achieves the objective of option 2 is the "money purchase" plan. A reader comments:

    "'Money purchase' plans restrict company contributions to a fixed amount; benefits are generally decided by a joint committee of management and union officials based on the value of the funds and the estimates of the actuary.... Since the company has no further interest in the dollars except the satisfaction and happiness of its employees, company trustees are generally quite fair in setting investment policies and return goals, and the pension fund no longer becomes a 'profit center' to the company. Here the problem is the union representatives who want to pay excessive amounts to retired union members in order to preserve their power and prestige in the union (e.g., John L. Lewis and the coal workers)—a different kind of conflict of interest."
4. The author has been advised that the duPont Corporation actually gives pension beneficiaries creditor status.
5. If pension beneficiaries and security analysts are to be able to make this reckoning, it is of course necessary that the market value of the pension portfolio be published at frequent intervals.
6. In making this reckoning it is, of course, necessary to take into account all the complications normally considered by the pension actuary, such as the age distribution of the work force, the extent of vesting, the probability of early retirement, and the probability of premature termination of the plan. The possibility of premature termination (as in liquidation of the corporation) complicates this determination. The Internal Revenue Service requires that a pension plan confer full vesting on its employees in the event of premature termination in order to be eligible for the usual tax treatment of pension contribution. Taken by itself, full vesting would of course increase the present value of the pension obligations. On the other hand, accrued service plans are worth less to the individual beneficiary in premature termination than in an ongoing plan. This effect, taken by itself, obviously tends to make the value of the plan in premature termination less than the value of an ongoing plan; whichever effect turns out to be more important will depend on the specifics of the individual pension plan.
7. Some pension actuaries feel very strongly that the discount rate should not be the riskless rate with inflationary expectations removed (3 percent) unless the terms of the pension contract specifically provide for cost of living adjustments.
8. In *real* terms, of course, there is no truly riskless investment since actual inflation rates often turn out to be different rates from the rates anticipated in yields on fixed-income securities at the time of purchase. There is, furthermore, uncertainty even in *nominal* terms regarding the rates of return at which any coupon income can be reinvested.
9. It has been pointed out to the author that class action suits by pension beneficiaries (construed as creditors) could hamstring the corporation's power to conduct its normal business affairs. It should be possible to give them the necessary priority as creditors without giving them power to interfere in the normal affairs of the corporation. One way to do this, of course, is to make them senior to all other creditors while giving them no legal power whatever. Then they are protected by the legal powers available to the other creditors.
10. The actuary normally reckons as part of cost in the current period any departure of actual events from the averages on which the plan was based.

11. Needless to say, diversification will not eliminate the risk in a portfolio containing risky assets but it will reduce the impact of that portion of the risk specific to the assets.
12. One reader comments on the ethics of the problem as follows:

> *You have not raised sufficient hell with the trustee who accepts either direction on investments from the company or accepts the pressures of the company to perform with the risk going to the beneficiaries. Legally, the trustee is trustee for the beneficiaries and not for the company or the 'fund'.*

# CHAPTER 72

# An Investor's Guide to the Index Fund Controversy

*An index fund that holds all available common stocks in proportion to their outstanding market values would provide the best possible tradeoff between expected return and risk for the investor who has no research advantage. A number of practical problems arise, however, when one attempts to translate this ideal into practice. The S&P 500, for example, is dominated by stocks of large American companies with a number of characteristics—industry representation, competitive position, financial strength, and exposure to government regulation—that make them unrepresentative of U.S. common stocks in general. Differences are even more marked when one compares the S&P companies with foreign ones.*

*Whether an index fund can actually economize on transaction costs depends on its size, the frequency of additions and withdrawals, and the techniques used by the manager to minimize these costs. If a very large index fund purchases 500 separate issues with the proceeds of each day's dividends, it will raise its transaction costs excessively. Yet any attempt to economize by making purchases less frequently, accumulating dividends in the interim, will move the client away from his desired objective. Holding substantially fewer than 500 stocks, on the other hand, will add to risk without adding to return.*

*Even in the absence of special investment insights, a managed portfolio can compete effectively with index funds in coping with these problems. But if such insights are available, the managed portfolio can take advantage of the opportunities they present.*

An investor seeking expert opinion on index funds might well be confused by what he hears. One conclusion, usually expressed with considerable feeling, is that

Copyright © CFA Institute. Reprinted from the *Financial Analysts Journal* with permission. November–December 1976.

Coauthored with Walter R. Good and Robert Ferguson.

The author of this article is Walter R. Good, Chairman of the Investment Policy Committee, Executive Vice-President and Director of Lionel D. Edie and Company. Appendix 72.1 was written by Robert Ferguson of Merrill Lynch, Pierce, Fenner & Smith, who advises institutional clients on the advantage of index funds and how to beat them, and Jack Treynor, who edits this magazine.

index funds are a "cop-out" and a fad that will soon disappear. Apparently only a very small minority hold the opposite point of view. They consider index funds the wave of the future, offering the best possible approach to investment. A third group is pragmatic, willing to keep an open mind on index funds as long as the record of the S&P 500 compares favorably with the experience of most other equity portfolios, as appears to have been the case over the last few years.

## OUR APPROACH

In view of the range of conflicting opinions already available, our effort seems best directed toward filling in the background needed to place index funds in perspective. The approach we have selected concentrates on three issues: (1) the index fund concept, or what index funds are intended to be; (2) how close the practical versions of index funds come to the theoretical model; and (3) what the managed portfolio can offer relative to index funds.

Our comparison of the managed portfolio with the index fund leaves the reader free to make his own assumptions concerning the contribution of management skill to investment performance. The word "skill," as used in this article, refers specifically to the ability to increase the value of an investment portfolio through judgments concerning whether market prices are too high or too low. Exercise of skill—in this sense—is distinguished from other activities (which may require skills of a different type) designed to adapt an investment portfolio to the risk objectives and other circumstances of the investor. Although we hold that management skill can add significantly to the value of an investment portfolio, specific consideration of this issue is confined to Appendix 72.1.

Because the subject involves both theory and its practical implications, our comments cannot completely avoid ranging between two extremes. On the one hand, a few basic points are made to assure common agreement on terminology. Such explanations, while necessary, will be brief. On the other hand, a part of the discussion requires consideration of statistical technique. The quantitative approach is limited to Appendix 72.1.

## INDEX FUND CONCEPT

The perfect index fund—if it were attainable—would, in theory, provide the best possible tradeoff between expected return and risk. In this sense, "risk" has a technical meaning broader than its meaning in common usage. Many investors think of risk as the chance of loss. In the technical sense, risk is the chance of securing a return either higher or lower than expected. (It is reflected in the variability of returns around the mean.) In effect, the holder of the perfect index fund would expect the same return expected by the total of all other investors, but his uncertainty concerning the expected return would be reduced to the lowest possible level. If it is assumed that the investor will always prefer the highest ratio of expected return to risk—an assumption considered applicable to most investors—the index fund would in theory be able to achieve this goal better than any other portfolio. By combining the index fund with "risk-free" Treasury bills or levering it through buying on margin, the investor could in theory secure the best portfolio for any return-risk objective.

To attain the theoretical ideal, the perfect equity index fund would hold all available common stocks in proportion to their market values outstanding. If a company issued additional stock or retired outstanding stock, the portfolio would be adjusted accordingly. Cash dividend payments would be reinvested as received. There would be no need, however, to adjust the portfolio for changes in market prices. The market value of holdings would automatically reflect the effect of price changes on the total market values outstanding.

Index fund theory is based on three assumptions which must be tested for relevance to the real world. First, the investor must believe that skill in evaluating stock prices will not contribute to investment success or, at least, that he does not have access to such skill. If he has the ability to identify one or more securities as overvalued or undervalued, the index fund is not the best portfolio. Second, there must be no penalties that discriminate among investors, causing a particular issue to be more attractive to one holder than to another. Consider, for example, two common stocks—one with a high dividend yield and the other with no dividend yield whatever—and two investors—one in a low tax bracket and the other in a high one. If the stocks are priced to be equally attractive to the high-bracket investor, they can scarcely be equally attractive to the one in the low bracket. Another example concerns differences in the scale of the portfolio: Transaction costs for the small portfolio, in percentage terms, should be the same as those for the large portfolio. The third assumption is applicable only to the investor who seeks through leverage a higher return than that offered by the index fund. There should be no difference between the risk-free interest rate provided by short-term Treasury bills and the interest rate on margin loans. Whether failure to meet any of the three assumptions would undermine the case for the index fund depends on the extent of the discrepancy between the actual situation and the theoretical model.

## PRACTICAL VERSIONS OF INDEX FUNDS

A practical version of an index fund can, of necessity, be only an approximation of the index fund concept, but it should come close to matching the stock market as a whole. As a crude test of how well this standard is met, the index fund should seldom seem to be providing a return much better or worse than the average for all investors. Investors sometimes indicate that they would be happy just to achieve the performance of the Standard & Poor's 500 or the Dow Jones Industrial Average—but they almost always make this point after the designated index seems to have provided for an extended period significantly better returns than those achieved by most investors. If recent superiority of the S&P's performance provides the main argument for its use as the basis for an index fund, then the adequacy of the S&P 500 as a means of implementing the index fund concept is questionable.

Among the currently available indexes that might serve as the basis for an index fund, the S&P 500 is usually preferred. It represents a practical tradeoff between the proportion of total market value reflected in the index and the number of issues that need to be included in the fund. The New York Stock Exchange Index, for example, is more comprehensive, but the advantage associated with more complete market representation is offset by the large increase in the number of issues the portfolio must hold. The DJIA would be much simpler to use, because it contains only

30 issues. A portfolio of stocks accurately matched to the DJIA, however, would violate the index fund concept, since the issues are not represented in proportion to their market values. The total market value of the 30 issues, meanwhile, is much less than that of the S&P 500.

While the precise percentage would vary with the situation of the investor, the S&P 500 accounts for the bulk of the market value of all common stocks that might be considered currently available to most American investors. It represents about 80 percent of the market value of the stocks listed on the NYSE. Although the market value of the additional stocks traded in both domestic and foreign markets approaches the total for those listed on the NYSE, not all of these stocks are practical alternatives for an investor, especially a fiduciary institution. A certain portion of foreign issues is precluded from consideration because of discriminatory taxes or other restrictions. A certain number of other issues, both domestic and foreign, are characterized by unacceptably thin trading markets.

Although selection of the S&P 500 as a proxy for the entire stock market is based on its large market value, it may still be subject to important shortcomings: (1) low covariance of market segments not included in the S&P 500 with the S&P 500 itself; (2) reduction in the ratio of expected return to risk resulting from special problems that affect different index funds differently; and (3) differences in nondiversifiable risk between the S&P 500 and the population of stocks outside the S&P 500. (The first two items concern primarily risks that can be eliminated through diversification, i.e., diversifiable risks; item three relates to risks unaffected by diversification, i.e., nondiversifiable risks.)

## Covariance

Despite its large market value, the usefulness of the S&P 500 as a proxy for all common stocks is limited by the problem of covariance. Covariance defines the degree to which stocks or groups of stocks tend to move together. A brief illustration indicates the importance of this problem to the construction of an index fund. Suppose Stock A offers exactly the same expected return that the S&P 500 offers and demonstrates a strong tendency to move in line with it. On the other hand, Stock B, also with the same expected return, is little influenced by movements of the S&P 500. According to the terms of the example, neither the addition of Stock A nor Stock B would change the expected return of the index fund portfolio. The addition of Stock B, however, would contribute more to reduction of risk, since, at any time, Stock B is more likely than Stock A to be moving differently to the S&P 500. In terms of index fund theory, omission of Stock B is more troublesome than omission of Stock A.

Even if the S&P 500 encompasses more than half the market value of stocks practically available, concentration of the index in a particular segment of the stock market suggests a covariance problem. The S&P 500 is dominated by stocks of large American companies having a number of characteristics in common. The industry pattern for the S&P 500, for example, is different from that of the aggregate of smaller domestic issues not included in the S&P 500, and there are also differences in competitive position, financial strength, and exposure to government regulation. Differences are even more marked when comparison is made with foreign issues because of variations in economic cycles from country to country, fluctuations in exchange rates, and independent changes in political environment. As a result, an index fund confined to the S&P 500 is characterized by a rate of risk relative to expected return higher than that of other carefully planned portfolios devised with fewer issues.

According to the index fund concept, the conventional index fund could be improved by diverting a portion of the funds from S&P 500 issues to other issues, both domestic and foreign. While this conclusion is acknowledged by current limited efforts to expand the application of the index fund concept beyond the S&P 500, its practical application runs into a dilemma. On the one hand, reduction of the number of issues represented in the S&P 500 to, say, 300, in order to add an additional 200 outside the S&P 500, would complicate communications with clients and prospective clients. The index fund would no longer track the S&P 500, and the selection of both the sample of the S&P 500 and the sample of other stocks would require the application of additional technical expertise to the management of the portfolio. On the other hand, supplementing the 500 stocks included in the S&P 500 with an additional 300 to 500 issues outside the index would increase the expenses of operating the fund to levels unacceptable to all but the largest pools of money. Moreover, it would not avoid the problem of diversifying without the aid of a ready-made index a large portion of the fund.

## Special Factors

In practice, the ratio of expected return to risk for the index fund may be reduced by several special factors that affect different index funds differently. These include limitation of the number of issues in the index fund because of the limited size of the fund, mandatory elimination of weak issues, and differences in transaction costs.

For all but very large index funds, a representative sample of issues must be used in order to control transaction costs. The limitation on the number of issues will moderately increase the risk that returns will vary from the S&P 500. The extent of any additional risk depends on the number of issues used and the quality of the sampling. Other things equal, a larger number of issues results in better representation of the index. In any event, use of a sample moves the index fund further from its intended role (under the assumptions of index fund theory) of maximizing expected return relative to risk.

Mandatory elimination of weak issues can further interfere with the effectiveness of the index fund in meeting the theoretical objective. At least for pension funds, legal considerations may be interpreted to require elimination of issues in jeopardy of financial failure. Elimination of such issues may reduce risk for the index fund but—where the covariance with the S&P 500 is low—it may not. In either case, the return expected under the assumptions of index fund theory will be decreased by elimination of volatile, risky issues. Because it reduces expected return without a fully compensating reduction in risk, elimination of weak issues degrades the ratio of expected return to risk. When the covariance of such issues with the S&P 500 is low, the effect may be stronger than the relative market value of the issues might infer.

The index fund approach can offer low transaction costs but, in practice, it may not. Much depends on the size of the index fund, the frequency of additions and withdrawals, and the techniques used by the manager to minimize transaction costs. Initial distribution of fund assets among 500 issues—or even a sample of 200 issues—would be more expensive than for a more typical managed portfolio of

20 to 60 issues. Subsequent transaction costs may be relatively low or relatively high for the index fund, depending on the size of the fund and frequency of additions and withdrawals. Substitutions in the S&P 500—or major revisions, which recently occurred—represent unexpected charges. Dividend reinvestment results in a small but recurring problem, since purchase of 500 issues with the proceeds of each day's dividends would raise transaction costs excessively. Any attempt to economize on transaction costs by accumulating dividends and involving even short delays introduces a systematic bias that moves the client away from his desired return objective.

## Adjusting Return-Risk Objectives

Practical versions of index funds, unlike the perfect index fund in theory, are not well situated to accommodate investors who aim at a higher return objective. The expected return and risk levels of the index fund are tied, in an approximate way, to those of the S&P 500. Risk, along with expected return, can be lowered relative to the S&P 500 by shifting a portion of the fund assets to short-term Treasury bills, which are regarded as risk-free. According to index fund theory, such action does not represent slippage in the ratio of expected return to risk, since both are reduced in the same proportion.

It is less practical to raise expected return through leverage without lowering the ratio of expected return to risk. For most institutions, buying on margin is inappropriate. In addition to legal prohibitions against the practice in many cases, there may also be firmly established policies that cannot be easily changed. Even where there are no restrictions, use of margin would involve interest-rate premiums not contemplated in theory. To the extent the margin rate is above the risk-free rate, expected return is reduced without compensating reduction in risk. For clients who desire an expected return higher than that of the S&P 500, the levered index fund represents a further step away from the theoretical objective.

Since the practical problems posed by the levered index fund are formidable, the investor who seeks a higher level of return than what the S&P 500 affords may consider combining the index fund with a much more aggressive common stock fund. While this approach may avoid the obvious problems associated with levering the index fund, it is likely to be a haphazard solution. Evaluation of the overall investment program in terms of index fund theory depends on the ratio of expected return to risk for the combined portfolios. Unless careful attention is directed to the covariance of the combined portfolios, the overall ratio of expected return to risk can hardly be the best available. In terms of index fund theory, the combination would probably be less efficient than a single portfolio not limited to issues in the S&P 500.

## MANAGED PORTFOLIOS

In order to meet the challenge of the index fund, the managed portfolio must show how it can provide a better ratio of expected return to risk. The case for the managed portfolio is strengthened to the extent the practical version of the index fund falls short of its theoretical objective. As indicated in the preceding sections, the problems are readily identifiable even if often overlooked; (1) Risk is higher than it need be relative to expected return because the S&P 500 excludes issues characterized by low covariance with the S&P 500 itself. (2) The covariance problem is further increased to the extent that weak issues in the S&P 500 must be eliminated. (3) Use of substantially fewer than 500 stocks, because of the size of the fund, also adds to risk. The degree of additional risk depends on the number of issues and the adequacy of the sampling technique. (4) The expected return of the index fund is limited by below-average emphasis on more dynamic issues through exclusion of those not in the S&P 500 and, in certain cases, mandatory elimination of certain volatile issues in the S&P 500. (5) Efforts to increase expected return by combining an aggressive portfolio with an index fund may result in more risk than necessary unless the characteristics of the total investment program are carefully planned. (6) Transaction costs—depending on the size of the fund, frequency of withdrawals and additions, and the skill of the manager—may in some cases be as large as or larger than those of a managed portfolio.

## Managing the Return-Risk Ratio

The point of departure for the investment manager is to make sure risks are under control. Without the special skill that would be exercised in evaluating stock prices and before allowance for special client circumstances, expected return relative to risk would be maximized by a portfolio that best represented the available issues in the entire stock market—not just the S&P 500. Consequently, the investment manager must recognize the range of practical alternatives—including domestic stocks not included in the S&P 500 and foreign issues. Whether or not a specific market segment is represented in the portfolio at a particular point in time, it must be considered part of the market population.

With this broader market framework clearly identified, the investment manager is in a position to apply his resources—economic forecasting, financial analysis, and capital market research—to efforts to improve the ratio of expected return to risk through exercise of investment skill. He will overweight or underweight the portfolio in those areas where he has strong reason to consider present market prices out of line with future values. He will attempt to approximate a neutral weighting for a market segment where he has no conviction. This approach differs sharply from the practice of including only those issues designated especially attractive.

Armed with a wide range of diversification tools, the investment manager is able to control risk with a relatively small number of stock positions compared to an index fund. He will use industry diversification, the traditional method, and also diversification by investment characteristics. Now receiving increasing attention in both the academic and professional communities, diversification by investment characteristics provides a means of identifying groups of stocks that tend to move together irrespective of industry classification. Criteria for classification include such company characteristics as financial stength, competitive position, consistency of earnings, and rate of earnings growth, along with such stock characteristics as market value and historical evidence of covariance. This dual approach to diversification facilitates emphasis on areas where the ratio of expected return to risk is judged favorable while avoiding unnecessary exposure to risk where conviction is low.

Selection of individual stocks will involve more than judgments concerning future returns. The first consideration will be the effect of the addition of a stock on the return-risk characteristics of the portfolio. Along with efforts to forecast the most probable returns, attention will be devoted to determining the risk associated with each forecast.[1] Based on the indicated relationship between expected return and risk, issues selected to implement the diversification strategy can aim to improve future returns without entailing unintended exposure to risk.

## Controlling Transaction Costs

Careful design of the managed portfolio will help to control transaction costs. Because of effective diversification planning within a market framework larger than the S&P 500, the managed portfolio can use a smaller number of issues than an index fund uses without losing control of risk. A systematic program of planning portfolio structure in terms of economic and financial fundamentals will tend to reduce the need for rapid turnover in response to day-to-day events. Where adjustments are required in the light of new information, they will continue to be made. Although transaction costs will almost certainly remain higher than those of the better situated index funds, the overall difference, narrowed by the shift to negotiated commissions, is likely to be modest. Transaction costs of active management could actually be lower than those of a poorly planned index fund when the portfolio is of limited size or subject to unexpectedly frequent additions or withdrawals.

## Management Skill

For the investment manager who is able to implement the program outlined above, the theoretical controversy concerning the value of management skill diminishes in significance. He knows that his portfolio will compete effectively with index funds without allowance for special skill in evaluating stock prices. Assuming he shares our position that management skill can add substantially to the value of the portfolio, the door is open to take advantage of the opportunity.

Our appendix deals with the relevance of statistical tests to the identification of management skill in the context of a specific portfolio. If management skill were a constant that showed up in returns for each successive time period, it would be relatively easy to identify its presence by standard statistical techniques. Few successful long-term investors, however, would agree that the real world conforms to this simple assumption. Instead, they accept the likelihood that skill, especially when applied to complex problems, may not be validated by the market for a considerable period, with the precise timing subject to uncertainty. If so, statistical analysis will have great difficulty identifying the contribution of management skill, even when the long-term record is highly favorable.

## CONCLUSION

Index funds represent an effort to apply sophisticated capital market theory to practical investment problems, but in a world that does not conform exactly to theory. The theory on which the index fund concept rests provides a major contribution to understanding the investment process. The issue is not the importance of the theory, but whether the mechanical commitment of funds to an arbitrarily selected stock index is the best way to make use of it.

Apart from the issue of the value of skill in the evaluation of stock prices, practical versions of index funds fall significantly short of the theoretical model. For the index fund based on the S&P 500, risk is not the least possible relative to expected return—for all the reasons we have listed. Expected return, meanwhile, is not the average expected for all investors. Under favorable conditions, savings in transaction costs are attainable, but the anticipated advantage may be negated by insufficient size of the fund, unexpectedly frequent withdrawals or additions, or a poorly implemented trading program.

The complex problems encountered by the index fund provide a background for examining what the professionally managed portfolio, properly directed, can offer. Carefully planned, the managed portfolio can provide a program that competes effectively with the index fund in terms of controlling risk and holding down transaction costs. Diversification opportunities for the managed portfolio benefit from an available market of stocks larger than the S&P 500. The managed portfolio can also be more flexible than the index fund in adjusting the return objective upward in cases where such is appropriate for the client. At the same time, it can continue to do what the index fund is not intended to do—seek to benefit from the application of skill to the evaluation of stock prices.

A number of professional managers will continue to achieve long-term records of above-average investment success—to the benefit of their clients. The long-standing statistical argument concerning the significance of such records will continue, but as suggested by Appendix 72.1, it is very difficult for statistical tests to identify the value of management skill when investment strategy may not be validated by the stock market for up to several years. In short, the investment manager, with adequate planning, can achieve most of the advantages expected of an index fund without foregoing the opportunity to add to the value of the portfolio through the application of skill.

For pragmatists who are reserving judgment on index funds until more performance data are available, it should be pointed out that the answer is already in. Apart from possible savings in transaction costs, the index fund is not intended to provide higher returns than the average for other investors. If, in a given period, the S&P 500 appears to have produced substantially better results than the total for other investors, it is because the S&P 500 falls short of the index fund goal of representing the entire market. There is no reason in index fund theory to expect that the situation will not be reversed in another period. Comparison of index funds with managed portfolios, moreover, must distinguish between the performance of the index and the performance of the index fund. Because of cumulative slippage resulting from transaction costs, an index fund based on the S&P 500 has no hope of keeping pace with the performance of the S&P 500 itself.

## APPENDIX 72.1

The purpose of this appendix is to illustrate the difficulty of identifying by statistical tests the contribution of skill, in the special sense used in this article, to investment performance. The assumptions we make for portfolios are too simple to reflect exactly how long-term insights can be expected to operate. Adjustment of our assumptions to bring them closer to the real-world situation might reduce the assumed contribution

**EXHIBIT 72.1**　Representative Values of the Appraisal Ratio

| $\sigma = 0.15$ | | $\dfrac{V'}{V} = 10$ |
|---|---|---|
| $P^2$ | P Annual | P Daily |
| 0.3000 | 0.5477 | 0.02867 |
| 0.1000 | 0.31623 | 0.01655 |
| 0.01660 | 0.12883 | 0.00674 |
| 0.00427 | 0.06537 | 0.00342 |

of investment management, but it would also further limit the ability of the statistical tests to achieve significance. The conclusion would still be the same: Statistical tests are unlikely to prove anything, one way or another, about the value of long-term stock market strategy.

The contribution of skill to portfolio performance is not, as is sometimes supposed, meaningfully measured in terms of incremental return. Rather, it is the extra return realized *per unit of extra risk incurred* that is the meaningful measure.[2] Since the only risk an investor need incur in the absence of research is nondiversifiable, or market, risk, the extra risk to which the abnormal return garnered by research must be related is the diversifiable, or specific, risk in the portfolio. The square of the ratio of average independent return to the standard deviation of that return is called the appraisal ratio; it is the contribution of active management to the so-called Sharpe ratio, which relates average return to risk for the overall (i.e., active plus passive) portfolio.

Exhibit 72.1 displays values of the appraisal ratio and its square root for four cases spanning a wide range of levels of research contribution. That this range is a plausible range to consider for long-term investment insights is argued in Section II of this appendix. At this point, however, in order to give the reader some standard by which to judge the reasonableness of these numbers, we merely point out that the Sharpe ratio ($p^2$) of a well diversified index fund is roughly 0.1—equal to the contribution of research at the level corresponding to the second case in Exhibit 72.1.

Of course, both risk and reward enter into active portfolio decisions, hence influence portfolio results, not only through the behavior of a security, but also through the size of the portfolio's position in that security. Thus, as the profusion of symbols in Exhibit 72.1 suggests, the interaction can get very complicated. (The symbols are defined below.) It is simple, however, if unique returns are statistically independent, one security from another. In what follows, therefore, we shall make this simplifying assumption (the key assumption in Sharpe's famous Diagonal Model).

**I**

Suppose an experimenter observed the daily unique returns of a portfolio and tried to determine whether or not the portfolio's true appraisal ratio was greater than zero. He might begin by calculating the square root of the appraisal ratio of his sample of unique returns—the mean return divided by the sample standard deviation. A positive sample ratio would be suggestive of a positive true ratio.

Even if the true appraisal ratio ($p^2$) is zero, however, chance may well lead to a positive sample ratio. The question the experimenter will ask then is: Assuming the true appraisal ratio is zero, what is the probability of a sample ratio at least as large as the one I observe? If this probability is sufficiently small—say, one percent or less—he will reject the hypothesis that the portfolio's true appraisal ratio is zero, concluding, instead, that the sample ratio is more likely to have come from a portfolio with a positive true appraisal ratio. (The hypothesis that the true appraisal ratio is zero is called the "null hypothesis." The hypothesis that it is positive is called the "alternate hypothesis.")

To see how this might work in practice, suppose that the portfolio's unique returns, $x_i$, are distributed normally, with mean $\mu_x$ and standard deviation $\sigma_x$. Suppose, further, that the sample is so large that the sample standard deviation is a good approximation of $\sigma_x$. Then, under the hypothesis that the true appraisal ratio ($\mu_x/\sigma_x$) is zero (which is equivalent to the hypothesis that $\mu_x$ is zero), the sample mean unique return, $\bar{x}$, has a normal distribution with mean $\mu_{\bar{x}} = $ zero and known standard deviation $\sigma_{\bar{x}} = \sigma_x\sqrt{N}$ (where N is the number of observations). Assuming that the experimenter requires a sample ratio whose probability of occurrence is one percent or less under the null hypothesis in order to reject that hypothesis, then if $\bar{x}$ turns out to be greater than $2.33\,\sigma_{\bar{x}}$, he will reject the null hypothesis. (He obtains the number 2.33 from a table of the normal distribution; the probability that a normal variable with mean zero will take on a value larger than 2.33 times its standard deviation is 1 percent.)

Thus the experimenter's procedure will consist of the following steps:

1. Obtain a sample of N daily unique returns; $x_1, \ldots, x_N$.
2. Calculate the sample mean $\bar{x} \equiv \sum_I^N x_i$. This is an estimate of $\mu_x$.
3. Calculate the sample standard deviation $S_x \equiv \left[\frac{1}{(N-1)}\sum_1^N (x_i - \bar{x})^2\right]^{1/2}$. This is an estimate of $\sigma_x$. It is assumed that N is large enough to ensure that $S_x$ can replace $\sigma_x$.
4. Calculate $S_{\bar{x}} = S_{\bar{x}}/\sqrt{N}$. This is an estimate of $\sigma_x$. By the assumption in (3), $S_{\bar{x}}$ is close enough to $\sigma_{\bar{x}}$ to be used in its place.
5. Calculate $\bar{x}_{0.01} = 2.33 S_{\bar{x}}$.
6. Reject the null hypothesis if $\bar{x} \geq \bar{x}_{0.01}$.

An investor may view this process with a jaundiced eye. What, he may ask the experimenter, is the probability that you will reject the null hypothesis if in fact the true appraisal ratio is actually positive? The experimenter's answer would be something like: If the ratio is large enough and if there are enough data, then the null hypothesis will almost certainly be rejected. The investor, with long experience in recognizing qualifications from his own line of work, will then ask something like: Suppose $\mu_x$ and $\sigma_x$ are really 4.74 and 15 percent annually, respectively. Then the true ratio is 0.316 annually, or 0.0166 daily. What is the probability that you will reject the null hypothesis if I give you five years of data (N = 1825)? Considering how attractive a bonus return of almost 5 percent annually is, the investor is not likely to be happy unless the probability of rejecting the null hypothesis is at least 50 percent.

He can calculate this probability as follows:

1. Accept the experimenter's assumption that the unique returns are distributed normally.
2. Accept the experimenter's estimate of $S_x$ and his assumption that N is large enough to permit using $S_x$ in place of $\sigma_x$.
3. Accept the experimenter's estimate of $S_{\bar{x}}$ and his assumption that N is large enough to permit using $S_{\bar{x}}$ in place of $\sigma_{\bar{x}}$.
4. Assume the true mean $\mu_x$ is really $0.0166 \, S_x$.
5. Calculate the difference between $0.0166 \, S_x$ and $\bar{x}_{0.01}$, measured in standard deviations of $\bar{x}$. Call this number $K_A$. The actual calculation follows:

$$K_A \equiv \frac{x_{0.01} - 0.0166 S_x}{S_{\bar{x}}}$$

$$K_A = \frac{2.33 S_x/\sqrt{N} - 0.0166 S_x}{S_x/\sqrt{N}}$$

$$K_A = 2.33 - 0.0166\sqrt{N}$$

$$K_A = 1.62 \tag{72.1}$$

6. Use a table of the standard normal distribution to find the probability that a normal variable would lie at least $K_A$ standard deviations to the right of its mean. This is the probability of rejecting the null hypothesis when the stated alternate hypothesis is true. In this case the probability is about 5.2 percent, somewhat discouraging at best.

The interesting thing about Equation 72.1 is that it is independent of $S_x$. Thus, for large samples, this procedure is really a check on a test of a hypothesis about the appraisal ratio, not the mean $\mu_x$. More generally, if (1) the one percent rejection criterion is replaced by a $100\alpha$ percent criterion; (2) the $100\alpha$ percent point on the standard normal distribution is $K\alpha$; and (3) the true daily appraisal ratio is P, Equation 72.1 becomes:

$$K_A = K\alpha - P\sqrt{N} \tag{72.2}$$

Exhibit 72.2 contains the results of applying Equation 72.2 to the values of P in Exhibit 72.1 for time samples of the lengths indicated. (The value of $\alpha$ is set equal to 0.01.)

**EXHIBIT 72.2** Percentage Probability of Rejecting the Null Hypothesis When the Alternate Hypothesis is True

| P | 1 | 5 | 10 | 15 | 20 | 25 | 50 |
|---------|------|------|------|------|------|------|------|
| 0.02867 | 3.8 | 13.6 | 27.7 | 40.7 | 54.5 | 66.1 | 93.2 |
| 0.01655 | 2.2 | 5.2 | 9.2 | 13.4 | 18.0 | 22.7 | 46.2 |
| 0.00674 | 1.4 | 2.1 | 2.7 | 3.4 | 4.0 | 4.6 | 7.8 |
| 0.00342 | 1.2 | 1.4 | 1.7 | 1.9 | 2.1 | 2.3 | 3.1 |

Exhibit 72.2 shows clearly that the investor's suspicion is justified. Valuable levels of talent for identifying attractive investment opportunities are likely to go undetected by conventional statistical tests—unless, of course, the investor is exceedingly old. Perhaps the Chinese were right after all: Age does deserve respect.

## II

Perhaps the simplest way to distinguish between long-term and short-term investment ideas or insights is in terms of the probability that the market consensus will react to (and incorporate) the insight in the next period. Thus if the insight is relatively obvious, with broad intellectual appeal, that probability will be high, whereas if the insight is subtle, sophisticated, and requires a high level of training for its comprehension, that probability will be low.

If the probability with which the market consensus reacts to an investor's long-term investment insights is low enough and the frequency with which he apprehends such insights is high enough, the chances are excellent that there will be a number of such insights as yet unrecognized by the market, hence a number of positions in his active portfolio at any point in time. In the following period the market may react to several of these insights or none. Whether there is one or several, however, the probabilistic nature of the market's reaction to long-term investment insights is significant, not only for the investor's expected return, but also for his risk.

Assume that market discovery has the same probability of occurring (when it has not previously occurred) in every period. Let that probability be "g." (One would expect intuitively that, the higher this probability, the more the insight contributes to the active portfolio on a risk-reward basis. As we will show, this intuition is correct.) Then the probability of discovery in period n is:

$$(1 - g)^n g$$

In each period prior to discovery, the distribution of incremental return has mean $gV$, where $V$ is the value of the information, second moment $gV^2$, and variance

$$gV^2 - (gV)^2 = V^2(g - g^2) = V^2 g(1 - g)$$

In Treynor-Black, the contribution of an insight to portfolio performance depends on (1) whether the insight can be isolated, rather than embedded in a mass of irrelevant uncertainties and (2) the appraisal ratio, which equals the ratio of the expected return, squared, to the variance. If the insight can indeed be isolated, the value of the appraisal ratio, $P^2$ is:

$$P^2 = \frac{g^2 V^2}{g(1 - g)V^2} = \frac{g}{1 - g}^3$$

(Note that we are treating as certain what is in practice one of the major investment uncertainties—whether the market had reacted to the insight before the investor got it.) Under these admittedly rather special circumstances, the contribution of the insight to risk-adjusted portfolio performance depends only on the probability of market reaction in the next period.[4]

It will, of course, more commonly be the case that an insight cannot be isolated; the only vehicle with which to capitalize on the insight will be individual securities with characteristic residual variance $\sigma^2 V'^2$, say, where V' is the current value of the security. The question immediately arises whether the insight reduces this (historical) level of residual variance. The answer depends on what one assumes about the statistical character of the process generating events that change the value of the security. If, as we prefer to assume, the process is one in which the occurrence of one such event alters not at all the probability of occurrence of subsequent events (i.e., if the process is Poisson), then the answer is clear: Possessing the insight leaves the level of residual variance (excluding the variance of the insight) unchanged.

In this case, the relevant variance for assessing the contribution of the insight to portfolio performance is the variance of the historical uncertainty and the uncertainty whether the market consensus will discover the insight, combined. If we make the further assumption that these two uncertainties are statistically independent, then the variance of the combination is the sum of the respective variances, or:

$$g(1-g)V^2 + \sigma^2 V'^2$$

The corresponding value of the appraisal ratio is:

$$P^2 = \frac{g^2 V^2}{g(1-g)V^2 + \sigma^2 V'^2}$$

$$= \frac{g^2}{g(1-g) + \sigma^2 (V'/V)^2}$$

Exhibit 72.3 displays computations of values of the appraisal ratio for a wide range of values of g, the probability that the market will react to the insights in question in the next year. Although Exhibit 72.3 is based on the assumption that a single insight is outstanding, it can be applied to the case of multiple insights (provided the insights are statistically independent) by multiplying the indicated values of the appraisal ratio by the number of insights (see Exhibit 72.4). Exhibit 72.5 is based on the computations in Exhibits 72.3 and 72.4. The reader can use Exhibit 72.5 to

**EXHIBIT 72.3**  Calculation of Appraisal Ratios for Single Insights

| g | 1−g | g(1−g) | $g^2$ | $g(1-g) + \sigma^2(V'/V)^2 = D$ | $\frac{g^2}{D}$ |
|---|-----|--------|-------|------------------------------------|------------------|
| 0.1 | 0.9 | 0.09 | 0.01 | 2.26 | 0.0044 |
| 0.2 | 0.8 | 0.16 | 0.04 | 2.29 | 0.0175 |
| 0.3 | 0.7 | 0.21 | 0.09 | 2.46 | 0.0366 |
| 0.4 | 0.6 | 0.24 | 0.16 | 2.49 | 0.0643 |
| 0.5 | 0.5 | 0.25 | 0.25 | 2.50 | 0.1 |

Assume: $\sigma = 0.15$, $\sigma^2 = 0.0225$   $V'/V = 10$   $\sigma^2(V'/V^2) = 2.25$

**EXHIBIT 72.4** How the Number of Independent Insights Outstanding Affects the Appraisal Ratio

| | | Appraisal Ratio | | | |
|---|---|---|---|---|---|
| g | No. of Insights | 1 | 2 | 4 | 10 |
| 0.1 | | 0.0044 | 0.0088 | 0.0176 | 0.0440 |
| 0.2 | | 0.0175 | 0.0350 | 0.0700 | 0.1750 |
| 0.3 | | 0.0366 | 0.0732 | 0.1464 | 0.3660 |
| 0.4 | | 0.0643 | 0.1286 | 0.2572 | 0.6430 |
| 0.5 | | 0.1000 | 0.2000 | 0.4000 | 1.0000 |

Assumptions: See Exhibit 72.3

deduce various combinations of (1) probability of market reaction and (2) number of long-term investment insights simultaneously outstanding that are consistent with the appraisal ratios assumed in Exhibit 72.2 (Section I).

We have assumed, as noted, that the uncertainties associated with the investor's several insights are statistically independent. When they aren't, the effective number of uncertainties is reduced. Thus the relevant row in Exhibit 72.4, for example, if the investor has 10 insights, some of which are strongly correlated, might be the row

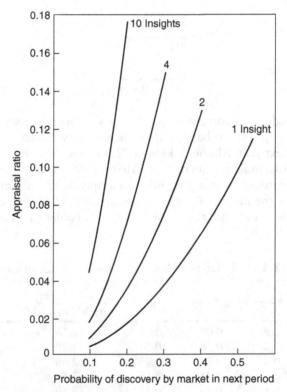

**EXHIBIT 72.5** Probability of Discovery by Market in the Next Period

corresponding to four strictly independent insights. Correlation, hence the absence of strict independence, would arise, for example, if the investor had one "dominant" investment insight on which the validity of several of his other insights depended.

On the other hand, it is sobering to reflect on what an appraisal ratio of 0.3 (generated, for example, by an average of 10 independent insights outstanding when odds of reaction by the market consensus in any one year are roughly one in four) means for performance: *At the same level of risk* an equity portfolio containing both an active element based on these insights and a passive element, efficiently balanced, would generate twice the annual excess return of an index fund. Thus, for example, if the famous Lorie-Fisher 9 percent annual return on a market portfolio included an average of roughly 5 percent return in excess of the riskless rate, then the return on the managed portfolio with the same overall risk would average 14 percent per annum. Whereas, on the average, with dividends reinvested, the index fund will double in eight years, the managed fund will double in a little over, five years (and redouble in a little over 10). Yet, as Exhibit 72.2 shows, it takes between 15 and 20 years of experience to have a better-than-even chance of detecting this level of skill. As Exhibit 72.2 also shows, it takes still longer to detect the levels of skill that most fund managers and clients would consider more realistic—even though those lower levels can nevertheless make a meaningful difference in investment performance (see Exhibit 72.4).

## Notes

1. Walter R. Good, "Interpreting Analysts' Recommendations," *Financial Analysts Journal* (May–June 1975).
2. See Jack L. Treynor and Fischer Black, "How to Use Security Analysis to Improve Portfolio Selection," *Journal of Business* (January 1973).
3. For an explanation of the meaning of the appraisal ratio, see Robert Ferguson, "How to Beat the Index Funds," *Financial Analysts Journal* (May–June 1975).
4. What do our assumptions about investment insights imply for the level of portfolio turnover? Broadly speaking, portfolio turnover depends on two things: (1) the rate of turnover in the active portfolio and (2) the relative importance of the active portfolio in the total portfolio. Once the market consensus has reacted to an investment insight, there is no point retaining in the active portfolio any longer the security serving as the vehicle for that insight. Hence the turnover rate for the active portfolio is simply the average level of probability that the market will react to an insight in the next period. When that probability is 0.5, for example, the implied turnover rate for the active portfolio is 50 percent per period. This rate is diluted, however, when the active portfolio is combined with a passive portfolio. (Note that the logic presented here regarding the turnover rate in the active portfolio applies only if short selling is not employed; if short positions are employed as actively as long positions, the turnover rate in the active portfolio can be infinite.)

# CHAPTER 73

# The Principles of Corporate Pension Finance

The key to understanding the financial implications of corporate pension plans— before and after the passage of ERISA—is the economic value of claims on a pension plan. Beneficiaries have regarded their claims as a bona fide retirement fund. On the other hand, sponsoring companies, their actuaries, their accountants, their creditors, and their stockholders have regarded pension claims lightly. Thus corporate pension plans have traditionally had a "something for nothing" aspect about them, whereby their value to beneficiaries seemed to exceed the financial burden they imposed on the sponsoring company. What are pension claims really worth?[1]

Although pension claims are not strictly lenders' claims, we can learn something about their worth from both parties' points of view by thinking of them as such. Because his entire principal, as well as current interest, is at risk, a lender cannot safely confine himself to looking at current flows (e.g., to comparisons of earnings before interest and taxes with interest expense, or even with debt service). The basic question of security for a lender is one of stocks, rather than flows. The basic issue is: How does the "contractual" value of the lender's claim compare with what he could sell the underlying security for in foreclosure?

If we assume that markets are reasonably efficient, then current market prices will be useful guides in answering this question. This is true even when the loan in question is secured by the general credit of the borrower, in which case it is the value of the borrowing corporation itself to which the lender must look for his protection. (If his claim is junior to other claims on the general credit then, of course, it is the value of the corporation *less* the value of the senior claims to which he must look.) The fluctuations in the market value of the corporation from day to day do not diminish its relevance for the lender, because this value impounds everything known about the borrower, including all past market values. The fluctuations raise the possibility, however, that *future* market values will be less than the current market value—a possibility that constitutes the fundamental risk for a lender.

Unless the lender's claim is a demand note, its present contractual value has to be reckoned. The rate at which future obligations are discounted back to the present is thus critical. The appropriate discount rate is the riskless interest rate; the present value that results from discounting at the riskless rate is an estimate of the market value of the assets on which lenders must have a claim if they are not to be subjected

---

Reprinted from the *Journal of Finance*, Volume 32, No. 2, 1977.

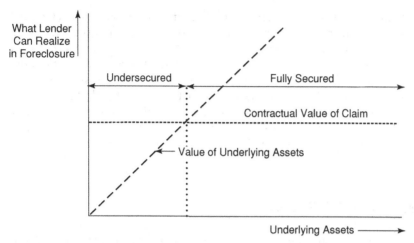

**EXHIBIT 73.1**   Instant Foreclosure

to investment risk. If the assets available exceed the present value of future claims only when the latter are discounted at a higher rate, the expected proceeds from the assets will fail to meet the claims unless the assets are invested aggressively, with the attendant possibility of loss.

Exhibit 73.1 shows the relationship between the value of a lender's claim and the value of the underlying security in the case of instant foreclosure. The horizontal line in Exhibit 73.1 represents the contractual payoff terms of the loan—periodic coupon plus return of principal—discounted at the riskless rate. No matter how valuable the security underlying the claim—measured along the horizontal axis—the current value of the claim can never exceed this amount: If the value of the security equals or exceeds this amount—in other words, if the claim is "fully secured"—then the value of the claim equals this amount. On the other hand, if the value of the security underlying the claim is less than the contractual value of the claim—if the claim is "undersecured"—then the value of the claim is equal to the value of the underlying security. When he is able, an alert lender will foreclose while his claim is still fully secured.

When the lender no longer has access to instantaneous foreclosure his lending ceases to be riskless, because he no longer knows what the value of the security underlying his claim will be when foreclosure proceedings are complete. The value of most economic assets tends of course to be continuous, with today's value commonly being close to our best guess about tomorrow's value. But other values are possible, even though less probable. If the lender's claim is fully secured today it may not be fully secured by the time he can foreclose; thus the economic value of his claim when the "foreclosure horizon" is no longer zero is always less than the contractual, or pure discount, value of his claim. On the other hand, because the upside potential in the underlying security belongs, not to him, but to the corporate shareholders, the value of his claim is always less than the value of the underlying security.

Black and Scholes have argued that the curve describing the value of the lender's claim as a function of the underlying security is in fact the option curve.[2] When the foreclosure interval exceeds zero, the lender is subject to an option held by the corporate shareholder.

Like all claims with an option aspect, a lender's claim can be construed in terms of either a put or a call. Under the put construction, the shareholders put the underlying value of the company to the lender if, at the end of the foreclosure interval, it falls short of the pure discount value of the lender's claim. Under the call construction, the underlying security belongs to the lender unless at the end of the foreclosure interval it exceeds the pure discount value of his claim—in which case the shareholders call the security away from the lender. In each case the "exercise price" is the pure discount value of the claim, the maturity of the option is the length of the foreclosure interval, and the optioned asset is the value of the company before deducting the lender's claim.

## IMPLICATIONS FOR PENSION CLAIMS

Very commonly pension claims are "under-funded." Does that mean that they are undersecured? It clearly means that the ostensible value of the claim exceeds the value of the underlying pension assets: If the pension fund were the only relevant security for a pension claim, the aggregate value of pension claims would exceed the value of the pension fund.

If that were true, and pension claimants knew it, they would be deeply unhappy. Even before ERISA, however, most companies felt an obligation not quite tantamount to a common-law obligation—certainly not a statutory obligation—to make contributions to a pension plan that would at least enable the plan to meet those benefits coming due. As long as the company was solvent, it felt obliged to draw against its own assets to meet those claims. Although the corporate creditor was clearly senior to the pension claimant, the net assets of the company itself were effectively behind the pension claims.

On the other hand, the pension claimant could be sure of getting paid in full only if the assets available to meet his claim exceeded their present value *at every point in time*. Any corporation that was insolvent in this special sense was imposing risks on the claimant for which he is unlikely to get fully rewarded. Pension beneficiaries have been virtually powerless to prevent employers from sliding into insolvency in this case—even though in many cases this kind of insolvency has prevented them from collecting their pension benefits. Although, of course, lender's claims do not permit instant foreclosure, they do permit foreclosure in a few months or at most a few years. But foreclosure, so to speak, in the case of a pension claim, would be as much as 40 years away. Thus the fundamental difference between pension claims and the more conventional lender's claims was really one of degree, rather than kind. The pension claimant was *optioned* in relation to his claim on the corporation in the same way as a conventional corporate lender, but often with a much longer "foreclosure" time.

The point of viewing pension claims in these terms is, of course, that it reduces any pension claim to two elements, each of which can be analyzed in terms of conventional financial theory: (1) the pension claim itself, discounted at the riskless rate—the contractual, or "gross" value, of the claim; and (2) the so-called "pension put" on the assets underlying the claim, with a strike price equal to the gross value of the claim. Viewed this way, the pension claim is a claim against the employer, rather than a claim against the pension fund, and the present value of that claim reckoned on a riskless basis represents a subtraction from the employer's equity. The pension put, on the other hand, is a claim against the pension beneficiary by the employer corporation and represents an asset of the employer. Thus the "net" value of a pension claim is the contractual (gross) value, suitably discounted, less the value of the put option on the assets underlying the claim.

If one considers that the corporation has no obligation to protect pension beneficiaries against inflation, then the appropriate discount rate is the rate on government obligations of comparable maturity. If, on the other hand, one considers that the current statement of future pension obligations is really a statement expressed in current dollars of future obligations, the real value of which is fixed, then the appropriate discount rate is the riskless interest rate with inflationary expectations removed—a rate commonly estimated at roughly 3 percent.

If we construct an economic balance sheet for the employer corporation it will show the pension claims as corporate liabilities (and the pension assets as corporate assets) but will also show the put against the pension claimants as an offsetting corporate asset (see Exhibit 73.2). Like the value of all options, the value of the pension put depends on the uncertainty surrounding the future value of the optioned asset. In the case of pension claims the relevant risky assets are the employer's equity in economic terms and the market value of the pension portfolio. Thus the value of the pension put to the employer corporation increases as the uncertainty surrounding the value of these two (positively correlated) assets increases.

Exhibit 73.3 shows how the value of the pension put is related to the value of the underlying assets (the sum of the net assets of the corporation proper and the pension assets) on one hand and the pension claim on the other. As the pension claim approaches its due date the value of the claim net of the pension put approaches the kinked line shown in the figure. On the other hand, the longer until the pension claim falls due, the larger the uncertainty surrounding the value of the underlying assets at the due date, and the more gradually curved is the line describing the value of the pension put. The more gradual the curvature, the less the pension claim net of the pension put will be worth for any given value of the underlying assets.

One can see that, if the riskiness of the relevant assets is large enough, and the time to foreclose is long enough—and, as noted, it may be up to 40 years—the option curvature can be very gradual indeed—particularly for a weak corporation with a weak pension plan. In such cases the value of a pension put may be of the same order of magnitude as, though never larger than, the face value of the pension claim itself.

The pension put fairs into the 45-degree line when the underlying assets approach zero. Thus, for employers whose net assets barely exceed the amount by which their pension plan is underfunded, a loss suffered investing in risky pension assets is borne almost entirely by pension claimants. On the other hand, when the underlying assets

**EXHIBIT 73.2**  Employer Balance Sheet

| | |
|---|---|
| Corporate Assets | Corporate Liabilities |
| Pension Assets | Pension Liabilities |
| Pension Put | True Employer Equity |

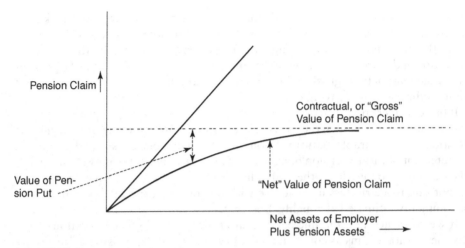

**EXHIBIT 73.3** Behavior of Put

are large in comparison with the face value of the pension claim, the curve describing the value of the claim net of the pension put is almost equal to the nominal value of the pension claim and parallel to it. In this circumstance, investment losses in the pension assets are borne almost entirely by the employer.

## THE PENSION ACTUARY'S APPROACH

How does the preceding discussion relate to the actuary's determination of the present value of the pension liability? It is well known that his choice of a discount rate depends in some way upon the past or future investment performance of the pension assets.

We have argued, however, that a fixed benefit pension plan cannot meaningfully be analyzed in isolation. It has to be analyzed in the context of the corporate balance sheet. When one does so the corporation has some new assets—the pension assets—and a new liability. The pension put also becomes an asset in that balance sheet. The only unusual item in this, the "economic" balance sheet for the corporation, is the presence of the pension put among the assets. Thus there is no more reason for looking to the return on a particular pension asset to determine how to discount the pension liability than there is for looking at the return on any other corporate assets to determine how to discount any other corporate liability—hence there is no more reason to single out pension liabilities for this bizarre treatment than, say, the employer's term loan with its local bank.

The actuary may argue in his defense that he is actually trying to estimate the value of the pension liability net of the pension put. To this rejoinder, we would have three objections: (1) In order to know the value of the pension put, one has first to know the contractual value of the pension liability; (2) the value of the put depends on the riskiness of the corporate assets as well as the riskiness of the pension assets; and (3) in any case, determination of the proper discount lies in the realm of option theory, rather than conventional capital budgeting. In short, there is no justification for the present actuarial practice of discounting pension liabilities at a rate somehow related to the historical rate of return on the pension assets.

What is really needed from the pension actuary is something much simpler, much more straightforward than he now provides—namely, the present value of expected pension benefits discounted at the riskless rate. Although the actuary must still make assumptions about the rates at which workers at different ages and skills leave prior to vesting or die, he has relatively little latitude for judgment. Thus the number comes close to being an objective measure of the financial burden of the company's pension liability. It is the relevant number, not only for the pension claimant, but also for private creditors of the company and, finally, for the analyst of the employer's equity shares.

What is the impact of a pension contribution by the employer? The effect of a contribution is always to increase the pension assets while either reducing corporate assets or increasing corporate liabilities, without reducing the aggregate risk in the corporate assets. In other words, corporations don't liquidate inventory or sell off plant to pay their pension contributions; nor do they issue stock. Rather, they liquidate their cash or expand creditors' claims against themselves.

Either way, the pension contribution leaves the value of the assets—corporate and pension combined—underlying pension claims unchanged. Unless the pension assets are completely riskless, however, the pension contribution always increases the absolute risk characterizing the underlying assets. Thus the impact of pension contributions when the pension assets are at least partly risky is to increase the value of the pension put, reduce the net value of the pension claim, and increase the value of the equity shares in the employer corporation. In no sense is the pension contribution an expense to the employer as represented in conventional accounting. Conversely, the beneficiary should concern himself not with putting a floor under the pension contribution, but with putting a ceiling on the corporate dividend; the dividend reduces the assets securing his claim.

It is now possible to understand three widely observed features of corporate pension plans:

1. Why employer corporations urge pension fund managers to invest pension funds in risky assets
2. Why conventional corporate claimants have traditionally disregarded the pension plan in evaluating their claims
3. Why, prior to ERISA, even vested beneficiaries sometimes failed to collect their full pension claims

## ENTER ERISA

We are now in a position to consider the impact of the Employee Retirement Income Security Act (ERISA) of 1974. Broadly speaking, the impact of the act is very simple. It creates an entity called the Pension Benefit Guaranty Corporation and interposes this corporation between the employer and the pension beneficiary. In effect, the Guaranty Corporation is charged with paying off the beneficiary, on one hand, and collecting from the employer on the other. The effect of charging it with these responsibilities is to transfer pension risk from the beneficiary to the Guaranty Corporation.

Under the provisions of ERISA, there is no longer any question whether, up to fairly generous statutory limits, the pension beneficiaries will get their benefits. The old question, "Will the employee get his benefits?" is replaced by a new question: "Who will bear the burden?" In the stead of the impotent, uninformed, unsophisticated beneficiary, the Pension Act has placed a new government agency with enormous powers—the Pension Benefit Guaranty Corporation.[3] On the other hand, it gives the Guaranty Corporation the power of a tax lien over the assets of corporations that terminate their pension plans with unfunded liabilities. These liabilities, most of which were incurred prior to the passage of the Pension Act and at a time when pension liabilities were merely "paper promises," threaten to be an onerous burden for many corporations.

To prevent such corporations from foundering at the outset, the Pension Act provides two kinds of protection to companies with pension plans: (1) a provision restricting the Guaranty Corporation's lien to 30 percent of the "net assets" of the terminating company and (2) liability insurance. In the absence of insurance, what kind of protection would the so-called "30 percent" provision afford the company whose pension plan terminates with unfunded liabilities? The relevant provisions of the Pension Act of 1974 are these:

1. The Guaranty Corporation can terminate a pension plan at its discretion, and is charged with responsibility to do so "if risk to the Corporation begins to increase unreasonably."
2. The Corporation can recover up to 30 percent of the net assets of the terminated corporation to help defray unfunded pension liabilities. "Net assets" apparently means "equity"—presumably in economic, rather than accounting, terms.[4]

If the Guaranty Corporation must wait until the employer is bankrupt before terminating, then, even if its claim on the corporation has the priority of a tax lien (i.e., precedes all creditors except employees owed) the amount of its claim will be roughly zero: Other creditors will get what they would get in the absence of a pension plan, hence will not force bankruptcy until they normally would—which is when corporation assets are just sufficient to secure conventional creditors, with little or nothing left over for either shareholders or the Guaranty Corporation.

On the other hand, the act charges the Guaranty Corporation with the responsibility of enforcing voluntary termination "whenever its risk begins to increase unreasonably." Because of the 30 percent rule, that point is reached long before conventional bankruptcy: In order to be able to defray the unfunded liability with the proceeds of its claim on the company's assets, the Guaranty Corporation must force involuntary termination while 30 percent of the company's net assets still exceeds the unfunded pension liability—which is to say, while the company's net assets still exceed 3.3 times the unfunded pension liability. This becomes the critical number for the Guaranty Corporation.

If the 30 percent provision is to protect the net assets against the claims of the Guaranty Corporation, the Guaranty Corporation must wait until the company is conventionally bankrupt. Will it do so? Or will it act soon enough to recover from the terminating company's assets the entire value of the unfunded pension liability? In view of the fact that it has both the power to terminate a pension plan any time it wants to and the responsibility to terminate "before the risk to its own assets begins to increase unreasonably," can there be any doubt how the Guaranty Corporation will behave?

In this case, other creditors must reckon with a senior claim equal to the unfunded liability. The other two-thirds of the net assets at termination are of course available to secure these creditors. Needless to say, extracting the Guaranty Corporation's "pound of flesh" from the company may undermine its continued viability. If private creditors lack confidence that the necessary financing can be found, they may have to consider that reorganization—or liquidation—is likely to be precipitated by termination of the pension plan. It is not unlikely, therefore, that we will see private creditors of sponsoring corporations shifting the focus of their attention from the conditions of conventional bankruptcy to the conditions of pension plan termination. The 30 percent provision has some significant implications, but probably not the implications supposed by the legislators who wrote the provision into the act.

## ARE PRIVATE CREDITORS WORSE OFF UNDER ERISA?

It does not follow, however, that private creditors are necessarily worse off under the Pension Act of 1974 than previously. Despite the fact that, under the act, they are junior to the Guaranty Corporation, they can actually benefit from the fact that the Guaranty Corporation has more power to force termination than they have to force bankruptcy—and from the fact that it is in the Guaranty Corporation's interest to force termination sooner than private creditors can force a conventional bankruptcy.

To demonstrate this, let $(a)$ represent gross assets, $(c)$ employer's corporate liabilities and $(u)$ the unfunded pension liability. In order to get out whole, the Guaranty Corporation must force termination of the pension plan when:

$$u \le 0.30(a - c) \tag{73.1}$$

Because the Guaranty Corporation is senior to almost all private creditors, the assets available to the latter will then equal or exceed:

$$a - 0.30(a - c) = 0.70a + 0.30c \tag{73.2}$$

For private creditors to get out whole, these assets must satisfy:

$$0.70a + 0.30c \ge c \tag{73.3}$$

But this condition is equivalent to:

$$0.70a \ge 0.70c \tag{73.4}$$

$a \ge c$, which under the condition expressed in Equation (73.1), is always satisfied. If the Guaranty Corporation terminates quickly enough to protect itself, therefore, the employer's private creditors will always be protected—so much so, in fact, that passage of the Pension Act may eventually improve the quality of many corporate bonds.

## LIABILITY INSURANCE

As we have seen, the Guaranty Corporation has the power to reach beyond the assets in a company pension fund to the assets of the sponsoring company itself. This power represents a potential revolution in the significance of pension liabilities for pension sponsors. One of the most important muddles in the Pension Act is the introduction, however, in parallel with the enormous powers granted to the Guaranty Corporation, of the concept of liability insurance, under which insured pension sponsors have their company assets protected from the depradations of the Guaranty Corporation. Unfortunately, there is typically market risk in the pension assets, market risk in the corporate assets, and the same market risk in the pension assets and corporate assets of every other pension plan: Because no law of large numbers operates with respect to market risk, it cannot be pooled away. Anybody foolish enough to undertake to insure against that risk will ultimately go broke. And when private insurers go broke, the PBGC will become the insurer of last resort. Actually, the early evidence suggests that the task of insuring corporate assets against claims in plan termination will fall on the PBGC sooner, rather than later: Private insurers are proving too smart to offer this kind of insurance.

If the PBGC insures companies against having their assets reached under this provision, it effectively reduces its own ability to get enough money to pay off pension claims as they fall due. ERISA has perpetuated virtually the same kind of situation employers enjoyed prior to ERISA. Under these circumstances the Guaranty Corporation gets the face value of the due claim or whatever the employer is able to pay—the sum of his corporate equity and the value of the corporate pension fund— whichever is less. In effect, if the employer's resources exceed the claim, he pays the claim whereas, if the claim exceeds his resources he "puts" the resources to the Guaranty Corporation in return for cancellation of the claim. In sum, the effect of the liability insurance provisions of the act is to preserve intact the pension put, greatly reducing the value to the Guaranty Corporation of its claims on employers with pension plans.

Exhibit 73.4 displays the balance sheet relationships among the employer, the Guaranty Corporation, and the pension beneficiary under ERISA. The employer's balance sheet has the same items (though possibly different entry values) it had prior to ERISA: the pension liability, the pension assets, and the pension put. The Guaranty Corporation has the employer's pension liability and the pension put on *its* balance sheet (on, of course, the reverse sides) *plus* a liability to the pension beneficiary equal in amount to the employer's liability. Because ERISA preserves the position of the employer company virtually unchanged from what it was prior to the new legislation, it still pays the employer to make overgenerous pension promises. And, despite the elaborate fiduciary responsibility provisions in the act, it still pays the employer to put heavy pressure on the manager of his pension funds to manage them aggressively.

Like any private insurer who would undertake to insure employer's assets under ERISA, the Guaranty Corporation will be highly diversified, whether or not individual pension portfolios are diversified. On the other hand, the level of market risk in the Guaranty Corporation's portfolio will be the average of the levels of market risk in the individual pension portfolios. No amount of diversification in

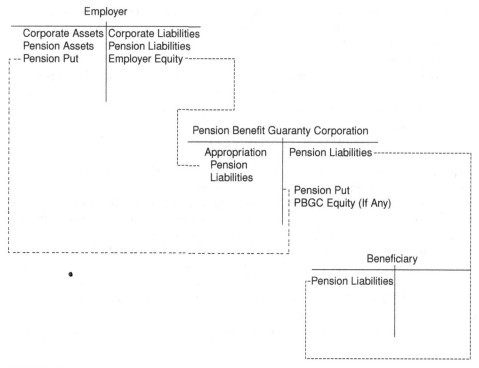

**EXHIBIT 73.4** ERISA Balance Sheet

individual pension portfolios will eliminate the market risk in the Guaranty Corporation's portfolio. Thus, when losses arise, the Guaranty Corporation is likely to find itself faced with losses in a great many pension plans simultaneously. It is hard to see how those fiduciary responsibility provisions of ERISA concerned with diversification can protect the Guaranty Corporation from this kind of loss. (Although, by reducing the level of nonmarket risk in individual pension funds, these provisions reduce the value of the puts associated with individual plans, hence the collective value of these puts.)

Since the impact on the Guaranty Corporation's equity of the pension liability from the employer to the Guaranty Corporation is equal and opposite to the impact of the liability from the Guaranty Corporation to the beneficiary, the net effect of the pension plan is to reduce the Guaranty Corporation's equity by the value of the pension put. As noted, the value of the pension put is sometimes of the same order of magnitude as, although smaller than, the pension liability itself. In aggregate terms, therefore, the consequence of liability insurance (which, as noted, creates the pension put) is probably a charge against the Guaranty Corporation's equity of some dozens of billions of dollars.

If, on the other hand, Congress eliminated the liability insurance provisions of ERISA, the Guaranty Corporation would be able to exercise its power to reach corporate assets. The power of a tax lien makes it senior to virtually all corporate creditors. As noted, the law says that it can go after corporate assets when it thinks the risk to its own claim is beginning to increase unreasonably, which is the classic situation for intervention by a conventional lender. If the PBGC behaves like a conventional lender: (1) there is no put (to the extent that the put can be regarded as negligible—more precisely, a small put); (2) every loss in its pension fund is a loss, dollar for dollar, to the shareholders of the corporation; (3) every increase in the present value of pension promises is a loss, dollar for dollar, to the shareholders of the corporation. In short, without liability insurance, pension sponsors would find it in their own interest to behave responsibly.

Up to fairly generous limits specified by ERISA, it is no longer the claimants' money that is at risk; it is the Pension Benefit Guaranty Corporation's money. Thus, if Congress's intention in writing the elaborate fiduciary responsibility and prudent-man provisions into the Act was to protect the individual claimant, it was probably misguided. On the other hand, without liability insurance one wouldn't need these provisions to protect the Pension Benefit Guaranty Corporation, any more than one needs them now to protect conventional corporate creditors. Because any losses in the pension portfolio will be borne primarily by the sponsoring company, it would then have as much to lose as gain by encouraging the fund manager to take large risks with its pension portfolio, and the conflict between its demands and the standards of prudence laid down by the Act will disappear. If the employer were to bear the primary investment risk in the pension fund, the fund manager's responsibility would be no different from any other professional investor's to his client.

## SUMMARY

We noted at the outset that corporate fixed benefit pension plans have traditionally had a "something for nothing" aspect about them. We saw subsequently that, whereas the pension put will sometimes be large enough to justify corporate sponsors treating these claims as "nothing," conventional analysis of pension plans encourages the beneficiary to treat these claims as "something." On the other hand, it also encourages sponsoring employers to treat pension claims as "nothing" even when the pension put against these claims is negligible.

We have argued that private underwriters are unlikely to offer liability insurance. When, as provided by the Act, the Guaranty Corporation assumes this burden as insurer of last resort, it assumes a position analogous to that of the individual claimant prior to ERISA. The liability insurance provisions of the Act perpetuate the fruits of the "something for nothing" game for the sponsoring employer.

Unfortunately, the resulting put on the Guaranty Corporation is huge compared to its capital. If the put is exercised then, of course, the United States government— which is to say, the U.S. taxpayer—can step in. The beneficiaries looking to a bankrupt Pension Benefit Guaranty Corporation to pay their pension claims will be very angry if it doesn't. On the other hand, many of the taxpayers called on to provide the necessary funds don't belong to a private pension plan. The financial burden they will be asked to assume is enormous, and it will benefit only that special group of people who do happen to belong to a private pension plan. The potential strain on the body politic is frightening to contemplate.[5]

## Notes

1. The author is greatly indebted to his co-authors of the book *The Financial Reality of Pension Funding under ERISA* (Dow-Jones, Irwin/Homewood: IL, 1976) Patrick Regan and William Priest, and to Joseph Spigelman, Fischer Black, and William F. Sharpe for their many helpful suggestions.
2. Fischer Black and Myron Scholes, "The Pricing of Options and Corporate Liabilities," *The Journal of Political Economy*, May–June 1973, pp. 637–654.
3. Up to the statutory limits mentioned above, the beneficiary's money is no longer at risk. Up to those limits, the elaborate "fiduciary responsibility" provisions of the act are protecting whoever provides the sponsoring employer with liability insurance, rather than the beneficiary these provisions were presumably intended to protect.
4. What will "net assets" reflect?
   1. corporate assets – corporate liabilities;
   2. corporate assets + pension assets – (corporate liabilities + pension liabilities; or
   3. corporate assets + pension assets + put – (corporate liabilities + pension liabilities)?

   William F. Sharpe points out that if, for purposes of determining this threshold, the equity of the corporation is used, then it is likely to reflect, not the difference between conventional corporate assets and liabilities, but rather (2), or even (3). (Actually, if our interpretation of the way the Guaranty Corporation will behave under the 30 percent rule is correct, in the absence of liability insurance, the value of the pension put will be negligible—hence the real issue is between (1) and (2).

   But, if anything in ERISA is clear, it is the intent of the Congress on this point: The "net assets" *they* had in mind were *conventional* corporate assets less *conventional* corporate liabilities. We can be sure this is what they had in mind because we know that they didn't view pension assets and liabilities as elements in the balance sheet of the employer corporation. Thus the problem that Sharpe identifies is essentially one of measuring the difference intended by Congress—i.e., (1)—when the market value of the equity reflects (3), and when book values of everything but corporate liabilities and the pension assets are commonly so misleading as to be irrelevant. We shall not, however, attempt to solve this measurement problem here.
5. This was pointed out to the author by Dr. Joseph Spigelman.

# CHAPTER 74

# Pension Claims and Corporate Assets

**B**ecause a lender's entire principal is at risk, he cannot safely confine himself to looking at current flows. Rather he must ask how the value of his claim compares with what the underlying security could be sold for in foreclosure. This is true even when his loan is secured by the general credit of the borrower, in which case he must look to the value of the borrowing corporation itself for protection.

For purposes of comparison with the underlying security, the appropriate value of pension beneficiaries' claims is the present value of future benefits, discounted at the riskless interest rate. If the assets available exceed the present value of the claims only when the latter are discounted at a higher rate, the proceeds from the underlying security will prove inadequate—unless the underlying assets are invested aggressively, with the attendant possibility of losses leading to a still greater inadequacy.

The beneficiary of a pension plan that is "underfunded" in this special sense must look beyond the pension assets to the sponsoring corporation for the security underlying his claim. Whether pension claims are "fully secured"—as opposed to "fully funded"—depends on whether the corporation is solvent in terms of an *augmented corporate balance sheet* that includes pension claims, discounted at the riskless rate, as a corporate liability and pension assets, valued at market, as a corporate asset.

> *The book value of a common stock was originally the most important element in its financial exhibit. It was supposed to show the value of the shares in the same way a merchant's balance sheet shows him the value of his business. This idea has almost completely disappeared from the financial horizon. The value of a company's assets as carried in its balance sheet has lost practically all its significance. This change arose from the fact, first, that the value of the fixed assets, as stated, frequently bore no relationship to the actual cost and, second, that in an even larger proportion of cases these values bore no relationship to the figure at which they could be sold or the figure which would be justified by the earnings* (Graham and Dodd).[1]

The potential burden of the pension plan is important.[2] But *how* important and *who* bears the burden? That depends on how pension claims are treated. We

Coauthored with P. J. Regan and W. W. Priest.

are fully aware that, before ERISA, a pension beneficiary's legal claim was against the pension fund and not the assets of the employer corporation. Yet, in practice, the system generally functioned as if the claim did extend to corporate assets. The beneficiary expected sufficient employer contributions to fund his or her claim, and society expected the company to pay such claims as they fell due.

On the other hand, the pension beneficiary's claim was not a conventional lender's claim against the corporation. Until ERISA, it was virtually ignored by corporate lenders and security analysts (as we shall see, for good reason). With ERISA they can no longer afford to do so. But to understand why, we must first understand the nature of a lender's claim against a corporation:

1. Because a lender's entire principal, as well as current interest, is at risk, a lender cannot safely confine himself to looking at current flows (e.g., to comparing the annual interest expense or the debt service to earnings before interest and taxes). The basic question of security for a lender is one of stocks rather than flows.
2. The lender must ask himself: How does the value of the lender's claim compare with what the underlying security could be sold for in foreclosure? If we assume that markets are reasonably efficient, then current market prices will be useful guides in answering this question.
3. This is true even when the loan in question is secured by the general credit of the borrower, in which case it is the value of the borrowing corporation itself to which the lender must look for protection. If the lender's claim is junior to other claims on the general credit, then it is the value of the corporation *less* the value of the senior claims to which the lender must look.
4. The market value of a corporation fluctuates from day to day. This does not diminish the relevance of current market value for the lender, because this value impounds everything known about the borrower, including all past market values. This does raise the possibility, however, that *future* market values will be less than the current market value—a possibility that constitutes the fundamental risk for a lender.
5. In bankruptcy, a borrower will sometimes be worth more as a going concern, sometimes more with his assets liquidated piecemeal. It may or may not be true that market value reflects the worth of the firm on a going-concern rather than a piecemeal basis, but the value relevant to creditors (i.e., the greater of these two values) will never be *less* than the market value.

How much his claim is really worth (as opposed to its cost or its face value) is of critical importance to the lender. But what is the relevance of this question for the executive of the borrowing corporation?

In arm's-length dealing, a rational lender will be unwilling to accommodate a borrower unless the value of the claim created by the loan exceeds the amount of the loan. But the corporation's ability to borrow is measured by the lender's willingness to lend. The value of the residual equity remaining after *existing* lenders' claims are deducted measures what the corporation can give *future* lenders in return for still further loans to the corporation. Thus the residual equity at market value is an upper limit on the corporation's as yet untapped borrowing power—a number of more than token interest to corporate executives. Since this number fluctuates unpredictably from day to day, the corporation's future borrowing power is to this extent also unpredictable.

In sum, although there are several ways to view the worth of the assets underlying claims on a corporation, there is only one pertinent way—market value. An asset is worth only what a willing buyer will pay for it. It is the relevant number even though it depends in part on economic and market forces wholly external to the assets being valued.

Whether the security in question is an entire firm or a specific asset, accounting book value will rarely, if ever, be superior to current market value as an estimate of what a lender could sell his security for, if he were to foreclose today. Book value is irrelevant, for it is an accountant's concept based on an entirely different premise— that of historical cost. The accountant's principal concern is the amortization of cost over the useful life of the asset, which rarely relates to economic reality. When valuing pension claims and assets—and particularly in making the actuarial interest assumption—the actuaries tend to assume a correlation between past returns and future returns, applying "smoothing techniques" to the valuation of pension portfolios, and basing their assumptions about future portfolio returns on past history. Yet, almost all studies of financial markets indicate that there is no correlation between historical returns and future returns and that asset prices tend to fluctuate unpredictably.[3] Because of the unpredictable character of market value fluctuations, today's value is the best basis for an estimate of tomorrow's value, and so on.

In a period of rising interest rates companies often take advantage of differences between book and market values and reduce debt outstanding by purchasing in the open market their own bonds selling at deep discounts. In 1973 and 1974, companies such as General Host, United Brands, and Western Union engineered debenture swaps that required minimal cash outlays but cleared the books of millions of dollars of debt. In June 1973, Western Union offered holders of its 5-1/4 percent debentures $100 cash and $560 principal amount of a new 10-3/4 percent debenture for each $1,000 principal amount of their 5-1/4 percent debentures. Because the market value of the latter was only $570 at the time of the offering, eager bondholders swapped $62 million of the old bonds for six million in cash and $35 million of the new bonds. In effect, Western Union wrote down some of its outstanding debt from book to market value, and thereby reduced its debt load by $21 million.

## THE PENSION BURDEN PRIOR TO ERISA

Since corporate pension assets were commonly invested at least in part in risky assets (i.e., common stocks), were the beneficiaries automatically in jeopardy?

Consider the analogy between pension beneficiaries and bank deposits. Loan defaults occur, and the rate of default is sensitive to economic and market conditions overall, so that even a highly diversified loan portfolio is risky. Yet in a properly run bank, depositors' claims can truly be said to be virtually riskless—even in the absence of a Federal Deposit Insurance Corporation. The reason is that a well-run bank maintains equity capital sufficiently large in relation to its deposits to absorb any losses incurred in the loan portfolio.

In similar fashion, the corporation can encourage risk-taking in its pension portfolio without jeopardizing the beneficiaries as long as:

**EXHIBIT 74.1**

Augmented Balance Sheet
(All Assets at Current Market Value)

| Assets | Liabilities |
| --- | --- |
| Pension portfolio | Present value of pension obligations |
| Corporate assets | Corporate liabilities |
| | Corporate equity* (plugged figure) |

*Because equity is a residual, it will generally be different for the augmented and original corporate balance sheets.

1. Pension beneficiaries are considered to have a claim on the general credit of the corporation in the event that assets in the pension portfolio prove inadequate.
2. The going-concern value of the corporation is adequate to meet the pension and other claims.

Whether the second condition is satisfied is most easily determined in terms of what we may call the *augmented corporate balance sheet* (see Exhibit 74.1), which includes pension and corporate assets, and pension and corporate liabilities.[4] On the left-hand side of the balance sheet we have the assets of the corporation—measured, however, at market rather than book value and augmented by the current market value of the pension portfolio. On the right-hand side of the balance sheet we have the usual claims of corporate creditors, but augmented by the present value of the pension obligations. In the augmented balance sheet the residual equity available to corporate shareholders is the margin of protection for the pension beneficiaries. (The introduction of the pension assets on the left side and the present value of pension claims on the right will generally change the residual equity.)

The key to interpreting the augmented balance sheet is the present value of the pension claims. The rate at which future obligations are discounted back to the present is critical. The appropriate discount rate is the riskless interest rate. If one considers that the corporation has no obligation to protect pension beneficiaries against inflation, then the appropriate discount rate is the rate on government obligations of comparable maturity. If, on the other hand, one considers that the current statement of future pension obligations is really a statement expressed in current dollars of future obligations, the real value of which is understood to be fixed, then the appropriate discount rate is the riskless interest rate with inflationary expectations removed—a rate commonly estimated at roughly 3 percent. A more common way to take inflationary expectations into account is to adjust both the wage and asset return assumptions. It is critical, however, that the gap between the wage and return assumptions not exceed three percentage points, for the reason cited previously. Thus, a company that uses a 6 percent interest rate assumption should apply at least a 3 percent wage assumption, so as to maintain the 3 percent spread.[5]

The present value that results from discounting at the appropriate rate is an estimate of the market value of the assets on which the beneficiaries must have a claim if they are not to be subjected to investment risk. If the assets available exceed the present value of future pension claims only when the latter are discounted at a higher rate, the expected proceeds from the assets will fail to meet the claims unless the assets are invested aggressively, with the attendant possibility of loss. Because the riskless rate represents the highest return one can be certain of getting, it enables us to calculate the magnitude of current pension assets necessary to *guarantee* that future obligations can be met.

Under defined benefit pension plans, the corporation guarantees, not its contributions, but the payment of the future obligations. The only way this guarantee can be meaningful is if the assets available to meet these obligations exceed this magnitude *at every point in time*. Any corporation that is insolvent in the sense of the augmented corporate balance sheet is imposing risks on the beneficiaries for which they are unlikely to get fully rewarded.

Unlike conventional corporate creditors, pension beneficiaries are not in a position to force reorganization of the corporation whenever the margin is threatened by suspending their willingness to lend. Hence pension beneficiaries have been virtually powerless to prevent employers from sliding into insolvency in this sense—even though in some cases it ultimately prevented them from collecting their pension benefits.

## A PRACTICAL EXAMPLE

Consider the application of the augmented balance sheet to a real, though slightly disguised, example. Exhibit 74.2 displays the conventional corporate balance sheet of firm ABC, with all figures at book value. The market value balance sheet, shown in Exhibit 74.3, is the second step. By adding stockholders' equity ($717.8 million) and long-term debt ($592 million), both at market value, to current liabilities ($359.5 million), we have the market value of the right-hand side of the balance sheet ($1,699.3 million). Since current assets are essentially valued at market (the inventory question aside), we can subtract the current asset total ($694.1 million) from the sum that appears on the right-hand side of the balance sheet to derive the implied market value of all noncurrent assets (in this case, largely plant and equipment, equal to $975.2 million). These changes are reflected in Exhibit 74.3.

To that balance sheet we now add the market value of the pension fund as an asset ($421.5 million) and the present value of the pension obligations as a liability ($1,070 million). To make the balance sheet balance, we then adjust the market value for the stockholders' equity downward (by $648.5 million) to reflect the difference between the market value of the pension fund and the present value of the pension obligation. The shrinkage in the equity section of the balance sheet is striking; nearly 90 percent of the market value of the company on 12/31/75 was accounted for by the unfunded vested pension obligation. Moreover, the debt-to-equity ratio rises from 0.48 to 1.00 in Exhibit 78.2 to 0.82 to 1.00 in Exhibit 74.3 and finally to 8.5 to 1.00 in Exhibit 74.4. The augmented balance sheet illustrates the considerable increase in leverage that results if pension obligations are treated like conventional corporate liabilities.

The framework of the augmented balance sheet enables us to understand why, for many weak companies with poorly funded pension plans, the pension claim can be worth much less than its face value. Because the market value of the underlying assets is inadequate, the face value of the pension claim overstates its true economic

```
                        ABC CORPORATION
                      Augmented Balance Sheet
                        December 31, 1975
                   (all figures in millions of dollars)

    Assets                        Liabilities and Stockholders' Equities

Current assets . . . . . . . . . . . . . . . . .$ 694.1    Current liabilities . . . . . . . . . . . . . . . . . .$  359.5
                                                           Long-term debt . . . . . . . . . . . . . . . . .    630.3
Fixed assets . . . . . . . . . . . . . . . . . . .1,601.7  Stockholders' equity* . . . . . . . . . . . . . . .1,306.0
    Total assets . . . . . . . . . . . . . . . . . $2,295.8    Total Liabilities and
                                                               Stockholders' Equity . . . . . . . . . .$2,295.8

* Twenty-three million common shares outstanding.
```

**EXHIBIT 74.2**

```
                        ABC CORPORATION
                          Balance Sheet
                        December 31, 1975
                   (all figures in millions of dollars)

    Assets                        Liabilities and Stockholders' Equity

Current assets . . . . . . . . . . . . . . . . .$ 694.1    Current liabilities . . . . . . . . . . . . . . . . . .$  359.5
                                                           Long-term debt (m.v.) . . . . . . . . . . . . . .    592.0
Fixed assets . . . . . . . . . . . . . . . . . . . . . 975.2  Stockholders' equity (m.v.)* . . . . . . . . . . .    717.8
    Total assets . . . . . . . . . . . . . . . . . $1,669.3    Total Liabilities and
                                                               Stockholders' Equity
                                                               (m.v.) . . . . . . . . . . . . . . . . . . . . . . .$1,669.3

* Market price of common stock 12/31/75 was $33 per share.
```

**EXHIBIT 74.3**

```
                        ABC CORPORATION
                      Augmented Balance Sheet
                        December 31, 1975
                   (all figures in millions of dollars)

    Assets                        Liabilities and Stockholders' Equity

Pension fund assets . . . . . . . . . . . . . . . . .$  421.5   Present value of vested
Current assets . . . . . . . . . . . . . . . . . . . . . . 694.1   pension liabilities* . . . . . . . . . . . . . . . .$1,070.0
Fixed assets . . . . . . . . . . . . . . . . . . . . . . . 975.2   Current liabilities. . . . . . . . . . . . . . . . . . .    359.5
                                                                  Long-term debt . . . . . . . . . . . . . . . . . .    592.0
                                                                  Stockholders' equity . . . . . . . . . . . . . . .     69.3
    Total assets . . . . . . . . . . . . . . . . . . $2,090.8      Total Liabilities and
                                                                   Stockholders' Equity . . . . . . . . . .$2,090.8

* Note: The present value of this obligation no doubt would be substantially greater if one were to use the risk-free rate as the discount rate
applied to the gross vested liability.
```

**EXHIBIT 74.4**

value. Because a key element is still missing, however, this framework does not yet enable us to determine the economic value of a pension claim.

## Notes

1. Benjamin Graham and David L. Dodd, *Security Analysis* (New York: McGraw-Hill Book Co., 1940). pp. 573–74.
2. See Patrick J. Regan. "Potential Corporate Liabilities under ERISA," *Financial Analysts Journal* (March–April 1976). pp. 26–32.
3. In an efficient market where information is freely available, the market price of a security can be expected to approximate its "intrinsic" value because of competition among investors. Intrinsic values can change as a result of new information. If, however, there is only gradual propagation of new information and awareness of its implications, past asset price changes will be correlated with future ones. If the adjustment to information is virtually instantaneous, successive price changes will be random.

   Random does not mean uncaused; nor does it mean that returns on average will be zero. Historically, returns have been randomly distributed around a nonzero mean—something akin to a coin so constructed that on average heads come up six times in ten, but with the probability of a head on any loss totally unaffected by the outcome of previous tosses. We are not concerned with the average magnitude of price changes, only their sequence.

   For further discussion, see the following: James Lorie and Mary Hamilton, *The Stock Market—Theories and Evidence* (Homewood, Ill.: Richard D. Irwin, Inc., 1973); and Richard A. Brealey, *An Introduction to Risk and Return from Common Stocks* (MIT Press, 1969; 3d printing, 1972).
4. The augmented balance sheet presentation here recapitulates Walter Bagehot, "Risk in Corporate Pension Funds," *Financial Analysts Journal* (January–February 1972). Walter Bagehot is the pseudonym of one of the authors of this book.
5. Some companies argue that the riskless rate for them is the rate guaranteed by major insurance companies. Indeed, several firms noted in their 1974 annual reports that their unfunded vested pension liabilities would have been much smaller if they had liquidated the pension assets and used the proceeds to purchase contracts from insurance companies. The latter were able to guarantee annual rates of 8 to 9 percent only because bond yields were in the 9 to 10 percent range, implying expected rates of inflation of 6 to seven percent. To be sure, if a plan terminates, the dollar value of pension claims is frozen, and no adjustment in the nominal value of the claim for depreciation in the value of the dollar subsequent to termination is required. If, on the other hand, the plan does not terminate, it is usually the real, rather than the nominal, value of the claim that must be paid. Thus, the insurance contract is more likely to cover the ultimate value of the claim if termination occurs soon enough to prevent the nominal value of the claim from reflecting the full impact of inflation.

# Ten

# Cases

The purpose of the case method is to teach students to make connections that others don't see—a valuable skill for the administrator. Because I came from a family of doctors, I had to work harder than my classmates to acquire this skill. But when I graduated, three of my professors asked me to stay on and write cases. I've never regretted choosing for my mentor, the late, great Robert N. Anthony.

J.L.T.

# CHAPTER 75

# Feathered Feast

**F**eathered Feast is a case about disclosure—about the relation between the reporting accountant and the outside user and about the framework within which these professionals perform mutually complementary roles. Like all cases, it confers little or no insight on those who merely read it. Rather, one has to live the case—to feel the frustration and anguish of the protagonist, Shepard Saunders.

Background readings for Feathered Feast include "The Trouble with Earnings" (*Financial Analysts Journal*, September–October 1972) and "A Hard Look at Traditional Disclosure" (*Financial Analysts Journal*, January–February 1993).

## FEATHERED FEAST, INC.

In May 1993, Shepard Saunders, manager of the Amalgamated Iceman's Pension Fund, was reviewing certain purchases that, in retrospect, had not worked out as successfully as he had originally hoped. Among these was Feathered Feast, Inc., purchased for the fund in December 1991.[1]

Feathered Feast, Inc. (FF) was at that time one of a number of rapidly growing fast-food chains specializing in fried chicken. FF was distinguished by the fact that, instead of selling franchises, it retained complete control of all FF retail outlets, owning them outright. Management argued that outright ownership gave them better control over the quality of the final product. But outright ownership, together with management's effort to keep pace with its rapidly growing competition, had also led to a heavy demand for funds.

Despite FF's rapid growth, its management had controlled costs very successfully, maintaining profit margins virtually constant until 1992. In order to conserve funds, management had subcontracted the warehousing, distribution, and food-preparation functions. New funds were mainly used for the construction of new outlets, which were built on leased land.

Each outlet was basically a standardized, sheet-metal structure fabricated in the shape of a giant chicken, with integral refrigeration, deep-fry vats, and warming ovens. Standing nearly 30 feet high, these structures served to excite the eating

---

Copyright © CFA Institute. Reprinted from the *Financial Analysts Journal* with permission. November–December 1993.

**EXHIBIT 75.1**   Foresight Depreciation and Profit Analysis for Feathered Feast
(dollars in millions)

|                              | 1987  | 1988 | 1989 | 1990 | 1991 (est.) |
|------------------------------|-------|------|------|------|-------------|
| Net Income (after taxes)     | $58   | 64   | 71   | 78   | 85          |
| Net Income Plus Depreciation | $100  | 110  | 121  | 133  | 146         |
| Dividends                    | $50   | 55   | 60   | 67   | 73          |
| Capital Investment           | $-    | 50   | 55   | 60   | 67          |
| Gross Plant                  | $500  | 550  | 605  | 665  | 732         |
| Dividends/Net Income         | 0.86  | 0.86 | 0.85 | 0.86 | 0.86        |

public's interest in FF's principal product, the Featherburger. They were, in fact, rapidly becoming a familiar sight along heavily traveled suburban arteries when fast-food retailing margins collapsed in 1992.

The shock and disappointment of FF shareholders was heightened by the fact that, until that time, FF's profit performance had been spectacular (see Exhibit 75.1). It was, in fact, the profit performance that had induced Shepard Saunders to "swing a little bit," as the institutional salesman from the First Hoboken Corporation had put it, cashing in Treasury bills amounting to roughly 5 percent of the fund's portfolio and devoting the proceeds to FF shares.

The salesman from First Hoboken had explained why Feathered Feast, selling at 40 times earnings, was a bargain: Since the company, with its aggressive merchandising and innovative product concept, had burst onto the fast-food service scene in 1987, earnings had grown steadily at 10 percent per year (see Exhibit 75.1). The performance was all the more impressive because, as the First Hoboken research report had made clear, the quality of earnings was high. The growth was entirely genuine, internal, organic growth, unadulterated by "dirty pooling" acquisitions. There were no franchise contracts to be taken into sales at inflated figures. Depreciation was conservative: The retail structures were fully depreciated in 12 years on a straight-line basis, despite the fact that, with proper maintenance, they would easily last 40 or 50 years.

In view of this rapid yet steady growth, coupled with the demonstrably high quality of earnings, a discount rate (total return) of 12 percent was surely conservative. Feathered Feast had consistently succeeded in paying out over 85 percent of its earnings in dividends, and it had achieved this high dividend payout without borrowing to finance its rapid expansion. Using the famous Gordon-Shapiro formula to translate these assumptions about growth rate, discount rate and dividend payout rate into an estimate of the investment value of Feathered Feast (see Exhibit 75.2), the salesman had argued that Feathered Feast was worth at least a price/earnings ratio of 43, in contrast to the ratio of 40, at which it was selling in December of 1991.[2] Although Saunders had never entirely bought the salesman's argument that these achievements made Feathered Feast the "bluest of the blue chips," he had been prepared to believe that it was a far sounder investment than many of the "story stocks" that lacked its tangible assets and record of solid earnings growth.

Shepard Saunders' first inkling that all was not well with FF came when he read in the *Wall Street Journal* that FF was defaulting on some of the lease contracts for retail sites (these contracts had 12 years' duration, with subsequent options to renew).

**EXHIBIT 75.2** Salesman's Estimate of the Investment Value of Feathered Feast (year-end 1991)

*Basic Assumptions*

| | |
|---|---|
| Five-Year Growth Rate (see Exhibit 75.1) | 10% |
| Discount Rate | 12% |

*Dividend Payout Detail*

| | |
|---|---|
| Depreciation (12 years, straight-line) | 5/12 of gross |
| Earnings after Depreciation | 7/12 of gross |
| Cash Investment | 6/12 of gross |
| Cash Available for Dividends | 6/12 of gross |
| Dividends/Earnings | 6/7 of net |

*Note:* The Gordon-Shapiro Formula is:

$$Price/Earnings\ Ratio = \frac{Dividend\ Payout\ Fraction}{Discount\ Rate - Growth\ Rate}$$

$$= \frac{6/7}{0.12 - 0.10}$$

$$= \frac{0.86}{0.02} = \underline{43.0}$$

Declining unit volume and cut-throat price cutting quickly transformed formerly profitable outlets into money losers. The problem, which appeared first in California and then spread across the country, was—at least in hindsight—clearly excess capacity. At the end of 1992, most of FF's retail outlets were barely covering out-of-pocket costs of operation. Unable to cover corporate overhead costs, FF auctioned off its assets for scrap value.

Although most of FF's competition had encountered the same problem at about the same time, it was hard to understand how a company that sold at 40 times earnings one year could be broke the next. In his attempt to understand why Feathered Feast had been such a disappointment, Saunders developed the figures shown in Exhibit 75.3. He noted that, by 1992, Feathered Feast's existing outlets, being scarcely able to cover out-of-pocket operating costs, were essentially worthless. That meant, he reasoned, that the outlets that came into operation at the beginning of 1987 had, at least in hindsight, a five-year economic life. In similar fashion, he reasoned that the outlets that went into operation in 1988 had a four-year economic life, and so forth. Using these new assumptions about the economic lives of units coming into operation in each of the years from 1987 through 1991, Saunders recalculated earnings after depreciation (see Exhibit 75.3).

When depreciation was adjusted with the benefit of hindsight, Feathered Feast still displayed a rapid earnings growth rate—but the earnings and the growth were negative.

If Exhibit 75.3 rather than Exhibit 75.1 represented the true earnings history for Feathered Feast, Saunders reasoned, then it had not been worth 43 times 1991 earnings (estimated) in December 1991. But it had not been until 1992 when fast-food margins collapsed, that it became clear that Exhibit 75.3 was a better representation of the earnings history than Exhibit 75.1.

**EXHIBIT 75.3**  Hindsight Depreciation and Profit Analysis for Feathered Feast (dollars in millions)

|  | 1987 | 1988 | 1989 | 1990 | 1991 (est.) |
|---|---|---|---|---|---|
| Gross Plant | $500 | 550 | 605 | 665 | 732 |
| New Investment | $– | 50 | 55 | 60 | 67 |
| Restated Depreciation | $100 | 112 | 131 | 161 | 228 |
| Net Plant | $400 | 338 | 262 | 161 | 0 |
| Net Income (after taxes plus depreciation) | $100 | 110 | 121 | 133 | 146 |
| Depreciation | $100 | 112 | 131 | 161 | 228 |
| Net Income | $0 | (2) | (10) | (28) | (82) |

Perhaps Saunders was misusing historical earnings data. Perhaps he didn't understand what the data meant. He decided to go to a well-recognized accountant, someone who had given a lot of thought to the objectives of financial statements and the conceptual framework for accounting. The obvious choice was the noted accounting theorist, Stamford Ridges. Saunders was delighted when Ridges granted him an interview. A transcript of Saunders' questions and Ridges' answers follows.

**Saunders:** Was I wrong to rely on the earnings history of Feathered Feast in estimating the value of its common stock?

**Ridges:** Earnings for an enterprise for a period measured by accrual accounting are generally considered to be the most relevant indicator of relative success or failure of the earnings process of an enterprise in bringing in needed cash. Measures of periodic earnings are widely used by investors, creditors, security analysts, and others.[3]

**Saunders:** Is it appropriate to extrapolate historical earnings trends into the future?

**Ridges:** The most important single factor determining a stock's value is now held to be the indicated future earning power—that is, the estimated average earnings for a future span of years. Intrinsic value would then be found by first forecasting this earning power and then multiplying that prediction by an appropriate "capitalization factor." "Earning power" means the long-term average ability of an enterprise to produce earnings and is estimated by normalizing or averaging reported earnings and projecting the resulting trend into the future.

**Saunders:** My experience with Feathered Feast suggests that earnings, earnings trend, and estimates of investment value based on these numbers can be very sensitive to the life of fixed assets.

**Ridges:** Assets are not inherently tangible or physical. An asset is an economic *quantum*. It may be attached to or represented by some physical object, or it may not. One of the common mistakes we all tend to make is that of attributing too much significance to the molecular concept of property. A brick wall is nothing but mud on edge if its capacity to render economic service has disappeared; the molecules are still there, and the wall may be as solid as ever, but the value has gone.

**Saunders:** So it's the economic, rather than the physical, life that matters. How is the outside user to know whether reported earnings are true earnings and reported earnings trend true trend unless he knows the economic life of major assets?

**Ridges:** The success or failure of a business enterprise's efforts to earn more cash than it spends on resources can be known with certainty only when the enterprise is liquidated.

**Saunders:** How, then, does the accountant arrive at the figures he reports?

**Ridges:** In the purest, or ideal, form of accrual accounting, sometimes called direct valuation, each noncash asset represents expected future cash receipts and each liability represents expected future cash outlays.

**Saunders:** Wouldn't I be better off if I focused on financial data that were untainted by the subjectivity of an accountant's expectations?

**Ridges:** The standard of verifiability is a necessary attribute of accounting information, allowing persons who have neither access to the underlying records nor the competence to audit them to rely on those records.

**Saunders:** If I wanted to base my analysis on numbers relatively free from the influence of an accountant's expectations regarding the future, what numbers might I use?

**Ridges:** The fundamental concern of investors and creditors with an enterprise's cash flows might suggest that financial statements that report cash receipts and cash disbursements of an enterprise during a period would provide the most useful information for investor and creditor analyses. That information is readily available, can be reported on a timely basis at minimum cost, and is essentially factual because it involves a minimum of judgment and assumption.

**Saunders:** Would you mind telling me again why outside users like myself are supposed to pay so much attention to earnings?

**Ridges:** The relation between cash flows to an enterprise and the market price of its securities, especially that of common stock, is complex, and there are significant gaps in the knowledge of how the market determines the prices of individual securities. Moreover, the prices of individual securities are affected by numerous other factors that affect market prices in general. Nevertheless, the expected cash inflows to the enterprise are the ultimate source of value for its securities, and major changes in expectations about these cash inflows immediately affect market prices significantly.

Instrinsic value is the value that the security ought to have and will have when other investors have the same insight and knowledge as the analyst. Because the intrinsic value of a stock usually cannot be measured directly, given the uncertainty of its future cash dividends and market prices, investors and security analysts commonly attempt to estimate it indirectly or to estimate some surrogate for intrinsic value, such as what a stock's price ought to be in a price/earnings ratio. The procedure involves estimating average earnings for a future span of years—the indicated future average earning power—and multiplying that prediction by an appropriate "capitalization" to obtain intrinsic value. For example, estimated average earnings per share may be multiplied by a price/earnings ratio to obtain a price that reflects intrinsic value. If that price is higher than the market price, the analysis advises the investor to buy; if it is less than the market price, the analysis advises the investor to sell.

**Saunders:** So that's why you accountants place heavy emphasis on reported earnings.

**Ridges:** Decisions about what information should be included in financial statements and what information should be excluded or summarized should depend primarily on what is relevant to investors' and creditors' decisions.

Sensing that he had gone about as far as he could go with Ridges, Saunders thanked him and brought the interview to a close. Although he found Ridges' answers enigmatic and mildly confusing, he had the feeling that they held the key to his problems with Feathered Feast.

In a few days, Saunders would be meeting with the trustees of the Amalgamated Iceman's Pension Fund to explain its investment performance since 1991. They had selected him to manage the portfolio largely because of his reputation for emphasizing tangible earning assets, rather than "stories." He was sure the trustees would ask him to defend the Feathered Feast decision and to explain the subsequent investment disappointment. Should he show them Exhibit 75.1 and 75.2? Or should he show them Exhibit 75.3? Saunders was uncertain exactly what to say.

## QUESTIONS

1. What accounts for the difference between the earnings pictures presented in Exhibits 75.1 and 75.3?
2. Was the earnings history of Feathered Feast as presented in Exhibit 75.1 really history?
3. Does Exhibit 75.1 present a true earnings picture for Feathered Feast?
4. In terms of the information available in December 1991, was Feathered Feast a growth company?
5. What information available in December 1991 should Saunders have relied on in his assessment of the investment worth of Feathered Feast?

### Notes

1. Feathered Feast is a case prepared by Jack Treynor.
2. Professors Gordon and Shapiro are the authors of a widely used formula according to which the appropriate price/earnings ratio for a common stock is equal to the proportion of earnings paid out in dividends divided by the appropriate discount rate (or total return) minus the expected growth rate.
3. All of Ridges' answers are excerpted, out of context and with malice aforethought, from two documents—*Tentative Conclusions on Objectives of Financial Statements of Business Enterprises* and (the discussion memorandum) *Conceptual Framework for Financial Accounting and Reporting*, published December 2, 1976, by the Financial Accounting Standards Board.

# CHAPTER 76

# An Extraordinarily Cheap Trade

Surely there was something to learn from the experience. The stock had collapsed dramatically right after his purchase for Buckingham Fund. Had he, Zoltan Kulak, the managing partner of Buckingham Advisors, expected too much from Dynamax?

Buckingham prided itself on its imagination, its special insights, its ability to see the future before investors who lacked its boldness could act. When Buckingham's pharmaceuticals analyst learned that the company's dynamic CEO, Felton Spackling, was presenting an ambitious plan for nationwide promotion of a product that had previously been a cult favorite of health clubs and fitness emporiums, he tried to gather as much information as he could. The promotions would feature Spackling, a former NFL linebacker who, with his booming voice and erect posture, was the living embodiment of the benefits of Dynamax.

No one knew exactly why the proprietary drug product was so effective. But Buckingham's analyst had satisfied himself that it contained no amphetamines. Spackling was no Dr. Feelgood. Nor was Dynamax another Hadacol; in fact, it contained no alcohol whatsoever.

Kulak knew that the prospect of a nationwide promotion would be exciting to investors. His trader had advised him that the stock was trading at 5-$\frac{1}{2}$ bid, 6-$\frac{1}{2}$ ask. Because speed was important, he was prepared to pay more than the asking price in order to acquire 500,000 shares. But Kulak instructed his trader to begin with a limit order, bidding 5-$\frac{1}{2}$ for 100,000 shares.

When, contrary to their expectations, the order executed quickly, Kulak suggested another order for 200,000 at 5-$\frac{1}{2}$. When the elated trader reported that this order had also executed quickly. Kulak hesitated.

His hesitation had been wise, Kulak reflected. With the stock currently trading at 1-$\frac{1}{4}$ bid, 2-$\frac{1}{4}$ ask, his shrewd hesitation had saved Buckingham's shareholders a lot of money.

His pharmaceuticals analyst had ultimately pieced together the real story. After Spackling's voice failed him during the presentation, he had stumbled badly coming down from the podium. Several directors had excused themselves from the boardroom.

Now, several months later, Spackling's obituary in the *New York Times* reminded Kulak of the Dynamax investment. Luck was a big part of investing, as he often cautioned his shareholders. It did not pay to dwell on the bad luck. And, Kulak told himself, let us face it: Dynamax was an extraordinarily cheap trade.

---

Reprinted from the *Journal of Investment Management*, Vol. 1, No. 1, 2003.

## QUESTIONS

1. Is it possible for a trade to be too easy?
2. Bad research cannot be worse than random. But some funds underperform their passive benchmark consistently. Why?
3. For such funds, what is the cost of failing to trade?
4. Some investment insights are more persuasive, more compelling, than others. Should such differences affect the trading decision?
5. Was Dynamax an unlucky investment or an expensive trade?
6. If you could change just one thing about the way Zoltan Kulak manages money, what would it be?

CHAPTER **77**

# The Gauntlet

The morning meeting was an institution at Grosvenor Capital. Each analyst and portfolio manager had his (her) appointed place at the long boardroom table. Each was given the opportunity to speak, starting with the most junior and proceeding around the table to the most senior.

It was, as the professional staff all recognized, an opportunity to make an impression. On the other hand, many a junior analyst's brain child had failed to make it around the table. One way to make an impression, after all, was to point out flaws an idea's author had failed to recognize.

The whole point of the exercise, of course, was to screen out all but the most practical of the staff's ideas. In this way, Grosvenor minimized the risk of trading on ideas that were conceptually flawed.

Grosvenor's holdings were often popular with other investment institutions who were, in effect, expressing a vote of confidence in Grosvenor's judgment. But, of course, when a popular idea was invalidated by developments none of these investors had anticipated, the price impact was dramatic.

To demonstrate the soundness of Grosvenor's approach to clients, senior management had asked Diogenes Smith, a young addition to the professional staff, to compare the performance of accepted ideas and rejected ideas. His preliminary review had yielded two surprises:

1. The "practical" ideas Grosvenor accepted got into market price almost before the firm could trade on them.
2. In contrast to the practical ideas, there was almost no market reaction when the rejected ideas failed.

Recognizing that one could easily jump to the wrong conclusion, Smith resolved to broaden his study before seeking an audience with management. But he was uncertain how to proceed.

---

Reprinted from the *Journal of Investment Management,* Vol. 1, No. 2, 2003.
I would like to thank the following people for their input in forming the gauntlet piece: Peter Williamson (discussion leader), Jim Farrell, Bob Hagin, and Walter French.

## QUESTIONS

1. What determines how fast an idea gets into the consensus?
2. Why is it that the prices of the affected stocks do not collapse when the "impractical" ideas fail?
3. How big is the risk in trading in an impractical idea?
4. If one divides the population of investors into *other directed* and *inner directed,* which group will be more successful?
5. Which kind will get promoted at a firm like Grosvenor?
6. What kind of ideas would Grosvenor's clients like?
7. Which kind of investor will Grosvenor's clients be more comfortable with?
8. You are Diogenes Smith, ambitious for advancement and eager to fit in. What do you tell management?

## DISCUSSION

Let

$p$ be the fraction of investors who respond to the new insight and think it is going to succeed,

$g$ the insight's actual degree of success,

$V$ the value of an insight if it succeeds, and

$x$ the price adjustment that reflects the two kinds of active investors: those betting on the success of the new insight and those betting against it.

The former's position is

$$p(V - x)$$

The latter's is

$$-(1 - p)x$$

The market clears when the two active positions sum to zero:

$$p(V - x) - (1 - p)x = 0$$
$$x = pV$$
$$\frac{x}{V} = p$$

Evidently, the fraction of the insight's value already reflected in the share price equals the fraction $p$ of investors who are betting on it.

If in the event the insight actually achieves a fraction $g$ of its anticipated value $V$, then the investor who bet on it realizes $(gV)$ less what he paid $(x)$ or

$$gV - pV = (g - p)V$$

Whether he gains or loses on his bet depends on

$$g - p$$

This suggests that the fraction of investors already on board is as important to the investor as the insight's ultimate degree of success.

To pay off now, an idea must be technically and economically feasible now. Is the economic potential big? Have some tough technological problems been solved? Then, investors can be understandably excited. But it takes only one unsolved problem to defeat (or indefinitely delay) an exciting new idea. And unsolved problems are not solved by appeals to economic arguments: The probability of solution next year (if they are not solved this year) is the same as the probability of a solution this year. A classic example is fusion power: enormous economic potential, safe (no Chernobyls), clean (no radioactive waste), great for the environment (no global warming). When fusion's last problem is ultimately solved, however, investors will be as surprised as everyone else.

These considerations suggest that the gauntlet is probably not very useful for predicting whether a new idea will have an early investment payoff. But it can still be useful for sampling an idea's popularity with investors. The payoff to Grosvenor depends on which way it uses the gauntlet.

Consider the simplified case where the insight either

1. Fails or succeeds ($g = 1$ or $0$), and
2. Is either fully in the price or not in the price ($p = 1$ or $0$). Then, the outcomes are as follows:

|  |  | $p$ | $p$ |
|---|---|---|---|
|  |  | 0 | 1 |
| $g$ | 0 | 0 | −1 |
| $g$ | 1 | 1 | 0 |

If it equates popularity with the gauntlet as measuring the likelihood of success, Grosvenor will bet only when the insight is popular. The table shows that, if the insight nevertheless fails, the best possible outcome is breakeven; the worst is a big loss. If instead Grosvenor interprets popularity with the gauntlet to mean the insight is already in the price, it will bet only when the insight is unpopular. Then, the best outcome is a big gain; the worst is breakeven.

As a device for making investment decisions, the gauntlet is neither good nor bad. But clients may not understand how to use it. Then, the best *marketing* use of the gauntlet may be in direct conflict with the best *investment* use.

But is that a problem? If the clients do not know what the outcome of the gauntlet was, is not the firm then free to make the best investment decision? Young Diogenes should explain to his superiors that he now understands why the gauntlet is such a powerful research tool, that institutional investing is even more subtle than he realized, and that he is thrilled to be associated with a firm that has so much to teach him.

# CHAPTER 78

# A Prudent Man

U nlike many small software companies, Postulation managed its fixed benefit pension fund in house. Assistant Treasurer Neville "Nervous" Nelson was very sensitive to the importance of satisfying the Prudent Man stipulation of ERISA.

He observed what the larger companies in his industry were doing with their pension funds, and then bought (and sold) what they bought (and sold). He had concluded that he was not the only small pension fund manager who was echoing the big funds' trades, because his buy prices were higher and his sell prices were lower.

At an industry trade show, Nelson had confided somewhat apologetically to his counterpart from one of the big firms that he, Nelson, was echoing his counterpart's pension fund trades. But the man had responded very generously, offering to give Nelson monthly updates of his holdings.

Nelson was especially grateful because, as the manager of a small fund, he had relatively limited access to important new research ideas. He knew many of his counterparts in the small companies were eager to find out what the big boys were holding.

> How is Nelson's focus on the Prudent Man requirement affecting his performance?
>
> How is it affecting the "big boys'" performance?
>
> Is Nelson trading prudently?
>
> How grateful should Nelson be?
>
> Is prudent holding consistent with prudent trading?
>
> Which is more important?
>
> Has modern capital theory made the prudent man obsolete, or worse?

---

Reprinted form the *Journal of Investment Management*. Vol. 1, No. 3, 2003.

# CHAPTER 79

# Default—Shawnee Manufacturing

**W**hen he took the job as the loan officer at the Red River Bank, Franklin Shedd had promised himself to bring modern ideas to the lending function. In particular, he was uncomfortable with the bank's traditional classification of loans in its portfolio into Performing and Nonperforming.

Shawnee Manufacturing, for example, was the largest employer in Red River. It had never failed to pay the interest on its revolving line of credit. But demand for Shawnee's products—milking machines and related electrical equipment—was sensitive to the vicissitudes of the dairy industry.

The sensitivity was evident in Shawnee's share price which, in recent years, had fluctuated widely between $25 and last week's close of $2.10. (Using weekly quotes, Shedd estimated a standard deviation around share price change of $10.00.) He recognized that the value of the two million shares outstanding would fluctuate less than the value of Shawnee's assets. But, given even rough indicators of the underlying asset risk, Shedd was troubled by the fact that Shawnee's current borrowings had nearly exhausted its line of credit with the bank ($10,000,000).

The line of credit was coming up for annual review next week. Masten Titus, Shawnee's chairman, was an outspoken and influential member of the bank's board of directors. He was proud of the fact that, although its line of credit had grown rapidly over the years, Shawnee had never defaulted.

## QUESTIONS

1. How much weight should Shedd give to the fact that Shawnee has never missed an interest payment?
2. That Shawnee has never defaulted?
3. How should risk factor into Shedd's lending decisions?
4. Into the bank examiner's determinations?
5. Into the bank's financial reporting?
6. If Titus asks for another increase in Shawnee's line of credit at the annual review, how should Shedd respond?

---

Reprinted from the *Journal of Investment Management*, Vol. 1, No. 4, 2003.

# DEFAULT DISCUSSION

*J. Peter Williamson, Discussion Leader*
*H. Russell Fogler, James H. Scott, Dave E. Tierney*

It is essential for the bank to go into next week's meeting with Titus with a clear-cut decision, presented by the bank's CEO. Shedd will have a busy weekend preparing him for that presentation.

Shedd needs to realize that the proper way to approach his recommendation is in three stages:

1. An analytical stage, considering all the available data
2. A rounded consideration of the human implications of the decision to Shawnee's stakeholders, the bank, and the town of Red River
3. A creative stage, in which Shedd turns problems into opportunities that will intrigue even Titus

Has the loan to Shawnee degenerated into a "workout?" Shedd should recognize that, if his recommendation is tough on Titus, the bank's CEO will probably identify Shedd as its author. If the boss does make him the goat, his job is probably in jeopardy.

But Shedd's first task is the analytical one. If Red River Bank is the only significant lender to Shawnee (apart from trade creditors) then he cannot look to others to determine whether it is in default. Instead, his analysis must begin with a clear understanding of the concept.

A loan has a value that reflects the borrower's option against the lender. The lender will not renew unless the value of his claim net of the option exceeds the new loan. Because the value of the option increases with time to maturity, a claim approaching maturity is worth more to the lender than the same claim after it is renewed (just before renewal, face value; after renewal, face value less the value of the borrower's new option). So, at renewal, the borrower will experience a cash loss equal to the difference.

Enlarging the borrower's line of credit can be a way of providing the needed cash. Alas, it also increases the value of the borrower's option, hence the size of the crisis at the next renewal. Shawnee can avoid the crisis if it has accumulated enough cash from operations between renewals. Otherwise . . .

## Prudent Man (Third Quarter 2003)—Discussion Notes

Is the Prudent Man just a nonquantitative way of arguing for diversification? For emphasizing the passive part of the portfolio rather than the active? If so, it protects the principal from the agent who gets a reputation as an investment genius if an improbable bet succeeds, while losing someone else's money if it fails.

Nelson's problem is that he can't tell the passive part of the portfolio he is emulating from the active part. So when its active holdings change, he trades, incurring unnecessary costs.

On the other hand, Nelson's trading is improving the performance of the portfolio he is emulating. Over time, this improvement may attract other emulators. It may even persuade the portfolio manager to shift assets away from the passive part of his portfolio, which isn't benefiting from Nelson's trading, to the active part, which is. Ultimately, he may even acquire a reputation for being an investment genius. Then again . . .

# CHAPTER 80

# Public Voting

The San Andreas Club had inserted a proposal into Mountain Lumber's proxy statement to limit its operations to forests below 3,000 feet. It argued that leaves of the aspen above 3,000 feet were the staple diet of the rare Hungarian Bobcat moth. The Prides Crossing Group owned Mountain Lumber's shares in several of its no-load mutual funds, amounting in the aggregate to about 4 percent of the company's equity.

Management knew from previous experience that the San Andreas Club would attack investment institutions that failed to support its proposals in their proxy voting, listing their names in emotional full page ads in the print media. In the past, management had avoided the hassle by selling its shares. But when other complexes did the same with an institutional favorite like Mountain Lumber, their share prices took a beating.

The management of Prides Crossing Group admired Mountain Lumber's management. But the Street was abuzz with rumors that "Chainsaw Chuck" Sylvan, CEO of the Clearcut Corporation, was interested in acquiring Mountain Lumber.

The Prides Crossing management had three choices:

1. Vote for the San Andreas proposal and inflict losses on fund shareholders if the proposal hurts Mountain Lumber's business.
2. Vote against the proposal, and lose some ecology-minded clients.
3. Sell the shares.

## QUESTIONS

1. What will Prides Crossing do?
2. What will other institutional owners of Mountain Lumber do?
3. How will Mountain Lumber's management be spending its time?
4. How much clout does the San Andreas Club have with Mountain Lumber?
5. Will other special-interest groups follow San Andreas Club's example?

## PUBLIC VOTING—DISCUSSION

Environment is an example of a corporate issue that will elicit organized, enthusiastic (vocal?) support for one side and apathy for the other. If management is obliged to

Reprinted from the *Journal of Investment Management*, Vol. 2, No. 1, 2004.

make its vote public, it has to justify voting against the ostensible majority in such cases.

But why, in a country that cherishes the secret ballot, should proxy voting be public? We like the secret ballot, not because it is good for voters, but because it is good for the country. The argument for public voting of proxies has to be that the votes belong to the owner of the shares—not the manager. An obvious problem with this argument: Although the client has entrusted his money to the manager, he does not expect a public justification for every investment decision. If he is willing to entrust his money to the manager, why should he not be willing to entrust his vote?

Prides Crossing's management feared that making their proxy voting positions public would attract more media attention. With more media attention, the issues would be more numerous as well as more controversial. They were thinking of creating a unit, staffed with lawyers, devoted full time to assessing the various kinds of exposure that Prides Crossing was likely to encounter.

The alternative is selling the shares. What would it cost fund shareholders if Prides Crossing sells its positions in Mountain Lumber? Less, if it is not trying to exit the revolving door at the same time as other institutional owners. Surely, it is better to be early than late. Maybe Prides Crossing should sell now, before the issue attracts more public attention. Some of the other fund complexes have itchy trigger fingers. Maybe it is worth a small price penalty to sell quickly.

But every time Prides Crossing sells its position in an embattled portfolio company, the management is nagged by the same troubling question: At what point does selling the shares become *de facto* social investing?

# CHAPTER 81

# Fiduciary Funds

Oscar Johnson was a portfolio manager with Fiduciary Funds, a mutual fund complex. He was pleased when his employer asked him to develop a type of mutual fund that would be new for them. The complex had an investment philosophy that emphasized bargain hunting rather than betting on new investment insights. What his bosses wanted was a global fund, new to them, that would include both

1. An actively managed piece that would be consistent with their investment philosophy
2. A passively managed piece that provided a high degree of diversification

To help organize his ideas, Johnson had drawn up two lists of potential industries:

1. Industries whose market was basically local, whose prosperity was presumably tied to the host country's prosperity. He called these industries "home goods" industries
2. Industries whose market was global. He called these industries "tradable goods" industries

Johnson did not want to rule out any industries that were big and mature enough to have well-developed securities markets. On the other hand, he had several questions he was anxious to resolve:

1. For companies in the same home goods industry, but different countries: if the countries were at different stages of the business cycle, would he encounter timing problems in making value comparisons?
2. Would tradables industries, with their global markets, pose any diversification problems?
3. Some of his shareholders would be nervous about currency risk. Should he hedge
   a. All the non-U.S. positions?
   b. All the non-U.S. home goods positions?
   c. All the non-U.S. tradables funds positions?
   d. None of his positions?

Johnson would be meeting with his bosses next week. He knew they would be curious about his preliminary thinking.

---

Reprinted from the *Journal of Investment Management*, Vol. 2, No. 2, 2004.
I would like to thank the following people for their input in forming this piece: Frank Jones, Ken Barker, Brett Hammond, and Peter Williamson.

## DISCUSSION

A global fund opens up new opportunities for diversification, for investment comparisons, for bets on currencies. Oscar has a lot to think about.

### Active Bets

Bargain hunting is a species of active management in which decisions to buy and sell are based on analysis of a company's investment value. As Sidney Cottle pointed out, such analysis entails *comparison*. If Johnson is going to base the active positions in his global fund on comparisons he should use a single valuation model, rather than different models for different countries. But the valuation model should allow for the differences between home goods industries and tradables industries. The former depend on local economic prospects, the latter on global economic prospects.

### Home Goods Plant versus Tradables Plant

The value of home goods plant, for example, will be driven by local developments in

currency value
central bank policy
inflation
fiscal policy
political climate

On the other hand, the price of a tradable product will be determined globally—by reconciling global supply with global demand. And its manufacturing cost in the different countries should be easy to compare, with one important caveat: Different countries have different real wages. A convenient measure of the difference is the "real exchange rate"—the "nominal," or conventional, exchange rate, adjusted for the two countries' money wages.

### Brand Franchise

Brand franchise is an important source of both value and risk. Not all tradables industries are commodity industries—industries where brand is relatively unimportant. Franchise is intrinsically local, in the sense that its value depends on the prosperity of the country where the franchise is located, rather than where the company's manufacturing plant or headquarters is located. But if the life of franchise is an order-of-magnitude shorter than the life of plant, then their relevant economic prospects may be different even when they are located in the same country.

### Hedging

When the value of the local currency changes, the dollar value of its (tradable) raw materials and tradable products do not change. Only the labor costs of a foreign tradables company change. Currency hedging the investment in such a company can consequently increase, rather than reduce, the exchange risk. And because of interactions with inflation, interest rates, and so forth currency change can have complicated consequences for the local demand for foreign home goods.

Reductions in currency value consequently affect different companies differently—reducing the real wage for tradables manufacturers, and raising the inflation rate, hence dimming local prospects, for home goods plant and franchise. On the other hand, big international companies with assets in lots of foreign countries will be less dependent on particular currencies.

Accumulating inflation will affect the money wage element in the real exchange rate. But the nominal exchange rate is obviously the principal source of sudden changes. Exchange rates and currency values are relative, not absolute, numbers. Do such changes merely *redistribute* the value of tradables plant between countries? Is a global portfolio of tradables plant, which depends on the prospects for global demand, less diversified than a global portfolio of home goods plant, which depends on the prospects for many individual countries?

## Oscar's Options

Clearly one way to address the need for both core and active segments is to use home goods companies for a highly diversified passive core, where investment comparison would not be necessary, and to use tradables companies, which were hard to diversify and easy to compare, for the active segment.

But whatever basic architecture he chooses for the portfolio, Oscar will need expertise on

currencies

countries

industry sectors

companies and their management

Is he going to need subadvisors to complement his own employer's special research strengths? Conceivably, he could divide the responsibilities in various ways:

active—passive

home goods—tradables

plant value—franchise value

local—foreign

Oscar can probably expect to have both active and passive holdings in many of the same countries. Will the client understand what Oscar is doing? Are there different kinds of global equity funds? Will the client understand the differences? And who is Oscar's intended client? How should he market the fund to this client? And the client will probably want him to measure his tracking error. But relative to what? Who is his real competition?

Oscar may want to ask his secretary to hold incoming phone calls while he considers his options.

# CHAPTER 82

# Poosha-Carta Food Stores

The board of Poosha-Carta Food Stores believed that instead of being stampeded into trading its stock by every rumor, by every provocative story in the media, institutional investors would take the time and trouble to understand their business. That's why they wanted to make its stock attractive to institutional investors.

The board had come to the conclusion that one way to increase the stock's appeal to institutions was to give it a stable risk character. But the board split on how to do that. While some argued for maintaining constant leverage, others argued, instead, for maintaining a constant beta. And some board members argued that this was a distinction without a difference—that constant leverage would assure a constant beta.

Expecting that the controversies would come up again at the next board meeting, CFO John Roselli wanted to be ready. To this end he had prepared a list of questions.

Was it really useful to measure leverage in accounting terms—in book values? Unlike book values, market values fluctuated constantly. What would a policy of constant leverage really mean? What is the nature of the link between leverage and beta? Specifically, is it true that constant leverage will produce a constant beta?

## DISCUSSION

Leverage is a simple concept when it is measured using the book values of debt and equity. But if the relevant values are market values, then leverage is not so simple. Instead, it entails two different processes:

1. Random, continuous fluctuations in market values
2. Adjusting transactions that exchange debt for equity, or equity for debt

When the first process moves the company's leverage away from the intended value, management can use the second to bring it back. By the time management has completed the adjusting transaction, however, the randomly fluctuating market values have moved on. Far from being a simple concept, leverage entailed endless pursuit of an elusive target.

The "market" is itself a collection of levered companies. When the general level of stock prices is rising, the "market" is becoming less levered. So, if the ultimate goal

Reprinted from the *Journal of Investment Management*, Vol. 2, No. 3, 2004.

is stabilizing beta, it's not clear that stabilizing leverage is the way to do it. Indeed, stabilizing Poosha-Carta's leverage is almost certain to destabilize its beta.

It is clear that constant leverage is

1. Not a simple idea
2. Not even strictly attainable
3. Probably not even desirable, once one focuses on beta

But most investors probably don't expect either constant leverage or constant beta. Is either goal meaningful enough to preoccupy Poosha-Carta's board?

# CHAPTER 83

# The Fed Watchers

**A**gile Fund promised its shareholders that its managers would make a genuine effort to avoid catastrophic market collapses. To this end, the managers included some high-beta stocks in the portfolio, which they stood ready to sell at the slightest hint of trouble (or buy back at the slightest encouragement).

They combed the media for clues, including data on

jobs

business investment

government fiscal policy

op-ed pieces by prominent economists

consumer spending

inflation

decisions of the Federal Reserve Board

pronouncements of the Fed chairman

The managers had all taken economics courses in college. Their teachers, who divided their time between teaching and Washington, had explained that the private sector was intrinsically unstable and that only a mixed economy with a large government sector had any hope of avoiding periodic collapses.

On the one hand, the managers of Agile Fund were determined to avoid the investment consequences of market collapses for their shareholders. On the other hand, they were equally determined that their shareholders not miss out on the investment consequences of good times.

The managers of Agile Fund knew from bitter experience that the price of avoiding the two kinds of failure was eternal vigilance. Sometimes the various kinds of information would be in conflict. Sometimes information would shift from bullish to bearish, or bearish to bullish in the space of a few hours. Fortunately, their trading desk understood the importance of being able to act quickly and decisively.

The managers paid special attention to the Fed's constant struggle to keep the economy on an even keel—to the decisions of the Federal Reserve Board and the pronouncements of its chairman.

---

Reprinted from the *Journal of Investment Management*, Vol. 2, No. 4, 2004.

## DISCUSSION

1. When does the market react to news about the economy?
2. How will the Fed react to bad news? To good news?
3. What should Agile focus on—the news, or the Fed's reaction to it?
4. If the Fed's action lags the economic news, should Agile attempt to anticipate the Fed?
5. What will the Fed do if its action turns out to be too little? Too much?
6. What is the role of economists in a mixed economy?

# CHAPTER 84

# Betting on Management

At the time it seemed like a good idea to Harley Pinkett, Chairman and CEO of Endless Chain. His executive vice-president and all three group vice presidents had been enthusiastic. The investment bankers who brought the idea to him termed it "bold, visionary" and had called him a "decisive, forward-looking leader" for going ahead. Mary ("Mamie") Persons, the chairman and CEO of Precision Sprocket, was clearly ready to hang up her pedal pushers. But now, three years later, Pinkett was still trying to understand exactly what happened.

Precision Sprocket had a reasonably good track record. And the acquisition had seemed to promise marketing synergies. Who could have foreseen that bicycle chains, which wore out, were sold primarily to repair shops, whereas sprockets, which did not, were sold primarily to manufacturers?

Yet, instead of rising when Pinkett announced the intended acquisition, the share price of Endless Chain had fallen—almost as if the shareholders, most of whom did not know one end of an Allen wrench from the other, had foreseen the problem.

## DISCUSSION

Those who make essential contributions to a company but do not want to bear its risks—including the risk of bad management decisions—are looking for a margin of protection. The purpose of a corporation's equity is to provide that margin. In the long run, good decisions do not reduce the equity. But active investors in the company's stock, who determine its value, are often obliged to evaluate management decisions long before the consequences are clear.

It does not, of course, consume equity to make decisions investors like. The problem is that corporate management and the investors use different decision processes. Consider on one hand the large, public companies where there is little communication between shareholders who have little say over boards of directors, and managers, who own a small fraction of the stock. There are often thousands of active investors with little or no opportunity to confer, so their assessments benefit from Francis Galton's discovery about independently formed opinions.[1] On the other hand, management is a small, closely knit group with a shared culture, deference to authority—the antithesis of Galton's "crowd."

Reprinted from the *Journal of Investment Management*, Vol. 3, No. 1, 2005.

When management bases decisions on its own evaluations of the gain or loss rather than the shareholders' evaluations, projects shareholders like do not get done; projects shareholders dislike do get done. So share value suffers *two* kinds of damage. Consider the following four quadrants.

1. *Quadrant I.* Management approves all projects. Shareholder's evaluation can be more or less favorable than management's but is still positive.
2. *Quadrant II.* Projects management undertakes, but shareholders disapprove. Damaging to share price.
3. *Quadrant III.* Projects shareholders disapprove, but management rejects. No change to share price.
4. *Quadrant IV.* Projects shareholders approve, but management rejects. Damaging to share price.

Whereas Quadrants I and II merely confirm shareholders' expectations, Quadrants II and IV are *bad news* quadrants (Figure 84.1).

Sometimes, however, management knows something the shareholders do not know. Then management can be right even when the shareholders disagree with management. Because shareholders never know how complete their own information is, they have to consider two possibilities:

1. Management is wrong.
2. It has more information.

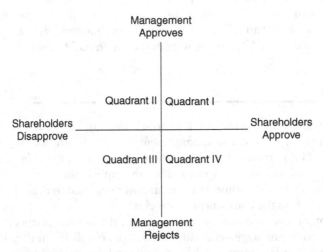

**EXHIBIT 84.1**  The Four Quadrants

They will divide into two groups, depending whether they choose to give management the benefit of a doubt. Some active investors will translate their opinions into action—the first group selling shares, the second group buying—in effect, trading with each other. The skeptics will hurt the share price. When the truth emerges

1. If the skeptics are right, the price will fall further.
2. If the skeptics are wrong, it will rise.

The price action will reward one group and penalize the other.

## Equity and Management's Power

When management's decision is actually justified by private information, wealth will transfer from the first group to the second, reducing the skeptics' future influence on share price. Unlike decisions based on public information which, on the average and over time, can only be a losing game, private information can consequently be a winning game for management.

We see that, with regard to such decisions, management and Wall Street have conflicting objectives. Every action will generate trading between the skeptics and the believers—and that is good for Wall Street. But only actions justified by private information benefit management.

## Note

1. Bernstein, P. (2000). *Against the Gods*. New York: Wiley, pp. 151–152.

# CHAPTER 85

# Financial Literacy

**A**ll the employees of the state had their retirement funds managed by a single entity. Its staff had played an active role in the governance of corporations whose shares it owned on behalf of state employees. One of its frequent complaints was that most members of corporate boards did not have the training or background to understand the impact of corporate decisions on the shareholders.

In order to increase awareness of the problem, the staff had approached business faculties in the colleges around the state asking for their suggestions regarding what board members of publicly held corporations ought to know. From their suggestions, the staff had compiled a tentative series of questions.

## DISCUSSION

1. Name the three potential nonfinancial sources of a company's investment value.
2. What market statistic is the best measure of investors' expectations for inflation?
3. What are the two macroeconomic variables with the broadest investment impact?
4. What are the two main limitations on a country's sustainable output and employment?
5. How does a widely publicized research report affect the accuracy of a company's stock price?
6. True or false: The best way to measure performance of a professionally managed fund is to consider the rate of return, not merely for last year, but for the last 2-, 3-, 4-, and 5-year periods.
7. Lenders require higher yields to maturity on junk bonds because the borrower enjoys a special advantage over the lender. Explain.
8. When a fund manager makes bigger bets on the same information his performance/turnover/beta increases.
9. The main cost of trading is

   Commissions
   Dealer spread
   Bid–ask bounce
   None of the above

---

Reprinted from the *Journal of Investment Management*, Vol. 3, No. 2, 2005.

10. "Although active investors couch their trades in the prices of specific securities, they are actually buying and selling time." Explain.

11. As investors' estimates of its value improve, the liquidity of a stock gets better. True or false?

12. How does the value of a publicly held company typically divide between shareholders and management? How will a change in the dividend yield affect that division?

13. How does a change in a company's debt–equity ratio affect its market value? Ignore taxes.

14. How does a change in the rate at which it is produced affect the current value of a capital good?

15. How does a company's growth rate affect its investment value?

16. List some examples of "commodity" stocks. How will the economic outlook affect their value?

17. The staff wondered if they were on the right track. Were some of these questions too tough for the average director? Or should they be confined to the chairman of the audit committee? And had they overlooked some important questions? The staff was uncertain how to proceed.

# CHAPTER 86

# Cereal Mergers

In a few days, Rex Mooring would be visiting the new CEO of Amalgamated Cereals. The purpose of his visit is to gather information that might help him appraise Amalgamated's latest acquisition. The CEO, who had been hired a few months before the acquisition was announced, was enthusiastic. But Mooring was skeptical: Would it prove to be merely the most recent in a long series of acquisitions that had followed the same depressing pattern:

1. A new CEO, hired with fanfare
2. An acquisition announcement
3. An enthusiastic CEO
4. Ultimate disappointment
5. Sudden departure of the CEOs, some fired outright, some "leaving to spend more time with their family"

In every case, the financial media had blamed the CEO for botching a promising acquisition.

To be sure, Almagamated's acquisitions had posed special challenges:

Rice Crunchies had defied all attempts to control manufacturing costs.

The marketing synergies promised for Oat Mealies had never materialized.

Corn Plasters had encountered unanticipated image problems with the consumers.

But now the latest CEO, Farley Boscombe, was touting the exciting possibilities of Wheat Crispies: Would he achieve the success that had eluded his predecessors or, like them, would he end up taking personal responsibility for a failed acquisition?

Mooring was discouraged by Amalgamated's record. On the other hand, in every case the departing CEO had taken full responsibility for the failure. Its highly touted new CEO had compiled an impressive record in agricultural pesticides. Would he put Amalgamated's pattern of failed acquisitions behind it? Mooring's clients needed a tough-minded appraisal from him. He felt that, if he asked the right questions, his interview with the new CEO could be helpful.

---

Reprinted from the *Journal of Investment Management*, Vol. 3, No. 3, 2005.

## QUESTIONS

1. What is the new CEO's take on the breakfast food business?
2. Was the acquisition the new CEO's idea? If not, was the new CEO nevertheless hired to manage an as yet unspecified acquisition?
3. What sort of compensation will he receive if he is fired? Is the compensation subject to any special conditions?
4. How long does he expect to be with Amalgamated?
5. How does he feel about the relevance of his previous work experience?
6. Are there influential investment bankers on the board?
7. Were they involved in finding and hiring him?
8. Has he talked to any of his predecessors?
9. Does he have any comments on Amalgamated's record?

# CHAPTER 87

# Quiz for Fed Candidates

In a short time Alan Greenspan will be retiring: Washington has the unenviable task of choosing his successor. There is no shortage of candidates. But chairman of the Fed is not, of course, just another important Washington job.

Expert students of the Fed have given us important clues in considering candidates.[1]

"We have had 12 chairmen . . . and some of them have made expensive blunders."—Allen H. Meltzer

He should be able to distinguish "between the economic models we construct and the real world."—Alan Greenspan

He shouldn't be "brainwashed into use of the doctrines."—Allen Sinai

The next chairman will undoubtedly be diplomatic with congressmen and other central bankers, articulate in his public utterances, perspicacious and discreet in his defense of the Fed's independence. But has he been so thoroughly brainwashed that he cannot see the real world beyond the academic models?

We have put together a brief quiz intended to reveal the inner applicant.

## Quiz for Candidates for Fed Chairman

Do you think "money matters"? How would you measure the degree of monetary ease or restraint?

How well would the U.S. economy function under hyperinflation?

What are the main limits on the sustainable level of prosperity?

True or false: Inflation results from a failure to invest in home goods plant.

True or false: Trade deficits result from a failure to invest in tradables plant.

What is the primary lesson from the great panics of the last two centuries? What do they tell us about demand failure?

Explain the significance of the *term premium*. Estimate its size.

To other countries, the United States is an independent economic entity. How should they determine whether we are pulling our weight? Should they be willing to make investments in the United States that increase our home goods plant?

---

Reprinted from the *Journal of Investment Management*, Vol. 3, No. 4, 2005.

Estimate what it costs the private sector to create one job. $5,000? $50,000? $500,000? What is the role in the country's saving of households with a low marginal propensity to consume? In its risk taking? In the distribution of the country's wealth? Will raising their taxes reduce consumption?

True or false: In contributing to the volume of our country's output, labor and capital are substitutes for each other.

How would you go about calculating the effect of a change in domestic demand on the trade balance?

Define *liquidity trap*. Explain why the concept is important to the Fed.

Discuss the impact of the spot inflation rate on the long Treasury rate. Assume that the U.S. economy is at least partly open.

## Special Difficulty—Double Points:

Explain how the value of the dollar is determined in a *pure float* (as distinguished from a dirty float, or flexible exchange rates). Assume that

1. U.S. economy is at least partly open.
2. Interest-rate parity holds.

The level of consideration that you give to policy suggestions from other members of the Board will be

1. About the same as your predecessors,
2. Even less.

In your view, how important to the Fed is its independence? What are the implications for its transactions in the capital markets? Can the Fed afford to be transparent with journalists? With legislators? With investors?

McChesney Martin dealt with the transparency problem by drawing on a pipe, Volcker by chewing on a cigar. Or would you adopt Greenspan's solution? (Please limit your answer to 500 words.)

    Answers will be revealed after the new chairman is chosen.

## Note

1. *New York Times*, Friday, August 26, 2005, p. 1.

# CHAPTER 88

# When Plant Wears Out

Thruway King was an interstate trucker. One of its major expense items was maintenance. With a few exceptions, trucks are like cars: They do not wear out if they are maintained. But for trucks, as for cars, technological progress is inevitable: Sooner or later a truck becomes marginal, with operating costs that eat up all the revenues.

"Spats" Luciano, the vice president for operations, made three points about maintenance:

1. It was a big enough cost item that a marginal truck's *economic* life could be prolonged by suspending it.
2. If Thruway suspended maintenance the truck would wear out, ending the truck's *physical* life.
3. Demand for interstate trucking was sensitive to prosperity, and future prosperity was uncertain. A truck that was marginal today might be profitable tomorrow.

A worn-out truck would not be profitable, no matter how prosperous tomorrow was. Luciano argued that a marginal truck was an option on the level of future demand for interstate trucking. On the other hand, he conceded that some trucks were so old that the option they represented was too far out of the money to justify continued maintenance. When they consequently wore out, he would consign them to the scrapyard.

## DISCUSSION

1. Presumably, idle trucks do not wear; their technological inferiority to new trucks depends instead on time. On the other hand, the maintenance issue does not arise, as long as a truck is idle.
2. Is there any economic advantage to using the marginal trucks for occasional peak demand? For shorter trips?
3. Should only worn-out trucks be scrapped?
4. Does Luciano's reasoning apply to other kinds of industrial machinery?

---

Reprinted from the *Journal of Investment Finance*, Vol. 4, No. 1, 2006.

5. How will uncertainty about future manufacturing margins affect the life of such machinery?
6. What role should the scrap value of machinery play in the maintenance decision?
7. How will the level of prosperity affect the supply of scrap?
8. Does industrial machinery "wear out?"

# CHAPTER 89

# Answers to Quiz for Fed Candidates

**Question:** Do you think that "money matters?" How would you measure the degree of monetary ease or restraint?

**Answer:** Although the scarcity of money is measured by the nominal overnight rate, the reward to consumers for delaying their consumption is measured by the real overnight rate—the nominal rate less inflation.

But when consumers are responsive, albeit with some lags and uncertainties, to the real rate, the Fed controls the level of domestic demand. The main concern for policy makers then becomes, not increasing the level of demand, but rather increasing the level the country can afford.

**Question:** How well would the U.S. economy function under hyperinflation?

**Answer:** If consumers respond to the real rate then, when it chooses the nominal rate, the Fed must allow for inflation. But the nominal rate determines how expensive money is to hold, therefore to use.

Specialization is the whole point of cities. But transactions between specialties require money. So, as it becomes more urbanized, hence more specialized, the United States has progressively less tolerance for high inflation rates, and even less for hyperinflation (Exhibit 89.1).

**Question:** What are the main limits on the sustainable level of prosperity? True or False: Inflation results from a failure to invest in home goods plant.

**Answer:** True. When domestic demand increases, home goods producers respond by activating an obsolete plant. But employers can afford to use their obsolete plant only at higher real prices. When workers attempt to recapture in money wages the resulting increase in money prices, inflation accelerates.

Moral: when inflation prevents policy makers from expanding domestic demand to the full employment level, the missing jobs must be provided by new home goods plant. But because investment in home goods plant does not improve the trade balance, it cannot reward the foreign investor. So the investment that relaxes the inflation constraint must be financed by local savings.

**Question:** True or false: Trade deficits result from a failure to invest in tradables plant.

---

Reprinted from the *Journal of Investment Management*, Vol. 4, No. 2, 2006.
The author is convinced that this insight originated with the late, great MIT professor, Rudiger Dornbush. But in which book? When you own so many of professor Dornbush's books, an idea can be tough to locate.

**EXHIBIT 89.1** Urbanization

| Year | Percent of Population in Agriculture |
|------|--------------------------------------|
| 1790 | 0.967 |
| 1820 | 0.80 |
| 1860 | 0.67 |
| 1929 | 0.25 |
| 1980 | 0.04 |

**Answer:** True. Trade deficits are another obstacle to full employment. The problem is that, although an increase in domestic demand increases local output of home goods, it does not increase local output of tradable goods. However, foreign investors *can* justify investment in tradable goods plant—provided the currency is not too strong. That is good news, because it improves the trade balance.

**Question:** What is the primary lesson from the great panics of the last two centuries? What do they tell us about demand failure?
**Answer:** Thanks to Sidney Homer, we have nominal interest rates before, during, and after the seven great panics. By this measure, money was tight in all seven. But if they were caused by tight money, the panics are not examples of the sort of spontaneous, self-reinforcing collapse of business confidence textbook writers call "demand failure" (Exhibit 89.2).

**Question:** Explain the significance of the term premium. Estimate its size.
**Answer:** The term premium compensates investors for the extra risk they incur by holding long maturities rather than short. But why, if there is a borrower for every lender, hence no net contribution to the riskiness of the market portfolio, should investors require any risk premium from long bonds? The answer lies in the correlation of long bonds with systematic risk in common stocks.

Over the life of the long Treasury bond, the average value of short rates must be neutral—reflecting neither ease nor restraint. But then the difference between the

**EXHIBIT 89.2** U.S. Commercial Paper Rates[*]

| Panic Year | Two Years Before | Year Before | Panic Year | Year After | Two Years After |
|------------|------------------|-------------|------------|------------|-----------------|
| 1837 | 1000 | 3600 | 3200 | 1800 | 3600 |
| 1857 | 1500 | 1200 | 2400 | 750 | 704 |
| 1873 | 1003 | 1162 | 1650 | 744 | 661 |
| 1893 | 583 | 550 | 1088 | 348 | 475 |
| 1907 | 675 | 721 | 733 | 670 | 598 |
| 1921 | 588 | 813 | 788 | 500 | 538 |
| 1929 | 425 | 563 | 625 | 488 | 400 |

All figures are averages for the highest month in the indicated year.
[*] *A History of Interest Rates*, Sidney Homer.

long rate and the neutral short rate reduces to two elements: the term premium and any inflation differential.

**Question:** To other countries, the United States is an independent economic entity. How should they determine whether we are pulling our weight?

**Answer:** If we choose to view the United States as a stand-alone business, buying and selling with the rest of the world, one useful measure is our *operating cash flow*— what our trade balance would be if we were not making substantial investments intended to benefit our *future* cash flows. Taking a leaf from corporate accountants, we can "capitalize" these investments, adding them back to the trade balance.

Needless to say, foreign lenders to the United States hope that our investments will improve future operating cash flows enough to pay them back.

**Question:** Estimate what it costs the private sector to create one job: $5,000? $50,000? $500,000?

**Answer:** Consider an historical interval with the special property that the identity of the marginal plant was the same at the end as at the beginning. Because at the end of the interval, the number of jobs provided by old plant will be the same as at the beginnning, any increase will be due entirely to new plant. By dividing the incremental jobs by the incremental dollars (gross private capital formation), we get a crude estimate of the cost of one job. It is obviously an average across a wide variety of investments.

To minimize sample error, we want the longest possible period for measuring the respective increments in jobs and investment. But, by the end of long time samples, the original marginal plant has usually been retired. So it is not easy to find periods with the special property. Limited evidence suggests that a new job costs $500,000.

**Question:** True or false: In contributing to the volume of our country's output, labor and capital are substitutes for each other.

**Answer:** False. It is a rare economics textbook that does not have a handsome graph demonstrating how various proportions of capital and labor can produce the same output. In industry, however, labor and capital are complements—not substitutes. Putting more people to work takes more machines. The explanation for chronic joblessness is machinelessness.

**Question:** How would you go about calculating the effect of an increase in domestic demand on the trade balance?

**Answer:** Consumers buy two kinds of goods: tradable goods and home goods. An increase in domestic demand will be partly tradable goods and partly home goods. The latter will increase domestic output and employment. The former will degrade the trade balance.

**Question:** Define liquidity trap. Explain why the concept is important to the Fed.

**Answer:** In fairness to the textbook writers, let us concede that liquidity traps are a species of demand failure. But it is a kind of demand failure in which, although money matters as much as ever, the real rate is out of the Fed's control.

The real interest rate is the algebraic difference between the nominal rate and inflation. So, when inflation is negative, the real rate is the sum of the absolute value of inflation and the nominal rate. And although the nominal rate falls when the velocity of money falls, there is no velocity so low that the nominal rate can be negative.

If inflation gets too negative, even the easiest monetary policy can result in real interest rates high enough to slow the economy. But then inflation may get even more negative. This is the "trap" in a liquidity trap.

**Question:** Discuss the impact of the spot inflation rate on the long Treasury rate. Assume that the U.S. economy is at least partly open.

**Answer:** The spot inflation rate is a weighted average of the home goods and tradable goods inflation rates. Because the worker's market basket contains both home goods and tradable goods, both rates influence inflation in his money wage. But, although the money wage influences home goods prices, it does not influence tradables prices. So, barring new information, tradables inflation will tend over time to dominate home goods inflation. But investors in the long Treasuries cannot foresee new information. So the yield on long Treasuries will *also* be dominated by tradables inflation—unlike the spot inflation rate.

## Special Difficulty—Double Points

**Question:** Explain how the value of the dollar is determined in a pure float (as distinguished from a dirty float, or flexible exchange rates). Assume that the U.S. economy is at least partly open and that interest-rate parity holds.

**Answer:** In a pure float, the value of the currency will not be changing. But then the forward value will be the same as the spot. If interest-rate parity holds, the domestic (nominal, short) rate must equal the foreign (nominal, short) rate.

For every possible value of the currency there will be a different local price of tradable goods—hence a different velocity of money, given the money stock. But the nominal short interest rate is determined by the velocity of money. The value of the dollar will be the one value for which the resulting velocity is consistent with the short rate determined by interest-rate parity.

# CHAPTER 90

# Gas Caps and the Sherman Act

**W**hen gas stations switched to self-service, it was a bonanza for manufacturers of replacement gas caps. Employees of gas stations who forgot to replace the cap when they had finished pumping gas did not remain employees. But some customers never learned. Harried, hurried, distracted, they regularly drove off without their gas caps. And when it came to buying a replacement, they were in no position to bargain.

The bonanza was shared by the manufacturer of the molding machines that combined the essential metal parts with a sturdy plastic body. There were enough manufacturers of replacement caps that their industry was competitive. But there was only one manufacturer of the molding machines. He suspected that, because demand for replacement caps was not responsive to price, every new molding machine he manufactured displaced an old molding machine.

But then the economic life of his molding machine would go down, if his production rate went up. And the shorter its life, the smaller the difference in technology between the new machines and the marginal machines—hence the smaller the scarcity rent on the new machines. But their value to his customers depended on the product of scarcity rent and economic life.

And the value of the old but not yet marginal machines in the hands of his customers depended on a similar product: When they bought his new machines were they counting on him not to increase his production rate?

What had provoked those thoughts was a call from a Washington law firm. The law firm argued that he was an "imperfect competitor" whose output affected his price, and said it was incumbent on imperfect competitors to demonstrate that they were pushing their output levels to the point where marginal cost equaled price.

The law firm mentioned something about treble damages.

Many of his customers had borrowed to buy his machines. How many would be bankrupted if he increased his output rate? He was uncertain what to tell the lawyers.

## DISCUSSION

1. If the manufacturer of the molding machine doubles his output, what happens to his prices?

---

Reprinted from the *Journal of Investment Management*, Vol. 4, No. 3, 2006.

2. What happens to his revenue?
3. If the manufacturer of the molding machines is offered the chance to buy additional capacity at a bargain price, how should he respond?
4. If demand for gas caps were price elastic, how would your answers change?
5. What should he tell the lawyers?

# CHAPTER 91

# The Worldwide Financier

**B**ecause he was the manager of Global Fund, his shareholders expected Ole "Bud" Carlson to be alert to investment opportunities all over the world, in small as well as large countries. His job offered special problems and special opportunities. In some countries, class or ethnic distinction created problems for business. Some countries had trouble getting along with their neighbors. Some countries were hostile to business, some were friendly. Some countries could handle prosperity, some couldn't. Some leaders understood the importance of the private sector, some didn't. Some leaders were so corrupt that they couldn't put their country's problems first; other leaders grew visibly in their job.

The investor who confined himself to a single country couldn't escape its problems. But global investing was an opportunity, either to

1. Diversify across many countries.
2. Attempt to distinguish the countries that were enjoying clear sailing from the countries that were encountering heavy weather.

Bud recognized that small countries are sometimes riskier than big countries. He also recognized the danger that local investors would know more about their country than he did. In his effort to increase his understanding, he used a wide variety of information sources.

One of these sources was *Worldwide Financier*. The *Financier* was the creation of Sir Henry Hepplewhite, the sole owner, editor, and publisher. Because Bud had found the magazine informative, his ears perked up when he heard it had been sold. The new owner, Lord Watford, promised readers that the magazine wouldn't change— that he wouldn't have bought it unless Sir Henry had agreed to stay on. Lord Watford added that only a fool would tinker with the cash cow Sir Henry had created.

Newspaper articles on the sale had provided profiles of Sir Henry. Bud was reassured that the lifelong bachelor planned to continue living in his modest flat in one of the less expensive sections of Liverpool with his faithful pit bull, Fang, and his collection of toy Matchbox cars.

But Bud was puzzled by Sir Henry's need to sell. Had he been so absorbed with the periodical that he neglected his own affairs? Certainly there was no shortage of investment ideas in Sir Henry's own magazine.

---

Reprinted from the *Journal of Investment Management*, Vol. 4, No. 4, 2006.

## QUESTIONS

1. Is Bud Carlson right to be worried?
2. If Sir Henry *was* using the investment ideas in his own periodical, why wasn't he more prosperous?
3. Will Bud be successful using the ideas in the magazine?
4. What should Bud learn from Sir Henry's experience?

# CHAPTER 92

# Reifen AG

It was Thornton Smith's first chance to manage a mutual fund. Because Active Fund had a reputation for being opportunistic, Smith wanted to demonstrate that he could be as bold and innovative as his predecessor. In casting about for fresh ideas, he remembered a point made by the teacher in his investment course: A fund could significantly improve its diversification by owning foreign stocks. But Active Fund had never owned any foreign stocks. He supposed that this was merely an oversight. But when he broached the idea to/with his predecessor, she explained that her omission was deliberate.

The shareholders of Active Fund were mostly U.S. citizens. She pointed out that they felt more comfortable owning U.S. companies and she was deeply interested in owning stocks her shareholders were comfortable with.

Smith had to admit that he too was interested in owning stocks that would appeal to U.S. shareholders. But then a salesman from a Wall Street firm brought to his attention a foreign company whose product was well known to U.S. investors: Reifen AG, which specialized in the manufacture of replacement tires for big American sportutes.

Heavily loaded sportutes, traveling at freeway speeds, put special stresses on their tires. By coupling high-tech development with extensive testing on the autobahn, Reifen AG had designed tires for these special stresses. With its catchy marketing slogan, "Lebensraum for the entire family," it had achieved wide recognition in the United States, even among families that did not drive sportutes.

But diversification was an abstraction to the salesman; he was focused on making a sale. He pointed out that, should the dollar devalue, the same earnings in Euros would be worth more in dollars.

Smith remonstrated that neither he nor the salesman was an expert on currencies. If the value of the dollar increased relative to the Euro, the same earnings in Euros would be worth *less* in dollars.

But he was not trying to start an argument with the salesman. He conceded Reifen AG was a foreign company that his U.S. shareholders clearly could feel comfortable with.

---

Reprinted from the *Journal of Investment Management*, Vol. 5, No. 1, 2007.

## QUESTIONS FOR DISCUSSION

1. Smith knows that, in order to maintain its U.S. market, Reifen's dollar price must remain competitive with the dollar price of U.S. tire manufacturers. When the value of the dollar changes:
   - Will Reifen AG have to adjust its prices to be competitive with them?
   - Will U.S. manufacturers adjust their prices?
   - How will Reifen's sales volume change? Its manufacturing margins?
2. Reifen AG appears to have a valuable franchise with U.S. consumers. What will happen to its value?
3. Should Smith simply follow the salesman's suggestion and assume that Reifen's Euro earnings will be unchanged?

# Miscellaneous

...is a catch-all category for papers that don't fit readily in the previous categories. It includes a paper on one of the cleverest investment ideas the author has ever encountered, Rob Arnott's fundamental indexation™.

J.L.T.

# CHAPTER 93

# Wha' Hoppen'?

This comment will avoid addressing such fascinating issues as why the October market reaction was so big and why it was so broad, focusing instead on the simpler question: What was the trigger? The answer is closely linked to the great bull market that preceded the collapse and to the unprecedented devaluation of the dollar that preceded the bull market.

Broadly speaking, the devaluation had three kinds of effects—

- Economic effects, both good and bad, most of which have yet to be reflected in securities prices and consequently require no explanation here
- Effects on portfolio balance with the Japanese investor, who now dominates world capital markets, finding himself with a smaller weighting in U.S. assets after the devaluation than before
- Effects on investors' perception of exchange risk

Investors view exchange risk as an extra element in foreign investments that is absent from domestic investments. In their new book, *Investment Markets*, authors Roger Ibbotson and Gary Brinson document a low degree of correlation across the major stock markets. When investors perceive exchange risk as small, they tend to find the advantages of international diversification compelling. When investors perceive exchange risk as large, however, foreign investments lose much of their appeal.

When investors perceive exchange risk as large, therefore, they will tend to invest domestically. A U.S. dollar devaluation will have little effect on their portfolio balance. But when investors perceive exchange risk as small, they will want substantial foreign holdings; a currency change will upset the balance in their portfolios. This imbalance cannot be corrected by trading.

The devaluation of the U.S. dollar not only left the Japanese wanting more U.S. risk, it also left Americans wanting less Japanese risk. Thus, even if (contrary to fact) U.S. investors' holdings were large enough to enable them to oblige the Japanese, the two could not solve their respective balance problems by trading with each other. Under these circumstances there was only one way to reestablish market equilibrium: In terms of their respective domestic currencies, the levels of the markets themselves had to change.

---

If, in the wake of the devaluation, Japanese investors had wanted to restore the balance in a portfolio diversified between U.S. and Japanese holdings, a likely result would have been an instantaneous jump in the U.S. stock market. But they didn't, and no such jump occurred. The Japanese didn't want to restore portfolio balance because the devaluation also raised their perception of the exchange risk, making diversification into U.S. assets less attractive.

Only when the devaluation had apparently run its course, with the dollar settling down to a new range of 140 to 150 yen, did investors' heightened perception of the yen/dollar exchange risk begin to subside. The longer the dollar persisted in the new range, the more investors' perception of the risk subsided and the more attractive diversification back into U.S. assets became.

This explains why the bull market occurred, not while the dollar was falling, but after it had stopped falling. It also explains why, in a world of ostensibly efficient capital markets, the great bull market of 1987 was so protracted. It was a response, not to changing expectations, but to changing perceptions of the risk surrounding those expectations.

But enough of history. What about the market collapse? Did Secretary Baker cause it by threatening to abandon the dollar to "free-fall"? Yes, because he raised investors' perceptions of exchange risk, undermining the appeal of diversifying into U.S. assets, hence the bull market caused by the portfolio-balance effects of the devaluation.

Should Secretary Baker be blamed for failing to see the consequences of his threat? Only if they were obvious. That, of course, is something each investor must judge for himself.

# CHAPTER 94

# Portfolio Insurance and Market Volatility

The key to understanding why the Black Monday crash was so deep is the model of dealer behavior described in "The Economics of the Dealer Function."[1] That model distinguishes between two fundamentally different kinds of investors, who transact with dealers in fundamentally different ways:

- The information-motivated transactor (IBT) is in a hurry to transact before this information gets impounded in price. Investors who believe, rightly or wrongly, that they have information are one of the dealer's most important customers. They are sufficiently anxious to transact that they pay a price of the dealer's choosing in order to transact at a time of their choosing.
- The value-motivated transactor (VBT) is a bargain hunter. When he perceives a big enough discrepancy between price and value, he transacts. In no hurry to transact, he waits until someone meets his price.

In a market without dealers, transactors in a hurry would trade with value-based transactors, paying whatever difference between price and value (perhaps 15 to 20 percent) is required to motivate the VBT to trade. The function of the dealer is to mediate between buyers in a hurry and sellers in a hurry, sparing both the high cost of trading with the VBT.

Even if buy and sell orders arrive randomly (as indeed they will if the dealer's price is close to the equilibrium price), the dealer will experience runs of buys and runs of sells. Because the dealer accommodates his customers by transacting for his own account, these runs result in big changes in his own position. When the dealer's position gets too long or short for comfort, he lays off or buys in from the only investor willing to transact at a time of someone else's choosing—the value-based transactor. To do so, of course, the dealer must meet the VBT's price.

To avoid accommodating a customer at one price and turning around and laying off (or buying in) at a different, less favorable price, the dealer adjusts his own price to reflect the likelihood of his having to lay off or buy in—which is to say, to reflect his position. Thus the dealer's price can range from the VBT's bid when the dealer is close to laying off to the VBT's ask when the dealer is close to buying in—a range of

---

perhaps 30 to 40 percent of the security's value—without any change in the VBT's appraisal of the true value.

Enter the portfolio insurer (PI). His trading behavior differs from that of either the IBT or the VBT. Unlike the IBT, he is price, rather than information, motivated. But unlike the VBT, who is also price-motivated, he is in a hurry to trade because he needs to track market-level changes fairly closely. And his trading behavior is unique in that he buys when price rises and sells when it falls.

Professor Hayne Leland of the University of California at Berkeley (and a principal of Leland O'Brien Rubinstein, purveyors of portfolio insurance) was quoted in the *New York Times* as arguing that, even with $60 to $90 billion in assets, portfolio insurance had an insignificant impact on equilibrium prices, compared with the impact of orthodox investors (with their $1,000 to $2,000 billion). The problem with this argument is that, within the widely separated prices at which the enormous assets of VBTs come into play, there are, broadly speaking, only three kinds of transactors:

- Information-based and other nonprice-motivated transactors in a hurry
- Portfolio insurers, who are price-motivated, but perversely
- Dealers, whose price rises as their position falls and falls as their position rises

In adjusting their portfolios to changing market levels, portfolio insurers do not distinguish—indeed, cannot distinguish—between changes in equilibrium price and changes in dealer price due purely to changes in dealer position. A drop in the dealer's position leads to an increase in the dealer's price, to which the portfolio insurer responds by quickly buying more, lowering the dealer's position still further, and so on. The result of this process, which under certain circumstances can be unstable, is an increase in the volatility of dealer price. (The effect is obviously symmetric.)

## CALCULATING THE IMPACT

To explore the impact of portfolio insurance on price volatility, let

$x$ = the combined holdings of portfolio insurers and dealers (stock and futures combined),

$x_1$ = the dealer's position,

$x_2$ = the portfolio insurer's position,

$p^*$ = the fair price according to value-based investors, and

$p$ = the mean of the dealer's current bid and ask prices.

For the dealer, a long position corresponds to a mean dealer price p low in relation to $p^*$—what value-based investors think the security is worth. For some positive constant $X_1$, therefore, we have:

$$x_1 = -X_1(p - p^*) \qquad (94.1)$$

But the higher the price level p, the more shares (or share equivalents) portfolio insurers want to hold. For another positive constant $X_2$ we have, then:

$$\frac{dx_2}{dp} = X_2 \tag{94.2}$$

From our definition of x we have

$$x = x_1 + x_2 \tag{94.3}$$

These three equations determine the behavior of dealer price p as a function of the demands of the dealer's other customers as reflected in x and the value $p^*$ of the security according to value-based investors. Differentiating the first and third equations with respect to p we have

$$\frac{dx_1}{dp} = -X_1 \tag{94.4}$$

and

$$\frac{dx}{dp} = \frac{dx_1}{dp} + \frac{dx_2}{dp} \tag{94.5}$$

respectively. Substituting Equations 94.2 and 94.4 in Equation 94.5, we have:

$$\frac{dx}{dp} = -X_1 + X_2; \quad -\frac{dp}{dx} = \frac{1}{X_1 - X_2} \tag{94.6}$$

When $X_2$ is zero, this result simplifies to Equation 94.4; in the absence of portfolio insurance, price sensitivity to trading pressure is the same as if the dealer were functioning alone.

Recalling that $X_1$ and $X_2$ are both positive, we can see that as portfolio insurance catches on, and $X_2$ grows, the sensitivity of dealer price to net demands for rapid accommodation also grows, blowing up when:

$$X_2 = X_1$$

What about the response of dealer price p to changes in the value-based transactor's estimate of value $p^*$? Differentiating Equations 94.1 and 94.3 with respect to $p^*$, we have, respectively

$$\frac{dx_1}{dp^*} = X_1\left(\frac{dp}{dp^*} - 1\right) \tag{94.7}$$

and

$$\frac{dx_1}{dp^*} + \frac{dx_2}{dp^*} = 0 \tag{94.8}$$

noting that x is unaffected by a change in p*. Substituting from Equation 94.8 into Equation 94.7, we have:

$$-\frac{dx_2}{dp^*} = -X_1\left(\frac{dp}{dp^*} - 1\right)$$

$$-\frac{dx_2}{dp}\frac{dp}{dp^*} = -X_1\frac{dp}{dp^*} + X_1$$

Substituting from Equation 94.2, we have:

$$X_1\frac{dp}{dp^*} - X_2\frac{dp}{dp^*} = X_1$$

$$\frac{dp}{dp^*} = \frac{X_1}{X_1 - X_2} \tag{94.9}$$

Absent portfolio insurance, $X_2$ is zero, and the change in dealer price (excluding effects of dealer position) equals the change in the value-based investor's appraisal. As portfolio insurance catches on, $X_2$ increases. The denominator falls (as previously noted, $X_1$ and $X_2$ are always positive), and the value of the fraction rises. Dealer price p becomes more volatile, blowing up when $X_2$ equals $X_1$.

As noted, portfolio insurance at its apogee controlled $60 to $90 billion of assets. NYSE specialist firms control perhaps $1 to $2 billion. Does this mean $X_2$ was not merely equal to $X_1$, but far larger? No, because the specialist commits a vastly larger fraction of his capital for a given price change than the portfolio insurer does.

Does a blow-up in the volatility of dealer price mean market chaos? No—it only means that the dealer price oscillates between the value-based transaction's bid and ask. Still, given a 30 to 40 percent spread between the outside bid and ask, the resulting price volatility will be spectacular—as indeed it was on Black Monday.

## Note

1. J.L. Treynor, "The Economics of the Dealer Function," *Financial Analysts Journal*, November–December 1987.

# CHAPTER 95

# Betting on Good Management

Some investors bet on their appraisals of management, buying shares in firms whose managements they rate as good and selling (or shorting) shares in firms whose managements they rate as bad, without any overt comparison of the share prices of the respective companies. If these bets are to succeed, companies with good managements must be underpriced and companies with bad managements must be overpriced.

This can happen if the investor typical of the consensus makes his appraisal by combining his observations of the management in question with his general view on corporate management, based on experience with other companies. A statistician would describe this approach as an example of "Bayesian" estimation. In such estimation, the average error in a properly weighted combination will always be smaller than the error in an estimate based on specifics alone. But the management in question will rarely be average. To state the paradox as baldly as possible: In order to appraise a *specific* management with the smallest possible error, the investor must combine a weighted average of his appraisals of the specific management and of the *average* management. If the investor is truly typical, the stock prices will also be a weighted average of these two appraisals.

If the typical investor ignores prior experience, then his errors will be (1) larger—maybe much larger—but (2) centered on the specific management, rather than on some blend of the specific and the average; market price will also be centered on the specific management, rather than on some blend of the specific and the average. Now the investor betting on his appraisal of the specific management has a problem: He can no longer assume that a management he appraises as better than average will automatically be underpriced, or that a management he appraises as worse than average will automatically be overpriced. Now he is betting the accuracy of his appraisal against the accuracy of the consensus. (My *FAJ* piece, "Market Efficiency and the Bean Jar Experiment" (May–June 1987), spells out the difficulty of trying to win that game.)

Which way do uninformed investors make their appraisals? The uninformed investor loses only modestly when he invests on his own error, because its impact on price will be negligible. He loses big only when his error is shared by enough other investors to influence price.

If uninformed investors use a Bayesian approach to appraising management, they will all make a common error—namely, the error that results from blending into their appraisal of the specific management their experience with the average. (Actually, of course, different uninformed investors will appraise the average management differently, with errors centered around a true appraisal of the average management. On average, those errors won't hurt them because they won't affect price. But the true appraisal of the average *will* hurt them, because it injects a common error into their appraisal, hence distorts price.) Uninformed investors are better off ignoring the information in their priors—in other words, their appraisal of the average management—even though this information can reduce substantially their error in appraising the specific management. If they do, equilibrium prices will reflect only their appraisals of the specific management, not their appraisals of the average management.

Equilibrium share price will then center on a true appraisal of the specific management, rather than on some blend of the specific and the average. The investor specializing in appraisals of management won't be able to rely on share prices of firms with good management being too low, or on share prices of firms with bad management being too high. The rationale for betting on management disappears. In sum:

1. Investors who bet on their appraisals of management are assuming that the market consensus is influenced by its appraisal of the average management.
2. Although this approach to appraisal will reduce most investors' appraisal errors, it will actually increase the error in market price.
3. Betting on one's errors costs very little if the errors aren't in the price (i.e., aren't shared by other investors), whereas shared errors are very costly.
4. Thus the great mass of investors are better off making big errors in appraisals that ignore the average quality of management than making smaller errors that reflect it.
5. If investors omit any consideration of the average quality of management in forming their appraisal, the consensus price will too.
6. Those who bet on good management are assuming that uninformed investors are minimizing their errors, rather than their losses.

# CHAPTER 96

# Remembering Fischer Black

It is pretty well-known that Fischer Black never took a course in economics or finance. At Harvard his undergraduate major was physics, and his doctorate was in math. Perhaps I had some small role in getting Fischer interested in finance.

We met when Fischer came to Arthur D. Little in 1965, having completed his doctoral work at Harvard in 1964. My recollection, possibly faulty, is that he came from Bolt, Beranek, and Newman. I don't think Fischer and I ever worked on a case together at ADL, but he took an interest in what I was doing, which developed into some serious, albeit extracurricular, conversations on finance.

Before Franco Modigliani persuaded me to take a sabbatical from ADL and go to MIT for the 1962–1963 school year, I had worked for several institutional clients on investment problems, and I was used to looking at security markets from their viewpoint, one period at a time. On the other hand, I had become fascinated with the capital budgeting problem as a student at Harvard Business School. We were taught (and I believed) that the proper rate of return for judging capital projects should reflect their risk. I *wasn't* taught, but came to believe, that the relevant rate was the one the capital markets would use to discount the project's future cash flows. Needless to say, I found Modigliani and Miller's 1958 publication very exciting.

The problem I wanted to solve was a multiperiod problem. Yet it seemed plausible that the discounting problem could be solved one period at a time, working back from the future cash flows to the present. By the time Stephen Sobotka, a Chicago Ph.D. in economics, came to ADL in 1961, I had drafted a paper that attempted to deal with the capital budgeting problem in two stages—solving the one-period problem, and then extending the one-period result to multiple periods. Steve sent the draft (which I had already given to John Lintner) to Merton Miller, who sent it to Franco.

Franco suggested separating the paper into two parts. His suggested title for the one-period paper was "Toward a Theory of the Market Value of Risky Assets." I used that title when I redrafted both pieces and presented them to the finance seminar at MIT.

The first presentation got a reasonably sympathetic hearing from Franco, Paul Cootner, and Ed Kuh, I thought, but the second got a stormy reception, particularly from Franco. Of course, Franco was right: I was trying to derive and solve partial differential equations that required a far better mathematician than I—and Itô's Lemma.

Reprinted with permission from *Institutional Investor Journals*. Please visit www.iijpm.com.

When I returned to ADL in the summer of 1963, my boss, Martin Ernst, asked: "What can you do with your stuff? Does it have any practical value?" I gave him a list of possible applications that included risk and performance measurement. From the list he chose performance measurement, and I wrote the two *Harvard Business Review* papers (the second with Kay Mazuy) that appeared in 1965 and 1966.

Fischer and I collaborated on two papers. The first was based on a joint presentation to Jim Lorie's CRESP seminar in 1967 ("How to Use Security Analysis to Improve Portfolio Selection," *Journal of Business*, 1973). The second, in which Fischer attacks the multiperiod continuous-time problem I had failed to solve, appears in *Modern Developments in Financial Management*, a compendium edited by Stewart Myers (New York: Praeger, 1976).

> In a field full of accomplished learners, Fischer Black was an accomplished thinker.
>
> In a field now full of talented mathematicians, Fischer was a mathematically talented physicist.
>
> In a field where so many profit from confusion, Fischer made a career out of analytical precision.

It's easy to forget that over Fischer's career finance changed:

- From a verbal to a mathematical discipline
- From accounting-centered to economics-centered
- From suppressing uncertainty to giving it a central role

Thirty years ago, nobody would have defined finance as the economics of uncertainty. Risk was a cop-out—for explaining why the future had departed from deterministic forecasts. Before the revolution, we regarded randomly fluctuating markets as evidence of the irrationality of market prices. Now we view departures from random fluctuation as "anomalies." In a Copernican turn, market prices have become more factual, more real, than accounting numbers.

Like most revolutions, this one had its casualties. Financial decisions tend to make some people richer and some people poorer. Confusion accelerates these wealth transfers. People with a professional stake in this confusion have fought the revolution—using the stick on recalcitrant teachers and the carrot (of large donations) on complaisant deans. Thoughtful researchers, such as John Burr Williams, find their teaching careers terminated on pretexts.

Faced with tough career choices, many teachers compromised their teaching, learning the hard way what Vaclav Havel learned from his experience with the Communists: You can't be cowardly in what you say, and still be courageous in what you think. Because Fischer was forthright about saying what he thought, he was a beacon to harried finance teachers, who loved him for his courage.

Some will say Fischer's greatest contribution to finance is his work on the Black-Scholes model. The partial differential equation developed in the Black-Scholes papers applies to any claim on an underlying asset. So it applies to all the claims in a complex corporate capital structure—and indeed, to all the individual claims on the underlying company.

In assigning market values to these claims, it represents a culmination of our understanding of corporate finance, which began with J.B. Williams's conservation of value principle, and took a giant leap forward with Modigliani and Miller's 1958 publication. Before Black-Scholes, we talked about bond quality; after Black-Scholes, we talked about the borrower's option against the lender. The old way was verbal rather than mathematical, vague about the nature of the lender's risk, and hopeless on the role of time.

Time has always been a pesky problem for economists, who have dealt with it by:

1. Restricting their model to perpetuities (Modigliani and Miller)
2. Focusing on one-period problems (Markowitz's portfolio balancing model)
3. Reducing the dynamic flow of economic events to a static long run and a static short run (Alfred Marshall)

That these pioneers in quantifying the previously unquantifiable ducked the problem is a measure of what Black-Scholes accomplished.

Fischer's research was about developing clever models—insightful, elegant models that changed the way we look at the world. They have more in common with the models of physics—Newton's laws of motion, or Maxwell's equations—than with the econometric "models"—lists of loosely plausible explanatory variables—that now dominate the finance journals.

Fischer's models share with great music and great literature an essential quality—improbability. One thousand monkeys typing on personal computers for one thousand years are unlikely to come up with any of Fischer's models.

It's easy to forget now that, when Black-Scholes was new, there were murmurs of dismay that it omitted any reference to a risk premium, or to the expected value of the underlying asset at the expiration of the option. It may be fair to conjecture that any attempt to solve the problem of option value using an *econometric* model would have included these variables, along with the proverbial kitchen sink.

Fischer resisted the argument that, if you can't run controlled experiments, you should restrict your models to linear, or log linear, regression models so you can bring the full panoply of econometric technique to bear on your tests. Never uncomfortable being a minority of one, Fischer wasn't alone in resisting this argument. Astrophysicists, who also have to forgo controlled experiments, are still unpersuaded.

Why did Fischer, working in finance, prefer the approach of the astrophysicists? It's tempting to argue that Fischer's *problem-solving* approach to finance was influenced by

- His undergraduate physics major
- His Ph.D. in math
- The absence of any formal study in economics or finance

There are two ways to interpret Fischer's career:

1. He succeeded *despite* his unusual training and career path, because of his extraordinary ability.
2. He succeeded in part *because of* his unusual training and career path.[1]

There's a problem with Fischer's obituary in the *New York Times*. It's the picture. The problem is not that the *Times* used an old picture; Fischer always looked like that. And, anyway, the *Times* obituaries print pictures of movie actors taken in their silent film days that don't jar the way Fischer's picture does.

No, what is jarring about Fischer's picture is that his expression shows the kind of joy, curiosity, anticipation, and love of life that we normally see only in babies. It reminds us of the rewards to living a life like Fischer's.

When I met Fischer, he was dating a woman who contracted one of the hopelessly incurable wasting diseases. Because she had an unhappy home life, she didn't want to go home to die. Fischer took her into his apartment and personally nursed her through her long terminal illness.

Fischer's surrender to intellectual curiosity was as complete as his surrender to conscience. He never said, "That's a deeply troubling idea. Maybe some day, when I have more time, I'll think about it." (I suspect most of us would say, like St. Augustine: "Lord, let me live a life as virtuous as Fischer Black's—but not yet.")

For most people, ideas scarcely exist until they are reduced to symbols—to words or mathematics. But Fischer's greatest contributions were in a far country beyond the symbols. For him, research meant abandoning the comfortable, familiar forms rather than merely refining or extending them—letting go of the old, in order to grasp the new. Research was a lonely journey into that far country—a journey from which one can never really go home again.

For Fischer, death was just another journey.

## Note

1. It doesn't hurt a student's career to accept received ideas he should have rejected. If, on the other hand, his capacity to reject bad ideas has been trained out of him, then, when he becomes a teacher (1) he won't know where the cracks in the edifice of received wisdom are, and (2) he won't have any basis for discriminating between ideas that are worth developing and ideas that aren't.

   But if he doesn't publish, he will perish. He can take refuge in either (1) some arcane technology relating to math, statistics, or computer science, or (2) econometric models. If the latter, he can let the econometric tests do the rejecting for him.

# CHAPTER 97

# Why Market-Valuation-Indifferent Indexing Works

**B**y the end of the Twentieth century, even casual investors had become comfortable with the idea of index funds. The idea of a *better* index fund (see Arnott, Hsu, and Moore 2005), however, is mind-boggling. This article offers one man's view of why it will actually work. He defines market-valuation-indifferent (MVI) indexing to be indexing in which the index is built on any weights that avoid the problem with market capitalization.

The bad news about stock markets is that they price stocks imperfectly. The good news is that the mispricings are always relative. Not only will overpriced stocks be counterbalanced by underpriced stocks, but the distribution of error at any point in time will be symmetrical. We can picture this distribution as a bell-shaped curve with "error" on the horizontal axis and some measure of "frequency" on the vertical axis. Because it reflects both the number of companies and their size, aggregate value is the appropriate measure of frequency.

But which measure of aggregate value—true value or market value? If we use market value, then, alas, it will make bigger bets on overpriced stocks and smaller bets on underpriced stocks.

To get a handle on how much error, we begin by defining

$u$ = relative error (expressed as a fraction of true value) and

$v(u)$ = amount of *true* value with error.

When we consider the thousands of stocks in the market, the randomness of particular stocks is submerged in a density function that associates a relatively stable amount of density $v(u)$ with relative error $u$ to satisfy

$$v(u) = v(-u) \qquad (97.1)$$

But $1 + u$ is the *market* value of $1.00 of *true* value with relative error $u$. So the amount of market value with error $u$ is $(1 + u)v(u)$; then the error distribution satisfies

$$(1 + u) v(u) > (1 - u)v(-u) \qquad (97.2)$$

---

Unlike the distribution of the pricing error that uses true value, the error distribution for market values is skewed to the right. This lack of symmetry is the problem with capitalization weighting: By using market values to determine its weights, a cap-weighted index fund will invest more money in overpriced stocks than in underpriced stocks.

Consider a symmetrical distribution of market errors $u$ around a mean error $\overline{u}$. For each stock whose error exceeds the mean by $u - \overline{u}$, there will tend to be a stock whose error falls short of the mean by $\overline{u} - u$. Expressed in terms of a frequency function $v(\ )$ of true values, the original symmetry condition is obviously satisfied by

$$v(u - \overline{u}) = v(\overline{u} - u) \tag{97.3}$$

because the second argument is indeed minus the first, as we specified. On the other hand, if we expect market errors to be symmetrical around a mean error of zero, we need to add the following condition: Weighted by the true values, the mean of the errors in market price is zero. In terms of our symbols, we can express the new condition:

$$\sum uv(u) = 0 \tag{97.4}$$

Obviously, the sum over all stocks—underpriced and overpriced—is zero.

## THE BASIC EQUATION

How does MVI indexing avoid cap-weighted indexing's problem? The key is a simple equation linking the covariances of portfolio weights with

- Market price per share
- True value per share
- Errors in market price per share

If, as before, $u$ is the relative error, then $1 + u$ is the ratio of market to true value $v$ and

$$v(1 + u) = v + vu \tag{97.5}$$

is market price. So, to a common divisor equal to the number of stocks, the covariance of portfolio weights $w$ with share prices is

$$\sum wv(1 + u) - \sum w \sum u(1 + u)$$
$$= \sum wv + \sum wvu - \sum w \sum v \tag{97.6}$$
$$= \left[\sum wv - \sum w \sum v\right] + \sum wvu$$

The expression in brackets is the covariance of portfolio weights with the true share values. Now, consider the covariance of portfolio weights with dollar errors in share price,

$$\text{cov } w(uv) = \sum wuv - \sum w \sum uv$$

$$\sum wuv = \text{cov } w(uv) + \sum w \sum uv \tag{97.7}$$

We see that the expression $\sum wuv$ equals this covariance plus the product $\sum w \sum uv$. But under our expanded symmetry condition, we have

$$\sum uv = \sum w \sum uv = 0 \tag{97.8}$$

So the first of the three covariances equals the algebraic sum of the second and third. The second is the covariance of portfolio weights with true values, and the third is the covariance of the weights with the dollar errors in prices.

## IMPLICATIONS FOR MVI INDEXING

One application of MVI indexing is weighting schemes in which the covariance of weights with market values is zero. In this case, to satisfy Equation 97.6, either the other two covariances must offset exactly—which is highly improbable—or both must be zero.

An extreme example is a portfolio with equal weights. On average, the number of overpriced stocks will be the same as the number of underpriced stocks. But if all the stocks are assigned the same weight, the investment in the overpriced segment will depend only on that number and the investment in the underpriced segment will depend only on that same number. So the two investments will tend to be equal—in contrast to the cap-weighted index fund, which pays more for the overpriced segment and less for the underpriced segment. Alas, a scheme that weights large-cap and small-cap stocks the same is going to have small-cap market bias, however, relative to many benchmark portfolios, hence more sensitivity to any systematic small-cap factor (as discussed in, for example, Fama and French 1973).

The equation relating the three covariances can be applied in other ways. For example, instead of demonstrating empirically that a given set of weights has zero covariance with market prices, we can appeal to *a priori* reasons why certain sets of weights will have a zero covariance with the errors. We have seen that if the portfolio gives the same weight to underpricing errors it gives to overpricing errors, the third covariance vanishes.

But then the other two covariances in the equation must be equal. So we can use market values, which are observable, rather than true values, which are not, to estimate the small-cap bias in such sets of weights.

## ELIMINATING SMALL-CAP BIAS

Is the constant-weight portfolio the best MVI indexing can do? Does it have the smallest tracking error *versus* a conventional cap-weighted index? Some weighting schemes will have less small-cap bias than others. Examples include weighting by number of employees, number of customers, or sales. And some schemes may actually weight large caps more heavily than the market indexes do. Suppose we used the number of corporate jets or corporate limousines. Readers are encouraged to give free rein to their imagination.

A different approach is to rank stocks by capitalization. Form cap-weighted portfolios that start with the biggest single stock, the biggest two stocks, and so on, up to 500 stocks. Every one of these portfolios except the last will have a large-cap bias relative to the S&P 500 Index. But each MVI portfolio will have a small-cap bias relative to its corresponding cap-weighted counterpart. Thus there will always be a unique number of stocks for which the MVI portfolio has the same small-cap bias as the cap-weighted S&P 500. If this breakeven portfolio includes enough stocks, it can still be satisfactorily diversified.

We have still other ways to remove small-cap bias. Consider a cap-weighted portfolio of the 100 smallest companies in the Wilshire 5000 Index. It will have

- No alpha resulting from MVI indexing
- A lot of small-cap bias

A short position in this portfolio will offset a lot of small-cap bias without reducing the MVI alpha.

An appropriate blend of any two schemes with opposite biases will always eliminate bias relative to any given benchmark. And if different clients have different benchmarks, the blend can be tailored to their benchmarks.

## THE SOURCE OF MVI'S ADVANTAGE

Stocks in the MVI portfolio with a given true value may get a large weight or a small weight. Because they are as likely to be underpriced as overpriced, however, whatever weight the method assigns is as likely to contribute to the underpriced stock as to the overpriced stock. Averaged across all the stocks in the MVI portfolio, the aggregate dollar investments will tend to be the same.

Of course, at a point in time, real stocks won't oblige the author by falling into exactly counterbalancing pairs. But the easiest way to explain how MVI capitalizes on the tendency for pricing errors to be symmetric is to focus on such an idealized pair.

Because of the errors in market price, the corresponding underpriced or overpriced stocks in a *cap-weighted* portfolio will have different market values even if they have the same true values. Let the true values of those stocks be $v$, and let the aggregate pricing errors be $+e$ and $-e$.

If cap-weighted investors spend $v + e$ dollars on the former and $v - e$ dollars on the latter, they will spend a total of

$$(v + e) + (v - e) = 2v \tag{97.9}$$

dollars and get

$$(v + e)\left(\frac{v}{v + e}\right) + (v - e)\left(\frac{v}{v - e}\right) = 2v \tag{97.10}$$

worth of true value.

On the other hand, the MVI investors spend the same number of dollars on the underpriced as they spend on the overpriced stocks. But a dollar spent on overpriced securities buys less true value than a dollar spent on underpriced securities. For example, a dollar spent on a stock with true value $v$ and market price $v + e$ buys $v/(v + e)$ of the true value; a dollar spent on a stock with true value $v$ and market price $v - e$ buys $v/(v - e)$ of the true value. If the MVI investors spend $v$ dollars on each stock, they make the same total investment as the cap-weighted investors and get

$$v\left(\frac{v}{v + e}\right) + v\left(\frac{v}{v - e}\right)$$

worth of true value, or

$$v\left[\frac{v(v - e) + v(v + e)}{v^2 - e^2}\right] = v^2\left(\frac{2v}{v^2 - e^2}\right)$$

$$= \left(\frac{v^2}{v^2 - e^2}\right)2v \qquad (97.11)$$

$$= \left[\frac{1}{1 - \left(\frac{e}{v}\right)^2}\right]2v$$

where the expression in brackets is always greater than zero. (The expression $e/v$ is what we previously called $u$—price error relative to true value.)

Thus for the same total investment, the MVI investors own more true value than the cap-weighted investors, with a difference that depends only on the relative size of the aggregate pricing error. The gain for the whole market sums across errors occurring with a wide range of frequencies. If the frequency function is $f(e/v)$, then the gain can be expressed as

$$\int_{-\infty}^{\infty} \frac{f(e/v)d(e/v)}{1 - (e/v)^2} \qquad (97.12)$$

For small errors, we can approximate this integral by

$$\int_{-\infty}^{\infty}\left[1 + \left(\frac{e}{v}\right)^2\right]f\left(\frac{e}{v}\right)d\left(\frac{e}{v}\right)$$

$$= \int_{-\infty}^{\infty} f\left(\frac{e}{v}\right)d\left(\frac{e}{v}\right) + \int_{-\infty}^{\infty}\left(\frac{e}{v}\right)^2 f\left(\frac{e}{v}\right)d\left(\frac{e}{v}\right) \qquad (97.13)$$

The value of the first integral is 1. If, as we have assumed for the frequency distribution of true values, the mean of the errors is 0, then the second integral is the variance of the errors.

When stocks are accurately priced, the MVI portfolio realizes no gain relative to the price-weighted portfolio. But when the error in market prices is expressed as a fraction of the true value, then the gain from MVI is the square of the standard error, $\sigma$. Exhibit 97.1 displays a range of possible values of $\sigma$, $\sigma^2$, $1 + \sigma^2$, and (for reasons to be explained) $1/(1 - \sigma^2)$. MVI investors realize this benefit even if mispriced stocks never revert to their true values. If reversion occurs, it offers an additional benefit (see Appendix 97.1).

To be sure, the correct integral is not as simply related to the standard error of stock prices as our crude approximation is. But in the event, small pricing errors will be much more frequent than large pricing errors. The reader can get some sense of how bad our approximation is by imagining that, instead of being sample averages, the numbers in the "$\sigma$" column are price errors on a specific stock, in which that stock's contribution to the approximation error is the difference between the right-hand columns. It takes a 31 percent pricing error to produce a 1 percent error in such a stock's contribution to the integral. And all individual stock errors, small or large, positive or negative, cause the author's approximation to understate the true gain from MVI. But that's the only purpose in including the right-hand column. The author trusts nobody will think it is an estimate of the true value of the integral for the indicated variance.

**EXHIBIT 97.1** MVI's Advantage for Indicated Standard Errors in Market Price

| $\sigma$ | $\sigma^2$ | $1 + \sigma^2$ | $\frac{1}{1-\sigma^2}$ |
|---|---|---|---|
| 0.01 | 0.0001 | 1.0001 | 1.0001 |
| 0.02 | 0.0004 | 1.0004 | 1.0004 |
| 0.04 | 0.0016 | 1.0016 | 1.0016 |
| 0.08 | 0.0064 | 1.0064 | 1.0064 |
| 0.12 | 0.0144 | 1.0144 | 1.0146 |
| 0.14 | 0.0196 | 1.0196 | 1.0200 |
| 0.16 | 0.0256 | 1.0256 | 1.0263 |
| 0.18 | 0.0324 | 1.0324 | 1.0335 |
| 0.20 | 0.0400 | 1.0400 | 1.0417 |
| 0.22 | 0.0484 | 1.0484 | 1.0509 |
| 0.24 | 0.0576 | 1.0576 | 1.0611 |
| 0.26 | 0.0676 | 1.0676 | 1.0725 |
| 0.28 | 0.0784 | 1.0784 | 1.0851 |
| 0.30 | 0.0900 | 1.0900 | 1.0989 |
| 0.32 | 0.1024 | 1.1024 | 1.1141 |
| 0.34 | 0.1156 | 1.1156 | 1.1307 |
| 0.36 | 0.1296 | 1.1296 | 1.1489 |
| 0.38 | 0.1444 | 1.1444 | 1.1688 |
| 0.40 | 0.1600 | 1.1600 | 1.1905 |
| 0.42 | 0.1764 | 1.1764 | 1.2142 |
| 0.44 | 0.1936 | 1.1936 | 1.2401 |
| 0.46 | 0.2116 | 1.2116 | 1.2684 |
| 0.48 | 0.2304 | 1.2304 | 1.2994 |
| 0.50 | 0.2500 | 1.2500 | 1.3333 |

Because we can't observe the market's pricing errors, we can't readily resolve debates about their magnitude. Eugene Fama has one view; Fischer Black had another. A 1 percent standard error in stock prices produces a gain relative to cap weighting of 0.0001—surely too small to warrant interest in MVI weighting. But the gain increases rapidly as the standard error increases, being 400 times as big for a 20 percent standard error. Can we afford to be wrong about our preconceptions?

## TRADING COSTS

MVI portfolio managers trade more than managers of cap-weighted portfolios, although how much more depends on the price discrepancies the MVI managers choose to tolerate before trading back to the prescribed weights. The trade size will increase with $\sqrt{t}$, so volume will be proportional to

$$\frac{size}{t} = \frac{\sqrt{t}}{t} = \frac{1}{\sqrt{t}} = \frac{1}{size} \tag{97.14}$$

The cost of increasing the trigger size is a departure from the portfolio proportions prescribed by MVI. Trading lags bring MVI closer to the cap-weighted result.

When all prices rise or fall in proportion to the MVI portfolio manager's weights, however, no trading is needed.

## CONCLUSION

The author has argued that one doesn't need to know true values in order to avoid the problem with cap-weighted index funds. One can still enjoy all the benefits of an index fund—a high level of diversification and low trading costs—by investing randomly with respect to the market's pricing errors.

## APPENDIX 97.1: REVERSION TO TRUE VALUE

The rate of return from the reversion of market value to true value depends on the *reversion rate*. Is the average time to reversion 1 year or 10 years? We do not know.

Presumably, resulting rates of return are also proportional to the initial pricing error. Assume over- and underpriced stocks have the same absolute error $e$; then, for an overpriced stock with true value $v_1$ and market price $p_1$, the rate of return is proportional to

$$\frac{v_1 - p_1}{p_1} = \frac{-e}{p_1} \tag{97.15}$$

and for an underpriced stock with true value $v_2$ and market price $p_2$, the rate of return is proportional to

$$\frac{v_2 - p_2}{p_2} = \frac{e}{p_2} \tag{97.16}$$

For the MVI investor with equal positions in the two stocks, the average return is

$$\frac{1}{2}\left(\frac{e}{p_2} - \frac{e}{p_1}\right) = \frac{e}{2}\left(\frac{1}{p_2} - \frac{1}{p_1}\right)$$

$$= \frac{e}{2}\left(\frac{p_1 - p_2}{p_1 p_2}\right)\frac{e}{2}\left(\frac{2e}{p_1 p_2}\right)$$

$$= \frac{e^2}{p_1 p_2} \approx \left(\frac{e}{v}\right)^2 \tag{97.17}$$

before dividing by the effective reversion time.
  For the whole portfolio, the return is

$$\frac{1}{T}\int_{-\infty}^{\infty} \left(\frac{e}{v}\right)^2 f\left(\frac{e}{v}\right) d\left(\frac{e}{v}\right) = \frac{1}{T}\left(\mathrm{var}\frac{e}{v}\right) \tag{97.18}$$

again assuming a mean of zero.

### References

Arnott, Robert D., Jason Hsu, and Philip Moore. 2005. "Fundamental Indexation." *Financial Analysts Journal*, vol. 61, no. 2 (March–April):83–99.

Fama, Eugene, and Kenneth French. 1973. "The Cross-Section of Expected Returns." *Journal of Finance*, vol. 47, no. 2 (June):427–465.

# Index